SEVEN CENTURIES

of
POETRY
in
ENGLISH

Fourth Edition

EDITED BY JOHN LEONARD

Melbourne

OXFORD UNIVERSITY PRESS

Oxford   Auckland   New York

OXFORD UNIVERSITY PRESS AUSTRALIA

Oxford New York
Athens Auckland Bangkok Bogotá
Buenos Aires Calcutta Cape Town Chennai
Dar es Salaam Delhi Florence Hong Kong
Istanbul Karachi Kuala Lumpur Madrid
Melbourne Mexico City Mumbai Nairobi
Paris Port Moresby São Paulo Singapore
Taipei Tokyo Toronto Warsaw

and associated companies in
Berlin Ibadan

OXFORD is a trade mark of Oxford University Press

© This collection John Leonard 1998
First published 1987
Reprinted with corrections 1988
Reprinted 1989
Revised edition 1991
Reprinted 1991, 1992
Third edition 1994
Reprinted 1997
Fourth edition 1998

National Library of Australia
Cataloguing-in-Publication data:

Seven centuries of poetry in English.

  4th ed.
  Includes indexes.
  ISBN 0 19 550780 0.

  1. English poetry. I. Leonard, John, 1940– .

  821.008

Typeset by Solo Typesetting, South Australia
Printed through Bookpac Production Services,
Singapore
Published by Oxford University Press,
253 Normanby Road, South Melbourne, Australia

Cover illustration: The cover shows a detail of a copper engraving by William Walker,
c. 1795, reproduced from Sigfred Talbert, *Bilder und Texte auf der Welt des Buchhandels*,
vol. 2, published by E. Hauswedell and Co. and Allen Lane/Penguin Press.

CONTENTS

JOHN WILMOT, EARL OF ROCHESTER *1647–80*
To A Lady, in A Letter 395
Upon Nothing 396

APHRA BEHN *1640–89*
Love Arm'd 397
Epilogue 398
And forgive us our Trespasses 399

THOMAS TRAHERNE *1636–74*
The Salutation 399

KATHERINE PHILIPS *1632–64*
Against Love 400
To the truly noble Mr Henry Lawes 401

JOHN DRYDEN *1631–1700*
From Mac Flecknoe lines 1–63 402
From Absalom and Achitophel lines 1–66; 150–74; 543–68 403
From Religio Laici lines 1–41 406
To the Memory of Mr Oldham 407
A Song for St Cecilia's Day, 1687 408

HENRY VAUGHAN *1622–95*
The World 409
Man 411
Quickness 411
They are all gone into the world of light 412

ANDREW MARVELL *1621–78*
A Dialogue between the Soul and Body 413
The Garden 414
An Horation Ode upon Cromwel's Return from Ireland 416
To his Coy Mistress 419
Bermudas 420

ANNE BRADSTREET *1612–72*
A Letter to her Husband, absent upon Publick employment 421
In reference to her Children, 23 June, 1656 422

JOHN MILTON *1608–74*
Lycidas 424
On the late Massacher in Piemont 429
When I consider how my light is spent 429
Lawrence of vertuous Father vertuous Son 429
Methought I saw my late espoused Saint 430
From Paradise Lost *IV*, lines 1–408 430

EDMUND WALLER *1606–87*
Song Go lovely Rose 439
Of the last Verses in the Book 440

THOMAS CAREW *1598–1639*
A Song Aske me no more where Jove bestowes 440
Maria Wentworth 441

PREFACE

The aim of this anthology is to delight. It is designed for all those who wish to explore and enjoy poetry, student and general reader alike. Exploration is of the essence. The reader tempted to a wide reading will discover continual contrast and change—the perspectives of comparison which are the strongest stimulus to thought. The selection from seven centuries of poetry composed in English is wide in terms of poets and their themes; and also poetic forms, metres and voices.

The first third of the book may be considered an anthology of modern poetry in its own right. The opening forty pages comprise recent poetry from eleven countries where English is spoken: Ireland, the United States of America, Canada, Australia, Great Britain, Nigeria, India, New Zealand, Uganda, Barbados and Trinidad. All the principal modern poets are present, with strong attention in this fourth edition to Dickinson, Yeats, Eliot, Auden and Plath.

Most of the remaining two thirds comprise six centuries of poetry composed in one northern European island. For modern readers and writers in the English language, this heritage, at once familiar and strange, is extraordinarily rich.

The selection offers many opportunities for comparison. A number of major poets are represented extensively to display their scope. Thematic and genre links among poems by different authors should be easy to find; the poems will fall readily into any number of groupings that an interested reader or teacher may devise. For example, the first pages open into themes of war and sexual love; in the modern period there are key meditations from a moving vehicle by Murray, Larkin, Purdy, Wright, Bishop, Roethke and Whitman. The chronological arrangement traces backwards towards origins rather than forwards to the present, to provide the perspective of looking into the past, of opening out to a knowledge of earlier themes and styles.

Two poets and thirty-three poems have been added for the expanded, fourth edition and a rather smaller number of poems have been omitted. The section on Rhythm, Form and Metre has been lightly revised for clarity. The anthology now includes five diverse long narratives, 'Goblin Market', the Julia section from *Don Juan*, 'The Rime of the Ancient Mariner', *The Rape of the Lock* and 'The Nun's Priest's Tale' (in addition to that modern refraction of narratives *The Waste Land*). With the inclusion of Charlotte Smith and the strengthening of the selections from Shelley, Coleridge, Wordsworth and Blake, it now provides a substantial introduction to Romantic poetry.

For each poem the date of first publication is given at the foot in normal type; the date of composition, where known, is given beside it in italics. There are biographical notes on each poet; although minimal, these are intended to give a sense of time and place, to make the writing not entirely anonymous. Also, since poetry in its brevity is often less self-explanatory than prose, there are occasional footnotes and marginal glosses. At first reading, however, it may be useful simply to savour an unfamiliar word or reference for its strangeness. When, in time, our curiosity finds out explanations, we may discover that the poem comes out of an experience which is genuinely unfamiliar to us, and valuable for that. Some poems may also be unclear at first reading because of the density of their language. It is natural to let such poems clarify their connections by familiarity—by several readings, preferably aloud. In fact readers often remark not only at the pleasure but also at the understanding that can result from putting a poem on the tongue. Silent reading of a poem, of course, is done at speaking pace, hearing it in the head. There is little value in reading it quickly, since the sense of a poem is bound closely with its rhythm.

The text of each poem is as close as possible to the final (or latest) version which would be recognised by the author. In the preparation of texts earlier than the twentieth century, the editorial work of others has been followed in a few cases, but most have been edited anew for this anthology. It should be realised that editing involves making choices, and sometimes reconstructions, from competing versions. Author's revisions, printers' errors and the alterations made by transcribers, publishers and later editors may all need to be sifted, and, with older poetry especially, the idea of a completely definitive text is not quite practical. Indeed this anthology adds its own small changes to original spelling and punctuation in order to avoid distraction. Modern equivalents have been used for the medieval letters þ and ȝ, and for other letters which survived into the seventeenth century—*i* (for *j*) and *u* and *v* (for each other)—and into the eighteenth century—ʃ (for non-final *s*). The early spellings *of, to, the, whether* and *then* have been modernised when their meaning is *off, too, thee, whither* and *than*. Apostrophes before *s* have been suppressed in the few instances where they were originally used in a plural, or in the genitive *its*. Quotation marks have occasionally been added to aid the sense. Punctuation as we know it did not exist until the sixteenth century; hence, from Wyatt back, and including the anonymous ballads, the punctuation is added. In four poems (two by Bronte, one each by Clare and Blake) where authorial manuscripts are used which lack punctuation entirely, none is added. Generally, original punctuation has been retained because of the clues which it so often gives as to how a poem was read in its time.

Original spelling has also been retained to maintain the sense of a living and changing language, which modernising would have tended to repress. Any strangeness in the spelling can be largely dispelled by reading aloud. Custom allows us to read poetry in our own accents, more or less; old spelling on the page can translate into familiar words in the mouth with a shock of delight, yet remains a visual indication of historical difference. It should be noted that the frequent use of capitals and italics in the seventeenth and early eighteenth centuries is not a rhythmical notation but a signalling of key words to the eye.

Until well into the nineteenth century, a poet could presume on the familiarity of many readers with the classical myths found in Homer and Virgil, in Greek drama and in the *Metamorphoses* of Ovid. These were taught at school. For the modern reader, a general note may be useful: Zeus is the chief of the Greek gods (his Roman equivalent is Jupiter or Jove); Dionysus (Roman Bacchus) is the god of wine and misrule; Phoebus Apollo is the sun god and god of poetry; and the laurel tree, or bay, sacred to Apollo, provides the garland awarded to those who excel in poetry, sport or battle. Footnotes in this anthology generally use the Greek names for the sake of simplicity, even when the reader is referred to a Roman author, such as Ovid.

I am deeply indebted for help received in preparing this anthology. My thanks are due to Monash University for a Special Research Grant and to the Monash Publications Committee for generous financial assistance with the first edition; to Dianne Heriot, who was an invaluable research assistant in the preparation of the first edition; to Shona Dewar, who did research for all four editions and prepared the index and assisted with proofreading for the first; to the always helpful staff at the Monash University Library; to Pauline Amphlett, who typed most of the first manuscript; to Ev Beissbarth of Oxford University Press for the finest editorial sense and skill in the preparation of the first two editions, and to Bette Moore and Lucy Davison for their very careful assistance with the third and fourth; and to my colleagues. The latter include many tertiary teachers whose answers to a questionnaire in the early preparation stages were practical and encouraging. For discussions and assistance I am particularly indebted to Elaine Barry, for whose experience and generosity in partnering this project in its preliminary stage I will always be grateful; also to Peter Groves, Geoffrey Hiller, Harold Love, Virginia Lowe, Evan Jones, Philip Martin, Susan Moore, Peter Naish, Elizabeth Perkins, Clive Probyn, Stephen Torre, Chris Wallace-Crabbe and Lyn Wilson; and finally, for discussion and support over many years, to Shona Dewar, Robert Moore and Charles Pullen.

MEDBH McGUCKIAN

(pron. 'Maeve') b 1950 Belfast, where she lives and writes.

The War Ending

In the still world
Between the covers of a book,
Silk glides through your name
Like a bee sleeping in a flower
Or a seal that turns its head to look   5
At a boy rowing a boat.

The fluttering motion of your hands
Down your body presses into my thoughts
As an enormous broken wave,
A rainbow or a painting being torn   10
Within me. I remove the hand
And order it to leave.

Your passion for light
Is so exactly placed,
I read them as eyes, mouth, nostrils,   15
Disappearing back into their mystery
Like the war that has gone
Into us ending;

There you have my head,
A meeting of Irish eyes   20
With something English:
And now,
Today,
It bursts.

                                                            1991

A Different Same

Moonlight is the clearest eye:
Moonlight as you know enlarges everything.
It occupies a pool so naturally
It might have grown there.
Its stoniness makes stones look less than us.   5
Our hands begin to feel like hooves
Deep in this life and not in any other.
It can free the crossed arms from the body
Where time has fitted them without question,
And place them once random in a swimming   10
Position, so it seems you have opened
Without sound. There are figures standing
On steps, and figures reading. Not one
Walks past without being blurred
Like bronze snapshots. The church bell hangs   15
In the swirling porthole of the yew tree,
Pierced by a sea as abstract and tough
As the infant around the next corner.

Morning, mid-morning, afternoon and evening,
The rose that is like a pink satin theatre   20
Programme spreads to three gardens
With her roots in one. Her gaze, from the intersection
Of the terrace, gathers in the horizon,
A ceiling of translucent planes
With paintings of fruit in each. Awake at night   25
Uprooted me from some last minute shoulder.
I came out of the photograph
With that year underneath this dream;
It met with his mouth.

          1991

PAUL DURCAN

b 1944 Dublin, where he lives. He is a full-time poet.

In Memory of Those Murdered in the Dublin Massacre, May 1974

In the grime-ridden sunlight in the downtown Wimpy bar
I think of all the crucial aeons—and of the labels
That freedom fighters stick onto the lost destinies of unborn children;
The early morning sunlight carries in the whole street from outside;
The whole wide street from outside through the plate-glass windows; 5
Wholly, sparklingly, surgingly, carried in from outside;
And the waitresses cannot help but be happy and gay
As they swipe at the tabletops with their dishcloths—
Such a moment as would provide the heroic freedom fighter
With his perfect meat.   10
And I think of those heroes—heroes?—heroes.

And as I stand up to walk out—
The aproned old woman who's been sweeping the floor
Has mop stuck in bucket, leaning on it;
And she's trembling all over, like a flower in the breeze.   15
She'd make a mighty fine explosion now, if you were to blow her up;
An explosion of petals, of aeons, and the waitresses too, flying breasts and
    limbs,
For a free Ireland.

          1976

Irish Church Comes in From the Cold

It was on an Air Canada flight from London to Montreal
That I learned, quite by chance, from a Redemptorist priest
Who was sitting in a non-smoking seat across the aisle from me
Of the good news that in a chapel in Limerick
There had been installed a rack of contraceptives—   5
In a profane world I could feel the heartbeat of the sacred.

'Candles: Ten Pence Each'—it is written—and I insert
A tenpenny coin into the lip of the moneybox

And I light a candle off another candle
And I plant it in the top rung thinking of the woman I love   10
And likewise I insert a second coin in the adjacent rack
And piously put in my pocket a packet of condoms.
I return to my pew and sit there praying and daydreaming.
I find sitting, rather than kneeling,
More conducive to praying and daydreaming.   15
I pray to St John of the Cross and to all the great lovers
And to all the women of the world who have had rhyme and reason,
As well as good cause, to love and to cherish their men.

                                                             1987

SHARON OLDS

b 1942 San Francisco. She lives in New York, where she teaches writing.

The Connoisseuse of Slugs

When I was a connoisseuse of slugs
I would part the ivy leaves, and look for the
naked jelly of those gold bodies,
translucent strangers glistening along
the stones, slowly, their gelatinous bodies   5
at my mercy. Made mostly of water, they would shrivel
to nothing if they were sprinkled with salt,
but I was not interested in that. What I liked
was to draw aside the ivy, breathe the
odour of the wall, and stand there in silence   10
until the slug forgot I was there
and sent its antennae up out of its
head, the glimmering umber horns
rising like telescopes, until finally the
sensitive knobs would pop out the ends,   15
delicate and intimate. Years later,
when I first saw a naked man,
I gasped with pleasure to see that quiet
mystery re-enacted, the slow
elegant being coming out of hiding and   20
gleaming in the dark air, eager and so
trusting you could weep.
                                                             1984

The Food-Thief

(Uganda, drought)

They drive him along the road in the steady
conscious way they drove their cattle
when they had cattle, when they had homes and

---

16 St John of the Cross (1542–91) a Spanish mystic who wrote religious poetry in sensual and often erotic language. A Carmelite friar, he was persecuted for supporting reform of his order.

living children. They drive him with pliant
peeled sticks, snapped from trees
whose bark cannot be eaten—snapped,   5
not cut, no one has a knife, and the trees that can be
eaten have been eaten leaf and trunk and the
long roots pulled from the ground and eaten.
They drive him and beat him, a loose circle of
thin men with sapling sticks,   10
driving him along slowly, slowly
beating him to death. He turns to them
with all the eloquence of the body, the
wrist turned out and the vein up his forearm
running like a root just under the surface, the   15
wounds on his head ripe and wet as a
rich furrow cut back and cut back at
plough-time to farrow a trench for the seed, his
eye pleading, the iris black and
gleaming as his skin, the white a dark   20
occluded white like cloud-cover on the
morning of a day of heavy rain.
His lips are open to his brothers as the body of a
woman might be open, as the earth itself was
split and folded back and wet and   25
seedy to them once, the lines on his lips
fine as the thousand tributaries of a
root-hair, a river, he is asking them for life
with his whole body, and they are driving his body   30
all the way down the road because
they know the life he is asking for—
it is their life.

                                                          1987

SEAMUS HEANEY

b 1939 in rural Derry, where he grew up. After living for some years in Belfast, he moved
to the Republic of Ireland in 1972. Based in Dublin, he teaches for part of each year at
Harvard.

Homecomings

I

Fetch me the sandmartin
skimming and veering
breast to breast with himself
in the clouds in the river.

II

At the worn mouth of the hole
flight after flight after flight   5
the swoop of his wings
gloved and kissed home.

III

A glottal stillness. An eardrum.
Far in, featherbrains tucked in silence,   10
a silence of water
lipping the bank.

IV

Mould my shoulders inward to you.
Occlude me.
Be damp clay pouting.   15
Let me listen under your eaves.

                                        1979

Casualty

I

He would drink by himself
And raise a weathered thumb
Towards the high shelf,
Calling another rum
And blackcurrant, without   5
Having to raise his voice,
Order a quick stout
By a lifting of the eyes
And a discreet dumb-show
Of pulling off the top;   10
At closing time would go
In waders and peaked cap
Into the showery dark,
A dole-kept breadwinner
But a natural for work.   15
I loved his whole manner,
Sure-footed but too sly,
His deadpan sidling tact,
His fisherman's quick eye
And turned observant back.   20

Incomprehensible
To him, my other life.
Sometimes, on his high stool,
Too busy with his knife
At a tobacco plug   25
And not meeting my eye,
In the pause after a slug
He mentioned poetry.
We would be on our own
And, always politic   30
And shy of condescension,
I would manage by some trick
To switch the talk to eels
Or lore of the horse and cart
Or the Provisionals.   35

---

35 the Provisionals   members of the Provisional IRA, the dominant IRA organisation

But my tentative art
His turned back watches too:
He was blown to bits
Out drinking in a curfew
Others obeyed, three nights   40
After they shot dead
The thirteen men in Derry.
PARAS THIRTEEN, the walls said,
BOGSIDE NIL. That Wednesday
Everybody held   45
His breath and trembled.

II
It was a day of cold
Raw silence, wind-blown
Surplice and soutane:
Rained-on, flower-laden   50
Coffin after coffin
Seemed to float from the door
Of the packed cathedral
Like blossoms on slow water.
The common funeral   55
Unrolled its swaddling band,
Lapping, tightening
Till we were braced and bound
Like brothers in a ring.

But he would not be held   60
At home by his own crowd
Whatever threats were phoned,
Whatever black flags waved.
I see him as he turned
In that bombed offending place,   65
Remorse fused with terror
In his still knowable face,
His cornered outfaced stare
Blinding in the flash.

He had gone miles away   70
For he drank like a fish
Nightly, naturally
Swimming towards the lure
Of warm lit-up places,
The blurred mesh and murmur   75
Drifting among glasses
In the gregarious smoke.
How culpable was he
That last night when he broke
Our tribe's complicity?   80
'Now you're supposed to be
An educated man,'

42–44 thirteen men   killed by British paratroopers in a confrontation with a civil rights march on
'Bloody Sunday', 30 January 1972. **Bogside**   Catholic area of Belfast

I hear him say. 'Puzzle me
The right answer to that one.'

III

I missed his funeral,   85
Those quiet walkers
And sideways talkers
Shoaling out of his lane
To the respectable
Purring of the hearse...   90
They move in equal pace
With the habitual
Slow consolation
Of a dawdling engine,
The line lifted, hand   95
Over fist, cold sunshine
On the water, the land
Banked under fog: that morning
I was taken in his boat,
The screw purling, turning   100
Indolent fathoms white,
I tasted freedom with him.
To get out early, haul
Steadily off the bottom,
Dispraise the catch, and smile   105
As you find a rhythm
Working you, slow mile by mile,
Into your proper haunt
Somewhere, well out, beyond...

Dawn-sniffing revenant,   110
Plodder through midnight rain,
Question me again.   1979

The Railway Children

When we climbed the slopes of the cutting
We were eye-level with the white cups
Of the telegraph poles and the sizzling wires.

Like lovely freehand they curved for miles   5
East and miles west beyond us, sagging
Under their burden of swallows.

We were small and thought we knew nothing
Worth knowing. We thought words travelled the wires
In the shiny pouches of raindrops,

Each one seeded full with the light   10
Of the sky, the gleam of the lines, and ourselves
So infinitesimally scaled

We could stream through the eye of a needle.

1984

MARGARET ATWOOD

b 1939 Ottawa. She is also a novelist and critic.

She considers evading him

I can change my-
self more easily
than I can change you

I could grow bark and
become a shrub   5

or switch back in time
to the woman image left
in cave rubble, the drowned
stomach bulbed with fertility,
face a tiny bead, a   10
lump, queen of the termites

or (better) speed myself up,
disguise myself in the knuckles
and purple-veined veils of old ladies,
become arthritic and genteel   15

or one twist further:
collapse across your
bed clutching my heart
and pull the nostalgic sheet up over
my waxed farewell smile   20

which would be inconvenient
but final.

                                               1971

You Begin

You begin this way:
this is your hand,
this is your eye,
that is a fish, blue and flat
on the paper, almost   5
the shape of an eye.
This is your mouth, this is an O
or a moon, whichever
you like. This is yellow.

Outside the window   10
is the rain, green
because it is summer, and beyond that
the trees and then the world,
which is round and has only
the colors of these nine crayons.   15

This is the world, which is fuller
and more difficult to learn than I have said.
You are right to smudge it that way
with the red and then
the orange: the world burns.   20

Once you have learned these words
you will learn that there are more
words than you can ever learn.
The word *hand* floats above your hand
like a small cloud over a lake.   25
The word *hand* anchors
your hand to this table,
your hand is a warm stone
I hold between two words.

This is your hand, these are my hands, this is the world,   30
which is round but not flat and has more colors
than we can see.

It begins, it has an end,
this is what you will
come back to, this is your hand.   35

                       1978

LES MURRAY

b 1938 Bunyah, northern NSW, where he grew up. After a period in Sydney he is now
based again at Bunyah, where his main occupation is poetry.

Driving Through Sawmill Towns

1

In the high cool country,
having come from the clouds,
down a tilting road
into a distant valley,
you drive without haste. Your windscreen parts the forest,   5
swaying and glancing, and jammed midday brilliance
crouches in clearings . . .
then you come across them,
the sawmill towns, bare hamlets built of boards
with perhaps a store,   10
perhaps a bridge beyond
and a little sidelong creek alive with pebbles.

2

The mills are roofed with iron, have no walls:
you look straight in as you pass, see lithe men working,

the swerve of a winch,   15
dim dazzling blades advancing
through a trolley-borne trunk
till it sags apart
in a manifold sprawl of weatherboards and battens.

The men watch you pass: 20
when you stop your car and ask them for directions,
tall youths look away—
it is the older men who
come out in blue singlets and talk softly to you.

Beside each mill, smoke trickles out of mounds   25
of ash and sawdust.

3

You glide on through town,
your mudguards damp with cloud.
The houses there wear verandahs out of shyness,
all day in calendared kitchens, women listen   30
for cars on the road,
lost children in the bush,
a cry from the mill, a footstep—
nothing happens.

The half-heard radio sings   35
its song of sidewalks.

Sometimes a woman, sweeping her front step,
or a plain young wife at a tankstand fetching water
in a metal bucket will turn round and gaze
at the mountains in wonderment,   40
looking for a city.

4

Evenings are very quiet. All around
the forest is there.
As night comes down, the houses watch each other:
a light going out in a window here has meaning.   45

You speed away through the upland,
glare through towns
and are gone in the forest, glowing on far hills.

On summer nights
ground-crickets sing and pause.   50
In the dark of winter, tin roofs sough with rain,
downpipes chafe in the wind, agog with water.
Men sit after tea
by the stove while their wives talk, rolling a dead match
between their fingers,   55
thinking of the future.

                                                  1965

The Conquest

Phillip was a kindly, rational man:
Friendship and Trust will win the natives, Sir.
Such was the deck the Governor walked upon.

One deck below, lieutenants hawked and spat.   5
One level lower, and dank nightmares grew.
Small floating Englands where our world began.

⋆

And what was trust when the harsh dead swarmed ashore
and warriors, trembling, watched the utterly strange
hard clouds, dawn beings, down there where time began,

so alien the eye could barely fix   10
blue parrot-figures wrecking the light with change,
man-shapes digging where no yam roots were?

⋆

The Governor proffers cloth and English words,
the tribesmen defy him in good Dhuruwal.
Marines stand firm, known warriors bite their beards.   15

Glass beads are scattered in that gulf of style
but pickpockets squeal, clubbed in imagination
as naked Indians circle them like birds.

⋆

They won't Respond. They threaten us. Drive them off.
In genuine grief, the Governor turns away.   20
Blowflies form trinkets for a harsher grief.

As the sickness of the earth bites into flesh
trees moan like women, striplings collapse like trees—
fever of Portsmouth hulks, the Deptford cough.

⋆

It makes dogs furtive, what they find to eat   25
but the noonday forest will not feed white men.
Capture some Natives, quick. Much may be learned

indeed, on both Sides. Sir! And Phillip smiles.
Two live to tell the back lanes of his smile
and the food ships come, and the barracks rise as planned.   30

⋆

And once again the Governor goes around
with his Amity. The yeasts of reason work,
triangle screams confirm the widening ground.

---

1 Phillip Arthur Phillip, first governor of the penal colony of New South Wales, 1788–92
7 dead Local Aboriginal people thought that the Europeans were ghosts of their ancestors.
24 Before transportation, many convicts were kept in prison hulks moored at **Portsmouth** on the
English Channel or at **Deptford** on the Thames.

No one records what month the first striped men
mounted a clawing child, then slit her throat   35
but the spear hits Phillip with a desperate sound.

*

The thoughtful savage with Athenian flanks
fades from the old books here. The sketchers draw
pipe-smoking cretins jigging on thin shanks

poor for the first time, learning the Crown Lands tune.   40
The age of unnoticed languages begins
and Phillip, recovering, gives a nodded thanks.

*

McEntire speared! My personal huntsman, Speared!
Ten Heads for this, and two alive to hang!
A brave lieutenant cools it, bid by bid,   45

to a decent six. The punitive squads march off
without result, but this quandong of wrath
ferments in slaughters for a hundred years.

*

They couldn't tell us how to farm their skin.
They camped with dogs in the rift glens of our mind   50
till their old men mumbled who the stars had been.

They had the noon trees' spiritual walk.
Pathetic with sores, they could be suddenly not,
the low horizon strangely concealing them.

*

A few still hunt way out beyond philosophy   55
where nothing is sacred till it is your flesh
and the leaves, the creeks shine through their poverty

or so we hope. We make our conquests, too.
The ruins at our feet are hard to see.
For all the generous Governor tried to do   60

the planet he had touched began to melt
though he used much Reason, and foreshadowed more
before he recoiled into his century.

                                                                                    1972

The Broad Bean Sermon

Beanstalks, in any breeze, are a slack church parade
without belief, saying *trespass against us* in unison,
recruits in mint Air Force dacron, with unbuttoned leaves.

Upright with water like men, square in stem-section
they grow to great lengths, drink rain, keel over all ways,   5
kink down and grow up afresh, with proffered new greenstuff.

---

36 The **spear** recalls another event, when Phillip was speared in the shoulder by a bystander as he
negotiated with two Aboriginal men who had been kidnapped (lines 27–29) and had then escaped.
He forbade reprisals.
47 quandong (pron. quondong) an edible berry sometimes used to make wine
1 church parade military assembly preceding a church service; here extended to the service itself

Above the cat-and-mouse floor of a thin bean forest
snails hang rapt in their food, ants hurry through several dimensions,
spiders tense and sag like little black flags in their cordage.

Going out to pick beans with the sun high as fence-tops, you find   10
plenty, and fetch them. An hour or a cloud later
you find shirtfulls more. At every hour of daylight

appear more than you missed: ripe, knobbly ones, flesh-sided,
thin-straight, thin-crescent, frown-shaped, bird-shouldered, boat-keeled ones,
beans knuckled and single-bulged, minute green dolphins at suck,   15

beans upright like lecturing, outstretched like blessing fingers
in the incident light, and more still, oblique to your notice
that the noon glare or cloud-light or afternoon slants will uncover

till you ask yourself Could I have overlooked so many, or
do they form in an hour? unfolding into reality   20
like templates for subtly broad grins, like unique caught expressions,

like edible meanings, each sealed around with a string
and affixed to its moment, an unceasing colloquial assembly,
the portly, the stiff, and those lolling in pointed green slippers...

Wondering who'll take the spare bagfulls, you grin with happiness   25
—it is your health—you vow to pick them all
even the last few, weeks off yet, misshapen as toes.

                                                          1974

MUDROOROO

b 1938 Narrogin, Western Australia, of the Bibbulmun people: novelist and poet. In his early
adult years he studied Buddhism in south-east Asia and India.

A Mouth

Being formed completely and utterly as a syllogism;
Being hounded and betrayed as a speaking voice;
Being defined and branded by my own words,
My own sex, my own skin, my own tones,
I can only gasp a drying mouth   5
Uttering silences readily interpreted as an insolence
To be tackled, to be stretched taunt
Into maps and charts of my out-dying breath.
'Hallelujah', there are no more cries for penitence;
But that gasping mouth is disturbing.   10
It is surrounded by teeth clicking sounds;
It is surrounded by lips dryly rasping:
It may tear, it may suckle;
It may give forth only that ceasing breath,
Smelling of cigarettes and other vices to be pitied   15
As the good folk busy themselves in forming the headstone
For a grave bereft of body and saving graces.

                                                          1991

Aussie Dreams a Wakey-wake Time 2

Suburban house wiles the time in fitful dozes of Nyoongah
Dodging how it is as the flowers grow scattering sleep-seeds
Over my faint snores mowing the lawns and stretching out lines
Jailing the quietness, sunny Aussie dream fought over,
Punching out sneerers, king-hitting the cynical bastards.   5
Holding on to my dream in my sleek arms, in my limp fists,
In my growing belly spawning the Aussie dream,
Life-time mortgage dream, earthquaking titles to my dream
In which insecurity lurks, in which adventures huddle,
Though the sounds of midnight blows sweeten my desire for   10
A city street rancid with a beer-smell of wilderness.
I'll seek a bridge to shelter my shivering body,
My vomit will stream away the debris of the gutters,
My saliva will rain down over this city blurring
The dancing lights hazy in my bleary eyes,   15
Playing over the loneliness of an old man's room
In which my toothless gums mutter dribbling past dentures.
Some folk don't make it to the suburbs,
Some folk one day button their jackets over past sorrows,
Holding out against excessive dreams and penthouse posturings.   20

(Chapel Hill, Brisbane, August 1988)

1991

TONY HARRISON

b 1937 Leeds; now based in Newcastle upon Tyne. He is also a translator of drama.

Divisions (I)

All aggro in tight clothes and skinhead crops
they think that like themselves I'm on the dole.
Once in the baths that mask of 'manhood' drops.
Their decorated skins lay bare a soul.

Teenage dole-wallah piss-up, then tattoos.   5
Brown Ale and boys' bravado numbs their fright—
MOTHER in ivy, blood reds and true blues
against that North East skin so sunless white.

When next he sees United lose a match,
his bovvers on, his scarf tied round his wrist,   10
his rash NEWCASTLE RULES will start to scratch,
he'll aerosol the walls, then go get pissed...

1 **Nyoongah**   a term used regionally in south-west Western Australia to denote Aboriginal people.
The biographical note in the poet's 1991 collection refers to him as 'Mudrooroo Nyoongah'.
Postscript   1988 was the bicentennial year of European invasion and settlement in Australia.

So I hope the TRUE LOVE on your arm stays true,
the MOTHER on your chest stays loved, not hated.

But most I hope for jobs for all of you—

next year your tattooed team gets relegated!

1981

Book Ends (I)

Baked the day she suddenly dropped dead
we chew it slowly that last apple pie.

Shocked into sleeplessness you're scared of bed.
We never could talk much, and now don't try.

You're like book ends, the pair of you, she'd say,
Hog that grate, say nothing, sit, sleep, stare . . .

The 'scholar' me, you, worn out on poor pay,
only our silence made us seem a pair.

Not as good for staring in, blue gas,
too regular each bud, each yellow spike.

A night you need my company to pass
and she not here to tell us we're alike!

Your life's all shattered into smithereens.

Back in our silences and sullen looks,
for all the Scotch we drink, what's still between's
not the thirty or so years, but books, books, books.

1981

WOLE SOYINKA

b 1934 western Nigeria. Also a playwright whose work is a meeting place of European and African forms, he teaches at the university in Ife.

Telephone Conversation

The price seemed reasonable, location
Indifferent. The landlady swore she lived
Off premises. Nothing remained
But self-confession. 'Madam,' I warned,
'I hate a wasted journey—I am African.'
Silence. Silenced transmission of
Pressurized good-breeding. Voice, when it came,
Lipstick coated, long gold-rolled
Cigarette-holder pipped. Caught I was, foully.
'HOW DARK?' . . . I had not misheard. . . . 'ARE YOU LIGHT
OR VERY DARK?' Button B. Button A. Stench
Of rancid breath of public hide-and-speak.
Red booth. Red pillar-box. Red double-tiered

---

11 **Button B. Button A**   phone-booth apparatus

Omnibus squelching tar. It *was* real! Shamed
By ill-mannered silence, surrender   15
Pushed dumbfoundment to beg simplification.
Considerate she was, varying the emphasis—
'ARE YOU DARK? OR VERY LIGHT?' Revelation came.
'You mean—like plain or milk chocolate?'
Her assent was clinical, crushing in its light   20
Impersonality. Rapidly, wave-length adjusted,
I chose. 'West African sepia'—and as afterthought,
'Down in my passport.' Silence for spectroscopic
Flight of fancy, till truthfulness clanged her accent
Hard on the mouthpiece. 'WHAT'S THAT?' conceding   25
'DON'T KNOW WHAT THAT IS.' 'Like brunette.'
'THAT'S DARK, ISN'T IT?' 'Not altogether.
Facially, I am brunette, but madam, you should see
The rest of me. Palm of my hand, soles of my feet
Are a peroxide blonde. Friction, caused—   30
Foolishly madam—by sitting down, has turned
My bottom raven black—One moment madam!'—sensing
Her receiver rearing on the thunderclap
About my ears—'Madam,' I pleaded, 'wouldn't you rather
See for yourself?'   35

                                                    1963

Civilian and Soldier

My apparition rose from the fall of lead,
Declared, 'I'm a civilian.' It only served
To aggravate your fright. For how could I
Have risen, a being of this world, in that hour
Of impartial death! And I thought also: nor is   5
Your quarrel of this world.
                              You stood still
For both eternities, and oh I heard the lesson
Of your training sessions, cautioning—
Scorch earth behind you, do not leave   10
A dubious neutral to the rear. Reiteration
Of my civilian quandary, burrowing earth
From the lead festival of your more eager friends
Worked the worse on your confusion, and when
You brought the gun to bear on me, and death   15
Twitched me gently in the eye, your plight
And all of you came clear to me.
                              I hope some day
Intent upon my trade of living, to be checked
In stride by *your* apparition in a trench,   20
Signalling, I am a soldier. No hesitation then
But I shall shoot you clean and fair
With meat and bread, a gourd of wine
A bunch of breasts from either arm, and that
Lone question—do you friend, even now, know   25
What it is all about?

                                                    1967

AUDRE LORDE

1934–1992 b New York. An African American of West Indian parents, she lived in New York for much of her life, in later years as a university teacher.

Coal

I
is the total black, being spoken
from the earth's inside.
There are many kinds of open
how a diamond comes into a knot of flame   5
how sound comes into a word, colored
by who pays what for speaking.
Some words are open like a diamond
on glass windows
singing out within the passing crash of sun
Then there are words like stapled wagers   10
in a perforated book—buy and sign and tear apart—
and come whatever wills all chances
the stub remains
an ill-pulled tooth with a ragged edge.
Some words live in my throat   15
breeding like adders. Others know sun
seeking like gypsies over my tongue
to explode through my lips
like young sparrows bursting from shell.
Some words   20
bedevil me.

Love is a word, another kind of open.
As the diamond comes into a knot of flame
I am Black because I come from the earth's inside
now take my word for jewel in the open light.   25

                                                        1968

The Art of Response

The first answer was incorrect
the second was
sorry   the third trimmed its toenails
on the Vatican steps
the fourth went mad   5
the fifth
nursed a grudge until it bore twins
that drank poisoned grape juice in Jonestown
the sixth   wrote a book about it
the seventh   10
argued a case before the Supreme Court
against taxation on Girl Scout Cookies
the eighth held a news conference

8 **Jonestown**   the site in Guyana of the mass suicide in 1977 of over 900 members of an American religious group

while four Black babies
and one other   picketed New York City   15
for a hospital bed to die in
the ninth and tenth swore
Revenge on the Opposition
and the eleventh dug their graves
next to Eternal Truth   20
the twelfth
processed funds from a Third World country
that provides doctors for Central Harlem
the thirteenth
refused
the fourteenth sold cocaine and shamrocks   25
near a toilet in the Big Apple circus
the fifteenth
changed the question.

                                                   1986

KAMALA DAS

b 1934 Malabar, south India. She writes in Malayalam (under the pseudonym
Madhavikutty) and English, and is engaged in regional politics as a conservationist.

An Introduction

I don't know politics but I know the names
Of those in power, and can repeat them like
Days of week, or names of months, beginning with
Nehru. I am Indian, very brown, born in
Malabar, I speak three languages, write in   5
Two, dream in one. Don't write in English, they said,
English is not your mother-tongue. Why not leave
Me alone, critics, friends, visiting cousins,
Every one of you? Why not let me speak in
Any language I like? The language I speak   10
Becomes mine, its distortions, its queernesses
All mine, mine alone. It is half English, half
Indian, funny perhaps, but it is honest,
It is as human as I am human, don't
You see? It voices my joys, my longings, my   15
Hopes, and it is useful to me as cawing
Is to crows or roaring to the lions, it
Is human speech, the speech of the mind that is
Here and not there, a mind that sees and hears and
Is aware. Not the deaf, blind speech   20
Of trees in storm or of monsoon clouds or of rain or the
Incoherent mutterings of the blazing
Funeral pyre. I was child, and later they
Told me I grew, for I became tall, my limbs
Swelled and one or two places sprouted hair. When   25
I asked for love, not knowing what else to ask
For, he drew a youth of sixteen into the

Bedroom and closed the door. He did not beat me
But my sad woman-body felt so beaten.
The weight of my breasts and womb crushed me. I shrank   30
Pitifully. Then . . . I wore a shirt and my
Brother's trousers, cut my hair short and ignored
My womanliness. Dress in saris, be girl,
Be wife, they said. Be embroiderer, be cook,
Be a quarreller with servants. Fit in. Oh,   35
Belong, cried the categorisers. Don't sit
On walls or peep in through our lace-draped windows.

Be Amy, or be Kamala. Or, better
Still, be Madhavikutty. It is time to
Choose a name, a role. Don't play pretending games.   40
Don't play at schizophrenia or be a
Nympho. Don't cry embarrassingly loud when
Jilted in love . . . I met a man, loved him. Call
Him not by any name, he is every man
Who wants a woman, just as I am every   45
Woman who seeks love. In him . . . the hungry haste
Of rivers, in me . . . the ocean's tireless
Waiting. Who are you, I ask each and everyone,
The answer is, it is I. Anywhere and
Everywhere, I see the one who calls himself   50
I; in this world, he is tightly packed like the
Sword in its sheath. It is I who drink lonely
Drinks at twelve, midnight, in hotels of strange towns,
It is I who laugh, it is I who make love
And then feel shame, it is I who lie dying   55
With a rattle in my throat. I am sinner,
I am saint. I am the beloved and the
Betrayed. I have no joys which are not yours, no
Aches which are not yours. I too call myself I.

                                                        1965

The Inheritance

This then was our only inheritance, this ancient
Virus that we nurtured in the soul so
That when at sundown, the Muezzin's high wail sounded from
The mosque, the chapel-bells announced the angelus, and
From the temple rose the Brahmin's assonant chant, we   5
Walked with hearts grown scabrous with a hate, illogical,
And chose not to believe—what we perhaps vaguely sensed—
That it was only our fathers' lunacy speaking,
In three different tones, babbling: Slay them who do not
Believe, or better still, disembowel their young ones   10
And scatter on the streets the meagre innards. Oh God,
Blessed be your fair name, blessed be the religion
Purified in the unbelievers' blood, blessed be
Our sacred city, blessed be its incarnadined glory. . . .

                                                        1973

FLEUR ADCOCK

b 1934 near Auckland. She has lived in England since 1963, working first as a librarian and now as a freelance writer.

The Soho Hospital for Women

1

Strange room, from this angle:
white door open before me,
strange bed, mechanical hum, white lights.
There will be stranger rooms to come.

As I almost slept I saw the deep flower opening   5
and leaned over into it, gratefully.
It swimmingly closed in my face. I was not ready.
It was not death, it was acceptance.

⁎

Our thin patient cat died purring,
her small triangular head tilted back,
the nurse's fingers caressing her throat,   10
my hand on her shrunken spine; the quick needle.
That was the second death by cancer.
The first is not for me to speak of.
It was telephone calls and brave letters
and a friend's hand bleeding under the coffin.   15

⁎

Doctor, I am not afraid of a word.
But neither do I wish to embrace that visitor,
to engulf it as Hine-Nui-te-Po
engulfed Maui; that would be the way of it.   20

And she was the winner there: her womb crushed him.
Goddesses can do these things.
But I have admitted the gloved hands and the speculum
and must part my ordinary legs to the surgeon's knife.

2

Nellie has only one breast   25
ample enough to make several.
Her quilted dressing-gown softens
to semi-doubtful this imbalance
and there's no starched vanity
in our abundant ward-mother: 30
her silvery hair's in braids, her slippers
loll, her weathered smile holds true.
When she dresses up in her black
with her glittering marcasite brooch on

19–22 Hine-Nui-te-Po   Maori death-goddess, who engulfed the hero, **Maui**, between her thighs as he entered to kill her

to go for the weekly radium treatment   35
she's the bright star of the taxi-party—
whatever may be growing under her ribs.

       *

Doris hardly smokes in the ward—
and hardly eats more than a dreamy spoonful—
but the corridors and bathrooms   40
reek of her Players Number 10,
and the drug-trolley pauses
for long minutes by her bed.
Each week for the taxi-outing
she puts on her skirt again   45
and has to pin the slack waistband
more tightly over her scarlet sweater.
Her face, a white shadow through smoked glass,
lets Soho display itself unregarded.

       *

Third in the car is Mrs Golding   50
who never smiles. And why should she?

3

The senior consultant on his rounds
murmurs in so subdued a voice
to the students marshalled behind
that they gather in, forming a cell,   55
a cluster, a rosette around him
as he stands at the foot of my bed
going through my notes with them,
half-audibly instructive, grave.

The slight ache as I strain forward   60
to listen still seems imagined.

Then he turns his practised smile on me:
'How are you this morning?' 'Fine,
very well, thank you.' I smile too.
And possibly all that murmurs within me   65
is the slow dissolving of stitches.

4

I am out in the supermarket choosing—
this very afternoon, this day—
picking up tomatoes, cheese, bread,

things I want and shall be using   70
to make myself a meal, while they
eat their stodgy suppers in bed:

Janet with her big freckled breasts,
her prim Scots voice, her one friend,
and never in hospital before,   75

who came in to have a few tests
and now can't see where they'll end;
and Coral in the bed by the door

who whimpered and gasped behind a screen
with nurses to and fro all night   80
and far too much of the day;

pallid, bewildered, nineteen.
And Mary, who will be all right
but gradually. And Alice, who may.

Whereas I stand almost intact,   85
giddy with freedom, not with pain,
I lift my light basket, observing

how little I needed in fact;
and move to the checkout, to the rain,
to the lights and the long street curving.   90

1979

Crab

Late at night we wrench open a crab;
flesh bursts out of its cup

in pastel colours. The dark fronds attract me:
Poison, you say, Dead Men's Fingers —

don't put them in your mouth, stop!   5
They brush over my tongue, limp and mossy,

until you snatch them from me, as you snatch
yourself, gently, if I come too close.

Here are the permitted parts of the crab,
wholesome on their nests of lettuce   10

and we are safe again in words.
All day the kitchen will smell of sea.

1983

SYLVIA PLATH

1932–63 b Boston. From 1955 she lived in England. After a history of intermittent mental illness she took her own life. A large number of increasingly personal poems date from the two years before her death.

Mushrooms

Overnight, very
Whitely, discreetly,
Very quietly

Our toes, our noses
Take hold on the loam,   5
Acquire the air.

Nobody sees us,
Stops us, betrays us;
The small grains make room.

Soft fists insist on   10
Heaving the needles,
The leafy bedding,

Even the paving.
Our hammers, our rams,
Earless and eyeless,   15

Perfectly voiceless,
Widen the crannies,
Shoulder through holes. We

Diet on water,
On crumbs of shadow,   20
Bland-mannered, asking

Little or nothing.
So many of us!
So many of us!

We are shelves, we are   25
Tables, we are meek,
We are edible,

Nudgers and shovers
In spite of ourselves.
Our kind multiplies: 30

We shall by morning
Inherit the earth.
Our foot's in the door.

                                                          1959   1960

Morning Song

Love set you going like a fat gold watch.
The midwife slapped your footsoles, and your bald cry
Took its place among the elements.

Our voices echo, magnifying your arrival. New statue.
In a drafty museum, your nakedness   5
Shadows our safety. We stand round blankly as walls.

I'm no more your mother
Than the cloud that distills a mirror to reflect its own slow
Effacement at the wind's hand.

All night your moth-breath   10
Flickers among the flat pink roses. I wake to listen:
A far sea moves in my ear.

One cry, and I stumble from bed, cow-heavy and floral
In my Victorian nightgown.
Your mouth opens clean as a cat's. The window square   15

Whitens and swallows its dull stars. And now you try
Your handful of notes;
The clear vowels rise like balloons.

                                                          1961   1965

Tulips

The tulips are too excitable, it is winter here.
Look how white everything is, how quiet, how snowed-in.
I am learning peacefulness, lying by myself quietly
As the light lies on these white walls, this bed, these hands.
I am nobody; I have nothing to do with explosions.   5
I have given my name and my day-clothes up to the nurses
And my history to the anesthetist and my body to surgeons.

They have propped my head between the pillow and the sheet-cuff
Like an eye between two white lids that will not shut.
Stupid pupil, it has to take everything in.   10
The nurses pass and pass, they are no trouble,
They pass the way gulls pass inland in their white caps,
Doing things with their hands, one just the same as another,
So it is impossible to tell how many there are.

My body is a pebble to them, they tend it as water   15
Tends to the pebbles it must run over, smoothing them gently.
They bring me numbness in their bright needles, they bring me sleep.
Now I have lost myself I am sick of baggage—
My patent leather overnight case like a black pillbox,
My husband and child smiling out of the family photo;   20
Their smiles catch onto my skin, little smiling hooks.

I have let things slip, a thirty-year-old cargo boat
Stubbornly hanging on to my name and address.
They have swabbed me clear of my loving associations.
Scared and bare on the green plastic-pillowed trolley   25
I watched my teaset, my bureaus of linen, my books
Sink out of sight, and the water went over my head.
I am a nun now, I have never been so pure.

I didn't want any flowers, I only wanted
To lie with my hands turned up and be utterly empty.   30
How free it is, you have no idea how free—
The peacefulness is so big it dazes you,
And it asks nothing, a name tag, a few trinkets.
It is what the dead close on, finally; I imagine them
Shutting their mouths on it, like a Communion tablet.   35

The tulips are too red in the first place, they hurt me.
Even through the gift paper I could hear them breathe
Lightly, through their white swaddlings, like an awful baby.
Their redness talks to my wound, it corresponds.
They are subtle: they seem to float, though they weigh me down,   40
Upsetting me with their sudden tongues and their color,
A dozen red lead sinkers round my neck.

Nobody watched me before, now I am watched.
The tulips turn to me, and the window behind me
Where once a day the light slowly widens and slowly thins,   45
And I see myself, flat, ridiculous, a cut-paper shadow
Between the eye of the sun and the eyes of the tulips,
And I have no face, I have wanted to efface myself.
The vivid tulips eat my oxygen.

Before they came the air was calm enough,   50
Coming and going, breath by breath, without any fuss.
Then the tulips filled it up like a loud noise.
Now the air snags and eddies round them the way a river
Snags and eddies round a sunken rust-red engine.
They concentrate my attention, that was happy   55
Playing and resting without committing itself.

The walls, also, seem to be warming themselves.
The tulips should be behind bars like dangerous animals;
They are opening like the mouth of some great African cat,
And I am aware of my heart: it opens and closes   60
Its bowl of red blooms out of sheer love of me.
The water I taste is warm and salt, like the sea,
And comes from a country far away as health.

1961   1965

The Arrival of the Bee Box

I ordered this, this clean wood box
Square as a chair and almost too heavy to lift.
I would say it was the coffin of a midget
Or a square baby
Were there not such a din in it.   5

The box is locked, it is dangerous.
I have to live with it overnight
And I can't keep away from it.
There are no windows, so I can't see what is in there.
There is only a little grid, no exit.   10

I put my eye to the grid.
It is dark, dark,
With the swarmy feeling of African hands
Minute and shrunk for export,
Black on black, angrily clambering.   15

How can I let them out?
It is the noise that appalls me most of all,
The unintelligible syllables.
It is like a Roman mob,
Small, taken one by one, but my god, together!   20

I lay my ear to furious Latin.
I am not a Caesar.
I have simply ordered a box of maniacs.
They can be sent back.
They can die, I need feed them nothing, I am the owner.   25

I wonder how hungry they are.
I wonder if they would forget me
If I just undid the locks and stood back and turned into a tree.
There is the laburnum, its blond colonnades,
And the petticoats of the cherry.   30

They might ignore me immediately
In my moon suit and funeral veil.
I am no source of honey
So why should they turn on me?
Tomorrow I will be sweet God, I will set them free.   35

The box is only temporary.

                                                    1962   1965

The Applicant

First, are you our sort of person?
Do you wear
A glass eye, false teeth or a crutch,
A brace or a hook,
Rubber breasts or a rubber crotch,   5

Stitches to show something's missing? No, no? Then
How can we give you a thing?
Stop crying.
Open your hand.
Empty? Empty. Here is a hand   10

To fill it and willing
To bring teacups and roll away headaches
And do whatever you tell it.
Will you marry it?
It is guaranteed   15

To thumb shut your eyes at the end
And dissolve of sorrow.
We make new stock from the salt.
I notice you are stark naked.
How about this suit—   20

Black and stiff, but not a bad fit.
Will you marry it?
It is waterproof, shatterproof, proof
Against fire and bombs through the roof.
Believe me, they'll bury you in it.   25

Now your head, excuse me, is empty.
I have the ticket for that.
Come here, sweetie, out of the closet.
Well, what do you think of *that*?
Naked as paper to start   30

But in twenty-five years she'll be silver,
In fifty, gold.
A living doll, everywhere you look.
It can sew, it can cook,
It can talk, talk, talk.   35

---

35 Bees that have travelled in a box are normally given time to settle before they are set free to hive.

It works, there is nothing wrong with it.
You have a hole, it's a poultice.
You have an eye, it's an image.
My boy, it's your last resort.
Will you marry it, marry it, marry it.   40

1962   1965

The Night Dances

A smile fell in the grass.
Irretrievable!

And how will your night dances
Lose themselves. In mathematics?

Such pure leaps and spirals—   5
Surely they travel

The world forever, I shall not entirely
Sit emptied of beauties, the gift

Of your small breath, the drenched grass
Smell of your sleeps, lilies, lilies.   10

Their flesh bears no relation.
Cold folds of ego, the calla,

And the tiger, embellishing itself—
Spots, and a spread of hot petals.

The comets   15
Have such a space to cross,

Such coldness, forgetfulness.
So your gestures flake off—

Warm and human, then their pink light
Bleeding and peeling   20

Through the black amnesias of heaven.
Why am I given

These lamps, these planets
Falling like blessings, like flakes

Six-sided, white   25
On my eyes, my lips, my hair

Touching and melting.
Nowhere.

1962   1965

The Night Dances   dances performed in his cot by Plath's baby son
12–13 calla, tiger   kinds of lily

Winter Trees

The wet dawn inks are doing their blue dissolve.
On their blotter of fog the trees
Seem a botanical drawing—
Memories growing, ring on ring,
A series of weddings.   5

Knowing neither abortions nor bitchery,
Truer than women,
They seed so effortlessly!
Tasting the winds, that are footless,
Waist-deep in history—   10

Full of wings, otherworldliness.
In this, they are Ledas.
O mother of leaves and sweetness
Who are these pietas?
The shadows of ringdoves chanting, but easing nothing.   15

26 November 1962   1971

Mystic

The air is a mill of hooks—
Questions without answer,
Glittering and drunk as flies
Whose kiss stings unbearably
In the fetid wombs of black air under pines in summer.   5

I remember
The dead smell of sun on wood cabins,
The stiffness of sails, the long salt winding sheets.
Once one has seen God, what is the remedy?
Once one has been seized up   10

Without a part left over,
Not a toe, not a finger, and used,
Used utterly, in the sun's conflagrations, the stains
That lengthen from ancient cathedrals
What is the remedy?   15

The pill of the Communion tablet,
The walking beside still water? Memory?
Or picking up the bright pieces
Of Christ in the faces of rodents,
The tame flower-nibblers, the ones   20

---

12 **Ledas**   In Greek myth, Leda was raped by Zeus, who appeared to her in the form of a swan.

Whose hopes are so low they are comfortable—
The humpback in her small, washed cottage
Under the spokes of the clematis.
Is there no great love, only tenderness?
Does the sea   25

Remember the walker upon it?
Meaning leaks from the molecules.
The chimneys of the city breathe, the window sweats,
The children leap in their cots.
The sun blooms, it is a geranium.   30

The heart has not stopped.

1 February 1963   1971

Words

Axes
After whose stroke the wood rings,
And the echoes!
Echoes travelling
Off from the centre like horses.   5

The sap
Wells like tears, like the
Water striving
To re-establish its mirror
Over the rock   10

That drops and turns,
A white skull,
Eaten by weedy greens.
Years later I
Encounter them on the road—   15

Words dry and riderless,
The indefatigable hoof-taps.
While
From the bottom of the pool, fixed stars
Govern a life.   20

1 February 1963   1965

Balloons

Since Christmas they have lived with us,
Guileless and clear,
Oval soul-animals,
Taking up half the space,
Moving and rubbing on the silk   5

Invisible air drifts,
Giving a shriek and pop
When attacked, then scooting to rest, barely trembling.
Yellow cathead, blue fish—
Such queer moons we live with   10

Instead of dead furniture!
Straw mats, white walls
And these travelling
Globes of thin air, red, green,
Delighting   15

The heart like wishes or free
Peacocks blessing
Old ground with a feather
Beaten in starry metals.
Your small   20

Brother is making
His balloon squeak like a cat.
Seeming to see
A funny pink world he might eat on the other side of it,
He bites,   25

Then sits
Back, fat jug
Contemplating a world clear as water,
A red
Shred in his little fist.   30

5 February 1963   1965

OKOT P'BITEK

1931–82 b Gulu, northern Uganda. He wrote poetry in both Acoli and English and taught African studies at universities in Kampala and Nairobi.

Return the Bridewealth

I

I go to my old father
He is sitting in the shade at the foot of the simsim granary,
His eyes are fixed on the three graves of his grandchildren
He is silent.

Father, I say to him,   5
Father, gather the bridewealth so that I may marry the girl of my bosom!

Bridewealth   dowry, paid by the family of the groom to that of the bride. Traditionally, it would not be repaid in the circumstances described here.
2 simsim   sesame

My old father rests his bony chin in the broken cups of his withered hands,
His long black finger-nails vainly digging into the tough dry skin of his cheeks
He keeps staring at the graves of his grandchildren,
Some labikka weeds and obiya grasses are growing on the mounds.   10
My old father does not answer me, only two large clotting tears crawl down his
    wrinkled cheeks,
And a faint half smile alights on his lips, causing them to quiver and part slightly.

He reaches out for his walking staff, oily with age and smooth like the long teeth
    of an old elephant.
One hand on his broken hip, he heaves himself up on the three stilts,
His every joint crackling and the bones breaking!   15
Hm! he sighs, and staggers towards the graves of his grandchildren,
And with the bony-dry staff he strikes the mounds: One! Two! Three!
He bends to pluck the labikka weeds and the obiya grasses,
But he cannot reach the ground, his stone-stiff back cracks like dry firewood.
Hm! he sighs again, he turns around and walks past me.   20
He does not speak to me.
There are more clotting tears on his glassy eyes,
The faint smile on his broken lips has grown bigger.

II

My old mother is returning from the well
The water-pot sits on the pad on her grey wet head.   25
One hand fondles the belly of the water-pot, the other strangles the walking staff.
She pauses briefly by the graves of her grandchildren and studies the labikka
    weeds and the obiya grasses waving like feathers atop the mounds.

Hm! she sighs
She walks past me;
She does not greet me.   30
Her face is wet, perhaps with sweat, perhaps with water from the water-pot
Perhaps some tears mingle with the water and sweat
The thing on her face is not a smile,
Her lips are tightly locked.

She stops before the door of her hut   35
She throws down the wet walking staff, klenky, klenky!
A little girl in green frock runs to her assistance;
Slowly, slowly, steadily she kneels down;
Together, slowly, slowly, gently they lift the water-pot and put it down.
My old mother says, Thank you!   40

Some water splashes onto the earth, and wets the little girl's school books.
She bursts into tears, and rolls on the earth, soiling her beautiful green frock,
A little boy giggles.
He says, All women are the same aren't they?
Another little boy consoles his sister.   45

III

I go to the Town
I see a man and a woman
He wears heavy boots, his buttocks are like sacks of cotton

His chest resembles the simsim granary,
His head is hidden under a broad-rimmed hat.   50

In one hand he holds a loaded machine-gun, his fingers at the trigger
His other hand coils round the waist of the woman like a starving python.
They part after a noisy kiss
Hm! he sighs!
Hm! she sighs!   55

He marches past me, stumping the earth in anger, like an elephant with a bullet
        in his bony head!
He does not look at me
He does not touch me, only the butt of his weapon touches my knee lightly,
He walks away, the sacks of cotton on his behind rising and falling alternately,
Like a bull hippo returning to the river after grazing in the fresh grasses.   60
Hm! I sigh!

I go to the woman,
She does not look up to me,
She writes things in the sand.
She says, How are my children?   65
I say, Three are dead, and some labikka weeds and obiya grasses grow on
        their graves.
She is silent!
I say, your daughter is now in Primary Six, and your little boys ask after you!

The woman says, My mother is dead!
I am silent!   70
The agoga bird flies overhead
He cries his sorrowful message:
        She is dead! She is dead!
The guinea-fowl croaks in the tree near by
        Sorrow is part of me,   75
        Sorrow is part of me. How can I escape
        The boldness on my head?
She is silent!
Hm! I sigh!
She says, I want to see my children!   80

I tell the woman I cannot trace her father.
I say to her I want back the bridewealth that my father paid when we wedded
        some years ago,
When she was full of charm, a sweet innocent little hospital ward-maid.
She is silent!
I tell the woman I will marry the girl of my bosom   85
I tell her the orphans she left behind will be mothered, and the labikka weeds and
        obiya grasses that grow on the graves of her children will be weeded,
And the ground around the mounds will be kept tidy.
Hm! she sighs!
She is silent!
I am silent!   90

The woman reaches out for her handbag.
It is not the one I gave her as a gift last Christmas.
She opens it,

She takes out a new purse,
She takes out a cheque.   95

She looks up to me, our eyes meet again after many months.
There are two deep valleys on her cheeks that were not there before
There is some water in the valleys.
The skin on her neck is rotting away,
They say the doctor has cut open her stomach and removed the bag of her eggs 100
So that she may remain a young woman for ever.

I am silent!
A broad witch-smile darkens her wet face,
She screams,
Here, take it! Go and marry your bloody woman!   105
I open the cheque
It reads,
Shillings One thousand four hundred only!

                                                      1971

TED HUGHES

b 1930 Yorkshire. He is also a children's writer. Currently poet laureate, he lives in Devon.

The Thought-Fox

I imagine this midnight moment's forest:
Something else is alive
Beside the clock's loneliness
And this blank page where my fingers move.

Through the window I see no star: 5
Something more near
Though deeper within darkness
Is entering the loneliness:

Cold, delicately as the dark snow
A fox's nose touches twig, leaf;   10
Two eyes serve a movement, that now
And again now, and now, and now

Sets neat prints into the snow
Between trees, and warily a lame
Shadow lags by stump and in hollow   15
Of a body that is bold to come

Across clearings, an eye,
A widening deepening greenness,
Brilliantly, concentratedly,
Coming about its own business   20

Till, with a sudden sharp hot stink of fox
It enters the dark hole of the head.
The window is starless still; the clock ticks,
The page is printed.

                                                      1957

Full Moon and Little Frieda

A cool small evening shrunk to a dog bark and the clank of a bucket—

And you listening.
A spider's web, tense for the dew's touch.
A pail lifted, still and brimming—mirror
To tempt a first star to a tremor.   5

Cows are going home in the lane there, looping the hedges with
      their warm wreaths of breath—
A dark river of blood, many boulders,
Balancing unspilled milk.

'Moon!' you cry suddenly, 'Moon! Moon!'

The moon has stepped back like an artist gazing amazed at a work   10

That points at him amazed.

                                                      1967

Bride and Groom Lie Hidden for Three Days

She gives him his eyes, she found them
Among some rubble, among some beetles

He gives her her skin
He just seemed to pull it down out of the air and lay it over her
She weeps with fearfulness and astonishment   5

She has found his hands for him, and fitted them freshly at the wrists
They are amazed at themselves, they go feeling all over her

He has assembled her spine, he cleaned each piece carefully
And sets them in perfect order
A superhuman puzzle but he is inspired   10
She leans back twisting this way and that, using it and laughing, incredulous

Now she has brought his feet, she is connecting them
So that his whole body lights up

And he has fashioned her new hips
With all fittings complete and with newly wound coils, all shiningly oiled   15
He is polishing every part, he himself can hardly believe it

They keep taking each other to the sun, they find they can easily
To test each new thing at each new step

And now she smooths over him the plates of his skull
So that the joints are invisible   20
And now he connects her throat, her breasts and the pit of her stomach
With a single wire

She gives him his teeth, tying their roots to the centrepin of his body

He sets the little circlets on her fingertips

She stitches his body here and there with steely purple silk   25

He oils the delicate cogs of her mouth

She inlays with deep-cut scrolls the nape of his neck

He sinks into place the inside of her thighs

So, gasping with joy, with cries of wonderment
Like two gods of mud   30
Sprawling in the dirt, but with infinite care

They bring each other to perfection.

                                                    1978

Ravens

As we came through the gate to look at the few new lambs
On the skyline of lawn smoothness,
A raven bundled itself into air from midfield
And slid away under hard glistenings, low and guilty.
Sheep nibbling, kneeling to nibble the reluctant nibbled grass.   5
Sheep staring, their jaws pausing to think, then chewing again,
Then pausing. Over there a new lamb
Just getting up, bumping its mother's nose
As she nibbles the sugar coating off it
While the tattered banners of her triumph swing and drip from her rear-end.   10
She sneezes again and again, till she's emptied.
She carries on investigating her new present and seeing how it works.
Over here is something else. But you are still interested
In that new one, and its new spark of voice,
And its tininess.   15
Now over here, where the raven was,
Is what interests you next. Born dead,
Twisted like a scarf, a lamb of an hour or two,
Its insides, the various jellies and crimsons and transparencies
And threads and tissues pulled out   20
In straight lines, like tent ropes
From its upward belly opened like a lamb-wool slipper,
The fine anatomy of silvery ribs on display and the cavity,
The head also emptied through the eye-sockets,
The woolly limbs swathed in birth-yolk and impossible   25
To tell now which in all this field of quietly nibbling sheep
Was its mother. I explain
That it died being born. We should have been here, to help it.
So it died being born. 'And did it cry?' you cry.
I pick up the dangling greasy weight by the hooves soft as dogs' pads   30
That had trodden only womb-water
And its raven-drawn strings dangle and trail,
Its loose head joggles, and 'Did it cry?' you cry again.
Its two-fingered feet splay in their skin between the pressures
Of my finger and thumb. And there is another,   35
Just born, all black, splaying its tripod, inching its new points
Towards its mother, and testing the note
It finds in its mouth. But you have eyes now

Only for the tattered bundle of throwaway lamb.
'Did it cry?' you keep asking, in a three-year-old field-wide   40
Piercing persistence. 'Oh yes' I say 'it cried.'

Though this one was lucky insofar
As it made the attempt into a warm wind
And its first day of death was blue and warm
The magpies gone quiet with domestic happiness   45
And skylarks not worrying about anything
And the blackthorn budding confidently
And the skyline of hills, after millions of hard years,
Sitting soft.

1979

KAMAU BRATHWAITE

b 1930 Barbados. A poet whose work explores the African and local origins of West Indian
culture, he teaches history at the university in Jamaica.

Ogun

My uncle made chairs, tables, balanced doors on, dug out
coffins, smoothing the white wood out

with plane and quick sandpaper until
it shone like his short-sighted glasses.

The knuckles of his hands were sil-   5
vered knobs of nails hit, hurt and flat-

tened out with blast of heavy hammer. He was knock-knee'd, flat-
footed and his clip clop sandals slapped across the concrete

flooring of his little shop where canefield mulemen and a fleet
of Bedford lorry drivers dropped in to scratch themselves and talk.   10

There was no shock of wood, no beam
of light mahogany his saw teeth couldn't handle.

When shaping squares for locks, a key hole
care tapped rat tat tat upon the handle

of his humpbacked chisel. Cold   15
world of wood caught fire as he whittled: rectangle

window frames, the intersecting x of folding chairs, triangle

trellises, the donkey
box-cart in its squeaking square.   20

But he was poor and most days he was hungry.
Imported cabinets with mirrors, formica table

Ogun   Yoruba (West African) and Caribbean god of creation and patron of artisans; but also a reckless destroyer

tops, spine-curving chairs made up of tubes, with hollow
steel-like bird bones that sat on rubber ploughs,

thin beds, stretched not on boards, but blue high-tensioned cables,   25
were what the world preferred.

And yet he had a block of wood that would have baffled them.
With knife and gimlet care he worked away at this on Sundays,

explored its knotted hurts, cutting his way
along its yellow whorls until his hands could feel   30

how it had swelled and shivered, breathing air,
its weathered green burning to rings of time,

its contoured grain still tuned to roots and water.
And as he cut, he heard the creak of forests:

green lizard faces gulped, grey memories with moth   35
eyes watched him from their shadows, soft

liquid tendrils leaked among the flowers
and a black rigid thunder he had never heard within his hammer

came stomping up the trunks. And as he worked within his shattered
Sunday shop, the wood took shape: dry shuttered   40

eyes, slack anciently everted lips, flat
ruined face, eaten by pox, ravaged by rat

and woodworm, dry cistern mouth, cracked
gullet crying for the desert, the heavy black

enduring jaw; lost pain, lost iron;   45
emerging woodwork image of his anger.

                                        1969

From Sun Poem

22

i

Soon after the blacks arrived plantations prospered
rivers of green flowered through valleys and up into the hills

white stone houses with green roof tops appeared
windmills retaining walls aqueducts

the slaves built themselves boxes of limestone   5
with black wooden shutters

pumpkin became divine
eke eat edge yourself slowly towards the borders of freedom and love-vine

in the grey cage of razor blade heat they sometimes glimpsed the sea
but the sky was too hot to be heaven   10

only at evening: the thin shave ice of the moon
the leaves of wind tinkling like glass in the cool of the seven stars

sun have you forgotten your brother
sun have you forgotten my mother
sun who gave birth to shango my uncle   15
   who was fixed in his place by ogoun the master of iron

sun who blows the elephant trumpets
sun whose hot nostril bellows in the bull
   testicle birth-sperm love-shout origin

sun who has clothed arethas voice in dark gospel   20
   who works on the railroad tracks
   who gave jesse owens his engine
   who blue coltranes crippled train

   remember us now in this sweat juiced jail
   in this hail of cutlass splinters of cane   25
   in this pale sail of soil

ii

but fear of the rat
   of the black
   wrack of africa

   ruins of dreamers   30
   conrad and kurtz

   rat-a-tap rat-a-tap rat-a-tap tappin

fear of the past
   not

   knowing it per-   35
   fumed or nas-

   ty: hear-
   ing about it

   only in whispers
   bound to the mast   40

   of streetcorners
   barbershop rumshop

   gossip in
   pissicle places

   after the sea-surge   45
   of young women's thighs

   combing hair
   between old women's sighs

---

16 ogoun   Ogun. See note to the previous poem.
20–23 Three notable African Americans are mentioned: Aretha Franklin (b. 1942), soul and gospel singer; Jesse Owens (1913–80), champion sprinter at the Olympic Games in Berlin in 1936; and John Coltrane (1926–67), jazz saxophonist.
31 conrad and kurtz   Kurtz, a sinister white trader, is a central figure in Joseph Conrad's novel of European incursion into Africa, *Heart of Darkness* (1902).

in the spittle of grandfather's pipe
   in his sneezes of snuff

fear of the graveyard ships
   clink coffle coffin

fear of the benin bronze
   of ifa's divination
   of maasai's mask of milk and bleeds

   running all life from the waves
   from the silver shadow of strife-
   heavy water

   turning the houses away from the landscrape
   ignoring the language of beach bus and gutter
   scavenging utters that were always our own

   like a rat like a rat like a rat-a-tap tappin

the sun is a curved glass that smokes
that bores holes in leaf and paper
that destroys archives and the parchments of industry

it is a baas eyed gaoler keeping our people back

   like a rat like a rat like a rat-a-tap tappin
   like a rat like a rat like a rat-a-tap tappin

   an we burnin babylone . . .

50

55

60

65

1982

DEREK WALCOTT

b 1930 St Lucia. He is also a dramatist. For many years he lived partly in Trinidad and partly in Boston, where he is a university teacher. His West Indian base is now St Lucia.

From Midsummer

VI

Midsummer stretches beside me with its cat's yawn.
Trees with dust on their lips, cars melting down
in its furnace. Heat staggers the drifting mongrels.
The capitol has been repainted rose, the rails
round Woodford Square the color of rusting blood.
Casa Rosada, the Argentinian mood,
croons from the balcony. Monotonous lurid bushes

5

---

53 benin   Benin in west Africa was famous from the thirteenth century for its crafts in wood, ivory and bronze.
54 ifa   Ife, a city of the Yoruba in south-west Nigeria; from the eleventh century the centre of a kingdom which influenced the culture of nearby Benin
55 maasai   Masai: an east African warrior and pastoralist people
66 baas   boss (Afrikaans)
VI   Title of an earlier version: 'Port of Spain'

brush the damp clouds with the ideograms of buzzards
over the Chinese groceries. The oven alleys stifle.
In Belmont, mournful tailors peer over old machines,   10
stitching June and July together seamlessly.
And one waits for midsummer lightning as the armed sentry
in boredom waits for the crack of a rifle.
But I feed on its dust, its ordinariness,
on the faith that fills its exiles with horror,   15
on the hills at dusk with their dusty orange lights,
even on the pilot light in the reeking harbor
that turns like a police car's. The terror
is local, at least. Like the magnolia's whorish whiff.
All night, the barks of a revolution crying wolf.   20
The moon shines like a lost button.
The yellow sodium lights on the wharf come on.
In streets, dishes clatter behind dim windows.
The night is companionable, the future as fierce as
tomorrow's sun everywhere. I can understand   25
Borges's blind love for Buenos Aires,
how a man feels the streets of a city swell in his hand.

XXV

The sun has fired my face to terra-cotta.
It carries the heat from his kiln all through the house.
But I cherish its wrinkles as much as those on blue water.
Gnats drill little holes around a saw-toothed cactus,
a furnace has curled the knives of the oleander,   5
and a branch of the logwood blurs with wild characters.
A stone house waits on the steps. Its white porch blazes.
I tell you a promise brought to me by the surf:
You shall see transparent Helen pass like a candle
flame in sunlight, weightless as woodsmoke that hazes   10
the sand with no shadow. My palms have been sliced by the twine
of the craft I have pulled at for more than forty years.
My Ionia is the smell of burnt grass, the scorched handle
of a cistern in August squeaking to rusty islands;
the lines I love have all their knots left in.   15
Through the stunned afternoon, when it's too hot to think
and the muse of this inland ocean still waits for a name,
and from the salt, dark room, the tight horizon line
catches nothing, I wait. Chairs sweat. Paper crumples the floor.
A lizard gasps on the wall. The sea glares like zinc.   20
Then, in the door light: not Nike loosening her sandal,
but a girl slapping sand from her foot, one hand on the frame.

                                                    1984

---

26 Borges   Jorge Luis Borges (1899–1986), Argentinian poet
9 The phantom image of **Helen** of Troy is summoned for the gaze of Faustus in a famous scene in Marlowe's play, *Dr Faustus* (c. 1594).
13 Ionia   the name for two areas in classical times: the islands west of Greece and a Greek settlement on the coast of Asia Minor
21 Nike   Greek goddess of victory

BRUCE DAWE

b 1930 Geelong. He lives in Toowoomba, where he taught literature in the university.

Soliloquy for One Dead

Ah, no, Joe, you never knew
the whole of it, the whistling
which is only the wind in the chimney's
smoking belly, the footsteps on the muddy
path that are always somebody else's.   5
I think of your limbs down there, softly
becoming mineral, the life of grasses,
and the old love of you thrusts the tears
up into my eyes, with the family aware
and looking everywhere else.   10
Sometimes when summer is over the land,
when the heat quickens the deaf timbers,
and birds are thick in the plums again,
my heart sickens, Joe, calling
for the water of your voice and the gone   15
agony of your nearness. I try hard
to forget, saying: If God wills,
it must be so, because of
His goodness, because—
but the grasshopper memory leaps   20
in the long thicket, knowing no ease. Ah, Joe,
you never knew the whole of it. . .

                                                        1955   1962

Drifters

One day soon he'll tell her it's time to start packing,
and the kids will yell 'Truly?' and get wildly excited for no reason,
and the brown kelpie pup will start dashing about, tripping everyone up,
and she'll go out to the vegetable-patch and pick all the green tomatoes from the
        vines,
and notice how the oldest girl is close to tears because she was happy here,   5
and how the youngest girl is beaming because she wasn't.
And the first thing she'll put on the trailer will be the bottling-set she never
                unpacked from Grovedale,
and when the loaded ute bumps down the drive past the blackberry-canes
                with their last shrivelled fruit,
she won't even ask why they're leaving this time, or where they're heading for
—she'll only remember how, when they came here,   10
she held out her hands bright with berries,
the first of the season, and said:
'Make a wish, Tom, make a wish.'

                                                        1968   1968

PETER PORTER

b 1929 Brisbane. Since 1951 he has lived in London, from 1968 as a freelance writer.

An Angel in Blythburgh Church

Shot down from its enskied formation,
This stern-faced plummet rests against the wall;
Cromwell's soldiers peppered it and now the death-
        watch beetle has it in thrall.

If you make fortunes from wool, along   5
The weeping winter foreshores of the tide,
You build big churches with clerestories
        And place angels high inside.

Their painted faces guard and guide. Now or
Tomorrow or whenever is the promise—   10
The resurrection comes: fix your eyes halfway
        Between Heaven and Diss.

The face is crudely carved, simplified by wind;
It looks straight at God and waits for orders,
Buffeted by the organ militant, and blasted   15
        By choristers and recorders.

Faith would have our eyes as wooden and as certain.
It might be worth it, to start the New Year's hymn
Allowing for death as a mere calculation,
        A depreciation, entered in.   20

Or so I fancy looking at the roof beams
Where the dangerous beetle sails. What is it
Turns an atheist's mind to prayer in almost
        Any church on a country visit?

Greed for love or certainty or forgiveness?   25
High security rising with the sea birds?
A theology of self looking for precedents?
        A chance to speak old words?

Rather, I think of a woman lying on her bed
Staring for hours up to the ceiling where   30
Nothing is projected—death the only angel
        To shield her from despair.

                                   1978

Blythburgh   a market town in Suffolk
12 Diss   a market town in Norfolk

What I Have Written I Have Written

It is the little stone of unhappiness
which I keep with me. I had it as a child
and put it in a drawer. There came
a heap of paper to put beside it,
letters, poems, a brittle dust   5
of affection, sallowed by memory.

Aphorisms came. Not evil, but
the competition of two goods
brings you to the darkened room.
I gave the stone to a woman   10
and it glowed. I set my mind
to hydraulic work, lifting words
from their swamp. In the light from the stone
her face was bloated. When she died
the stone returned to me, a present   15
from reality. The two goods
were still contending. From wading pools
the children grew to darken
gardens with their shadows. Duty
is better than love, it suffers no betrayal.   20

Beginning again, I notice
I have less breath but the joining
is more golden. There is a long way to go,
among gardens and alarms,
after-dinner sleeps peopled by toads   25
and all the cries of childhood.
Someone comes to say my name
has been removed from the Honourable
Company of Scribes. Books in the room
turn their backs on me.   30

Old age will be the stone and me together.
I have become used to its weight
in my pocket and my brain.
To move it from lining to lining
like Beckett's tramp,   35
to modulate it to the major
or throw it at the public—
all is of no avail. But I'll add
to the songs of the stone. These words
I take from my religious instruction,   40
complete responsibility—
let them be entered in the record,
What I have written I have written.

                                                        1981

What I have written I have written   Pilate's words: see John 19:22.

A.K. RAMANUJAN

1929–93 b Mysore, southern India; Tamil. From 1962 he was a university teacher in south
Asian studies in Chicago.

Love Poem for a Wife

Really what keeps us apart
at the end of years is unshared
childhood. You cannot, for instance,
meet my father. He is some years
dead. Neither can I meet yours: 5
he has lately lost his temper
and mellowed.

In the transverse midnight gossip
of cousins' reunions among
brandy fumes, cashews and the Absences   10
of grandparents, you suddenly grow
nostalgic for my past and I
envy you your village dog-ride
and the mythology

of the seven crazy aunts.   15
You begin to recognize me
as I pass from ghost to real
and back again in the albums
of family rumours, in brothers'
anecdotes of how noisily   20
father bathed,

slapping soap on his back;
find sources for a familiar
sheep-mouth look in a sepia wedding
picture of father in a turban,   25
mother standing on her bare
splayed feet, silver rings
on her second toes;

and reduce the entire career
of my recent unique self   30
to the compulsion of some high
sentence in His Smilesian diary.
And your father, gone irrevocable
in age, after changing every day
your youth's evenings,   35

he will acknowledge the wickedness
of no reminiscence: no, not
the burning end of the cigarette

---

32 Smilesian   Samuel Smiles was the author of *Self-Help* (1859), a popular book recommending
thrift. It was translated into several Indian languages.

in the balcony, pacing
to and fro as you came to the gate,   40
late, after what you thought
was an innocent

date with a nice Muslim friend
who only hinted at touches.
Only two weeks ago, in Chicago,   45
you and brother James started
one of your old drag-out fights
about where the bathroom was
in the backyard,

north or south of the well   50
next to the jackfruit tree
in your father's father's house
in Alleppey. Sister-in-law
and I were blank cut-outs
fitted to our respective   55
slots in a room

really nowhere as the two of you
got down to the floor to draw
blueprints of a house from memory
on everything, from newspapers   60
to the backs of envelopes
and road-maps of the United States
that happened

to flap in the other room
in a midnight wind: you wagered heirlooms   65
and husband's earnings on what
the Uncle in Kuwait
would say about the Bathroom
and the Well, and the dying,
by now dead,   70

tree next to it. Probably
only the Egyptians had it right:
their kings had sisters for queens
to continue the incests
of childhood into marriage.   75
Or we should do as well-meaning
hindus did,

betroth us before birth,
forestalling separate horoscopes
and mothers' first periods,   80
and wed us in the oral cradle
and carry marriage back into
the namelessness of childhoods.

                                                        1971

---

53 **Alleppey** a city in the state of Kerala, India

ADRIENNE RICH

b 1929 Baltimore. A noted writer on feminist issues, she has been a university teacher in New York, and at Stanford in California.

Aunt Jennifer's Tigers

Aunt Jennifer's tigers prance across a screen,
Bright topaz denizens of a world of green.
They do not fear the men beneath the tree;
They pace in sleek chivalric certainty.

Aunt Jennifer's fingers fluttering through her wool   5
Find even the ivory needle hard to pull.
The massive weight of Uncle's wedding band
Sits heavily upon Aunt Jennifer's hand.

When Aunt is dead, her terrified hands will lie
Still ringed with ordeals she was mastered by.   10
The tigers in the panel that she made
Will go on prancing, proud and unafraid.

                                                  1951

After Twenty Years

Two women sit at a table by a window. Light breaks
unevenly on both of them.
Their talk is a striking of sparks
which passers-by in the street observe
as a glitter in the glass of that window.   5
Two women in the prime of life.
Their babies are old enough to have babies.
Loneliness has been part of their story for twenty years,
the dark edge of the clever tongue,
the obscure underside of the imagination.   10
It is snow and thunder in the street.
While they speak the lightning flashes purple.
It is strange to be so many women,
eating and drinking at the same table,
those who bathed their children in the same basin   15
who kept their secrets from each other
walked the floors of their lives in separate rooms
and flow into history now as the woman of their time
living in the prime of life
as in a city where nothing is forbidden   20
and nothing permanent.

                                                  1973

ANNE SEXTON

1928–74 b Massachusetts. She taught writing and wrote poetry which often attends to raw personal feelings. She took her own life.

Woman with Girdle

Your midriff sags toward your knees;
your breasts lie down in air,
their nipples as uninvolved
as warm starfish.
You stand in your elastic case,   5
still not giving up the new-born
and the old-born cycle.
Moving, you roll down the garment,
down that pink snapper and hoarder,
as your belly, soft as pudding,   10
slops into the empty space;
down, over the surgeon's careful mark,
down over hips, those head cushions
and mouth cushions,
slow motion like a rolling pin,   15
over crisp hairs, that amazing field
that hides your genius from your patron;
over thighs, thick as young pigs,
over knees like saucers,
over calves, polished as leather,   20
down toward the feet.
You pause for a moment,
tying your ankles into knots.
Now you rise,
a city from the sea,   25
born long before Alexandria was,
straightway from God you have come
into your redeeming skin.

         1962

Pain for a Daughter

Blind with love, my daughter
has cried nightly for horses,
those long-necked marchers and churners
that she has mastered, any and all,
reining them in like a circus hand—   5
the excitable muscles and the ripe neck;
tending this summer, a pony and a foal.
She who is too squeamish to pull
a thorn from the dog's paw,
watched her pony blossom with distemper,   10

the underside of the jaw swelling
like an enormous grape.
Gritting her teeth with love,
she drained the boil and scoured it
with hydrogen peroxide until pus
ran like milk on the barn floor.   15

Blind with loss all winter,
in dungarees, a ski jacket and a hard hat,
she visits the neighbors' stable,
our acreage not zoned for barns;   20
they who own the flaming horses
and the swan-whipped thoroughbred
that she tugs at and cajoles,
thinking it will burn like a furnace
under her small-hipped English seat.   25

Blind with pain she limps home.
The thoroughbred has stood on her foot.
He rested there like a building.
He grew into her foot until they were one.
The marks of the horseshoe printed   30
into her flesh, the tips of her toes
ripped off like pieces of leather,
three toenails swirled like shells
and left to float in blood in her riding boot.

Blind with fear, she sits on the toilet,   35
her foot balanced over the washbasin,
her father, hydrogen peroxide in hand,
performing the rites of the cleansing.
She bites on a towel, sucked in breath,
sucked in and arched against the pain,   40
her eyes glancing off me where
I stand at the door, eyes locked
on the ceiling, eyes of a stranger,
and then she cries...
Oh my God, help me!   45
Where a child would have cried *Mama!*
Where a child would have believed *Mama!*
she bit the towel and called on God
and I saw her life stretch out...
I saw her torn in childbirth,   50
and I saw her, at that moment,
in her own death and I knew that she
knew.

1965   1966

GALWAY KINNELL

b 1927 Providence, Rhode Island. He has taught poetry and creative writing at many universities in the USA and elsewhere; currently in New York.

After Making Love We Hear Footsteps

For I can snore like a bullhorn
or play loud music
or sit up talking with any reasonably sober Irishman
and Fergus will only sink deeper
into his dreamless sleep, which goes by all in one flash,   5
but let there be that heavy breathing
or a stifled come-cry anywhere in the house
and he will wrench himself awake
and make for it on the run—as now, we lie together,
after making love, quiet, touching along the length of our bodies,   10
familiar touch of the long-married,
and he appears—in his baseball pajamas, it happens,
the neck opening so small
he has to screw them on, which one day may make him wonder
about the mental capacity of baseball players—   15
and flops down between us and hugs us and snuggles himself to sleep,
his face gleaming with satisfaction at being this very child.

In the half darkness we look at each other
and smile
and touch arms across his little, startlingly muscled body—   20
this one whom habit of memory propels to the ground of his making,
sleeper only the mortal sounds can sing awake,
this blessing love gives again into our arms.

                                        1980

The Man Splitting Wood in the Daybreak

The man splitting wood in the daybreak
looks strong, as though, if one weakened,
one could turn to him and he would help.
Gus Newland was strong. When he split wood
he struck hard, flashing the bright steel   5
through air of daybreak so fast rock maple
leapt apart—as they think marriages will
in countries about to institute divorce—
and even willow, which, though stacked
to dry a full year, on separating   10
actually weeps—totem wood, therefore,
to the married-until-death—miseried asunder
with many small lip-smacking gasp-noises.
But Gus is dead. We could turn to our fathers,
but they protect us only through the unperplexed   15
looking-back of the numerals cut into their headstones.
Or to our mothers, whose love, so devastated,
can't, even in spring, break through the hard earth.

Our spouses weaken at the same rate we do.
We have to hold our children up to lean on them.   20
Everyone who could help goes or hasn't arrived.
What about the man splitting wood in the daybreak,
who looked strong? That was years ago. That was me.

                                                        1985

Prayer

Whatever happens. Whatever
what is is is what
I want. Only that. But that.

                                                        1985

JOHN ASHBERY

b 1927 Rochester, NY. He works as an art editor and university teacher in New York.

Some Trees

These are amazing: each
Joining a neighbor, as though speech
Were a still performance.
Arranging by chance

To meet as far this morning   5
From the world as agreeing
With it, you and I
Are suddenly what the trees try

To tell us we are:
That their merely being there   10
Means something; that soon
We may touch, love, explain.

And glad not to have invented
Such comeliness, we are surrounded:
A silence already filled with noises,   15
A canvas on which emerges

A chorus of smiles, a winter morning.
Placed in a puzzling light, and moving,
Our days put on such reticence
These accents seem their own defense.   20

                                                        1956

Paradoxes and Oxymorons

This poem is concerned with language on a very plain level.
Look at it talking to you. You look out a window
Or pretend to fidget. You have it but you don't have it.
You miss it, it misses you. You miss each other.

The poem is sad because it wants to be yours, and cannot.   5
What's a plain level? It is that and other things,
Bringing a system of them into play. Play?
Well, actually, yes, but I consider play to be

A deeper outside thing, a dreamed role-pattern,
As in the division of grace these long August days   10
Without proof. Open-ended. And before you know
It gets lost in the steam and chatter of typewriters.

It has been played once more. I think you exist only
To tease me into doing it, on your level, and then you aren't there
Or have adopted a different attitude. And the poem   15
Has set me softly down beside you. The poem is you.

                                                        1981

ALLEN GINSBERG

1926–97 Newark, NJ. He made his reputation with *Howl* and *Kaddish*, which were influential
in the Beat movement and with the generation of the sixties. He lives in New York.

An Open Window on Chicago

Midwinter night,
   Clark & Halstead brushed with this week's snow
  grill lights blinking at the corner
      decades ago
Smokestack poked above roofs & watertower   5
    standing still above the blue
       lamped boulevards,
  sky blacker than th' east
   for all the steel smoke
      settled in heaven from South.   10
Downtown—like Batman's Gotham City
    battleshipped with Lights,
  towers winking under clouds,
    police cars blinking on Avenues,
      space above city misted w / fine soot   15
cars crawling past redlites down Avenue,
      exuding white wintersmoke—
Eat Eat said the sign, so I went in the Spanish Diner
The girl at the counter, whose yellow Bouffant roots
    grew black over her pinch'd face,   20
    spooned her coffee with knuckles
      puncture-marked,
  whose midnight wrists had needletracks,
    scars inside her arms:
   'Wanna go get a Hotel Room with me?'   25
    The Heroin Whore
thirty years ago come haunting Chicago's midnite streets,
  me come here so late with my beard!

Corner Grill-lights blink, police car turned
      & took away its load of bum to jail,   30
         black uniforms patrolling streets
   where suffering
         lifts a hand palsied by Parkinson's Disease
            to beg a cigarette.

The psychiatrist came visiting this Hotel 12th floor—   35
         Where does the Anger come from?
         Outside! Radio messages, images on Television,
                     Electric Networks spread
         fear of murder on the streets—
            'Communications Media'   40
inflict the Vietnam War & its anxiety on every private skin
         in hotel room or bus—
Sitting, meditating quietly on Great Space outside—
Bleep Bleep dit dat dit radio on, Television
                murmuring,   45
     bombshells crash on flesh
       his flesh my flesh all the same.—
The Dakini in the hotel room turns in her sleep
           while War news flashes thru Aether—
     Shouts at streetcorners as bums   50
          crawl in the metal policevan.
And there's a tiny church in middle Chicago
         with its black spike to the black air
And there's the new Utensil Towers round on horizon.
And there's red glow of Central Neon   55
         on hushed building walls at 4 A.M.,
And there's proud Lights & Towers of Man's Central City
      looking pathetic at 4 A.M., traveler passing through,
      staring outa hotel window under Heaven—
Is this tiny city the best we can do?   60
     These tiny reptilian towers
       so proud of their Executives
   they haveta build a big sign in middle downtown
              to Advertise
     old Connor's Insurance sign fading on brick   65
                  building side—
     Snow on deserted roofs & parkinglots—
Hog Butcher to the World!?
      Taxi-Harmonious Modernity grown rusty-old—
The prettiness of Existence! To sit at the window   70
      & moan over Chicago's stone & brick
        lifting itself vertical tenderly,
           hanging from the sky.

Elbow on windowsill,
     I lean and muse, taller than any building here   75

---

48 Dakini Buddhist sky goddess, a bringer of knowledge

Steam from my head
    wafting into the smog
      Elevators running up & down my leg
Couples copulating in hotelroom beds in my belly
          & bearing children in my heart,   80
    Eyes shining like warning-tower Lights,
      Hair hanging down like a black cloud—
Close your eyes on Chicago and be God,
    all Chicago is, is what you see—
That row of lights Finance Building   85
    sleeping on its bottom floors,
    Watchman stirring
paper coffee cups by bronzed glass doors—
and under the bridge, brown water
    floats great turds of ice beside buildings' feet   90
    in windy metropolis
        waiting for a Bomb.

8 January 1967   1972

FRANK O'HARA

1926–66 b Baltimore. He settled in New York in 1951, where he became a curator at the Museum of Modern Art.

Why I Am Not a Painter

I am not a painter, I am a poet.
Why? I think I would rather be
a painter, but I am not. Well,

for instance, Mike Goldberg
is starting a painting. I drop in.   5
'Sit down and have a drink' he
says. I drink; we drink. I look
up. 'You have SARDINES in it.'
'Yes, it needed something there.'
'Oh.' I go and the days go by   10
and I drop in again. The painting
is going on, and I go, and the days
go by. I drop in. The painting is
finished. 'Where's SARDINES?'
All that's left is just   15
letters, 'It was too much,' Mike says.

But me? One day I am thinking of
a color: orange. I write a line
about orange. Pretty soon it is a
whole page of words, not lines.   20
Then another page. There should be
so much more, not of orange, of
words, of how terrible orange is

and life. Days go by. It is even in
prose, I am a real poet. My poem   25
is finished and I haven't mentioned
orange yet. It's twelve poems, I call
it ORANGES. And one day in a gallery
I see Mike's painting, called SARDINES.

1956   1960

The Day Lady Died

It is 12:20 in New York a Friday
three days after Bastille day, yes
it is 1959 and I go get a shoeshine
because I will get off the 4:19 in Easthampton
at 7:15 and then go straight to dinner   5
and I don't know the people who will feed me

I walk up the muggy street beginning to sun
and have a hamburger and a malted and buy
an ugly NEW WORLD WRITING to see what the poets
in Ghana are doing these days
                              I go on to the bank
and Miss Stillwagon (first name Linda I once heard)   10
doesn't even look up my balance for once in her life
and in the GOLDEN GRIFFIN I get a little Verlaine
for Patsy with drawings by Bonnard although I do
think of Hesiod, trans. Richmond Lattimore or
Brendan Behan's new play or *Le Balcon* or *Les Nègres*   15
of Genet, but I don't, I stick with Verlaine
after practically going to sleep with quandariness

And for Mike I just stroll into the PARK LANE
Liquor Store and ask for a bottle of Strega and
then I go back where I came from to 6th Avenue   20
and the tobacconist in the Ziegfeld Theatre and
casually ask for a carton of Gauloises and a carton
of Picayunes, and a NEW YORK POST with her face on it

And I am sweating a lot by now and thinking of
leaning on the john door in the 5 SPOT   25
while she whispered a song along the keyboard
to Mal Waldron and everyone and I stopped breathing

17 July 1959   1960

Lady   Billie Holiday (1915–59) blues singer, known as Lady Day
28 Mal Waldron   Billie Holiday's pianist

JAMES K. BAXTER

1926–72 b Dunedin. He lived there and in Wellington until 1969, when he made his home at an alternative community at Jerusalem on the Wanganui river.

Lament for Barney Flanagan

Licensee of the Hesperus Hotel

Flanagan got up on a Saturday morning,
Pulled on his pants while the coffee was warming;
He didn't remember the doctor's warning,
   'Your heart's too big, Mr Flanagan.'

Barney Flanagan, sprung like a frog   5
From a wet root in an Irish bog—
May his soul escape from the tooth of the dog!
    God have mercy on Flanagan.

Barney Flanagan R.I.P.
Rode to his grave on Hennessy's   10
Like a bottle-cork boat in the Irish Sea.
    The bell-boy rings for Flanagan.

Barney Flanagan, ripe for a coffin,
Eighteen stone and brandy-rotten,
Patted the housemaid's velvet bottom—   15
    'Oh, is it you, Mr Flanagan?'

The sky was bright as a new milk token.
Bill the Bookie and Shellshock Hogan
Waited outside for the pub to open—
    'Good day, Mr Flanagan.'   20

At noon he was drinking in the lounge bar corner
With a sergeant of police and a racehorse owner
When the Angel of Death looked over his shoulder—
    'Could you spare a moment, Flanagan?'

Oh the deck was cut; the bets were laid;   25
But the very last card that Barney played
Was the Deadman's Trump, the bullet of Spades—
    'Would you like more air, Mr Flanagan?'

The priest came running but the priest came late
For Barney was banging at the Pearly Gate.   30
St Peter said, 'Quiet! You'll have to wait
    For a hundred masses, Flanagan.'

The regular boys and the loud accountants
Left their nips and their seven-ounces
As chickens fly when the buzzard pounces—   35
    'Have you heard about old Flanagan?'

Cold in the parlour Flanagan lay
Like a bride at the end of her marriage day.
The Waterside Workers' Band will play
   A brass goodbye to Flanagan.   40

While publicans drink their profits still,
While lawyers flock to be in at the kill,
While Aussie barmen milk the till
   We will remember Flanagan.

For Barney had a send-off and no mistake.   45
He died like a man for his country's sake;
And the Governor-General came to his wake.
   Drink again to Flanagan!

Despise not, O Lord, the work of Thine own hands
And let light perpetual shine upon him.   50

                                1954

The Beach House

The wind outside this beach house
Shaking the veranda rail
Has the weight of the sky behind its blows,
A violence stronger than the fable

Of life and art. Sitting alone   5
Late at the plywood table,
I have become a salt-scoured bone
Tumbling in the drifted rubble,

And you, my love, sleep under quilts within
The square bunk-room. When I was young   10
(Hot words and brandy on my tongue)
Only the grip of breast, mouth, loin,

Could ward off the incubus
Of night's rage. Now I let
The waters grind me, knowing well that the sweet   15
Daybreak behind your eyes

Will not be struck dead by any wind,
And we will walk on the shore
A day older, while the yoked waves thunder,
As if the storm were a dream. Sleep sound.   20

          1963–64   1966

Tomcat

This tomcat cuts across the
zones of the respectable
through fences, walls, following
other routes, his own. I see
the sad whiskered skull-mouth fall   5
wide, complainingly, asking

to be picked up and fed, when
I thump up the steps through bush
at 4 p.m. He has no
dignity, thank God! has grown   10
older, scruffier, the ash-
black coat sporting one or two

flowers like round stars, badges
of bouts and fights. The snake head
is seamed on top with rough scars: 15
old Samurai! He lodges
in cellars, and the tight furred
scrotum drives him into wars

as if mad, yet tumbling on
the rug looks female, Turkish-   20
trousered. His bagpipe shriek at
sluggish dawn dragged me out in
pyjamas to comb the bush
(he being under the vet

for septic bites): the old fool   25
stood, body hard as a board,
heart thudding, hair on end, at
the house corner, terrible,
yelling at something. They said,
'Get him doctored.' I think not.   30

1966

The Ikons

Hard, heavy, slow, dark,
Or so I find them, the hands of Te Whaea

Teaching me to die. Some lightness will come later
When the heart has lost its unjust hope

For special treatment. Today I go with a bucket   5
Over the paddocks of young grass,

So delicate like fronds of maidenhair,
Looking for mushrooms. I find twelve of them,

Most of them little, and some eaten by maggots,
But they'll do to add to the soup. It's a long time now   10

Since the great ikons fell down,
God, Mary, home, sex, poetry,

Whatever one uses as a bridge
To cross the river that only has one beach,

And even one's name is a way of saying—   15
'This gap inside a coat'—the darkness I call God,

---

2 **Te Whaea** Mother of God, or Source (Maori)

The darkness I call Te Whaea, how can they translate
The blue calm evening sky that a plane tunnels through

Like a little wasp, or the bucket in my hand,
Into something else? I go on looking   20

For mushrooms in the field, and the fist of longing
Punches my heart, until it is too dark to see.

                                                    1971

FRANCIS WEBB

1925–73 b Adelaide. He lived and worked variously in Australia, Canada and England.
Much of his later life was spent in psychiatric hospitals.

Five Days Old

(For Christopher John)

Christmas is in the air.
You are given into my hands
Out of quietest, loneliest lands.
My trembling is all my prayer.
To blown straw was given   5
All the fullness of Heaven.

The tiny, not the immense,
Will teach our groping eyes.
So the absorbed skies
Bleed stars of innocence.   10
So cloud-voice in war and trouble
Is at last Christ in the stable.

Now wonderingly engrossed
In your fearless delicacies,
I am launched upon sacred seas,   15
Humbly and utterly lost
In the mystery of creation,
Bells, bells of ocean.

Too pure for my tongue to praise,
That sober, exquisite yawn   20
Or the gradual, generous dawn
At an eyelid, maker of days:
To shrive my thought for perfection
I must breathe old tempests of action

For the snowflake and face of love,   25
Windfall and word of truth,
Honour close to death.
O eternal truthfulness, Dove,
Tell me what I hold—
Myrrh? Frankincense? Gold?   30

If this is man, then the danger
And fear are as lights of the inn,
Faint and remote as sin
Out here by the manger.
In the sleeping, weeping weather   35
We shall all kneel down together.

                                                                1961

The Old Women

From social ellipses, from actual weight and mass
They are disembarking, from age and weight and sex,
Floating among us this Sunday afternoon,
Ugly, vague, tiny as the vagrant island of gas
Embracing, nosing certain unthinkable wrecks,   5
Sunken faces like the face of the cretin moon.
Son, husband, lover, have spun out of orbit; this place
Holds the fugitive vessel to be kissed; and the rest is space.

They wait in the visitors' room: archaic clothing,
Reading-glass, patois of tin, rigmarole hair.   10
Men like meteorites enter their atmosphere:
The bombast, the wake of fire, the joy, the nothing,
Known strata of repartee unveiled with care,
Ice Age of the cherished calculated fear.
Gravity bends to an earlier law in this place: 15
Comes a lifting of heads among grazing herds of space.

The grazing herds are all for a foundering
Old planet borne in the omnibus of the sun
Patchy and coughing in all its wheels and wild
About the roof. They watch her blundering   20
While gravity pauses, down to clipped hedges, mown
Grasses, ferrying pastries for her child.
So this is earth, the worn stockings in this place.
They are chewing and swishing, the startled herds of space.

They have missed her absurd mimesis of cosmic war;   25
Her rain of trivial shapely missiles; the pimple
Of the megaton explosion upon her brow;
Her deaths by the spadeful; her dancing orator.
Missed the man punchdrunk, grappling with a simple
Colour or stone or song that might disavow   30
His midget mother tumbling in metre, displace
The ancient entente between earth and space and space.

Giggling, squinting, with laundry, confectioneries,
Old women bear fodder for the universe, add their spark
To a train of time that blows open the infinite.   35
It is blackness about them discloses our galaxies.
Look on these faces: now look out at the dark:
It was always and must be always the stuff of light.
The decrepit persistent folly within this place
Will sow with itself the last paddock of space.   40

                                                                1964

DENNIS BRUTUS

b 1924 Salisbury, Southern Rhodesia (now Zimbabwe), of mixed race. He taught in schools in South Africa for 14 years. His prominent anti-apartheid activities led to a gaol sentence, and then to exile in the late 1960s. He settled in the USA, where he taught literature and African studies at Northwestern and Pittsburgh universities.

From Letters to Martha

1

After the sentence
mingled feelings:
sick relief,   *loins*
the load of the approaching days
apprehension —   5
the hints of brutality
have a depth of personal meaning;

exultation —
the sense of challenge,
of confrontation,   10
vague heroism
mixed with self-pity
and tempered by the knowledge of those
who endure much more
and endure . . .   15

2

One learns quite soon
that nails and screws
and other sizeable bits of metal
must be handed in;

and seeing them shaped and sharpened   20
one is chilled, appalled
to see how vicious it can be
—this simple, useful bit of steel:

and when these knives suddenly flash
—produced perhaps from some disciplined anus—   25
one grasps at once the steel-bright horror
in the morning air
and how soft and vulnerable is naked flesh.

3

Suddenly one is tangled
in a mesh of possibilities: 30
notions cobweb around your head,
tendrils sprout from your guts in a hundred directions:
why did this man stab this man for that man?

Letters to Martha   a series of 18 poems written after release from gaol for anti-apartheid activity, in the form of private letters to the poet's sister-in-law to circumvent a ban on his writing any poetry intended for publication

what was the nature of the emotion
and how did it grow?   35
was this the reason for a warder's unmotived senseless brutality?
by what shrewdness was it instigated?

desire for prestige or lust for power?
Or can it—strange, most strange!—be love, strange love?
And from what human hunger was it born?   40

4

Particularly in a single cell,
but even in the sections
the religious sense asserts itself;

perhaps a childhood habit of nightly prayers
the accessibility of Bibles,   45
or awareness of the proximity of death:

and, of course, it is a currency—
pietistic expressions can purchase favours
and it is a way of suggesting reformation
(which can procure promotion);   50

and the resort of the weak
is to invoke divine revenge
against a rampaging injustice;

but in the grey silence of the empty afternoons
it is not uncommon   55
to find oneself talking to God.

5

In the greyness of isolated time
which shafts down into the echoing mind,
wraiths appear, and whispers of horrors
that people the labyrinth of self.   60

Coprophilism; necrophilism; fellatio;
penis-amputation;
and in this gibbering society
hooting for recognition as one's other selves
suicide, self-damnation, walks   65
if not a companionable ghost
then a familiar familiar,
a doppelgänger
not to be shaken off.

                                                        1965   1968

[A simple lust is all my woe]

A simple lust is all my woe:
the thin thread of agony
that runs through the reins

after the flesh is overspent
in over-taxing acts of love: 5

only I speak the others' woe:
those congealed in concrete
or rotting in rusted ghetto-shacks;
only I speak their wordless woe,
their unarticulated simple lust.   10

1971   1973

NISSIM EZEKIEL

b 1924 Bombay, into a Jewish Indian family. He taught literature there in the university.

Background, Casually

1

A poet-rascal-clown was born,
The frightened child who would not eat
Or sleep, a boy of meagre bone.
He never learnt to fly a kite,
His borrowed top refused to spin.   5

I went to Roman Catholic school,
A mugging Jew among the wolves.   *swotting*
They told me I had killed the Christ,
That year I won the scripture prize.
A Muslim sportsman boxed my ears.   10

I grew in terror of the strong
But undernourished Hindu lads,
Their prepositions always wrong,
Repelled me by passivity.
One noisy day I used a knife.   15

At home on Friday nights the prayers
Were said. My morals had declined.
I heard of Yoga and of Zen.
Could I, perhaps, be rabbi-saint?
The more I searched, the less I found.   20

Twenty-two: time to go abroad.
First, the decision, then a friend
To pay the fare. Philosophy,
Poverty and Poetry, three
Companions shared my basement room.   25

2

The London seasons passed me by.
I lay in bed two years alone,
And then a Woman came to tell
My willing ears I was the Son
Of Man. I knew that I had failed   30

In everything, a bitter thought.
So, in an English cargo-ship
Taking French guns and mortar shells
To Indo-China, scrubbed the decks,
And learned to laugh again at home.   35

How to feel it home, was the point.
Some reading had been done, but what
Had I observed, except my own
Exasperation? All Hindus are
Like that, my father used to say,   40

When someone talked too loudly, or
Knocked at the door like the Devil.
They hawked and spat. They sprawled around.
I prepared for the worst. Married,
Changed jobs, and saw myself a fool.   45

The song of my experience sung,
I knew that all was yet to sing.
My ancestors, among the castes,
Were aliens crushing seed for bread
(The hooded bullock made his rounds).   50

3

One among them fought and taught,
A Major bearing British arms.
He told my father sad stories
Of the Boer War. I dreamed that
Fierce men had bound my feet and hands.   55

The later dreams were all of words.
I did not know that words betray
But let the poems come, and lost
That grip on things the worldly prize.
I would not suffer that again.   60

I look about me now, and try
To formulate a plainer view:
The wise survive and serve—to play
The fool, to cash in on
The inner and the outer storms.   65

The Indian landscape sears my eyes.
I have become a part of it
To be observed by foreigners.
They say that I am singular,
Their letters overstate the case.   70

I have made my commitments now.
This is one: to stay where I am,
As others choose to give themselves
In some remote and backward place.
My backward place is where I am.   75

1965 1976

HONE TUWHARE

b 1922 Kaikohe, north of Auckland; Maori. He worked as a boilermaker, turning to
professional writing in his forties.

Rain

I can hear you
making small holes
in the silence
rain

If I were deaf   5
the pores of my skin
would open to you
and shut

And I
should know you   10
by the lick of you
if I were blind

the something
special smell of you
when the sun cakes   15
the ground

the steady
drum-roll sound
you make
when the wind drops   20

But if I
should not hear
smell or feel or see
you

you would still   25
define me
disperse me
wash over me
rain

                                                            1970

Who Tests Today?

Something stirs in the night
A cat? A fish? A rat?
How strange. Am I dreaming?
Rain-pimples on glass: are they real?
Is the door unhinged?   5

It is not a cat. It is not a fish
Neither rat door-bang nor trickle
of rain on the windows

It is the void: the stillness in the void
emptied of all sound. There is no human cry   10
glad or sad: cat-spit fish-burp rat-squeal

The door you see has quite effaced itself
and is at one with the molten glass
and hinge
The houses are as powder sweet smelling   15
talcum-dust: there is nothing

And the stillness? Ah yes
The stillness may I say is Absolute
The Ascension is complete: and the people
long gone to Christ knows where   20
with a whopping great hallelujah shout: this

is no dream
Something stirs in the night
A cat-fish-rat? A door slammed shut?
And the rain? What of the rain?   25

It is silent. It is insidious
It falls: there is no comment

1982

PHILIP LARKIN

1922–85 b Coventry. He worked as a senior librarian in the university at Hull in Yorkshire.

Going

There is an evening coming in
Across the fields, one never seen before,
That lights no lamps.

Silken it seems at a distance, yet
When it is drawn up over the knees and breast   5
It brings no comfort.

Where has the tree gone, that locked
Earth to the sky? What is under my hands,
That I cannot feel?

What loads my hands down?   10

1946 1955

Lines on a Young Lady's Photograph Album

At last you yielded up the album, which,
Once open, sent me distracted. All your ages
Matt and glossy on the thick black pages!
Too much confectionery, too rich:
I choke on such nutritious images.   5

My swivel eye hungers from pose to pose—
In pigtails, clutching a reluctant cat;
Or furred yourself, a sweet girl-graduate;
Or lifting a heavy-headed rose
Beneath a trellis, or in a trilby hat   10

(Faintly disturbing, that, in several ways)—
From every side you strike at my control,
Not least through these disquieting chaps who loll
At ease about your earlier days:
Not quite your class, I'd say, dear, on the whole.   15

But o, photography! as no art is,
Faithful and disappointing! that records
Dull days as dull, and hold-it smiles as frauds,
And will not censor blemishes
Like washing-lines, and Hall's-Distemper boards,   20

But shows the cat as disinclined, and shades
A chin as doubled when it is, what grace
Your candour thus confers upon her face!
How overwhelmingly persuades
That this is a real girl in a real place,   25

In every sense empirically true!
Or is it just *the past?* Those flowers, that gate,
These misty parks and motors, lacerate
Simply by being over; you
Contract my heart by looking out of date.   30

Yes, true; but in the end, surely, we cry
Not only at exclusion, but because
It leaves us free to cry. We know *what was*
Won't call on us to justify
Our grief, however hard we yowl across   35

The gap from eye to page. So I am left
To mourn (without a chance of consequence)
You, balanced on a bike against a fence;
To wonder if you'd spot the theft
Of this one of you bathing; to condense,   40

In short, a past that no one now can share,
No matter whose your future; calm and dry,
It holds you like a heaven, and you lie
Unvariably lovely there,
Smaller and clearer as the years go by.   45

                                        1953   1955

The Whitsun Weddings

That Whitsun, I was late getting away: *Whit Sunday*
   Not till about
One-twenty on the sunlit Saturday
Did my three-quarters-empty train pull out,
All windows down, all cushions hot, all sense   5
Of being in a hurry gone. We ran
Behind the backs of houses, crossed a street
Of blinding windscreens, smelt the fish-dock; thence
The river's level drifting breadth began,
Where sky and Lincolnshire and water meet.   10

All afternoon, through the tall heat that slept
   For miles inland,
A slow and stopping curve southwards we kept.
Wide farms went by, short-shadowed cattle, and
Canals with floatings of industrial froth;   15
A hothouse flashed uniquely: hedges dipped
And rose: and now and then a smell of grass
Displaced the reek of buttoned carriage-cloth
Until the next town, new and nondescript,
Approached with acres of dismantled cars.   20

At first, I didn't notice what a noise
   The weddings made
Each station that we stopped at: sun destroys
The interest of what's happening in the shade,
And down the long cool platforms whoops and skirls   25
I took for porters larking with the mails,
And went on reading. Once we started, though,
We passed them, grinning and pomaded, girls
In parodies of fashion, heels and veils,
All posed irresolutely, watching us go,   30

As if out on the end of an event
   Waving goodbye
To something that survived it. Struck, I leant
More promptly out next time, more curiously,
And saw it all again in different terms: 35
The fathers with broad belts under their suits
And seamy foreheads; mothers loud and fat;
An uncle shouting smut; and then the perms,
The nylon gloves and jewellery-substitutes,
The lemons, mauves, and olive-ochres that   40

Marked off the girls unreally from the rest.
   Yes, from cafés
And banquet-halls up yards, and bunting-dressed
Coach-party annexes, the wedding-days
Were coming to an end. All down the line   45
Fresh couples climbed aboard: the rest stood round;
The last confetti and advice were thrown,
And, as we moved, each face seemed to define

Just what it saw departing: children frowned
At something dull; fathers had never known   50

Success so huge and wholly farcical;
    The women shared
The secret like a happy funeral;
While girls, gripping their handbags tighter, stared
At a religious wounding. Free at last,   55
And loaded with the sum of all they saw,
We hurried towards London, shuffling gouts of steam.
Now fields were building-plots, and poplars cast
Long shadows over major roads, and for
Some fifty minutes, that in time would seem   60

Just long enough to settle hats and say
    I nearly died,
A dozen marriages got under way.
They watched the landscape, sitting side by side
—An Odeon went past, a cooling tower,   65
And someone running up to bowl—and none
Thought of the others they would never meet
Or how their lives would all contain this hour.
I thought of London spread out in the sun,
Its postal districts packed like squares of wheat: 70

There we were aimed. And as we raced across
    Bright knots of rail
Past standing Pullmans, walls of blackened moss
Came close, and it was nearly done, this frail
Travelling coincidence; and what it held   75
Stood ready to be loosed with all the power
That being changed can give. We slowed again,
And as the tightened brakes took hold, there swelled
A sense of falling, like an arrow-shower
Sent out of sight, somewhere becoming rain.   80

                                                1958 1964

The Explosion

On the day of the explosion
Shadows pointed towards the pithead:
In the sun the slagheap slept.

Down the lane came men in pitboots
Coughing oath-edged talk and pipe-smoke,   5
Shouldering off the freshened silence.

One chased after rabbits; lost them;
Came back with a nest of lark's eggs;
Showed them; lodged them in the grasses.

So they passed in beards and moleskins,   10
Fathers, brothers, nicknames, laughter,
Through the tall gates standing open.

At noon, there came a tremor; cows
Stopped chewing for a second; sun,
Scarfed as in a heat-haze, dimmed.

The dead go on before us, they
Are sitting in God's house in comfort,
We shall see them face to face—

Plain as lettering in the chapels
It was said, and for a second
Wives saw men of the explosion

Larger than in life they managed—
Gold as on a coin, or walking
Somehow from the sun towards them,

One showing the eggs unbroken.

15

20

25

1970 1974

Aubade

I work all day, and get half-drunk at night.
Waking at four to soundless dark, I stare.
In time the curtain-edges will grow light.
Till then I see what's really always there:
Unresting death, a whole day nearer now,
Making all thought impossible but how
And where and when I shall myself die.
Arid interrogation: yet the dread
Of dying, and being dead,
Flashes afresh to hold and horrify.

5

10

The mind blanks at the glare. Not in remorse
—The good not done, the love not given, time
Torn off unused—nor wretchedly because
An only life can take so long to climb
Clear of its wrong beginnings, and may never;
But at the total emptiness for ever,
The sure extinction that we travel to
And shall be lost in always. Not to be here,
Not to be anywhere,
And soon; nothing more terrible, nothing more true.

15

20

This is a special way of being afraid
No trick dispels. Religion used to try,
That vast moth-eaten musical brocade
Created to pretend we never die,
And specious stuff that says *No rational being*
Can fear a thing it will not feel, not seeing
That this is what we fear—no sight, no sound,
No touch or taste or smell, nothing to think with,
Nothing to love or link with,
The anaesthetic from which none come round.

25

30

Aubade   dawn poem, usually joyful (French)

And so it stays just on the edge of vision,
A small unfocused blur, a standing chill
That slows each impulse down to indecision.
Most things may never happen: this one will,
And realisation of it rages out
In furnace-fear when we are caught without   35
People or drink. Courage is no good:
It means not scaring others. Being brave
Lets no one off the grave.
Death is no different whined at than withstood.   40

Slowly light strengthens, and the room takes shape.
It stands plain as a wardrobe, what we know,
Have always known, know that we can't escape,
Yet can't accept. One side will have to go.
Meanwhile telephones crouch, getting ready to ring   45
In locked-up offices, and all the uncaring
Intricate rented world begins to rouse.
The sky is white as clay, with no sun.
Work has to be done.
Postmen like doctors go from house to house.   50

1977 1988

RICHARD WILBUR

b 1921 New York. He was a teacher of literature from 1950 to 1986 at several universities. He is known also as a librettist and translater of drama.

'A World without Objects Is a Sensible Emptiness'

    The tall camels of the spirit
  Steer for their deserts, passing the last groves loud
With the sawmill shrill of the locust, to the whole honey of the arid
    Sun. They are slow, proud,

    And move with a stilted stride   5
  To the land of sheer horizon, hunting Traherne's
Sensible emptiness, there where the brain's lantern-slide
    Revels in vast returns.

    O connoisseurs of thirst,
  Beasts of my soul who long to learn to drink
Of pure mirage, those prosperous islands are accurst   10
    That shimmer on the brink

    Of absence; auras, lustres,
  And all shinings need to be shaped and borne.
Think of those painted saints, capped by the early masters 15
    With bright, jauntily-worn

'A World without Objects' See Thomas Traherne (1636–74), *The Second Century*, 65: 'The Whole World ministers to you as the Theatre of your Lov.... Life without Objects is Sensible Emptiness. Objects without Lov are the Delusion of Life.'

Aureate plates, or even
Merry-go-round rings. Turn, O turn
From the fine sleights of the sand, from the long empty oven
Where flames in flamings burn   20

Back to the trees arrayed
In bursts of glare, to the halo-dialing run
Of the country creeks, and the hills' bracken tiaras made
Gold in the sunken sun,

Wisely watch for the sight   25
Of the supernova burgeoning over the barn,
Lampshine blurred in the steam of beasts, the spirit's right
Oasis, light incarnate.

                                                                    1950

Shame

It is a cramped little state with no foreign policy,
Save to be thought inoffensive. The grammar of the language
Has never been fathomed, owing to the national habit
Of allowing each sentence to trail off in confusion.
Those who have visited Scusi, the capital city,   5
Report that the railway-route from Schuldig passes
Through country best described as unrelieved.
Sheep are the national product. The faint inscription
Over the city gates may perhaps be rendered,
'I'm afraid you won't find much of interest here.'   10
Census-reports which give the population
As zero are, of course, not to be trusted,
Save as reflecting the natives' flustered insistence
That they do not count, as well as their modest horror
Of letting one's sex be known in so many words.   15
The uniform grey of the nondescript buildings, the absence
Of churches or comfort-stations, have given observers
An odd impression of ostentatious meanness,
And it must be said of the citizens (muttering by
In their ratty sheepskins, shying at cracks in the sidewalk)   20
That they lack the peace of mind of the truly humble.
The tenor of life is careful, even in the stiff
Unsmiling carelessness of the border-guards
And *douaniers*, who admit, whenever they can,
Not merely the usual carloads of deodorant   25
But gypsies, g-strings, hasheesh, and contraband pigments.
Their complete negligence is reserved, however,
For the hoped-for invasion, at which time the happy people
(Sniggering, ruddily naked, and shamelessly drunk)
Will stun the foe by their overwhelming submission,   30
Corrupt the generals, infiltrate the staff,
Usurp the throne, proclaim themselves to be sun-gods,
And bring about the collapse of the whole empire.

                                                                    1961

EDWIN MORGAN

b 1920 Glasgow, where he was a teacher of literature at the university.

Opening the Cage:

14 variations on 14 words
I have nothing to say and I am saying it and that is poetry.
John Cage

I have to say poetry and is that nothing and am I saying it
I am and I have poetry to say and is that nothing saying it
I am nothing and I have poetry to say and that is saying it
I that am saying poetry have nothing and it is I and to say
And I say that I am to have poetry and saying it is nothing   5
I am poetry and nothing and saying it is to say that I have
To have nothing is poetry and I am saying that and I say it
Poetry is saying I have nothing and I am to say that and it
Saying nothing I am poetry and I have to say that and it is
It is and I am and I have poetry saying say that to nothing   10
It is saying poetry to nothing and I say I have and am that
Poetry is saying I have it and I am nothing and to say that
And that nothing is poetry I am saying and I have to say it
Saying poetry is nothing and to that I say I am and have it

1968

GWEN HARWOOD

1920–95 Brisbane. She has lived in Hobart since 1945. She is also a librettist and musician.

Suburban Sonnet

She practises a fugue, though it can matter
to no one now if she plays well or not.
Beside her on the floor two children chatter,
then scream and fight. She hushes them. A pot
boils over. As she rushes to the stove   5
too late, a wave of nausea overpowers
subject and counter-subject. Zest and love
drain out with soapy water as she scours
the crusted milk. Her veins ache. Once she played
for Rubinstein, who yawned. The children caper   10
round a sprung mousetrap where a mouse lies dead.
When the soft corpse won't move they seem afraid.
She comforts them; and wraps it in a paper
featuring: *Tasty dishes from stale bread.*

1968

---

10 Rubinstein   Artur Rubinstein (1887–1982), Polish concert pianist

An Impromptu for Ann Jennings

Sing, memory, sing those seasons in the freezing
    suburb of Fern Tree, a rock-shaded place
with tree ferns, gullies, snowfalls and eye-pleasing
    prospects from paths along the mountain-face.

Nursing our babies by huge fires of wattle,   5
    or pushing them in prams when it was fine,
exchanging views on diet, or Aristotle,
    discussing Dr Spock or Wittgenstein,

cleaning up infants and the floors they muddied,
    bandaging, making ends and tempers meet—   10
sometimes I'd mind your children while you studied,
    or you'd take mine when I felt near defeat;

keeping our balance somehow through the squalling
    disorder, or with anguish running wild
when sickness, a sick joke from some appalling   15
    orifice of the nightwatch, touched a child;

think of it, woman: each of us gave birth to
    four children, our new lords whose beautiful
tyrannic kingdom might restore the earth to
    that fullness we thought lost beyond recall   20

when, in the midst of life, we could not name it,
    when spirit cried in darkness, '*I will have. . .*'
but what? have what? There was no word to frame it,
    though spirit beat at flesh as in a grave

from which it could not rise. But we have risen.   25
    Caesar's we were, and wild, though we seemed tame.
Now we move where we will. Age is no prison
    to hinder those whose joy has found its name.

We are our own. All Caesar's debts are rendered
    in full to Caesar. Time has given again   30
a hundredfold those lives that we surrendered,
    the love, the fruitfulness; but not the pain.

Before the last great fires we two went climbing
    like gods or blessed spirits in summer light
with the quiet pulse of mountain water chiming   35
    as if twenty years were one long dreaming night,

above the leafy dazzle of the streams
    to fractured rock, where water had its birth,
and stood in silence, at the roots of dreams,
    content to know: our children walk the earth.   40

                                           1975

---

8 Wittgenstein Ludwig Wittgenstein (1889–1951), Austrian-born philosopher
29–30 See Mark, 12:17: 'Render to Caesar the things that are Caesar's, and to God the things that are
God's'.

The Sea Anemones

Grey mountains, sea and sky. Even the misty
seawind is grey. I walk on lichened rock
in a kind of late assessment, call it peace.
Then the anemones, scarlet, gouts of blood.
There is a word I need, and earth was speaking.   5
I cannot hear. These seaflowers are too bright.
Kneeling on rock, I touch them through cold water.
My fingers meet some hungering gentleness.
A newborn child's lips moved so at my breast.
I woke, once, with my palm across your mouth.   10
      The word is: *ever*. Why add salt to salt?
      Blood drop by drop among the rocks they shine.
      Anemos, wind. The spirit, where it will.
Not flowers, no, animals that must eat or die.

                                                          1981

From The Sharpness of Death

Nasturtiums

Purest of colours, how they shone
while we talked in your studio.
Light like a noble visitor
stayed with us briefly and moved on.
A schoolgirl bringing flowers, an artist   5
accepting colour and crazy love,
we stand among the plaster mouldings
of figures from an earlier time.
How would you ever know me now
if I came to your grave and called you,   10
unless I brought those flowers, those colours,
that ray of light descending through
the room's eccentric fenestration?
Seed of the seed of countless seasons
blossoms to hold the light that's gone.   15

Death, I will tell you now:
my love and I stood still
in the roofless chapel. My
body was full of him, my
tongue sang with his juices, I   5
grew ripe in his blond light.
If I fall from that time,
then set your teeth in me.

                                                          1981

---

13 **Anemos**   wind (Greek: anemone means 'daughter of the wind').   **The spirit** See John 3:8
(Revised Standard Version): 'The wind blows where it wills, and you hear the sound of it, but you
do not know whence it comes or whither it goes; so it is with every one who is born of the Spirit'. In
Latin, 'spiritus' can denote spirit, wind, or breath. See also John 3:5.
The Sharpness of Death   four poems on a theme, of which 'Nasturtiums' and the untitled 'Death,
I will tell you now', are the final two.

ELMA MITCHELL

b 1919 Airdrie, Scotland. She worked in London variously in publishing, journalism and libraries until 1961 and now lives in Somerset.

Thoughts After Ruskin

Women reminded him of lilies and roses.
Me they remind rather of blood and soap,
Armed with a warm rag, assaulting noses,
Ears, neck, mouth and all the secret places:

Armed with a sharp knife, cutting up liver, 5
Holding hearts to bleed under a running tap,
Cutting and stuffing, pickling and preserving,
Scalding, blanching, broiling, pulverising,
—All the terrible chemistry of their kitchens.

Their distant husbands lean across mahogany 10
And delicately manipulate the market,
While safe at home, the tender and the gentle
Are killing tiny mice, dead snap by the neck,
Asphyxiating flies, evicting spiders,
Scrubbing, scouring aloud, disturbing cupboards, 15
Committing things to dustbins, twisting, wringing,
Wrists red and knuckles white and fingers puckered,
Pulpy, tepid. Steering screaming cleaners
Around the snags of furniture, they straighten
And haul out sheets from under the incontinent 20
And heavy old, stoop to importunate young,
Tugging, folding, tucking, zipping, buttoning,
Spooning in food, encouraging excretion,
Mopping up vomit, stabbing cloth with needles,
Contorting wool around their knitting needles, 25
Creating snug and comfy on their needles.

Their huge hands! their everywhere eyes! their voices
Raised to convey across the hullabaloo.
Their massive thighs and breasts dispensing comfort,
Their bloody passages and hairy crannies, 30
Their wombs that pocket a man upside down!

And when all's over, off with overalls,
Quickly consulting clocks, they go upstairs,
Sit and sigh a little, brushing hair,
And somehow find, in mirrors, colours, odours, 35
Their essences of lilies and of roses.

                                                    1976

At First, My Daughter

She is world without understanding.
She is made of sound.
She drinks me.

Ruskin John Ruskin (1819–1900), influential British art critic

We laugh when I lift her by the feet.
She is new as a petal.   5
Water comes out of her mouth and her little crotch.

She gives the crook of my arm
A weight of delight.
I stare in her moving mirror of untouched flesh.

Absurd, but verifiable,   10
These words — mother, daughter —
They taste of receiving and relinquishing.

She will never again be quite so novel and lovely
Nor I so astonished.
In touch, we are celebrating   15

The first and last moments
Of being together and separate
Indissolute — till we are split

By time, and growth, and man,
The things I made her with.   20

                                                              1979

AL PURDY

---

b 1918 Ontario. Since 1960 he has lived at Roblin Lake in rural Ontario.

Old Alex

"85 years old, that miserable alcoholic
old bastard is never gonna die," the man said
where he got bed and board. But he did.
I'll say this for Alex's immortality tho:
if they dig him up in a thousand years,   5
and push a spigot into his belly why
his fierce cackle'll drive a nail in silence,
his laugh split cordwood and trees kowtow
like green butlers, the staggering world
get drunk and sober men run scared.   10

So you say: was I fond of him?
No – not exactly anyhow. Once
he told his sons and daughters to bugger off,
and then vomited on their memory. It'd be
like liking toadstools or a gun pointing at you –   15
He sat home three weeks drinking whiskey,
singing harsh songs and quoting verse and chapter
from the Bible: his mean and privileged piety
dying slowly: they rolled him onto a stretcher
like an old pig and prettied him with cosmetics,   20
sucked his blood out with a machine and
dumped him into the ground like garbage.

I don't mourn. Nobody does. Like mourning an ulcer.
Why commemorate disease in a poem then?
I don't know. But his hate was lovely,   25
given freely and without stint. His smallness
had the quality of making everyone else feel noble,
and thus fools. I search desperately
for good qualities, and end up crawling
inside that decaying head and wattled throat   30
to scream obscenities like papal blessings,
knowing now and again I'm at least God.
Well, who remembers a small purple and yellow bruise long?
But when he was here he was a sunset!

                                            1965

The Road to Newfoundland

My foot has pushed a fire ahead of me
for a thousand miles
my arms' response to hills and stones
has stated parallel green curves
deep in my unknown country   5
the clatter of gravel on fenders registers
on a ghostly player piano
inside my head with harsh fraying music
I'm lost to reality
but turn the steering wheel a quarter   10
inch to avoid a bug on the road
A long time's way here since stone
age man carried the fire-germ
in a moss-lined basket
from camp to camp   15
and prayed to it
as I shall solemnly hold Henry Ford
and all his descendants accountable
to the 24,000 mile guarantee
Well there are many miles left   20
before it expires and several
more to the next rest
stop and I kick the fire
ahead of me with one foot
even harder than before   25
hearing the sound of burning
forests muffled in steel
toppling buildings
history accelerating
racing up and down   30
hills with my flesh grown captive
of a steel extension of myself
hauling down the sun and stars
for mileposts going nowhere fast
wanting speed and more Speed   35
—Stop

at a calm lake
embossed with 2-inch waves
sit there a few minutes
without getting out of the car   40
my heart a hammering drum
among the trees' and grass roots'
August diminuendo
watching the composed landscape
the sun where it's supposed to be   45
in its deliberate dance thru space
then drive steadily north
with the captive fire
in cool evening
towards the next camp   50
                                          1968

ROBERT LOWELL

1917–77 b Boston, where he lived for periods of his life. He taught writing, but mainly was a full-time poet, who used a large canvas of family and public history.

Memories of West Street and Lepke

Only teaching on Tuesdays, book-worming
in pajamas fresh from the washer each morning,
I hog a whole house on Boston's
'hardly passionate Marlborough Street,'
where even the man   5
scavenging filth in the back alley trash cans,
has two children, a beach wagon, a helpmate,
and is a 'young Republican.'
I have a nine months' daughter,
young enough to be my granddaughter.   10
Like the sun she rises in her flame-flamingo infants' wear.

These are the tranquillized *Fifties*,
And I am forty. Ought I to regret my seedtime?
I was a fire-breathing Catholic C.O.,
and made my manic statement,   15
telling off the state and president, and then
sat waiting sentence in the bull pen
beside a Negro boy with curlicues
of marijuana in his hair.

Given a year,   20
I walked on the roof of the West Street Jail, a short
enclosure like my school soccer court,
and saw the Hudson River once a day
through sooty clothesline entanglements

14 C.O.   Lowell, at the time a Catholic, was a conscientious objector to military service in 1943.

and bleaching khaki tenements.   25
Strolling, I yammered metaphysics with Abramowitz,
a jaundice-yellow ('it's really tan')
and fly-weight pacifist,
so vegetarian,
he wore rope shoes and preferred fallen fruit.   30
He tried to convert Bioff and Brown,
the Hollywood pimps, to his diet.
Hairy, muscular, suburban,
wearing chocolate double-breasted suits,
they blew their tops and beat him black and blue.   35

I was so out of things, I'd never heard
of the Jehovah's Witnesses.
'Are you a C.O.?' I asked a fellow jailbird.
'No,' he answered, 'I'm a J.W.'
He taught me the 'hospital tuck,'   40
and pointed out the T-shirted back
of *Murder Incorporated's* Czar Lepke,
there piling towels on a rack,
or dawdling off to his little segregated cell full
of things forbidden the common man: 45
a portable radio, a dresser, two toy American
flags tied together with a ribbon of Easter palm.
Flabby, bald, lobotomized,
he drifted in a sheepish calm,
where no agonizing reappraisal   50
jarred his concentration on the electric chair—
hanging like an oasis in his air
of lost connections. . . .

                                                                1959

For the Union Dead

'Relinquunt Omnia Servare Rem Publicam.'

The old South Boston Aquarium stands
in a Sahara of snow now. Its broken windows are boarded.
The bronze weathervane cod has lost half its scales.
The airy tanks are dry.

Once my nose crawled like a snail on the glass;   5
my hand tingled
to burst the bubbles
drifting from the noses of the cowed, compliant fish.

My hand draws back. I often sigh still
for the dark downward and vegetating kingdom   10
of the fish and reptile. One morning last March,
I pressed against the new barbed and galvanized

Epigraph: 'They relinquish everything to serve the republic': motto on the monument discussed in the poem (altered by Lowell to the plural)

fence on the Boston Common. Behind their cage,
yellow dinosaur steamshovels were grunting
as they cropped up tons of mush and grass   15
to gouge their underworld garage.

Parking spaces luxuriate like civic
sandpiles in the heart of Boston.
A girdle of orange, Puritan-pumpkin colored girders
braces the tingling Statehouse,   20

shaking over the excavations, as it faces Colonel Shaw
and his bell-cheeked Negro infantry
on St Gaudens' shaking Civil War relief,
propped by a plank splint against the garage's earthquake.

Two months after marching through Boston,   25
half the regiment was dead;
at the dedication,
William James could almost hear the bronze Negroes breathe.

Their monument sticks like a fishbone
in the city's throat.   30
Its Colonel is as lean
as a compass-needle.

He has an angry wrenlike vigilance,
a greyhound's gentle tautness;
he seems to wince at pleasure,   35
and suffocate for privacy.

He is out of bounds now. He rejoices in man's lovely,
peculiar power to choose life and die—
when he leads his black soldiers to death,
he cannot bend his back.   40

On a thousand small town New England greens,
the old white churches hold their air
of sparse, sincere rebellion; frayed flags
quilt the graveyards of the Grand Army of the Republic.

The stone statues of the abstract Union Soldier   45
grow slimmer and younger each year—
wasp-waisted, they doze over muskets
and muse through their sideburns . . .

Shaw's father wanted no monument
except the ditch,
where his son's body was thrown   50
and lost with his 'niggers.'

---

21 Colonel Shaw   Robert Gould Shaw (1837–63), white commander of the 'Negro' 54th Massachusetts regiment during the American civil war. He died, with many of his troops, in an attack on Fort Wagner, South Carolina.
23 St Gaudens   Augustus Saint-Gaudens (1848–1907), sculptor
28 William James   (1842–1910), American philosopher, who was present at the dedication of Saint-Gaudens' bronze relief in 1897

The ditch is nearer.
There are no statues for the last war here;
on Boylston Street, a commercial photograph   55
shows Hiroshima boiling

over a Mosler Safe, the 'Rock of Ages'
that survived the blast. Space is nearer.
When I crouch to my television set,
the drained faces of Negro school-children rise like balloons.   60

Colonel Shaw
is riding on his bubble,
he waits
for the blessèd break.

The Aquarium is gone. Everywhere,   65
giant finned cars nose forward like fish;
a savage servility
slides by on grease.

                                                    1959

Fourth of July in Maine

(For Harriet Winslow)

Another summer! Our Independence
Day Parade, all innocence
of children's costumes, helps resist
the communist and socialist.
Five nations: Dutch, French, Englishmen,   5
Indians, and we, who held Castine,
rise from their graves in combat gear—
world-losers elsewhere, conquerors here!

Civil Rights clergy face again
the scions of the good old strain,   10
the poor who always must remain
poor and Republicans in Maine,
upholders of the American Dream,
who will not sink and cannot swim—
Emersonian self-reliance,   15
lethargy of Russian peasants!

High noon. Each child has won his blue,
red, yellow ribbon, and our statue,
a dandyish Union Soldier, sees
his fields reclaimed by views and spruce—   20
he seems a convert to old age,
small, callous, elbowed off the stage,
while the canned martial music fades
from scene and green—no more parades!

---

6 Castine   the town in Maine where the poem is set
15 Emersonian   i.e. as taught by the nineteenth-century New England writer, Ralph Waldo
Emerson

Blue twinges of mortality   25
remind us the theocracy
drove in its stakes here to command
the infinite, and gave this land
a ministry that would have made
short work of Christ, the Son of God,   30
and then exchanged His crucifix,
hardly our sign, for politics.

This white Colonial frame house,
willed downward, Dear, from you to us,
still matters—the Americas'
best artifact produced en masse.   35
The founders' faith was in decay,
and yet their building seems to say:
'Every time I take a breath,
my God you are the air I breathe.'   40

New England, everywhere I look,
old letters crumble from the Book,
China trade rubble, one more line
unravelling from the dark design
spun by God and Cotton Mather—   45
our *bel età dell' oro*, another
bright thing thinner than a cobweb,
caught in Calvinism's ebb.

Dear Cousin, life is much the same,
though only fossils know your name   50
here since you left this solitude,
gone, as the Christians say, for good.
Your house, still outwardly in form
lasts, though no emissary come
to watch the garden running down,   55
or photograph the propped-up barn.

If memory is genius, you
had Homer's, enough gossip to
repeople Trollope's Barchester,
nurses, Negro, diplomat, down-easter,
cousins kept up with, nipped, corrected,   60
kindly, majorfully directed,
though family furniture, decor,
and rooms redone meant almost more.

How often when the telephone
brought you to us from Washington,   65

---

45 Cotton Mather (1663–1728) a theologian associated with the New England Puritan **theocracy** (line 26), in which moral and political authority resided in the leading laity and clergy of the church
46 bel età dell' oro fine age of gold (Italian)
59 Trollope Anthony Trollope (1815–82), the prolific author of a series of novels set in a town which he called Barchester

we had to look around the room
to find the objects you would name—
lying there, ten years paralyzed,
half blind, no voice unrecognized,
not trusting in the afterlife,
teasing us for a carving knife.

70

High New England summer, warm
and fortified against the storm
by nightly nips you once adored,
though never going overboard,
Harriet, when you used to play
your chosen Nadia Boulanger
Monteverdi, Purcell, and Bach's
precursors on the Magnavox.

75

80

Blue-ribboned, blue-jeaned, named for you,
our daughter cartwheels on the blue—
may your proportion strengthen her
to live through the millennial year
Two Thousand, and like you possess
friends, independence, and a house,
herself God's plenty, mistress of
your tireless sedentary love.

85

Her two angora guinea pigs
are nibbling seed, the news, and twigs—
untroubled, petrified, atremble,
a mother and her daughter, so humble,
giving, idle and sensitive,
few animals will let them live,
and only a vegetarian God
could look on them and call them good.

90

95

Man's poorest cousins, harmonies
of lust and appetite and ease,
little pacific things, who graze
the grass about their box, they praise
whatever stupor gave them breath
to multiply before their death—
Evolution's snails, by birth,
outrunning man who runs the earth.

100

And now the frosted summer night-dew
brightens, the north wind rushes through
your ailing cedars, finds the gaps;
thumbtacks rattle from the white maps,
food's lost sight of, dinner waits,
in the cold oven, icy plates—
repeating and repeating, one
Joan Baez on the gramophone.

105

110

---

78 Nadia Boulanger   (1887–1979) French conductor, who revived interest in early classical music

And here in your converted barn,
we burn our hands a moment, borne
by energies that never tire
of piling fuel on the fire;
monologue that will not hear,
logic turning its deaf ear,
wild spirits and old sores in league
with inexhaustible fatigue.

Far off that time of gentleness,
when man, still licensed to increase,
unfallen and unmated, heard
only the uncreated Word—
when God the Logos still had wit
to hide his bloody hands, and sit
in silence, while his peace was sung.
Then the universe was young.

We watch the logs fall. Fire once gone,
we're done for: we escape the sun,
rising and setting, a red coal,
until it cinders like the soul.
Great ash and sun of freedom, give
us this day the warmth to live,
and face the household fire. We turn
our backs, and feel the whiskey burn.

115

120

Word 125

130

135

1967

JAMES McAULEY

1917–76 b Sydney. He was an influential literary editor and, from 1961, a teacher of literature at the university in Hobart.

Because

My father and my mother never quarrelled.
They were united in a kind of love
As daily as the *Sydney Morning Herald*,
Rather than like the eagle or the dove.

I never saw them casually touch,
Or show a moment's joy in one another.
Why should this matter to me now so much?
I think it bore more hardly on my mother,

5

Who had more generous feeling to express.
My father had dammed up his Irish blood
Against all drinking praying fecklessness,
And stiffened into stone and creaking wood.

10

His lips would make a switching sound, as though
Spontaneous impulse must be kept at bay.
That it was mainly weakness I see now,
But then my feelings curled back in dismay.

15

Small things can pit the memory like a cyst:
Having seen other fathers greet their sons,
I put my childish face up to be kissed
After an absence. The rebuff still stuns   20

My blood. The poor man's curt embarrassment
At such a delicate proffer of affection
Cut like a saw. But home the lesson went:
My tenderness thenceforth escaped detection.

My mother sang *Because*, and *Annie Laurie*,   25
White Wings, and other songs; her voice was sweet.
I never gave enough, and I am sorry;
But we were all closed in the same defeat.

People do what they can; they were good people,
They cared for us and loved us. Once they stood   30
Tall in my childhood as the school, the steeple.
How can I judge without ingratitude?

Judgment is simply trying to reject
A part of what we are because it hurts.
The living cannot call the dead collect: 35
They won't accept the charge, and it reverts.

It's my own judgment day that I draw near,
Descending in the past, without a clue,
Down to that central deadness: the despair
Older than any hope I ever knew.   40

                                        1969

JUDITH WRIGHT

b 1915 near Armidale, NSW. She lives in the Monaro near Canberra, and is an activist in the causes of conservation and Aboriginal rights.

Woman to Man

The eyeless labourer in the night,
the selfless, shapeless seed I hold,
builds for its resurrection day—
silent and swift and deep from sight
foresees the unimagined light.   5

This is no child with a child's face;
this has no name to name it by:
yet you and I have known it well.
This is our hunter and our chase,
the third who lay in our embrace.   10

This is the strength that your arm knows,
the arc of flesh that is my breast,
the precise crystals of our eyes.
This is the blood's wild tree that grows
the intricate and folded rose.   15

This is the maker and the made;
this is the question and reply;
the blind head butting at the dark,
the blaze of light along the blade.
Oh hold me, for I am afraid.   20

                                                              1949

Train Journey

Glassed with cold sleep and dazzled by the moon,
out of the confused hammering dark of the train
I looked and saw under the moon's cold sheet
your delicate dry breasts, country that built my heart;

and the small trees on their uncoloured slope   5
like poetry moved, articulate and sharp
and purposeful under the great dry flight of air,
under the crosswise currents of wind and star.

Clench down your strength, box-tree and ironbark.
Break with your violent root the virgin rock.
Draw from the flying dark its breath of dew   10
till the unliving come to life in you.

Be over the blind rock a skin of sense,
under the barren height a slender dance...

I woke and saw the dark small trees that burn   15
suddenly into flowers more lovely than the white moon.

                                                              1953

Naked Girl and Mirror

This is not I. I had no body once—
only what served my need to laugh and run
and stare at stars and tentatively dance
on the fringe of foam and wave and sand and sun.
Eyes loved, hands reached for me, but I was gone   5
on my own currents, quicksilver, thistledown.
Can I be trapped at last in that soft face?

I stare at you in fear, dark brimming eyes.
Why do you watch me with that immoderate plea—
'Look under these curled lashes, recognize   10
that you were always here; know me—be me.'
Smooth once-hermaphrodite shoulders, too tenderly
your long slope runs, above those sudden shy
curves furred with light that spring below your space.

No, I have been betrayed. If I had known   15
that this girl waited between a year and a year,
I'd not have chosen her bough to dance upon.
Betrayed, by that little darkness here, and here
this swelling softness and that frightened stare
from eyes I will not answer; shut out here   20
from my own self, by its new body's grace—

for I am betrayed by someone lovely. Yes,
I see you are lovely, hateful naked girl.
Your lips in the mirror tremble as I refuse
to know or claim you. Let me go—let me be gone.   25
You are half of some other who may never come.
Why should I tend you? You are not my own;
you seek that other—he will be your home.

Yet I pity your eyes in the mirror, misted with tears;
I lean to your kiss. I must serve you; I will obey.   30
Some day we may love. I may miss your going, some day,
though I shall always resent your dumb and fruitful years.
Your lovers shall learn better, and bitterly too,
if their arrogance dares to think I am part of you.

                                                    1966

Smalltown Dance

Two women find the square-root of a sheet.
That is an ancient dance;
arms wide; together; again; two forward steps; hands meet
your partner's once and twice.
That white expanse   5
reduces to a neat
compression fitting in the smallest space
a sheet can pack in on a cupboard shelf.

High scented walls there were of flapping white
when I was small, myself.   10
I walked between them, playing Out of Sight.
Simpler than arms, they wrapped and comforted—
clean corridors of hiding, roofed with blue—
saying, Your sins too are made Monday-new;
and see, ahead,   15
that glimpse of unobstructed waiting green.
Run, run before you're seen.

But women know the scale of possibility,
the limit of opportunity,
the fence,   20
how little chance
there is of getting out. The sheets that tug
sometimes struggle from the peg,
don't travel far. Might symbolize
something. Knowing where danger lies   25
you have to keep things orderly.
The household budget will not stretch to more.

And they can demonstrate it in a dance.
First pull those wallowing white dreamers down,
spread arms, then close them. Fold   30
those beckoning roads to some impossible world,
put them away and close the cupboard door.

                                                    1985

RANDALL JARRELL

1914–65 b Nashville. He taught literature at the university in Greensboro, NC.

The Death of the Ball Turret Gunner

From my mother's sleep I fell into the State,
And I hunched in its belly till my wet fur froze.
Six miles from earth, loosed from its dream of life,
I woke to black flak and the nightmare fighters.
When I died they washed me out of the turret with a hose.   5

1945

The Truth

When I was four my father went to Scotland.
They *said* he went to Scotland.

When I woke up I think I thought that I was dreaming—
I was so little then that I thought dreams
Are in the room with you, like the cinema.   5
That's why you don't dream when it's still light—
They pull the shades down when it is, so you can sleep.
I thought that then, but that's not right.
Really it's in your head.

And it was light then—light at *night*.   10
I heard Stalky bark outside.
But really it was Mother crying—
She coughed so hard she cried.
She kept shaking Sister,
She shook her and shook her.   15
I thought Sister had had her nightmare.
But he wasn't barking, he had died.
There was dirt all over Sister.
It was all streaks, like mud. I cried.
She didn't, but she was older.
                    I thought she didn't   20
Because she was older, I thought Stalky had just gone.
I got *everything* wrong.
I didn't get one single thing right.
It seems to me that I'd have thought
It didn't happen, like a dream,   25
Except that it was light. At night.
They burnt our house down, they burnt down London.
Next day my mother cried all day, and after that
She said to me when she would come to see me:
'Your father has gone away to Scotland.   30
He will be back after the war.'

The war then was different from the war now.
The war now is *nothing*.

I used to live in London till they burnt it.
What was it like? It was just like here.   35
No, that's the truth.
My mother would come here, some, but she would cry.
She said to Miss Elise, 'He's not himself';
She said, 'Don't you love me any more at all?'
I was *my*self.   40
Finally she wouldn't come at all.
She never said one thing my father said, or Sister.
Sometimes she did,
Sometimes she was the same, but that was when I dreamed it.
I could tell I was dreaming, she was just the same.   45

That Christmas she bought me a toy dog.

I asked her what was its name, and when she didn't know
I asked her over, and when she didn't know
I said, 'You're not my mother, you're not my mother.
She *hasn't* gone to Scotland, she is dead!'   50
And she said, 'Yes, he's dead, he's dead!'
And cried and cried; she *was* my mother,
She put her arms around me and we cried.

                                                                      1945

DYLAN THOMAS

1914–53 b Wales, where he grew up. He moved to London and became well known through recitations of his work.

The Hand that Signed the Paper

The hand that signed the paper felled a city;
Five sovereign fingers taxed the breath,
Doubled the globe of dead and halved a country;
These five kings did a king to death.

The mighty hand leads to a sloping shoulder,   5
The finger joints are cramped with chalk;
A goose's quill has put an end to murder
That put an end to talk.

The hand that signed the treaty bred a fever,
And famine grew, and locusts came;   10
Great is the hand that holds dominion over
Man by a scribbled name.

The five kings count the dead but do not soften
The crusted wound nor stroke the brow;
A hand rules pity as a hand rules heaven;   15
Hands have no tears to flow.

                                                        1933   1936

The Force that through the Green Fuse Drives the Flower

The force that through the green fuse drives the flower
Drives my green age; that blasts the roots of trees
Is my destroyer.
And I am dumb to tell the crooked rose
My youth is bent by the same wintry fever.   5

The force that drives the water through the rocks
Drives my red blood; that dries the mouthing streams
Turns mine to wax.
And I am dumb to mouth unto my veins
How at the mountain spring the same mouth sucks.   10

The hand that whirls the water in the pool
Stirs the quicksand; that ropes the blowing wind
Hauls my shroud sail.
And I am dumb to tell the hanging man
How of my clay is made the hangman's lime.   15

The lips of time leech to the fountain head;
Love drips and gathers, but the fallen blood
Shall calm her sores.
And I am dumb to tell a weather's wind
How time has ticked a heaven round the stars.   20

And I am dumb to tell the lover's tomb
How at my sheet goes the same crooked worm.

                                        1933   1934

Fern Hill

Now as I was young and easy under the apple boughs
About the lilting house and happy as the grass was green,
    The night above the dingle starry,
        Time let me hail and climb
    Golden in the heydays of his eyes,   5
And honoured among wagons I was prince of the apple towns
And once below a time I lordly had the trees and leaves
        Trail with daisies and barley
    Down the rivers of the windfall light.

And as I was green and carefree, famous among the barns   10
About the happy yard and singing as the farm was home,
    In the sun that is young once only,
        Time let me play and be
    Golden in the mercy of his means,
And green and golden I was huntsman and herdsman, the calves   15
Sang to my horn, the foxes on the hills barked clear and cold,
        And the sabbath rang slowly
    In the pebbles of the holy streams.

All the sun long it was running, it was lovely, the hay
Fields high as the house, the tunes from the chimneys, it was air   20
   And playing, lovely and watery
     And fire green as grass.
   And nightly under the simple stars
As I rode to sleep the owls were bearing the farm away,
All the moon long I heard, blessed among stables, the nightjars   25
   Flying with the ricks, and the horses
     Flashing into the dark.

And then to awake, and the farm, like a wanderer white
With the dew, come back, the cock on his shoulder; it was all
   Shining, it was Adam and maiden,   30
     The sky gathered again
   And the sun grew round that very day.
So it must have been after the birth of the simple light
In the first, spinning place, the spellbound horses walking warm
   Out of the whinnying green stable   35
     On to the fields of praise.

And honoured among foxes and pheasants by the gay house
Under the new made clouds and happy as the heart was long,
   In the sun born over and over,
     I ran my heedless ways,   40
   My wishes raced through the house high hay
And nothing I cared, at my sky blue trades, that time allows
In all his tuneful turning so few and such morning songs
   Before the children green and golden
     Follow him out of grace,   45

Nothing I cared, in the lamb white days, that time would take me
Up to the swallow thronged loft by the shadow of my hand,
   In the moon that is always rising,
     Nor that riding to sleep
   I should hear him fly with the high fields   50
And wake to the farm forever fled from the childless land.
Oh as I was young and easy in the mercy of his means,
     Time held me green and dying
   Though I sang in my chains like the sea.

1945 1946

Do not go gentle into that good night

Do not go gentle into that good night,
Old age should burn and rave at close of day;
Rage, rage against the dying of the light.

Though wise men at their end know dark is right,
Because their words had forked no lightning they   5
Do not go gentle into that good night.

Good men, the last wave by, crying how bright
Their frail deeds might have danced in a green bay,
Rage, rage against the dying of the light.

Wild men who caught and sang the sun in flight,   10
And learn, too late, they grieved it on its way,
Do not go gentle into that good night.

Grave men, near death, who see with blinding sight
Blind eyes could blaze like meteors and be gay,
Rage, rage against the dying of the light.   15

And you, my father, there on the sad height,
Curse, bless, me now with your fierce tears, I pray.
Do not go gentle into that good night.
Rage, rage against the dying of the light.

                                              1951   1952

DENIS GLOVER

1912–80 b Dunedin. A typographer and printer, he lived in Christchurch and Wellington.

The Magpies

When Tom and Elizabeth took the farm
The bracken made their bed,
And *Quardle oodle ardle wardle doodle*
The magpies said.

Tom's hand was strong to the plough   5
Elizabeth's lips were red,
And *Quardle oodle ardle wardle doodle*
The magpies said.

Year in year out they worked
While the pines grew overhead,   10
And *Quardle oodle ardle wardle doodle*
The magpies said.

But all the beautiful crops soon went
To the mortgage-man instead,
And *Quardle oodle ardle wardle doodle*   15
The magpies said.

Elizabeth is dead now (it's years ago);
Old Tom went light in the head;
And *Quardle oodle ardle wardle doodle*
The magpies said.   20

The farm's still there. Mortgage corporations
Couldn't give it away.
And *Quardle oodle ardle wardle doodle*
The magpies say.

                                              1941

ALLEN CURNOW

b 1911 Timaru. He taught literature at the university in Auckland.

House and Land

Wasn't this the site, asked the historian,
Of the original homestead?
Couldn't tell you, said the cowman;
I just live here, he said,
Working for old Miss Wilson   5
Since the old man's been dead.

Moping under the bluegums
The dog trailed his chain
From the privy as far as the fowlhouse
And back to the privy again,   10
Feeling the stagnant afternoon
Quicken with the smell of rain.

There sat old Miss Wilson,
With her pictures on the wall,
The baronet uncle, mother's side,   15
And one she called The Hall;
Taking tea from a silver pot
For fear the house might fall.

People in the *colonies*, she said,
Can't quite understand...   20
Why, from Waiau to the mountains
It was all father's land.

She's all of eighty said the cowman,
Down at the milking-shed.
I'm leaving here next winter.   25
Too bloody quiet, he said.

The spirit of exile, wrote the historian,
Is strong in the people still.
He reminds me rather, said Miss Wilson,
Of Harriet's youngest, Will.   30

The cowman, home from the shed, went drinking
With the rabbiter home from the hill.

The sensitive nor'west afternoon
Collapsed, and the rain came;
The dog crept into his barrel   35
Looking lost and lame.
But you can't attribute to either
Awareness of what great gloom
Stands in a land of settlers
With never a soul at home.   40

                                            1941

Wild Iron

Sea go dark, dark with wind,
Feet go heavy, heavy with sand,
Thoughts go wild, wild with the sound
Of iron on the old shed swinging, clanging:
Go dark, go heavy, go wild, go round,   5
    Dark with the wind,
    Heavy with the sand,
Wild with the iron that tears at the nail
And the foundering shriek of the gale.

                                    1941

The Kitchen Cupboard

Sun, moon, and tides.
With the compliments of the *New Zealand Herald*
and Donaghy's Industries Limited makers
of the finest cordage since 1876.
Look on the inside of the cupboard door,   5
the middle one, on the left of the sink-bench.

All the bays are empty, a quick-drying wind
from the south-west browns the grey silt
the ebb-tide printed sexily, opulently,
making Nature's art nouveau, little as it matters   10
to mudlarking crabs and the morning's blue heron.

Olive, olive-budded, mangroves wait for the turn,
little as it means, to call that waiting.

A green car follows a blue car passing a brown car
on the Shore Road beyond the mangroves which wait   15
no more than the tide does because nothing waits.
Everything happens at once. It is enough.

That is not to say there is nothing to cry about,
only that the poetry of tears is a dead cuckoo.

The middle one, on the left of the sink-bench.   20
I stuck it on with sellotape. Not quite straight.

                                    1972

Continuum

The moon rolls over the roof and falls behind
my house, and the moon does neither of these things,
I am talking about myself.

It's not possible to get off to sleep or
the subject or the planet, nor to think thoughts.   5
Better barefoot it out the front

door and lean from the porch across the privets
and the palms into the washed-out creation,
a dark place with two particular

bright clouds dusted (query) by the moon, one's mine   10
the other's an adversary, which may depend
on the wind, or something.

A long moment stretches, the next one is not
on time. Not unaccountably the chill of
the planking underfoot rises   15

in the throat, for its part the night sky empties
the whole of its contents down. Turn on a bare
heel, close the door behind

on the author, cringing demiurge, who picks up
his litter and his tools and paces me back   20
to bed, stealthily in step.

                                            1988

ELIZABETH BISHOP

1911–79 b Massachusetts; grew up in Nova Scotia. She taught literature for a time in universities. In the latter part of her life, she spent 17 years in Brazil.

Sestina

September rain falls on the house.
In the failing light, the old grandmother
sits in the kitchen with the child
beside the Little Marvel Stove,
reading the jokes from the almanac,   5
laughing and talking to hide her tears.

She thinks that her equinoctial tears
and the rain that beats on the roof of the house
were both foretold by the almanac,
but only known to a grandmother.   10
The iron kettle sings on the stove.
She cuts some bread and says to the child,

It's time for tea now; but the child
is watching the teakettle's small hard tears
dance like mad on the hot black stove,   15
the way the rain must dance on the house.
Tidying up, the old grandmother
hangs up the clever almanac

on its string. Birdlike, the almanac
hovers half open above the child,   20
hovers above the old grandmother
and her teacup full of dark brown tears.
She shivers and says she thinks the house
feels chilly, and puts more wood in the stove.

---

19 demiurge an ancient Greek word meaning craftsman; also magistrate; also creator of the universe—as the supreme being (in Plato) or as a subordinate deity (in Gnostic thought)

It was to be, says the Marvel Stove.   25
I know what I know, says the almanac.
With crayons the child draws a rigid house
and a winding pathway. Then the child
puts in a man with buttons like tears
and shows it proudly to the grandmother.   30

But secretly, while the grandmother
busies herself about the stove,
the little moons fall down like tears
from between the pages of the almanac
into the flower bed the child   35
has carefully placed in the front of the house.

Time to plant tears, says the almanac.
The grandmother sings to the marvellous stove
and the child draws another inscrutable house.

                                                       1965

The Moose

From narrow provinces
of fish and bread and tea,
home of the long tides
where the bay leaves the sea
twice a day and takes   5
the herrings long rides,

where if the river
enters or retreats
in a wall of brown foam
depends on if it meets   10
the bay coming in,
the bay not at home;

where, silted red,
sometimes the sun sets
facing a red sea,   15
and others, veins the flats'
lavender, rich mud
in burning rivulets;

on red, gravelly roads,
down rows of sugar maples,   20
past clapboard farmhouses
and neat, clapboard churches,
bleached, ridged as clamshells,
past twin silver birches,

through late afternoon   25
a bus journeys west,
the windshield flashing pink,
pink glancing off of metal,
brushing the dented flank
of blue, beat-up enamel;   30

down hollows, up rises,
and waits, patient, while
a lone traveller gives
kisses and embraces
to seven relatives
and a collie supervises.

Goodbye to the elms,
to the farm, to the dog.
The bus starts. The light
grows richer; the fog,
shifting, salty, thin,
comes closing in.

Its cold, round crystals
form and slide and settle
in the white hens' feathers,
in gray glazed cabbages,
on the cabbage roses
and lupins like apostles;

the sweet peas cling
to their wet white string
on the whitewashed fences;
bumblebees creep
inside the foxgloves,
and evening commences.

One stop at Bass River.
Then the Economies—
Lower, Middle, Upper;
Five Islands, Five Houses,
where a woman shakes a tablecloth
out after supper.

A pale flickering. Gone.
The Tantramar marshes
and the smell of salt hay.
An iron bridge trembles
and a loose plank rattles
but doesn't give way.

On the left, a red light
swims through the dark:
a ship's port lantern.
Two rubber boots show,
illuminated, solemn.
A dog gives one bark.

A woman climbs in
with two market bags,
brisk, freckled, elderly.
'A grand night. Yes, sir,
all the way to Boston.'
She regards us amicably.

Moonlight as we enter
the New Brunswick woods,
hairy, scratchy, splintery;   80
moonlight and mist
caught in them like lamb's wool
on bushes in a pasture.

The passengers lie back.
Snores. Some long sighs.   85
A dreamy divagation
begins in the night,
a gentle, auditory,
slow hallucination. . . .   90

In the creakings and noises,
an old conversation
—not concerning us,
but recognizable, somewhere,
back in the bus: 95
Grandparents' voices

uninterruptedly
talking, in Eternity:
names being mentioned,
things cleared up finally;   100
what he said, what she said,
who got pensioned;

deaths, deaths and sicknesses;
the year he remarried;
the year (something) happened.   105
She died in childbirth.
That was the son lost
when the schooner foundered.

He took to drink. Yes.
She went to the bad.   110
When Amos began to pray
even in the store and
finally the family had
to put him away.

'Yes. . .' that peculiar   115
affirmative. 'Yes. . .'
A sharp, indrawn breath,
half groan, half acceptance,
that means 'Life's like that.
We know *it* (also death).'   120

Talking the way they talked
in the old featherbed,
peacefully, on and on,
dim lamplight in the hall,
down in the kitchen, the dog   125
tucked in her shawl.

Now, it's all right now
even to fall asleep
just as on all those nights.
—Suddenly the bus driver
stops with a jolt,
turns off his lights.

130

A moose has come out of
the impenetrable wood
and stands there, looms, rather,
in the middle of the road.
It approaches; it sniffs at
the bus's hot hood.

135

Towering, antlerless,
high as a church,
homely as a house
(or, safe as houses).
A man's voice assures us
'Perfectly harmless. . . .'

140

Some of the passengers
exclaim in whispers,
childishly, softly,
'Sure are big creatures.'
'It's awful plain.'
'Look! It's a she!'

145

150

Taking her time,
she looks the bus over,
grand, otherworldly.
Why, why do we feel
(we all feel) this sweet
sensation of joy?

155

'Curious creatures,'
says our quiet driver,
rolling his *r*'s.
'Look at that, would you.'
Then he shifts gears.
For a moment longer,

160

by craning backward,
the moose can be seen
on the moonlit macadam;
then there's a dim
smell of moose, an acrid
smell of gasoline.

165

1976

One Art

The art of losing isn't hard to master;
so many things seem filled with the intent
to be lost that their loss is no disaster.

Lose something every day. Accept the fluster
of lost door keys, the hour badly spent.   5
The art of losing isn't hard to master.

Then practice losing farther, losing faster:
places, and names, and where it was you meant
to travel. None of these will bring disaster.

I lost my mother's watch. And look! my last, or   10
next-to-last, of three loved houses went.
The art of losing isn't hard to master.

I lost two cities, lovely ones. And, vaster,
some realms I owned, two rivers, a continent.
I miss them, but it wasn't a disaster.   15

—Even losing you (the joking voice, a gesture
I love) I shan't have lied. It's evident
the art of losing's not too hard to master
though it may look like (*Write* it!) like disaster.

                                                            1976

THEODORE ROETHKE

1908–63 b Michigan. He taught literature and writing at the university in Seattle.

My Papa's Waltz

The whiskey on your breath
Could make a small boy dizzy;
But I hung on like death:
Such waltzing was not easy.

We romped until the pans   5
Slid from the kitchen shelf;
My mother's countenance
Could not unfrown itself.

The hand that held my wrist
Was battered on one knuckle;   10
At every step you missed
My right ear scraped a buckle.

You beat time on my head
With a palm caked hard by dirt,
Then waltzed me off to bed   15
Still clinging to your shirt.

                                                            1948

Child on Top of a Greenhouse

The wind billowing out the seat of my britches,
My feet crackling splinters of glass and dried putty,
The half-grown chrysanthemums staring up like accusers,
Up through the streaked glass, flashing with sunlight,
A few white clouds all rushing eastward,   5
A line of elms plunging and tossing like horses,
And everyone, everyone pointing up and shouting!

1948

Journey to the Interior

1

In the long journey out of the self,
There are many detours, washed-out interrupted raw places
Where the shale slides dangerously
And the back wheels hang almost over the edge
At the sudden veering, the moment of turning.   5
Better to hug close, wary of rubble and falling stones.
The arroyo cracking the road, the wind-bitten buttes, the canyons,
Creeks swollen in midsummer from the flash-flood roaring into the
    narrow valley.
Reeds beaten flat by wind and rain,
Grey from the long winter, burnt at the base in late summer.   10
—Or the path narrowing,
Winding upward toward the stream with its sharp stones,
The upland of alder and birchtrees,
Through the swamp alive with quicksand,
The way blocked at last by a fallen fir-tree,   15
The thickets darkening,
The ravines ugly.

2

I remember how it was to drive in gravel,
Watching for dangerous down-hill places, where the wheels whined
    beyond eighty—
When you hit the deep pit at the bottom of the swale,   20
The trick was to throw the car sideways and charge over the hill, full of
    the throttle.
Grinding up and over the narrow road, spitting and roaring.
A chance? Perhaps. But the road was part of me, and its ditches,
And the dust lay thick on my eyelids,—Who ever wore goggles?—
Always a sharp turn to the left past a barn close to the roadside,   25
To a scurry of small dogs and a shriek of children,
The highway ribboning out in a straight thrust to the North,
To the sand dunes and fish flies, hanging, thicker than moths,
Dying brightly under the street lights sunk in coarse concrete,
The towns with their high pitted road-crowns and deep gutters,   30
Their wooden stores of silvery pine and weather-beaten red courthouses,
An old bridge below with a buckled iron railing, broken by some idiot
    plunger;

Underneath, the sluggish water running between weeds, broken wheels,
      tires, stones.
And all flows past—
The cemetery with two scrubby trees in the middle of the prairie,   35
The dead snakes and muskrats, the turtles gasping in the rubble,
The spikey purple bushes in the winding dry creek bed—
The floating hawks, the jackrabbits, the grazing cattle—
I am not moving but they are,
And the sun comes out of a blue cloud over the Tetons,   40
While, farther away, the heat-lightning flashes.
I rise and fall in the slow sea of a grassy plain,
The wind veering the car slightly to the right,
Whipping the line of white laundry, bending the cottonwoods apart,
The scraggly wind-break of a dusty ranch-house.   45
I rise and fall, and time folds
Into a long moment;
And I hear the lichen speak,
And the ivy advance with its white lizard feet—
On the shimmering road,   50
On the dusty detour.

3

I see the flower of all water, above and below me, the never receding,
Moving, unmoving in a parched land, white in the moonlight:
The soul at a still-stand,
At ease after rocking the flesh to sleep,   55
Petals and reflections of petals mixed on the surface of a glassy pool,
And the waves flattening out when the fishermen drag their nets over the stones.

In the moment of time when the small drop forms, but does not fall,
I have known the heart of the sun,—
In the dark and light of a dry place,
In a flicker of fire brisked by a dusty wind.   60
I have heard, in a drip of leaves,
A slight song,
After the midnight cries.
I rehearse myself for this: 65
The stand at the stretch in the face of death,
Delighting in surface change, the glitter of light on waves,
And I roam elsewhere, my body thinking,
Turning toward the other side of light,
In a tower of wind, a tree idling in air,   70
Beyond my own echo,
Neither forward nor backward,
Unperplexed, in a place leading nowhere.

As a blind man, lifting a curtain, knows it is morning,
I know this change: 75
On one side of silence there is no smile;
But when I breathe with the birds,
The spirit of wrath becomes the spirit of blessing,
And the dead begin from their dark to sing in my sleep.

                                                                          1964

A.D. HOPE

(Alec Derwent) b 1907 Cooma, NSW. He lives in Canberra, where he taught literature in the university.

X-Ray Photograph

Mapped by its panoply of shade
There is the skull I shall not see
—Dark hollow in its galaxy
From which the blazing eye must fade—

And, though I cannot see it plain,   5
Within those stellar spaces roll
The countless sparks and whorls of soul:
My constellation of the brain.

These bones are calm and beautiful;
The flesh, like water, strains and clears   10
To show the face my future wears
Drowned at the bottom of its pool.

Then I am full of rage and bliss,
For in our naked bed I feel,
Mate of your panting mouth as well,   15
The deathshead lean toward your kiss;

And I am mad to have you here,
Now, Now, the instant shield of lust,
Deep in your flesh my flesh to thrust
Against a more tremendous fear.   20

For in a last analysis
The mind has finer rays that show
The woof of atoms, and below
The mathematical abyss;

The solid bone dissolving just   25
As this dim pulp about the bone;
And whirling in its void alone
Yearns a fine interstitial dust.

The ray that melts away my skin   30
Pales at that sub-atomic wave:
This shows my image in the grave,
But that the emptiness within

By which I know our contacts are
Delusive as a point of light   35
That froths against my shores of sight
Sent out from the remotest star,

So spent, that great sun's fiery head
Is scarcely visible; a ray
So ancient that it brings today   40
Word from a world already dead.

1944   1955

The Death of the Bird

For every bird there is this last migration:
Once more the cooling year kindles her heart;
With a warm passage to the summer station
Love pricks the course in lights across the chart.

Year after year a speck on the map, divided
By a whole hemisphere, summons her to come;
Season after season, sure and safely guided,
Going away she is also coming home.

And being home, memory becomes a passion
With which she feeds her brood and straws her nest,
Aware of ghosts that haunt the heart's possession
And exiled love mourning within the breast.

The sands are green with a mirage of valleys;
The palm-tree casts a shadow not its own;
Down the long architrave of temple or palace
Blows a cool air from moorland scarps of stone.

And day by day the whisper of love grows stronger;
That delicate voice, more urgent with despair,
Custom and fear constraining her no longer,
Drives her at last on the waste leagues of air.

A vanishing speck in those inane dominions,
Single and frail, uncertain of her place,
Alone in the bright host of her companions,
Lost in the blue unfriendliness of space,

She feels it close now, the appointed season:
The invisible thread is broken as she flies;
Suddenly, without warning, without reason,
The guiding spark of instinct winks and dies.

Try as she will, the trackless world delivers
No way, the wilderness of light no sign,
The immense and complex map of hills and rivers
Mocks her small wisdom with its vast design.

And darkness rises from the eastern valleys,
And the winds buffet her with their hungry breath,
And the great earth, with neither grief nor malice,
Receives the tiny burden of her death.

1948   1955

Paradise Saved

(*another version of the Fall*)

Adam, indignant, would not eat with Eve,
They say, and she was driven from his side.
Watching the gates close on her tears, his pride
Upheld him, though he could not help but grieve

And climbed the wall, because his loneliness   5
Pined for her lonely figure in the dust:
Lo, there were two! God who is more than just
Sent her a helpmeet in that wilderness.

Day after day he watched them in the waste
Grow old, breaking the harsh unfriendly ground,   10
Bearing their children, till at last they died;
While Adam, whose fellow God had not replaced,
Lived on immortal, young, with virtue crowned,
Sterile and impotent and justified.

                                                              1967   1970

W.H. AUDEN

(Wystan Hugh) 1907–73 b York; grew up in Birmingham. A full-time poet, he was also a librettist and noted critic. He emigrated to the USA in 1939, where he lived in New York, after the war spending half of each year in Europe.

Song

For what as easy
For what though small,
For what is well
Because between,
To you simply   5
From me I mean.

Who goes with who
The bedclothes say,
As I and you
Go kissed away,   10
The data given,
The senses even.

Fate is not late,
Nor the speech rewritten,
Nor one word forgotten,   15
Said at the start
About heart,
By heart, for heart.

                                                              1932   1945

A New Age

So an age ended, and its last deliverer died
In bed, grown idle and unhappy; they were safe:
The sudden shadow of a giant's enormous calf
Would fall no more at dusk across their lawns outside.

W. H. Auden   'A New Age' and 'Refugee Blues' are here given the titles that Auden used for these poems' individual publication; he also included them, untitled, within longer sequences.

They slept in peace: in marshes here and there no doubt   5
A sterile dragon lingered to a natural death,
But in a year the slot had vanished from the heath;
A kobold's knocking in the mountain petered out.   *cave goblin*

Only the sculptors and the poets were half-sad,
And the pert retinue from the magician's house   10
Grumbled and went elsewhere. The vanquished powers were glad

To be invisible and free; without remorse
Struck down the silly sons who strayed into their course,
And ravished the daughters, and drove the fathers mad.

                                                    1936   1939

Lullaby

Lay your sleeping head, my love,
Human on my faithless arm;
Time and fevers burn away
Individual beauty from
Thoughtful children, and the grave   5
Proves the child ephemeral:
But in my arms till break of day
Let the living creature lie,
Mortal, guilty, but to me
The entirely beautiful.   10

Soul and body have no bounds:
To lovers as they lie upon
Her tolerant enchanted slope
In their ordinary swoon,
Grave the vision Venus sends   15
Of supernatural sympathy,
Universal love and hope;
While an abstract insight wakes
Among the glaciers and the rocks
The hermit's carnal ecstasy.   20

Certainty, fidelity
On the stroke of midnight pass
Like vibrations of a bell
And fashionable madmen raise
Their pedantic boring cry: 25
Every farthing of the cost,
All the dreaded cards foretell,
Shall be paid, but from this night
Not a whisper, not a thought,
Not a kiss nor look be lost.   30

Beauty, midnight, vision dies:
Let the winds of dawn that blow
Softly round your dreaming head
Such a day of welcome show
Eye and knocking heart may bless,   35
Find our mortal world enough;
Noons of dryness find you fed

By the involuntary powers,
Nights of insult let you pass
Watched by every human love.   40

                                        1937   1940

As I Walked Out One Evening

As I walked out one evening,
    Walking down Bristol Street,
The crowds upon the pavement
    Were fields of harvest wheat.

And down by the brimming river   5
    I heard a lover sing
Under an arch of the railway:
    'Love has no ending.

'I'll love you, dear, I'll love you
    Till China and Africa meet,   10
And the river jumps over the mountain
    And the salmon sing in the street,

'I'll love you till the ocean
    Is folded and hung up to dry
And the seven stars go squawking   15
    Like geese about the sky.

'The years shall run like rabbits,
    For in my arms I hold
The Flower of the Ages,
    And the first love of the world.'   20

But all the clocks in the city
    Began to whirr and chime:
'O let not Time deceive you,
    You cannot conquer Time.

'In the burrows of the Nightmare   25
    Where Justice naked is,
Time watches from the shadow
    And coughs when you would kiss.

'In headaches and in worry
    Vaguely life leaks away,   30
And Time will have his fancy
    To-morrow or to-day.

'Into many a green valley
    Drifts the appalling snow;
Time breaks the threaded dances   35
    And the diver's brilliant bow.

'O plunge your hands in water,
    Plunge them in up to the wrist;
Stare, stare in the basin
    And wonder what you've missed.   40

'The glacier knocks in the cupboard,
    The desert sighs in the bed,
And the crack in the tea-cup opens
    A lane to the land of the dead.

'Where the beggars raffle the banknotes   45
    And the Giant is enchanting to Jack,
And the Lily-white Boy is a Roarer,   *tearaway*
    And Jill goes down on her back.

'O look, look in the mirror,
    O look in your distress;   50
Life remains a blessing
    Although you cannot bless.

'O stand, stand at the window
    As the tears scald and start;
You shall love your crooked neighbour   55
    With your crooked heart.'

It was late, late in the evening,
    The lovers they were gone;
The clocks had ceased their chiming,
    And the deep river ran on.   60

                                              1937   1940

Musée des Beaux Arts

About suffering they were never wrong,
The Old Masters: how well they understood
Its human position; how it takes place
While someone else is eating or opening a window or just walking dully along;
How, when the aged are reverently, passionately waiting   5
For the miraculous birth, there always must be
Children who did not specially want it to happen, skating
On a pond at the edge of the wood:
They never forgot
That even the dreadful martyrdom must run its course   10
Anyhow in a corner, some untidy spot
Where the dogs go on with their doggy life and the torturer's horse
Scratches its innocent behind on a tree.

In Breughel's *Icarus*, for instance: how everything turns away
Quite leisurely from the disaster; the ploughman may   15
Have heard the splash, the forsaken cry,
But for him it was not an important failure; the sun shone
As it had to on the white legs disappearing into the green
Water; and the expensive delicate ship that must have seen
Something amazing, a boy falling out of the sky,   20
Had somewhere to get to and sailed calmly on.

                                              1938   1940

Musee des Beaux Arts   Museum of Fine Arts, Brussels
14 Breughel's Icarus   *The Fall of Icarus*, painted by Pieter Breughel (*c.* 1525–69). In Greek myth,
Daedalus, imprisoned on the island of Crete with his son Icarus, made wings of feathers and wax for
their escape. Icarus, however, flew too near the sun, the wax melted, and he fell to the sea and
drowned. A ploughman dominates the foreground of the painting.

In Memory of W.B. Yeats

(d. Jan. 1939)

I

He disappeared in the dead of winter:
The brooks were frozen, the airports almost deserted,
And snow disfigured the public statues;
The mercury sank in the mouth of the dying day.
What instruments we have agree   5
The day of his death was a dark cold day.

Far from his illness
The wolves ran on through the evergreen forests,
The peasant river was untempted by the fashionable quays;
By mourning tongues   10
The death of the poet was kept from his poems.

But for him it was his last afternoon as himself,
An afternoon of nurses and rumours;
The provinces of his body revolted,
The squares of his mind were empty,   15
Silence invaded the suburbs,
The current of his feeling failed; he became his admirers.

Now he is scattered among a hundred cities
And wholly given over to unfamiliar affections,
To find his happiness in another kind of wood   20
And be punished under a foreign code of conscience.
The words of a dead man
Are modified in the guts of the living.

But in the importance and noise of to-morrow
When the brokers are roaring like beasts on the floor of the Bourse,   25
And the poor have the sufferings to which they are fairly accustomed,
And each in the cell of himself is almost convinced of his freedom,
A few thousand will think of this day
As one thinks of a day when one did something slightly unusual.
What instruments we have agree   30
The day of his death was a dark cold day.

II

You were silly like us; your gift survived it all:
The parish of rich women, physical decay,
Yourself. Mad Ireland hurt you into poetry.
Now Ireland has her madness and her weather still,   35
For poetry makes nothing happen: it survives
In the valley of its making where executives
Would never want to tamper, flows on south
From ranches of isolation and the busy griefs,
Raw towns that we believe and die in; it survives,   40
A way of happening, a mouth.

---

25 Bourse   Paris stock exchange

III

Earth, receive an honoured guest:
William Yeats is laid to rest.
Let the Irish vessel lie
Emptied of its poetry.   45

In the nightmare of the dark
All the dogs of Europe bark,
And the living nations wait,
Each sequestered in its hate;

Intellectual disgrace   50
Stares from every human face,
And the seas of pity lie
Locked and frozen in each eye.

Follow, poet, follow right
To the bottom of the night,   55
With your unconstraining voice
Still persuade us to rejoice;

With the farming of a verse
Make a vineyard of the curse,
Sing of human unsuccess   60
In a rapture of distress;

In the deserts of the heart
Let the healing fountain start,
In the prison of his days
Teach the free man how to praise.   65

                                        February 1939   1940

Refugee Blues

Say this city has ten million souls,
Some are living in mansions, some are living in holes:
Yet there's no place for us, my dear, yet there's no place for us.

Once we had a country and we thought it fair,
Look in the atlas and you'll find it there: 5
We cannot go there now, my dear, we cannot go there now.

In the village churchyard there grows an old yew,
Every spring it blossoms anew:
Old passports can't do that, my dear, old passports can't do that.

The consul banged the table and said: 10
'If you've got no passport you're officially dead':
But we are still alive, my dear, but we are still alive.

Went to a committee; they offered me a chair;
Asked me politely to return next year:
But where shall we go to-day, my dear, but where shall we go to-day?   15

Came to a public meeting; the speaker got up and said:
'If we let them in, they will steal our daily bread';
He was talking of you and me, my dear, he was talking of you and me.

Thought I heard the thunder rumbling in the sky;
It was Hitler over Europe, saying: 'They must die';   20
We were in his mind, my dear, we were in his mind.

Saw a poodle in a jacket fastened with a pin,
Saw a door opened and a cat let in:
But they weren't German Jews, my dear, but they weren't German Jews.

Went down to the harbour and stood upon the quay,   25
Saw the fish swimming as if they were free:
Only ten feet away, my dear, only ten feet away.

Walked through a wood, saw the birds in the trees;
They had no politicians and sang at their ease:
They weren't the human race, my dear, they weren't the human race.   30

Dreamed I saw a building with a thousand floors,
A thousand windows and a thousand doors;
Not one of them was ours, my dear, not one of them was ours.

Stood on a great plain in the falling snow;
Ten thousand soldiers marched to and fro: 35
Looking for you and me, my dear, looking for you and me.

March 1939   1940

In Praise of Limestone

If it form the one landscape that we, the inconstant ones,
   Are consistently homesick for, this is chiefly
Because it dissolves in water. Mark these rounded slopes
   With their surface fragrance of thyme and, beneath,
A secret system of caves and conduits; hear the springs   5
   That spurt out everywhere with a chuckle,
Each filling a private pool for its fish and carving
   Its own little ravine whose cliffs entertain
The butterfly and the lizard; examine this region
   Of short distances and definite places: 10
What could be more like Mother or a fitter background
   For her son, the flirtatious male who lounges
Against a rock in the sunlight, never doubting
   That for all his faults he is loved; whose works are but
Extensions of his power to charm? From weathered outcrop   15
   To hill-top temple, from appearing waters to
Conspicuous fountains, from a wild to a formal vineyard,
   Are ingenious but short steps that a child's wish
To receive more attention than his brothers, whether
   By pleasing or teasing, can easily take.   20
Watch, then, the band of rivals as they climb up and down
   Their steep stone gennels in twos and threes, at times   *alleys*
Arm in arm, but never, thank God, in step; or engaged
   On the shady side of a square at midday in
Voluble discourse, knowing each other too well to think   25
   There are any important secrets, unable

To conceive a god whose temper-tantrums are moral
  And not to be pacified by a clever line
Or a good lay: for, accustomed to a stone that responds,
  They have never had to veil their faces in awe   30
Of a crater whose blazing fury could not be fixed;
  Adjusted to the local needs of valleys
Where everything can be touched or reached by walking,
  Their eyes have never looked into infinite space
Through the lattice-work of a nomad's comb; born lucky,   35
  Their legs have never encountered the fungi
And insects of the jungle, the monstrous forms and lives
  With which we have nothing, we like to hope, in common.
So, when one of them goes to the bad, the way his mind works
  Remains comprehensible: to become a pimp   40
Or deal in fake jewellery or ruin a fine tenor voice
  For effects that bring down the house, could happen to all
But the best and the worst of us . . .
                   That is why, I suppose,
  The best and worst never stayed here long but sought   45
Immoderate soils where the beauty was not so external,
  The light less public and the meaning of life
Something more than a mad camp. 'Come!' cried the granite wastes,
  'How evasive is your humor, how accidental
Your kindest kiss, how permanent is death.' (Saints-to-be   50
  Slipped away sighing.) 'Come!' purred the clays and gravels,
'On our plains there is room for armies to drill; rivers
  Wait to be tamed and slaves to construct you a tomb
In the grand manner: soft as the earth is mankind and both
  Need to be altered.' (Intendant Caesars rose and   55
Left, slamming the door.) But the really reckless were fetched
  By an older colder voice, the oceanic whisper:
'I am the solitude that asks and promises nothing;
  That is how I shall set you free. There is no love;
There are only the various envies, all of them sad.'   60

  They were right, my dear, all those voices were right
And still are; this land is not the sweet home that it looks,
  Nor its peace the historical calm of a site
Where something was settled once and for all: A backward
  And dilapidated province, connected   65
To the big busy world by a tunnel, with a certain
  Seedy appeal, is that all it is now? Not quite:
It has a worldly duty which in spite of itself
  It does not neglect, but calls into question
All the Great Powers assume; it disturbs our rights. The poet, 70
  Admired for his earnest habit of calling
The sun the sun, his mind Puzzle, is made uneasy
  By these marble statues which so obviously doubt
His antimythological myth; and these gamins,   *urchins*
  Pursuing the scientist down the tiled colonnade   75
With such lively offers, rebuke his concern for Nature's
  Remotest aspects: I, too, am reproached, for what

And how much you know. Not to lose time, not to get caught,
  Not to be left behind, not, please! to resemble
The beasts who repeat themselves, or a thing like water   80
  Or stone whose conduct can be predicted, these
Are our Common Prayer, whose greatest comfort is music
  Which can be made anywhere, is invisible,
And does not smell. In so far as we have to look forward
  To death as a fact, no doubt we are right: But if   85
Sins can be forgiven, if bodies rise from the dead,
  These modifications of matter into
Innocent athletes and gesticulating fountains,
  Made solely for pleasure, make a further point:
The blessed will not care what angle they are regarded from,   90
  Having nothing to hide. Dear, I know nothing of
Either, but when I try to imagine a faultless love
  Or the life to come, what I hear is the murmur
Of underground streams, what I see is a limestone landscape.

                                          1948 1951

Prime

Simultaneously, as soundlessly,
  Spontaneously, suddenly
As, at the vaunt of the dawn, the kind
  Gates of the body fly open
To its world beyond, the gates of the mind,   5
  The horn gate and the ivory gate
Swing to, swing shut, instantaneously
  Quell the nocturnal rummage
Of its rebellious fronde, ill-favored,
  Ill-natured and second-rate,   10
Disenfranchised, widowed and orphaned
  By an historical mistake:
Recalled from the shades to be a seeing being,
  From absence to be on display,
Without a name or history I wake   15
  Between my body and the day.

Holy this moment, wholly in the right,
  As, in complete obedience
To the light's laconic outcry, next
  As a sheet, near as a wall,   20
Out there as a mountain's poise of stone,
  The world is present, about,
And I know that I am, here, not alone
  But with a world and rejoice

Prime   the hour of morning prayer, at dawn
6 Homer relates how dreams of truth issue from a **gate** made of **horn**, and dreams of fantasy from
one of **ivory**. See *Odyssey* XIX.
9 fronde   violent opposition party (French)

Unvexed, for the will has still to claim   25
   This adjacent arm as my own,
The memory to name me, resume
   Its routine of praise and blame,
And smiling to me is this instant while
   Still the day is intact, and I   30
The Adam sinless in our beginning,
   Adam still previous to any act.

I draw breath; that is of course to wish
   No matter what, to be wise,
To be different, to die and the cost,   35
   No matter how, is Paradise
Lost of course and myself owing a death:
   The eager ridge, the steady sea,
The flat roofs of the fishing village
   Still asleep in its bunny,   40
Though as fresh and sunny still, are not friends
   But things to hand, this ready flesh
No honest equal, but my accomplice now,
   My assassin to be, and my name
Stands for my historical share of care   45
   For a lying self-made city,
Afraid of our living task, the dying
   Which the coming day will ask.

                1949   1951

The Shield of Achilles

    She looked over his shoulder
      For vines and olive trees,
    Marble well-governed cities
      And ships upon untamed seas,
    But there on the shining metal   5
      His hands had put instead
    An artificial wilderness
      And a sky like lead.

A plain without a feature, bare and brown,
   No blade of grass, no sign of neighbourhood,   10
Nothing to eat and nowhere to sit down,
   Yet, congregated on its blankness, stood
   An unintelligible multitude,
A million eyes, a million boots in line,
Without expression, waiting for a sign.   15

---

40 bunny   small ravine opening onto the sea
The Shield of Achilles   Homer relates that, during the siege of Troy, **Thetis** (line 62), goddess mother of the Greek warrior Achilles, had a shield made for him by the lame blacksmith god, **Hephaestos** (line 61). It was decorated with scenes of human community (one of which involved war) in an ordered cosmos. See *Odyssey* XVIII.

Out of the air a voice without a face
   Proved by statistics that some cause was just
In tones as dry and level as the place:
   No one was cheered and nothing was discussed;
   Column by column in a cloud of dust   20
They marched away enduring a belief
Whose logic brought them, somewhere else, to grief.

       She looked over his shoulder
          For ritual pieties,
       White flower-garlanded heifers,   25
          Libation and sacrifice,
       But there on the shining metal
          Where the altar should have been,
       She saw by his flickering forge-light
          Quite another scene.   30

Barbed wire enclosed an arbitrary spot
   Where bored officials lounged (one cracked a joke)
And sentries sweated for the day was hot:
   A crowd of ordinary decent folk
   Watched from without and neither moved nor spoke   35
As three pale figures were led forth and bound
To three posts driven upright in the ground.

The mass and majesty of this world, all
   That carries weight and always weighs the same
Lay in the hands of others; they were small   40
   And could not hope for help and no help came:
   What their foes liked to do was done, their shame
Was all the worst could wish; they lost their pride
And died as men before their bodies died.

       She looked over his shoulder   45
          For athletes at their games,
       Men and women in a dance
          Moving their sweet limbs
       Quick, quick, to music,
          But there on the shining shield   50
       His hands had set no dancing-floor
          But a weed-choked field.

A ragged urchin, aimless and alone,
   Loitered about that vacancy; a bird
Flew up to safety from his well-aimed stone: 55
   That girls are raped, that two boys knife a third,
   Were axioms to him, who'd never heard
Of any world where promises were kept,
Or one could weep because another wept.

       The thin-lipped armorer,   60
          Hephaestos, hobbled away,
       Thetis of the shining breasts
          Cried out in dismay

At what the god had wrought
   To please her son, the strong   65
Iron-hearted man-slaying Achilles
   Who would not live long.

                                      1952   1955

Since

On a mid-December day,
frying sausages
for myself, I abruptly
felt under fingers
thirty years younger the rim   5
of a steering-wheel,
on my cheek the parching wind
of an August noon,
as passenger beside me
You as then you were.   10

Slap across a veg-growing
alluvial plain
we raced in clouds of white dust,
and geese fled screaming
as we missed them by inches,   15
making a bee-line
for mountains gradually
enlarging eastward,
joyfully certain nightfall
would occasion joy.   20

It did. In a flagged kitchen
we were served broiled trout
and a rank cheese: for a while
we talked by the fire,
then, carrying candles, climbed   25
steep stairs. Love was made
then and there: so halcyoned,
soon we fell asleep
to the sound of a river
swabbling through a gorge.   30

Since then, other enchantments
have blazed and faded,
enemies changed their address,
and War made ugly
an uncountable number   35
of unknown neighbors,
precious as us to themselves:
but round your image
there is no fog, and the Earth
can still astonish.   40

Of what, then, should I complain,
pottering about
a neat suburban kitchen?
Solitude? Rubbish!
It's social enough with real   45
faces and landscapes
for whose friendly countenance
I at least can learn
to live with obesity
and a little fame.   50

                                        1965   1969

Old People's Home

      All are limitory, but each has her own
nuance of damage. The elite can dress and decent themselves,
      are ambulant with a single stick, adroit
to read a book all through, or play the slow movements of
      easy sonatas. (Yet, perhaps their very   5
carnal freedom is their spirit's bane: intelligent
      of what has happened and why, they are obnoxious
to a glum beyond tears.) Then come those on wheels, the average
      majority, who endure T.V. and, led by
lenient therapists, do community-singing, then   10
      the loners, muttering in Limbo, and last
the terminally incompetent, as improvident,
      unspeakable, impeccable as the plants
they parody. (Plants may sweat profusely but never
      sully themselves.) One tie, though, unites them: all   15
appeared when the world, though much was awry there, was more
      spacious, more comely to look at, its Old Ones
with an audience and secular station. Then a child,
      in dismay with Mamma, could refuge with Gran
to be revalued and told a story. As of now,   20
      we all know what to expect, but their generation
is the first to fade like this, not at home but assigned
      to a numbered frequent ward, stowed out of conscience
as unpopular luggage.
                    As I ride the subway   25
      to spend half-an-hour with one, I revisage
who she was in the pomp and sumpture of her hey-day,
      when week-end visits were a presumptive joy,
not a good work. Am I cold to wish for a speedy
      painless dormition, pray, as I know she prays,   30
that God or Nature will abrupt her earthly function?

                                        1970   1972

---

30 dormition   death as going to sleep

LOUIS MACNEICE

1907–63 b Belfast. He lived much of his life in London, working for the BBC.

Bagpipe Music

It's no go the merrygoround, it's no go the rickshaw,
All we want is a limousine and a ticket for the peepshow.
Their knickers are made of crêpe-de-chine, their shoes are made
    of python,
Their halls are lined with tiger rugs and their walls with heads of bison.

John MacDonald found a corpse, put it under the sofa,   5
Waited till it came to life and hit it with a poker,
Sold its eyes for souvenirs, sold its blood for whiskey,
Kept its bones for dumb-bells to use when he was fifty.

It's no go the Yogi-Man, it's no go Blavatsky,
All we want is a bank balance and a bit of skirt in a taxi.   10

Annie MacDougall went to milk, caught her foot in the heather,
Woke to hear a dance record playing of Old Vienna.
It's no go your maidenheads, it's no go your culture,
All we want is a Dunlop tyre and the devil mend the puncture.

The Laird o' Phelps spent Hogmanay declaring he was sober,   15
Counted his feet to prove the fact and found he had one foot over.
Mrs. Carmichael had her fifth, looked at the job with repulsion,
Said to the midwife 'Take it away; I'm through with over-production'.

It's no go the gossip column, it's no go the Ceilidh,
All we want is a mother's help and a sugar-stick for the baby.   20

Willie Murray cut his thumb, couldn't count the damage,
Took the hide of an Ayrshire cow and used it for a bandage.
His brother caught three hundred cran when the seas were lavish,
Threw the bleeders back in the sea and went upon the parish.

It's no go the Herring Board, it's no go the Bible,   25
All we want is a packet of fags when our hands are idle.

It's no go the picture palace, it's no go the stadium,
It's no go the country cot with a pot of pink geraniums,   *cottage*
It's no go the Government grants, it's no go the elections,
Sit on your arse for fifty years and hang your hat on a pension.   30

It's no go my honey love, it's no go my poppet;
Work your hands from day to day, the winds will blow the profit.
The glass is falling hour by hour, the glass will fall for ever,   *barometer*
But if you break the bloody glass you won't hold up the weather.

        1938

---

9 Blavatsky   Madame Helena Blavatsky (1831–91), Russian founder of the occultist Theosophical
Society
19 Ceilidh   (pron. kayley) a small gathering for traditional music, dancing or stories
23 cran   a measure of about 750 herrings

Conversation

Ordinary people are peculiar too:
Watch the vagrant in their eyes
Who sneaks away while they are talking with you
Into some black wood behind the skull,
Following un-, or other, realities,   5
Fishing for shadows in a pool.

But sometimes the vagrant comes the other way
Out of their eyes and into yours
Having mistaken you perhaps for yesterday
Or for to-morrow night, a wood in which   10
He may pick up among the pine-needles and burrs
The lost purse, the dropped stitch.

Vagrancy however is forbidden; ordinary men
Soon come back to normal, look you straight
In the eyes as if to say 'It will not happen again',   15
Put up a barrage of common sense to baulk
Intimacy but by mistake interpolate
Swear-words like roses in their talk.

                                            1940   1941

SIR JOHN BETJEMAN

1906–84 b London, where he lived. He was poet laureate and also a well-known conservationist in the area of English architecture and locality.

Indoor Games near Newbury

In among the silver birches winding ways of tarmac wander
  And the signs to Bussock Bottom, Tussock Wood and Windy Brake,
Gabled lodges, tile-hung churches, catch the lights of our Lagonda
  As we drive to Wendy's party, lemon curd and Christmas cake.
      Rich the makes of motor whirring,   5
      Past the pine-plantation purring
         Come up, Hupmobile, Delage!
      Short the way your chauffeurs travel,
      Crunching over private gravel
         Each from out his warm garáge.   10

Oh but Wendy, when the carpet yielded to my indoor pumps
    There you stood, your gold hair streaming,
    Handsome in the hall-light gleaming
There you looked and there you led me off into the game of clumps
    Then the new Victrola playing   15
    And your funny uncle saying

'Choose your partners for a fox-trot! Dance until it's *tea* o'clock!
   'Come on, young 'uns, foot it featly!'
   Was it chance that paired us neatly,
   I, who loved you so completely,   20
You, who pressed me closely to you, hard against your party frock?

'Meet me when you've finished eating!' So we met and no one found us.
  Oh that dark and furry cupboard while the rest played hide and seek!
Holding hands our two hearts beating in the bedroom silence round us,
  Holding hands and hardly hearing sudden footstep, thud and shriek.   25
    Love that lay too deep for kissing—
    'Where *is* Wendy? Wendy's missing!'
    Love so pure it *had* to end,
    Love so strong that I was frighten'd
    When you gripped my fingers tight and   30
    Hugging, whispered 'I'm your friend.'

Good-bye Wendy! Send the fairies, pinewood elf and larch tree gnome,
   Spingle-spangled stars are peeping
   At the lush Lagonda creeping
Down the winding ways of tarmac to the leaded lights of home.   35
   There, among the silver birches,
   All the bells of all the churches
Sounded in the bath-waste running out into the frosty air.
   Wendy speeded my undressing,
   Wendy is the sheet's caressing   40
   Wendy bending gives a blessing,
Holds me as I drift to dreamland, safe inside my slumberwear.

              1948

Devonshire Street W.1

The heavy mahogany door with its wrought-iron screen
  Shuts. And the sound is rich, sympathetic, discreet.
The sun still shines on this eighteenth-century scene
  With Edwardian faience adornments— Devonshire Street.

No hope. And the X-ray photographs under his arm   5
  Confirm the message. His wife stands timidly by.
The opposite brick-built house looks lofty and calm
  Its chimneys steady against a mackerel sky.

No hope. And the iron knob of his palisade
  So cold to the touch, is luckier now than he
'Oh merciless, hurrying Londoners! Why was I made   10
  For the long and the painful deathbed coming to me?'

She puts her fingers in his as, loving and silly,
  At long-past Kensington dances she used to do
'It's cheaper to take the tube to Piccadilly   15
  And then we can catch a nineteen or a twenty-two.'

              1954

STEVIE SMITH

1902–71 b Hull. She was also a novelist, and worked as a private secretary in London.

Not Waving but Drowning

Nobody heard him, the dead man,
But still he lay moaning:
I was much further out than you thought
And not waving but drowning.

Poor chap, he always loved larking   5
And now he's dead
It must have been too cold for him his heart gave way,
They said.

Oh, no no no, it was too cold always
(Still the dead one lay moaning)   10
I was much too far out all my life
And not waving but drowning.

                                              1957

Away, Melancholy

Away, melancholy,
Away with it, let it go.

Are not the trees green,
The earth as green?
Does not the wind blow,   5
Fire leap and the rivers flow?
Away melancholy.

The ant is busy
He carrieth his meat,
All things hurry   10
To be eaten or eat.
Away, melancholy.

Man, too, hurries,
Eats, couples, buries,
He is an animal also   15
With a hey ho melancholy,
Away with it, let it go.

Man of all creatures
Is superlative
(Away melancholy)   20
He of all creatures alone
Raiseth a stone
(Away melancholy)
Into the stone, the god,
Pours what he knows of good   25
Calling, good, God.
Away melancholy, let it go.

Speak not to me of tears,
Tyranny, pox, wars,
Saying, Can God
Stone of man's thought, be good?   30

Say rather it is enough
That the stuffed
Stone of man's good, growing,
By man's called God.
Away, melancholy, let it go.   35

Man aspires
To good,
To love
Sighs;   40

Beaten, corrupted, dying
In his own blood lying
Yet heaves up an eye above
Cries, Love, love.
It is his virtue needs explaining,   45
Not his failing.

Away, melancholy,
Away with it, let it go.

                                          1957

A House of Mercy

It was a house of female habitation,
Two ladies fair inhabited the house,
And they were brave. For although Fear knocked loud
Upon the door, and said he must come in,
They did not let him in.   5

There were also two feeble babes, two girls,
That Mrs S. had by her husband had,
He soon left them and went away to sea,
Nor sent them money, nor came home again
Except to borrow back   10
Her Naval Officer's Wife's Allowance from Mrs S.
Who gave it him at once, she thought she should.

There was also the ladies' aunt
And babes' great aunt, a Mrs Martha Hearn Clode,
And she was elderly.   15
These ladies put their money all together
And so we lived.

I was the younger of the feeble babes
And when I was a child my mother died
And later Great Aunt Martha Hearn Clode died   20
And later still my sister went away.

Now I am old I tend my mother's sister
The noble aunt who so long tended us,
Faithful and True her name is. Tranquil.
Also Sardonic. And I tend the house.   25

It is a house of female habitation
A house expecting strength as it is strong
A house of aristocratic mould that looks apart
When tears fall; counts despair
Derisory. Yet it has kept us well. For all its faults,   30
If they are faults, of sternness and reserve,
It is a Being of warmth I think; at heart
A house of mercy.
                                                                1966

ROY CAMPBELL

1901–1957 Durban. He was a soldier, horse breeder, polemicist and poet; based in England from 1928 and also, later, in Spain and Portugal.

The Zulu Girl

When in the sun the hot red acres smoulder,
Down where the sweating gang its labour plies,
A girl flings down her hoe, and from her shoulder
Unslings her child tormented by the flies.

She takes him to a ring of shadow pooled   5
By thorn-trees: purpled with the blood of ticks,
While her sharp nails, in slow caresses ruled,
Prowl through his hair with sharp electric clicks,

His sleepy mouth plugged by the heavy nipple,
Tugs like a puppy, grunting as he feeds: 10
Through his frail nerves her own deep languors ripple
Like a broad river sighing through its reeds.

Yet in that drowsy stream his flesh imbibes
An old unquenched unsmotherable heat—
The curbed ferocity of beaten tribes,   15
The sullen dignity of their defeat.

Her body looms above him like a hill
Within whose shade a village lies at rest,
Or the first cloud so terrible and still
That bears the coming harvest in its breast.   20
                                                                1930

The Serf

His naked skin clothed in the torrid mist
That puffs in smoke around the patient hooves,
The ploughman drives, a slow somnambulist,
And through the green his crimson furrow grooves.

His heart, more deeply than he wounds the plain,   5
Long by the rasping share of insult torn,
Red clod, to which the war-cry once was rain
And tribal spears the fatal sheaves of corn,
Lies fallow now. But as the turf divides
I see in the slow progress of his strides   10
Over the toppled clods and falling flowers,
The timeless, surly patience of the serf
That moves the nearest to the naked earth
And ploughs down palaces, and thrones, and towers.

1930

KENNETH SLESSOR

1901–71 b and lived in Sydney. He worked as a journalist and war correspondent.

Five Bells

Time that is moved by little fidget wheels
Is not my Time, the flood that does not flow.
Between the double and the single bell
Of a ship's hour, between a round of bells
From the dark warship riding there below,
I have lived many lives, and this one life   5
Of Joe, long dead, who lives between five bells.

Deep and dissolving verticals of light
Ferry the falls of moonshine down. Five bells
Coldly rung out in a machine's voice. Night and water   10
Pour to one rip of darkness, the Harbour floats
In air, the Cross hangs upside-down in water.

Why do I think of you, dead man, why thieve
These profitless lodgings from the flukes of thought
Anchored in Time? You have gone from earth,   15
Gone even from the meaning of a name;
Yet something's there, yet something forms its lips
And hits and cries against the ports of space,
Beating their sides to make its fury heard.

Are you shouting at me, dead man, squeezing your face   20
In agonies of speech on speechless panes?
Cry louder, beat the windows, bawl your name!

But I hear nothing, nothing . . . only bells,
Five bells, the bumpkin calculus of Time.
Your echoes die, your voice is dowsed by Life,   25
There's not a mouth can fly the pygmy strait—

Five Bells   ship's signal for ten-thirty

Nothing except the memory of some bones
Long shoved away, and sucked away, in mud;
And unimportant things you might have done,
Or once I thought you did; but you forgot,   30
And all have now forgotten—looks and words
And slops of beer; your coat with buttons off,
Then I saw the road, I heard the thunder
Tumble, and felt the talons of the rain
The night we came to Moorebank in slab-dark,   35
So dark you bore no body, had no face,
But a sheer voice that rattled out of air
(As now you'd cry if I could break the glass),
A voice that spoke beside me in the bush,
Loud for a breath or bitten off by wind,   40
Of Milton, melons, and the Rights of Man,
And blowing flutes, and how Tahitian girls
Are brown and angry-tongued, and Sydney girls
Are white and angry-tongued, or so you'd found.
But all I heard was words that didn't join   45
So Milton became melons, melons girls,
And fifty mouths, it seemed, were out that night,
And in each tree an Ear was bending down,
Or something had just run, gone behind grass,
When, blank and bone-white, like a maniac's thought,   50
The naphtha-flash of lightning slit the sky,
Knifing the dark with deathly photographs.
There's not so many with so poor a purse
Or fierce a need, must fare by night like that,
Five miles in darkness on a country track,   55
But when you do, that's what you think.
                                    Five bells.

In Melbourne, your appetite had gone,
Your angers too; they had been leeched away
By the soft archery of summer rains   60
And the sponge-paws of wetness, the slow damp
That stuck the leaves of living, snailed the mind,
And showed your bones, that had been sharp with rage,
The sodden ecstasies of rectitude.
I thought of what you'd written in faint ink,   65
Your journal with the sawn-off lock, that stayed behind
With other things you left, all without use,
All without meaning now, except a sign
That someone had been living who now was dead:
'At Labassa. Room 6 x 8   70
On top of the tower; because of this, very dark
And cold in winter. Everything has been stowed
Into this room—500 books all shapes
And colours, dealt across the floor
And over sills and on the laps of chairs;   75
Guns, photoes of many differant things
And differant curioes that I obtained. . . .'

In Sydney, by the spent aquarium-flare
Of penny gaslight on pink wallpaper,
We argued about blowing up the world,   80
But you were living backward, so each night
You crept a moment closer to the breast,
And they were living, all of them, those frames
And shapes of flesh that had perplexed your youth,
And most your father, the old man gone blind,   85
With fingers always round a fiddle's neck,
That graveyard mason whose fair monuments
And tablets cut with dreams of piety
Rest on the bosoms of a thousand men
Staked bone by bone, in quiet astonishment   90
At cargoes they had never thought to bear,
These funeral-cakes of sweet and sculptured stone.   .

Where have you gone? The tide is over you,
The turn of midnight water's over you,
As Time is over you, and mystery,   95
And memory, the flood that does not flow.
You have no suburb, like those easier dead
In private berths of dissolution laid—
The tide goes over, the waves ride over you
And let their shadows down like shining hair,   100
But they are Water; and the sea-pinks bend
Like lilies in your teeth, but they are Weed;
And you are only part of an Idea.
I felt the wet push its black thumb-balls in,
The night you died, I felt your eardrums crack,   105
And the short agony, the longer dream,
The Nothing that was neither long nor short;
But I was bound, and could not go that way,
But I was blind, and could not feel your hand.
If I could find an answer, could only find   110
Your meaning, or could say why you were here
Who now are gone, what purpose gave you breath
Or seized it back, might I not hear your voice?

I looked out of my window in the dark
At waves with diamond quills and combs of light   115
That arched their mackerel-backs and smacked the sand
In the moon's drench, that straight enormous glaze,
And ships far off asleep, and Harbour-buoys
Tossing their fireballs wearily each to each,
And tried to hear your voice, but all I heard   120
Was a boat's whistle, and the scraping squeal
Of seabirds' voices far away, and bells,
Five bells. Five bells coldly ringing out.
                                    Five bells.

                                                    1939

Beach Burial

Softly and humbly to the Gulf of Arabs
The convoys of dead sailors come;
At night they sway and wander in the waters far under,
But morning rolls them in the foam.

Between the sob and clubbing of the gunfire   5
Someone, it seems, has time for this,
To pluck them from the shallows and bury them in burrows
And tread the sand upon their nakedness;

And each cross, the driven stake of tidewood,
Bears the last signature of men,   10
Written with such perplexity, with such bewildered pity,
The words choke as they begin—

'*Unknown seaman*'—the ghostly pencil
Wavers and fades, the purple drips,
The breath of the wet season has washed their inscriptions   15
As blue as drowned men's lips,

Dead seamen, gone in search of the same landfall,
Whether as enemies they fought,
Or fought with us, or neither; the sand joins them together,
Enlisted on the other front.   20

El Alamein.
                                        1942   1944

HART CRANE

1899–1932 b Ohio. He led an unsettled existence in Ohio and New York, and died young, taking his own life.

From Voyages

I

Above the fresh ruffles of the surf
Bright striped urchins flay each other with sand.
They have contrived a conquest for shell shucks,
And their fingers crumble fragments of baked weed
Gaily digging and scattering.   5

And in answer to their treble interjections
The sun beats lightning on the waves,
The waves fold thunder on the sand;
And could they hear me I would tell them:

O brilliant kids, frisk with your dog,   10
Fondle your shells and sticks, bleached
By time and the elements; but there is a line
You must not cross nor ever trust beyond it

Spry cordage of your bodies to caresses
Too lichen-faithful from too wide a breast.   15
The bottom of the sea is cruel.

II

—And yet this great wink of eternity,
Of rimless floods, unfettered leewardings,
Samite sheeted and processioned where
Her undinal vast belly moonward bends,
Laughing the wrapt inflections of our love;   5

Take this Sea, whose diapason knells
On scrolls of silver snowy sentences,
The sceptred terror of whose sessions rends
As her demeanors motion well or ill,
All but the pieties of lovers' hands.   10

And onward, as bells off San Salvador
Salute the crocus lustres of the stars,
In these poinsettia meadows of her tides,—
Adagios of islands, O my Prodigal,
Complete the dark confessions her veins spell.   15

Mark how her turning shoulders wind the hours,
And hasten while her penniless rich palms
Pass superscription of bent foam and wave,—
Hasten, while they are true,—sleep, death, desire,
Close round one instant in one floating flower.   20

Bind us in time, O Seasons clear, and awe.
O minstrel galleons of Carib fire,
Bequeath us to no earthly shore until
Is answered in the vortex of our grave
The seal's wide spindrift gaze toward paradise.   25

                                                    1926

ROBERT GRAVES

1895–1985 b London; father Irish. From the late twenties he lived in Majorca as a
professional writer.

The Cool Web

Children are dumb to say how hot the day is,
How hot the scent is of the summer rose,
How dreadful the black wastes of evening sky,
How dreadful the tall soldiers drumming by.

But we have speech, to chill the angry day,   5
And speech, to dull the rose's cruel scent.
We spell away the overhanging night,
We spell away the soldiers and the fright.

There's a cool web of language winds us in,
Retreat from too much joy or too much fear: 10
We grow sea-green at last and coldly die
In brininess and volubility.

But if we let our tongues lose self-possession,
Throwing off language and its watery clasp
Before our death, instead of when death comes,   15
Facing the wide glare of the children's day,
Facing the rose, the dark sky and the drums,
We shall go mad no doubt and die that way.

                                                1927

Nature's Lineaments

When mountain rocks and leafy trees
And clouds and things like these,
With edges,

Caricature the human face,
Such scribblings have no grace   5
Nor peace—

The bulbous nose, the sunken chin,
The ragged mouth in grin
Of cretin.

Nature is always so: you find   10
That all she has of mind
Is wind,

Retching among the empty spaces,
Ruffling the idiot grasses,
The sheeps' fleeces.   15

Whose pleasures are excreting, poking,
Havocking and sucking,
Sleepy licking.

Whose griefs are melancholy,
Whose flowers are oafish,   20
Whose waters, silly,
Whose birds, raffish,
Whose fish, fish.   1938

With a Gift of Rings

It was no costume jewellery I sent:
True stones cool to the tongue, their settings ancient,
Their magic evident.
Conceal your pride, accept them negligently
But, naked on your couch, wear them for me.   5

                                                1972

E.E. CUMMINGS

(Edward Estlin) 1894–1962 b Massachusetts. He lived in New York, earning a frugal living as a writer and painter.

[my sweet old etcetera]

my sweet old etcetera
aunt lucy during the recent

war could and what
is more did tell you just
what everybody was fighting   5

for,
my sister

isabel created hundreds
(and
hundreds)of socks not to   10
mention shirts fleaproof earwarmers
etcetera wristers etcetera, my
mother hoped that

i would die etcetera
bravely of course my father used   15
to become hoarse talking about how it was
a privilege and if only he
could meanwhile my

self etcetera lay quietly
in the deep mud et   20

cetera
(dreaming,
et
    cetera, of
Your smile   25
eyes knees and of your Etcetera)

                                                    1926

[next to of course god america i]

'next to of course god america i
love you land of the pilgrims' and so forth oh
say can you see by the dawn's early my
country 'tis of centuries come and go
and are no more what of it we should worry   5
in every language even deafanddumb
thy sons acclaim your glorious name by gorry
by jingo by gee by gosh by gum

why talk of beauty what could be more beautiful than these heroic happy dead
who rushed like lions to the roaring slaughter
they did not stop to think they died instead
then shall the voice of liberty be mute?'

He spoke. And drank rapidly a glass of water

1926

[these children singing in stone a]

these children singing in stone a
silence of stone these
little children wound with stone
flowers opening for

ever these silently lit
tle children are petals
their song is a flower
always their flowers

of stone are
silently singing
a song more silent
than silence these always

children forever
singing wreathed with singing
blossoms children of
stone with blossoming

eyes
know if a
lit tle
tree listens

forever to always children singing forever
a song made
of silent as stone silence of
song

1940

[l(a]

l(a

le
af
fa

ll

s)
one
l

iness

1958

WILFRED OWEN

1893–1918 b Shropshire. He fought in France in 1917, from which period his war poetry
derives. Returning to the Front late in 1918, he was killed a week before the armistice.

Strange Meeting

It seemed that out of battle I escaped
Down some profound dull tunnel, long since scooped
Through granites which titanic wars had groined.
Yet also there encumbered sleepers groaned,
Too fast in thought or death to be bestirred.   5
Then, as I probed them, one sprang up, and stared
With piteous recognition in fixed eyes,
Lifting distressful hands as if to bless.
And by his smile, I knew that sullen hall,
By his dead smile I knew we stood in Hell.   10
With a thousand pains that vision's face was grained;
Yet no blood reached there from the upper ground,
And no guns thumped, or down the flues made moan.
'Strange friend,' I said, 'here is no cause to mourn.'
'None,' said that other, 'save the undone years,   15
The hopelessness. Whatever hope is yours,
Was my life also; I went hunting wild
After the wildest beauty in the world,
Which lies not calm in eyes, or braided hair,
But mocks the steady running of the hour,   20
And if it grieves, grieves richlier than here.
For by my glee might many men have laughed,
And of my weeping something had been left,
Which must die now. I mean the truth untold,
The pity of war, the pity war distilled.   25
Now men will go content with what we spoiled,
Or, discontent, boil bloody, and be spilled.
They will be swift with swiftness of the tigress.
None will break ranks, though nations trek from progress.
Courage was mine, and I had mystery,   30
Wisdom was mine, and I had mastery:
To miss the march of this retreating world
Into vain citadels that are not walled.
Then, when much blood had clogged their chariot-wheels,
I would go up and wash them from sweet wells,   35
Even with truths that lie too deep for taint.
I would have poured my spirit without stint
But not through wounds; not on the cess of war.
Foreheads of men have bled where no wounds were.
I am the enemy you killed, my friend.   40
I knew you in this dark: for so you frowned
Yesterday through me as you jabbed and killed.
I parried; but my hands were loath and cold.
Let us sleep now....'

1920

Dulce et Decorum Est

Bent double, like old beggars under sacks,
Knock-kneed, coughing like hags, we cursed through sludge,
Till on the haunting flares we turned our backs
And towards our distant rest began to trudge.
Men marched asleep. Many had lost their boots   5
But limped on, blood-shod. All went lame; all blind;
Drunk with fatigue; deaf even to the hoots
Of tired, outstripped Five-Nines that dropped behind.   *gas shells*

Gas! GAS! Quick, boys!—An ecstasy of fumbling,
Fitting the clumsy helmets just in time,   10
But someone still was yelling out and stumbling
And flound'ring like a man in fire or lime . . .
Dim, through the misty panes and thick green light,
As under a green sea, I saw him drowning.

In all my dreams, before my helpless sight,   15
He plunges at me, guttering, choking, drowning.

If in some smothering dreams, you too could pace
Behind the wagon that we flung him in,
And watch the white eyes writhing in his face,
His hanging face, like a devil's sick of sin;   20
If you could hear, at every jolt the blood
Come gargling from the froth-corrupted lungs,
Obscene as cancer, bitter as the cud
Of vile, incurable sores on innocent tongues,—
My friend, you would not tell with such high zest   25
To children ardent for some desperate glory,
The old Lie: Dulce et decorum est
Pro patria mori.
                                                        1920

Futility

Move him into the sun—
Gently its touch awoke him once,
At home, whispering of fields unsown.
Always it woke him, even in France,
Until this morning and this snow.   5
If anything might rouse him now
The kind old sun will know.

Think how it wakes the seeds,—
Woke, once, the clays of a cold star.
Are limbs, so dear-achieved, are sides,   10
Full-nerved,—still warm,—too hard to stir?
Was it for this the clay grew tall?
—O what made fatuous sunbeams toil
To break earth's sleep at all?
                                                        1920

27–28 From Horace: *Odes* III, ii, 13: 'It is sweet and honourable to die for one's country'.

HUGH MACDIARMID

(Christopher Murray Grieve) 1892–1978 b Dumfriesshire. Also a literary editor, he was a prominent communist and Scottish nationalist. He wrote poetry in both Scots and English.

Another Epitaph on an Army of Mercenaries

It is a God-damned lie to say that these
Saved, or knew, anything worth any man's pride.
They were professional murderers and they took
Their blood money and impious risks and died.
In spite of all their kind some elements of worth   5
With difficulty persist here and there on earth.

1935

Crystals like Blood

I remember how, long ago, I found
Crystals like blood in a broken stone.

I picked up a broken chunk of bed-rock
And turned it this way and that,
It was heavier than one would have expected   5
From its size. One face was caked
With brown limestone. But the rest
Was a hard greenish-grey quartz-like stone
Faintly dappled with darker shadows,
And in this quartz ran veins and beads   10
Of bright magenta.

And I remember how later on I saw
How mercury is extracted from cinnebar
—The double ring of iron piledrivers
Like the multiple legs of a fantastically symmetrical spider   15
Rising and falling with monotonous precision,
Marching round in an endless circle
And pounding up and down with a tireless, thunderous force,
While, beyond, another conveyor drew the crumbled ore
From the bottom and raised it to an opening high   20
In the side of a gigantic grey-white kiln.

So I remember how mercury is got
When I contrast my living memory of you
And your dear body rotting here in the clay
—And feel once again released in me   25
The bright torrents of felicity, naturalness, and faith
My treadmill memory draws from you yet.

1949

Another Epitaph   A reply to Housman's poem (p. 191)

T.S. ELIOT

(Thomas Stearns) 1888–1965 b St Louis; moved to Massachusetts as a child. In 1914 he settled in London, later becoming a British citizen. He was an influential critic and playwright as well as poet.

The Love Song of J. Alfred Prufrock

S'io credessi che mia risposta fosse
a persona che mai tornasse al mondo,
questa fiamma staria senza più scosse.
Ma per ciò che giammai di questo fondo
non tornò vivo alcun, s'i'odo il vero,
senza tema d'infamia ti rispondo.

Let us go then, you and I,
When the evening is spread out against the sky
Like a patient etherised upon a table;
Let us go, through certain half-deserted streets,
The muttering retreats   5
Of restless nights in one-night cheap hotels
And sawdust restaurants with oyster-shells:
Streets that follow like a tedious argument
Of insidious intent
To lead you to an overwhelming question. . .   10
Oh, do not ask, 'What is it?'
Let us go and make our visit.

In the room the women come and go
Talking of Michelangelo.

The yellow fog that rubs its back upon the window-panes,   15
The yellow smoke that rubs its muzzle on the window-panes,
Licked its tongue into the corners of the evening,
Lingered upon the pools that stand in drains,
Let fall upon its back the soot that falls from chimneys,
Slipped by the terrace, made a sudden leap,   20
And seeing that it was a soft October night,
Curled once about the house, and fell asleep.

And indeed there will be time
For the yellow smoke that slides along the street
Rubbing its back upon the window-panes;   25
There will be time, there will be time
To prepare a face to meet the faces that you meet;
There will be time to murder and create,
And time for all the works and days of hands
That lift and drop a question on your plate;   30

Epigraph: from Dante, *Inferno* XXVII, 61–66. The words are spoken in tongues of flame by Guido da Montefeltro in the eighth circle of hell, that of the evil counsellors: 'If I thought that my answer were to a person who would ever return to the world, this flame would stand still and not move. But since from this abyss no one ever returned alive, if what I hear is true, without fear of disgrace I reply.' **23–24** See Eccles. 3:1 'a time to every purpose under the heaven'.

Time for you and time for me,
And time yet for a hundred indecisions,
And for a hundred visions and revisions,
Before the taking of a toast and tea.

    In the room the women come and go   35
Talking of Michelangelo.

    And indeed there will be time
To wonder, 'Do I dare?' and, 'Do I dare?'
Time to turn back and descend the stair,
With a bald spot in the middle of my hair—   40
(They will say: 'How his hair is growing thin!')
My morning coat, my collar mounting firmly to the chin,
My necktie rich and modest, but asserted by a simple pin—
(They will say: 'But how his arms and legs are thin!')
Do I dare   45
Disturb the universe?
In a minute there is time
For decisions and revisions which a minute will reverse.

    For I have known them all already, known them all—
Have known the evenings, mornings, afternoons,   50
I have measured out my life with coffee spoons;
I know the voices dying with a dying fall
Beneath the music from a farther room.
    So how should I presume?

    And I have known the eyes already, known them all—   55
The eyes that fix you in a formulated phrase,
And when I am formulated, sprawling on a pin,
When I am pinned and wriggling on the wall,
Then how should I begin
To spit out all the butt-ends of my days and ways?   60
    And how should I presume?

    And I have known the arms already, known them all—
Arms that are braceleted and white and bare
(But in the lamplight, downed with light brown hair!)
Is it perfume from a dress   65
That makes me so digress?
Arms that lie along a table, or wrap about a shawl.
    And should I then presume?
    And how should I begin?

        . . . . .

    Shall I say, I have gone at dusk through narrow streets   70
And watched the smoke that rises from the pipes
Of lonely men in shirt-sleeves, leaning out of windows? . . .

    I should have been a pair of ragged claws
Scuttling across the floors of silent seas.

        . . . . .

    And the afternoon, the evening, sleeps so peacefully!   75
Smoothed by long fingers,
Asleep. . .tired. . .or it malingers,
Stretched on the floor, here beside you and me.

Should I, after tea and cakes and ices,
Have the strength to force the moment to its crisis?   80
But though I have wept and fasted, wept and prayed,
Though I have seen my head (grown slightly bald) brought in upon a platter,
I am no prophet—and here's no great matter;
I have seen the moment of my greatness flicker,
And I have seen the eternal Footman hold my coat, and snicker,   85
And in short, I was afraid.

    And would it have been worth it, after all,
After the cups, the marmalade, the tea,
Among the porcelain, among some talk of you and me,
Would it have been worth while,   90
To have bitten off the matter with a smile,
To have squeezed the universe into a ball
To roll it towards some overwhelming question,
To say: 'I am Lazarus, come from the dead,
Come back to tell you all, I shall tell you all'—   95
If one, settling a pillow by her head,
       Should say: 'That is not what I meant at all.
       That is not it, at all.'

    And would it have been worth it, after all,
Would it have been worth while,   100
After the sunsets and the dooryards and the sprinkled streets,
After the novels, after the teacups, after the skirts that trail along the floor—
And this, and so much more?—
It is impossible to say just what I mean!
But as if a magic lantern threw the nerves in patterns on a screen: 105
Would it have been worth while
If one, settling a pillow or throwing off a shawl,
And turning toward the window, should say:
       'That is not it at all,
       That is not what I meant, at all.'
                    . . . . . .

    No! I am not Prince Hamlet, nor was meant to be;
Am an attendant lord, one that will do
To swell a progress, start a scene or two,
Advise the prince; no doubt, an easy tool,
Deferential, glad to be of use,   115
Politic, cautious, and meticulous;
Full of high sentence, but a bit obtuse;
At times, indeed, almost ridiculous—
Almost, at times, the Fool.

    I grow old...I grow old...   120
I shall wear the bottoms of my trousers rolled.
    Shall I part my hair behind? Do I dare to eat a peach?
I shall wear white flannel trousers, and walk upon the beach.
I have heard the mermaids singing, each to each.

---

82 See Matt. 14:1–12, where Salome is granted her request for the head of St John the Baptist on a platter.
92 See Marvell, 'To his Coy Mistress', lines 41–44 (p. 420).
94 **Lazarus** was raised from the dead by Christ. See John 2:1–44.

I do not think that they will sing to me.   125

I have seen them riding seaward on the waves
Combing the white hair of the waves blown back
When the wind blows the water white and black.

We have lingered in the chambers of the sea
By sea-girls wreathed with seaweed red and brown   130
Till human voices wake us, and we drown.

                                          1910–11   *1917*

The Waste Land

1922

> 'Nam Sibyllam quidem Cumis ego ipse oculis meis
> vidi in ampulla pendere, et cum illi pueri dicerent:
> Σίβνλλα τί θέλεις; respondebat illa: ἀποθανεῖν θέλω.'

For Ezra Pound
il miglior fabbro.

I. The Burial of the Dead

   April is the cruellest month, breeding
Lilacs out of the dead land, mixing
Memory and desire, stirring
Dull roots with spring rain.
Winter kept us warm, covering   5
Earth in forgetful snow, feeding
A little life with dried tubers.
Summer surprised us, coming over the Starnbergersee

The Waste Land   The energy of this poem derives firstly from the immediacy of its abruptly mixed voices and images of postwar England and Europe. These, being modern, require few explanatory notes. However, jostling with such voices, and often within them, are literary and religious fragments from the past: pieces of earlier attempts by the cultures of Europe to make or find meaning (this includes engagement with Eastern religions). Necessary notes are provided for these. The poem has many motifs, hints at a pattern in the collage, none of which is necessarily pre-eminent. One is traditionally noted, however: the frequent image of a land laid waste and its possible return to fertility. In regard to this motif, Eliot's published notes to the poem mention the influence of two books on the recurrence of myths. The first is *The Golden Bough* (1890–1915) by Sir James Frazer, whose *Attis, Adonis, Osiris* volumes discuss myths of the dismemberment of a god and its rebirth in spring. The other is *From Ritual to Romance* (1920) by Jessie Weston, which examines connections between ancient myths of a maimed or ill, impotent Fisher King and medieval myths of the search for the Holy Grail, whose finding is similarly restorative. The Fisher King and Grail stories both involve a virtuous quester who asks the right ritual questions.
Epigraph: From the first-century Roman novel by Petronius, the *Satyricon*: 'For I saw the Sybil with these very eyes at Cumae, suspended in a jar, and when the children said, Sybil, what do you want, she replied, I want to die'. The Sybil, the oracle at Cumae near Naples, was granted perpetual life, but in a body which decayed with age until there was little left of it. See *Metamorphoses* XIV.
il miglior fabbro   the better craftsman: Dante's tribute to the twelfth century poet, Arnaut Daniel (*Purgatorio*, XXVI, 117) and Eliot's to Pound, who edited his manuscript, reducing it by half
8–18 Derived from the autobiography (1913) of Marie Larisch, niece of Empress Elizabeth of Austria.
8–10 Starnbergersee   a lake near Munich   **Hofgarten**   a public park in Munich

With a shower of rain; we stopped in the colonnade,
And went on in sunlight, into the Hofgarten,   10
And drank coffee, and talked for an hour.
Bin gar keine Russin, stamm' aus Litauen, echt deutsch.
And when we were children, staying at the arch-duke's,
My cousin's, he took me out on a sled,
And I was frightened. He said, Marie,   15
Marie, hold on tight. And down we went.
In the mountains, there you feel free.
I read, much of the night, and go south in the winter.

    What are the roots that clutch, what branches grow
Out of this stony rubbish? Son of man,   20
You cannot say, or guess, for you know only
A heap of broken images, where the sun beats,
And the dead tree gives no shelter, the cricket no relief,
And the dry stone no sound of water. Only
There is shadow under this red rock,   25
(Come in under the shadow of this red rock),
And I will show you something different from either
Your shadow at morning striding behind you
Or your shadow at evening rising to meet you;
I will show you fear in a handful of dust.   30
           Frisch weht der Wind
           Der Heimat zu
           Mein Irisch Kind,
           Wo weilest du?
'You gave me hyacinths first a year ago;   35
'They called me the hyacinth girl.'
—Yet when we came back, late, from the hyacinth garden,
Your arms full, and your hair wet, I could not
Speak, and my eyes failed, I was neither
Living nor dead, and I knew nothing,   40
Looking into the heart of light, the silence.
Oed' und leer das Meer.

    Madame Sosostris, famous clairvoyante,
Had a bad cold, nevertheless
Is known to be the wisest woman in Europe,   45
With a wicked pack of cards. Here, said she,
Is your card, the drowned Phoenician Sailor,
(Those are pearls that were his eyes. Look!)
Here is Belladonna, the Lady of the Rocks,

---

12 'I'm not at all Russian, I come from Lithuania, real German.'
20 **Son of man**   form of address used to the prophet Ezekiel by his God: see Ezekiel 2 ff.
31–34 The sailor's love song in Wagner's *Tristan und Isolde*, I, 58: 'Fresh blows the wind towards home: my Irish child, where are you lingering?'
42 Ibid. III, 24: 'Bleak and empty the sea'—the report to the dying Tristan that the ship of his love, Isolde, is not in sight
46–55 **pack of cards**   the Tarot, used for divination. Some of the cards can be associated with figures in this poem; but there is no **Phoenician Sailor**, **Belladonna** or **one-eyed merchant** in the Tarot pack.
48 From Ariel's song to Ferdinand on the (supposed) drowning of his father, the king of Naples: *The Tempest*, I, iii, 401 (see p. 481).

The lady of situations.   50
Here is the man with three staves, and here the Wheel,
And here is the one-eyed merchant, and this card,
Which is blank, is something he carries on his back,
Which I am forbidden to see. I do not find
The Hanged Man. Fear death by water.   55
I see crowds of people, walking round in a ring.
Thank you. If you see dear Mrs Equitone,
Tell her I bring the horoscope myself:
One must be so careful these days.

    Unreal City,   60
Under the brown fog of a winter dawn,
A crowd flowed over London Bridge, so many,
I had not thought death had undone so many.
Sighs, short and infrequent, were exhaled,
And each man fixed his eyes before his feet.   65
Flowed up the hill and down King William Street,
To where Saint Mary Woolnoth kept the hours
With a dead sound on the final stroke of nine.
There I saw one I knew, and stopped him, crying: 'Stetson!
'You who were with me in the ships at Mylae!   70
'That corpse you planted last year in your garden,
'Has it begun to sprout? Will it bloom this year?
'Or has the sudden frost disturbed its bed?
'O keep the Dog far hence, that's friend to men,
'Or with his nails he'll dig it up again!   75
'You! hypocrite lecteur!—mon semblable,—mon frère!'

II. A Game of Chess

    The Chair she sat in, like a burnished throne,
Glowed on the marble, where the glass
Held up by standards wrought with fruited vines
From which a golden Cupidon peeped out   80
(Another hid his eyes behind his wing)
Doubled the flames of sevenbranched candelabra
Reflecting light upon the table as
The glitter of her jewels rose to meet it,
From satin cases poured in rich profusion.   85
In vials of ivory and coloured glass
Unstoppered, lurked her strange synthetic perfumes,
Unguent, powdered, or liquid—troubled, confused
And drowned the sense in odours; stirred by the air
That freshened from the window, these ascended   90

---

55 Hanged Man   a Tarot card which depicts a serene, sacrificial victim hanging upside down
63 See Dante's vision of the mediocre, *Inferno* III, 55–57: 'So long a procession of people, that I would never have believed that death had undone so many.'
70 Mylae   the site, in Sicily, of a naval battle between Rome and Carthage in 260 BC
76 From Charles Baudelaire, 'Au Lecteur' (1857): 'Hypocrite Reader! my mirror-image, my brother!'
77ff Compare the description of Cleopatra on her royal barge, *Antony and Cleopatra* II, ii, 191–218.

In fattening the prolonged candle-flames,
Flung their smoke into the laquearia,
Stirring the pattern on the coffered ceiling.
Huge sea-wood fed with copper
Burned green and orange, framed by the coloured stone,   95
In which sad light a carvèd dolphin swam.
Above the antique mantel was displayed
As though a window gave upon the sylvan scene
The change of Philomel, by the barbarous king
So rudely forced; yet there the nightingale   100
Filled all the desert with inviolable voice
And still she cried, and still the world pursues,
'Jug Jug' to dirty ears.
And other withered stumps of time
Were told upon the walls; staring forms   105
Leaned out, leaning, hushing the room enclosed.
Footsteps shuffled on the stair.
Under the firelight, under the brush, her hair
Spread out in fiery points
Glowed into words, then would be savagely still.   110

　'My nerves are bad to-night. Yes, bad. Stay with me.
'Speak to me. Why do you never speak. Speak.
　'What are you thinking of? What thinking? What?
'I never know what you are thinking. Think.'

　I think we are in rats' alley   115
Where the dead men lost their bones.

　'What is that noise?'
　　　　　　　The wind under the door.
'What is that noise now? What is the wind doing?'
　　　　　　　Nothing again nothing.   120

　　　　　　　　　　　　　　'Do
'You know nothing? Do you see nothing? Do you remember
'Nothing?'

　　　I remember
Those are pearls that were his eyes.   125
'Are you alive, or not? Is there nothing in your head?'
　　　　　　　　　　　　But

O O O O that Shakespeherian Rag—
It's so elegant
So intelligent   130
'What shall I do now? What shall I do?'

---

92 laquearia panelled ceiling
98 sylvan scene See *Paradise Lost* IV, 140 (p. 433).
99–101 Philomel in Greek myth, raped by King Tereus, husband of her sister, Procne, and imprisoned by him with her tongue cut out. She sent a tapestry of the event to Procne, who rescued her, then presented Tereus with their son served as a meal in revenge. Procne and Philomel escaped his fury by being changed respectively into a swallow and a nightingale. See *Metamorphoses* VI.
103 Jug jug the nightingale's sound as it is sometimes represented in Renaissance poetry, e.g. John Lyly's *Campaspe* (1584): 'Jug, Jug, Jug, tereu, shee cryes'

'I shall rush out as I am, and walk the street
'With my hair down, so. What shall we do tomorrow?
'What shall we ever do?'
                    The hot water at ten.   135
And if it rains, a closed car at four.
And we shall play a game of chess,
Pressing lidless eyes and waiting for a knock upon the door.

    When Lil's husband got demobbed, I said—
I didn't mince my words, I said to her myself,   140
HURRY UP PLEASE ITS TIME
Now Albert's coming back, make yourself a bit smart.
He'll want to know what you done with that money he gave you
To get yourself some teeth. He did, I was there.
You have them all out, Lil, and get a nice set,   145
He said, I swear, I can't bear to look at you.
And no more can't I, I said, and think of poor Albert,
He's been in the army four years, he wants a good time,
And if you don't give it him, there's others will, I said.
Oh is there, she said. Something o' that, I said.   150
Then I'll know who to thank, she said, and give me a straight look.
HURRY UP PLEASE ITS TIME
If you don't like it you can get on with it, I said.
Others can pick and choose if you can't.
But if Albert makes off, it won't be for lack of telling.   155
You ought to be ashamed, I said, to look so antique.
(And her only thirty-one.)
I can't help it, she said, pulling a long face,
It's them pills I took, to bring it off, she said.
(She's had five already, and nearly died of young George.)   160
The chemist said it would be all right, but I've never been the same.
You *are* a proper fool, I said.
Well, if Albert won't leave you alone, there it is, I said,
What you get married for if you don't want children?
HURRY UP PLEASE ITS TIME   165
Well, that Sunday Albert was home, they had a hot gammon,
And they asked me in to dinner, to get the beauty of it hot—
HURRY UP PLEASE ITS TIME
HURRY UP PLEASE ITS TIME
Goonight Bill. Goonight Lou. Goonight May. Goonight.   170
Ta ta. Goonight. Goonight.
Good night, ladies, good night, sweet ladies, good night, good night.

III. The Fire Sermon

    The river's tent is broken; the last fingers of leaf
Clutch and sink into the wet bank. The wind
Crosses the brown land, unheard. The nymphs are departed.   175

---

172 Ophelia's last words in *Hamlet*: IV, v, 73
The Fire Sermon   title of a sermon preached by the Buddha, warning against the fires of human
senses and emotions

Sweet Thames, run softly, till I end my song.
The river bears no empty bottles, sandwich papers,
Silk handkerchiefs, cardboard boxes, cigarette ends
Or other testimony of summer nights. The nymphs are departed.
And their friends, the loitering heirs of City directors;   180
Departed, have left no addresses.
By the waters of Leman I sat down and wept...
Sweet Thames, run softly till I end my song,
Sweet Thames, run softly, for I speak not loud or long.
But at my back in a cold blast I hear   185
The rattle of the bones, and chuckle spread from ear to ear.

A rat crept softly through the vegetation
Dragging its slimy belly on the bank
While I was fishing in the dull canal
On a winter evening round behind the gashouse   190
Musing upon the king my brother's wreck
And on the king my father's death before him.
White bodies naked on the low damp ground
And bones cast in a little low dry garret,
Rattled by the rat's foot only, year to year.   195
But at my back from time to time I hear
The sound of horns and motors, which shall bring
Sweeney to Mrs Porter in the spring.
O the moon shone bright on Mrs Porter
And on her daughter   200
They wash their feet in soda water
Et O ces voix d'enfants, chantant dans la coupole!

Twit twit twit
Jug jug jug jug jug jug
So rudely forc'd.   205
Tereu

   Unreal City
Under the brown fog of a winter noon
Mr Eugenides, the Smyrna merchant
Unshaven, with a pocket full of currants   210
C.i.f. London: documents at sight,
Asked me in demotic French
To luncheon at the Cannon Street Hotel
Followed by a weekend at the Metropole.

---

176 the refrain from Spenser's 'Prothalamion' (see p. 491)
182 See Psalm 137:1: 'By the waters of Babylon ...'   **Leman**   Lac Leman, at Geneva, near where
Eliot worked on this poem
185 See Marvell, 'To his Coy Mistress', line 21 (p. 421).
191–92 See *The Tempest* I, ii, 393.
199–201 From a popular song of the First World War
202 From Paul Verlaine's sonnet, 'Parsifal' (1886): 'And O these children's voices, singing in the
dome'. Sir Parsifal, a quester for the Holy Grail, has proved his virtue with a temptress and healed the
wounded king. Wagner's opera, *Parsifal*, ends with an uplifting children's choir, which in Verlaine's
version ironically becomes for the knight a new temptation of the flesh.
211 **C.i.f.**   carriage and insurance free

At the violet hour, when the eyes and back   215
Turn upward from the desk, when the human engine waits
Like a taxi throbbing waiting,
I Tiresias, though blind, throbbing between two lives,
Old man with wrinkled female breasts, can see
At the violet hour, the evening hour that strives   220
Homeward, and brings the sailor home from sea,
The typist home at teatime, clears her breakfast, lights
Her stove, and lays out food in tins.
Out of the window perilously spread
Her drying combinations touched by the sun's last rays,   225
On the divan are piled (at night her bed)
Stockings, slippers, camisoles, and stays.
I Tiresias, old man with wrinkled dugs
Perceived the scene, and foretold the rest—
I too awaited the expected guest.   230
He, the young man carbuncular, arrives,
A small house agent's clerk, with one bold stare,
One of the low on whom assurance sits
As a silk hat on a Bradford millionaire.
The time is now propitious, as he guesses,   235
The meal is ended, she is bored and tired,
Endeavours to engage her in caresses
Which still are unreproved, if undesired.
Flushed and decided, he assaults at once;
Exploring hands encounter no defence;   240
His vanity requires no response,
And makes a welcome of indifference.
(And I Tiresias have foresuffered all
Enacted on this same divan or bed;
I who have sat by Thebes below the wall   245
And walked among the lowest of the dead.)
Bestows one final patronising kiss,
And gropes his way, finding the stairs unlit...

She turns and looks a moment in the glass,
Hardly aware of her departed lover;   250
Her brain allows one half-formed thought to pass:
'Well now that's done: and I'm glad it's over.'

---

218 Tiresias   the blinded seer of Greek legend, who had been both man and woman. Eliot notes: 'Tiresias, although a mere spectator and not indeed a "character", is yet the most important personage in the poem, uniting all the rest. Just as the one-eyed merchant, seller of currants, melts into the Phoenician Sailor, and the latter is not wholly distinct from Ferdinand Prince of Naples, so all the women are one woman, and the two sexes meet in Tiresias. What Tiresias *sees*, in fact, is the substance of the poem.'
220–22   These lines imitate the mood and patterning of Fragment 104a by the Greek poet Sappho (c. 600 BC).
234 Bradford   the prosperous centre of the British woollen industry, in Yorkshire
245 Thebes   In the play *King Oedipus* by Sophocles (?496–406 BC), Tiresias is aware of the parricide and incest, committed unconsciously by Oedipus, which have laid a curse on the city of Thebes.
246   Tiresias was visited by Odysseus in the underworld. See *Odyssey* II.

When lovely woman stoops to folly and
Paces about her room again, alone,
She smoothes her hair with automatic hand,   255
And puts a record on the gramophone.

'This music crept by me upon the waters'
And along the Strand, up Queen Victoria Street.
O City city, I can sometimes hear
Beside a public bar in Lower Thames Street,   260
The pleasant whining of a mandoline
And a clatter and a chatter from within
Where fishmen lounge at noon: where the walls
Of Magnus Martyr hold
Inexplicable splendour of Ionian white and gold.   265

    The river sweats
    Oil and tar
    The barges drift
    With the turning tide
    Red sails   270
    Wide
    To leeward, swing on the heavy spar.
    The barges wash
    Drifting logs
    Down Greenwich reach   275
    Past the Isle of Dogs.
        Weialala leia
        Wallala leialala

    Elizabeth and Leicester
    Beating oars   280
    The stern was formed
    A gilded shell
    Red and gold
    The brisk swell
    Rippled both shores   285
    Southwest wind
    Carried down stream
    The peal of bells
    White towers
        Weialala leia   290
        Wallala leialala

    'Trams and dusty trees.
    Highbury bore me. Richmond and Kew

---

253 **When lovely woman**   From a song by Oliver Goldsmith (see p. 351).
257 From *The Tempest*, I, ii, 394
258–65 The places mentioned are in the business centre of London.
292–306 Eliot, in a note, refers to the women who speak in turn here as 'the Thames-daughters'. They recall the Rhine-daughters who, in Wagner's *Götterdämmerung* III, i, lament the loss of their treasure of gold: **Weialala**.
275–76 **Greenwich ... Isle of Dogs**   a busy stretch of the Thames
279 The Earl of **Leicester** was a frequent companion of Queen **Elizabeth** I.
293 **Highbury**   a London suburb   **Richmond and Kew**   places of recreation on the Thames

Undid me. By Richmond I raised my knees
Supine on the floor of a narrow canoe.'   295

'My feet are at Moorgate, and my heart
Under my feet. After the event
He wept. He promised "a new start."
I made no comment. What should I resent?'

'On Margate Sands.   300
I can connect
Nothing with nothing.
The broken fingernails of dirty hands.
My people humble people who expect
Nothing.'   305
                    la la

To Carthage then I came

Burning burning burning burning
O Lord Thou pluckest me out
O Lord Thou pluckest   310

burning

IV. Death by Water

Phlebas the Phoenician, a fortnight dead,
Forgot the cry of gulls, and the deep sea swell
And the profit and loss.
                            A current under sea   315
Picked his bones in whispers. As he rose and fell
He passed the stages of his age and youth
Entering the whirlpool.
                            Gentile or Jew
O you who turn the wheel and look to windward,   320
Consider Phlebas, who was once handsome and tall as you.

V. What the Thunder said

    After the torchlight red on sweaty faces
After the frosty silence in the gardens
After the agony in stony places
The shouting and the crying   325
Prison and palace and reverberation
Of thunder of spring over distant mountains

---

296 Moorgate   a working-class district in London
300 Margate   a holiday resort on the Thames estuary
307 See the opening of Book III of the *Confessions* of St Augustine (354–430): 'To Carthage then I
came, where a cauldron of unholy loves sang all about mine ears'.
309 From *Confessions*, X, 34: 'I entangle my steps with these outward beauties, but thou pluckest me
out, O Lord, thou pluckest me out!'
312 Phoenician   The Phoenicians of the tenth century BC traded in the Mediterranean and beyond.
322ff   The images in these lines recall the Gospel accounts of Christ's agony and arrest in the garden
of Gethsemane and his subsequent trial and crucifixion.

He who was living is now dead
We who were living are now dying
With a little patience   330

    Here is no water but only rock
Rock and no water and the sandy road
The road winding above among the mountains
Which are mountains of rock without water
If there were water we should stop and drink   335
Amongst the rock one cannot stop or think
Sweat is dry and feet are in the sand
If there were only water amongst the rock
Dead mountain mouth of carious teeth that cannot spit
Here one can neither stand nor lie nor sit   340
There is not even silence in the mountains
But dry sterile thunder without rain
There is not even solitude in the mountains
But red sullen faces sneer and snarl
From doors of mudcracked houses
                                If there were water   345

    And no rock
    If there were rock
    And also water
    And water
    A spring   350
    A pool among the rock
    If there were the sound of water only
    Not the cicada
    And dry grass singing
    But sound of water over a rock   355
    Where the hermit-thrush sings in the pine trees
    Drip drop drip drop drop drop drop
    But there is no water

    Who is the third who walks always beside you?
When I count, there are only you and I together   360
But when I look ahead up the white road
There is always another one walking beside you
Gliding wrapt in a brown mantle, hooded
I do not know whether a man or a woman
—But who is that on the other side of you?   365

    What is that sound high in the air
Murmur of maternal lamentation
Who are those hooded hordes swarming
Over endless plains, stumbling in cracked earth
Ringed by the flat horizon only   370
What is the city over the mountains

---

359 In the context of lines 322ff, this line hints at the anonymous appearance of the resurrected Christ to his disciples travelling to Emmaus: see Luke 24:13–31.
360ff A note by Eliot states that this passage was stimulated by an account of the 'constant delusion', experienced by stressed Antarctic explorers, that their expedition had an extra member.

Cracks and reforms and bursts in the violet air
Falling towers
Jerusalem Athens Alexandria
Vienna London   375
Unreal

    A woman drew her long black hair out tight
And fiddled whisper music on those strings
And bats with baby faces in the violet light
Whistled, and beat their wings   380
And crawled head downward down a blackened wall
And upside down in air were towers
Tolling reminiscent bells, that kept the hours
And voices singing out of empty cisterns and exhausted wells.

    In this decayed hole among the mountains   385
In the faint moonlight, the grass is singing
Over the tumbled graves, about the chapel
There is the empty chapel, only the wind's home.
It has no windows, and the door swings,
Dry bones can harm no one.
Only a cock stood on the rooftree   390
Co co rico co co rico
In a flash of lightning. Then a damp gust
Bringing rain

    Ganga was sunken, and the limp leaves   395
Waited for rain, while the black clouds
Gathered far distant, over Himavant.
The jungle crouched, humped in silence.
Then spoke the thunder
D A
Datta: what have we given?   400
My friend, blood shaking my heart
The awful daring of a moment's surrender
Which an age of prudence can never retract
By this, and this only, we have existed
Which is not to be found in our obituaries   405
Or in memories draped by the beneficent spider
Or under seals broken by the lean solicitor
In our empty rooms
D A
Dayadhvam: I have heard the key   410
Turn in the door once and turn once only
We think of the key, each in his prison

---

387 chapel   Legends of the search for the Holy Grail include a visit to the Chapel Perilous, where the knight's courage is tested by hallucinations.
395 Ganga   Ganges, a holy river for Hindus and Buddhists
397 Himavant   a Himalayan peak
399–422   In the Hindu sacred text, the *Brihad-aranyaka Upanishad* V, 2, **Da** is the exhortation of the lord of creation, Prajapati, to men, daemons and gods. These respectively interpret it as meaning **Datta** (give), **Dayadhvam** (sympathize) and **Damyata** (control the self). He tells each that they have interpreted correctly.

Thinking of the key, each confirms a prison
Only at nightfall, aethereal rumours   415
Revive for a moment a broken Coriolanus
DA
Damyata: The boat responded
Gaily, to the hand expert with sail and oar
The sea was calm, your heart would have responded   420
Gaily, when invited, beating obedient
To controlling hands

                   I sat upon the shore
Fishing, with the arid plain behind me
Shall I at least set my lands in order?   425
London Bridge is falling down falling down falling down
Poi s'ascose nel foco che gli affina
Quando fiam uti chelidon—O swallow swallow
Le Prince d'Aquitaine à la tour abolie
These fragments I have shored against my ruins   430
Why then Ile fit you. Hieronymo's mad againe.
Datta. Dayadhvam. Damyata.
           Shantih shantih shantih

                           1922

Journey of the Magi

   'A cold coming we had of it,
Just the worst time of the year
For a journey, and such a long journey:
The ways deep and the weather sharp,
The very dead of winter.'   5
And the camels galled, sore-footed, refractory,
Lying down in the melting snow.
There were times we regretted
The summer palaces on slopes, the terraces,
And the silken girls bringing sherbet.   10
Then the camel men cursing and grumbling
And running away, and wanting their liquor and women,
And the night-fires going out, and the lack of shelters,

---

416 Coriolanus in Shakespeare's tragedy, a leader of Rome who was ruined for despising the people
427 The poet, Arnaud Daniel, has asked Dante to remember him and his sufferings for his sins of lust: 'Then he hid himself in the fire that purified him' (*Purgatorio* XXVI, 148).
428 From *Pervigilium Veneris* (The Vigil of Venus, anonymous, *c.* third century): 'When will I become like the swallow?' Hearing the song of 'the daughter of Tereus', the speaker longs for his own spring.
429 From Gerard de Nerval's sonnet, 'El Desdichado' ('The Disinherited', 1853): 'The Prince of Aquitaine of the ruined tower'
431 Hieronymo's mad againe sub-title of Thomas Kyd's play, *The Spanish Tragedy* (1592). **Why then Ile fit you** are Hieronymo's words to his son's murderers, whom he is casting for a play in which they are to be killed.
433 Shantih The formal ending to an Upanishad, interpreted by Eliot as equivalent to the phrase, 'The peace which passeth understanding'. See Phil. 4:7.
Magi wise men. See Matt. 2.
1–5 adapted from a Christmas sermon of 1622, by Launcelot Andrewes.

And the cities hostile and the towns unfriendly
And the villages dirty and charging high prices: 15
A hard time we had of it.
At the end we preferred to travel all night,
Sleeping in snatches,
With the voices singing in our ears, saying
That this was all folly.   20
    Then at dawn we came down to a temperate valley,
Wet, below the snow line, smelling of vegetation,
With a running stream and a water-mill beating the darkness,
And three trees on the low sky.
And an old white horse galloped away in the meadow.   25
Then we came to a tavern with vine-leaves over the lintel,
Six hands at an open door dicing for pieces of silver,
And feet kicking the empty wine-skins.
But there was no information, and so we continued
And arrived at evening, not a moment too soon   30
Finding the place; it was (you may say) satisfactory.

    All this was a long time ago, I remember,
And I would do it again, but set down
This set down
This: were we led all that way for   35
Birth or Death? There was a Birth, certainly,
We had evidence and no doubt. I had seen birth and death,
But had thought they were different; this Birth was
Hard and bitter agony for us, like Death, our death.
We returned to our places, these Kingdoms,   40
But no longer at ease here, in the old dispensation,
With an alien people clutching their gods.
I should be glad of another death.

                                                                 1927

Marina

> *Quis hic locus, quae*
> *regio, quae mundi plaga?*

    What seas what shores what grey rocks and what islands
What water lapping the bow
And scent of pine and the woodthrush singing through the fog
What images return
O my daughter.   5

    Those who sharpen the tooth of the dog, meaning
Death

Marina See Shakespeare's *Pericles*: Marina (who was born at sea) is lost as a baby and restored to her father as an adult.
Epigraph: the words of Hercules as he wakes from insanity and discovers that he has murdered his wife and children; from *Hercules Furens* a play by Seneca (55 BC–AD 37): 'What place is this, what country, what region of the world?'

Those who glitter with the glory of the hummingbird, meaning
Death
Those who sit in the sty of contentment, meaning   10
Death
Those who suffer the ecstasy of the animals, meaning
Death
   Are become unsubstantial, reduced by a wind,
A breath of pine, and the woodsong fog   15
By this grace dissolved in place

   What is this face, less clear and clearer
The pulse in the arm, less strong and stronger—
Given or lent? more distant than stars and nearer than the eye

   Whispers and small laughter between leaves and hurrying feet   20
Under sleep, where all the waters meet.

   Bowsprit cracked with ice and paint cracked with heat.
I made this, I have forgotten
And remember.
The rigging weak and the canvas rotten   25
Between one June and another September.
Made this unknowing, half conscious, unknown, my own.
The garboard strake leaks, the seams need caulking.
This form, this face, this life
Living to live in a world of time beyond me; let me   30
Resign my life for this life, my speech for that unspoken,
The awakened, lips parted, the hope, the new ships.

   What seas what shores what granite islands towards my timbers
And woodthrush calling through the fog
My daughter.   35
                   1930

MARIANNE MOORE

1887–1972 b St Louis. She lived in New York from 1918 and was an influential poetry editor during the 1920s.

Bird-Witted

With innocent wide penguin eyes, three
  large fledgling mockingbirds below
the pussy-willow tree,
  stand in a row,
wings touching, feebly solemn,   5
till they see
    their no longer larger
    mother bringing
something which will partially
feed one of them.   10

Toward the high-keyed intermittent squeak
  of broken carriage springs, made by
the three similar, meek-
    coated bird's-eye
freckled forms she comes; and when   15
from the beak
      of one, the still living
      beetle has dropped
out, she picks it up and puts
it in again.   20

Standing in the shade till they have dressed
  their thickly filamented, pale
pussy-willow-surfaced
    coats, they spread tail
and wings, showing one by one,   25
the modest
      white stripe lengthwise on the
      tail and crosswise
underneath the wing, and the
accordion   30

is closed again. What delightful note
  with rapid unexpected flute
sounds leaping from the throat
    of the astute
grown bird, comes back to one from   35
the remote
      unenergetic sun-
      lit air before
the brood was here? How harsh
the bird's voice has become.   40

A piebald cat observing them,
  is slowly creeping toward the trim
trio on the tree stem.
    Unused to him
the three make room—uneasy   45
new problem.
      A dangling foot that missed
      its grasp, is raised
and finds the twig on which it
planned to perch. The   50

parent darting down, nerved by what chills
  the blood, and by hope rewarded—
of toil—since nothing fills
    squeaking unfed
mouths, wages deadly combat,   55
and half kills
      with bayonet beak and
      cruel wings, the
intellectual cautious-
ly creeping cat.   60

1941

The Mind Is an Enchanting Thing

is an enchanted thing
    like the glaze on a
katydid-wing
        subdivided by sun
        till the nettings are legion.   5
Like Gieseking playing Scarlatti;

like the apteryx-awl
    as a beak, or the
kiwi's rain-shawl
        of haired feathers, the mind   10
        feeling its way as though blind,
walks along with its eyes on the ground.

It has memory's ear
    that can hear without
having to hear.   15
        Like the gyroscope's fall,
        truly unequivocal
because trued by regnant certainty,

it is a power of
        strong enchantment. It   20
is like the dove-
        neck animated by
        sun; it is memory's eye;
it's conscientious inconsistency.

                                   25
It tears off the veil; tears
    the temptation, the
mist the heart wears,
        from its eyes—if the heart
        has a face; it takes apart
dejection. It's fire in the dove-neck's   30

iridescence; in the
    inconsistencies
of Scarlatti.
        Unconfusion submits
        its confusion to proof; it's   35
not a Herod's oath that cannot change.

                                  1944

---

6 Gieseking Walter Gieseking (1895–1956), German classical pianist **Scarlatti** Domenico
Scarlatti (1685–1757), Italian composer and harpsichordist
36 Herod's oath the injudicious oath of the tetrarch of Galilee, Herod Antipas (21 BC–AD 39),
which led to the execution of John the Baptist. See Mark 6.17–28.

H. D.

(Hilda Doolittle) 1886–1961 b Pennsylvania. Also a novelist, she was a pioneer of literary modernism. From 1911 she lived mostly in Switzerland and England.

From Toward the Piraeus

5

It was not chastity that made me cold nor fear,
only I knew that you, like myself, were sick
of the puny race that crawls and quibbles and lisps
of love and love and lovers and love's deceit.

It was not chastity that made me wild, but fear   5
that my weapon, tempered in different heat,
was over-matched by yours, and your hand
skilled to yield death-blows, might break

With the slightest turn — no ill will meant —
my own lesser, yet still somewhat fine-wrought,   10
fiery-tempered, delicate, over-passionate steel.

                                                        1924

From The Master

V

She is a woman,
yet beyond woman,
yet in woman,
her feet are the delicate pulse of the narcissus bud,
pushing from earth   5
(ah, where is your man-strength?)
her arms are the waving of the young
male,
tentative,
reaching out   10
that first evening
alone in a forest;

she is woman,
her thighs are frail yet strong,
she leaps from rock to rock   15
(it was only a small circle for her dance)
and the hills dance,

she conjures the hills;
'rhododendrons
awake,'   20
her feet
pulse,
the rhododendrons
wake
there is purple flower   25
between her marble, her birch-tree white
thighs,
or there is a red flower,

there is a rose flower
parted wide,   30
as her limbs fling wide in dance
ecstatic
Aphrodite,
there is a frail lavender flower
hidden in grass;   35

O God, what is it,
this flower
that in itself had power over the whole earth?
for she needs no man,
herself   40
is that dart and pulse of the male,
hands, feet, thighs,
herself perfect.

                                        c. 1935   1984

EZRA POUND

1885–1972 b Idaho; grew up in Philadelphia. In 1908 he settled in London, where he was a catalyst in the development of literary modernism. From 1924 he lived in Italy. Arrested at the end of the war for his support of fascism, he spent 12 years confined as insane in the USA before returning to Italy.

In a Station of the Metro

The apparition of these faces in the crowd;
Petals on a wet, black bough.

                                        c. *1911*   1916

Alba

As cool as the pale wet leaves
           of lily-of-the-valley
She lay beside me in the dawn.

                                        c. *1912*   1916

The River-Merchant's Wife: A Letter

While my hair was still cut straight across my forehead
I played about the front gate, pulling flowers.
You came by on bamboo stilts, playing horse,
You walked about my seat, playing with blue plums.
And we went on living in the village of Chokan: 5
Two small people, without dislike or suspicion.

At fourteen I married My Lord you.
I never laughed, being bashful.

Alba   dawn poem (Provencal)

Lowering my head, I looked at the wall.
Called to, a thousand times, I never looked back.   10

At fifteen I stopped scowling,
I desired my dust to be mingled with yours
Forever and forever and forever.
Why should I climb the look out?

At sixteen you departed,   15
You went into far Ku-to-yen, by the river of swirling eddies,
And you have been gone five months.
The monkeys make sorrowful noise overhead.

You dragged your feet when you went out.
By the gate now, the moss is grown, the different mosses,   20
Too deep to clear them away!
The leaves fall early this autumn, in wind.
The paired butterflies are already yellow with August
Over the grass in the West garden;
They hurt me. I grow older.   25
If you are coming down through the narrows of the river Kiang,
Please let me know beforehand,
And I will come out to meet you
              As far as Cho-fu-Sa.

  By Rihaku
                                              1914   1915

The Temperaments

Nine adulteries, 12 liaisons, 64 fornications and something approaching a rape
Rest nightly upon the soul of our delicate friend Florialis,
And yet the man is so quiet and reserved in demeanour
That he passes for both bloodless and sexless.
Bastidides, on the contrary, who both talks and writes of nothing save   5
        copulation,
Has become the father of twins,
But he accomplished this feat at some cost;
He had to be four times cuckold.
                                              1917

From The Cantos

From *Canto LXXXIII*

Will I ever see the Giudecca again?
      or the lights against it, Ca' Foscari, Ca' Giustinian
or the Ca', as they say, of Desdemona

Rihaku Japanese name for the eighth-century Chinese poet, Li Po. Pound wrote this version of a
poem by Li Po from a rough transcription into English of a Japanese translation of the Chinese.
The Cantos an eclectic epic of ideas, of which *The Pisan Cantos* (LXXIV–LXXXIV), written in the
six months that Pound spent in an American prison camp at Pisa after his arrest in 1945, are the most
personal
1–6 The places mentioned are in Venice, where Pound had lived.

or the two towers where are the cypress no more
    or the boats moored off le Zattere _   5
or the north quai of the Sensaria DAKRUŌN ΔΑΚΡΥΩΝ   *tears*

    and Brother Wasp is building a very neat house
    of four rooms, one shaped like a squat indian bottle
    La vespa, *la* vespa, mud, swallow system
so that dreaming of Bracelonde and of Perugia   10
and the great fountain in the Piazza
or of old Bulagaio's cat that with a well timed leap
    could turn the lever-shaped door handle
It comes over me that Mr Walls must be a ten-strike
with the signorinas   15
and in the warmth after chill sunrise
an infant, green as new grass,
has stuck its head or tip
out of Madame La Vespa's bottle

mint springs up again   20
    in spite of Jones' rodents
as had the clover by the gorilla cage
    with a four-leaf

When the mind swings by a grass-blade
    an ant's forefoot shall save you   25
the clover leaf smells and tastes as its flower

    The infant has descended,
    from mud on the tent roof to Tellus,
like to like colour he goes amid grass-blades
    greeting them that dwell under XTHONOS ΧΘΟΝΟΣ   30
ΟΙ ΧΘΟΝΙΟΙ;   to carry our news
    εἰς χθονίους   to them that dwell under the earth,
begotten of air, that shall sing in the bower
    of Kore,   Περσεφονεια
and have speech with Tiresias, Thebae   35

    Cristo Re, Dio Sole

in about ½ a day she has made her adobe
(la vespa) the tiny mud-flask

    and that day I wrote no further

                1945 1948

---

9 la vespa the wasp
10 Bracelonde Braceliande, an enchanted forest in *Yvain* (c. 1173), by Crétien de Troyes
21 Jones' rodents inmates who cleared grass under the command of the provost officer, Jones
28 Tellus earth (Latin)
30 ΧΘΟΝΟΣ earth (Greek)
31 ΟΙ ΧΘΟΝΙΟΙ those of the earth
32 εἰς χθονίους to those under the earth
34 Kore or Persephone (Περσεφονεια): a goddess abducted by the god of the underworld, the realm
of the dead, to be his queen; she returns to the world every spring. See *Metamorphoses* V.
35 Tiresias, Thebae Tiresias of Thebes. See the notes to lines 218 and 245 of *The Waste Land*.
36 Christ the king, God the sun

D.H. LAWRENCE

1885–1930 b Nottinghamshire. A novelist and poet, he travelled widely, staying for periods in Italy, Mexico and New Mexico.

Snake

A snake came to my water-trough
On a hot, hot day, and I in pyjamas for the heat,
To drink there.

In the deep, strange-scented shade of the great dark carob-tree
I came down the steps with my pitcher   5
And must wait, must stand and wait, for there he was at the trough before me.

He reached down from a fissure in the earth-wall in the gloom
And trailed his yellow-brown slackness soft-bellied down, over the edge of the
          stone trough
And rested his throat upon the stone bottom,
And where the water had dripped from the tap, in a small clearness,   10
He sipped with his straight mouth,
Softly drank through his straight gums, into his slack long body,
Silently.

Someone was before me at my water-trough,
And I, like a second comer, waiting.   15

He lifted his head from his drinking, as cattle do,
And looked at me vaguely, as drinking cattle do,
And flickered his two-forked tongue from his lips, and mused a moment,
And stooped and drank a little more,
Being earth-brown, earth-golden from the burning bowels of the earth   20
On the day of Sicilian July, with Etna smoking.

The voice of my education said to me
He must be killed,
For in Sicily the black, black snakes are innocent, the gold are venomous.

And voices in me said, If you were a man   25
You would take a stick and break him now, and finish him off.

But must I confess how I liked him,
How glad I was he had come like a guest in quiet, to drink at my water-trough
And depart peaceful, pacified, and thankless,
Into the burning bowels of this earth?   30

Was it cowardice, that I dared not kill him?
Was it perversity, that I longed to talk to him?
Was it humility, to feel so honoured?
I felt so honoured.

And yet those voices: 35
If you were not afraid, you would kill him!

And truly I was afraid, I was most afraid,
But even so, honoured still more
That he should seek my hospitality
From out the dark door of the secret earth.   40

He drank enough
And lifted his head, dreamily, as one who has drunken,
And flickered his tongue like a forked night on the air, so black;
Seeming to lick his lips,
And looked around like a god, unseeing, into the air,   45
And slowly turned his head,
And slowly, very slowly, as if thrice adream,
Proceeded to draw his slow length curving round
And climb again the broken bank of my wall-face.

And as he put his head into that dreadful hole,   50
And as he slowly drew up, snake-easing his shoulders, and entered farther,
A sort of horror, a sort of protest against his withdrawing into that horrid black
      hole,
Deliberately going into the blackness, and slowly drawing himself after,
Overcame me now his back was turned.

I looked round, I put down my pitcher,   55
I picked up a clumsy log
And threw it at the water-trough with a clatter.
I think it did not hit him,
But suddenly that part of him that was left behind convulsed in undignified haste,
Writhed like lightning, and was gone   60
Into the black hole, the earth-lipped fissure in the wall-front,
At which, in the intense still noon, I stared with fascination.

And immediately I regretted it.
I thought how paltry, how vulgar, what a mean act!
I despised myself and the voices of my accursed human education.   65

And I thought of the albatross,
And I wished he would come back, my snake.

For he seemed to me again like a king,
Like a king in exile, uncrowned in the underworld,
Now due to be crowned again.   70

And so, I missed my chance with one of the lords
Of life.
And I have something to expiate;
A pettiness.

   Taormina
                                                                                1923

After All Saints' Day

Wrapped in the dark-red mantle of warm memories
the little, slender soul sits swiftly down, and takes the oars
and draws away, away, towards dark depths
wafting with warm love from still-living hearts
breathing on his small frail sail, and helping him on   5
to the fathomless deeps ahead, far, far from the grey shores
of marginal existence.

                                                                                1929

---

66 albatross   See 'The Rime of the Ancient Mariner', p. 287 ff.

WILLIAM CARLOS WILLIAMS

1883–1963 b Rutherford, NJ; mother Puerto Rican. He lived in Rutherford for most of his life, practising as a physician.

Poem

As the cat
climbed over
the top of

the jamcloset   5
first the right
forefoot

carefully
then the hind
stepped down

into the pit of   10
the empty
flowerpot

                                                          1934

The Last Words of My English Grandmother

1920

There were some dirty plates
and a glass of milk
beside her on a small table
near the rank, disheveled bed—

Wrinkled and nearly blind   5
she lay and snored
rousing with anger in her tones
to cry for food,

Gimme something to eat—
They're starving me—   10
I'm all right I won't go
to the hospital. No, no, no

Give me something to eat
Let me take you
to the hospital, I said   15
and after you are well

you can do as you please.
She smiled, Yes
you do what you please first
then I can do what I please—   20

Oh, oh, oh! she cried
as the ambulance men lifted
her to the stretcher—
Is this what you call

making me comfortable?   25
By now her mind was clear—
Oh you think you're smart
you young people,

she said, but I'll tell you
you don't know anything.   30
Then we started.
On the way

we passed a long row
of elms. She looked at them
awhile out of   35
the ambulance window and said,

What are all those
fuzzy-looking things out there?
Trees? Well, I'm tired
of them and rolled her head away.   40

                                                            1941

The Dance

In Breughel's great picture, The Kermess,
the dancers go round, they go round and
around, the squeal and the blare and the
tweedle of bagpipes, a bugle and fiddles
tipping their bellies (round as the thick-   5
sided glasses whose wash they impound)
their hips and their bellies off balance
to turn them. Kicking and rolling about
the Fair Grounds, swinging their butts, those
shanks must be sound to bear up under such   10
rollicking measures, prance as they dance
in Breughel's great picture, The Kermess.

                                                            1944

A Sort of a Song

Let the snake wait under
his weed
and the writing
be of words, slow and quick, sharp
to strike, quiet to wait,   5
sleepless.

—through metaphor to reconcile
the people and the stones.
Compose. (No ideas
but in things) Invent!   10
Saxifrage is my flower that splits
the rocks.

                                                            1944

---

1 **Breughel**   Pieter Breughel (Flemish, *c.* 1525–69)

The Sparrow

(To My Father)

This sparrow
          who comes to sit at my window
                    is a poetic truth
more than a natural one.
          His voice,   5
                    his movements,
his habits—
          how he loves to
                    flutter his wings
in the dust—   10
          all attest it;
                    granted, he does it
to rid himself of lice
          but the relief he feels
                    makes him   15
cry out lustily—
          which is a trait
                    more related to music
than otherwise.
          Wherever he finds himself   20
                    in early spring,
on back streets
          or beside palaces,
                    he carries on
unaffectedly   25
          his amours.
                    It begins in the egg,
his sex genders it:
          What is more pretentiously
                    useless   30
or about which
          we more pride ourselves?
                    It leads as often as not
to our undoing.
          The cockerel, the crow   35
                    with their challenging voices
cannot surpass
          the insistence
                    of his cheep!
Once   40
          at El Paso
                    toward evening,
I saw—and heard!—
          ten thousand sparrows
                    who had come in from   45
the desert
          to roost. They filled the trees
                    of a small park. Men fled

(with ears ringing!)
        from their droppings,   50
           leaving the premises
to the alligators
    who inhabit
        the fountain. His image
is familiar   55
    as that of the aristocratic
        unicorn, a pity
there are not more oats eaten
    nowadays
        to make living easier   60
for him.
    At that,
        his small size,
keen eyes,
    serviceable beak   65
        and general truculence
assure his survival—
    to say nothing
        of his innumerable
brood.   70
    Even the Japanese
        know him
and have painted him
    sympathetically,
        with profound insight   75
into his minor
    characteristics.
        Nothing even remotely
subtle
    about his lovemaking.   80
        He crouches
before the female,
    drags his wings,
        waltzing,
throws back his head   85
    and simply—
        yells! The din
is terrific.
    The way he swipes his bill
        across a plank   90
to clean it,
    is decisive.
        So with everything
he does. His coppery
    eyebrows   95
        give him the air
of being always
    a winner—and yet
        I saw once,

the female of his species   100
            clinging determinedly
                        to the edge of
a water pipe,
            catch him
                        by his crown-feathers   105
to hold him
            silent,
                        subdued,
hanging above the city streets
            until   110
                        she was through with him.
What was the use
            of that?
                        She hung there
herself,   115
            puzzled at her success.
                        I laughed heartily.
Practical to the end,
            it is the poem
                        of his existence   120
that triumphed
            finally;
                        a wisp of feathers
flattened to the pavement,
            wings spread symmetrically   125
                        as if in flight,
the head gone,
            the black escutcheon of the breast
                        undecipherable,
an effigy of a sparrow,   130
            a dried wafer only,
                        left to say
and it says it
            without offense,
                        beautifully;   135
This was I,
            a sparrow.
                        I did my best;
farewell.

                                                            1955

JAMES JOYCE

1882–1941 b Dublin. Principally a novelist, he lived in Trieste, Zurich and Paris.

Ecce Puer

Of the dark past
A child is born
With joy and grief
My heart is torn

Calm in his cradle   5
The living lies.
May love and mercy
Unclose his eyes!

Young life is breathed
On the glass;   10
The world that was not
Comes to pass.

A child is sleeping:
An old man gone.
O, father forsaken,   15
Forgive your son!

1932   1936

WALLACE STEVENS

1879–1955 b Pennsylvania. He worked for much of his life as a senior insurance executive
in Hartford, Conn.

Disillusionment of Ten O'clock

The houses are haunted
By white night-gowns.
None are green,
Or purple with green rings,
Or green with yellow rings,   5
Or yellow with blue rings.
None of them are strange,
With socks of lace
And beaded ceintures.
People are not going   10
To dream of baboons and periwinkles.
Only, here and there, an old sailor,
Drunk and asleep in his boots,
Catches tigers
In red weather.   15

1915   1923

Ecce Puer   'Behold the boy.' Joyce, whose father had recently died, wrote this poem for the birth of
his grandson.

Thirteen Ways of Looking at a Blackbird

I
Among twenty snowy mountains,
The only moving thing
Was the eye of the blackbird.
II
I was of three minds,
Like a tree   5
In which there are three blackbirds.
III
The blackbird whirled in the autumn winds.
It was a small part of the pantomime.
IV
A man and a woman
Are one.   10
A man and a woman and a blackbird
Are one.
V
I do not know which to prefer,
The beauty of inflections
Or the beauty of innuendoes,   15
The blackbird whistling
Or just after.
VI
Icicles filled the long window
With barbaric glass.
The shadow of the blackbird   20
Crossed it, to and fro.
The mood
Traced in the shadow
An indecipherable cause.
VII
O thin men of Haddam,   25
Why do you imagine golden birds?
Do you not see how the blackbird
Walks around the feet
Of the women about you?
VIII
I know noble accents   30
And lucid, inescapable rhythms;
But I know, too,
That the blackbird is involved
In what I know.
IX
When the blackbird flew out of sight,   35
It marked the edge
Of one of many circles.
X
At the sight of blackbirds
Flying in a green light,
Even the bawds of euphony   40
Would cry out sharply.

XI

He rode over Connecticut
In a glass coach.
Once, a fear pierced him,
In that he mistook   45
The shadow of his equipage
For blackbirds.

XII

The river is moving.
The blackbird must be flying.

XIII

It was evening all afternoon.   50
It was snowing
And it was going to snow.
The blackbird sat
In the cedar-limbs.

                                        1917 1923

The Snow Man

One must have a mind of winter
To regard the frost and the boughs
Of the pine-trees crusted with snow;

And have been cold a long time
To behold the junipers shagged with ice,   5
The spruces rough in the distant glitter

Of the January sun; and not to think
Of any misery in the sound of the wind,
In the sound of a few leaves,

Which is the sound of the land   10
Full of the same wind
That is blowing in the same bare place

For the listener, who listens in the snow,
And, nothing himself, beholds
Nothing that is not there and the nothing that is.   15

                                        1921 1923

On the Road Home

It was when I said,
'There is no such thing as the truth,'
That the grapes seemed fatter.
The fox ran out of his hole.

You . . . You said,   5
'There are many truths,
But they are not parts of a truth.'
Then the tree, at night, began to change,

Smoking through green and smoking blue.
We were two figures in a wood.   10
We said we stood alone.

It was when I said,
'Words are not forms of a single word.
In the sum of the parts, there are only the parts.
The world must be measured by eye';   15

It was when you said,
'The idols have seen lots of poverty,
Snakes and gold and lice,
But not the truth';

It was at that time, that the silence was largest   20
And longest, the night was roundest,
The fragrance of the autumn warmest,
Closest and strongest.

                                            1938   1942

Men Made Out of Words

What should we be without the sexual myth,
The human revery or poem of death?

Castratos of moon-mash—Life consists
Of propositions about life. The human

Revery is a solitude in which   5
We compose these propositions, torn by dreams,

By the terrible incantations of defeats
And by the fear that defeats and dreams are one.

The whole race is a poet that writes down
The eccentric propositions of its fate.   10

                                            1946   1947

Of Mere Being

The palm at the end of the mind,
Beyond the last thought, rises
In the bronze decor,

A gold-feathered bird
Sings in the palm, without human meaning,   5
Without human feeling, a foreign song.

You know then that it is not the reason
That makes us happy or unhappy.
The bird sings. Its feathers shine.

The palm stands on the edge of space.   10
The wind moves slowly in the branches.
The bird's fire-fangled feathers dangle down.

                                            1955   1957

EDWARD THOMAS

1878–1917 b London; Welsh. He worked as a freelance writer and took up poetry relatively late. He was killed at Arras in the First World War.

Adlestrop

Yes. I remember Adlestrop—
The name, because one afternoon
Of heat the express-train drew up there
Unwontedly. It was late June.

The steam hissed. Someone cleared his throat.   5
No one left and no one came
On the bare platform. What I saw
Was Adlestrop—only the name

And willows, willow-herb, and grass,
And meadowsweet, and haycocks dry,   10
No whit less still and lonely fair
Than the high cloudlets in the sky.

And for that minute a blackbird sang
Close by, and round him, mistier,
Farther and farther, all the birds   15
Of Oxfordshire and Gloucestershire.

                                          1915   1917

Cock-Crow

Out of the wood of thoughts that grows by night
To be cut down by the sharp axe of light,—
Out of the night, two cocks together crow,
Cleaving the darkness with a silver blow:
And bright before my eyes twin trumpeters stand,   5
Heralds of splendour, one at either hand,
Each facing each as in a coat of arms:
The milkers lace their boots up at the farms.

                                          1915   1916

ROBERT FROST

1874–1963 b San Francisco; moved to Massachusetts as a child. He farmed there briefly, then in 1911 went to England, where his first book of poetry was published. On his return to the USA he settled in New England, earning a living from his poetry and by lecturing.

'Out, Out—'

The buzz saw snarled and rattled in the yard
And made dust and dropped stove-length sticks of wood,
Sweet-scented stuff when the breeze drew across it.
And from there those that lifted eyes could count

Five mountain ranges one behind the other   5
Under the sunset far into Vermont.
And the saw snarled and rattled, snarled and rattled,
As it ran light, or had to bear a load.
And nothing happened: day was all but done.
Call it a day, I wish they might have said   10
To please the boy by giving him the half hour
That a boy counts so much when saved from work.
His sister stood beside them in her apron
To tell them 'Supper.' At the word, the saw,
As if to prove saws knew what supper meant,   15
Leaped out at the boy's hand, or seemed to leap—
He must have given the hand. However it was,
Neither refused the meeting. But the hand!
The boy's first outcry was a rueful laugh,
As he swung toward them holding up the hand,   20
Half in appeal, but half as if to keep
The life from spilling. Then the boy saw all—
Since he was old enough to know, big boy
Doing a man's work, though a child at heart—
He saw all spoiled. 'Don't let him cut my hand off—   25
The doctor, when he comes. Don't let him, sister!'
So. But the hand was gone already.
The doctor put him in the dark of ether.
He lay and puffed his lips out with his breath.
And then—the watcher at his pulse took fright.   30
No one believed. They listened at his heart.
Little—less—nothing!—and that ended it.
No more to build on there. And they, since they
Were not the one dead, turned to their affairs.

                                                        1916

Neither Out Far Nor In Deep

The people along the sand
All turn and look one way.
They turn their back on the land.
They look at the sea all day.

As long as it takes to pass   5
A ship keeps raising its hull;
The wetter ground like glass
Reflects a standing gull.

The land may vary more;
But wherever the truth may be—   10
The water comes ashore,
And the people look at the sea.

They cannot look out far.
They cannot look in deep.
But when was that ever a bar   15
To any watch they keep?

                                                        1936

Design

I found a dimpled spider, fat and white,
On a white heal-all, holding up a moth
Like a white piece of rigid satin cloth—
Assorted characters of death and blight
Mixed ready to begin the morning right,   5
Like the ingredients of a witches' broth—
A snow-drop spider, a flower like a froth,
And dead wings carried like a paper kite.
What had that flower to do with being white,
The wayside blue and innocent heal-all?   10
What brought the kindred spider to that height,
Then steered the white moth thither in the night?
What but design of darkness to appall?—
If design govern in a thing so small.

                                                        1936

The Most of It

He thought he kept the universe alone;
For all the voice in answer he could wake
Was but the mocking echo of his own
From some tree-hidden cliff across the lake.
Some morning from the boulder-broken beach   5
He would cry out on life, that what it wants
Is not its own love back in copy speech,
But counter-love, original response.
And nothing ever came of what he cried
Unless it was the embodiment that crashed   10
In the cliff's talus on the other side,
And then in the far-distant water splashed,
But after a time allowed for it to swim,
Instead of proving human when it neared
And someone else additional to him,   15
As a great buck it powerfully appeared,
Pushing the crumpled water up ahead,
And landed pouring like a waterfall,
And stumbled through the rocks with horny tread,
And forced the underbrush—and that was all.   20
                                        c. *1929*   1942

The Subverted Flower

She drew back; he was calm:
'It is this that had the power.'
And he lashed his open palm
With the tender-headed flower.
He smiled for her to smile,   5
But she was either blind
Or willfully unkind.
He eyed her for a while
For a woman and a puzzle.

He flicked and flung the flower,   10
And another sort of smile
Caught up like fingertips
The corners of his lips
And cracked his ragged muzzle.
She was standing to the waist   15
In goldenrod and brake,
Her shining hair displaced.
He stretched her either arm
As if she made it ache
To clasp her—not to harm;   20
As if he could not spare
To touch her neck and hair.
'If this has come to us
And not to me alone—'
So she thought she heard him say;   25
Though with every word he spoke
His lips were sucked and blown
And the effort made him choke
Like a tiger at a bone.
She had to lean away.   30
She dared not stir a foot,
Lest movement should provoke
The demon of pursuit
That slumbers in a brute.
It was then her mother's call   35
From inside the garden wall
Made her steal a look of fear
To see if he could hear
And would pounce to end it all
Before her mother came.   40
She looked and saw the shame:
A hand hung like a paw,
An arm worked like a saw
As if to be persuasive,
An ingratiating laugh   45
That cut the snout in half,
An eye become evasive.
A girl could only see
That a flower had marred a man,
But what she could not see   50
Was that the flower might be
Other than base and fetid:
That the flower had done but part,
And what the flower began
Her own too meager heart   55
Had terribly completed.
She looked and saw the worst.
And the dog or what it was,
Obeying bestial laws,
A coward save at night,   60
Turned from the place and ran.

She heard him stumble first
And use his hands in flight.
She heard him bark outright.
And oh, for one so young   65
The bitter words she spit
Like some tenacious bit
That will not leave the tongue.
She plucked her lips for it,
And still the horror clung.   70
Her mother wiped the foam
From her chin, picked up her comb,
And drew her backward home.

                                        1912–42   1942

EDGAR LEE MASTERS

1868–1950 b Kansas; lived in Chicago. His *Spoon River Anthology* is famous for its portraits
of small-town America.

The Hill

Where are Elmer, Herman, Bert, Tom and Charley,
The weak of will, the strong of arm, the clown, the boozer, the fighter?
All, all, are sleeping on the hill.

One passed in a fever,
One was burned in a mine,   5
One was killed in a brawl,
One died in a jail,
One fell from a bridge toiling for children and wife—
All, all are sleeping, sleeping, sleeping on the hill.

Where are Ella, Kate, Mag, Lizzie and Edith,   10
The tender heart, the simple soul, the loud, the proud, the happy one?—
All, all, are sleeping on the hill.

One died in shameful child-birth,
One of a thwarted love,
One at the hands of a brute in a brothel,   15
One of a broken pride, in the search for heart's desire,
One after life in far-away London and Paris
Was brought to her little space by Ella and Kate and Mag—
All, all are sleeping, sleeping, sleeping on the hill.

Where are Uncle Isaac and Aunt Emily,   20
And old Towny Kincaid and Sevigne Houghton,
And Major Walker who had talked
With venerable men of the revolution?—
All, all, are sleeping on the hill.

They brought them dead sons from the war,   25
And daughters whom life had crushed,
And their children fatherless, crying—
All, all are sleeping, sleeping, sleeping on the hill.

Where is Old Fiddler Jones
Who played with life all his ninety years,   30
Braving the sleet with bared breast,
Drinking, rioting, thinking neither of wife nor kin,
Nor gold, nor love, nor heaven?
Lo! he babbles of the fish-frys of long ago,
Of the horse-races of long ago at Clary's Grove,   35
Of what Abe Lincoln said
One time at Springfield.

                                                                    1915

HENRY LAWSON

1867–1922 b Grenfell, NSW, and grew up near Mudgee. A short-story writer and poet, he
lived mainly in Sydney.

Middleton's Rouseabout

Tall and freckled and sandy,
    Face of a country lout;
This was the picture of Andy,
    Middleton's Rouseabout.

Type of a coming nation,   5
    In the land of cattle and sheep,
Worked on Middleton's station,
    'Pound a week and his keep.'

On Middleton's wide dominions
    Plied the stockwhip and shears;   10
Hadn't any opinions,
    Hadn't any 'idears.'

Swiftly the years went over,
    Liquor and drought prevailed;
Middleton went as a drover   15
    After his station had failed.

Type of a careless nation,
    Men who are soon played out,
Middleton was:—and his station
    Was bought by the Rouseabout.   20

Flourishing beard and sandy,
    Tall and solid and stout;
This is the picture of Andy,
    Middleton's Rouseabout.

Now on his own dominions   25
    Works with his overseers;
Hasn't any opinions,
    Hasn't any idears.

                                                        1890   1896

W.B. YEATS

1865–1939 b Dublin; childhood spent in London and Sligo. He was also a playwright involved in the founding of an Irish national theatre, and a senator in the Irish parliament, 1922–28.

The Song of Wandering Aengus

I went out to the hazel wood,
Because a fire was in my head,
And cut and peeled a hazel wand,
And hooked a berry to a thread;
And when white moths were on the wing,   5
And moth-like stars were flickering out,
I dropped the berry in a stream
And caught a little silver trout.

When I had laid it on the floor
I went to blow the fire aflame,   10
But something rustled on the floor,
And some one called me by my name:
It had become a glimmering girl
With apple blossom in her hair
Who called me by my name and ran   15
And faded through the brightening air.

Though I am old with wandering
Through hollow lands and hilly lands,
I will find out where she has gone,
And kiss her lips and take her hands;   20
And walk among long dappled grass,
And pluck till time and times are done
The silver apples of the moon,
The golden apples of the sun.
                                        1893   1899

Easter 1916

I have met them at close of day
Coming with vivid faces
From counter or desk among grey
Eighteenth-century houses.
I have passed with a nod of the head   5
Or polite meaningless words,
Or have lingered awhile and said
Polite meaningless words,
And thought before I had done
Of a mocking tale or a gibe   10

Easter 1916   date of a republican uprising in Dublin against British rule. It was suppressed after some days and the leaders, including those named in lines 75–76, were shot.

To please a companion
Around the fire at the club,
Being certain that they and I
But lived where motley is worn:
All changed, changed utterly: 15
A terrible beauty is born.

That woman's days were spent
In ignorant good-will,
Her nights in argument
Until her voice grew shrill.   20
What voice more sweet than hers
When, young and beautiful,
She rode to harriers?
This man had kept a school
And rode our wingèd horse;   25
This other his helper and friend
Was coming into his force;
He might have won fame in the end,
So sensitive his nature seemed,
So daring and sweet his thought.   30
This other man I had dreamed
A drunken, vainglorious lout.
He had done most bitter wrong
To some who are near my heart,
Yet I number him in the song;   35
He, too, has resigned his part
In the casual comedy;
He, too, has been changed in his turn,
Transformed utterly:
A terrible beauty is born.   40

Hearts with one purpose alone
Through summer and winter seem
Enchanted to a stone
To trouble the living stream.
The horse that comes from the road,   45
The rider, the birds that range
From cloud to tumbling cloud,
Minute by minute they change;
A shadow of cloud on the stream
Changes minute by minute;   50
A horse-hoof slides on the brim,
And a horse plashes within it;

---

17 That woman Constance Markiewicz, a friend of Yeats. Her death sentence was commuted.
24 This man Padraic Pearse, a schoolteacher and poet
25 wingèd horse Pegasus, associated in Greek mythology with poetic inspiration
26 This other Thomas MacDonagh, a university teacher and writer
31 This other man Major John MacBride, who had had a brief, unhappy marriage with Yeats' friend, Maud Gonne

The long-legged moor-hens dive,
And hens to moor-cocks call;
Minute by minute they live: 55
The stone's in the midst of all.

Too long a sacrifice
Can make a stone of the heart.
O when may it suffice?
That is Heaven's part, our part   60
To murmur name upon name,
As a mother names her child
When sleep at last has come
On limbs that had run wild.
What is it but nightfall?   65
No, no, not night but death;
Was it needless death after all?
For England may keep faith
For all that is done and said.
We know their dream; enough   70
To know they dreamed and are dead;
And what if excess of love
Bewildered them till they died?
I write it out in a verse—
MacDonagh and MacBride   75
And Connolly and Pearse
Now and in time to be,
Wherever green is worn,
Are changed, changed utterly:
A terrible beauty is born.

                                      25 September 1916   1916

The Wild Swans at Coole

The trees are in their autumn beauty,
The woodland paths are dry,
Under the October twilight the water
Mirrors a still sky;
Upon the brimming water among the stones   5
Are nine-and-fifty swans.

The nineteenth autumn has come upon me
Since I first made my count;
I saw, before I had well finished,
All suddenly mount   10
And scatter wheeling in great broken rings
Upon their clamorous wings.

---

68 The British had started legislation for Irish home rule before World War I intervened.
76 Connolly James Connolly, a trade union leader
Coole Coole Park, the estate in Galway of Yeats' friend and patron, Lady Augusta Gregory

I have looked upon those brilliant creatures,
And now my heart is sore.
All's changed since I, hearing at twilight,   15
The first time on this shore,
The bell-beat of their wings above my head,
Trod with a lighter tread.

Unwearied still, lover by lover,
They paddle in the cold   20
Companionable streams or climb the air;
Their hearts have not grown old;
Passion or conquest, wander where they will,
Attend upon them still.

But now they drift on the still water,   25
Mysterious, beautiful;
Among what rushes will they build,
By what lake's edge or pool
Delight men's eyes when I awake some day
To find they have flown away?   30

                                            1916   1917

The Second Coming

Turning and turning in the widening gyre
The falcon cannot hear the falconer;   *spiral*
Things fall apart; the centre cannot hold;
Mere anarchy is loosed upon the world,
The blood-dimmed tide is loosed, and everywhere
The ceremony of innocence is drowned;   5
The best lack all conviction, while the worst
Are full of passionate intensity.

Surely some revelation is at hand;
Surely the Second Coming is at hand.
The Second Coming! Hardly are those words out   10
When a vast image out of *Spiritus Mundi*
Troubles my sight: somewhere in sands of the desert
A shape with lion body and the head of a man,
A gaze blank and pitiless as the sun,
Is moving its slow thighs, while all about it   15
Reel shadows of the indignant desert birds.
The darkness drops again; but now I know
That twenty centuries of stony sleep
Were vexed to nightmare by a rocking cradle,
And what rough beast, its hour come round at last,   20
Slouches towards Bethlehem to be born?

                                            1918   1921

Second Coming   See the prophecy of Christ's second coming, Matt. 24; also the prophecy of an
anti-Christ, 1 John 2:18.
12 Spiritus Mundi   'spirit of the world': for Yeats, the store of images of collective human experience

A Prayer for my Daughter

Once more the storm is howling, and half hid
Under this cradle-hood and coverlid
My child sleeps on. There is no obstacle
But Gregory's wood and one bare hill
Whereby the haystack- and roof-levelling wind,   5
Bred on the Atlantic, can be stayed;
And for an hour I have walked and prayed
Because of the great gloom that is in my mind.

I have walked and prayed for this young child an hour
And heard the sea-wind scream upon the tower,   10
And under the arches of the bridge, and scream
In the elms above the flooded stream;
Imagining in excited reverie
That the future years had come,
Dancing to a frenzied drum,   15
Out of the murderous innocence of the sea.

May she be granted beauty and yet not
Beauty to make a stranger's eye distraught,
Or hers before a looking-glass, for such,
Being made beautiful overmuch,   20
Consider beauty a sufficient end,
Lose natural kindness and maybe
The heart-revealing intimacy
That chooses right, and never find a friend.

Helen being chosen found life flat and dull   25
And later had much trouble from a fool,
While that great Queen, that rose out of the spray,
Being fatherless could have her way
Yet chose a bandy-leggèd smith for man.
It's certain that fine women eat   30
A crazy salad with their meat
Whereby the Horn of Plenty is undone.

In courtesy I'd have her chiefly learned;
Hearts are not had as a gift but hearts are earned
By those that are not entirely beautiful;   35
Yet many, that have played the fool

---

10 Tower a ruined Norman tower which Yeats had refurbished for habitation, at Coole Park
25–26 In Greek myth, Helen left her husband, Menelaus, to go with her lover, Paris, to Troy. Menelaus, with his fellow Greeks, besieged Troy for ten years to bring her back. Homer's *Iliad* relates that she grew to despise Paris.
32 Horn of Plenty or cornucopia: in Greek myth, a horn taken from the goat which suckled the infant Zeus, filled with an abundance of everything desired
27–9 Queen Aphrodite, Greek goddess of love. Hesiod, in *Theogony* (*c.* eighth century BC), relates how she was conceived from foam of the severed genitals of the deposed sky-god, Uranus, after they were cast into the sea. See also Botticelli's painting, *The Birth of Venus*. Aphrodite was married to the lame blacksmith god, Hephaestos.

For beauty's very self, has charm made wise,
And many a poor man that has roved,
Loved and thought himself beloved,
From a glad kindness cannot take his eyes.   40

May she become a flourishing hidden tree
That all her thoughts may like the linnet be,
And have no business but dispensing round
Their magnanimities of sound,
Nor but in merriment begin a chase,   45
Nor but in merriment a quarrel.
O may she live like some green laurel
Rooted in one dear perpetual place.

My mind, because the minds that I have loved,
The sort of beauty that I have approved,   50
Prosper but little, has dried up of late,
Yet knows that to be choked with hate
May well be of all evil chances chief.
If there's no hatred in a mind
Assault and battery of the wind   55
Can never tear the linnet from the leaf.

An intellectual hatred is the worst,
So let her think opinions are accursed.
Have I not seen the loveliest woman born
Out of the mouth of Plenty's horn,   60
Because of her opinionated mind
Barter that horn and every good
By quiet natures understood
For an old bellows full of angry wind?

Considering that, all hatred driven hence,   65
The soul recovers radical innocence
And learns at last that it is self-delighting,
Self-appeasing, self-affrighting,
And that its own sweet will is Heaven's will;
She can, though every face should scowl   70
And every windy quarter howl
Or every bellows burst, be happy still.

And may her bridegroom bring her to a house
Where all's accustomed, ceremonious;
For arrogance and hatred are the wares   75
Peddled in the thoroughfares.
How but in custom and in ceremony
Are innocence and beauty born?
Ceremony's a name for the rich horn,
And custom for the spreading laurel tree.   80

                                    1919   1921

59–64 A reference to Maud Gonne (1865–1953) for whom Yeats had maintained strong feelings, unreturned, since first meeting her in 1889. She was a feminist and revolutionary Irish republican.

The Road at My Door

An affable Irregular,
A heavily-built Falstaffian man,
Comes cracking jokes of civil war
As though to die by gunshot were
The finest play under the sun.   5

A brown Lieutenant and his men,
Half dressed in national uniform,
Stand at my door, and I complain
Of the foul weather, hail and rain,
A pear-tree broken by the storm.   10

I count those feathered balls of soot
The moor-hen guides upon the stream,
To silence the envy in my thought;
And turn towards my chamber, caught
In the cold snows of a dream.   15
                                                1922 1928

The Stare's Nest by My Window   *starling*

The bees build in the crevices
Of loosening masonry, and there
The mother birds bring grubs and flies.
My wall is loosening; honey-bees,
Come build in the empty house of the stare.   5

We are closed in, and the key is turned
On our uncertainty; somewhere
A man is killed, or a house burned,
Yet no clear fact to be discerned:
Come build in the empty house of the stare.   10

A barricade of stone or of wood;
Some fourteen days of civil war;
Last night they trundled down the road
That dead young soldier in his blood:
Come build in the empty house of the stare.   15

We had fed the heart on fantasies,
The heart's grown brutal from the fare;
More substance in our enmities
Than in our love; O honey-bees,
Come build in the empty house of the stare.   20
                                                1922 1928

The Road at My Door This and the following poem refer to Yeats' refurbished Norman tower at
Coole Park. He grouped them with five other poems under the heading, 'Meditations in Time of Civil
War', in reference to the armed conflict in 1922 between Irish government forces and the more
uncompromising 'Irregulars' over the terms of independence in the Anglo-Irish treaty of December,
1921.
2 Falstaffian like Falstaff in Shakespeare's *Henry IV* plays
6 brown Lieutenant member of the army of the provisional government

Leda and the Swan

A sudden blow: the great wings beating still
Above the staggering girl, her thighs caressed
By the dark webs, her nape caught in his bill,
He holds her helpless breast upon his breast.

How can those terrified vague fingers push   5
The feathered glory from her loosening thighs,
And how can body, laid in that white rush,
But feel the strange heart beating where it lies?

A shudder in the loins engenders there
The broken wall, the burning roof and tower   10
And Agamemnon dead.
                    Being so caught up,
So mastered by the brute blood of the air,
Did she put on his knowledge with his power
Before the indifferent beak could let her drop?   15

                              1923   1924

Among School Children

                    I
I walk through the long schoolroom questioning;
A kind old nun in a white hood replies;
The children learn to cipher and to sing,
To study reading-books and histories,
To cut and sew, be neat in everything
In the best modern way—the children's eyes   5
In momentary wonder stare upon
A sixty-year-old smiling public man.

                    II
I dream of a Ledaean body, bent
Above a sinking fire, a tale that she
Told of a harsh reproof, or trivial event   10
That changed some childish day to tragedy—
Told, and it seemed that our two natures blent
Into a sphere from youthful sympathy,
Or else, to alter Plato's parable,
Into the yolk and white of the one shell.   15

                    III
And thinking of that fit of grief or rage
I look upon one child or t'other there
And wonder if she stood so at that age—
For even daughters of the swan can share
                                                     20

Leda and the Swan   In Greek myth, Leda conceived her daughter, Helen of Troy, when raped by Zeus, who appeared to her in the form of a swan.
11 Agamemnon dead   In Greek myth, Agamemnon, the leader of the Greek army of Troy, sacrificed his daughter, Iphigenia, for fair winds. His wife, Clytemnestra, killed him upon his return.
9 Ledaean   i.e. like Leda or (as in line 20) her daughter Helen. Yeats has in mind his early love, Maud Gonne.
15 Plato's parable   i.e. of how both sexes were once in one body, but were divided by Zeus as one might divide an egg, since when they have always sought to re-unite. See *Symposium*, 190.

Something of every paddler's heritage—
And had that colour upon cheek or hair,
And thereupon my heart is driven wild:
She stands before me as a living child.

IV
Her present image floats into the mind—
Did Quattrocento finger fashion it
Hollow of cheek as though it drank the wind
And took a mess of shadows for its meat?
And I though never of Ledaean kind
Had pretty plumage once—enough of that,
Better to smile on all that smile, and show
There is a comfortable kind of old scarecrow.

V
What youthful mother, a shape upon her lap
Honey of generation had betrayed,
And that must sleep, shriek, struggle to escape
As recollection or the drug decide,
Would think her son, did she but see that shape
With sixty or more winters on its head,
A compensation for the pang of his birth,
Or the uncertainty of his setting forth?

VI
Plato thought nature but a spume that plays
Upon a ghostly paradigm of things;
Solider Aristotle played the taws
Upon the bottom of a king of kings;
World-famous golden-thighed Pythagoras
Fingered upon a fiddle-stick or strings
What a star sang and careless Muses heard:
Old clothes upon old sticks to scare a bird.

VII
Both nuns and mothers worship images,
But those the candles light are not as those
That animate a mother's reveries,
But keep a marble or a bronze repose.
And yet they too break hearts—O Presences
That passion, piety or affection knows,
And that all heavenly glory symbolise—
O self-born mockers of man's enterprise;

VIII
Labour is blossoming or dancing where
The body is not bruised to pleasure soul,

25
30
35
40
45
50
55

---

26 **Quattrocento** the fifteenth century, great period of Italian art
41 **Plato** (? 427–347 BC) Greek philosopher, who taught that the physical world is merely an image of a permanent spiritual pattern (**ghostly paradigm**)
43 **Aristotle** (384–322 BC) Plato's pupil, who was more interested in the nature of the physical world **taws** strap. Aristotle was tutor to the young Alexander the Great.
45–47 **Pythagoras** (Greek, sixth century BC) discoverer of the mathematical ratios of musical intervals. His followers postulated a mathematical unity for the cosmos. **golden-thighed** Pythagoras was reported to have shown his golden thigh to Abaris, a priest of Apollo, as evidence of his divinity.

Nor beauty born out of its own despair,
Nor blear-eyed wisdom out of midnight oil.   60
O chestnut tree, great rooted blossomer,
Are you the leaf, the blossom or the bole?
O body swayed to music, O brightening glance,
How can we know the dancer from the dance?

                                                    1926   1928

Sailing to Byzantium

I

That is no country for old men. The young
In one another's arms, birds in the trees,
—Those dying generations—at their song,
The salmon-falls, the mackerel-crowded seas,
Fish, flesh, or fowl, commend all summer long   5
Whatever is begotten, born, and dies.
Caught in that sensual music all neglect
Monuments of unageing intellect.

II

An aged man is but a paltry thing,
A tattered coat upon a stick, unless   10
Soul clap its hands and sing, and louder sing
For every tatter in its mortal dress,
Nor is there singing school but studying
Monuments of its own magnificence;
And therefore I have sailed the seas and come   15
To the holy city of Byzantium.

III

O sages standing in God's holy fire
As in the gold mosaic of a wall,
Come from the holy fire, perne in a gyre,
And be the singing-masters of my soul.   20
Consume my heart away; sick with desire
And fastened to a dying animal
It knows not what it is; and gather me
Into the artifice of eternity.

IV

Once out of nature I shall never take   25
My bodily form from any natural thing,
But such a form as Grecian goldsmiths make
Of hammered gold and gold enamelling
To keep a drowsy Emperor awake;
Or set upon a golden bough to sing   30
To lords and ladies of Byzantium
Of what is past, or passing, or to come.

                                                    1926   1928

---

16 **Byzantium** (now Istanbul) at its height in the sixth century as the centre both of the Roman
Empire and of the church. Its art was stylised and almost impersonal in the service of a spiritual reality.
18 **perne** spool **gyre** spiral, as of a thread unwinding from a spool. The speaker is asking the
sages in eternity briefly to enter the cycles of time.

Crazy Jane Talks with the Bishop

I met the Bishop on the road
And much said he and I.
'Those breasts are flat and fallen now
Those veins must soon be dry;
Live in a heavenly mansion,   5
Not in some foul sty.'

'Fair and foul are near of kin,
And fair needs foul,' I cried.
'My friends are gone, but that's a truth
Nor grave nor bed denied,   10
Learned in bodily lowliness
And in the heart's pride.

'A woman can be proud and stiff
When on love intent;
But Love has pitched his mansion in   15
The place of excrement;
For nothing can be sole or whole
That has not been rent.'

                                         1931   1933

The Circus Animals' Desertion

I

I sought a theme and sought for it in vain,
I sought it daily for six weeks or so.
Maybe at last, being but a broken man
I must be satisfied with my heart, although
Winter and summer till old age began   5
My circus animals were all on show,
Those stilted boys, that burnished chariot,
Lion and woman and the Lord knows what.

II

What can I but enumerate old themes?
First that sea-rider Oisin led by the nose   10
Through three enchanted islands, allegorical dreams,
Vain gaiety, vain battle, vain repose,
Themes of the embittered heart, or so it seems,
That might adorn old songs or courtly shows;
But what cared I that set him on to ride,   15
I, starved for the bosom of his faery bride?

And then a counter-truth filled out its play,
The Countess Cathleen was the name I gave it;

6–8 Although the images here loosely allude to early works by Yeats (e.g. his play, *The Unicorn from the Stars*, 1908), the idea of them as circus entertainment is unique to this poem.
10–16 Oisin (pron. 'Usheen') hero of Yeats' poem, *The Wanderings of Oisin* (1889) who is led by a **faery** to three islands, of Dancing, Victories and Forgetfulness.

She, pity-crazed, had given her soul away
But masterful Heaven had intervened to save it.   20
I thought my dear must her own soul destroy,
So did fanaticism and hate enslave it,
And this brought forth a dream and soon enough
This dream itself had all my thought and love.

And when the Fool and Blind Man stole the bread   25
Cuchulain fought the ungovernable sea;
Heart-mysteries there, and yet when all is said
It was the dream itself enchanted me:
Character isolated by a deed
To engross the present and dominate memory.   30
Players and painted stage took all my love,
And not those things that they were emblems of.

III

Those masterful images because complete
Grew in pure mind, but out of what began?
A mound of refuse or the sweepings of a street,   35
Old kettles, old bottles, and a broken can,
Old iron, old bones, old rags, that raving slut
Who keeps the till. Now that my ladder's gone,
I must lie down where all the ladders start,
In the foul rag-and-bone shop of the heart.   40

                                        c. *1937–8*   1939

Long-legged Fly

That civilisation may not sink
Its great battle lost,
Quiet the dog, tether the pony
To a distant post.
Our master Caesar is in the tent   5
Where the maps are spread,
His eyes fixed upon nothing,
A hand under his head.

Like a long-legged fly upon the stream
His mind moves upon silence.   10

That the topless towers be burnt
And men recall that face,
Move most gently if move you must
In this lonely place.

17–24 In Yeats' first play, **The Countess Cathleen** (1892), the heroine, seeing people selling their souls for food during a famine, sells her own to save them: she is forgiven by heaven when she dies.
21 **my dear**   Yeats' friend, Maud Gonne, who was dedicated to Irish independence
25–32 In Yeats' play, *On Baile's Strand* (1903) **Cuchulain** (pron. 'Cuhoolin') fights the sea in a frenzy upon discovering that he has killed his son. The **Fool** and **Blind Man** steal bread from the ovens when the villagers run to watch.
12 **that face**   i.e. Helen of Troy, as addressed in Christopher Marlowe's play, *Doctor Faustus* (c. 1594): 'Was this the face that Launcht a thousand ships, / And burnt the toplesse Towers of Ilium?'

She thinks, part woman, three parts a child,   15
That nobody looks; her feet
Practise a tinker shuffle
Picked up on the street.

Like a long-legged fly upon the stream
Her mind moves upon silence.   20

That girls at puberty may find
The first Adam in their thought,
Shut the door of the Pope's chapel,
Keep those children out.
There on that scaffolding reclines   25
Michael Angelo.
With no more sound than the mice make
His hand moves to and fro.

Like a long-legged fly upon the stream
His mind moves upon silence.   30

1938 1939

RUDYARD KIPLING

1865–1936 b Bombay; educated in England. After publishing his first stories and poems while a journalist in India 1882–87, he settled in England.

Danny Deever

'What are the bugles blowin' for?' said Files-on-Parade.
'To turn you out, to turn you out,' the Colour-Sergeant said.
'What makes you look so white, so white?' said Files-on-Parade.
'I'm dreadin' what I've got to watch,' the Colour-Sergeant said.
 For they're hangin' Danny Deever, you can hear the Dead March play,   5
 The Regiment's in 'ollow square—they're hangin' him to-day;
 They've taken of his buttons off an' cut his stripes away,
 An' they're hangin' Danny Deever in the mornin'.

'What makes the rear-rank breathe so 'ard?' said Files-on-Parade.
'It's bitter cold, it's bitter cold,' the Colour-Sergeant said.   10
'What makes that front-rank man fall down?' says Files-on-Parade.
'A touch o' sun, a touch o' sun,' the Colour-Sergeant said.
 They are hangin' Danny Deever, they are marchin' of 'im round,
 They 'ave 'alted Danny Deever by 'is coffin on the ground;
 An' 'e'll swing in 'arf a minute for a sneakin' shootin' hound—   15
 O they're hangin' Danny Deever in the mornin'!

''Is cot was right-'and cot to mine,' said Files-on-Parade.
''E's sleepin' out an' far to-night,' the Colour-Sergeant said.
'I've drunk 'is beer a score o' times,' said Files-on-Parade.
''E's drinkin' bitter beer alone,' the Colour-Sergeant said.   20
 They are hangin' Danny Deever, you must mark 'im to 'is place,
 For 'e shot a comrade sleepin'—you must look 'im in the face;
 Nine 'undred of 'is county an' the regiment's disgrace,
 While they're hangin' Danny Deever in the mornin'.

'What's that so black agin the sun?' said Files-on-Parade.   25
'It's Danny fightin' 'ard for life,' the Colour-Sergeant said.
'What's that that whimpers over'ead?' said Files-on-Parade.
'It's Danny's soul that's passin' now,' the Colour-Sergeant said.
    For they're done with Danny Deever, you can 'ear the quickstep play,
    The regiment's in column, an' they're marchin' us away;   30
    Ho! the young recruits are shakin', an' they'll want their beer to-day,
    After hangin' Danny Deever in the mornin'.

                            1892

The Ballad of the 'Bolivar'

   Seven men from all the world back to Docks again,
   Rolling down the Ratcliffe Road drunk and raising Cain:
   Give the girls another drink 'fore we sign away—
   We that took the 'Bolivar' out across the Bay!

We put out from Sunderland loaded down with rails;   5
   We put back to Sunderland 'cause our cargo shifted;
We put out from Sunderland—met the winter gales—
   Seven days and seven nights to the Start we drifted.

   Racketing her rivets loose, smoke-stack white as snow,
   All the coals adrift adeck, half the rails below,   10
   Leaking like a lobster-pot, steering like a dray—
   Out we took the 'Bolivar,' out across the Bay!

One by one the Lights came up, winked and let us by;
   Mile by mile we waddled on, coal and fo'c'sle short;
Met a blow that laid us down, heard a bulkhead fly;
   Left the 'Wolf' behind us with a two-foot list to port.   15

   Trailing like a wounded duck, working out her soul;
   Clanging like a smithy-shop after every roll;
   Just a funnel and a mast lurching through the spray—
   So we threshed the 'Bolivar' out across the Bay!

Felt her hog and felt her sag, betted when she'd break;   20
   Wondered every time she raced if she'd stand the shock;
Heard the seas like drunken men pounding at her strake;
   Hoped the Lord 'ud keep his thumb on the plummer-block.

   Banged against the iron decks, bilges choked with coal;
   Flayed and frozen foot and hand, sick of heart and soul;   25
   Last we prayed she'd buck herself into Judgment Day—
   Hi! we cursed the 'Bolivar' knocking round the Bay!

O her nose flung up to sky, groaning to be still—
   Up and down and back we went, never time for breath;
Then the money paid at Lloyd's caught her by the heel,   30
   And the stars ran round and round dancin' at our death.

   Aching for an hour's sleep, dozing off between;
   Heard the rotten rivets draw when she took it green;
   Watched the compass chase its tail like a cat at play—
   That was on the 'Bolivar,' south across the Bay.   35

Once we saw between the squalls, lyin' head to swell—
  Mad with work and weariness, wishin' they was we—
Some damned Liner's lights go by like a grand hotel;
  Cheered her from the 'Bolivar' swampin' in the sea.

    Then a greyback cleared us out, then the skipper laughed;   40
    'Boys, the wheel has gone to Hell—rig the winches aft!
    'Yoke the kicking rudder-head—get her under way!'
    So we steered her, pully-haul, out across the Bay!

Just a pack o' rotten plates puttied up with tar,
  In we came, an' time enough, 'cross Bilbao Bar.   45
Overloaded, undermanned, meant to founder, we
  Euchred God Almighty's storm, bluffed the Eternal Sea!

Seven men from all the world, back to town again,
Rollin' down the Ratcliffe Road drunk and raising Cain:
Seven men from out of Hell. Ain't the owners gay,   50
'Cause we took the 'Bolivar' safe across the Bay?

                          1892

A.B. PATERSON

(Andrew Barton—'The Banjo') 1864–1941 b Orange, NSW. A lawyer by training, he
worked as a journalist in Sydney.

The Travelling Post Office

The roving breezes come and go, the reed-beds sweep and sway,
The sleepy river murmurs low, and loiters on its way,
It is the land of lots o' time along the Castlereagh.
    .   .   .   .

The old man's son had left the farm, he found it dull and slow,
He drifted to the great North-west where all the rovers go.   5
'He's gone so long,' the old man said, 'he's dropped right out of mind,
But if you'd write a line to him I'd take it very kind;
He's shearing here and fencing there, a kind of waif and stray,
He's droving now with Conroy's sheep along the Castlereagh.
The sheep are travelling for the grass, and travelling very slow;   10
They may be at Mundooran now, or past the Overflow,
Or tramping down the black-soil flats across by Waddiwong,
But all those little country towns would send the letter wrong,
The mailman, if he's extra tired, would pass them in his sleep,
It's safest to address the note to "Care of Conroy's sheep,"   15
For five and twenty thousand head can scarcely go astray,
You write to "Care of Conroy's sheep along the Castlereagh."'

By rock and ridge and riverside the western mail has gone,
Across the great Blue Mountain Range to take that letter on.
A moment on the topmost grade, while open fire doors glare,   20
She pauses like a living thing to breathe the mountain air,
Then launches down the other side across the plains away
To bear the note to 'Conroy's sheep along the Castlereagh.'
    .   .   .   .   .

And now by coach and mailman's bag it goes from town to town,
And Conroy's Gap and Conroy's Creek have marked it 'Further down.'   25
Beneath a sky of deepest blue where never cloud abides,
A speck upon the waste of plain the lonely mailman rides.
Where fierce hot winds have set the pine and myall boughs asweep
He hails the shearers passing by for news of Conroy's sheep.
By big lagoons where wildfowl play and crested pigeons flock,   30
By camp fires where the drovers ride around their restless stock,
And past the teamster toiling down to fetch the wool away
My letter chases Conroy's sheep along the Castlereagh.

                                                          1895

A.E. HOUSMAN

(Alfred Edward) 1859–1936 b Worcestershire. He was a scholar and editor of Latin texts for most of his life, mainly in Cambridge.

[Loveliest of trees, the cherry now]

Loveliest of trees, the cherry now
Is hung with bloom along the bough,
And stands about the woodland ride
Wearing white for Eastertide.

Now, of my threescore years and ten,   5
Twenty will not come again,
And take from seventy springs a score,
It only leaves me fifty more.

And since to look at things in bloom
Fifty springs are little room,   10
About the woodlands I will go
To see the cherry hung with snow.

                                                          1896

[On Wenlock Edge the wood's in trouble]

On Wenlock Edge the wood's in trouble;
    His forest fleece the Wrekin heaves;
The gale, it plies the saplings double,
    And thick on Severn snow the leaves.

'Twould blow like this through holt and hanger   5
    When Uricon the city stood:
'Tis the old wind in the old anger,
    But then it threshed another wood.

---

1 **Wenlock Edge**   a range of hills in Shropshire
2 **the Wrekin**   a hill in the vicinity
5 **holt**   wood   **hanger**   wooded slope
6 **Uricon**   a town of Roman times, on the site of Wroxeter

Then, 'twas before my time, the Roman
    At yonder heaving hill would stare: 10
The blood that warms an English yeoman,
    The thoughts that hurt him, they were there.

There, like the wind through woods in riot,
    Through him the gale of life blew high;
The tree of man was never quiet: 15
    Then 'twas the Roman, now 'tis I.

The gale, it plies the saplings double,
    It blows so hard, 'twill soon be gone:
To-day the Roman and his trouble
    Are ashes under Uricon.   20

                          1896

Epitaph on an Army of Mercenaries

These, in the day when heaven was falling,
    The hour when earth's foundations fled,
Followed their mercenary calling
    And took their wages and are dead.

Their shoulders held the sky suspended;   5
    They stood, and earth's foundations stay;
What God abandoned, these defended,
    And saved the sum of things for pay.

                          1922

GERARD MANLEY HOPKINS

1844–89 b London. He became a Catholic while at Oxford and, in 1868, a Jesuit. His poems, written amidst pastoral work and the teaching of classics, were published in 1918.

The Windhover: *kestrel*

To Christ our Lord

I caught this morning morning's minion, king-   *darling*
    dom of daylight's dauphin, dapple-dawn-drawn Falcon, in his riding
    Of the rolling level underneath him steady air, and striding
High there, how he rung upon the rein of a wimpling wing
In his ecstasy! then off, off forth on swing,   5
    As a skate's heel sweeps smooth on a bow-bend: the hurl and gliding
    Rebuffed the big wind. My heart in hiding
Stirred for a bird,—the achieve of, the mastery of the thing!

Brute beauty and valour and act, oh, air, pride, plume, here
    Buckle! AND the fire that breaks from thee then, a billion   10
Times told lovelier, more dangerous, O my chevalier!

Epitaph See MacDiarmid's reply (p. 134).
Gerard Manley Hopkins Hopkins' poems in manuscript often include various marks to indicate prosody. A handful of these are retained here to assist reading.

No wonder of it: shéer plód makes plough down sillion   *furrow*
Shine, and blue-bleak embers, ah my dear,
    Fall, gall themselves, and gash gold-vermilion.

                                                          1877   1918

God's Grandeur

The world is charged with the grandeur of God.
    It will flame out, like shining from shook foil;
    It gathers to a greatness, like the ooze of oil
Crushed. Why do men then now not reck his rod?
Generations have trod, have trod, have trod;   5
    And all is seared with trade; bleared, smeared with toil;
    And wears man's smudge and shares man's smell: the soil
Is bare now, nor can foot feel, being shod.

And for all this, nature is never spent;
    There lives the dearest freshness deep down things;   10
And though the last lights off the black West went
    Oh, morning, at the brown brink eastward, springs—
Because the Holy Ghost over the bent
    World broods with warm breast and with ah! bright wings.

                                                          1877   1895

[As kingfishers catch fire, dragonflies draw flame]

As kingfishers catch fire, dragonflies draw flame;
    As tumbled over rim in roundy wells
    Stones ring; like each tucked string tells, each hung bell's
Bow swung finds tongue to fling out broad its name;
Each mortal thing does one thing and the same: 5
    Deals out that being indoors each one dwells;
    Selves—goes its self; *myself* it speaks and spells,
Crying *What I do is me: for that I came.*

I say more: the just man justices;
    Keeps grace: thát keeps all his goings graces;   10
Acts in God's eye what in God's eye he is—
    Christ. For Christ plays in ten thousand places,
Lovely in limbs, and lovely in eyes not his
    To the Father through the features of men's faces.

                                                          ?1877   1918

Pied Beauty

Glory be to God for dappled things—
    For skies of couple-colour as a brinded cow;   *streaked*
        For rose-moles all in stipple upon trout that swim;
Fresh-firecoal chestnut-falls; finches' wings;
    Landscape plotted and pieced—fold, fallow, and plough;   5
        And áll trádes, their gear and tackle and trim.

All things counter, original, spare, strange;
　Whatever is fickle, freckled (who knows how?)
　　With swift, slow; sweet, sour; adazzle, dim;
He fathers-forth whose beauty is past change:　　　　　　　　10
　　　　　Praise him.

　　　　　　　　　　　　　　　　1877　1918

Binsey Poplars

felled 1879

My aspens dear, whose airy cages quelled,
　Quelled or quenched in leaves the leaping sun,
All felled, felled, are all felled;
　　Of a fresh and following folded rank
　　　　Not spared, not one　　　　　　　　5
　　　　That dandled a sandalled
　　　Shadow that swam or sank
On meadow and river and wind-wandering weed-winding bank.

O if we but knew what we do
　　　When we delve or hew—　　　　　　　10
　　Hack and rack the growing green!
　　　Since country is so tender
　To touch, her being só slender,
　That, like this sleek and seeing ball
　But a prick will make no eye at all,　　　　　15
　Whére we, even where we mean
　　　　To mend her we end her,
　　　When we hew or delve:
After-comers cannot guess the beauty been.
　Ten or twelve, only ten or twelve　　　　　20
　　　Strokes of havoc únselve
　　　　The sweet especial scene,
　　Rural scene, a rural scene,
　　Sweet especial rural scene.

　　　　　　　　　　　　　　　1879　1918

Spring and Fall:

to a young child

Márgarét, áre you gríeving
Over Goldengrove unleaving?
Leáves, líke the thíngs of mán, you
With your fresh thoughts care for, can you?
Áh! ás the héart grows ólder　　　　　　5
It will come to such sights colder
By and by, nor spare a sigh
Though worlds of wanwood leafmeal lie;
And yet you *will* weep and know why.
Now no matter, child, the name:　　　　　10
Sórrow's spríngs áre the sáme.

Nor mouth had, no nor mind, expressed
What heart heard of, ghost guessed:
It ís the blíght mán was bórn for,
It is Margaret you mourn for.   15

1880 1893

[No worst, there is none. Pitched past pitch of grief]

No worst, there is none. Pitched past pitch of grief,
More pangs will, schooled at forepangs, wilder wring.
Comforter, where, where is your comforting?
Mary, mother of us, where is your relief?
My cries heave, herds-long; huddle in a main, a chief-   5
Woe, wórld-sorrow; on an áge-old anvil wince and sing—
Then lull, then leave off. Fury had shrieked 'No ling-
ering! Let me be fell: force I must be brief'.
O the mind, mind has mountains; cliffs of fall
Frightful, sheer, no-man-fathomed. Hold them cheap   10
May who ne'er hung there. Nor does long our small
Durance deal with that steep or deep. Here! creep,
Wretch, under a comfort serves in a whirlwind: all
Life death does end and each day dies with sleep.

1885 1918

[I wake and feel the fell of dark, not day]

I wake and feel the fell of dark, not day.
What hours, O what black hoürs we have spent
This night! what sights you, heart, saw; ways you went!
And more must, in yet longer light's delay.
With witness I speak this. But where I say   5
Hours I mean years, mean life. And my lament
Is cries countless, cries like dead letters sent
To dearest him that lives alas! away.

I am gall, I am heartburn. God's most deep decree
Bitter would have me taste: my taste was me;   10
Bones built in me, flesh filled, blood brimmed the curse.

Selfyeast of spirit a dull dough sours. I see
The lost are like this, and their scourge to be
As I am mine, their sweating selves; but worse.

1885 1918

Harry Ploughman

Hard as hurdle arms, with a broth of goldish flue   *downy hair*
Breathed round; the rack of ribs; the scooped flank; lank
Rope-over thigh; knee-nave; and barrelled shank—
                Head and foot, shoulder and shank—

---

3 **Comforter** the Holy Spirit
8 **fell** fierce **force** perforce
1 **fell** animal skin, pelt; also cruel, fierce (as an adjective); also gall (archaic)

By a grey eye's heed steered well, one crew, fall to;   5
Stand at stress. Each limb's barrowy brawn, his thew
That onewhere curded, onewhere sucked or sank—   *knotted*
              Soared or sank—,
Though as a beechbole firm, finds his, as at a roll-call, rank
And features, in flesh, what deed he each must do—   10
              His sinew-service where do.
He leans to it, Harry bends, look. Back, elbow, and liquid waist
In him, all quail to the wallowing o' the plough. 'S cheek crimsons; curls
Wag or crossbridle, in a wind lifted, windlaced—
              See his wind- lilylocks -laced—;   15
Churlsgrace, too, child of Amansstrength, how it hangs or hurls
Them—broad in bluff hide his frowning feet lashed! raced
With, along them, cragiron under and cold furls—
              With-a-fountain's shining-shot furls.
                                                      1887   1918

That Nature is a Heraclitean Fire
and of the comfort of the Resurrection

Cloud-puffball, torn tufts, tossed pillows | flaunt forth, then chevy on an air-
Built thoroughfare: heaven-roysterers, in gay-gangs | they throng; they glitter
        in marches.
Down roughcast, down dazzling whitewash, | wherever an elm arches,
Shivelights and shadowtackle in long | lashes lace, lance, and pair.
Delightfully the bright wind boisterous | ropes, wrestles, beats earth bare   5
Of yestertempest's creases; in pool and rutpeel parches
Squandering ooze to squeezed | dough, crust, dust; stanches, starches
Squadroned masks and manmarks | treadmire toil there
Footfretted in it. Million-fuelèd, | nature's bonfire burns on.
But quench her bonniest, dearest | to her, her clearest-selvèd spark   10
Man, how fast his firedint, | his mark on mind, is gone!
Both are in an unfathomable, all is in an enormous dark
Drowned. O pity and indig | nation! Manshape, that shone
Sheer off, disseveral, a star, | death blots black out; nor mark
              Is any of him at all so stark   15
But vastness blurs and time | beats level. Enough! the Resurrection,
A heart's-clarion! Away grief's gasping, | joyless days, dejection.
              Across my foundering deck shone
A beacon, an eternal beam. | Flesh fade, and mortal trash
Fall to the residuary worm; | world's wildfire, leave but ash: 20
              In a flash, at a trumpet crash,
I am all at once what Christ is, | since he was what I am, and
This Jack, joke, poor potsherd, | patch, matchwood, immortal diamond,
              Is immortal diamond.
                                                      1888   1918

---

16 Churlsgrace 'Churl' is archaic English for man, or peasant.
Heraclitean The Greek philosopher Heraclitus (*c.* 500 BC) held that the world is made of fire, and
is continually changing.
1 chevy scamper
4 Shivelights splintered lights

THOMAS HARDY

1840–1928 b Dorset, where he lived as a novelist after several years practising architecture.
Much of his poetry was written after he stopped writing novels in 1896.

The Self-Unseeing

Here is the ancient floor,
Footworn and hollowed and thin,
Here was the former door
Where the dead feet walked in.

She sat here in her chair,   5
Smiling into the fire;
He who played stood there,
Bowing it higher and higher.

Childlike, I danced in a dream;
Blessings emblazoned that day;   10
Everything glowed with a gleam;
Yet we were looking away!

1892–1901   1901

The Ruined Maid

'O 'Melia, my dear, this does everything crown!
Who could have supposed I should meet you in Town?
And whence such fair garments, such prosperi-ty?'—
'O didn't you know I'd been ruined?' said she.

—'You left us in tatters, without shoes or socks,   5
Tired of digging potatoes, and spudding up docks;
And now you've gay bracelets and bright feathers three!'—
'Yes: that's how we dress when we're ruined,' said she.

—'At home in the barton you said 'thee' and 'thou',   *farm*
And 'thik oon', and 'theäs oon', and 't'other'; but now   *this / that* 10
Your talking quite fits 'ee for high compa-ny!'—
'Some polish is gained with one's ruin,' said she.

—'Your hands were like paws then, your face blue and bleak
But now I'm bewitched by your delicate cheek,
And your little gloves fit as on any la-dy!'—   15
'We never do work when we're ruined,' said she.

—'You used to call home-life a hag-ridden dream,
And you'd sigh, and you'd sock; but at present you seem   *sigh loudly*
To know not of megrims or melancho-ly!'—
'True. One's pretty lively when ruined,' said she.   20

—'I wish I had feathers, a fine sweeping gown,
And a delicate face, and could strut about Town!'—
'My dear—a raw country girl, such as you be,
Cannot quite expect that. You ain't ruined,' said she.

1866   1902

The Self-Unseeing A memory of Hardy's parents, written after a visit to his childhood home
3 former In later years this door had been made into a window.

During Wind and Rain

They sing their dearest songs—
He, she, all of them—yea,
Treble and tenor and bass,
   And one to play;
With the candles mooning each face....   5
   Ah, no; the years O!
How the sick leaves reel down in throngs!

They clear the creeping moss—
Elders and juniors—aye,
Making the pathways neat   10
   And the garden gay;
And they build a shady seat....
   Ah, no; the years, the years;
See, the white storm-birds wing across!

They are blithely breakfasting all—   15
Men and maidens—yea,
Under the summer tree,
   With a glimpse of the bay,
While pet fowl come to the knee....
   Ah, no; the years O!   20
And the rotten rose is ript from the wall.

They change to a high new house,
He, she, all of them—aye,
Clocks and carpets and chairs
   On the lawn all day,   25
And brightest things that are theirs....
   Ah, no; the years, the years;
Down their carved names the rain-drop ploughs.

                      ?1913   1917

At Castle Boterel

As I drive to the junction of lane and highway,
   And the drizzle bedrenches the waggonette,
I look behind at the fading byway,
   And see on its slope, now glistening wet,
      Distinctly yet   5

Myself and a girlish form benighted
   In dry March weather. We climb the road
Beside a chaise. We had just alighted
   To ease the sturdy pony's load
      When he sighed and slowed.   10

Castle Boterel   near St Juliot, in Cornwall, where Hardy first met his wife Emma in 1870. A visit to the area in March 1913, three months after her death, touched off a number of tender poems about their marriage which had for a long time been strained.

What we did as we climbed, and what we talked of
   Matters not much, nor to what it led,—
Something that life will not be balked of
   Without rude reason till hope is dead,
      And feeling fled.   15

It filled but a minute. But was there ever
   A time of such quality, since or before,
In that hill's story? To one mind never,
   Though it has been climbed, foot-swift, foot-sore,
      By thousands more.   20

Primaeval rocks form the road's steep border,
   And much have they faced there, first and last,
Of the transitory in Earth's long order;
   But what they record in colour and cast
      Is—that we two passed.   25

And to me, though Time's unflinching rigour,
   In mindless rote, has ruled from sight
The substance now, one phantom figure
   Remains on the slope, as when that night
      Saw us alight.   30

I look and see it there, shrinking, shrinking,
   I look back at it amid the rain
For the very last time; for my sand is sinking,
   And I shall traverse old love's domain
      Never again.   35

                       March 1913   1914

After a Journey

Hereto I come to view a voiceless ghost;
   Whither, O whither will its whim now draw me?
Up the cliff, down, till I'm lonely, lost,
   And the unseen waters' ejaculations awe me.
Where you will next be there's no knowing,   5
   Facing round about me everywhere,
      With your nut-coloured hair,
And gray eyes, and rose-flush coming and going.

Yes: I have re-entered your olden haunts at last;
   Through the years, through the dead scenes I have tracked you;   10
What have you now found to say of our past—
   Scanned across the dark space wherein I have lacked you?
Summer gave us sweets, but autumn wrought division?
   Things were not lastly as firstly well
      With us twain, you tell?   15
But all's closed now, despite Time's derision.

I see what you are doing: you are leading me on
   To the spots we knew when we haunted here together,
The waterfall, above which the mist-bow shone
   At the then fair hour in the then fair weather,   20

And the cave just under, with a voice still so hollow
  That it seems to call out to me from forty years ago,
      When you were all aglow,
And not the thin ghost that I now frailly follow!

Ignorant of what there is flitting here to see,   25
  The waked birds preen and the seals flop lazily;
Soon you will have, Dear, to vanish from me,
  For the stars close their shutters and the dawn whitens hazily.
Trust me, I mind not, though Life lours,
  The bringing me here; nay, bring me here again!   30
      I am just the same as when
Our days were a joy, and our paths through flowers.

Pentargan Bay   1914

Channel Firing

That night your great guns, unawares,
Shook all our coffins as we lay,
And broke the chancel window-squares,
We thought it was the Judgment-day

And sat upright. While drearisome   5
Arose the howl of wakened hounds:
The mouse let fall the altar-crumb,
The worms drew back into the mounds,

The glebe cow drooled. Till God called, 'No;
It's gunnery practice out at sea   10
Just as before you went below;
The world is as it used to be:

'All nations striving strong to make
Red war yet redder. Mad as hatters
They do no more for Christés sake   15
Than you who are helpless in such matters.

'That this is not the judgment-hour
For some of them's a blessed thing,
For if it were they'd have to scour
Hell's floor for so much threatening. . . .   20

'Ha, ha. It will be warmer when
I blow the trumpet (if indeed
I ever do; for you are men,
And rest eternal sorely need).'

So down we lay again. 'I wonder,   25
Will the world ever saner be,'
Said one, 'than when He sent us under
In our indifferent century!'

Pentargan Bay   near St Juliot, Cornwall
9 glebe cow   cow pastured in the glebe, a field attached to a vicarage

And many a skeleton shook his head.
'Instead of preaching forty year,'   30
My neighbour Parson Thirdly said,
'I wish I had stuck to pipes and beer.'

Again the guns disturbed the hour,
Roaring their readiness to avenge,
As far inland as Stourton Tower,   35
And Camelot, and starlit Stonehenge.

April 1914   1914

In Time of 'The Breaking of Nations'

I
Only a man harrowing clods
  In a slow silent walk
With an old horse that stumbles and nods
  Half asleep as they stalk.
II
Only thin smoke without flame   5
  From the heaps of couch-grass;
Yet this will go onward the same
  Though Dynasties pass.
III
Yonder a maid and her wight   *man*
  Come whispering by: 10
War's annals will cloud into night
  Ere their story die.

1915   1916

Ice on the Highway

Seven buxom women abreast, and arm in arm,
    Trudge down the hill, tip-toed,
        And breathing warm;
They must perforce trudge thus, to keep upright
    On the glassy ice-bound road,   5
And they must get to market whether or no,
    Provisions running low
        With the nearing Saturday night,
While the lumbering van wherein they mostly ride
        Can nowise go: 10
Yet loud their laughter as they stagger and slide!

1925

35–36 Stourton Tower   a memorial to King Alfred's victory over the Danes in 878, a few kilometres from the prehistoric monoliths at **Stonehenge**. Glastonbury and South Cadbury, two of
the candidates (in Hardy's time) for the site of King Arthur's legendary pre-Saxon court of **Camelot**,
are also nearby. All are in north Wiltshire, more than fifty kilometres from the English Channel.
Breaking of Nations   See Jer. 51:20: 'Thou art my battle axe and weapons of war: for with thee will I
break in pieces the nations.'

ALGERNON CHARLES SWINBURNE

1837–1909 b London. His poetry was popular for its musical rhythms. He was also a radical political writer.

Stage Love

When the game began between them for a jest,
He played king and she played queen to match the best;
Laughter soft as tears, and tears that turned to laughter,
These were things she sought for years and sorrowed after.

Pleasure with dry lips, and pain that walks by night;   5
All the sting and all the stain of long delight;
These were things she knew not of, that knew not of her,
When she played at half a love with half a lover.

Time was chorus, gave them cues to laugh or cry;
They would kill, befool, amuse him, let him die;   10
Set him webs to weave to-day and break to-morrow,
Till he died for good in play, and rose in sorrow.

What the years mean; how time dies and is not slain;
How love grows and laughs and cries and wanes again;
These were things she came to know, and take their measure,   15
When the play was played out so for one man's pleasure.

      1866

LEWIS CARROLL

(Charles L. Dodgson) 1832–98 b Cheshire. He was a lecturer in mathematics in Oxford as well as a writer of nonsense.

Jabberwocky

'Twas brillig, and the slithy toves
  Did gyre and gimble in the wabe;
All mimsy were the borogoves,
  And the mome raths outgrabe.

'Beware the Jabberwock, my son!   5
  The jaws that bite, the claws that catch!
Beware the Jubjub bird, and shun
  The frumious Bandersnatch!'

He took his vorpal sword in hand:
  Long time the manxome foe he sought—   10
So rested he by the Tumtum tree,
  And stood awhile in thought.

And as in uffish thought he stood,
  The Jabberwock, with eyes of flame,
Came whiffling through the tulgey wood,   15
  And burbled as it came!

One, two! One, two! And through and through
   The vorpal blade went snicker-snack!
He left it dead, and with its head
   He went galumphing back.   20

'And hast thou slain the Jabberwock?
   Come to my arms, my beamish boy!
O frabjous day! Callooh! Callay!'
   He chortled in his joy.

'Twas brillig, and the slithy toves   25
   Did gyre and gimble in the wabe;
All mimsy were the borogoves,
   And the mome raths outgrabe.

                                    1872

EMILY DICKINSON

1830–86 b Amherst, Mass., where she spent her life, and became a recluse in her mid-twenties. She kept her poetry private, and it was published after her death.

249

Wild Nights – Wild Nights!
Were I with thee
Wild Nights should be
Our luxury!

Futile – the Winds –   5
To a Heart in port –
Done with the Compass –
Done with the Chart!

Rowing in Eden –
Ah, the Sea!
Might I but moor – Tonight –   10
In Thee!

                          c. 1861   1891

280

I felt a Funeral, in my Brain,
And Mourners to and fro
Kept treading – treading – till it seemed
That Sense was breaking through –

And when they all were seated,   5
A Service, like a Drum –
Kept beating – beating – till I thought
My Mind was going numb –

And then I heard them lift a Box
And creak across my Soul
With those same Boots of Lead, again,   10
Then Space – began to toll,

As all the Heavens were a Bell,
And Being, but an Ear,
And I, and Silence, some strange Race   15
Wrecked, solitary, here –

And then a Plank in Reason, broke,
And I dropped down, and down –
And hit a World, at every plunge,
And Finished knowing – then –   20

                                    c. 1861   1896

303

The Soul selects her own Society –
Then – shuts the Door –
To her divine Majority –
Present no more –

Unmoved – she notes the Chariots – pausing –   5
At her low Gate –
Unmoved – an Emperor be kneeling
Upon her Mat –

I've known her – from an ample nation –
Choose One –   10
Then – close the Valves of her attention –
Like Stone –

                                    c. 1862   1890

341

After great pain, a formal feeling comes –
The Nerves sit ceremonious, like Tombs –
The stiff Heart questions was it He, that bore,
And Yesterday, or Centuries before?

The Feet, mechanical, go round –   5
Of Ground, or Air, or Ought –
A Wooden way
Regardless grown,
A Quartz contentment, like a stone –

This is the Hour of Lead –   10
Remembered, if outlived,
As Freezing persons, recollect the Snow –
First – Chill – then Stupor – then the letting go –

                                    c. 1862   1929

348

I dreaded that first Robin, so,
But He is mastered, now,
I'm some accustomed to Him grown,
He hurts a little, though –

I thought if I could only live   5
Till that first Shout got by –
Not all Pianos in the Woods
Had power to mangle me –

I dared not meet the Daffodils –
For fear their Yellow Gown   10
Would pierce me with a fashion
So foreign to my own –

I wished the Grass would hurry –
So when 'twas time to see –
He'd be too tall, the tallest one   15
Could stretch – to look at me –

I could not bear the Bees should come,
I wished they'd stay away
In those dim countries where they go,
What word had they, for me?   20

They're here, though; not a creature failed –
No Blossom stayed away
In gentle deference to me –
The Queen of Calvary –

Each one salutes me, as he goes,   25
And I, my childish Plumes,
Lift, in bereaved acknowledgement
Of their unthinking Drums –

                                              c. 1862   1891

401

What Soft – Cherubic Creatures –
These Gentlewomen are –
One would as soon assault a Plush –
Or violate a Star –

Such Dimity Convictions –   5
A Horror so refined
Of freckled Human Nature –
Of Deity – ashamed –

It's such a common – Glory –
A Fisherman's – Degree –   10
Redemption – Brittle Lady –
Be so – ashamed of Thee –

                                              c. 1862   1896

449

I died for Beauty – but was scarce
Adjusted in the Tomb
When One who died for Truth, was lain
In an adjoining Room –

---

5 Dimity   a cotton cloth with raised stripes and patterns
10 Fisherman's Degree   i.e. the degree, or social class, of a fisherman, such as several of Christ's
apostles were
12 See Luke 9:26: 'Whosoever shall be ashamed of me and of my words, of him shall the Son of man
be ashamed, when he shall come in his own glory, and in his Father's, and of the holy angels.'

He questioned softly 'Why I failed'?   5
'For Beauty', I replied –
'And I – for Truth – Themself are One –
We Brethren, are', He said –

And so, as Kinsmen, met a Night –
We talked between the Rooms –   10
Until the Moss had reached our lips –
And covered up – our names –

c. *1862*   1890

465

I heard a Fly buzz – when I died –
The Stillness in the Room
Was like the Stillness in the Air –
Between the Heaves of Storm –

The Eyes around – had wrung them dry –   5
And Breaths were gathering firm
For that last Onset – when the King
Be witnessed – in the Room –

I willed my Keepsakes – Signed away
What portion of me be   10
Assignable – and then it was
There interposed a Fly –

With Blue – uncertain – stumbling Buzz –
Between the light – and me –
And then the Windows failed – and then   15
I could not see to see –

c. *1862*   1896

580

I gave myself to Him –
And took Himself, for Pay,
The solemn contract of a Life
Was ratified, this way –

The Wealth might disappoint –   5
Myself a poorer prove
Than this great Purchaser suspect,
The Daily Own – of Love

Depreciate the Vision –
But till the Merchant buy –   10
Still Fable – in the Isles of Spice –
The subtle Cargoes – lie –

At least – 'tis Mutual – Risk –
Some – found it – Mutual Gain –
Sweet Debt of Life – Each Night to owe –   15
Insolvent – every Noon –

c. *1862*   1891

601

A still – Volcano – Life –
That flickered in the night –
When it was dark enough to do
Without erasing sight –

A quiet – Earthquake Style –   5
Too subtle to suspect
By natures this side Naples –
The North cannot detect

The Solemn – Torrid – Symbol –
The lips that never lie –   10
Whose hissing Corals part – and shut –
And Cities – ooze away –

                                        c. 1862   1929

640

I cannot live with You –
It would be Life –
And Life is over there –
Behind the Shelf

The Sexton keeps the Key to –   5
Putting up
Our Life – His Porcelain –
Like a Cup –

Discarded of the Housewife –
Quaint – or Broke –   10
A newer Sevres pleases –
Old Ones crack –

I could not die – with You –
For One must wait
To shut the Other's Gaze down –   15
You – could not –

And I – Could I stand by
And see You – freeze –
Without my Right of Frost –
Death's privilege?   20

Nor could I rise – with You –
Because Your Face
Would put out Jesus' –
That New Grace

Glow plain – and foreign   25
On my homesick Eye –
Except that You than He
Shone closer by –

They'd judge Us – How –
For You – served Heaven – You know,   30
Or sought to –
I could not –

Because You saturated Sight –
And I had no more Eyes
For sordid excellence   35
As Paradise

And were You lost, I would be –
Though My Name
Rang loudest
On the Heavenly fame –   40

And were You – saved –
And I – condemned to be
Where You were not –
That self – were Hell to Me –

So We must meet apart –   45
You there – I – here –
With just the Door ajar
That Oceans are – and Prayer –
And that White Sustenance –
Despair –   50

       c. 1862 1890

657

I dwell in Possibility –
A fairer House than Prose –
More numerous of Windows –
Superior – for Doors –

Of Chambers as the Cedars –   5
Impregnable of Eye –
And for an Everlasting Roof
The Gambrels of the Sky –   *curved roofs*

Of Visitors – the fairest –
For Occupation – This –   10
The spreading wide my narrow Hands
To gather Paradise –

       c. 1862 1929

712

Because I could not stop for Death –
He kindly stopped for me –
The Carriage held but just Ourselves –
And Immortality.

We slowly drove – He knew no haste   5
And I had put away
My labor and my leisure too,
For His Civility –

We passed the School, where Children strove
At Recess – in the Ring –
We passed the Fields of Gazing Grain –
We passed the Setting Sun –

Or rather – He passed Us –
The Dews drew quivering and chill –
For only Gossamer, my Gown –
My Tippet – only Tulle –

shoulder cape

We paused before a House that seemed
A Swelling of the Ground –
The Roof was scarcely visible –
The Cornice – in the Ground –

Since then – 'tis Centuries – and yet
Feels shorter than the Day
I first surmised the Horses' Heads
Were toward Eternity –

c. 1863   1890

764

Presentiment – is that long Shadow – on the Lawn –
Indicative that Suns go down –

The Notice to the startled Grass
That Darkness – is about to pass –

c. 1863   1890

1540

As imperceptibly as Grief
The Summer lapsed away –
Too imperceptible at last
To seem like Perfidy –
A Quietness distilled
As Twilight long begun,
Or Nature spending with herself
Sequestered Afternoon –
The Dusk drew earlier in –
The Morning foreign shone –
A courteous, yet harrowing Grace,
As Guest, that would be gone –
And thus, without a Wing
Or service of a Keel
Our Summer made her light escape
Into the Beautiful.

c. 1865   1891

1100

The last Night that She lived
It was a Common Night
Except the Dying – this to Us
Made Nature different

10

15

20

5

10

15

We noticed smallest things –   5
Things overlooked before
By this great light upon our Minds
Italicized – as 'twere.

As We went out and in
Between Her final Room   10
And Rooms where Those to be alive
Tomorrow were, a Blame

That Others could exist
While She must finish quite
A Jealousy for Her arose   15
So nearly infinite –

We waited while She passed –
It was a narrow time –
Too jostled were Our Souls to speak
At length the notice came.   20

She mentioned, and forgot –
Then lightly as a Reed
Bent to the Water, struggled scarce –
Consented, and was dead –

And We – We placed the Hair –   25
And drew the Head erect –
And then an awful leisure was
Belief to regulate –

                                                        c. 1866   1890

1593

There came a Wind like a Bugle –
It quivered through the Grass
And a Green Chill upon the Heat
So ominous did pass
We barred the Windows and the Doors   5
As from an Emerald Ghost –
The Doom's electric Moccasin
That very instant passed –
On a strange Mob of panting Trees
And Fences fled away   10
And Rivers where the Houses ran
Those looked that lived – that Day –
The Bell within the steeple wild
The flying tidings told –
How much can come   15
And much can go,
And yet abide the World!

                                                        c. 1883   1891

CHRISTINA ROSSETTI

1830–94 b and lived in London; father Italian. She was a central figure in the pre-Raphaelite movement.

A Birthday

My heart is like a singing bird
    Whose nest is in a watered shoot;
My heart is like an apple-tree
    Whose boughs are bent with thickset fruit;
My heart is like a rainbow shell   5
    That paddles in a halcyon sea;
My heart is gladder than all these
    Because my love is come to me.

Raise me a dais of silk and down;
    Hang it with vair and purple dyes;   10
Carve it in doves and pomegranates,
    And peacocks with a hundred eyes;
Work it in gold and silver grapes,
    In leaves and silver fleurs-de-lys;
Because the birthday of my life   15
    Is come, my love is come to me.

                      1857   1862

Goblin Market

Morning and evening
Maids heard the goblins cry:
'Come buy our orchard fruits,
Come buy, come buy:
Apples and quinces,   5
Lemons and oranges,
Plump unpecked cherries,
Melons and raspberries,
Bloom-down-cheeked peaches,
Swart-headed mulberries,   10
Wild free-born cranberries,
Crab-apples, dewberries,
Pine-apples, blackberries,
Apricots, strawberries;—
All ripe together   15
In summer weather,—
Morns that pass by,
Fair eves that fly;
Come buy, come buy:
Our grapes fresh from the vine,   20
Pomegranates full and fine,
Dates and sharp bullaces,
Rare pears and greengages,

Damsons and bilberries, 25
Taste them and try:
Currants and gooseberries,
Bright-fire-like barberries,
Figs to fill your mouth,
Citrons from the South, 30
Sweet to tongue and sound to eye;
Come buy, come buy.'

Evening by evening
Among the brookside rushes,
Laura bowed her head to hear, 35
Lizzie veiled her blushes:
Crouching close together
In the cooling weather,
With clasping arms and cautioning lips,
With tingling cheeks and finger tips. 40
'Lie close,' Laura said,
Pricking up her golden head:
'We must not look at goblin men,
We must not buy their fruits:
Who knows upon what soil they fed 45
Their hungry thirsty roots?'
'Come buy,' call the goblins
Hobbling down the glen.
'Oh,' cried Lizzie, 'Laura, Laura,
You should not peep at goblin men.' 50
Lizzie covered up her eyes,
Covered close lest they should look;
Laura reared her glossy head,
And whispered like the restless brook:
'Look, Lizzie, look, Lizzie, 55
Down the glen tramp little men.
One hauls a basket,
One bears a plate,
One lugs a golden dish
Of many pounds weight. 60
How fair the vine must grow
Whose grapes are so luscious;
How warm the wind must blow
Thro' those fruit bushes.'
'No,' said Lizzie: 'No, no, no; 65
Their offers should not charm us,
Their evil gifts would harm us.'
She thrust a dimpled finger
In each ear, shut eyes and ran:
Curious Laura chose to linger 70
Wondering at each merchant man.
One had a cat's face,
One whisked a tail,
One tramped at a rat's pace,
One crawled like a snail,

One like a wombat prowled obtuse and furry,   75
One like a ratel tumbled hurry skurry.
She heard a voice like voice of doves
Cooing all together:
They sounded kind and full of loves
In the pleasant weather.   80

Laura stretched her gleaming neck
Like a rush-imbedded swan,
Like a lily from the beck,
Like a moonlit poplar branch,
Like a vessel at the launch   85
When its last restraint is gone.

Backwards up the mossy glen
Turned and trooped the goblin men,
With their shrill repeated cry,
'Come buy, come buy.'   90
When they reached where Laura was
They stood stock still upon the moss,
Leering at each other,
Brother with queer brother;
Signalling each other,   95
Brother with sly brother.
One set his basket down,
One reared his plate;
One began to weave a crown
Of tendrils, leaves and rough nuts brown   100
(Men sell not such in any town);
One heaved the golden weight
Of dish and fruit to offer her:
'Come buy, come buy,' was still their cry.
Laura stared but did not stir,   105
Longed but had no money:
The whisk-tailed merchant bad her taste
In tones as smooth as honey,
The cat-faced purr'd,
The rat-paced spoke a word   110
Of welcome, and the snail-paced even was heard;
One parrot-voiced and jolly
Cried 'Pretty Goblin' still for 'Pretty Polly;'—
One whistled like a bird.

But sweet-tooth Laura spoke in haste: 115
'Good Folk, I have no coin;
To take were to purloin:
I have no copper in my purse,
I have no silver either,
And all my gold is on the furze   120
That shakes in windy weather
Above the rusty heather.'
'You have much gold upon your head,'
They answered all together:

'Buy from us with a golden curl.'   125
She clipped a precious golden lock,
She dropped a tear more rare than pearl,
Then sucked their fruit globes fair or red:
Sweeter than honey from the rock,
Stronger than man-rejoicing wine,   130
Clearer than water flowed that juice;
She never tasted such before,
How should it cloy with length of use?
She sucked and sucked and sucked the more
Fruits which that unknown orchard bore;   135
She sucked until her lips were sore;
Then flung the emptied rinds away
But gathered up one kernel stone,
And knew not was it night or day
As she turned home alone.   140

Lizzie met her at the gate
Full of wise upbraidings:
'Dear, you should not stay so late,
Twilight is not good for maidens;
Should not loiter in the glen   145
In the haunts of goblin men.
Do you not remember Jeanie,
How she met them in the moonlight,
Took their gifts both choice and many,
Ate their fruits and wore their flowers   150
Plucked from bowers
Where summer ripens at all hours?
But ever in the noonlight
She pined and pined away;
Sought them by night and day,   155
Found them no more, but dwindled and grew grey;
Then fell with the first snow,
While to this day no grass will grow
Where she lies low:
I planted daisies there a year ago   160
That never blow.
You should not loiter so.'
'Nay, hush,' said Laura:
'Nay, hush, my sister:
I ate and ate my fill,   165
Yet my mouth waters still;
To-morrow night I will
Buy more:' and kissed her:
'Have done with sorrow;
I'll bring you plums tomorrow   170
Fresh on their mother twigs,
Cherries worth getting;
You cannot think what figs
My teeth have met in,

What melons icy-cold   175
Piled on a dish of gold
Too huge for me to hold,
What peaches with a velvet nap,
Pellucid grapes without one seed:
Odorous indeed must be the mead   180
Whereon they grow, and pure the wave they drink
With lilies at the brink,
And sugar-sweet their sap.'

Golden head by golden head,
Like two pigeons in one nest   185
Folded in each other's wings,
They lay down in their curtained bed:
Like two blossoms on one stem,
Like two flakes of new-fall'n snow,
Like two wands of ivory   190
Tipped with gold for awful kings.
Moon and stars gazed in at them,
Wind sang to them lullaby,
Lumbering owls forbore to fly,
Not a bat flapped to and fro   195
Round their rest:
Cheek to cheek and breast to breast
Locked together in one nest.

Early in the morning
When the first cock crowed his warning,   200
Neat like bees, as sweet and busy,
Laura rose with Lizzie:
Fetched in honey, milked the cows,
Aired and set to rights the house,
Kneaded cakes of whitest wheat,   205
Cakes for dainty mouths to eat,
Next churned butter, whipped up cream,
Fed their poultry, sat and sewed;
Talked as modest maidens should:
Lizzie with an open heart,   210
Laura in an absent dream,
One content, one sick in part;
One warbling for the mere bright day's delight,
One longing for the night.

At length slow evening came: 215
They went with pitchers to the reedy brook;
Lizzie most placid in her look,
Laura most like a leaping flame.
They drew the gurgling water from its deep;
Lizzie plucked purple and rich golden flags,   220
Then turning homewards said: 'The sunset flushes
Those furthest loftiest crags;
Come, Laura, not another maiden lags,
No wilful squirrel wags,

The beasts and birds are fast asleep.'   225
But Laura loitered still among the rushes
And said the bank was steep.

And said the hour was early still,
The dew not fall'n, the wind not chill;
Listening ever, but not catching   230
The customary cry,
'Come buy, come buy,'
With its iterated jingle
Of sugar-baited words:
Not for all her watching   235
Once discerning even one goblin
Racing, whisking, tumbling, hobbling;
Let alone the herds
That used to tramp along the glen,
In groups or single,   240
Of brisk fruit-merchant men.
Till Lizzie urged, 'O Laura, come;
I hear the fruit-call, but I dare not look:
You should not loiter longer at this brook:
Come with me home.   245
The stars rise, the moon bends her arc,
Each glowworm winks her spark,
Let us get home before the night grows dark:
For clouds may gather
Tho' this is summer weather,   250
Put out the lights and drench us thro';
Then if we lost our way what should we do?'

Laura turned cold as stone
To find her sister heard that cry alone,
That goblin cry,   255
'Come buy our fruits, come buy.'
Must she then buy no more such dainty fruit?
Must she no more such succous pasture find,
Gone deaf and blind?
Her tree of life drooped from the root: 260
She said not one word in her heart's sore ache;
But peering thro' the dimness, nought discerning,
Trudged home, her pitcher dripping all the way;
So crept to bed, and lay
Silent till Lizzie slept;   265
Then sat up in a passionate yearning,
And gnashed her teeth for baulked desire, and wept
As if her heart would break.

Day after day, night after night,
Laura kept watch in vain   270
In sullen silence of exceeding pain.
She never caught again the goblin cry:
'Come buy, come buy;'—

She never spied the goblin men
Hawking their fruits along the glen: 275
But when the noon waxed bright
Her hair grew thin and gray;
She dwindled, as the fair full moon doth turn
To swift decay and burn
Her fire away.   280

One day remembering her kernel-stone
She set it by a wall that faced the south;
Dewed it with tears, hoped for a root,
Watched for a waxing shoot,
But there came none;   285
It never saw the sun,
It never felt the trickling moisture run:
While with sunk eyes and faded mouth
She dreamed of melons, as a traveller sees
False waves in desert drouth   290
With shade of leaf-crowned trees,
And burns the thirstier in the sandful breeze.

She no more swept the house,
Tended the fowls or cows,
Fetched honey, kneaded cakes of wheat,   295
Brought water from the brook:
But sat down listless in the chimney-nook
And would not eat.

Tender Lizzie could not bear
To watch her sister's cankerous care   300
Yet not to share.
She night and morning
Caught the goblins' cry:
'Come buy our orchard fruits,
Come buy, come buy:'—   305
Beside the brook, along the glen,
She heard the tramp of goblin men,
The voice and stir
Poor Laura could not hear;
Longed to buy fruit to comfort her,   310
But feared to pay too dear.
She thought of Jeanie in her grave,
Who should have been a bride;
But who for joys brides hope to have
Fell sick and died   315
In her gay prime,
In earliest Winter time,
With the first glazing rime,
With the first snow-fall of crisp Winter time.

Till Laura dwindling   320
Seemed knocking at Death's door:
Then Lizzie weighed no more

Better and worse;
But put a silver penny in her purse,
Kissed Laura, crossed the heath with clumps of furze   325
At twilight, halted by the brook:
And for the first time in her life
Began to listen and look.

Laughed every goblin
When they spied her peeping: 330
Came towards her hobbling,
Flying, running, leaping,
Puffing and blowing,
Chuckling, clapping, crowing,
Clucking and gobbling,   335
Mopping and mowing,
Full of airs and graces,
Pulling wry faces,
Demure grimaces,
Cat-like and rat-like,   340
Ratel- and wombat-like,
Snail-paced in a hurry,
Parrot-voiced and whistler,
Helter skelter, hurry skurry,
Chattering like magpies,   345
Fluttering like pigeons,
Gliding like fishes,—
Hugged her and kissed her:
Squeezed and caressed her:
Stretched up their dishes,   350
Panniers, and plates:
'Look at our apples
Russet and dun,
Bob at our cherries,
Bite at our peaches,   355
Citrons and dates,
Grapes for the asking,
Pears red with basking
Out in the sun,
Plums on their twigs;   360
Pluck them and suck them,
Pomegranates, figs.'—

'Good folk,' said Lizzie,
Mindful of Jeanie:
'Give me much and many:'—   365
Held out her apron,
Tossed them her penny.
'Nay, take a seat with us,
Honour and eat with us,'
They answered grinning: 370
'Our feast is but beginning.
Night yet is early,
Warm and dew-pearly,

Wakeful and starry:
Such fruits as these   375
No man can carry;
Half their bloom would fly,
Half their dew would dry,
Half their flavour would pass by.
Sit down and feast with us,   380
Be welcome guest with us,
Cheer you and rest with us.'—
'Thank you,' said Lizzie: 'But one waits
At home alone for me:
So without further parleying,   385
If you will not sell me any
Of your fruits tho' much and many,
Give me back my silver penny
I tossed you for a fee.'—
They began to scratch their pates,   390
No longer wagging, purring,
But visibly demurring,
Grunting and snarling.
One called her proud,
Cross-grained, uncivil;   395
Their tones waxed loud,
Their looks were evil.
Lashing their tails
They trod and hustled her,
Elbowed and jostled her,   400
Clawed with their nails,
Barking, mewing, hissing, mocking,
Tore her gown and soiled her stocking,
Twitched her hair out by the roots,
Stamped upon her tender feet,   405
Held her hands and squeezed their fruits
Against her mouth to make her eat.

White and golden Lizzie stood,
Like a lily in a flood,—
Like a rock of blue-veined stone   410
Lashed by tides obstreperously,—
Like a beacon left alone
In a hoary roaring sea,
Sending up a golden fire,—
Like a fruit-crowned orange-tree   415
White with blossoms honey-sweet
Sore beset by wasp and bee,—
Like a royal virgin town
Topped with gilded dome and spire
Close beleaguered by a fleet   420
Mad to tug her standard down.

One may lead a horse to water,
Twenty cannot make him drink.

Tho' the goblins cuffed and caught her,
Coaxed and fought her,   425
Bullied and besought her,
Scratched her, pinched her black as ink,
Kicked and knocked her,
Mauled and mocked her,
Lizzie uttered not a word;   430
Would not open lip from lip
Lest they should cram a mouthful in:
But laughed in heart to feel the drip
Of juice that syrupped all her face,
And lodged in dimples of her chin,   435
And streaked her neck which quaked like curd.
At last the evil people,
Worn out by her resistance,
Flung back her penny, kicked their fruit
Along whichever road they took,   440
Not leaving root or stone or shoot;
Some writhed into the ground,
Some dived into the brook
With ring and ripple,
Some scudded on the gale without a sound,   445
Some vanished in the distance.

In a smart, ache, tingle,
Lizzie went her way;
Knew not was it night or day;
Sprang up the bank, tore thro' the furze,   450
Threaded copse and dingle,
And heard her penny jingle
Bouncing in her purse,—
Its bounce was music to her ear.
She ran and ran   455
As if she feared some goblin man
Dogged her with gibe or curse
Or something worse:
But not one goblin skurried after,
Nor was she pricked by fear;   460
The kind heart made her windy-paced
That urged her home quite out of breath with haste
And inward laughter.

She cried, 'Laura,' up the garden,
'Did you miss me?   465
Come and kiss me.
Never mind my bruises,
Hug me, kiss me, suck my juices
Squeezed from goblin fruits for you,
Goblin pulp and goblin dew.   470
Eat me, drink me, love me;
Laura, make much of me;
For your sake I have braved the glen
And had to do with goblin merchant men.'

Laura started from her chair,   475
Flung her arms up in the air,
Clutched her hair:
'Lizzie, Lizzie, have you tasted
For my sake the fruit forbidden?
Must your light like mine be hidden,   480
Your young life like mine be wasted,
Undone in mine undoing,
And ruined in my ruin,
Thirsty, cankered, goblin-ridden?'—
She clung about her sister,   485
Kissed and kissed and kissed her:
Tears once again
Refreshed her shrunken eyes,
Dropping like rain
After long sultry drouth;   490
Shaking with aguish fear, and pain,
She kissed and kissed her with a hungry mouth.

Her lips began to scorch,
That juice was wormwood to her tongue,
She loathed the feast: 495
Writhing as one possessed she leaped and sung,
Rent all her robe, and wrung
Her hands in lamentable haste,
And beat her breast.
Her locks streamed like the torch   500
Borne by a racer at full speed,
Or like the mane of horses in their flight,
Or like an eagle when she stems the light
Straight toward the sun,
Or like a caged thing freed,   505
Or like a flying flag when armies run.

Swift fire spread thro' her veins, knocked at her heart,
Met the fire smouldering there
And overbore its lesser flame;
She gorged on bitterness without a name: 510
Ah! fool, to choose such part
Of soul-consuming care!
Sense failed in the mortal strife:
Like the watch-tower of a town
Which an earthquake shatters down,   515
Like a lightning-stricken mast,
Like a wind-uprooted tree
Spun about,
Like a foam-topped waterspout
Cast down headlong in the sea,   520
She fell at last;
Pleasure past and anguish past,
Is it death or is it life?

Life out of death.
That night long Lizzie watched by her,   525
Counted her pulse's flagging stir,
Felt for her breath,
Held water to her lips, and cooled her face
With tears and fanning leaves:
But when the first birds chirped about their eaves,   530
And early reapers plodded to the place
Of golden sheaves,
And dew-wet grass
Bowed in the morning winds so brisk to pass,
And new buds with new day   535
Opened of cup-like lilies on the stream,
Laura awoke as from a dream,
Laughed in the innocent old way,
Hugged Lizzie but not twice or thrice;
Her gleaming locks showed not one thread of grey,   540
Her breath was sweet as May
And light danced in her eyes.

Days, weeks, months, years
Afterwards, when both were wives
With children of their own;   545
Their mother-hearts beset with fears,
Their lives bound up in tender lives;
Laura would call the little ones
And tell them of her early prime,
Those pleasant days long gone   550
Of not-returning time:
Would talk about the haunted glen,
The wicked, quaint fruit-merchant men,
Their fruits like honey to the throat
But poison in the blood;   555
(Men sell not such in any town):
Would tell them how her sister stood
In deadly peril to do her good,
And win the fiery antidote:
Then joining hands to little hands   560
Would bid them cling together,
'For there is no friend like a sister
In calm or stormy weather;
To cheer one on the tedious way,
To fetch one if one goes astray,   565
To lift one if one totters down,
To strengthen whilst one stands.'

1859 1862

MATTHEW ARNOLD

1822–88 b Middlesex. An inspector of schools for much of his life, he wrote most of his poetry while young; from about 1865 he was an influential literary and cultural critic.

To Marguerite—Continued

Yes! in the sea of life enisled,
With echoing straits between us thrown,
Dotting the shoreless watery wild,
We mortal millions live *alone*.
The islands feel the enclasping flow,
And then their endless bounds they know.

But when the moon their hollows lights,
And they are swept by balms of spring,
And in their glens, on starry nights,
The nightingales divinely sing;
And lovely notes, from shore to shore,
Across the sounds and channels pour—

Oh! then a longing like despair
Is to their farthest caverns sent;
For surely once, they feel, we were
Parts of a single continent!
Now round us spreads the watery plain—
Oh might our marges meet again!

Who order'd, that their longing's fire
Should be, as soon as kindled, cool'd?
Who renders vain their deep desire?—
A God, a God their severance ruled!
And bade betwixt their shores to be
The unplumb'd, salt, estranging sea.

1852

The Buried Life

Light flows our war of mocking words, and yet,
Behold, with tears mine eyes are wet!
I feel a nameless sadness o'er me roll.
Yes, yes, we know that we can jest,
We know, we know that we can smile!
But there's a something in this breast,
To which thy light words bring no rest,
And thy gay smiles no anodyne.
Give me thy hand, and hush awhile,
And turn those limpid eyes on mine,
And let me read there, love! thy inmost soul.

To Marguerite   one of several poems addressed to a French woman whom Arnold met briefly on holiday in Switzerland in 1849

Alas! is even love too weak
To unlock the heart, and let it speak?
Are even lovers powerless to reveal
To one another what indeed they feel? 15
I knew the mass of men conceal'd
Their thoughts, for fear that if reveal'd
They would by other men be met
With blank indifference, or with blame reproved;
I knew they lived and moved 20
Trick'd in disguises, alien to the rest
Of men, and alien to themselves—and yet
The same heart beats in every human breast!

But we, my love! doth a like spell benumb
Our hearts, our voices?—must we too be dumb? 25

Ah! well for us, if even we,
Even for a moment, can get free
Our heart, and have our lips unchain'd;
For that which seals them hath been deep-ordain'd!

Fate, which foresaw 30
How frivolous a baby man would be—
By what distractions he would be possess'd,
How he would pour himself in every strife,
And well-nigh change his own identity—
That it might keep from his capricious play 35
His genuine self, and force him to obey
Even in his own despite his being's law,
Bade through the deep recesses of our breast
The unregarded river of our life
Pursue with indiscernible flow its way; 40
And that we should not see
The buried stream, and seem to be
Eddying at large in blind uncertainty,
Though driving on with it eternally.

But often, in the world's most crowded streets, 45
But often, in the din of strife,
There rises an unspeakable desire
After the knowledge of our buried life;
A thirst to spend our fire and restless force
In tracking out our true, original course; 50
A longing to inquire
Into the mystery of this heart which beats
So wild, so deep in us—to know
Whence our lives come and where they go.
And many a man in his own breast then delves, 55
But deep enough, alas! none ever mines.
And we have been on many thousand lines,
And we have shown, on each, spirit and power;
But hardly have we, for one little hour,
Been on our own line, have we been ourselves— 60
Hardly had skill to utter one of all

The nameless feelings that course through our breast,
But they course on for ever unexpress'd.

And long we try in vain to speak and act
Our hidden self, and what we say and do   65
Is eloquent, is well—but 'tis not true!
And then we will no more be rack'd
With inward striving, and demand
Of all the thousand nothings of the hour
Their stupifying power;   70
Ah yes, and they benumb us at our call!
Yet still, from time to time, vague and forlorn,
From the soul's subterranean depth upborne
As from an infinitely distant land,
Come airs, and floating echoes, and convey   75
A melancholy into all our day.

Only—but this is rare—
When a beloved hand is laid in ours,
When, jaded with the rush and glare
Of the interminable hours,   80
Our eyes can in another's eyes read clear,
When our world-deafen'd ear
Is by the tones of a loved voice caress'd—
A bolt is shot back somewhere in our breast,
And a lost pulse of feeling stirs again.   85
The eye sinks inward, and the heart lies plain,
And what we mean, we say, and what we would, we know.
A man becomes aware of his life's flow,
And hears its winding murmur; and he sees
The meadows where it glides, the sun, the breeze.   90

And there arrives a lull in the hot race
Wherein he doth for ever chase
That flying and elusive shadow, rest.
An air of coolness plays upon his face,
And an unwonted calm pervades his breast.   95
And then he thinks he knows
The hills where his life rose,
And the sea where it goes.

                                                          1852

Dover Beach

The sea is calm to-night.
The tide is full, the moon lies fair
Upon the straits;—on the French coast the light
Gleams and is gone; the cliffs of England stand,
Glimmering and vast, out in the tranquil bay.   5
Come to the window, sweet is the night-air!

Dover Beach   probably written in 1851, when Arnold and his wife twice visited Dover soon after
their marriage

Only, from the long line of spray
Where the sea meets the moon-blanch'd land,
Listen! you hear the grating roar
Of pebbles which the waves draw back, and fling,   10
At their return, up the high strand,
Begin, and cease, and then again begin,
With tremulous cadence slow, and bring
The eternal note of sadness in.

Sophocles long ago   15
Heard it on the Ægæan and it brought
Into his mind the turbid ebb and flow
Of human misery; we
Find also in the sound a thought,
Hearing it by this distant northern sea.   20

The Sea of Faith
Was once, too, at the full, and round earth's shore
Lay like the folds of a bright girdle furl'd.
But now I only hear
Its melancholy, long, withdrawing roar,   25
Retreating, to the breath
Of the night-wind, down the vast edges drear
And naked shingles of the world.

Ah, love, let us be true
To one another! for the world, which seems   30
To lie before us like a land of dreams,
So various, so beautiful, so new,
Hath really neither joy, nor love, nor light,
Nor certitude, nor peace, nor help for pain;
And we are here as on a darkling plain   35
Swept with confused alarms of struggle and flight,
Where ignorant armies clash by night.

                                                        1867

ARTHUR HUGH CLOUGH

1819–61 b Liverpool. He worked in the Education Office in London. Much of his poetry
was published posthumously.

From Amours de Voyage
II, v. Claude to Eustace

Yes, we are fighting at last, it appears. This morning, as usual,   95
Murray, as usual, in hand, I enter the Caffè Nuovo;
Seating myself with a sense as it were of a change in the weather,

---

15 Sophocles (?496–406 BC)   Greek tragic playwright. No specific play seems to be indicated.
Amours de Voyage   a verse novella in the form of letters written mostly by Claude, an Englishman
visiting Italy
95 fighting   the siege of Rome by French forces in 1849. Clough was present.

Not understanding, however, but thinking mostly of Murray,
And, for to-day is their day, of the Campidoglio Marbles,
Caffè-latte! I call to the waiter,—and *Non c' è latte*,   100
This is the answer he makes me, and this the sign of a battle.
So I sit; and truly they seem to think any one else more
Worthy than me of attention. I wait for my milkless *nero*,
Free to observe undistracted all sorts and sizes of persons,
Blending civilian and soldier in strangest costume, coming in, and   105
Gulping in hottest haste, still standing, their coffee,—withdrawing
Eagerly, jangling a sword on the steps, or jogging a musket
Slung to the shoulder behind. They are fewer, moreover, than usual,
Much, and silenter far; and so I begin to imagine
Something is really afloat. Ere I leave, the Caffè is empty,   110
Empty too the streets, in all its length the Corso
Empty, and empty I see to my right and left the Condotti.
    Twelve o'clock, on the Pincian Hill, with lots of English,
Germans, Americans, French,—The Frenchmen, too, are protected,—
So we stand in the sun, but afraid of a probable shower;   115
So we stand and stare, and see, to the left of St Peter's,
Smoke, from the cannon, white,—but that is at intervals only,—
Black, from a burning house, we suppose, by the Cavalleggieri;
And we believe we discern some lines of men descending
Down through the vineyard-slopes, and catch a bayonet gleaming.   120
Every ten minutes, however,—in this there is no misconception,—
Comes a great white puff from behind Michel Angelo's dome, and
After a space the report of a real big gun,—not the Frenchman's?—
That must be doing some work. And so we watch and conjecture.
    Shortly, an Englishman comes, who says he has been to St Peter's,   125
Seen the Piazza and troops, but that is all he can tell us;
So we watch and sit, and, indeed, it begins to be tiresome.—
All this smoke is outside; when it has come to the inside,
It will be time, perhaps, to descend and retreat to our houses.
    Half-past one, or two. The report of small arms frequent,   130
Sharp and savage indeed; that cannot all be for nothing:
So we watch and wonder; but guessing is tiresome, very.
Weary of wondering, watching, and guessing, and gossiping idly,
Down I go, and pass through the quiet streets with the knots of
National Guards patrolling, and flags hanging out at the windows,   135
English, American, Danish,—and, after offering to help an
Irish family moving *en masse* to the Maison Serny,
After endeavouring idly to minister balm to the trembling
Quinquagenarian fears of two lone British spinsters,
Go to make sure of my dinner before the enemy enter.   140
But by this there are signs of stragglers returning; and voices
Talk, though you don't believe it, of guns and prisoners taken;
And on the walls you read the first bulletin of the morning.—
This is all that I saw, and all I know of the battle.

                                      1849–58   1862

WALT WHITMAN

1819–92 b Long Island, New York. He worked as a printer, editor and clerk. The democratic
note in his poetry has been widely influential.

Crossing Brooklyn Ferry

1

Flood-tide below me! I see you face to face!
Clouds of the west-sun there half an hour high—I see you also face to face.

Crowds of men and women attired in the usual costumes, how curious you
    are to me!
On the ferry-boats the hundreds and hundreds that cross, returning home,
    are more curious to me than you suppose,
And you that shall cross from shore to shore years hence are more to me, and
    more in my meditations, than you might suppose.   5

2

The impalpable sustenance of me from all things at all hours of the day,
The simple, compact, well-join'd scheme, myself disintegrated, every one
    disintegrated yet part of the scheme,
The similitudes of the past and those of the future,
The glories strung like beads on my smallest sights and hearings, on the walk
    in the street and the passage over the river,
The current rushing so swiftly and swimming with me far away,   10
The others that are to follow me, the ties between me and them,
The certainty of others, the life, love, sight, hearing of others.

Others will enter the gates of the ferry and cross from shore to shore,
Others will watch the run of the flood-tide,
Others will see the shipping of Manhattan north and west, and the heights
    of Brooklyn to the south and east,   15
Others will see the islands large and small;
Fifty years hence, others will see them as they cross, the sun half an hour high,
A hundred years hence, or ever so many hundred years hence, others will see
    them,
Will enjoy the sunset, the pouring-in of the flood-tide, the falling-back to the
    sea of the ebb-tide.

3

It avails not, time nor place—distance avails not,   20
I am with you, you men and women of a generation, or ever so many
    generations hence,
Just as you feel when you look on the river and sky, so I felt,
Just as any of you is one of a living crowd, I was one of a crowd,
Just as you are refresh'd by the gladness of the river and the bright flow,
    I was refresh'd,
Just as you stand and lean on the rail, yet hurry with the swift current,
    I stood yet was hurried,   25
Just as you look on the numberless masts of ships and the thick-stemm'd
    pipes of steamboats, I look'd.

I too many and many a time cross'd the river of old,
Watched the Twelfth-month sea-gulls, saw them high in the air floating with
    motionless wings, oscillating their bodies,
Saw how the glistening yellow lit up parts of their bodies and left the rest in
    strong shadow,
Saw the slow-wheeling circles and the gradual edging toward the south,   30
Saw the reflection of the summer sky in the water,
Had my eyes dazzled by the shimmering track of beams,
Look'd at the fine centrifugal spokes of light round the shape of my head in the
    sunlit water,
Look'd on the haze on the hills southward and south-westward,
Look'd on the vapor as it flew in fleeces tinged with violet,   35
Look'd toward the lower bay to notice the vessels arriving,
Saw their approach, saw aboard those that were near me,
Saw the white sails of schooners and sloops, saw the ships at anchor,
The sailors at work in the rigging or out astride the spars,
The round masts, the swinging motion of the hulls, the slender serpentine
    pennants,
                                                                                      40
The large and small steamers in motion, the pilots in their pilot-houses,
The white wake left by the passage, the quick tremulous whirl of the wheels,
The flags of all nations, the falling of them at sunset,
The scallop-edged waves in the twilight, the ladled cups, the frolicsome
    crests and glistening,
The stretch afar growing dimmer and dimmer, the gray walls of the granite
    storehouses by the docks,
                                                                                      45
On the river the shadowy group, the big steam-tug closely flank'd on each
    side by the barges, the hay-boat, the belated lighter,
On the neighboring shore the fires from the foundry chimneys burning
    high and glaringly into the night,
Casting their flicker of black contrasted with wild red and yellow light
    over the tops of houses, and down into the clefts of streets.

4

These and all else were to me the same as they are to you,
I loved well those cities, loved well the stately and rapid river,   50
The men and women I saw were all near to me,
Others the same—others who look back on me because I look'd forward
    to them,
(The time will come, though I stop here to-day and to-night.)

5

What is it then between us?
What is the count of the scores or hundreds of years between us?   55
Whatever it is, it avails not—distance avails not, and place avails not,
I too lived, Brooklyn of ample hills was mine,
I too walk'd the streets of Manhattan island, and bathed in the waters
    around it,
I too felt the curious abrupt questionings stir within me,
In the day among crowds of people sometimes they came upon me,   60
In my walks home late at night or as I lay in my bed they came upon me,
I too had been struck from the float forever held in solution,

I too had receiv'd identity by my body,
That I was I knew was of my body, and what I should be I knew I should
    be of my body.

6

It is not upon you alone the dark patches fall,   65
The dark threw its patches down upon me also,
The best I had done seem'd to me blank and suspicious,
My great thoughts as I supposed them, were they not in reality meagre?
Nor is it you alone who know what it is to be evil,
I am he who knew what it was to be evil,   70
I too knitted the old knot of contrariety,
Blabb'd, blush'd, resented, lied, stole, grudg'd,
Had guile, anger, lust, hot wishes I dared not speak,
Was wayward, vain, greedy, shallow, sly, cowardly, malignant,
The wolf, the snake, the hog, not wanting in me,   75
The cheating look, the frivolous word, the adulterous wish, not wanting,
Refusals, hates, postponements, meanness, laziness, none of these wanting,
Was one with the rest, the days and haps of the rest,
Was call'd by my nighest name by clear loud voices of young men as they
    saw me approaching or passing,
Felt their arms on my neck as I stood, or the negligent leaning of their flesh
    against me as I sat,   80
Saw many I loved in the street or ferry-boat or public assembly, yet never
    told them a word,
Lived the same life with the rest, the same old laughing, gnawing, sleeping,
Play'd the part that still looks back on the actor or actress,
The same old role, the role that is what we make it, as great as we like,
Or as small as we like, or both great and small.   85

7

Closer yet I approach you,
What thought you have of me now, I had as much of you—I laid in my stores
    in advance,
I consider'd long and seriously of you before you were born.

Who was to know what should come home to me?
Who knows but I am enjoying this?   90
Who knows, for all the distance, but I am as good as looking at you now,
    for all you cannot see me?

8

Ah, what can ever be more stately and admirable to me than mast-hemm'd
    Manhattan?
River and sunset and scallop-edg'd waves of flood-tide?
The sea-gulls oscillating their bodies, the hay-boat in the twilight, and the
    belated lighter?
What gods can exceed these that clasp me by the hand, and with voices I love
    call me promptly and loudly by my nighest name as I approach?   95
What is more subtle than this which ties me to the woman or man that looks
    in my face?
Which fuses me into you now, and pours my meaning into you?

We understand then do we not?
What I promis'd without mentioning it, have you not accepted?
What the study could not teach—what the preaching could not accomplish
    is accomplish'd, is it not?   100

9

Flow on, river! flow with the flood-tide, and ebb with the ebb-tide!
Frolic on, crested and scallop-edg'd waves!
Gorgeous clouds of the sunset! drench with your splendor me, or the men
    and women generations after me!
Cross from shore to shore, countless crowds of passengers!
Stand up, tall masts of Mannahatta! stand up, beautiful hills of Brooklyn!   105
Throb, baffled and curious brain! throw out questions and answers!
Suspend here and everywhere, eternal float of solution!
Gaze, loving and thirsting eyes, in the house or street or public assembly!
Sound out, voices of young men! loudly and musically call me by my nighest
    name!
Live, old life! play the part that looks back on the actor or actress!   110
Play the old role, the role that is great or small according as one makes it!
Consider, you who peruse me, whether I may not in unknown ways be looking
    upon you;
Be firm, rail over the river, to support those who lean idly, yet haste with the
    hasting current;
Fly on, sea-birds! fly sideways, or wheel in large circles high in the air;
Receive the summer sky, you water, and faithfully hold it till all downcast eyes
    have time to take it from you!   115
Diverge, fine spokes of light, from the shape of my head, or any one's head,
    in the sunlit water!
Come on, ships from the lower bay! pass up or down, white-sail'd
    schooners, sloops, lighters!
Flaunt away, flags of all nations! be duly lower'd at sunset!
Burn high your fires, foundry chimneys! cast black shadows at nightfall!
    cast red and yellow light over the tops of the houses!
Appearances, now or henceforth, indicate what you are,   120
You necessary film, continue to envelop the soul,
About my body for me, and your body for you, be hung our divinest aromas,
Thrive, cities—bring your freight, bring your shows, ample and sufficient
    rivers,
Expand, being than which none else is perhaps more spiritual,
Keep your places, objects than which none else is more lasting.   125
You have waited, you always wait, you dumb, beautiful ministers,
We receive you with free sense at last, and are insatiate henceforward,
Not you any more shall be able to foil us, or withhold yourselves from us,
We use you, and do not cast you aside—we plant you permanently within us,
We fathom you not—we love you—there is perfection in you also,   130
You furnish your parts toward eternity,
Great or small, you furnish your parts toward the soul.

                                   1856

---

105 Mannahatta   Native American name for Manhattan.

This Compost

1

Something startles me where I thought I was safest,
I withdraw from the still woods I loved,
I will not go now on the pastures to walk,
I will not strip the clothes from my body to meet my lover the sea,   5
I will not touch my flesh to the earth as to other flesh to renew me.

O how can it be that the ground itself does not sicken?
How can you be alive you growths of spring?
How can you furnish health you blood of herbs, roots, orchards, grain?
Are they not continually putting distemper'd corpses within you?
Is not every continent work'd over and over with sour dead?   10

Where have you disposed of their carcasses?
Those drunkards and gluttons of so many generations?
Where have you drawn off all the foul liquid and meat?
I do not see any of it upon you to-day, or perhaps I am deceiv'd,
I will run a furrow with my plough, I will press my spade through
        the sod and turn it up underneath,   15
I am sure I shall expose some of the foul meat.

2

Behold this compost! behold it well!
Perhaps every mite has once form'd part of a sick person—yet behold!
The grass of spring covers the prairies,
The bean bursts noiselessly through the mould in the garden,   20
The delicate spear of the onion pierces upward,
The apple-buds cluster together on the apple-branches,
The resurrection of the wheat appears with pale visage out of its graves,
The tinge awakes over the willow-tree and the mulberry-tree,
The he-birds carol mornings and evenings while the she-birds sit on their
        nests,   25
The young of poultry break through the hatch'd eggs,
The new-born of animals appear, the calf is dropt from the cow, the colt from
        the mare,
Out of its little hill faithfully rise the potato's dark green leaves,
Out of its hill rises the yellow maize-stalk, the lilacs bloom in the dooryards,
The summer growth is innocent and disdainful above all those strata of sour
        dead.   30

What chemistry!
That the winds are really not infectious,
That this is no cheat, this transparent green-wash of the sea which is so
        amorous after me,
That it is safe to allow it to lick my naked body all over with its tongues,
That it will not endanger me with the fevers that have deposited themselves
        in it,   35
That all is clean forever and forever,
That the cool drink from the well tastes so good,
That blackberries are so flavorous and juicy,

That the fruits of the apple-orchard and the orange-orchard, that melons,
    grapes, peaches, plums, will none of them poison me,
That when I recline on the grass I do not catch any disease,   40
Though probably every spear of grass rises out of what was once a
    catching disease.

Now I am terrified at the Earth, it is that calm and patient,
It grows such sweet things out of such corruptions,
It turns harmless and stainless on its axis, with such endless successions
    of diseas'd corpses,
It distills such exquisite winds out of such infused fetor,   45
It renews with such unwitting looks its prodigal, annual, sumptuous crops,
It gives such divine materials to men, and accepts such leavings from them at
    last.

                                 1856

I Saw in Louisiana a Live-Oak Growing

I saw in Louisiana a live-oak growing,
All alone stood it and the moss hung down from the branches,
Without any companion it grew there uttering joyous leaves of dark green,
And its look, rude, unbending, lusty, made me think of myself,
But I wonder'd how it could utter joyous leaves standing alone there
    without its friend near, for I knew I could not,   5
And I broke off a twig with a certain number of leaves upon it, and twined
    around it a little moss,
And brought it away, and I have placed it in sight in my room,
It is not needed to remind me as of my own dear friends,
(For I believe lately I think of little else than of them,)
Yet it remains to me a curious token, it makes me think of manly love; 10
For all that, and though the live-oak glistens there in Louisiana solitary in
    a wide flat space,
Uttering joyous leaves all its life without a friend a lover near,
I know very well I could not.

                        1860   1867

EMILY BRONTË

1818–48 b Haworth, on the Yorkshire moors, the setting for *Wuthering Heights*. She
worked intermittently as a teacher and governess.

[The starry night shall tidings bring]

The starry night shall tidings bring
Go out upon the breezy moor
Watch for a bird with sable wing
And beak and talons dripping gore

Look not around look not beneath   5
But mutely trace its airy way
Mark where it lights upon the heath
Then wanderer kneel thee down and pray

What fortune may await thee there
I will not and I dare not tell   10
But Heaven is moved by fervent prayer
And God is mercy—fare thee well!

1839 1910

[There was a time when my cheek burned]

There was a time when my cheek burned
To give such scornful fiends the lie
Ungoverned nature madly spurned
The law that bade it not defy
O in the days of ardent youth   5
I would have given my life for truth

For truth for right for liberty
I would have gladly, freely died
And now I calmly hear and see
The vain man smile the fool deride   10
Though not because my heart is tame
Though not for fear though not for shame

My soul still chafes at every tone
Of selfish and self-blinded error
My breast still braves the world alone   15
Steeled as it ever was to terror
Only I know however I frown
The same world will go rolling on

1839 1910

Remembrance

Cold in the earth and the deep snow piled above thee!
Far, far removed, cold in the dreary grave!
Have I forgot, my Only Love, to love thee,
Severed at last by Time's all wearing wave?

Now, when alone, do my thoughts no longer hover   5
Over the mountains on Angora's shore;
Resting their wings where heath and fern-leaves cover
That noble heart for ever, ever more?

Cold in the earth, and fifteen wild Decembers
From those brown hills have melted into spring—   10
Faithful indeed is the spirit that remembers
After such years of change and suffering!

Sweet Love of youth, forgive if I forget thee
While the World's tide is bearing me along:
Sterner desires and darker hopes beset me,   15
Hopes which obscure but cannot do thee wrong.

Remembrance Title from 1846 publication; text from ms. of the unfinished Gondal saga, where it is designated 'R. Alcona to J. Brenzaida' and dated March 3, 1845.

No other sun has lightened up my heaven;
No other star has ever shone for me:
All my life's bliss from thy dear life was given—
All my life's bliss is in the grave with thee.   20

But when the days of golden dreams had perished
And even Despair was powerless to destroy,
Then did I learn how existence could be cherished,
Strengthened and fed without the aid of joy;

Then did I check the tears of useless passion,   25
Weaned my young soul from yearning after thine;
Sternly denied its burning wish to hasten
Down to that tomb already more than mine!

And even yet, I dare not let it languish,
Dare not indulge in Memory's rapturous pain,   30
Once drinking deep of that divinest anguish
How could I seek the empty world again?

                                                        1846

Stars

Ah! why, because the dazzling sun
Restored my earth to joy
Have you departed, every one,
And left a desert sky?

All through the night, your glorious eyes   5
Were gazing down in mine,
And with a full heart's thankful sighs
I blessed that watch divine!

I was at peace—and drank your beams
As they were life to me   10
And revelled in my changeful dreams
Like petrel on the sea.

Thought followed thought—star followed star
Through boundless regions on,
While one sweet influence, near and far,   15
Thrilled through and proved us one.

Why did the morning rise to break
So great, so pure a spell,
And scorch with fire the tranquil cheek
Where your cool radiance fell?   20

Blood red he rose, and arrow-straight
His fierce beams struck my brow:
The soul of Nature sprang elate,
But mine sank sad and low!

Stars   Title from 1846 publication; text from a ms. dated March 14, 1845.

My lids closed down—yet through their veil   25
I saw him blazing still;
And bathe in gold the misty dale
And flash upon the hill.

I turned me to the pillow then
To call back Night, and see   30
Your worlds of solemn light again
Throb with my heart and me!

It would not do—the pillow glowed
And glowed both roof and floor
And birds sang loudly in the wood   35
And fresh winds shook the door.

The curtains waved, the wakened flies
Were murmuring round my room,
Imprisoned there, till I should rise
And give them leave to roam.   40

O Stars and Dreams and Gentle Night,
O Night and Stars return!
And hide me from the hostile light
That does not warm, but burn—

That drains the blood of suffering men—   45
Drinks tears, instead of dew—
Let me sleep through his blinding reign
And only wake with you!

                                                              1846

ROBERT BROWNING

1812–89 b London. He mainly lived with his parents, writing poetry, until he married Elizabeth Barrett in 1846 and moved to Italy for 15 years. He returned to England when she died.

My Last Duchess

Ferrara

That's my last Duchess painted on the wall,
Looking as if she were alive. I call
That piece a wonder, now: Frà Pandolf's hands
Worked busily a day, and there she stands.
Will't please you sit and look at her? I said   5
'Frà Pandolf' by design, for never read
Strangers like you that pictured countenance,
The depth and passion of its earnest glance,

Ferrara a city in northern Italy. In 1561 the Duke of Ferrara's 17-year-old wife of three years died in suspicious circumstances, whereupon he sought the hand of the ward of the Count of Tyrol, of Innsbruck. The painting, **Frà Pandolf** (line 3) and **Claus** (line 56) are fictional.

But to myself they turned (since none puts by
The curtain I have drawn for you, but I)   10
And seemed as they would ask me, if they durst,
How such a glance came there; so, not the first
Are you to turn and ask thus. Sir, 't was not
Her husband's presence only, called that spot
Of joy into the Duchess' cheek: perhaps   15
Frà Pandolf chanced to say 'Her mantle laps
Over my lady's wrist too much,' or 'Paint
Must never hope to reproduce the faint
Half-flush that dies along her throat:' such stuff
Was courtesy, she thought, and cause enough   20
For calling up that spot of joy. She had
A heart—how shall I say?—too soon made glad,
Too easily impressed; she liked whate'er
She looked on, and her looks went everywhere.
Sir, 't was all one! My favour at her breast,   25
The dropping of the daylight in the West,
The bough of cherries some officious fool
Broke in the orchard for her, the white mule
She rode with round the terrace—all and each
Would draw from her alike the approving speech,   30
Or blush, at least. She thanked men,—good! but thanked
Somehow—I know not how—as if she ranked
My gift of a nine-hundred-years-old name
With anybody's gift. Who'd stoop to blame
This sort of trifling? Even had you skill   35
In speech—(which I have not)—to make your will
Quite clear to such an one, and say, 'Just this
Or that in you disgusts me; here you miss,
Or there exceed the mark'—and if she let
Herself be lessoned so, nor plainly set   40
Her wits to yours, forsooth, and made excuse,
—E'en then would be some stooping; and I choose
Never to stoop. Oh sir, she smiled, no doubt,
Whene'er I passed her; but who passed without
Much the same smile? This grew; I gave commands;   45
Then all smiles stopped together. There she stands
As if alive. Will 't please you rise? We'll meet
The company below, then. I repeat,
The Count your master's known munificence
Is ample warrant that no just pretence   50
Of mine for dowry will be disallowed;
Though his fair daughter's self, as I avowed
At starting, is my object. Nay, we'll go
Together down, sir. Notice Neptune, though,
Taming a sea-horse, thought a rarity,   55
Which Claus of Innsbruck cast in bronze for me!

1842 1842

Meeting at Night

I

The grey sea and the long black land;
And the yellow half-moon large and low;
And the startled little waves that leap
In fiery ringlets from their sleep,
As I gain the cove with pushing prow,   5
And quench its speed i' the slushy sand.

II

Then a mile of warm sea-scented beach;
Three fields to cross till a farm appears;
A tap at the pane, the quick sharp scratch
And blue spurt of a lighted match,   10
And a voice less loud, thro' its joys and fears,
Than the two hearts beating each to each!

                                                            1845

Parting at Morning

Round the cape of a sudden came the sea,
And the sun looked over the mountain's rim:
And straight was a path of gold for him,
And the need of a world of men for me.

                                                            1845

The Bishop Orders His Tomb
at Saint Praxed's Church

Rome, 15—

Vanity, saith the preacher, vanity!
Draw round my bed: is Anselm keeping back?
Nephews—sons mine. . .ah God, I know not! Well—
She, men would have to be your mother once,
Old Gandolf envied me, so fair she was!   5
What's done is done, and she is dead beside,
Dead long ago, and I am Bishop since,
And as she died so must we die ourselves,
And thence ye may perceive the world's a dream.
Life, how and what is it? As here I lie   10
In this state-chamber, dying by degrees,
Hours and long hours in the dead night, I ask
'Do I live, am I dead?' Peace, peace seems all.
Saint Praxed's ever was the church for peace;
And so, about this tomb of mine. I fought   15
With tooth and nail to save my niche, ye know:
—Old Gandolf cozened me, despite my care;   *cheated*

The Bishop Orders his Tomb   Both the Bishop and **Gandolf** are fictional. Santa Prassede was a
virgin saint whose church in Rome dates from the fifth century.
1 See Eccles. 1:2
3 Nephews   a common euphemism for illegitimate sons

Shrewd was that snatch from out the corner South
He graced his carrion with, God curse the same!
Yet still my niche is not so cramped but thence   20
One sees the pulpit o' the epistle-side,
And somewhat of the choir, those silent seats,
And up into the aery dome where live
The angels, and a sunbeam's sure to lurk:
And I shall fill my slab of basalt there,   25
And 'neath my tabernacle take my rest,   *canopy*
With those nine columns round me, two and two,
The odd one at my feet where Anselm stands:
Peach-blossom marble all, the rare, the ripe
As fresh-poured red wine of a mighty pulse.   30
—Old Gandolf with his paltry onion-stone,
Put me where I may look at him! True peach,
Rosy and flawless: how I earned the prize!
Draw close: that conflagration of my church
—What then? So much was saved if aught were missed!   35
My sons, ye would not be my death? Go dig
The white-grape vineyard where the oil-press stood,
Drop water gently till the surface sink,
And if ye find...Ah God, I know not, I!...
Bedded in store of rotten fig-leaves soft,   40
And corded up in a tight olive-frail,   *basket*
Some lump, ah God, of *lapis lazuli*,
Big as a Jew's head cut off at the nape,
Blue as a vein o'er the Madonna's breast...
Sons, all have I bequeathed you, villas, all,   45
That brave Frascati villa with its bath,
So, let the blue lump poise between my knees,
Like God the Father's globe on both his hands
Ye worship in the Jesu Church so gay,
For Gandolf shall not choose but see and burst!   50
Swift as a weaver's shuttle fleet our years:
Man goeth to the grave, and where is he?
Did I say basalt for my slab, sons? Black—
'Twas ever antique-black I meant! How else
Shall ye contrast my frieze to come beneath?   55
The bas-relief in bronze ye promised me,
Those Pans and Nymphs ye wot of, and perchance   *know*
Some tripod, thyrsus, with a vase or so,
The Saviour at his sermon on the mount,

21 **epistle side** the south side of a church
22 **choir** place for the singers
31 **onion stone** a marble which tends to flake
42 **lapis lazuli** a blue semi-precious stone
46 **Frascati** hill resort near Rome
49 **Jesu Church** Il Gesù, a baroque church completed in 1568; one of its sculptures is of the Trinity, with a globe carved of the largest known block of lapis lazuli.
51 See Job 7:6: 'My days are swifter than a weaver's shuttle, and are spent without hope.'
58 **tripod** three-legged throne of the Delphic oracle of ancient Greece **thyrsus** staff carried by the attendants of Dionysus
59 **sermon on the mount** preached by Christ. See Matt. chs 5–7.

Saint Praxed in a glory, and one Pan   *halo*   60
Ready to twitch the Nymph's last garment off,
And Moses with the tables...but I know
Ye mark me not! What do they whisper thee,
Child of my bowels, Anselm? Ah, ye hope   65
To revel down my villas while I gasp   *limestone*
Bricked o'er with beggar's mouldy travertine
Which Gandolf from his tomb-top chuckles at!
Nay, boys, ye love me—all of jasper, then!
'Tis jasper ye stand pledged to, lest I grieve   70
My bath must needs be left behind, alas!
One block, pure green as a pistachio-nut,
There's plenty jasper somewhere in the world—
And have I not Saint Praxed's ear to pray
Horses for ye, and brown Greek manuscripts,   75
And mistresses with great smooth marbly limbs?
—That's if ye carve my epitaph aright,
Choice Latin, picked phrase, Tully's every word,
No gaudy ware like Gandolf's second line—
Tully, my masters? Ulpian serves his need!   80
And then how I shall lie through centuries,
And hear the blessed mutter of the mass,
And see God made and eaten all day long,
And feel the steady candle-flame, and taste
Good strong thick stupefying incense-smoke!   85
For as I lie here, hours of the dead night,
Dying in state and by such slow degrees,
I fold my arms as if they clasped a crook,
And stretch my feet forth straight as stone can point,
And let the bedclothes, for a mortcloth, drop   90
Into great laps and folds of sculptor's-work:
And as yon tapers dwindle, and strange thoughts
Grow, with a certain humming in my ears,
About the life before I lived this life,
And this life too, popes, cardinals and priests,   95
Saint Praxed at his sermon on the mount,
Your tall pale mother with her talking eyes,
And new-found agate urns as fresh as day,
And marble's language, Latin pure, discreet,
—Aha, ELUCESCEBAT quoth our friend?   100
No Tully, said I, Ulpian at the best!
Evil and brief hath been my pilgrimage.
All *lapis*, all, sons! Else I give the Pope
My villas! Will ye ever eat my heart?
Ever your eyes were as a lizard's quick,

---

62 tables   stones inscribed with the Ten Commandments
77 Tully   Marcus Tullius Cicero (106–43 BC), recognized as a master of classical Latin
79 Ulpian   Domitius Ulpianus (AD 170–228), a writer of post-classical Latin, which was considered
an inferior style
87 crook   crozier: bishop's staff, shaped like a shepherd's crook as an emblem of pastoral care
99 elucescebat   'He was illustrious' (inscribed in post-classical Latin: Cicero would have written
'elucebat').

They glitter like your mother's for my soul,   105
Or ye would heighten my impoverished frieze,
Piece out its starved design, and fill my vase
With grapes, and add a vizor and a Term,
And to the tripod ye would tie a lynx
That in his struggle throws the thyrsus down,   110
To comfort me on my entablature
Whereon I am to lie till I must ask
'Do I live, am I dead?' There, leave me, there!
For ye have stabbed me with ingratitude
To death—ye wish it—God, ye wish it! Stone—   115
Gritstone, a-crumble! Clammy squares which sweat
As if the corpse they keep were oozing through—
And no more *lapis* to delight the world!
Well go! I bless ye. Fewer tapers there,
But in a row: and, going, turn your backs   120
—Ay, like departing altar-ministrants,
And leave me in my church, the church for peace,
That I may watch at leisure if he leers—
Old Gandolf, at me, from his onion-stone,
As still he envied me, so fair she was!   125

                                              1845   1849

Two in the Campagna

                    I
I wonder do you feel to-day
    As I have felt since, hand in hand,
We sat down on the grass, to stray
    In spirit better through the land,
This morn of Rome and May?   5
                    II
For me, I touched a thought, I know,
    Has tantalized me many times,
(Like turns of thread the spiders throw
    Mocking across our path) for rhymes
To catch at and let go.   10
                    III
Help me to hold it! First it left
    The yellowing fennel, run to seed
There, branching from the brickwork's cleft,
    Some old tomb's ruin: yonder weed
Took up the floating weft,   15
                    IV
Where one small orange cup amassed
    Five beetles,—blind and green they grope

---

106 **frieze**   carved stonework
108 **vizor**   mask   **Term**   bust, on top of a pillar
111 **entablature**   stonework above pillars, on which his effigy will lie
116 **Gritstone**   coarse sandstone
Campagna   name for the open grassland outside Rome; referred to as **champaign** in line twenty-one

Among the honey-meal: and last,
   Everywhere on the grassy slope
I traced it. Hold it fast!   20
        V
The champaign with its endless fleece
   Of feathery grasses everywhere!
Silence and passion, joy and peace,
   An everlasting wash of air—
Rome's ghost since her decease.   25
       VI
Such life here, through such lengths of hours,
   Such miracles performed in play,
Such primal naked forms of flowers,
   Such letting nature have her way
While heaven looks from its towers!   30
       VII
How say you? Let us, O my dove,
   Let us be unashamed of soul,
As earth lies bare to heaven above!
   How is it under our control
To love or not to love?   35
       VIII
I would that you were all to me,
   You that are just so much, no more.
Nor yours nor mine, nor slave nor free!
   Where does the fault lie? What the core
O' the wound, since wound must be?   40
       IX
I would I could adopt your will,
   See with your eyes, and set my heart
Beating by yours, and drink my fill
   At your soul's springs,—your part my part
In life, for good and ill.   45
       X
No. I yearn upward, touch you close,
   Then stand away. I kiss your cheek,
Catch your soul's warmth,—I pluck the rose
   And love it more than tongue can speak—
Then the good minute goes.   50
       XI
Already how am I so far
   Out of that minute? Must I go
Still like the thistle-ball, no bar,
   Onward, whenever light winds blow,
Fixed by no friendly star?   55
       XII
Just when I seemed about to learn!
   Where is the thread now? Off again!
The old trick! Only I discern—
   Infinite passion, and the pain
Of finite hearts that yearn.   60
               1855

A Toccata of Galuppi's

I

Oh Galuppi, Baldassaro, this is very sad to find!
I can hardly misconceive you; it would prove me deaf and blind;
But although I take your meaning, 'tis with such a heavy mind!

II

Here you come with your old music, and here's all the good it brings.
What, they lived once thus at Venice where the merchants were the kings,   5
Where Saint Mark's is, where the Doges used to wed the sea with rings?

III

Ay, because the sea's the street there; and 'tis arched by...what you call
...Shylock's bridge with houses on it, where they kept the carnival:
I was never out of England—it's as if I saw it all.

IV

Did young people take their pleasure when the sea was warm in May?   10
Balls and masks begun at midnight, burning ever to mid-day,
When they made up fresh adventures for the morrow, do you say?

V

Was a lady such a lady, cheeks so round and lips so red,—
On her neck the small face buoyant, like a bell-flower on its bed,
O'er the breast's superb abundance where a man might base his head?   15

VI

Well, and it was graceful of them—they'd break talk off and afford
—She, to bite her mask's black velvet—he, to finger on his sword,
While you sat and played Toccatas, stately at the clavichord?

VII

What? Those lesser thirds so plaintive, sixths diminished, sigh on sigh,
Told them something? Those suspensions, those solutions—'Must we die?'   20
Those commiserating sevenths—'Life might last! we can but try!'

VIII

'Were you happy?'—'Yes.'—'And are you still as happy?'—'Yes. And you?'
—'Then, more kisses!'—'Did *I* stop them, when a million seemed so few?'
Hark, the dominant's persistence till it must be answered to!

IX

So, an octave struck the answer. Oh, they praised you, I dare say!   25
'Brave Galuppi! that was music! good alike at grave and gay!
I can always leave off talking when I hear a master play!'

X

Then they left you for their pleasure: till in due time, one by one,
Some with lives that came to nothing, some with deeds as well undone,
Death stepped tacitly and took them where they never see the sun.   30

Toccata   a musical composition for virtuoso performance
Galuppi   Baldassare Galuppi, Venetian composer (1706–85)
6 St Marks'   cathedral in Venice. The **Doge** (elected ruler) annually threw a ring into the sea,
wedding it with the city.
8 Shylock's bridge   the Rialto, mentioned in *The Merchant of Venice*
18 clavichord   a small keyboard instrument
24–25 dominant's persistence   a sustained note on the dominant (the fifth note of the scale),
which requires resolution to the tonic (the first note of the scale)

XI
But when I sit down to reason, think to take my stand nor swerve,
While I triumph o'er a secret wrung from nature's close reserve,
In you come with your cold music till I creep thro' every nerve.

XII
Yes, you, like a ghostly cricket, creaking where a house was burned:
'Dust and ashes, dead and done with, Venice spent what Venice earned.   35
The soul, doubtless, is immortal—where a soul can be discerned.

XIII
'Yours for instance: you know physics, something of geology,
Mathematics are your pastime; souls shall rise in their degree;
Butterflies may dread extinction,—you'll not die, it cannot be!

XIV
'As for Venice and her people, merely born to bloom and drop,   40
Here on earth they bore their fruitage, mirth and folly were the crop:
What of soul was left, I wonder, when the kissing had to stop?

XV
'Dust and ashes!' So you creak it, and I want the heart to scold.
Dear dead women, with such hair, too—what's become of all the gold
Used to hang and brush their bosoms? I feel chilly and grown old.   45

c. *1847*   1855

EDWARD LEAR

1812–88 b London. A professional artist, he wrote his nonsense poems for the grandson of a patron.

The Dong with a Luminous Nose

When awful darkness and silence reign
Over the great Gromboolian plain,
    Through the long, long wintry nights;—
When the angry breakers roar
As they beat on the rocky shore;—   5
    When Storm-clouds brood on the towering heights
Of the Hills of the Chankly Bore:—

Then, through the vast and gloomy dark,
There moves what seems a fiery spark,
    A lonely spark with silvery rays   10
        Piercing the coal-black night,—
        A Meteor strange and bright:—
    Hither and thither the vision strays,
        A single lurid light.

Slowly it wanders,—pauses,—creeps,—   15
Anon it sparkles,—flashes and leaps;
And ever as onward it gleaming goes
A light on the Bong-tree stems it throws.
And those who watch at that midnight hour
From Hall or Terrace, or lofty Tower,   20

Cry, as the wild light passes along,—
    'The Dong!—the Dong!
  The wandering Dong through the forest goes!
    The Dong! the Dong!
  The Dong with a luminous Nose!'   25

    Long years ago
  The Dong was happy and gay,
Till he fell in love with a Jumbly Girl
  Who came to those shores one day.
For the Jumblies came in a sieve, they did,—   30
Landing at eve near the Zemmery Fidd
  Where the Oblong Oysters grow,
  And the rocks are smooth and gray.
And all the woods and the valleys rang
With the Chorus they daily and nightly sang,—   35
  'Far and few, far and few,
  Are the lands where the Jumblies live;
  Their heads are green, and their hands are blue
  And they went to sea in a sieve.'

Happily, happily passed those days!   40
  While the cheerful Jumblies staid;
  They danced in circlets all night long,
  To the plaintive pipe of the lively Dong,
  In moonlight, shine, or shade.
For day and night he was always there   45
By the side of the Jumbly Girl so fair,
With her sky-blue hands, and her sea-green hair.
Till the morning came of that hateful day
When the Jumblies sailed in their sieve away,
And the Dong was left on the cruel shore   50
Gazing—gazing for evermore,—
Ever keeping his weary eyes on
That pea-green sail on the far horizon,—
Singing the Jumbly Chorus still
As he sate all day on the grassy hill,—   55
  'Far and few, far and few,
  Are the lands where the Jumblies live;
  Their heads are green, and their hands are blue,
  And they went to sea in a sieve.'

But when the sun was low in the West,   60
  The Dong arose and said;—
  —'What little sense I once possessed
  Has quite gone out of my head!'—
And since that day he wanders still
By lake and forest, marsh and hill,   65
Singing—'O somewhere, in valley or plain
Might I find my Jumbly Girl again!
For ever I'll seek by lake and shore
Till I find my Jumbly Girl once more!'

Playing a pipe with silvery squeaks, 70
Since then his Jumbly Girl he seeks,
And because by night he could not see,
He gathered the bark of the Twangum Tree
   On the flowery plain that grows.
   And he wove him a wondrous Nose,— 75
  A Nose as strange as a Nose could be!
Of vast proportions and painted red,
And tied with cords to the back of his head.
    —In a hollow rounded space it ended
    With a luminous Lamp within suspended, 80
      All fenced about
      With a bandage stout
      To prevent the wind from blowing it out;—
    And with holes all round to send the light,
    In gleaming rays on the dismal night. 85

And now each night, and all night long,
Over those plains still roams the Dong;
And above the wail of the Chimp and Snipe
You may hear the squeak of his plaintive pipe
While ever he seeks, but seeks in vain 90
To meet with his Jumbly Girl again;
Lonely and wild—all night he goes,—
The Dong with a luminous Nose!
And all who watch at the midnight hour,
From Hall or Terrace, or lofty Tower, 95
Cry, as they trace the Meteor bright,
Moving along through the dreary night,—
    'This is the hour when forth he goes,
    The Dong with a luminous Nose!
    Yonder—over the plain he goes; 100
      He goes!
      He goes;
    The Dong with a luminous Nose!'

1877

ALFRED, LORD TENNYSON

1809–92 b Lincolnshire; made a peer in 1884. He lived on the Isle of Wight and in Surrey, a private man despite the adulation he received from about 1850 when he became poet laureate.

The Lady of Shalott

Part I

On either side the river lie
Long fields of barley and of rye,
That clothe the wold and meet the sky;   *open country*
And thro' the field the road runs by
   To many-tower'd Camelot; 5

And up and down the people go,
Gazing where the lilies blow
Round an island there below,
    The island of Shalott.

Willows whiten, aspens quiver,   10
Little breezes dusk and shiver
Thro' the wave that runs for ever
By the island in the river
        Flowing down to Camelot.
Four gray walls, and four gray towers,   15
Overlook a space of flowers,
And the silent isle imbowers
        The Lady of Shalott.

By the margin, willow-veil'd,
Slide the heavy barges trail'd
By slow horses; and unhail'd   20
The shallop flitteth silken-sail'd
        Skimming down to Camelot: *sloop*
But who hath seen her wave her hand?
Or at the casement seen her stand?
Or is she known in all the land,   25
        The Lady of Shalott?

Only reapers, reaping early
In among the bearded barley,
Hear a song that echoes cheerly   30
From the river winding clearly,
        Down to tower'd Camelot:
And by the moon the reaper weary,
Piling sheaves in uplands airy,
Listening, whispers ''Tis the fairy   35
        Lady of Shalott.'

Part II

There she weaves by night and day
A magic web with colours gay.
She has heard a whisper say,
A curse is on her if she stay   40
        To look down to Camelot.
She knows not what the curse may be,
And so she weaveth steadily,
And little other care hath she,
        The Lady of Shalott.   45

And moving thro' a mirror clear
That hangs before her all the year,
Shadows of the world appear.
There she sees the highway near
        Winding down to Camelot: 50

There the river eddy whirls,
And there the surly village-churls,
And the red cloaks of market girls,
    Pass onward from Shalott.

Sometimes a troop of damsels glad,   55
An abbot on an ambling pad,   *horse*
Sometimes a curly shepherd-lad,
Or long-hair'd page in crimson clad,
    Goes by to tower'd Camelot;
And sometimes thro' the mirror blue   60
The knights come riding two and two:
She hath no loyal knight and true,
    The Lady of Shalott.

But in her web she still delights
To weave the mirror's magic sights,   65
For often thro' the silent nights
A funeral, with plumes and lights
    And music, went to Camelot:
Or when the moon was overhead,   70
Came two young lovers lately wed;
'I am half sick of shadows,' said
    The Lady of Shalott.

Part III

A bow-shot from her bower-eaves,
He rode between the barley-sheaves,
The sun came dazzling thro' the leaves,   75
And flamed upon the brazen greaves
    Of bold Sir Lancelot.
A red-cross knight for ever kneel'd
To a lady in his shield,
That sparkled on the yellow field,   80
    Beside remote Shalott.

The gemmy bridle glitter'd free,
Like to some branch of stars we see
Hung in the golden Galaxy.
The bridle bells rang merrily   85
    As he rode down to Camelot:
And from his blazon'd baldric slung
A mighty silver bugle hung,
And as he rode his armour rung,   90
    Beside remote Shalott.

All in the blue unclouded weather
Thick-jewell'd shone the saddle-leather,
The helmet and the helmet-feather
Burn'd like one burning flame together,   95
    As he rode down to Camelot.

As often thro' the purple night,
Below the starry clusters bright,
Some bearded meteor, trailing light,
    Moves over still Shalott.

His broad clear brow in sunlight glow'd;   100
On burnish'd hooves his war-horse trode;
From underneath his helmet flow'd
His coal-black curls as on he rode,
    As he rode down to Camelot.
From the bank and from the river   105
He flash'd into the crystal mirror,
'Tirra lirra,' by the river
    Sang Sir Lancelot.

She left the web, she left the loom,
She made three paces thro' the room,   110
She saw the water-lily bloom,
She saw the helmet and the plume,
    She look'd down to Camelot.
Out flew the web and floated wide;
The mirror crack'd from side to side;   115
'The curse is come upon me,' cried
    The Lady of Shalott.

Part IV

In the stormy east-wind straining,
The pale yellow woods were waning,
The broad stream in his banks complaining,   120
Heavily the low sky raining
    Over tower'd Camelot;
Down she came and found a boat
Beneath a willow left afloat,
And round about the prow she wrote
    The Lady of Shalott.   125

And down the river's dim expanse
Like some bold seër in a trance,
Seeing all his own mischance—
With a glassy countenance   130
    Did she look to Camelot.
And at the closing of the day
She loosed the chain, and down she lay;
The broad stream bore her far away,
    The Lady of Shalott.   135

Lying, robed in snowy white
That loosely flew to left and right—
The leaves upon her falling light—
Thro' the noises of the night
    She floated down to Camelot: 140

And as the boat-head wound along
The willowy hills and fields among,
They heard her singing her last song,
    The Lady of Shalott.

Heard a carol, mournful, holy,   145
Chanted loudly, chanted lowly,
Till her blood was frozen slowly,
And her eyes were darken'd wholly,
    Turn'd to tower'd Camelot.
For ere she reach'd upon the tide   150
The first house by the water-side,
Singing in her song she died,
    The Lady of Shalott.

Under tower and balcony,
By garden-wall and gallery,   155
A gleaming shape she floated by,
Dead-pale between the houses high,
    Silent into Camelot.
Out upon the wharfs they came,
Knight and burgher, lord and dame,   160
And round the prow they read her name,
    The Lady of Shalott.

Who is this? and what is here?
And in the lighted palace near
Died the sound of royal cheer;   165
And they cross'd themselves for fear,
    All the knights at Camelot:
But Lancelot mused a little space;
He said, 'She has a lovely face;
God in his mercy lend her grace,   170
    The Lady of Shalott.'

                          1832   1842

Ulysses

It little profits that an idle king,
By this still hearth, among these barren crags,
Match'd with an aged wife, I mete and dole
Unequal laws unto a savage race,
That hoard, and sleep, and feed, and know not me.   5
I cannot rest from travel: I will drink
Life to the lees: all times I have enjoy'd
Greatly, have suffer'd greatly, both with those

Ulysses In Dante's *Inferno* XXVI, Ulysses (or Odysseus), the hero of Homer's *Odyssey*, tells how, after returning home to Ithaca from twenty years of war and wandering, he sought further experience and knowledge in a voyage into the unknown sea west of the Mediterranean. There he and his ship were engulfed.

That loved me, and alone; on shore, and when
Thro' scudding drifts the rainy Hyades   10
Vext the dim sea: I am become a name;
For always roaming with a hungry heart
Much have I seen and known; cities of men
And manners, climates, councils, governments,
Myself not least, but honour'd of them all;   15
And drunk delight of battle with my peers,
Far on the ringing plains of windy Troy.
I am a part of all that I have met;
Yet all experience is an arch wherethro'
Gleams that untravell'd world, whose margin fades   20
For ever and for ever when I move.
How dull it is to pause, to make an end,
To rust unburnish'd, not to shine in use!
As tho' to breathe were life! Life piled on life
Were all too little, and of one to me   25
Little remains: but every hour is saved
From that eternal silence, something more,
A bringer of new things; and vile it were
For some three suns to store and hoard myself,
And this gray spirit yearning in desire   30
To follow knowledge like a sinking star,
Beyond the utmost bound of human thought.
    This is my son, mine own Telemachus,
To whom I leave the sceptre and the isle—
Well-loved of me, discerning to fulfil   35
This labour, by slow prudence to make mild
A rugged people, and thro' soft degrees
Subdue them to the useful and the good.
Most blameless is he, centred in the sphere
Of common duties, decent not to fail   40
In offices of tenderness, and pay
Meet adoration to my household gods,
When I am gone. He works his work, I mine.
    There lies the port: the vessel puffs her sail:
There gloom the dark broad seas. My mariners,   45
Souls that have toil'd, and wrought, and thought with me—
That ever with a frolic welcome took
The thunder and the sunshine, and opposed
Free hearts, free foreheads—you and I are old;
Old age hath yet his honour and his toil;   50
Death closes all: but something ere the end,
Some work of noble note, may yet be done,
Not unbecoming men that strove with Gods.
The lights begin to twinkle from the rocks;
The long day wanes: the slow moon climbs: the deep   55
Moans round with many voices. Come, my friends.
'Tis not too late to seek a newer world.
Push off, and sitting well in order smite

---

10 Hyades a group of stars in the constellation Taurus whose appearance was thought to herald rain

The sounding furrows; for my purpose holds   60
To sail beyond the sunset, and the baths
Of all the western stars, until I die.
It may be that the gulfs will wash us down:
It may be we shall touch the Happy Isles,
And see the great Achilles, whom we knew.   65
Tho' much is taken, much abides; and tho'
We are not now that strength which in old days
Moved earth and heaven, that which we are, we are;
One equal temper of heroic hearts,
Made weak by time and fate, but strong in will   70
To strive, to seek, to find, and not to yield.

                                                              1833   1842

'Break, break, break'

Break, break, break,
   On thy cold gray stones, O Sea!
And I would that my tongue could utter
   The thoughts that arise in me.

O well for the fisherman's boy,   5
   That he shouts with his sister at play!
O well for the sailor lad,
   That he sings in his boat on the bay!

And the stately ships go on
   To their haven under the hill;   10
But O for the touch of a vanish'd hand,
   And the sound of a voice that is still!

Break, break, break,
   At the foot of thy crags, O Sea!
But the tender grace of a day that is dead   15
   Will never come back to me.

                                                              1834   1842

[Tears, idle tears, I know not what they mean]

   Tears, idle tears, I know not what they mean,
Tears from the depth of some divine despair
Rise in the heart, and gather to the eyes,
In looking on the happy Autumn-fields,
And thinking of the days that are no more.   5

   Fresh as the first beam glittering on a sail,
That brings our friends up from the underworld,
Sad as the last which reddens over one
That sinks with all we love below the verge;
So sad, so fresh, the days that are no more.   10

---

63 Happy Isles islands of the blessed, where, in Greek mythology, the heroic and virtuous dwell after death

Ah, sad and strange as in dark summer dawns
The earliest pipe of half-awaken'd birds
To dying ears, when unto dying eyes
The casement slowly grows a glimmering square;
So sad, so strange, the days that are no more.   15

Dear as remember'd kisses after death,
And sweet as those by hopeless fancy feign'd
On lips that are for others; deep as love,
Deep as first love, and wild with all regret;
O Death in Life, the days that are no more.   20

                                                        1847

From In Memoriam *A.H.H.*

II

Old Yew, which graspest at the stones
    That name the under-lying dead,
    Thy fibres net the dreamless head,
Thy roots are wrapt about the bones.

The seasons bring the flower again,   5
    And bring the firstling to the flock;
    And in the dusk of thee, the clock
Beats out the little lives of men.

O not for thee the glow, the bloom,
    Who changest not in any gale,   10
    Nor branding summer suns avail
To touch thy thousand years of gloom:

And gazing on thee, sullen tree,
    Sick for thy stubborn hardihood,
    I seem to fail from out my blood   15
And grow incorporate into thee.

VII

Dark house, by which once more I stand
    Here in the long unlovely street,
    Doors, where my heart was used to beat
So quickly, waiting for a hand,

A hand that can be clasp'd no more—   5
    Behold me, for I cannot sleep,
    And like a guilty thing I creep
At earliest morning to the door.

He is not here; but far away
    The noise of life begins again,   10
    And ghastly thro' the drizzling rain
On the bald street breaks the blank day.

In Memoriam A.H.H.   Written over some 17 years, this poem of 133 loosely joined lyrics explores the poet's grief at the sudden death of his friend, Arthur Henry Hallam (1811–33).

LIV

Oh yet we trust that somehow good
    Will be the final goal of ill,
    To pangs of nature, sins of will,
Defects of doubt, and taints of blood;

That nothing walks with aimless feet;   5
    That not one life shall be destroy'd,
    Or cast as rubbish to the void,
When God hath made the pile complete;

That not a worm is cloven in vain;
    That not a moth with vain desire   10
    Is shrivell'd in a fruitless fire,
Or but subserves another's gain.

Behold, we know not anything;
    I can but trust that good shall fall
    At last—far off—at last, to all,   15
And every winter change to spring.

So runs my dream; but what am I?
    An infant crying in the night:
    An infant crying for the light:
And with no language but a cry.   20

LV

The wish, that of the living whole
    No life may fail beyond the grave,
    Derives it not from what we have
The likest God within the soul?

Are God and Nature then at strife,   5
    That Nature lends such evil dreams?
    So careful of the type she seems,   *species*
So careless of the single life;

That I, considering everywhere
    Her secret meaning in her deeds,   10
    And finding that of fifty seeds,
She often brings but one to bear,

I falter where I firmly trod,
    And falling with my weight of cares
    Upon the great world's altar-stairs   15
That slope thro' darkness up to God,

I stretch lame hands of faith, and grope,
    And gather dust and chaff, and call
    To what I feel is Lord of all,
And faintly trust the larger hope.   20

LVI

'So careful of the type'? but no.
    From scarped cliff and quarried stone
    She cries, 'A thousand types are gone:
I care for nothing, all shall go.

'Thou makest thine appeal to me: 5
    I bring to life, I bring to death:
    The spirit does but mean the breath:
I know no more.' And he, shall he,

Man, her last work, who seem'd so fair,
    Such splendid purpose in his eyes,   10
    Who roll'd the psalm to wintry skies,
Who built him fanes of fruitless prayer,   *temples*

Who trusted God was love indeed
    And love Creation's final law —
    Tho' Nature, red in tooth and claw   15
With ravine, shriek'd against his creed —

Who loved, who suffer'd countless ills,
    Who battled for the True, the Just,
    Be blown about the desert dust,
Or seal'd within the iron hills?   20

No more? A monster then, a dream,
    A discord. Dragons of the prime,
    That tare each other in their slime,   *tore*
Were mellow music match'd with him.

O life as futile, then, as frail!   25
    O for thy voice to soothe and bless!
    What hope of answer, or redress?
Behind the veil, behind the veil.

           1833–50   1850

ELIZABETH BARRETT BROWNING

1806–61 b Durham; moved to London in her twenties. She was a semi-invalid from the age of 15. Upon marrying Robert Browning in 1846, she settled with him in Italy.

From Sonnets from the Portuguese

VI

Go from me. Yet I feel that I shall stand
Henceforward in thy shadow. Nevermore
Alone upon the threshold of my door
Of individual life, I shall command

Sonnets from the Portuguese   a sequence of 44 original sonnets (not translations) written at the time the poet met and married Robert Browning

The uses of my soul, nor lift my hand   5
Serenely in the sunshine as before,
Without the sense of that which I forebore—
Thy touch upon the palm. The widest land
Doom takes to part us, leaves thy heart in mine
With pulses that beat double. What I do   10
And what I dream include thee, as the wine
Must taste of its own grapes. And when I sue
God for myself, He hears that name of thine,
And sees within my eyes, the tears of two.

                                                    1845–46   1850

From Aurora Leigh

From *First Book*

I broke the copious curls upon my head   385
In braids, because she liked smooth-ordered hair.
I left off saying my sweet Tuscan words
Which still at any stirring of the heart
Came up to float across the English phrase
As lilies, (*Bene* or *Che che,*) because   390
She liked my father's child to speak his tongue.
I learnt the collects and the catechism,
The creeds, from Athanasius back to Nice,
The Articles, the Tracts *against* the times,
(By no means Buonaventure's 'Prick of Love,')   395
And various popular synopses of
Inhuman doctrines never taught by John,
Because she liked instructed piety.
I learnt my complement of classic French
(Kept pure of Balzac and neologism)   400
And German also, since she liked a range
Of liberal education,—tongues, not books.
I learnt a little algebra, a little
Of the mathematics,—brushed with extreme flounce
The circle of the sciences, because   405
She misliked women who are frivolous.
I learnt the royal genealogies
Of Oviedo, the internal laws
Of the Burmese empire,—by how many feet
Mount Chimborazo outsoars Teneriffe,   410
What navigable river joins itself

Aurora Leigh   a verse novel, which begins with Aurora, the daughter of a Tuscan mother and English father, leaving Italy upon being orphaned at the age of 13, and joining her aunt in England, the 'she' of this extract
392 collects   short liturgical prayers
393 The Athanasian and Nicene creeds were early summaries of Christian belief
394 The Articles   39 short statements of Anglican doctrines.
395–97 The Franciscan, St Bonaventure (1217–74), and St John the Evangelist both emphasized love as the basis of Christianity.
395 Prick   (archaic) spur. St Bonaventure was the reputed author of *Stimulus Divini Amoris* (The spur of divine love).

To Lara, and what census of the year five
Was taken at Klagenfurt,—because she liked
A general insight into useful facts.
I learnt much music,—such as would have been   415
As quite impossible in Johnson's day
As still it might be wished—fine sleights of hand
And unimagined fingering, shuffling off
The hearer's soul through hurricanes of notes
To a noisy Tophet; and I drew ... costumes   420
From French engravings, nereids neatly draped,
(With smirks of simmering godship)—I washed in
Landscapes from nature (rather say, washed out).
I danced the polka and Cellarius,
Spun glass, stuffed birds, and modelled flowers in wax,   425
Because she liked accomplishments in girls.
I read a score of books on womanhood
To prove, if women do not think at all,
They may teach thinking, (to a maiden-aunt
Or else the author)—books that boldly assert   430
Their right of comprehending husband's talk
When not too deep, and even of answering
With pretty 'may it please you,' or 'so it is,'—
Their rapid insight and fine aptitude,
Particular worth and general missionariness,   435
As long as they keep quiet by the fire
And never say 'no' when the world says 'ay,'
For that is fatal,—their angelic reach
Of virtue, chiefly used to sit and darn,
And fatten household sinners,—their, in brief,   440
Potential faculty in everything
Of abdicating power in it: she owned
She liked a woman to be womanly,
And English women, she thanked God and sighed,
(Some people always sigh in thanking God)   445
Were models to the universe. And last
I learnt cross-stitch, because she did not like
To see me wear the night with empty hands
A-doing nothing. So, my shepherdess
Was something after all, (the pastoral saints   450
Be praised for't) leaning lovelorn with pink eyes
To match her shoes, when I mistook the silks;
Her head uncrushed by that round weight of hat
So strangely similar to the tortoise-shell
Which slew the tragic poet.
                            By the way,   455
The works of women are symbolical.
We sew, sew, prick our fingers, dull our sight,
Producing what? A pair of slippers, sir,

---

420 Tophet   A place of child sacrifice in ancient Palestine, which became symbolic of hell; see Isa. 30:33; Jer. 7:31–32.
455 the tragic poet   Aeschylus (525–456 BC) reputedly killed by a tortoise falling from an eagle's talons

To put on when you're weary—or a stool
To stumble over and vex you ... 'curse that stool!'   460
Or else at best, a cushion, where you lean
And sleep, and dream of something we are not
But would be for your sake. Alas, alas!
This hurts most, this—that, after all, we are paid
The worth of our work, perhaps.
                  In looking down   465
Those years of education (to return)
I wonder if Brinvilliers suffered more
In the water-torture,... flood succeeding flood
To drench the incapable throat and split the veins
Than I did. Certain of your feebler souls   470
Go out in such a process; many pine
To a sick, inodorous light; my own endured:
I had relations in the Unseen, and drew
The elemental nutriment and heat
From nature, as earth feels the sun at nights,   475
Or as a babe sucks surely in the dark.
I kept the life thrust on me, on the outside
Of the inner life with all its ample room
For heart and lungs, for will and intellect
Inviolable by conventions. God,   480
I thank thee for that grace of thine!
                At first
I felt no life which was not patience,—did
The thing she bade me, without heed to a thing
Beyond it, sat in just the chair she placed,
With back against the window, to exclude   485
The sight of the great lime-tree on the lawn,
Which seemed to have come on purpose from the woods
To bring the house a message,—ay, and walked
Demurely in her carpeted low rooms,
As if I should not, hearkening my own steps,   490
Misdoubt I was alive.
                      1853–56   1857

RALPH WALDO EMERSON

1803–82 b Boston. Also an influential essayist and lecturer, he lived in Concord from 1834.

Give All to Love

Give all to love;
Obey thy heart;
Friends, kindred, days,
Estate, good-fame,

---

467 **Brinvilliers** Marie-Madeleine-Marguerite d'Aubray, Marquise de Brinvilliers (*c.* 1630–76) a multiple poisoner. Before execution, she was given the **water torture** in a vain attempt to identify her accomplices: sixteen pints of water poured into the stretched body.

Plans, credit and the Muse,—   5
Nothing refuse.

'Tis a brave master;
Let it have scope:
Follow it utterly,
Hope beyond hope: 10
High and more high
It dives into noon,
With wing unspent,
Untold intent;
But it is a god,   15
Knows its own path
And the outlets of the sky.

It was never for the mean;
It requireth courage stout.
Souls above doubt,   20
Valor unbending,
It will reward,—
They shall return
More than they were,
And ever ascending.   25

Leave all for love;
Yet, hear me, yet,
One word more thy heart behoved,
One pulse more of firm endeavor,—
Keep thee to-day,   30
To-morrow, forever,
Free as an Arab
Of thy beloved.

Cling with life to the maid;
But when the surprise,   35
First vague shadow of surmise
Flits across her bosom young,
Of a joy apart from thee,
Free be she, fancy-free;
Nor thou detain her vesture's hem,   40
Nor the palest rose she flung
From her summer diadem.

Though thou loved her as thyself,
As a self of purer clay,
Though her parting dims the day,   45
Stealing grace from all alive;
Heartily know,
When half-gods go,
The gods arrive.

                                                            1846

Brahma

If the red slayer think he slays,
  Or if the slain think he is slain,
They know not well the subtle ways
  I keep, and pass, and turn again.

Far or forgot to me is near;   5
  Shadow and sunlight are the same;
The vanished gods to me appear;
  And one to me are shame and fame.

They reckon ill who leave me out;
  When me they fly, I am the wings;   10
I am the doubter and the doubt,
  And I the hymn the Brahmin sings.

The strong gods pine for my abode,
  And pine in vain the sacred Seven;
But thou, meek lover of the good!   15
  Find me, and turn thy back on heaven.

                              1856   1857

WILLIAM BARNES

1801–86 b Dorset, where he worked as a schoolmaster and, in his later years, as an Anglican parish priest. He was an archaeologist and linguist.

My Orcha'd in Linden Lea

'Ithin the woodlands, flow'ry gleäded,
  By the woak tree's mossy moot,   *oak / stump*
The sheenèn grass-bleädes, timber-sheäded,
  Now do quiver under voot;
An' birds do whissle over head,   5
An' water's bubblèn in its bed,
An' there vor me the apple tree
Do leän down low in Linden Lea.

When leaves that leätely wer a-springèn
  Now do feäde 'ithin the copse,   10
An' päinted birds do hush their zingèn
  Up upon the timber's tops;
An' brown-leav'd fruit's a-turnèn red,
In cloudless zunsheen, over head,

Brahma in Hindu religion, the creative aspect of God. The poem also concerns Brahman, the supreme godhead which includes the universe, and through whom opposites are reconciled (as in lines 5–8) and killing or being killed is mere illusion (as in lines 1–4).
12 Brahmin member of the priestly caste
13 strong gods i.e. strongest of the many subsidiary Hindu gods
14 the sacred Seven the highest saints

Wi' fruit vor me, the apple tree   15
Do leän down low in Linden Lea.

Let other vo'k meäk money vaster
   In the aïr o' dark-room'd towns,
I don't dread a peevish meäster;
   Though noo man do heed my frowns,   20
I be free to goo abrode,
Or teäke ageän my hwomeward road
To where, vor me, the apple tree
Do leän down low in Linden Lea.

                                 1859

Woak Hill

When sycamore leaves wer a-spreadèn,
     Green-ruddy, in hedges,
Bezide the red doust o' the ridges,
     A-dried at Woak Hill;

I packed up my goods all a-sheenèn   5
     Wi' long years o' handlèn,
On dousty red wheels ov a waggon,
     To ride at Woak Hill.

The brown thatchen ruf o' the dwellèn
     I then wer a-leävèn,   10
Had shelter'd the sleek head o' Meäry,
     My bride at Woak Hill.

But now vor zome years, her light voot-vall
     'S a-lost vrom the vloorèn.   *floors*
Too soon vor my jaÿ an' my childern,   15
     She died at Woak Hill.

But still I do think that, in soul,
     She do hover about us;
To ho vor her motherless childern,   *be anxious for*
     Her pride at Woak Hill.   20

Zoo—lest she should tell me hereafter   *so*
     I stole off 'ithout her,
An' left her, uncall'd at house-riddèn,
     To bide at Woak Hill—

I call'd her so fondly, wi' lippèns   *speeches* 25
     All soundless to others,
An' took her wi' aïr-reachen hand,
     To my zide at Woak Hill.

On the road I did look round, a-talkèn
     To light at my shoulder,   30
An' then led her in at the door-way,
     Miles wide vrom Woak Hill.

An' that's why vo'k thought, vor a season,
    My mind wer a-wandrèn
Wi' sorrow, when I wer so sorely   35
    A-tried at Woak Hill.

But no; that my Meäry mid never
    Behold herzelf slighted,
I wanted to think that I guided
    My guide vrom Woak Hill.   40

                  1862

JOHN KEATS

1795–1821 b London. He studied medicine and qualified as an apothecary but did not practise. Discovering late in 1819 that he had TB, he travelled to Italy for his health, but died soon after arriving.

On First Looking into Chapman's Homer

Much have I travell'd in the realms of gold,
    And many goodly states and kingdoms seen;
    Round many western islands have I been
Which bards in fealty to Apollo hold.   *fidelity*
Oft of one wide expanse had I been told   5
    That deep-brow'd Homer ruled as his demesne;
    Yet did I never breathe its pure serene
Till I heard Chapman speak out loud and bold:
Then felt I like some watcher of the skies
    When a new planet swims into his ken;   10
Or like stout Cortez when with eagle eyes
    He star'd at the Pacific—and all his men
Look'd at each other with a wild surmise—
    Silent, upon a peak in Darien.

          October 1816   1816

[When I have fears that I may cease to be]

When I have fears that I may cease to be
    Before my pen has glean'd my teeming brain,
Before high-piled books, in charactry,
    Hold like rich garners the full ripen'd grain;   *granaries*
When I behold, upon the night's starr'd face,   5
    Huge cloudy symbols of a high romance,
And think that I may never live to trace
    Their shadows, with the magic hand of chance;

Chapman's Homer   the translation of Homer by George Chapman (1616)
7 serene   clear atmosphere
11–14 It was not **Cortez** (the conqueror of Mexico) but Balboa who in 1513 was the first of the Spanish explorers to see the Pacific, when he crossed the isthmus of Panama from the settlement of **Darien**.

And when I feel, fair creature of an hour!
  That I shall never look upon thee more,   10
Never have relish in the faery power   *magic*
  Of unreflecting love!—then on the shore
Of the wide world I stand alone, and think
Till love and fame to nothingness do sink.

                           January 1818   1848

La Belle Dame Sans Merci

A Ballad

I
O what can ail thee, knight-at-arms,
  Alone and palely loitering?
The sedge has wither'd from the lake,
  And no birds sing.
II
O what can ail thee, knight-at-arms,   5
  So haggard and so woe-begone?
The squirrel's granary is full,
  And the harvest's done.
III
I see a lilly on thy brow,
  With anguish moist and fever dew,   10
And on thy cheeks a fading rose
  Fast withereth too.
IV
I met a lady in the meads,
  Full beautiful—a faery's child,
Her hair was long, her foot was light,   15
  And her eyes were wild.
V
I made a garland for her head,
  And bracelets too, and fragrant zone;   *belt*
She look'd at me as she did love,
  And made sweet moan.   20
VI
I set her on my pacing steed,
  And nothing else saw all day long,
For sidelong would she bend, and sing
  A faery's song.
VII
She found me roots of relish sweet,   25
  And honey wild, and manna dew,
And sure in language strange she said—
  'I love thee true'.

La Belle Dame Sans Merci   Title taken from that of a poem of the fifteenth century by Alain
Chartier: 'The beautiful lady without pity'

VIII

She took me to her elfin grot,
   And there she wept, and sigh'd full sore,   30
And there I shut her wild wild eyes
   With kisses four.

IX

And there she lulled me asleep,
   And there I dream'd—Ah! woe betide!
The latest dream I ever dream'd   35
   On the cold hill side.

X

I saw pale kings and princes too,
   Pale warriors, death-pale were they all;
They cried—'La Belle Dame sans Merci
   Hath thee in thrall!'   40

XI

I saw their starved lips in the gloam,   *gloom*
   With horrid warning gaped wide,
And I awoke and found me here,
   On the cold hill's side.

XII

And this is why I sojourn here,   45
   Alone and palely loitering,
Though the sedge is wither'd from the lake,
   And no birds sing.

            April 1819   1848

Ode to Psyche

O Goddess! hear these tuneless numbers, wrung
   By sweet enforcement and remembrance dear,
And pardon that thy secrets should be sung
   Even into thine own soft-conched ear:
Surely I dreamt to-day, or did I see   5
   The winged Psyche with awaken'd eyes?
I wander'd in a forest thoughtlessly,
   And, on the sudden, fainting with surprise,
Saw two fair creatures, couched side by side
   In deepest grass, beneath the whisp'ring roof   10
   Of leaves and trembled blossoms, where there ran
      A brooklet, scarce espied:
'Mid hush'd, cool-rooted flowers, fragrant-eyed,
   Blue, silver-white, and budded Tyrian,
They lay calm-breathing on the bedded grass;   15
   Their arms embraced, and their pinions too;
   Their lips touch'd not, but had not bade adieu,

Psyche Greek for 'soul'. In the *Golden Ass* by the Roman writer, Apuleius (fl, c. 150) Psyche was a woman visited by an unknown lover. Lighting a lamp, she discovered that he was Cupid, god of love (the **winged boy** of line 21) but she injured him by spilling lamp oil in her agitation. The injury, the discovery and the hostility of Cupid's mother, Venus, all led to separation and suffering, but Psyche was finally reunited, as a goddess, with her lover. Since this story is from the late classical period, Psyche is **latest born** of the gods who dwell on Mount **Olympus** (lines 24–25).
14 Tyrian deep red, like the dyes of ancient Tyre

As if disjoined by soft-handed slumber,
And ready still past kisses to outnumber
  At tender eye-dawn of aurorean love: 20
      The winged boy I knew;
  But who wast thou, O happy, happy dove?
      His Psyche true!

O latest born and loveliest vision far
  Of all Olympus' faded hierarchy!   25
Fairer than Phoebe's sapphire-region'd star,   *moon goddess*
  Or Vesper, amorous glow-worm of the sky;   *evening star*
Fairer than these, though temple thou hast none,
      Nor altar heap'd with flowers;
Nor virgin-choir to make delicious moan   30
      Upon the midnight hours;
No voice, no lute, no pipe, no incense sweet
  From chain-swung censer teeming;
No shrine, no grove, no oracle, no heat
  Of pale-mouth'd prophet dreaming.   35

O brightest! though too late for antique vows,
  Too, too late for the fond believing lyre,
When holy were the haunted forest boughs,
  Holy the air, the water, and the fire;
Yet even in these days so far retir'd   40
  From happy pieties, thy lucent fans,   *wings*
  Fluttering among the faint Olympians,
I see, and sing, by my own eyes inspired.
So let me be thy choir, and make a moan
      Upon the midnight hours;   45
Thy voice, thy lute, thy pipe, thy incense sweet
  From swinged censer teeming;
Thy shrine, thy grove, thy oracle, thy heat
  Of pale-mouth'd prophet dreaming.

Yes, I will be thy priest, and build a fane   *temple* 50
  In some untrodden region of my mind,
Where branched thoughts, new grown with pleasant pain,
  Instead of pines shall murmur in the wind:
Far, far around shall those dark-cluster'd trees
  Fledge the wild-ridged mountains steep by steep;   · 55
And there by zephyrs, streams, and birds, and bees,   *warm breezes*
  The moss-lain Dryads shall be lull'd to sleep;   *tree nymphs*
And in the midst of this wide quietness
A rosy sanctuary will I dress
With the wreath'd trellis of a working brain,   60
  With buds, and bells, and stars without a name,
With all the gardener Fancy e'er could feign,
  Who breeding flowers, will never breed the same:
And there shall be for thee all soft delight
  That shadowy thought can win,   65
A bright torch, and a casement ope at night,
  To let the warm Love in!

      April 1819 1820

Ode to a Nightingale

1

My heart aches, and a drowsy numbness pains
  My sense, as though of hemlock I had drunk,
Or emptied some dull opiate to the drains
  One minute past, and Lethe-wards had sunk:
'Tis not through envy of thy happy lot,   5
  But being too happy in thine happiness,—
    That thou, light-winged Dryad of the trees,   *tree nymph*
      In some melodious plot
Of beechen green, and shadows numberless,
Singest of summer in full-throated ease.   10

2

O, for a draught of vintage! that hath been
  Cool'd a long age in the deep-delved earth,
Tasting of Flora and the country green,
  Dance, and Provencal song, and sunburnt mirth!
O for a beaker full of the warm South,   15
Full of the true, the blushful Hippocrene,
  With beaded bubbles winking at the brim,
    And purple-stained mouth;
That I might drink, and leave the world unseen,
And with thee fade away into the forest dim: 20

3

Fade far away, dissolve, and quite forget
  What thou among the leaves hast never known,
The weariness, the fever, and the fret
  Here, where men sit and hear each other groan;
Where palsy shakes a few, sad, last gray hairs,   25
  Where youth grows pale, and spectre-thin, and dies;
    Where but to think is to be full of sorrow
      And leaden-eyed despairs,
Where Beauty cannot keep her lustrous eyes,
  Or new Love pine at them beyond to-morrow.   30

4

Away! away! for I will fly to thee,
  Not charioted by Bacchus and his pards,   *leopards*
But on the viewless wings of Poesy,
  Though the dull brain perplexes and retards:
Already with thee! tender is the night,   35
  And haply the Queen-Moon is on her throne,   *perhaps*
    Cluster'd around by all her starry Fays;   *fairies*
      But here there is no light,

---

2 **hemlock** a herb whose sedative properties can be fatal
4 **Lethe** Roman name for the river of forgetfulness in the underworld, realm of the dead
13 **Flora** goddess of flowers
14 **Provencal song** i.e. of the troubadours of medieval Provence
16 **Hippocrene** spring of the muses at Mt Helicon in Greece

Save what from heaven is with the breezes blown
  Through verdurous glooms and winding mossy ways.   40

     5
I cannot see what flowers are at my feet,
  Nor what soft incense hangs upon the boughs,
But, in embalmed darkness, guess each sweet
  Wherewith the seasonable month endows
The grass, the thicket, and the fruit-tree wild;   45
  White hawthorn, and the pastoral eglantine;
    Fast fading violets cover'd up in leaves;
      And mid-May's eldest child,
  The coming musk-rose, full of dewy wine,
    The murmurous haunt of flies on summer eves.   50

     6
Darkling I listen; and, for many a time   *in the dark*
  I have been half in love with easeful Death,
Call'd him soft names in many a mused rhyme,
  To take into the air my quiet breath;
Now more than ever seems it rich to die,   55
  To cease upon the midnight with no pain,
    While thou art pouring forth thy soul abroad
      In such an ecstasy!
  Still wouldst thou sing, and I have ears in vain—
    To thy high requiem become a sod.   60

     7
Thou wast not born for death, immortal Bird!
  No hungry generations tread thee down;
The voice I hear this passing night was heard
  In ancient days by emperor and clown: *peasant*
Perhaps the self-same song that found a path   65
  Through the sad heart of Ruth, when, sick for home,
    She stood in tears amid the alien corn;
      The same that oft-times hath
  Charm'd magic casements, opening on the foam
    Of perilous seas, in faery lands forlorn.   70

     8
Forlorn! the very word is like a bell
  To toll me back from thee to my sole self!
Adieu! the fancy cannot cheat so well
  As she is fam'd to do, deceiving elf.
Adieu! adieu! thy plaintive anthem fades   75
  Past the near meadows, over the still stream,
    Up the hill-side; and now 'tis buried deep
      In the next valley-glades:
  Was it a vision, or a waking dream?
    Fled is that music:—Do I wake or sleep?   80

                      May 1819   1820

66–67 **Ruth** a widow stranded in a new country—a Moabite in Judah—who worked in corn-fields for a living and to find a new husband. See Ruth 2.

Ode on Melancholy

1

No, no, go not to Lethe, neither twist
  Wolf's-bane, tight-rooted, for its poisonous wine;
Nor suffer thy pale forehead to be kiss'd
  By nightshade, ruby grape of Proserpine;
Make not your rosary of yew-berries,   5
    Nor let the beetle, nor the death-moth be
      Your mournful Psyche, nor the downy owl
A partner in your sorrow's mysteries;
    For shade to shade will come too drowsily,
      And drown the wakeful anguish of the soul.   10

2

But when the melancholy fit shall fall
  Sudden from heaven like a weeping cloud,
That fosters the droop-headed flowers all,
  And hides the green hill in an April shroud;
Then glut thy sorrow on a morning rose,   15
  Or on the rainbow of the salt sand-wave,
  Or on the wealth of globed peonies;
Or if thy mistress some rich anger shows,
    Emprison her soft hand, and let her rave,
      And feed deep, deep upon her peerless eyes.   20

3

She dwells with Beauty—Beauty that must die;
  And Joy, whose hand is ever at his lips
Bidding adieu; and aching Pleasure nigh,
  Turning to poison while the bee-mouth sips:
Ay, in the very temple of Delight   25
  Veil'd Melancholy has her sovran shrine,
    Though seen of none save him whose strenuous tongue
Can burst Joy's grape against his palate fine;
  His soul shall taste the sadness of her might,
    And be among her cloudy trophies hung.   30

                           1819   1820

Ode on a Grecian Urn

1

Thou still unravish'd bride of quietness,
  Thou foster-child of silence and slow time,
Sylvan historian, who canst thus express
  A flowery tale more sweetly than our rhyme:
What leaf-fring'd legend haunts about thy shape   5
  Of deities or mortals, or of both,
    In Tempe or the dales of Arcady?

1–4 Lethe See note to 'Ode to a Nightingale'.   **Proserpine** queen of the underworld
6 beetle death-watch beetle   **death-moth** a large moth with skull-like markings
7 Psyche the Greek word for 'soul', whose emblem is a butterfly. See note to 'Ode to Psyche'.
7 Tempe, Arcady respectively a valley and a region in rural Greece which in the literary tradition of
Pastoral (line 45) symbolise an idyllic existence

What men or gods are these? What maidens loth?
  What mad pursuit? What struggle to escape?
    What pipes and timbrels? What wild ecstasy?   *tambourines* 10
        2
Heard melodies are sweet, but those unheard
  Are sweeter; therefore, ye soft pipes, play on;
Not to the sensual ear, but, more endear'd,
  Pipe to the spirit ditties of no tone:
Fair youth, beneath the trees, thou canst not leave   15
  Thy song, nor ever can those trees be bare;
    Bold Lover, never, never canst thou kiss,
Though winning near the goal—yet, do not grieve;
  She cannot fade, though thou hast not thy bliss,
    For ever wilt thou love, and she be fair!   20
        3
Ah, happy, happy boughs! that cannot shed
  Your leaves, nor ever bid the Spring adieu;
And, happy melodist, unwearied,
  For ever piping songs for ever new;
More happy love! more happy, happy love!   25
  For ever warm and still to be enjoy'd,
    For ever panting, and for ever young;
All breathing human passion far above,
  That leaves a heart high-sorrowful and cloy'd,
    A burning forehead, and a parching tongue.   30
        4
Who are these coming to the sacrifice?
  To what green altar, O mysterious priest,
Lead'st thou that heifer lowing at the skies,
  And all her silken flanks with garlands drest?
What little town by river or sea shore,   35
  Or mountain-built with peaceful citadel,
    Is emptied of its folk, this pious morn?
And, little town, thy streets for evermore
  Will silent be; and not a soul to tell
    Why thou art desolate, can e'er return.   40
        5
O Attic shape! Fair attitude! with brede   *embroidery*
  Of marble men and maidens overwrought,
With forest branches and the trodden weed;
  Thou, silent form, dost tease us out of thought
As doth eternity: Cold Pastoral!   45
  When old age shall this generation waste,
    Thou shalt remain, in midst of other woe
Than ours, a friend to man, to whom thou say'st,
  Beauty is truth, truth beauty.—That is all
    Ye know on earth, and all ye need to know.   50

                          1819   1820

---

41 Attic in the style of Attica, the region around Athens: simple and elegant
49–50 The first book publication of 1820 has quotation marks: 'Beauty . . . beauty'. However, there are none in any of the extant transcripts; or in the first printing (*Annals of the Fine Arts*, IV, Jan. 1820), the punctuation of which is adopted here.

To Autumn

1

Season of mists and mellow fruitfulness,
    Close bosom-friend of the maturing sun;
Conspiring with him how to load and bless
    With fruit the vines that round the thatch-eves run;
To bend with apples the moss'd cottage-trees,   5
    And fill all fruit with ripeness to the core;
        To swell the gourd, and plump the hazel shells
    With a sweet kernel; to set budding more,
And still more, later flowers for the bees,
Until they think warm days will never cease,   10
        For Summer has o'er-brimm'd their clammy cells.

2

Who hath not seen thee oft amid thy store?
    Sometimes whoever seeks abroad may find
Thee sitting careless on a granary floor,
    Thy hair soft-lifted by the winnowing wind;   15
Or on a half-reap'd furrow sound asleep,
    Drows'd with the fume of poppies, while thy hook
        Spares the next swath and all its twined flowers:
And sometimes like a gleaner thou dost keep
    Steady thy laden head across a brook;   20
    Or by a cyder-press, with patient look,
        Thou watchest the last oozings hours by hours.

3

Where are the songs of Spring? Ay, where are they?
    Think not of them, thou hast thy music too,—
While barred clouds bloom the soft-dying day,   25
    And touch the stubble-plains with rosy hue;
Then in a wailful choir the small gnats mourn
    Among the river sallows, borne aloft   *willows*
        Or sinking as the light wind lives or dies;
And full-grown lambs loud bleat from hilly bourn;   30
    Hedge-crickets sing; and now with treble soft
    The red-breast whistles from a garden-croft;   *enclosed plot*
        And gathering swallows twitter in the skies.

                      September 1819   1820

[Bright star, would I were stedfast as thou art]

Bright star, would I were stedfast as thou art—
    Not in lone splendor hung aloft the night
And watching, with eternal lids apart,
    Like nature's patient, sleepless Eremite,   *hermit*
The moving waters at their priestlike task   5
    Of pure ablution round earth's human shores,
Or gazing on the new soft-fallen mask
    Of snow upon the mountains and the moors;

---

30 bourn   either boundary or stream

No—yet still stedfast, still unchangeable,
  Pillow'd upon my fair love's ripening breast,   10
To feel for ever its soft swell and fall,
  Awake for ever in a sweet unrest,
Still, still to hear her tender-taken breath,
And so live ever—or else swoon to death.

                        1819   1848

JOHN CLARE

1793–1864 b Northamptonshire. Self-educated, he worked as a labourer to support a large family. From 1837 he was confined to mental asylums.

Winter Fields

O for a pleasant book to cheat the sway
Of winter—where rich mirth with hearty laugh
Listens and rubs his legs on corner seat
For fields are mire and sludge—and badly off
Are those who on their pudgy paths delay   *puddly* 5
There striding shepherd seeking driest way
Fearing nights wetshod feet and hacking cough
That keeps him waken till the peep of day
Goes shouldering onward and with ready hook
Progs oft to ford the sloughs that nearly meet   *pokes* 10
Accross the lands—croodling and thin to view   *hunching*
His loath dog follows—stops and quakes and looks
For better roads—till whistled to pursue
Then on with frequent jump he hirkles through   *crouches*

         c. 1832–5   1935

'I Am'

    1

I am—yet what I am, none cares or knows;
  My friends forsake me like a memory lost:—
I am the self-consumer of my woes;—
  They rise and vanish in oblivion's host,
Like shadows in love's frenzied stifled throes:—   5
And yet I am, and live—like vapours tost
    2
Into the nothingness of scorn and noise,—
  Into the living sea of waking dreams,
Where there is neither sense of life or joys,
  But the vast shipwreck of my lifes esteems;   10
Even the dearest, that I love the best
Are strange—nay, rather stranger than the rest.
    3
I long for scenes, where man hath never trod
  A place where woman never smiled or wept
There to abide with my Creator, God;
  And sleep as I in childhood, sweetly slept,   15
Untroubling, and untroubled where I lie,
The grass below—above the vaulted sky.

         c. 1844   1865

PERCY BYSSHE SHELLEY

1792–1822 b Sussex. He was an active republican and critic of moral convention. Living in Italy from 1818, he died in a sailing accident.

Ozymandias

I met a traveller from an antique land
Who said: Two vast and trunkless legs of stone
Stand in the desert. Near them, on the sand,
Half sunk, a shattered visage lies, whose frown,
And wrinkled lip, and sneer of cold command, 5
Tell that its sculptor well those passions read
Which yet survive, stamped on these lifeless things,
The hand that mocked them and the heart that fed;
And on the pedestal these words appear:
'My name is Ozymandias, king of kings: 10
Look on my works, ye Mighty, and despair!'
Nothing beside remains. Round the decay
Of that colossal wreck, boundless and bare
The lone and level sands stretch far away.

 1817 1819

England in 1819

An old, mad, blind, despised, and dying king,—
Princes, the dregs of their dull race, who flow
Through public scorn,—mud from a muddy spring,—
Rulers, who neither see, nor feel, nor know,
But leech-like to their fainting country cling, 5
Till they drop, blind in blood, without a blow;
A people starved and stabbed in the untilled field,—
An army, which liberticide and prey
Makes as a two-edged sword to all who wield;
Golden and sanguine laws which tempt and slay; 10
Religion Christless, Godless,—a book sealed;
A Senate,—Time's worst statute unrepealed,—
Are graves, from which a glorious Phantom may
Burst, to illumine our tempestuous day.

 1819 1839

Sonnet

Lift not the painted veil which those who live
Call Life: though unreal shapes be pictured there,
And it but mimic all we would believe
With colours idly spread,—behind, lurk Fear
And Hope, twin Destinies; who ever weave 5
Their shadows, o'er the chasm, sightless and drear.

---

1 king George III
7 In the Peterloo massacre of 16 August, 1819, a worker's meeting in St Peter's Field, Manchester, was charged by cavalry. Several died and hundreds were injured.
12 statute the law excluding Catholics from holding office

I knew one who had lifted it—he sought,
For his lost heart was tender, things to love,
But found them not, alas! nor was there aught
The world contains, the which he could approve.   10
Through the unheeding many he did move,
A splendour among shadows, a bright blot
Upon this gloomy scene, a Spirit that strove
For truth, and like the Preacher found it not.

?1819   1824

Ode to the West Wind

I

O, wild West Wind, thou breath of Autumn's being,
Thou, from whose unseen presence the leaves dead
Are driven, like ghosts from an enchanter fleeing,

Yellow, and black, and pale, and hectic red,
Pestilence-stricken multitudes: O, thou,   5
Who chariotest to their dark wintry bed

The winged seeds, where they lie cold and low,
Each like a corpse within its grave, until
Thine azure sister of the spring shall blow

Her clarion o'er the dreaming earth, and fill   10
(Driving sweet buds like flocks to feed in air)
With living hues and odours plain and hill:

Wild Spirit, which art moving every where;
Destroyer and preserver; hear, O, hear!

II

Thou on whose stream, 'mid the steep sky's commotion,   15
Loose clouds like earth's decaying leaves are shed,
Shook from the tangled boughs of Heaven and Ocean,

Angels of rain and lightning: there are spread
On the blue surface of thine airy surge,
Like the bright hair uplifted from the head   20

Of some fierce Mænad, even from the dim verge
Of the horizon to the zenith's height,
The locks of the approaching storm. Thou dirge

Of the dying year, to which this closing night
Will be the dome of a vast sepulchre,   25
Vaulted with all thy congregated might

Of vapours, from whose solid atmosphere
Black rain, and fire, and hail will burst: O, hear!

---

14 the Preacher   See Eccles. 1:2: 'Vanity of vanities, saith the Preacher.'
Ode to the West Wind   According to Shelley, this poem was 'conceived and chiefly written' on a day
of autumn wind outside Florence.
18 Angels   i.e. as messengers
21 Mænad   frenzied female follower of Dionysus

III

Thou who didst waken from his summer dreams
The blue Mediterranean, where he lay,   30
Lulled by the coil of his crystalline streams,

Beside a pumice isle in Baiæ's bay,
And saw in sleep old palaces and towers
Quivering within the wave's intenser day,

All overgrown with azure moss and flowers   35
So sweet, the sense faints picturing them! Thou
For whose path the Atlantic's level powers

Cleave themselves into chasms, while far below
The sea-blooms and the oozy woods which wear
The sapless foliage of the ocean, know   40

Thy voice, and suddenly grow grey with fear,
And tremble and despoil themselves: O, hear!

IV

If I were a dead leaf thou mightest bear;
If I were a swift cloud to fly with thee;
A wave to pant beneath thy power, and share   45

The impulse of thy strength, only less free
Than thou, O, uncontroulable! If even
I were as in my boyhood, and could be

The comrade of thy wanderings over heaven,
As then, when to outstrip thy skiey speed   50
Scarce seemed a vision; I would ne'er have striven

As thus with thee in prayer in my sore need.
Oh! lift me as a wave, a leaf, a cloud!
I fall upon the thorns of life! I bleed!

A heavy weight of hours has chained and bowed   55
One too like thee: tameless, and swift, and proud.

V

Make me thy lyre, even as the forest is:
What if my leaves are falling like its own!
The tumult of thy mighty harmonies

Will take from both a deep, autumnal tone,   60
Sweet though in sadness. Be thou, spirit fierce,
My spirit! Be thou me, impetuous one!

Drive my dead thoughts over the universe
Like withered leaves to quicken a new birth!
And, by the incantation of this verse,   65

---

32 Baiæ ancient coastal resort near Naples, now partly submerged
38–42 Shelley notes: 'The phenomenon ... is well known to naturalists. The vegetation at the bottom of the sea, of rivers and of lakes, sympathizes with that of the land in the change of seasons, and is consequently influenced by the winds which announce it.'

Scatter, as from an unextinguished hearth
Ashes and sparks, my words among mankind!
Be through my lips to unawakened earth

The trumpet of a prophecy! O, wind,
If Winter comes, can Spring be far behind?   70

1819 1820

To Night

I
Swiftly walk o'er the western wave,
    Spirit of Night!
Out of the misty eastern cave,
Where, all the long and lone daylight,
Thou wovest dreams of joy and fear,   5
Which make thee terrible and dear,—
    Swift be thy flight!

II
Wrap thy form in a mantle grey,
    Star-inwrought!
Blind with thine hair the eyes of Day,   10
Kiss her until she be wearied out,
Then wander o'er city, and sea, and land,
Touching all with thine opiate wand—
    Come, long-sought!

III
When I arose and saw the dawn,   15
    I sighed for thee;
When light rode high, and the dew was gone,
And noon lay heavy on flower and tree,
And the weary Day turned to his rest,
Lingering like an unloved guest,   20
    I sighed for thee.

IV
Thy brother Death came, and cried,
    Wouldst thou me?
Thy sweet child Sleep, the filmy-eyed,
Murmured like a noon-tide bee,   25
Shall I nestle near thy side?
Wouldst thou me?—And I replied,
    No, not thee!

V
Death will come when thou art dead,
    Soon, too soon—   30
Sleep will come when thou art fled;
Of neither would I ask the boon
I ask of thee, beloved Night—
Swift be thine approaching flight,
    Come soon, soon!   35

1821 1824

GEORGE GORDON, LORD BYRON

1788–1824 b London. He became a cult figure, who in his personal life seemed to match the extravagance of the heroes of his earlier poems. *Don Juan* is later, dating from a period in Italy, 1816–23, and its hero is more comically passive. Byron died of fever while taking part in the revolt of Greece against Turkey.

So we'll go no more a roving

I
So, we'll go no more a roving
   So late into the night,
Though the heart be still as loving,
   And the moon be still as bright.
II
For the sword outwears its sheath,   5
   And the soul wears out the breast,
And the heart must pause to breathe,
   And love itself have rest.

III
Though the night was made for loving,
   And the day returns too soon,   10
Yet we'll go no more a roving
   By the light of the moon.

                             1817 1836

From Don Juan

From *Canto the First*
LXIII
'Tis a sad thing, I cannot choose but say,
   And all the fault of that indecent sun,
Who cannot leave alone our helpless clay,
   But will keep baking, broiling, burning on,   500
That howsoever people fast and pray,
   The flesh is frail, and so the soul undone:
What men call gallantry, and gods adultery,
Is much more common where the climate's sultry.

LXIV
Happy the nations of the moral north!   505
   Where all is virtue, and the winter season
Sends sin, without a rag on, shivering forth;
   ('Twas snow that brought St. Anthony to reason);
Where juries cast up what a wife is worth
   By laying whate'er sum, in mulct, they please on   *as a fine* 510

---

508 St Anthony a mistake for St Francis of Assisi, who cooled temptation by throwing himself into snow

The lover, who must pay a handsome price,
Because it is a marketable vice.

LXV

Alfonso was the name of Julia's lord,
   A man well looking for his years, and who
Was neither much beloved, nor yet abhorr'd: 515
   They lived together as most people do,
Suffering each other's foibles by accord,
   And not exactly either *one* or *two*;
Yet he was jealous, though he did not show it,
For jealousy dislikes the world to know it.   520

LXVI

Julia was—yet I never could see why—
   With Donna Inez quite a favourite friend;
Between their tastes there was small sympathy,
   For not a line had Julia ever penn'd:
Some people whisper (but, no doubt, they lie,   525
   For malice still imputes some private end)
That Inez had, ere Don Alfonso's marriage,
Forgot with him her very prudent carriage;

LXVII

And that still keeping up the old connexion,
   Which time had lately render'd much more chaste,   530
She took his lady also in affection,
   And certainly this course was much the best:
She flatter'd Julia with her sage protection,
   And complimented Don Alfonso's taste;
And if she could not (who can?) silence scandal,   535
At least she left it a more slender handle.

LXVIII

I can't tell whether Julia saw the affair
   With other people's eyes, or if her own
Discoveries made, but none could be aware
   Of this, at least no symptom e'er was shown;   540
Perhaps she did not know, or did not care,
   Indifferent from the first, or callous grown:
I'm really puzzled what to think or say,
She kept her counsel in so close a way.

LXIX

Juan she saw, and, as a pretty child,   545
   Caress'd him often,—such a thing might be
Quite innocently done, and harmless styled,
   When she had twenty years, and thirteen he;
But I am not so sure I should have smiled
   When he was sixteen, Julia twenty-three;   550
These few short years make wondrous alterations,
Particularly amongst sun-burnt nations.

---

545 Juan Donna Inez' son

LXX
Whate'er the cause might be, they had become
   Changed; for the dame grew distant, the youth shy,
Their looks cast down, their greetings almost dumb,   555
   And much embarrassment in either eye;
There surely will be little doubt with some
   That Donna Julia knew the reason why,
But as for Juan, he had no more notion
Than he who never saw the sea of ocean.   560

LXXI
Yet Julia's very coldness still was kind,
   And tremulously gentle her small hand
Withdrew itself from his, but left behind
   A little pressure, thrilling, and so bland
And slight, so very slight, that to the mind   565
   'Twas but a doubt; but ne'er magician's wand
Wrought change with all Armida's fairy art
Like what this light touch left on Juan's heart.

LXXII
And if she met him, though she smiled no more,
   She look'd a sadness sweeter than her smile,   570
As if her heart had deeper thoughts in store
   She must not own, but cherish'd more the while,
For that compression in its burning core;
   Even innocence itself has many a wile,
And will not dare to trust itself with truth,   575
And love is taught hypocrisy from youth.

LXXIII
But passion most dissembles yet betrays
   Even by its darkness; as the blackest sky
Foretells the heaviest tempest, it displays
   Its workings through the vainly guarded eye,   580
And in whatever aspect it arrays
   Itself, 'tis still the same hypocrisy;
Coldness or anger, even disdain or hate,
Are masks it often wears, and still too late.

LXXIV
Then there were sighs, the deeper for suppression,   585
   And stolen glances, sweeter for the theft,
And burning blushes, though for no transgression,
   Tremblings when met, and restlessness when left;
All these are little preludes to possession,
   Of which young Passion cannot be bereft,   590
And merely tend to show how greatly Love is
Embarrass'd at first starting with a novice.

LXXV
Poor Julia's heart was in an awkward state;
   She felt it going, and resolved to make

---

567 **Armida**   a seductive sorceress in Tasso's *Jerusalem Delivered* (1581)

The noblest efforts for herself and mate,   595
  For honour's, pride's, religion's, virtue's sake;
Her resolutions were most truly great,
  And almost might have made a Tarquin quake;
She pray'd the Virgin Mary for her grace,
As being the best judge of a lady's case.   600
                    LXXVI
She vow'd she never would see Juan more,
  And next day paid a visit to his mother,
And look'd extremely at the opening door,
  Which, by the Virgin's grace, let in another;
Grateful she was, and yet a little sore—   605
  Again it opens, it can be no other,
'Tis surely Juan now—No! I'm afraid
That night the Virgin was no further pray'd.
                    LXXVII
She now determined that a virtuous woman
  Should rather face and overcome temptation,   610
That flight was base and dastardly, and no man
  Should ever give her heart the least sensation;
That is to say, a thought beyond the common
  Preference, that we must feel upon occasion,
For people who are pleasanter than others,   615
But then they only seem so many brothers.
                    LXXVIII
And even if by chance—and who can tell?
  The devil's so very sly—she should discover
That all within was not so very well,
  And, if still free, that such or such a lover   620
Might please perhaps, a virtuous wife can quell
  Such thought, and be the better when they're over;
And if the man should ask, 'tis but denial:
I recommend young ladies to make trial
                    LXXIX
And then there are such things as love divine,   625
  Bright and immaculate, unmix'd and pure,
Such as the angels think so very fine,
  And matrons, who would be no less secure,
Platonic, perfect, 'just such love as mine':
  Thus Julia said—and thought so, to be sure,   630
And so I'd have her think, were I the man
On whom her reveries celestial ran.
                    LXXX
Such love is innocent, and may exist
  Between young persons without any danger,
A hand may first, and then a lip be kist;   635
  For my part, to such doings I'm a stranger,
But *hear* these freedoms form the utmost list
  Of all o'er which such love may be a ranger:

---

598 **Tarquin**   a nobleman of a powerful family in ancient Rome, who raped Lucretia. Shakespeare uses the story in *The Rape of Lucrece.*

If people go beyond, 'tis quite a crime,
But not my fault—I tell them all in time.   640
          LXXXI
Love, then, but love within its proper limits,
   Was Julia's innocent determination
In young Don Juan's favour, and to him its
   Exertion might be useful on occasion;
And, lighted at too pure a shrine to dim its   645
   Etherial lustre, with what sweet persuasion
He might be taught, by love and her together—
I really don't know what, nor Julia either.
          LXXXII
Fraught with this fine intention, and well fenced
   In mail of proof—her purity of soul,   650
She, for the future of her strength convinced,
   And that her honour was a rock, or mole,
Exceeding sagely from that hour dispensed
   With any kind of troublesome control;
But whether Julia to the task was equal   655
Is that which must be mention'd in the sequel.
          LXXXIII
Her plan she deem'd both innocent and feasible,
   And, surely, with a stripling of sixteen
Not scandal's fangs could fix on much that's seizable,
   Or if they did so, satisfied to mean   660
Nothing but what was good, her breast was peaceable:
   A quiet conscience makes one so serene!
Christians have burnt each other, quite persuaded
That all the Apostles would have done as they did.
          LXXXIV
And if in the mean time her husband died,   665
   But heaven forbid that such a thought should cross
Her brain, though in a dream! (and then she sigh'd)
   Never could she survive that common loss;
But just suppose that moment should betide,
   I only say suppose it—*inter nos*.   670
(This should be *entre nous*, for Julia thought
In French, but then the rhyme would go for nought.)
          LXXXV
I only say suppose this supposition:
   Juan being then grown up to man's estate
Would fully suit a widow of condition,   675
   Even seven years hence it would not be too late;
And in the interim (to pursue this vision)
   The mischief, after all, could not be great,
For he would learn the rudiments of love,
I mean the seraph way of those above.   680
          LXXXVI
So much for Julia. Now we'll turn to Juan,
   Poor little fellow! he had no idea

---

670 inter nos 'between ourselves' (Latin)

Of his own case, and never hit the true one;
 In feelings quick as Ovid's Miss Medea,
He puzzled over what he found a new one,   685
 But not as yet imagined it could be a
Thing quite in course, and not at all alarming,
Which, with a little patience, might grow charming.
                    LXXXVII
Silent and pensive, idle, restless, slow,
 His home deserted for the lonely wood,   690
Tormented with a wound he could not know,
 His, like all deep grief, plunged in solitude:
I'm fond myself of solitude or so,
 But then, I beg it may be understood,
By solitude I mean a sultan's, not   695
A hermit's, with a haram for a grot.
                    LXXXVIII
'Oh Love! in such a wilderness as this,
 Where transport and security entwine,   *ecstasy*
Here is the empire of thy perfect bliss,
 And here thou art a god indeed divine.'   700
The bard I quote from does not sing amiss,
 With the exception of the second line,
For that same twining 'transport and security'
Are twisted to a phrase of some obscurity.
                    LXXXIX
The poet meant, no doubt, and thus appeals   705
 To the good sense and senses of mankind,
The very thing which every body feels,
 As all have found on trial, or may find,
That no one likes to be disturb'd at meals
 Or love.—I won't say more about 'entwined'   710
Or 'transport,' as we knew all that before,
But beg 'Security' will bolt the door.
                    XC
Young Juan wander'd by the glassy brooks,
 Thinking unutterable things; he threw
Himself at length within the leafy nooks   715
 Where the wild branch of the cork forest grew;
There poets find materials for their books,
 And every now and then we read them through,
So that their plan and prosody are eligible,
Unless, like Wordsworth, they prove unintelligible.   720
                    XCI
He, Juan (and not Wordsworth), so pursued
 His self-communion with his own high soul,
Until his mighty heart, in its great mood,
 Had mitigated part, though not the whole
Of its disease; he did the best he could   725
 With things not very subject to control,

---

684 Ovid's Miss Medea   i.e. Medea's sudden infatuation with Jason. See *Metamorphoses* VII.
697–700   Paraphrased from Thomas Campbell's *Gertrude of Wyoming* (1809)

And turn'd, without perceiving his condition,
Like Coleridge, into a metaphysician.
            XCII
He thought about himself, and the whole earth,
    Of man the wonderful, and of the stars,   730
And how the deuce they ever could have birth;
    And then he thought of earthquakes, and of wars,
How many miles the moon might have in girth,
    Of air-balloons, and of the many bars
To perfect knowledge of the boundless skies;   735
And then he thought of Donna Julia's eyes.
            XCIII
In thoughts like these true wisdom may discern
    Longings sublime, and aspirations high,
Which some are born with, but the most part learn
    To plague themselves withal, they know not why: 740
'Twas strange that one so young should thus concern
    His brain about the action of the sky;
If *you* think 'twas philosophy that this did,
I can't help thinking puberty assisted.
            XCIV
He pored upon the leaves, and on the flowers,   745
    And heard a voice in all the winds; and then
He thought of wood nymphs and immortal bowers,
    And how the goddesses came down to men:
He miss'd the pathway, he forgot the hours,
    And when he look'd upon his watch again,   750
He found how much old Time had been a winner—
He also found that he had lost his dinner.
            XCV
Sometimes he turn'd to gaze upon his book,
    Boscan, or Garcilasso;—by the wind
Even as the page is rustled while we look,   755
    So by the poesy of his own mind
Over the mystic leaf, his soul was shook,
    As if 'twere one whereon magicians bind
Their spells, and give them to the passing gale,
According to some good old woman's tale.   760
            XCVI
Thus would he while his lonely hours away
    Dissatisfied, nor knowing what he wanted;
Nor glowing reverie, nor poet's lay,
    Could yield his spirit that for which it panted,
A bosom whereon he his head might lay,   765
    And hear the heart beat with the love it granted,
With—several other things, which I forget,
Or which, at least, I need not mention yet.

---

754 Boscan ... Garcilasso Spanish poets of the sixteenth century

XCVII

Those lonely walks, and lengthening reveries,
  Could not escape the gentle Julia's eyes;   770
She saw that Juan was not at his ease;
  But that which chiefly may, and must surprise,
Is, that the Donna Inez did not tease
  Her only son with question or surmise;
Whether it was she did not see, or would not,   775
Or, like all very clever people, could not.

XCVIII

This may seem strange, but yet 'tis very common;
  For instance—gentlemen, whose ladies take
Leave to o'erstep the written rights of woman,
  And break the—Which commandment is't they break?   780
(I have forgot the number, and think no man
  Should rashly quote, for fear of a mistake.)
I say, when these same gentlemen are jealous,
They make some blunder, which their ladies tell us.

XCIX

A real husband always is suspicious,   785
  But still no less suspects in the wrong place,
Jealous of some one who had no such wishes,
  Or pandering blindly to his own disgrace
By harbouring some dear friend extremely vicious;
  The last indeed's infallibly the case: 790
And when the spouse and friend are gone off wholly,
He wonders at their vice, and not his folly.

C

Thus parents also are at times short-sighted;
  Though watchful as the lynx, they ne'er discover,
The while the wicked world beholds delighted,   795
  Young Hopeful's mistress, or Miss Fanny's lover,
Till some confounded escapade has blighted
  The plan of twenty years, and all is over;
And then the mother cries, the father swears,
And wonders why the devil he got heirs.   800

CI

But Inez was so anxious, and so clear
  Of sight, that I must think, on this occasion,
She had some other motive much more near
  For leaving Juan to this new temptation;
But what that motive was, I sha'n't say here;   805
  Perhaps to finish Juan's education,
Perhaps to open Don Alfonso's eyes,
In case he thought his wife too great a prize.

CII

It was upon a day, a summer's day;—
  Summer's indeed a very dangerous season,   810
And so is spring about the end of May;
  The sun, no doubt, is the prevailing reason;

But whatsoe'er the cause is, one may say,
   And stand convicted of more truth than treason,
That there are months which nature grows more merry in,   815
March has its hares, and May must have its heroine.
            CIII
'Twas on a summer's day—the sixth of June:—
   I like to be particular in dates,
Not only of the age, and year, but moon;
   They are a sort of post-house, where the Fates   820
Change horses, making history change its tune,
   Then spur away o'er empires and o'er states,
Leaving at last not much besides chronology,
Excepting the post-obits of theology.
            CIV
'Twas on the sixth of June, about the hour   825
   Of half-past six—perhaps still nearer seven—
When Julia sate within as pretty a bower
   As e'er held houri in that heathenish heaven
Described by Mahomet, and Anacreon Moore,
   To whom the lyre and laurels have been given,   830
With all the trophies of triumphant song—
He won them well, and may he wear them long!
            CV
She sate, but not alone; I know not well
   How this same interview had taken place,
And even if I knew, I should not tell—   835
   People should hold their tongues in any case;
No matter how or why the thing befel,
   But there were she and Juan, face to face—
When two such faces are so, 'twould be wise,
But very difficult, to shut their eyes.   840
            CVI
How beautiful she look'd! her conscious heart
   Glow'd in her cheek, and yet she felt no wrong.
Oh Love! how perfect is thy mystic art,
   Strengthening the weak, and trampling on the strong,
How self-deceitful is the sagest part   845
   Of mortals whom thy lure hath led along—
The precipice she stood on was immense,
So was her creed in her own innocence.
            CVII
She thought of her own strength, and Juan's youth,
   And of the folly of all prudish fears,   850
Victorious virtue, and domestic truth,
   And then of Don Alfonso's fifty years:
I wish these last had not occurr'd, in sooth,
   Because that number rarely much endears,

---

824 post-obits   loans due for repayment from an estate after death
828 houri   a beautiful woman in the Muslim heaven
829 Moore   Byron's friend, Thomas Moore, translator of love poems attributed to the Greek,
Anacreon (sixth century BC), and author of the oriental tales in *Lalla Rookh* (1817)

And through all climes, the snowy and the sunny,   855
Sounds ill in love, whate'er it may in money.

CVIII

When people say, 'I've told you *fifty* times,'
   They mean to scold, and very often do;
When poets say, 'I've written *fifty* rhymes,'
   They make you dread that they'll recite them too;   860
In gangs of *fifty* thieves commit their crimes;
   At *fifty* love for love is rare, 'tis true,
But then, no doubt, it equally as true is,
A good deal may be bought for *fifty* Louis.   *gold coins*

CIX

Julia had honour, virtue, truth, and love,   865
   For Don Alfonso; and she inly swore,
By all the vows below to powers above,
   She never would disgrace the ring she wore,
Nor leave a wish which wisdom might reprove;
   And while she ponder'd this, besides much more,   870
One hand on Juan's carelessly was thrown,
Quite by mistake—she thought it was her own;

CX

Unconsciously she lean'd upon the other,
   Which play'd within the tangles of her hair;
And to contend with thoughts she could not smother,   875
   She seem'd by the distraction of her air.
'Twas surely very wrong in Juan's mother
   To leave together this imprudent pair,
She who for many years had watch'd her son so—
I'm very certain *mine* would not have done so.   880

CXI

The hand which still held Juan's, by degrees
   Gently, but palpably confirm'd its grasp,
As if it said, 'detain me, if you please';
   Yet there's no doubt she only meant to clasp
His fingers with a pure Platonic squeeze;   885
   She would have shrunk as from a toad, or asp,
Had she imagined such a thing could rouse
A feeling dangerous to a prudent spouse.

CXII

I cannot know what Juan thought of this,
   But what he did, is much what you would do;   890
His young lip thank'd it with a grateful kiss,
   And then, abash'd at its own joy, withdrew
In deep despair, lest he had done amiss,
   Love is so very timid when 'tis new:
She blush'd, and frown'd not, but she strove to speak,   895
And held her tongue, her voice was grown so weak.

CXIII

The sun set, and up rose the yellow moon:
   The devil's in the moon for mischief; they
Who call'd her CHASTE, methinks, began too soon
   Their nomenclature; there is not a day,   900

The longest, not the twenty-first of June,
  Sees half the business in a wicked way
On which three single hours of moonshine smile—
And then she looks so modest all the while.
          CXIV

There is a dangerous silence in that hour,   905
  A stillness, which leaves room for the full soul
To open all itself, without the power
  Of calling wholly back its self-control;
The silver light which, hallowing tree and tower,
  Sheds beauty and deep softness o'er the whole,   910
Breathes also to the heart, and o'er it throws
A loving languor, which is not repose.
          CXV

And Julia sate with Juan, half embraced
  And half retiring from the glowing arm,
Which trembled like the bosom where 'twas placed;   915
  Yet still she must have thought there was no harm,
Or else 'twere easy to withdraw her waist;
  But then the situation had its charm,
And then—God knows what next—I can't go on;   920
I'm almost sorry that I e'er begun.
          CXVI

Oh Plato! Plato! you have paved the way,
  With your confounded fantasies, to more
Immoral conduct by the fancied sway
  Your system feigns o'er the controlless core
Of human hearts, than all the long array   925
  Of poets and romancers:—You're a bore,
A charlatan, a coxcomb—and have been,
At best, no better than a go-between.
          CXVII

And Julia's voice was lost, except in sighs,
  Until too late for useful conversation;   930
The tears were gushing from her gentle eyes,
  I wish, indeed, they had not had occasion,
But who, alas! can love, and then be wise?
  Not that remorse did not oppose temptation,
A little still she strove, and much repented,   935
And whispering 'I will ne'er consent'—consented.
          CXVIII

'Tis said that Xerxes offer'd a reward
  To those who could invent him a new pleasure;
Methinks, the requisition's rather hard,
  And must have cost his majesty a treasure: 940
For my part, I'm a moderate-minded bard,
  Fond of a little love (which I call leisure);
I care not for new pleasures, as the old
Are quite enough for me, so they but hold.

---

937 Xerxes King of Persia, 486–65 BC

CXIX

Oh Pleasure! you're indeed a pleasant thing,   945
  Although one must be damn'd for you, no doubt;
I make a resolution every spring
  Of reformation, ere the year run out,
But, somehow, this my vestal vow takes wing,
  Yet still, I trust, it may be kept throughout: 950
I'm very sorry, very much ashamed,
And mean, next winter, to be quite reclaim'd.

CXX

Here my chaste Muse a liberty must take—
  Start not! still chaster reader—she'll be nice hence-
Forward, and there is no great cause to quake;   955
  This liberty is a poetic licence,
Which some irregularity may make
  In the design, and as I have a high sense
Of Aristotle and the Rules, 'tis fit
To beg his pardon when I err a bit.   960

CXXI

This licence is to hope the reader will
  Suppose from June the sixth (the fatal day,
Without whose epoch my poetic skill
  For want of facts would all be thrown away),
But keeping Julia and Don Juan still   965
  In sight, that several months have pass'd; we'll say
'Twas in November, but I'm not so sure
About the day—the era's more obscure.

CXXII

We'll talk of that anon.—'Tis sweet to hear
  At midnight on the blue and moonlit deep   970
The song and oar of Adria's gondolier,
  By distance mellow'd, o'er the waters sweep;
'Tis sweet to see the evening star appear;
  'Tis sweet to listen as the nightwinds creep
From leaf to leaf; 'tis sweet to view on high   975
The rainbow, based on ocean, span the sky.

CXXIII

'Tis sweet to hear the watchdog's honest bark
  Bay deep-mouth'd welcome as we draw near home;
'Tis sweet to know there is an eye will mark
  Our coming, and look brighter when we come;   980
'Tis sweet to be awaken'd by the lark,
  Or lull'd by falling waters; sweet the hum
Of bees, the voice of girls, the song of birds,
The lisp of children, and their earliest words.

CXXIV

Sweet is the vintage, when the showering grapes   985
  In Bacchanal profusion reel to earth
Purple and gushing: sweet are our escapes
  From civic revelry to rural mirth;
Sweet to the miser are his glittering heaps,
  Sweet to the father is his first-born's birth,   990
Sweet is revenge—especially to women,
Pillage to soldiers, prize-money to seamen.

CXXV
Sweet is a legacy, and passing sweet
  The unexpected death of some old lady
Or gentleman of seventy years complete,   995
  Who've made 'us youth' wait too—too long already
For an estate, or cash, or country-seat,
  Still breaking, but with stamina so steady,
That all the Israelites are fit to mob its
Next owner for their double-damn'd post-obits.   1000

CXXVI
'Tis sweet to win, no matter how, one's laurels
  By blood or ink; 'tis sweet to put an end
To strife; 'tis sometimes sweet to have our quarrels,
  Particularly with a tiresome friend;
Sweet is old wine in bottles, ale in barrels;   1005
  Dear is the helpless creature we defend
Against the world; and dear the schoolboy spot
We ne'er forget, though there we are forgot.

CXXVII
But sweeter still than this, than these, than all,
  Is first and passionate love—it stands alone,   1010
Like Adam's recollection of his fall;
  The tree of knowledge has been pluck'd—all's known—
And life yields nothing further to recall
  Worthy of this ambrosial sin, so shown,
No doubt in fable, as the unforgiven   1015
Fire which Prometheus filch'd for us from heaven.

                                                          1819

SAMUEL TAYLOR COLERIDGE

1772–1834 b Ottery St Mary, Devon; settled in London in later years. His best poetry was written early, stimulated by his association with Wordsworth. His criticism has been influential.

The Rime of the Ancient Mariner

Part I

An ancient Mariner
meeteth three
gallants bidden to a
wedding-feast, and
detaineth one.

It is an ancient Mariner,
And he stoppeth one of three.
'By thy long grey beard and glittering eye,
Now wherefore stopp'st thou me?

---

996 us youth 'They hate us youth': Falstaff, in *Henry IV, Part I*, II, ii, 93
1016 Prometheus a god who was punished by Zeus for stealing fire from heaven for humankind
The Rime of the Ancient Mariner Coleridge added an epigraph (in Latin) from Thomas Burnet, *Archæologiæ Philosophicæ* (1692), along with the marginal commentary, in the edition of 1817: 'I readily believe that there are more invisible than visible beings in the universe. But who will describe for us the families of all these, the ranks, connections, distinctions and functions of each? What do they do? Where do they live? Human intelligence has always circled around a knowledge of these things but never attained it. Yet I do not doubt that sometimes it is good to contemplate in the mind, as in a picture, the image of a greater and better world: lest the mind, grown used to the trivia of daily life, contract itself too much and subside completely into petty thinking. Meanwhile, however, we must watch for the truth, keeping a sense of proportion so that we distinguish certain from uncertain and day from night.'

The Bridegroom's doors are opened wide,   5
And I am next of kin;
The guests are met, the feast is set:
May'st hear the merry din.'

He holds him with his skinny hand,
'There was a ship,' quoth he.   10
'Hold off! unhand me, grey-beard loon!'
Eftsoons his hand dropt he.   *at once*

The wedding guest is spellbound by the eye of the old seafaring man, and constrained to hear his tale.

He holds him with his glittering eye—
The wedding-guest stood still,
And listens like a three years' child: 15
The Mariner hath his will.

The wedding-guest sat on a stone:
He cannot choose but hear;
And thus spake on that ancient man,
The bright-eyed Mariner.   20

'The ship was cheered, the harbour cleared,
Merrily did we drop
Below the kirk, below the hill,
Below the light house top.

The Mariner tells how the ship sailed southward with a good wind and fair weather, till it reached the line.

The sun came up upon the left,   25
Out of the sea came he!
And he shone bright, and on the right
Went down into the sea.

Higher and higher every day,
Till over the mast at noon—'   30
The Wedding-Guest here beat his breast,
For he heard the loud bassoon.

The wedding guest heareth the bridal music; but the mariner continueth his tale.

The bride hath paced into the hall,
Red as a rose is she;
Nodding their heads before her goes   35
The merry minstrelsy.

The Wedding-Guest he beat his breast,
Yet he cannot choose but hear;
And thus spake on that ancient man,
The bright-eyed Mariner.   40

The ship drawn by a storm toward the south pole.

'And now the storm-blast came, and he
Was tyrannous and strong:
He struck with his o'ertaking wings,
And chased us south along.

With sloping masts and dipping prow,   45
As who pursued with yell and blow
Still treads the shadow of his foe,
And forward bends his head,
The ship drove fast, loud roared the blast,
And southward aye we fled.   50

And now there came both mist and snow,
And it grew wondrous cold:
And ice, mast-high, came floating by,
As green as emerald.

The land of ice,
and of fearful
sounds where no
living thing was to
be seen.

And through the drifts the snowy cliffs   55
Did send a dismal sheen:
Nor shapes of men nor beasts we ken—   *see*
The ice was all between.

The ice was here, the ice was there,
The ice was all around: 60
It cracked and growled, and roared and howled,
Like noises in a swound!   *swoon*

Till a great sea-
bird, called the
Albatross, came
through the snow-
fog, and was
received with great
joy and hospitality.

At length did cross an Albatross,
Thorough the fog it came;
As if it had been a Christian soul,   65
We hailed it in God's name.

It ate the food it ne'er had eat,
And round and round it flew.
The ice did split with a thunder-fit;
The helmsman steered us through!   70

And lo! the
Albatross proveth a
bird of good omen,
and followeth the
ship as it returned
northward through
fog and floating ice.

And a good south wind sprung up behind;
The Albatross did follow,
And every day, for food or play,
Came to the mariner's hollo!

In mist or cloud, on mast or shroud,   75
It perched for vespers nine;
Whiles all the night, through fog-smoke white,
Glimmered the white moon-shine.'

The ancient
Mariner
inhospitably killeth
the pious bird of
good omen.

'God save thee, ancient Mariner!
From the fiends, that plague thee thus!—   80
Why look'st thou so?'—With my cross-bow
I shot the Albatross.

Part II

The Sun now rose upon the right:
Out of the sea came he,
Still hid in mist, and on the left   85
Went down into the sea.

And the good south wind still blew behind,
But no sweet bird did follow,
Nor any day for food or play
Came to the mariner's hollo!   90

His shipmates cry
out against the
ancient Mariner,
for killing the bird
of good luck.

And I had done a hellish thing,
And it would work 'em woe:
For all averred, I had killed the bird
That made the breeze to blow.

Ah wretch! said they, the bird to slay,   95
That made the breeze to blow!

But when the fog
cleared off, they
justify the same,
and thus make
themselves
accomplices in the
crime.

Nor dim nor red, like God's own head,
The glorious Sun uprist:
Then all averred, I had killed the bird
That brought the fog and mist.   100
'Twas right, said they, such birds to slay,
That bring the fog and mist.

The fair breeze
continues; the ship
enters the Pacific
Ocean, and sails
northward, even till
it reaches the Line.

The fair breeze blew, the white foam flew,
The furrow followed free;
We were the first that ever burst   105
Into that silent sea.

The ship hath been
suddenly becalmed.

Down dropt the breeze, the sails dropt down,
'Twas sad as sad could be;
And we did speak only to break
The silence of the sea!   110

All in a hot and copper sky,
The bloody Sun, at noon,
Right up above the mast did stand,
No bigger than the Moon.

Day after day, day after day,   115
We stuck, nor breath nor motion;
As idle as a painted ship
Upon a painted ocean.

And the Albatross
begins to be
avenged.

Water, water, every where,
And all the boards did shrink;   120
Water, water, every where,
Nor any drop to drink.

The very deep did rot: O Christ!
That ever this should be!
Yea, slimy things did crawl with legs   125
Upon the slimy sea.

About, about, in reel and rout
The death-fires danced at night;
The water, like a witch's oils,
Burnt green, and blue and white.   130

A Spirit had
followed them; one
of the invisible
inhabitants of this
planet, neither
departed souls nor

And some in dreams assured were
Of the spirit that plagued us so;
Nine fathom deep he had followed us
From the land of mist and snow.

angels; concerning whom the learned Jew, Josephus, and the Platonic Constantinopolitan,
Michael Psellus, may be consulted. They are very numerous, and there is no climate or
element without one or more.

And every tongue, through utter drought,   135
Was withered at the root;
We could not speak, no more than if
We had been choked with soot.

Ah! well a-day! what evil looks
Had I from old and young!   140
Instead of the cross, the Albatross
About my neck was hung.

The shipmates, in their sore distress, would fain throw the whole guilt on the ancient Mariner: in sign whereof they hang the dead sea-bird round his neck.

Part III

There passed a weary time. Each throat
Was parched, and glazed each eye.
A weary time! a weary time!   145
How glazed each weary eye,
When looking westward, I beheld
A something in the sky.

The ancient Mariner beholdeth a sign in the element afar off.

At first it seemed a little speck,
And then it seemed a mist;   150
It moved and moved, and took at last
A certain shape, I wist.

A speck, a mist, a shape, I wist!   *knew*
And still it neared and neared: 155
As if it dodged a water-sprite,
It plunged and tacked and veered.

At its nearer approach, it seemeth him to be a ship; and at a dear ransom he freeth his speech from the bonds of thirst.

With throats unslaked, with black lips baked,
We could nor laugh nor wail;
Through utter drought all dumb we stood!
I bit my arm, I sucked the blood,   160
And cried, A sail! a sail!

A flash of joy;

With throats unslaked, with black lips baked,
Agape they heard me call:
Gramercy! they for joy did grin,   165
And all at once their breath drew in,
As they were drinking all.

And horror follows. For can it be a ship that comes onward without wind or tide?

See! see! (I cried) she tacks no more!
Hither to work us weal;   *good*
Without a breeze, without a tide,
She steadies with upright keel!   170

The western wave was all a-flame.
The day was well nigh done!
Almost upon the western wave
Rested the broad bright Sun;
When that strange shape drove suddenly   175
Betwixt us and the Sun.

It seemeth him but the skeleton of a ship.

And straight the Sun was flecked with bars,
(Heaven's Mother send us grace!)
As if through a dungeon-grate he peered
With broad and burning face.   180

Alas! (thought I, and my heart beat loud)
How fast she nears and nears!

Are those her sails that glance in the Sun,
Like restless gossameres?

And its ribs are
seen as bars on the
face of the setting
Sun. The spectre-
woman and her
death-mate, and no
other on board the
skeleton-ship.

Are those her ribs through which the Sun   185
Did peer, as through a grate?
And is that Woman all her crew?
Is that a Death? and are there two?
Is Death that woman's mate?

Like vessel, like
crew!

Her lips were red, her looks were free,   190
Her locks were yellow as gold:
Her skin was as white as leprosy,
The Night-mare Life-in-Death was she,
Who thicks man's blood with cold.

Death and Life-in-
death have diced
for the ship's crew,
and she (the latter)
winneth the ancient
Mariner.

The naked hulk alongside came,   195
And the twain were casting dice;
'The game is done! I've won! I've won!'
Quoth she, and whistles thrice.

No twilight within
the courts of the
sun.

The Sun's rim dips; the stars rush out:
At one stride comes the dark;   200
With far-heard whisper, o'er the sea,
Off shot the spectre-bark.

At the rising of the
Moon,

We listened and looked sideways up!
Fear at my heart, as at a cup,
My life-blood seemed to sip!   205
The stars were dim, and thick the night,
The steersman's face by his lamp gleamed white;
From the sails the dew did drip—
Till clomb above the eastern bar
The horned Moon, with one bright star   210
Within the nether tip.

One after another,

One after one, by the star-dogged Moon,
Too quick for groan or sigh,
Each turned his face with a ghastly pang,
And cursed me with his eye.   215

His shipmates drop
down dead.

Four times fifty living men,
(And I heard nor sigh nor groan)
With heavy thump, a lifeless lump,
They dropped down one by one.

But Life-in-Death
begins her work on
the ancient
Mariner.

The souls did from their bodies fly,—   220
They fled to bliss or woe!
And every soul, it passed me by,
Like the whizz of my cross-bow!'

Part IV

The wedding guest
feareth that a Spirit
is talking to him.

'I fear thee, ancient Mariner!
I fear thy skinny hand!   225
And thou art long, and lank, and brown,
As is the ribbed sea-sand.

I fear thee and thy glittering eye,
And thy skinny hand, so brown.'—

But the ancient
Mariner assureth
him of his bodily
life, and proceedeth
to relate his horrible
penance.

Fear not, fear not, thou wedding-guest!   230
This body dropt not down.

Alone, alone, all, all alone,
Alone on a wide wide sea!
And never a saint took pity on
My soul in agony.   235

He despiseth the
creatures of the
calm,

The many men, so beautiful!
And they all dead did lie:
And a thousand thousand slimy things
Lived on; and so did I.

And envieth that
they should live,
and so many lie
dead.

I looked upon the rotting sea,   240
And drew my eyes away;
I looked upon the rotting deck,
And there the dead men lay.

I looked to heaven, and tried to pray;
But or ever a prayer had gusht,   *before*   245
A wicked whisper came, and made
My heart as dry as dust.

I closed my lids, and kept them close,
And the balls like pulses beat;
For the sky and the sea, and the sea and the sky   250
Lay like a load on my weary eye,
And the dead were at my feet.

But the curse liveth
for him in the eye
of the dead men.

The cold sweat melted from their limbs,
Nor rot nor reek did they:
The look with which they looked on me   255
Had never passed away.

An orphan's curse would drag to hell
A spirit from on high;
But oh! more horrible than that
Is the curse in a dead man's eye!   260
Seven days, seven nights, I saw that curse,
And yet I could not die.

In his loneliness
and fixedness he
yearneth towards
the journeying
Moon, and the stars
that still sojourn,
yet still move
onward; and every
where the blue sky
belongs to them,
and is their
appointed rest, and
their native country
and their own
natural homes, which they enter unannounced, as lords that are certainly expected and
yet there is a silent joy at their arrival.

The moving Moon went up the sky,
And no where did abide:
Softly she was going up,   265
And a star or two beside—

Her beams bemocked the sultry main,
Like April hoar-frost spread;
But where the ship's huge shadow lay,
The charmed water burnt alway   270
A still and awful red.

By the light of the
Moon he beholdeth
God's creatures of
the great calm.

Beyond the shadow of the ship,
I watched the water-snakes:
They moved in tracks of shining white,
And when they reared, the elfish light   275
Fell off in hoary flakes.

Within the shadow of the ship
I watched their rich attire:
Blue, glossy green, and velvet black,
They coiled and swam; and every track   280
Was a flash of golden fire.

Their beauty and
their happiness.

O happy living things! no tongue
Their beauty might declare:
A spring of love gushed from my heart,

He blesseth them
in his heart.

And I blessed them unaware: 285
Sure my kind saint took pity on me,
And I blessed them unaware.

The spell begins to
break.

The selfsame moment I could pray;
And from my neck so free
The Albatross fell off, and sank   290
Like lead into the sea.

Part V

Oh sleep! it is a gentle thing,
Beloved from pole to pole!
To Mary Queen the praise be given!
She sent the gentle sleep from Heaven,   295
That slid into my soul.

By grace of the holy
Mother, the ancient
Mariner is
refreshed with rain.

The silly buckets on the deck,   *simple*
That had so long remained,
I dreamt that they were filled with dew;
And when I awoke, it rained.   300

My lips were wet, my throat was cold,
My garments all were dank;
Sure I had drunken in my dreams,
And still my body drank.

I moved, and could not feel my limbs: 305
I was so light—almost
I thought that I had died in sleep,
And was a blessed ghost.

He heareth sounds
and seeth strange
sights and
commotions in the
sky and the element.

And soon I heard a roaring wind:
It did not come anear;   310
But with its sound it shook the sails,
That were so thin and sere.   *worn*

The upper air burst into life!
And a hundred fire-flags sheen,
To and fro they were hurried about!   315
And to and fro, and in and out,
The wan stars danced between.

And the coming wind did roar more loud,
And the sails did sigh like sedge;
And the rain poured down from one black cloud;   320
The Moon was at its edge.

The thick black cloud was cleft, and still
The Moon was at its side:
Like waters shot from some high crag,
The lightning fell with never a jag,   325
A river steep and wide.

The bodies of the ship's crew are inspired, and the ship moves on;

The loud wind never reached the ship,
Yet now the ship moved on!
Beneath the lightning and the moon
The dead men gave a groan.   330

They groaned, they stirred, they all uprose,
Nor spake, nor moved their eyes;
It had been strange, even in a dream,
To have seen those dead men rise.

The helmsman steered, the ship moved on;   335
Yet never a breeze up blew;
The mariners all 'gan work the ropes,
Where they were wont to do;
They raised their limbs like lifeless tools—
We were a ghastly crew.   340

The body of my brother's son
Stood by me, knee to knee:
The body and I pulled at one rope,
But he said nought to me.

'I fear thee, ancient Mariner!'   345

But not by the souls of the men, nor by demons of earth or middle air, but by a blessed troop of angelic spirits, sent down by the invocation of the guardian saint.

Be calm, thou Wedding-Guest!
'Twas not those souls that fled in pain,
Which to their corses came again,   *corpses*
But a troop of spirits blest:

For when it dawned—they dropped their arms,   350
And clustered round the mast;
Sweet sounds rose slowly through their mouths,
And from their bodies passed.

Around, around, flew each sweet sound,
Then darted to the Sun;   355
Slowly the sounds came back again,
Now mixed, now one by one.

Sometimes a-dropping from the sky
I heard the sky-lark sing;

Sometimes all little birds that are,   360
How they seemed to fill the sea and air
With their sweet jargoning!

And now 'twas like all instruments,
Now like a lonely flute;
And now it is an angel's song,   365
That makes the heavens be mute.

It ceased; yet still the sails made on
A pleasant noise till noon,
A noise like of a hidden brook
In the leafy month of June,   370
That to the sleeping woods all night
Singeth a quiet tune.

Till noon we quietly sailed on,
Yet never a breeze did breathe:
Slowly and smoothly went the ship,   375
Moved onward from beneath.

The lonesome spirit from the south-pole carries on the ship as far as the line, in obedience to the angelic troop, but still requireth vengeance.

Under the keel nine fathom deep,
From the land of mist and snow,
The spirit slid: and it was he
That made the ship to go.   380
The sails at noon left off their tune,
And the ship stood still also.

The Sun, right up above the mast,
Had fixed her to the ocean:
But in a minute she 'gan stir,   385
With a short uneasy motion—
Backwards and forwards half her length
With a short uneasy motion.

Then like a pawing horse let go,
She made a sudden bound:
It flung the blood into my head,   390
And I fell down in a swound.

The Polar Spirit's fellow-demons, the invisible inhabitants of the element, take part in his wrong; and two of them relate, one to the other, that penance long and heavy for the ancient Mariner hath been accorded to the Polar Spirit, who returneth southward.

How long in that same fit I lay,
I have not to declare;   *am unable*
but ere my living life returned,   395
I heard and in my soul discerned
Two voices in the air.

'Is it he?' quoth one, 'Is this the man?
By him who died on cross,
With his cruel bow he laid full low   400
The harmless Albatross.

The spirit who bideth by himself
In the land of mist and snow,
He loved the bird that loved the man
Who shot him with his bow.'   405

The other was a softer voice,
As soft as honey-dew:
Quoth he, 'The man hath penance done,
And penance more will do.'

Part VI

FIRST VOICE
But tell me, tell me! speak again,   410
Thy soft response renewing—
What makes that ship drive on so fast?
What is the ocean doing?

SECOND VOICE
Still as a slave before his lord,
The ocean hath no blast;   415
His great bright eye most silently
Up to the Moon is cast—

If he may know which way to go;
For she guides him smooth or grim.
See, brother, see! how graciously   420
She looketh down on him.

FIRST VOICE
But why drives on that ship so fast,
Without or wave or wind?

SECOND VOICE
The air is cut away before,
And closes from behind.   425

Fly, brother, fly! more high, more high!
Or we shall be belated:
For slow and slow that ship will go,
When the Mariner's trance is abated.

I woke, and we were sailing on   430
As in a gentle weather:
'Twas night, calm night, the moon was high;
The dead men stood together.

All stood together on the deck,
For a charnel-dungeon fitter: 435
All fixed on me their stony eyes,
That in the Moon did glitter.

The pang, the curse, with which they died,
Had never passed away:
I could not draw my eyes from theirs,   440
Nor turn them up to pray.

And now this spell was snapt: once more
I viewed the ocean green,
And looked far forth, yet little saw
Of what had else been seen—   445

Marginal glosses:

The Mariner hath been cast into a trance; for the angelic power causeth the vessel to drive northward faster than human life could endure.

The supernatural motion is retarded; the Mariner awakes, and his penance begins anew.

The curse is finally expiated.

Like one, that on a lonesome road
Doth walk in fear and dread,
And having once turned round walks on,
And turns no more his head;
Because he knows, a frightful fiend   450
Doth close behind him tread.

But soon there breathed a wind on me,
Nor sound nor motion made:
Its path was not upon the sea,
In ripple or in shade.   455

It raised my hair, it fanned my cheek
Like a meadow-gale of spring—
It mingled strangely with my fears,
Yet it felt like a welcoming.

Swiftly, swiftly flew the ship,   460
Yet she sailed softly too:
Sweetly, sweetly blew the breeze—
On me alone it blew.

And the ancient
Mariner beholdeth
his native country.

Oh! dream of joy! is this indeed
The light-house top I see?   465
Is this the hill? is this the kirk?
Is this mine own countree?

We drifted o'er the harbour-bar,
And I with sobs did pray—
O let me be awake, my God!   470
Or let me sleep alway.

The harbour-bay was clear as glass,
So smoothly it was strewn!
And on the bay the moonlight lay,
And the shadow of the moon.   475

The rock shone bright, the kirk no less,
That stands above the rock:
The moonlight steeped in silentness
The steady weathercock.

And the bay was white with silent light,   480
Till rising from the same,

The angelic spirits
leave the dead
bodies,

Full many shapes, that shadows were,
In crimson colours came.

And appear in their
own forms of light.

A little distance from the prow
Those crimson shadows were: 485
I turned my eyes upon the deck—
Oh, Christ! what saw I there!

Each corse lay flat, lifeless and flat,
And, by the holy rood!   *cross*
A man all light, a seraph-man,   490
On every corse there stood.

This seraph-band, each waved his hand:
It was a heavenly sight!
They stood as signals to the land,
Each one a lovely light;   495

This seraph-band, each waved his hand,
No voice did they impart—
No voice; but oh! the silence sank
Like music on my heart.

But soon I heard the dash of oars,   500
I heard the Pilot's cheer;
My head was turned perforce away,
And I saw a boat appear.

The Pilot and the Pilot's boy,
I heard them coming fast: 505
Dear Lord in Heaven! it was a joy
The dead men could not blast.

I saw a third—I heard his voice:
It is the Hermit good!
He singeth loud his godly hymns   510
That he makes in the wood.
He'll shrieve my soul, he'll wash away
The Albatross's blood.

Part VII

The Hermit of the
wood,

This Hermit good lives in that wood
Which slopes down to the sea.   515
How loudly his sweet voice he rears!
He loves to talk with marineres
That come from a far countree.

He kneels at morn, and noon, and eve—
He hath a cushion plump: 520
It is the moss that wholly hides
The rotted old oak-stump.

The skiff-boat neared: I heard them talk,
'Why, this is strange, I trow!   *believe*
Where are those lights so many and fair,   525
That signal made but now?'

Approacheth the
ship with wonder.

'Strange, by my faith!' the Hermit said—
'And they answered not our cheer!
The planks looked warped! and see those sails,
How thin they are and sere!   530
I never saw aught like to them,
Unless perchance it were

Brown skeletons of leaves that lag
My forest-brook along;
When the ivy-tod is heavy with snow,   *clump* 535

And the owlet whoops to the wolf below,
That eats the she-wolf's young.'

'Dear Lord! it hath a fiendish look—
(The Pilot made reply)
I am a-feared'—'Push on, push on!'   540
Said the Hermit cheerily.

The boat came closer to the ship,
But I nor spake nor stirred;
The boat came close beneath the ship,
And straight a sound was heard.   545

The ship suddenly sinketh.

Under the water it rumbled on,
Still louder and more dread:
It reached the ship, it split the bay;
The ship went down like lead.

The ancient Mariner is saved in the Pilot's boat.

Stunned by that loud and dreadful sound,   550
Which sky and ocean smote,
Like one that hath been seven days drowned
My body lay afloat;
But swift as dreams, myself I found
Within the Pilot's boat.   555

Upon the whirl, where sank the ship,
The boat spun round and round;
And all was still, save that the hill
Was telling of the sound.

I moved my lips—the Pilot shrieked   560
And fell down in a fit;
The holy Hermit raised his eyes,
And prayed where he did sit.

I took the oars: the Pilot's boy,
Who now doth crazy go,   565
Laughed loud and long, and all the while
His eyes went to and fro.
'Ha! ha!' quoth he, 'full plain I see,
The Devil knows how to row.'

And now, all in my own countree,   570
I stood on the firm land!
The Hermit stepped forth from the boat,
And scarcely he could stand.

The ancient Mariner earnestly entreateth the Hermit to shrieve him; and the penance of life falls on him.

'O shrieve me, shrieve me, holy man!'
The Hermit crossed his brow.   575
'Say quick,' quoth he, 'I bid thee say—
What manner of man art thou?'

Forthwith this frame of mine was wrenched
With a woful agony,
Which forced me to begin my tale;   580
And then it left me free.

And ever and anon
throughout his
future life an agony
constraineth him to
travel from land to
land;

Since then, at an uncertain hour,
That agony returns:
And till my ghastly tale is told,
This heart within me burns.   585

I pass, like night, from land to land;
I have strange power of speech;
That moment that his face I see,
I know the man that must hear me:
To him my tale I teach.   590

What loud uproar bursts from that door!
The wedding-guests are there:
But in the garden-bower the bride
And bride-maids singing are:
And hark the little vesper bell,   595
Which biddeth me to prayer!

O Wedding-Guest! this soul hath been
Alone on a wide wide sea:
So lonely 'twas, that God himself
Scarce seemed there to be.   600

O sweeter than the marriage-feast,
'Tis sweeter far to me,
To walk together to the kirk
With a goodly company!—

To walk together to the kirk,   605
And all together pray,
While each to his great Father bends,
Old men, and babes, and loving friends
And youths and maidens gay!

And to teach, by
his own example,
love and reverence
to all things that
God made and
loveth.

Farewell, farewell! but this I tell   610
To thee, thou Wedding-Guest!
He prayeth well, who loveth well
Both man and bird and beast.

He prayeth best, who loveth best
All things both great and small;   615
For the dear God who loveth us,
He made and loveth all.'

The Mariner, whose eye is bright,
Whose beard with age is hoar,
Is gone: and now the Wedding-Guest   620
Turned from the bridegroom's door.

He went like one that hath been stunned,
And is of sense forlorn: *bereft*
A sadder and a wiser man,
He rose the morrow morn.   625

1797–98 1798

Frost at Midnight

The frost performs its secret ministry,
Unhelped by any wind. The owlet's cry
Came loud—and hark, again! loud as before.
The inmates of my cottage, all at rest,
Have left me to that solitude, which suits   5
Abstruser musings: save that at my side
My cradled infant slumbers peacefully.
'Tis calm indeed! so calm, that it disturbs
And vexes meditation with its strange
And extreme silentness. Sea, hill, and wood,   10
This populous village! Sea, and hill, and wood,
With all the numberless goings on of life,
Inaudible as dreams! the thin blue flame
Lies on my low burnt fire, and quivers not;
Only that film, which fluttered on the grate,   15
Still flutters there, the sole unquiet thing.
Methinks, its motion in this hush of nature
Gives it dim sympathies with me who live,
Making it a companionable form,
Whose puny flaps and freaks the idling Spirit   20
By its own moods interprets, every where
Echo or mirror seeking of itself,
And makes a toy of Thought.

                              But O! how oft,
How oft, at school, with most believing mind,
Presageful, have I gazed upon the bars,   25
To watch that fluttering stranger! and as oft
With unclosed lids, already had I dreamt
Of my sweet birth-place, and the old church tower
Whose bells, the poor man's only music, rang
From morn to evening, all the hot Fair-day,   30
So sweetly, that they stirred and haunted me
With a wild pleasure, falling on mine ear
Most like articulate sounds of things to come!
So gazed I, till the soothing things I dreamt
Lulled me to sleep, and sleep prolonged my dreams!   35
And so I brooded all the following morn,
Awed by the stern preceptor's face, mine eye
Fixed with mock study on my swimming book:
Save if the door half opened, and I snatched
A hasty glance, and still my heart leaped up.   40
For still I hoped to see the stranger's face,
Townsman, or aunt, or sister more beloved,
My play-mate when we both were clothed alike!

---

15 film   soot fluttering in the fireplace. Coleridge notes: 'In all parts of the kingdom these films are called *strangers* and supposed to portend the arrival of some absent friend.'
24 school   at Christ's Hospital school in London, where Coleridge went as a boarder at the age of nine

Dear Babe, that sleepest cradled by my side,
Whose gentle breathings, heard in this deep calm,   45
Fill up the interspersed vacancies
And momentary pauses of the thought!
My babe so beautiful! it thrills my heart
With tender gladness, thus to look at thee,
And think that thou shalt learn far other lore   50
And in far other scenes! For I was reared
In the great city, pent 'mid cloisters dim,
And saw nought lovely but the sky and stars.
But thou, my babe! shalt wander like a breeze
By lakes and sandy shores, beneath the crags   55
Of ancient mountain, and beneath the clouds,
Which image in their bulk both lakes and shores
And mountain crags: so shalt thou see and hear
The lovely shapes and sounds intelligible
Of that eternal language, which thy God   60
Utters, who from eternity doth teach
Himself in all, and all things in himself.
Great universal Teacher! he shall mould
Thy spirit, and by giving make it ask.

Therefore all seasons shall be sweet to thee,   65
Whether the summer clothe the general earth
With greenness, or the redbreast sit and sing
Betwixt the tufts of snow on the bare branch
Of mossy apple-tree, while the nigh thatch
Smokes in the sun-thaw; whether the eave-drops fall   70
Heard only in the trances of the blast,
Or if the secret ministry of frost
Shall hang them up in silent icicles,
Quietly shining to the quiet Moon.

1798   1798

Kubla Khan

In Xanadu did Kubla Khan
A stately pleasure-dome decree:
Where Alph, the sacred river, ran
Through caverns measureless to man
    Down to a sunless sea.   5
So twice five miles of fertile ground
With walls and towers were girdled round:

Kubla Khan first emperor of the Mogul dynasty in thirteenth century China. Samuel Purchas writes, in *Purchas His Pilgrimage* (1613): 'In Xamdu did Cublai Can build a stately Palace, encompassing sixteene miles of plaine ground with a wall, wherein are fertile meddowes, pleasant Springs, delightful Streames, and all sorts of beasts of chase and game, and in the middest thereof a sumptuous house of pleasure.' Coleridge states in a note that the whole poem came to him in two or three hundred lines in a 'profound sleep' into which he fell while reading this passage, after taking 'an anodyne' (possibly opium); and that, having written down upon waking 'the lines that are here preserved', he was interrupted by 'a person from Porlock' and forgot the remainder. **Alph** (line 3) recalls Alpheus (Milton's 'Lycidas', line 132, p. 427) and **Mount Abora** (line 41) recalls Mount Amara (*Paradise Lost* IV, 281, p. 436).

And there were gardens bright with sinuous rills
Where blossomed many an incense-bearing tree;
And here were forests ancient as the hills,   10
Enfolding sunny spots of greenery.

But oh! that deep romantic chasm which slanted
Down the green hill athwart a cedarn cover!
A savage place! as holy and enchanted
As e'er beneath a waning moon was haunted   15
By woman wailing for her demon-lover!
And from this chasm, with ceaseless turmoil seething,
As if this earth in fast thick pants were breathing,
A mighty fountain momently was forced:
Amid whose swift half-intermitted burst   20
Huge fragments vaulted like rebounding hail,
Or chaffy grain beneath the thresher's flail:
And mid these dancing rocks at once and ever
It flung up momently the sacred river.
Five miles meandering with a mazy motion   25
Through wood and dale the sacred river ran,
Then reached the caverns measureless to man,
And sank in tumult to a lifeless ocean:
And 'mid this tumult Kubla heard from far
Ancestral voices prophesying war!   30
    The shadow of the dome of pleasure
    Floated midway on the waves;
    Where was heard the mingled measure
    From the fountain and the caves.
It was a miracle of rare device,   35
A sunny pleasure-dome with caves of ice!

    A damsel with a dulcimer
    In a vision once I saw:
    It was an Abyssinian maid,
    And on her dulcimer she played,   40
    Singing of Mount Abora.
    Could I revive within me
    Her symphony and song,
    To such a deep delight 'twould win me,
That with music loud and long,   45
I would build that dome in air,
That sunny dome! those caves of ice!
And all who heard should see them there,
And all should cry, Beware! Beware!
His flashing eyes, his floating hair!   50
Weave a circle round him thrice,
And close your eyes with holy dread,
For he on honey-dew hath fed,
And drunk the milk of Paradise.

1798   1816

---

37 dulcimer   a stringed instrument played with two small hammers

Dejection: An Ode

Late, late yestreen I saw the new Moon,
With the old Moon in her arms;
And I fear, I fear, my Master dear!
We shall have a deadly storm.
BALLAD OF SIR PATRICK SPENCE

I

Well! If the Bard was weather-wise, who made
　　The grand old ballad of Sir Patrick Spence,
　　This night, so tranquil now, will not go hence
Unroused by winds, that ply a busier trade
Than those which mould yon cloud in lazy flakes,　　　　5
Or the dull sobbing draft, that moans and rakes
Upon the strings of this Æolian lute,
　　　　Which better far were mute.
　　For lo! the New-moon winter-bright!
　　And overspread with phantom light,　　　　10
　　(With swimming phantom light o'erspread
　　But rimmed and circled by a silver thread)
I see the old Moon in her lap, foretelling
　　The coming-on of rain and squally blast.
And oh! that even now the gust were swelling,　　　　15
　　And the slant night-shower driving loud and fast!
Those sounds which oft have raised me, whilst they awed,
　　　　And sent my soul abroad,
Might now perhaps their wonted impulse give,
Might startle this dull pain, and make it move and live!　　　　20

II

A grief without a pang, void, dark, and drear,
　　A stifled, drowsy, unimpassioned grief,
　　Which finds no natural outlet, no relief,
　　　　In word, or sigh, or tear—
O Lady! in this wan and heartless mood,　　　　25
To other thoughts by yonder throstle woo'd,
　　All this long eve, so balmy and serene,
Have I been gazing on the western sky,
　　And its peculiar tint of yellow green:
And still I gaze—and with how blank an eye!　　　　30
And those thin clouds above, in flakes and bars,
That give away their motion to the stars;
Those stars, that glide behind them or between,
Now sparkling, now bedimmed, but always seen;

Dejection: An Ode　Coleridge wrote this poem after hearing the first four sections of William Wordsworth's 'Ode: Intimations of Immortality' (see p. 322). An early unpublished version was in the form of a letter to 'Sara' (Sara Hutchinson, whom the poet loved without return). Rewritten as an ode, it was addressed in manuscript to 'William' (Wordsworth) and, in the *Morning Post* in 1802, to 'Edward' (a fiction). 'Lady' became the addressee in the book publication in 1817.
Epigraph　See p. 537 for the remainder of this poem.
7 Æolian lute　a soundbox with strings which was placed by an open window to be played by the wind

Yon crescent Moon, as fixed as if it grew   35
In its own cloudless, starless lake of blue;
I see them all so excellently fair,
I see, not feel, how beautiful they are!

III

    My genial spirits fail;
    And what can these avail   40
To lift the smothering weight from off my breast?
    It were a vain endeavour,
    Though I should gaze forever
On that green light that lingers in the west:
I may not hope from outward forms to win   45
The passion and the life, whose fountains are within.

IV

O Lady! we receive but what we give,
And in our life alone does Nature live:
Ours is her wedding garment, ours her shroud!
    And would we aught behold, of higher worth,   50
Than that inanimate cold world allowed
To the poor loveless ever-anxious crowd,
    Ah! from the soul itself must issue forth
A light, a glory, a fair luminous cloud
      Enveloping the Earth—   55
And from the soul itself must there be sent
    A sweet and potent voice, of its own birth,
Of all sweet sounds the life and element!

V

O pure of heart! thou need'st not ask of me
What this strong music in the soul may be!   60
What, and wherein it doth exist,
This light, this glory, this fair luminous mist,
This beautiful and beauty-making power.
    Joy, virtuous Lady! Joy that ne'er was given,
Save to the pure, and in their purest hour,   65
Life, and Life's effluence, cloud at once and shower,
Joy, Lady! is the spirit and the power,
Which wedding Nature to us gives in dower
    A new Earth and new Heaven,
Undreamt of by the sensual and the proud—   70
Joy is the sweet voice, Joy the luminous cloud—
      We in ourselves rejoice!
And thence flows all that charms or ear or sight,
    All melodies the echoes of that voice,
All colours a suffusion from that light.   75

---

39 **genial**   natural; also cheerful. See Wordsworth's 'Lines', line 113, p. 311.

VI

There was a time when, though my path was rough,
　This joy within me dallied with distress,
And all misfortunes were but as the stuff
　Whence Fancy made me dreams of happiness:
For hope grew round me, like the twining vine,   80
And fruits, and foliage, not my own, seemed mine.
But now afflictions bow me down to earth:
Nor care I that they rob me of my mirth;
　　But oh! each visitation
Suspends what nature gave me at my birth,   85
　My shaping spirit of Imagination.
For not to think of what I needs must feel,
　But to be still and patient, all I can;
And haply by abstruse research to steal
　From my own nature all the natural man—   90
　This was my sole resource, my only plan:
Till that which suits a part infects the whole,
And now is almost grown the habit of my soul.

VII

Hence, viper thoughts, that coil around my mind,
　　Reality's dark dream!   95
I turn from you, and listen to the wind,
　Which long has raved unnoticed. What a scream
Of agony by torture lengthened out
That lute sent forth! Thou Wind, that rav'st without,
　Bare crag, or mountain tairn, or blasted tree,   *pool*   100
Or pine-grove whither woodman never clomb,
Or lonely house, long held the witches' home,
　Methinks were fitter instruments for thee,
Mad Lutanist! who in this month of showers,
Of dark-brown gardens, and of peeping flowers,   105
Makest Devils' yule, with worse than wintry song,
The blossoms, buds, and timorous leaves among.
　Thou Actor, perfect in all tragic sounds!
Thou mighty Poet, e'en to frenzy bold!
　　What tell'st thou now about?   110
　　'Tis of the rushing of an host in rout,
　With groans, of trampled men, with smarting wounds—
At once they groan with pain, and shudder with the cold!
But hush! there is a pause of deepest silence!
　And all that noise, as of a rushing crowd,   115
With groans, and tremulous shudderings—all is over—
　It tells another tale, with sounds less deep and loud!
　　A tale of less affright,
　　And tempered with delight,
As Otway's self had framed the tender lay,—   *song*   120

---

106 Devils' yule devil's Christmas: a midwinter storm out of season

'Tis of a little child
  Upon a lonesome wild,
Not far from home, but she hath lost her way:
And now moans low in bitter grief and fear,
And now screams loud, and hopes to make her mother hear.   125

VIII

'Tis midnight, but small thoughts have I of sleep:
Full seldom may my friend such vigils keep!
Visit her, gentle Sleep! with wings of healing,
  And may this storm be but a mountain-birth,
May all the stars hang bright above her dwelling,   130
  Silent as though they watched the sleeping Earth!
    With light heart may she rise,
    Gay fancy, cheerful eyes,
  Joy lift her spirit, joy attune her voice;
To her may all things live, from pole to pole,   135
Their life the eddying of her living soul!
  O simple spirit, guided from above,
Dear Lady! friend devoutest of my choice,
Thus mayest thou ever, evermore rejoice.

1802   1817

WILLIAM WORDSWORTH

1770–1850 b Cumberland, near the Lake District where he spent much of his life. His poetry became an important source of the nineteenth century's understanding of an interaction between the natural world and human imagination.

Lines

*Composed a few miles above Tintern Abbey, on revisiting the banks
of the Wye during a tour. July 13, 1798.*

Five years have past; five summers, with the length
Of five long winters! and again I hear
These waters, rolling from their mountain-springs
With a soft inland murmur.—Once again
Do I behold these steep and lofty cliffs,   5
That on a wild secluded scene impress
Thoughts of more deep seclusion; and connect
The landscape with the quiet of the sky.
The day is come when I again repose
Here, under this dark sycamore, and view   10
These plots of cottage-ground, these orchard-tufts,
Which at this season, with their unripe fruits,

Tintern Abbey a ruined medieval abbey in the Wye valley, south Wales. Although not referred to in the poem itself, 'Tintern Abbey' has become the accepted short title. **tour** private walking holiday

Are clad in one green hue, and lose themselves
'Mid groves and copses. Once again I see
These hedge-rows, hardly hedge-rows, little lines   15
Of sportive wood run wild: these pastoral farms,
Green to the very door; and wreaths of smoke
Sent up, in silence, from among the trees!
With some uncertain notice, as might seem
Of vagrant dwellers in the houseless woods,   20
Or of some Hermit's cave, where by his fire
The Hermit sits alone.

           These beauteous forms,
Through a long absence, have not been to me
As is a landscape to a blind man's eye:
But oft, in lonely rooms, and 'mid the din   25
Of towns and cities, I have owed to them
In hours of weariness, sensations sweet,
Felt in the blood, and felt along the heart;
And passing even into my purer mind,
With tranquil restoration:—feelings too   30
Of unremembered pleasure: such, perhaps,
As have no slight or trivial influence
On that best portion of a good man's life,
His little, nameless, unremembered, acts
Of kindness and of love. Nor less, I trust,   35
To them I may have owed another gift,
Of aspect more sublime; that blessed mood,
In which the burthen of the mystery,
In which the heavy and the weary weight
Of all this unintelligible world,   40
Is lightened:—that serene and blessed mood,
In which the affections gently lead us on,—
Until, the breath of this corporeal frame
And even the motion of our human blood
Almost suspended, we are laid asleep   45
In body, and become a living soul:
While with an eye made quiet by the power
Of harmony, and the deep power of joy,
We see into the life of things.

                If this
Be but a vain belief, yet, oh! how oft—   50
In darkness and amid the many shapes
Of joyless daylight; when the fretful stir
Unprofitable, and the fever of the world,
Have hung upon the beatings of my heart—
How oft, in spirit, have I turned to thee,   55
O sylvan Wye! thou wanderer thro' the woods,
How often has my spirit turned to thee!

  And now, with gleams of half-extinguished thought,
With many recognitions dim and faint,
And somewhat of a sad perplexity,   60

The picture of the mind revives again:
While here I stand, not only with the sense
Of present pleasure, but with pleasing thoughts
That in this moment there is life and food
For future years. And so I dare to hope,   65
Though changed, no doubt, from what I was when first
I came among these hills; when like a roe
I bounded o'er the mountains, by the sides
Of the deep rivers, and the lonely streams,
Wherever nature led: more like a man   70
Flying from something that he dreads, than one
Who sought the thing he loved. For nature then
(The coarser pleasures of my boyish days,
And their glad animal movements all gone by)
To me was all in all.—I cannot paint   75
What then I was. The sounding cataract
Haunted me like a passion: the tall rock,
The mountain, and the deep and gloomy wood,
Their colours and their forms, were then to me
An appetite; a feeling and a love,   80
That had no need of a remoter charm,
By thought supplied, nor any interest
Unborrowed from the eye.—That time is past,
And all its aching joys are now no more,
And all its dizzy raptures. Not for this   85
Faint I, nor mourn nor murmur; other gifts
Have followed; for such loss, I would believe,
Abundant recompence. For I have learned
To look on nature, not as in the hour
Of thoughtless youth; but hearing oftentimes   90
The still, sad music of humanity,
Nor harsh nor grating, though of ample power
To chasten and subdue. And I have felt
A presence that disturbs me with the joy
Of elevated thoughts; a sense sublime   95
Of something far more deeply interfused,
Whose dwelling is the light of setting suns,
And the round ocean and the living air,
And the blue sky, and in the mind of man:
A motion and a spirit, that impels   100
All thinking things, all objects of all thought,
And rolls through all things. Therefore am I still
A lover of the meadows and the woods,
And mountains; and of all that we behold
From this green earth; of all the mighty world   105
Of eye, and ear,—both what they half create,
And what perceive; well pleased to recognise

66ff Wordsworth had first visited the Wye valley in 1793, and the experience had started a slow
process of regeneration of spirit. Still a very young man, he had been beset by isolation, poverty, an
uncertain future and disillusionment with the French revolution upon returning to England after
residing in revolutionary France, 1791–92.

73–74 A reference to a yet earlier time, his boyhood in the Lake District in north-west England

In nature and the language of the sense,
The anchor of my purest thoughts, the nurse,
The guide, the guardian of my heart, and soul   110
Of all my moral being.
                            Nor perchance,
If I were not thus taught, should I the more
Suffer my genial spirits to decay:
For thou art with me here upon the banks
Of this fair river; thou my dearest Friend,   115
My dear, dear Friend; and in thy voice I catch
The language of my former heart, and read
My former pleasures in the shooting lights
Of thy wild eyes. Oh! yet a little while
May I behold in thee what I was once,   120
My dear, dear Sister! and this prayer I make,
Knowing that Nature never did betray
The heart that loved her; 'tis her privilege,
Through all the years of this our life, to lead
From joy to joy: for she can so inform   125
The mind that is within us, so impress
With quietness and beauty, and so feed
With lofty thoughts, that neither evil tongues,
Rash judgments, nor the sneers of selfish men,
Nor greetings where no kindness is, nor all   130
The dreary intercourse of daily life,
Shall e'er prevail against us, or disturb
Our cheerful faith, that all which we behold
Is full of blessings. Therefore let the moon
Shine on thee in thy solitary walk;   135
And let the misty mountain-winds be free
To blow against thee: and, in after years,
When these wild ecstasies shall be matured
Into a sober pleasure; when thy mind
Shall be a mansion for all lovely forms,   140
Thy memory be as a dwelling-place
For all sweet sounds and harmonies; oh! then,
If solitude, or fear, or pain, or grief,
Should be thy portion, with what healing thoughts
Of tender joy wilt thou remember me,   145
And these my exhortations! Nor, perchance—
If I should be where I no more can hear
Thy voice, nor catch from thy wild eyes these gleams
Of past existence—wilt thou then forget
That on the banks of this delightful stream   150
We stood together; and that I, so long
A worshipper of Nature, hither came
Unwearied in that service: rather say
With warmer love—oh! with far deeper zeal

---

113 genial   natural; also cheerful
121 Sister   Dorothy Wordsworth (1771–1855), the author of *Journals* published after her death; close to William throughout their lives.

Of holier love. Nor wilt thou then forget,   155
That after many wanderings, many years
Of absence, these steep woods and lofty cliffs,
And this green pastoral landscape, were to me
More dear, both for themselves and for thy sake!

                                                          1798   1798

There Was a Boy

There was a Boy; ye knew him well, ye cliffs
And islands of Winander!—many a time,
At evening, when the earliest stars began
To move along the edges of the hills,
Rising or setting, would he stand alone,   5
Beneath the trees, or by the glimmering lake;
And there, with fingers interwoven, both hands
Pressed closely palm to palm and to his mouth
Uplifted, he, as through an instrument,
Blew mimic hootings to the silent owls,   10
That they might answer him.—And they would shout
Across the watery vale, and shout again,
Responsive to his call,—with quivering peals,
And long halloos, and screams, and echoes loud
Redoubled and redoubled; concourse wild   15
Of jocund din! And, when there came a pause
Of silence such as baffled his best skill:
Then, sometimes, in that silence, while he hung
Listening, a gentle shock of mild surprise
Has carried far into his heart the voice   20
Of mountain-torrents; or the visible scene
Would enter unawares into his mind
With all its solemn imagery, its rocks,
Its woods, and that uncertain heaven received
Into the bosom of the steady lake.   25
   This boy was taken from his mates, and died
In childhood, ere he was full twelve years old.
Pre-eminent in beauty is the vale
Where he was born and bred: the churchyard hangs
Upon a slope above the village-school;   30
And, through that churchyard when my way has led
On summer-evenings, I believe, that there
A long half-hour together I have stood
Mute—looking at the grave in which he lies!

                                                          1798   1800

Boy   In an early draft of the poem, the boy is Wordsworth himself.
2 **Winander**   a name for Lake Windermere, in the Lake District

From The Prelude

or, Growth of a Poet's Mind
An Autobiographical Poem

From *Book First*

Fair seed-time had my soul, and I grew up
Fostered alike by beauty and by fear:
Much favoured in my birth-place, and no less
In that beloved Vale to which erelong
We were transplanted—there were we let loose   305
For sports of wider range. Ere I had told
Ten birth-days, when among the mountain slopes
Frost, and the breath of frosty wind, had snapped
The last autumnal crocus, 'twas my joy
With store of springes o'er my shoulder hung   *snares*   310
To range the open heights where woodcocks ran
Along the smooth green turf. Through half the night,
Scudding away from snare to snare, I plied
That anxious visitation;—moon and stars
Were shining o'er my head. I was alone,   315
And seemed to be a trouble to the peace
That dwelt among them. Sometimes it befel
In these night wanderings, that a strong desire
O'erpowered my better reason, and the bird
Which was the captive of another's toil   320
Became my prey; and when the deed was done
I heard among the solitary hills
Low breathings coming after me, and sounds
Of undistinguishable motion, steps
Almost as silent as the turf they trod.   325

Nor less when spring had warmed the cultured Vale,
Roved we as plunderers where the mother-bird
Had in high places built her lodge; though mean
Our object and inglorious, yet the end
Was not ignoble. Oh! when I have hung   330
Above the raven's nest, by knots of grass
And half-inch fissures in the slippery rock
But ill-sustained, and almost (so it seemed)
Suspended by the blast that blew amain,
Shouldering the naked crag, oh, at that time   335
While on the perilous ridge I hung alone,
With what strange utterance did the loud dry wind
Blow through my ear! the sky seemed not a sky
Of earth—and with what motion moved the clouds!

The Prelude   a poem of book length which covers the period from Wordsworth's infancy to his early
twenties. The extract here is from the version published in 1850.
304 Vale   the valley of Esthwaite in the Lake District of north-west England. Wordsworth was born
not far away at Cockermouth.

Dust as we are, the immortal spirit grows   340
Like harmony in music; there is a dark
Inscrutable workmanship that reconciles
Discordant elements, makes them cling together
In one society. How strange that all
The terrors, pains, and early miseries,   345
Regrets, vexations, lassitudes interfused
Within my mind, should e'er have borne a part,
And that a needful part, in making up
The calm existence that is mine when I
Am worthy of myself! Praise to the end!   350
Thanks to the means which Nature deigned to employ;
Whether her fearless visitings, or those
That came with soft alarm, like hurtless light
Opening the peaceful clouds; or she may use
Severer interventions, ministry   355
More palpable, as best might suit her aim.

One summer evening (led by her) I found
A little boat tied to a willow tree
Within a rocky cave, its usual home.
Straight I unloosed her chain, and stepping in   360
Pushed from the shore. It was an act of stealth
And troubled pleasure, nor without the voice
Of mountain-echoes did my boat move on;
Leaving behind her still, on either side,
Small circles glittering idly in the moon,   365
Until they melted all into one track
Of sparkling light. But now, like one who rows,
Proud of his skill, to reach a chosen point
With an unswerving line, I fixed my view
Upon the summit of a craggy ridge,   370
The horizon's utmost boundary; for above
Was nothing but the stars and the grey sky.
She was an elfin pinnace; lustily   *small boat*
I dipped my oars into the silent lake,
And, as I rose upon the stroke, my boat   375
Went heaving through the water like a swan;
When, from behind that craggy steep till then
The horizon's bound, a huge peak, black and huge,
As if with voluntary power instinct
Upreared its head. I struck and struck again,   380
And growing still in stature the grim shape
Towered up between me and the stars, and still,
For so it seemed, with purpose of its own
And measured motion like a living thing,
Strode after me. With trembling oars I turned,   385
And through the silent water stole my way
Back to the covert of the willow tree;
There in her mooring-place I left my bark,—
And through the meadows homeward went, in grave
And serious mood; but after I had seen   390

That spectacle, for many days, my brain
Worked with a dim and undetermined sense
Of unknown modes of being; o'er my thoughts
There hung a darkness, call it solitude
Or blank desertion. No familiar shapes   395
Remained, no pleasant images of trees,
Of sea or sky, no colours of green fields;
But huge and mighty forms, that do not live
Like living men, moved slowly through the mind
By day, and were a trouble to my dreams.   400

    Wisdom and Spirit of the universe!
Thou Soul that art the eternity of thought,
That givest to forms and images a breath
And everlasting motion, not in vain
By day or star-light thus from my first dawn   405
Of childhood didst thou intertwine for me
The passions that build up our human soul;
Not with the mean and vulgar works of man,
But with high objects, with enduring things—
With life and nature, purifying thus   410
The elements of feeling and of thought,
And sanctifying, by such discipline,
Both pain and fear, until we recognise
A grandeur in the beatings of the heart.
Nor was this fellowship vouchsafed to me   415
With stinted kindness. In November days,
When vapours rolling down the valley made
A lonely scene more lonesome, among woods
At noon, and 'mid the calm of summer nights,
When, by the margin of the trembling lake,   420
Beneath the gloomy hills homeward I went
In solitude, such intercourse was mine;
Mine was it in the fields both day and night,
And by the waters, all the summer long.

    And in the frosty season, when the sun   425
Was set, and visible for many a mile
The cottage windows blazed through twilight gloom,
I heeded not their summons: happy time
It was indeed for all of us—for me
It was a time of rapture! Clear and loud   430
The village clock tolled six,—I wheeled about,
Proud and exulting like an untired horse
That cares not for his home. All shod with steel,
We hissed along the polished ice in games
Confederate, imitative of the chase   435
And woodland pleasures,—the resounding horn,
The pack loud chiming, and the hunted hare.
So through the darkness and the cold we flew,
And not a voice was idle; with the din

Smitten, the precipices rang aloud;   440
The leafless trees and every icy crag
Tinkled like iron; while far distant hills
Into the tumult sent an alien sound
Of melancholy not unnoticed, while the stars
Eastward were sparkling clear, and in the west   445
The orange sky of evening died away.
Not seldom from the uproar I retired
Into a silent bay, or sportively
Glanced sideway, leaving the tumultuous throng,
To cut across the reflex of a star   450
That fled, and, flying still before me, gleamed
Upon the glassy plain; and oftentimes,
When we had given our bodies to the wind,
And all the shadowy banks on either side
Came sweeping through the darkness, spinning still   455
The rapid line of motion, then at once
Have I, reclining back upon my heels,
Stopped short; yet still the solitary cliffs
Wheeled by me—even as if the earth had rolled
With visible motion her diurnal round!   *daily* 460
Behind me did they stretch in solemn train,
Feebler and feebler, and I stood and watched
Till all was tranquil as a dreamless sleep.

                                                      1798–1800   1850

[Three years she grew in sun and shower]

Three years she grew in sun and shower,
Then Nature said, 'A lovelier flower
On earth was never sown;
This Child I to myself will take;
She shall be mine, and I will make   5
A Lady of my own.

'Myself will to my darling be
Both law and impulse: and with me
The Girl, in rock and plain,
In earth and heaven, in glade and bower,   10
Shall feel an overseeing power
To kindle or restrain.

'She shall be sportive as the fawn
That wild with glee across the lawn
Or up the mountain springs;   15
And hers shall be the breathing balm,
And hers the silence and the calm
Of mute insensate things.

'The floating clouds their state shall lend
To her; for her the willow bend;   20
Nor shall she fail to see
Even in the motions of the Storm
Grace that shall mould the Maiden's form
By silent sympathy.

'The stars of midnight shall be dear   25
To her; and she shall lean her ear
In many a secret place
Where rivulets dance their wayward round,
And beauty born of murmuring sound
Shall pass into her face.   30

'And vital feelings of delight
Shall rear her form to stately height,
Her virgin bosom swell;
Such thoughts to Lucy I will give
While she and I together live   35
Here in this happy dell.'

Thus Nature spake—The work was done—
How soon my Lucy's race was run!
She died, and left to me
This heath, this calm, and quiet scene;   40
The memory of what has been,
And never more will be.

                          1799   1800

[A slumber did my spirit seal]

A slumber did my spirit seal;
   I had no human fears:
She seemed a thing that could not feel
   The touch of earthly years.

No motion has she now, no force;   5
   She neither hears nor sees;
Rolled round in earth's diurnal course,   *daily*
   With rocks, and stones, and trees.

                          1799   1800

Resolution and Independence

          I
There was a roaring in the wind all night;
The rain came heavily and fell in floods;
But now the sun is rising calm and bright;
The birds are singing in the distant woods;
Over his own sweet voice the Stock-dove broods;   5
The Jay makes answer as the Magpie chatters;
And all the air is filled with pleasant noise of waters.
          II
All things that love the sun are out of doors;
The sky rejoices in the morning's birth;
The grass is bright with rain-drops;—on the moors   10
The hare is running races in her mirth;
And with her feet she from the plashy earth

---

38 **Lucy** unidentified; as also 'she' in the following poem, with which this one is clearly to be linked.
There may be no specific reference.

Raises a mist; that, glittering in the sun,
Runs with her all the way, wherever she doth run.
III
I was a Traveller then upon the moor;   15
I saw the hare that raced about with joy;
I heard the woods and distant waters roar;
Or heard them not, as happy as a boy:
The pleasant season did my heart employ:
My old remembrances went from me wholly;   20
And all the ways of men, so vain and melancholy.
IV
But, as it sometimes chanceth, from the might
Of joy in minds that can no further go,
As high as we have mounted in delight
In our dejection do we sink as low;   25
To me that morning did it happen so;
And fears and fancies thick upon me came;
Dim sadness—and blind thoughts, I knew not, nor could name.
V
I heard the sky-lark warbling in the sky;
And I bethought me of the playful hare: 30
Even such a happy Child of earth am I;
Even as these blissful creatures do I fare;
Far from the world I walk, and from all care;
But there may come another day to me—
Solitude, pain of heart, distress, and poverty.   35
VI
My whole life I have lived in pleasant thought,
As if life's business were a summer mood;
As if all needful things would come unsought
To genial faith, still rich in genial good;
But how can He expect that others should   40
Build for him, sow for him, and at his call
Love him, who for himself will take no heed at all?
VII
I thought of Chatterton, the marvellous Boy,
The sleepless Soul that perished in his pride;
Of Him who walked in glory and in joy   45
Following his plough, along the mountain-side:
By our own spirits are we deified:
We Poets in our youth begin in gladness;
But thereof come in the end despondency and madness.
VIII
Now, whether it were by peculiar grace,   50
A leading from above, a something given,
Yet it befell that, in this lonely place,

---

39 genial   natural; also cheerful
43 Chatterton   Thomas Chatterton (1752–70), a promising poet who killed himself at seventeen.
45 Him   Robert Burns (1759–96), who left his farm (where, however, he had been poor and over-worked) for an often dissipated life as a poet

When I with these untoward thoughts had striven,
Beside a pool bare to the eye of heaven
I saw a Man before me unawares: 55
The oldest man he seemed that ever wore grey hairs.
                    IX
As a huge stone is sometimes seen to lie
Couched on the bald top of an eminence;
Wonder to all who do the same espy,
By what means it could thither come, and whence;   60
So that it seems a thing endued with sense:
Like a sea-beast crawled forth, that on a shelf
Of rock or sand reposeth, there to sun itself;
                    X
Such seemed this Man, not all alive nor dead,
Nor all asleep—in his extreme old age: 65
His body was bent double, feet and head
Coming together in life's pilgrimage;
As if some dire constraint of pain, or rage
Of sickness felt by him in times long past,
A more than human weight upon his frame had cast.   70
                    XI
Himself he propped, limbs, body, and pale face,
Upon a long grey staff of shaven wood:
And, still as I drew near with gentle pace,
Upon the margin of that moorish flood   *boggy*
Motionless as a cloud the old Man stood,   75
That heareth not the loud winds when they call;
And moveth all together, if it move at all.
                    XII
At length, himself unsettling, he the pond
Stirred with his staff, and fixedly did look
Upon the muddy water, which he conned,   *studied* 80
As if he had been reading in a book:
And now a stranger's privilege I took;
And, drawing to his side, to him did say,
'This morning gives us promise of a glorious day.'
                    XIII
A gentle answer did the old Man make,   85
In courteous speech which forth he slowly drew:
And him with further words I thus bespake,
'What occupation do you there pursue?
This is a lonesome place for one like you.'
Ere he replied, a flash of mild surprise   90
Broke from the sable orbs of his yet-vivid eyes.
                    XIV
His words came feebly, from a feeble chest,
But each in solemn order followed each,
With something of a lofty utterance drest—
Choice word and measured phrase, above the reach   95
Of ordinary men; a stately speech;
Such as grave Livers do in Scotland use,
Religious men, who give to God and man their dues.

XV

He told, that to these waters he had come
To gather leeches, being old and poor: 100
Employment hazardous and wearisome!
And he had many hardships to endure:
From pond to pond he roamed, from moor to moor;
Housing, with God's good help, by choice or chance;
And in this way he gained an honest maintenance.   105

XVI

The old Man still stood talking by my side;
But now his voice to me was like a stream
Scarce heard; nor word from word could I divide;
And the whole body of the Man did seem
Like one whom I had met with in a dream;   110
Or like a man from some far region sent,
To give me human strength, by apt admonishment.

XVII

My former thoughts returned: the fear that kills;
And hope that is unwilling to be fed;
Cold, pain, and labour, and all fleshly ills;   115
And mighty Poets in their misery dead.
—Perplexed, and longing to be comforted,
My question eagerly did I renew,
'How is it that you live, and what is it you do?'

XVIII

He with a smile did then his words repeat;   120
And said that, gathering leeches, far and wide
He travelled; stirring thus about his feet
The waters of the pools where they abide.
'Once I could meet with them on every side;
But they have dwindled long by slow decay;   125
Yet still I persevere, and find them where I may.'

XIX

While he was talking thus, the lonely place,
The old Man's shape, and speech—all troubled me:
In my mind's eye I seemed to see him pace
About the weary moors continually,   130
Wandering about alone and silently.
While I these thoughts within myself pursued,
He, having made a pause, the same discourse renewed.

XX

And soon with this he other matter blended,
Cheerfully uttered, with demeanour kind,   135
But stately in the main; and when he ended,
I could have laughed myself to scorn to find
In that decrepit Man so firm a mind.
'God,' said I, 'be my help and stay secure;
I'll think of the Leech-gatherer on the lonely moor!'   140

                                                          1802 1807

---

100 leeches   i.e. for use by physicians in drawing blood

Composed upon Westminster Bridge, September 3, 1802

Earth has not anything to show more fair:
Dull would he be of soul who could pass by
A sight so touching in its majesty:
This City now doth, like a garment, wear
The beauty of the morning; silent, bare,   5
Ships, towers, domes, theatres, and temples lie
Open unto the fields, and to the sky;
All bright and glittering in the smokeless air.
Never did sun more beautifully steep
In his first splendour, valley, rock, or hill;   10
Ne'er saw I, never felt, a calm so deep!
The river glideth at his own sweet will:
Dear God! the very houses seem asleep;
And all that mighty heart is lying still!

1802   1807

The Solitary Reaper

Behold her, single in the field,
Yon solitary Highland Lass!
Reaping and singing by herself;
Stop here, or gently pass!
Alone she cuts and binds the grain,   5
And sings a melancholy strain;
O listen! for the Vale profound
Is overflowing with the sound.

No Nightingale did ever chaunt
More welcome notes to weary bands   10
Of travellers in some shady haunt,
Among Arabian sands:
A voice so thrilling ne'er was heard
In spring-time from the Cuckoo-bird,
Breaking the silence of the seas   15
Among the farthest Hebrides.

Will no one tell me what she sings?—
Perhaps the plaintive numbers flow
For old, unhappy, far-off things,
And battles long ago: 20
Or is it some more humble lay,   *song*
Familiar matter of to-day?
Some natural sorrow, loss, or pain,
That has been, and may be again?

Whate'er the theme, the Maiden sang   25
As if her song could have no ending;
I saw her singing at her work,
And o'er the sickle bending:—
I listened, motionless and still;
And, as I mounted up the hill,   30
The music in my heart I bore,
Long after it was heard no more.

1805   1807

Ode

Intimations of Immortality from Recollections of Early Childhood

> *The Child is Father of the Man;*
> *And I could wish my days to be*
> *Bound each to each by natural piety.*

I

There was a time when meadow, grove, and stream,
The earth, and every common site,
    To me did seem
    Apparelled in celestial light,
The glory and the freshness of a dream.   5
It is not now as it hath been of yore;—
    Turn wheresoe'er I may,
      By night or day,
The things which I have seen I now can see no more.

II

    The Rainbow comes and goes,   10
    And lovely is the Rose;
    The Moon doth with delight
Look round her when the heavens are bare;
    Waters on a starry night
    Are beautiful and fair;   15
  The sunshine is a glorious birth;
  But yet I know, where'er I go,
That there hath past away a glory from the earth.

III

Now, while the birds thus sing a joyous song,
  And while the young lambs bound   20
    As to the tabor's sound,
To me alone there came a thought of grief:
A timely utterance gave that thought relief,
    And I again am strong:
The cataracts blow their trumpets from the steep;   25
No more shall grief of mine the season wrong;
I hear the Echoes through the mountains throng,
The Winds come to me from the fields of sleep,
    And all the earth is gay;
      Land and sea   30
  Give themselves up to jollity,
    And with the heart of May
Doth every Beast keep holiday;—
    Thou Child of Joy,
Shout round me, let me hear thy shouts, thou happy Shepherd-boy!   35

Ode The first four sections of this poem were written in 1802, and the remainder in 1804.
Epigraph from Wordsworth's poem 'My Heart Leaps Up' (1807)

IV

Ye blessèd Creatures, I have heard the call
  Ye to each other make; I see
The heavens laugh with you in your jubilee;
  My heart is at your festival,
    My head hath its coronal,   *garland of flowers*   40
The fulness of your bliss, I feel—I feel it all.
    Oh evil day! if I were sullen
    While Earth herself is adorning,
      This sweet May-morning,
    And the Children are culling   45
      On every side,
  In a thousand valleys far and wide,
  Fresh flowers; while the sun shines warm,
And the Babe leaps up on his Mother's arm:—
  I hear, I hear, with joy I hear!   50
  —But there's a Tree, of many, one,
A single Field which I have looked upon,
Both of them speak of something that is gone:
  The Pansy at my feet
  Doth the same tale repeat: 55
Whither is fled the visionary gleam?
Where is it now, the glory and the dream?

V

Our birth is but a sleep and a forgetting:
The Soul that rises with us, our life's Star,
  Hath had elsewhere its setting,   60
    And cometh from afar:
  Not in entire forgetfulness,
  And not in utter nakedness,
But trailing clouds of glory do we come
  From God, who is our home: 65
Heaven lies about us in our infancy!
Shades of the prison-house begin to close
  Upon the growing Boy,
But he beholds the light, and whence it flows,
  He sees it in his joy;   70
The Youth, who daily farther from the east
  Must travel, still is Nature's Priest,
    And by the vision splendid
    Is on his way attended;
At length the Man perceives it die away,   75
And fade into the light of common day.

VI

Earth fills her lap with pleasures of her own;
Yearnings she hath in her own natural kind,
And, even with something of a Mother's mind,
  And no unworthy aim,   80
  The homely Nurse doth all she can
To make her Foster-child, her Inmate Man,

Forget the glories he hath known,
And that imperial palace whence he came.

VII

Behold the Child among his new-born blisses,   85
A six years' Darling of a pigmy size!
See, where 'mid work of his own hand he lies,
Fretted by sallies of his mother's kisses,
With light upon him from his father's eyes!
See, at his feet, some little plan or chart,   90
Some fragment from his dream of human life,
Shaped by himself with newly-learned art;
    A wedding or a festival,
    A mourning or a funeral;
      And this hath now his heart,   95
    And unto this he frames his song:
      Then will he fit his tongue
To dialogues of business, love, or strife;
    But it will not be long
    Ere this be thrown aside,   100
    And with new joy and pride
The little Actor cons another part;
Filling from time to time his 'humorous stage'
With all the Persons, down to palsied Age,
That Life brings with her in her equipage;   105
    As if his whole vocation
    Were endless imitation.

VIII

Thou, whose exterior semblance doth belie
    Thy Soul's immensity;
Thou best Philosopher, who yet dost keep   110
Thy heritage, thou Eye among the blind,
That, deaf and silent, read'st the eternal deep,
Haunted for ever by the eternal mind,—
    Might Prophet! Seer blest!
    On whom those truths do rest,   115
Which we are toiling all our lives to find,
In darkness lost, the darkness of the grave;
Thou, over whom thy Immortality
Broods like the Day, a Master o'er a Slave,
A Presence which is not to be put by;   120
Thou little Child, yet glorious in the might
Of heaven-born freedom on thy being's height,
Why with such earnest pains dost thou provoke
The years to bring the inevitable yoke,
Thus blindly with thy blessedness at strife?   125

---

103 humorous stage as in some Elizabethan drama, where characters represent 'humours' (i.e. temperaments); quoted from a dedicatory sonnet by Samuel Daniel for *Musophilus* (1599)

Full soon thy Soul shall have her earthly freight,
And custom lie upon thee with a weight,
Heavy as frost, and deep almost as life!

IX

    O Joy! that in our embers
    Is something that doth live,   130
    That nature yet remembers
    What was so fugitive!
The thought of our past years in me doth breed
Perpetual benediction: not indeed
For that which is most worthy to be blest;   135
Delight and liberty, the simple creed
Of Childhood, whether busy or at rest,
With new-fledged hope still fluttering in his breast:—
    Not for these I raise
    The song of thanks and praise;   140
  But for those obstinate questionings
  Of sense and outward things,
  Fallings from us, vanishings;
  Blank misgivings of a Creature
Moving about in worlds not realized,   145
High instincts before which our mortal Nature
Did tremble like a guilty Thing surprised:
    But for those first affections,
    Those shadowy recollections,
  Which, be they what they may,   150
Are yet the fountain light of all our day,
Are yet a master light of all our seeing;
  Uphold us, cherish, and have power to make
Our noisy years seem moments in the being
Of the eternal Silence: truths that wake,   155
    To perish never;
Which neither listlessness, nor mad endeavour,
    Nor Man nor Boy,
Nor all that is at enmity with joy,
Can utterly abolish or destroy!   160
  Hence in a season of calm weather
    Though inland far we be,
Our Souls have sight of that immortal sea
    Which brought us hither,
    Can in a moment travel thither,   165
And see the Children sport upon the shore,
And hear the mighty waters rolling evermore.

X

Then sing, ye Birds, sing, sing a joyous song!
    And let the young Lambs bound
    As to the tabor's sound!   170
We in thought will join your throng,
    Ye that pipe and ye that play,
    Ye that through your hearts to-day

Feel the gladness of the May!
What though the radiance which was once so bright   175
Be now for ever taken from my sight,
  Though nothing can bring back the hour
Of splendour in the grass, of glory in the flower;
    We will grieve not, rather find
    Strength in what remains behind;   180
    In the primal sympathy
    Which having been must ever be;
    In the soothing thoughts that spring
    Out of human suffering;
    In the faith that looks through death,   185
In years that bring the philosophic mind.

XI

And O, ye Fountains, Meadows, Hills, and Groves,
Forebode not any severing of our loves!
Yet in my heart of hearts I feel your might;
I only have relinquished one delight   190
To live beneath your more habitual sway.
I love the Brooks which down their channels fret,
Even more than when I tripped lightly as they;
The innocent brightness of a new-born Day
    Is lovely yet;   195
The Clouds that gather round the setting sun
Do take a sober colouring from an eye
That hath kept watch o'er man's mortality;
Another race hath been, and other palms are won.
Thanks to the human heart by which we live,   200
Thanks to its tenderness, its joys, and fears,
To me the meanest flower that blows can give
Thoughts that do often lie too deep for tears.

                            1802–04   1807

[Surprised by joy—impatient as the Wind]

Surprised by joy—impatient as the Wind
I turned to share the transport—Oh! with whom   *ecstasy*
But Thee, deep buried in the silent tomb,
That spot which no vicissitude can find?
Love, faithful love, recalled thee to my mind—   5
But how could I forget thee? Through what power,
Even for the least division of an hour,
Have I been so beguiled as to be blind
To my most grievous loss!—That thought's return
Was the worst pang that sorrow ever bore,   10
Save one, one only, when I stood forlorn,
Knowing my heart's best treasure was no more;
That neither present time, nor years unborn
Could to my sight that heavenly face restore.

                                 1815

---

3 Thee   Wordsworth's second daughter, Catherine (1808–12)

ROBERT BURNS

1759–96 b Ayrshire. He was a tenant farmer until the success of his first book of poems (1786) brought an appointment as a customs officer in Dumfries. He was a pioneer collector of folk songs.

To a Mouse,

On turning her up in her Nest, with the Plough, November, 1785

Wee, sleeket, cowran, tim'rous *beastie*,	*sleek, cowering*
O, what a panic's in thy breastie!	
Thou need na start awa sae hasty,	
Wi' bickering brattle!	*hurrying scamper*
I wad be laith to rin an' chase thee,	5
Wi' murd'ring *pattle*!	*paddle*
I'm truly sorry Man's dominion	
Has broken Nature's social union,	
An' justifies that ill opinion,	
Which makes thee startle,	10
At me, thy poor, earth-born companion,	
An' *fellow-mortal*!	
I doubt na, whyles, but thou may *thieve*:	*sometimes*
What then? poor beastie, thou maun live!	*must*
A *daimen-icker* in a *thrave*	15
'S a sma' request:	
I'll get a blessin wi' the lave,	*remainder*
An' never miss't!	
Thy wee-bit *housie*, too, in ruin!	
Its silly wa's the win's are strewin!	*frail walls* 20
An' naething, now, to big a new ane,	*build*
O' foggage green!	*moss*
An' bleak *December's winds* ensuin,	
Baith snell an' keen!	
Thou saw the fields laid bare an' wast,	25
An' weary *Winter* comin fast,	
An' cozie here, beneath the blast,	
Thou thought to dwell,	
Till crash! the cruel *coulter* past	
Out thro' thy cell.	30
That wee-bit heap o' leaves an' stibble,	
Has cost thee monie a weary nibble!	
Now thou's turn'd out, for a' thy trouble,	
But house or hald,	
To thole the Winter's *sleety dribble*,	*endure* 35
An' *cranreuch* cauld!	*hoarfrost*

---

15 daimen random **icker** ear of corn **thrave** a measure of two stooks of corn
29 coulter advance blade attached to a plough.
34 But without

But Mousie, thou art no thy-lane,   *not alone*
In proving *foresight* may be vain:
The best laid schemes o' *Mice* an' *Men,*
      Gang aft agley,   *go often astray*   40
An' lea'e us nought but grief an' pain,
      For promis'd joy!

Still, thou art blest, compar'd wi' *me!*
The *present* only toucheth thee:
But Och! I *backward* cast my e'e,   45
      On prospects drear!
An' *forward,* tho' I canna *see,*
      I *guess* an' *fear!*

                             1786

Song—For a' that and a' that

Is there, for honest Poverty
    That hings his head, and a' that;
The coward-slave, we pass him by,
    We dare be poor for a' that!
  For a' that, and a' that,   5
    Our toils obscure, and a' that,
  The rank is but the guinea's stamp,
    The Man's the gowd for a' that.—   *gold*

What though on hamely fare we dine,
    Wear hoddin grey, and a' that.   *undyed wool*   10
Gie fools their silks, and knaves their wine,
    A Man's a Man for a' that.
  For a' that, and a' that,
    Their tinsel show, and a' that;
  The honest man, though e'er sae poor,   15
    Is king o' men for a' that.—

Ye see yon birkie ca'd a lord,   *brisk young man*
    Wha struts, and stares, and a' that,
Though hundreds worship at his word,
    He's but a coof for a' that.   *fool*   20
  For a' that, and a' that,
    His ribband, star and a' that,
  The man of independant mind,
    He looks and laughs at a' that.—

A prince can mak a belted knight,   25
    A marquis, duke, and a' that;
But an honest man's aboon his might,
    Gude faith he mauna fa' that!   *above*
  For a' that, and a' that,   *must not*
    Their dignities, and a' that,   30
  The pith o' Sense, and pride o' Worth,
    Are higher rank than a' that.—

Then let us pray that come it may,
    As come it will for a' that,
That Sense and Worth, o'er a' the earth   35
    Shall bear the gree, and a' that.   *victory*

For a' that, and a' that,
  Its comin yet for a' that,
That Man to Man the warld o'er,
  Shall brothers be for a' that.—

?1794   1805

A red red Rose

O my Luve's like a red, red rose,
  That's newly sprung in June;
O my Luve's like the melodie
  That's sweetly play'd in tune.

As fair art thou, my bonie lass,   5
  So deep in luve am I;
And I will love thee still, my Dear,
  Till a' the seas gang dry.   *go*

Till a' the seas gang dry, my Dear,
  And the rocks melt wi' the sun: 10
I will love thee still, my Dear,
  While the sands o' life shall run.

And fare thee weel, my only Luve!
  And fare thee weel, a while!
And I will come again, my Luve,   15
  Tho' it were ten thousand mile!

1796

WILLIAM BLAKE

1757–1828 b and lived in London, working in poverty as an illustrator and engraver; he published his own poems, the text and illustrations engraved together. He was a republican and a visionary with his own version of Christianity.

From The Marriage of Heaven and Hell

Without Contraries is no progression. Attraction and Repulsion, Reason and Energy, Love and Hate, are necessary to Human existence.

From these contraries spring what the religious call Good & Evil. Good is the passive that obeys Reason. Evil is the active springing from Energy.

Good is Heaven. Evil is Hell.   5

The voice of the Devil

All Bibles or sacred codes. have been the causes of the following Errors.

1. That Man has two real existing principles Viz: a Body & a Soul.

2. That Energy. calld Evil. is alone from the Body. & that Reason. calld Good. is alone from the Soul.   10

---

6 The voice of the Devil From other writings by Blake, it is clear that the ideas expounded by this 'voice' in lines 7–17 are in general accord with his own. However, its rhetoric of systematic exclusion is notably un-Blakean, and stands within the passage in ironic contrast to the more inclusive valuing of 'Contraries' in lines 1–2.

3. That God will torment Man in Eternity for following his Energies.
But the following Contraries to these are True
    1. Man has no Body distinct from his Soul for that calld Body is a portion
of Soul discernd by the five Senses. the chief inlets of Soul in this age
    2. Energy is the only life and is from the Body and Reason is the bound   15
or outward circumference of Energy.
    3. Energy is Eternal Delight

                                                                    1790–93   1793

The Book of Thel

Thel's Motto,

Does the Eagle know what is in the pit?
Or wilt thou go ask the Mole:
Can Wisdom be put in a silver rod?
Or Love in a golden bowl?

I

The daughters of Mne Seraphim led round their sunny flocks.   5
All but the youngest; she in paleness sought the secret air.
To fade away like morning beauty from her mortal day:
Down by the river of Adona her soft voice is heard:
And thus her gentle lamentation falls like morning dew.

O life of this our spring! why fades the lotus of the water?   10
Why fade these children of the spring? born but to smile & fall.
Ah! Thel is like a watry bow. and like a parting cloud.
Like a reflection in a glass. like shadows in the water.
Like dreams of infants. like a smile upon an infants face,
Like the doves voice, like transient day, like music in the air;   15
Ah! gentle may I lay me down, and gentle rest my head.
And gentle sleep the sleep of death. and gentle hear the voice
Of him that walketh in the garden in the evening time.

The Lilly of the valley breathing in the humble grass
Answer'd the lovely maid and said; I am a watry weed,   20
And I am very small, and love to dwell in lowly vales;
So weak, the gilded butterfly scarce perches on my head.
Yet I am visited from heaven and he that smiles on all.
Walks in the valley. and each morn over me spreads his hand
Saying, rejoice thou humble grass, thou new-born lilly flower,   25
Thou gentle maid of silent valleys. and of modest brooks;
For thou shalt be clothed in light, and fed with morning manna:
Till summers heat melts thee beside the fountains and the springs
To flourish in eternal vales: then why should Thel complain,

---

5 In the Bible, the **Seraphim** are the highest order of angels. **Mne** is an invented name, which has a
loose affinity of sound with several names from ancient mythologies.
8 Adona   an invented word, perhaps associated with Adonis
14 See Genesis 3:8; see also Blake's poem 'Introduction', p. 336.

Why should the mistress of the vales of Har, utter a sigh.
She ceasd & smild in tears, then sat down in her silver shrine.

Thel answered. O thou little virgin of the peaceful valley.
Giving to those that cannot crave, the voiceless, the o'ertired.
Thy breath doth nourish the innocent lamb, he smells thy milky garments,
He crops thy flowers, while thou sittest smiling in his face,   35
Wiping his mild and meekin mouth from all contagious taints.
Thy wine doth purify the golden honey, thy perfume,
Which thou dost scatter on every little blade of grass that springs
Revives the milked cow, & tames the fire-breathing steed.
But Thel is like a faint cloud kindled at the rising sun: 40
I vanish from my pearly throne, and who shall find my place.

Queen of the vales the Lilly answered, ask the tender cloud,
And it shall tell thee why it glitters in the morning sky,
And why it scatters its bright beauty thro' the humid air.
Descend O little cloud & hover before the eyes of Thel.   45

The Cloud descended, and the Lilly bowd her modest head:
And went to mind her numerous charge among the verdant grass.

II

O little Cloud the virgin said, I charge thee tell to me,
Why thou complainest not when in one hour thou fade away:
Then we shall seek thee but not find; ah Thel is like to thee.   50
I pass away. yet I complain, and no one hears my voice.

The Cloud then shew'd his golden head & his bright form emerg'd,
Hovering and glittering on the air before the face of Thel.

O virgin know'st thou not. our steeds drink of the golden springs
Where Luvah doth renew his horses: look'st thou on my youth,   55
And fearest thou because I vanish and am seen no more.
Nothing remains; O maid I tell thee, when I pass away,
It is to tenfold life, to love, to peace, and raptures holy:
Unseen descending, weigh my light wings upon balmy flowers;
And court the fair eyed dew. to take me to her shining tent;   60
The weeping virgin, trembling kneels before the risen sun,
Till we arise link'd in a golden band, and never part;
But walk united, bearing food to all our tender flowers

Dost thou O little Cloud? I fear that I am not like thee;
For I walk through the vales of Har. and smell the sweetest flowers;   65
But I feed not the little flowers: I hear the warbling birds,
But I feed not the warbling birds. they fly and seek their food;
But Thel delights in these no more because I fade away,
And all shall say, without a use this shining woman liv'd,
Or did she only live. to be at death the food of worms.   70

The Cloud reclind upon his airy throne and answer'd thus.

---

30 vales of Har in Blake's poem *Tiriel* (1789), a valley of infantile innocence; Har is its inchoate Adam figure.
55 In several later poems by Blake, **Luvah** is a mythic figure associated with sexual energy.

Then if thou art the food of worms. O virgin of the skies,
How great thy use. how great thy blessing; every thing that lives,
Lives not alone, nor for itself: fear not and I will call
The weak worm from its lowly bed, and thou shalt hear its voice.   75
Come forth worm of the silent valley, to thy pensive queen.

The helpless worm arose, and sat upon the Lillys leaf,
And the bright Cloud saild on. to find his partner in the vale.

III

Then Thel astonish'd view'd the Worm upon its dewy bed.

Art thou a Worm? image of weakness. art thou but a Worm?   80
I see thee like an infant wrapped in the Lillys leaf:
Ah weep not little voice, thou can'st not speak. but thou can'st weep;
Is this a Worm? I see thee lay helpless & naked: weeping,
And none to answer. none to cherish thee with mothers smiles.

The Clod of Clay heard the Worms voice, & raisd her pitying head;   85
She bow'd over the weeping infant, and her life exhal'd
In milky fondness, then on Thel she fix'd her humble eyes.

O beauty of the vales of Har. we live not for ourselves,
Thou seest me the meanest thing, and so I am indeed;
My bosom of itself is cold. and of itself is dark,   90
But he that loves the lowly, pours his oil upon my head.
And kisses me, and binds his nuptial bands around my breast.
And says; Thou mother of my children, I have loved thee.
And I have given thee a crown that none can take away
But how this is sweet maid, I know not, and I cannot know,   95
I ponder, and I cannot ponder; yet I live and love.

The daughter of beauty wip'd her pitying tears with her white veil,
And said. Alas! I knew not this, and therefore did I weep:
That God would love a Worm I knew, and punish the evil foot
That wilful, bruis'd its helpless form: but that he cherish'd it   100
With milk and oil, I never knew; and therefore did I weep,
And I complaind in the mild air, because I fade away,
And lay me down in thy cold bed, and leave my shining lot.
Queen of the vales, the matron Clay answerd; I heard thy sighs.
And all thy moans flew o'er my roof. but I have call'd them down: 105
Wilt thou O Queen enter my house. 'tis given thee to enter,
And to return; fear nothing. enter with thy virgin feet.

IV

The eternal gates terrific porter lifted the northern bar:
Thel enter'd in & saw the secrets of the land unknown;
She saw the couches of the dead, & where the fibrous roots   110
Of every heart on earth infixes deep its restless twists:
A land of sorrows & of tears where never smile was seen.

She wanderd in the land of clouds thro' valleys dark, listning
Dolours & lamentations: waiting oft beside a dewy grave
She stood in silence. listning to the voices of the ground,   115
Till to her own grave plot she came, & there she sat down.
And heard this voice of sorrow breathed from the hollow pit.

Why cannot the Ear be closed to its own destruction?
Or the glistning Eye to the poison of a smile!
Why are Eyelids stord with arrows ready drawn, 120
Where a thousand fighting men in ambush lie?
Or an Eye of gifts & graces, show'ring fruits & coined gold!
Why a Tongue impress'd with honey from every wind?
Why an Ear, a whirlpool fierce to draw creations in?
Why a Nostril wide inhaling terror trembling & affright. 125
Why a tender curb upon the youthful burning boy!
Why a little curtain of flesh on the bed of our desire?

The Virgin started from her seat, & with a shriek.
Fled back unhinderd till she came into the vales of Har

1789–91 1791

From *Songs of Innocence*

Introduction

Piping down the valleys wild
Piping songs of pleasant glee
On a cloud I saw a child.
And he laughing said to me.

Pipe a song about a Lamb; 5
So I piped with merry chear,
Piper pipe that song again—
So I piped, he wept to hear.

Drop thy pipe thy happy pipe
Sing thy songs of happy chear, 10
So I sung the same again
While he wept with joy to hear

Piper sit thee down and write
In a book that all may read—
So he vanish'd from my sight. 15
And I pluck'd a hollow reed.

And I made a rural pen,
And I stain'd the water clear,
And I wrote my happy songs
Every child may joy to hear 20

1789

Nurse's Song

When the voices of children are heard on the green
And laughing is heard on the hill,
My heart is at rest within my breast
And every thing else is still

The **Songs of Innocence** were composed *c.* 1784–90, the **Songs of Experience** mostly 1790–92. When published together in 1794 they bore the sub-title: 'Shewing the Two Contrary States of the Human Soul'. In *The Marriage of Heaven and Hell* Blake writes, 'Without Contraries is no progression'; i.e. each contrary provides a perspective that the other lacks. See p. 329.

Then come home my children, the sun is gone down   5
And the dews of night arise
Come come leave off play, and let us away
Till the morning appears in the skies

No no let us play, for it is yet day
And we cannot go to sleep   10
Besides in the sky, the little birds fly
And the hills are all coverd with sheep

Well well go & play till the light fades away
And then go home to bed
The little ones leaped & shouted & laugh'd   15
And all the hills ecchoed

                 1789

Holy Thursday

Twas on a Holy Thursday their innocent faces clean
The children walking two & two in red & blue & green
Grey headed beadles walkd before with wands as white as snow
Till into the high dome of Pauls they like Thames waters flow

O what a multitude they seemd these flowers of London town   5
Seated in companies they sit with radiance all their own
The hum of multitudes was there but multitudes of lambs
Thousands of little boys & girls raising their innocent hands

Now like a mighty wind they raise to heaven the voice of song
Or like harmonious thunderings the seats of heaven among   10
Beneath them sit the aged men wise guardians of the poor
Then cherish pity, lest you drive an angel from your door

                 1789

The Chimney Sweeper

When my mother died I was very young,
And my father sold me while yet my tongue,
Could scarcely cry weep weep weep weep.
So your chimneys I sweep & in soot I sleep.

Theres little Tom Dacre, who cried when his head   5
That curl'd like a lambs back, was shav'd, so I said.
Hush Tom never mind it, for when your head's bare,
You know that the soot cannot spoil your white hair.

And so he was quiet, & that very night,
As Tom was a sleeping he had such a sight,   10
That thousands of sweepers Dick, Joe, Ned & Jack
Were all of them lock'd up in coffins of black,

And by came an Angel who had a bright key,
And he open'd the coffins & set them all free.
Then down a green plain leaping laughing they run   15
And wash in a river and shine in the Sun.

Holy Thursday   feast of Christ's ascension into Heaven

Then naked & white, all their bags left behind,
They rise upon clouds, and sport in the wind.
And the Angel told Tom if he'd be a good boy,
He'd have God for his father & never want joy.   20

And so Tom awoke and we rose in the dark
And got with our bags & our brushes to work.
Tho' the morning was cold, Tom was happy & warm,
So if all do their duty, they need not fear harm.

                                                1789

The Lamb

   Little Lamb who made thee
   Dost thou know who made thee
Gave thee life & bid thee feed.
By the stream & o'er the mead;
Gave thee clothing of delight,   5
Softest clothing wooly bright;
Gave thee such a tender voice,
Making all the vales rejoice:
   Little Lamb who made thee
   Dost thou know who made thee   10

   Little Lamb I'll tell thee,
   Little Lamb I'll tell thee
He is called by thy name,
For he calls himself a Lamb:
He is meek & he is mild,   15
He became a little child:
I a child & thou a lamb,
We are called by his name.
   Little Lamb God bless thee.
   Little Lamb God bless thee.   20
                                                1789

The Divine Image

To Mercy Pity Peace and Love,
All pray in their distress:
And to these virtues of delight
Return their thankfulness.

For Mercy Pity Peace and Love,   5
Is God our father dear:
And Mercy Pity Peace and Love,
Is Man his child and care.

For Mercy has a human heart
Pity, a human face: 10
And Love, the human form divine,
And Peace, the human dress.

Then every man of every clime,
That prays in his distress,
Prays to the human form divine   15
Love Mercy Pity Peace.

And all must love the human form,
In heathen, turk or jew.
Where Mercy, Love & Pity dwell,
There God is dwelling too   20

1789

From *Songs of Experience*

Introduction

Hear the voice of the Bard!
Who Present, Past, & Future sees
Whose ears have heard,
The Holy Word,
That walk'd among the ancient trees.   5

Calling the lapsed Soul
And weeping in the evening dew:
That might controll,
The starry pole;
And fallen fallen light renew!   10

O Earth O Earth return!
Arise from out the dewy grass;
Night is worn,
And the morn
Rises from the slumberous mass.   15

Turn away no more:
Why wilt thou turn away
The starry floor
The watry shore
Is giv'n thee till the break of day.   20

1794

Earth's Answer

Earth rais'd up her head,
From the darkness dread & drear.
Her light fled:
Stony dread!
And her locks cover'd with grey despair.   5

4–5 See Gen. 3:8: 'And they heard the voice of the Lord God walking in the garden in the cool of the day: and Adam and his wife hid themselves from the presence of the Lord God amongst the trees of the garden.'
18 starry   symbolic of the rigid ordering of reason
19 watry   symbolic of materialism

Prison'd on watry shore
Starry Jealousy does keep my den
Cold and hoar
Weeping o'er
I hear the Father of the ancient men   10

Selfish father of men
Cruel jealous selfish fear
Can delight
Chain'd in night
The virgins of youth and morning bear.   15

Does spring hide its joy
When buds and blossoms grow?
Does the sower
Sow by night?
Or the plowman in darkness plow?   20

Break this heavy chain,
That does freeze my bones around
Selfish! vain!
Eternal bane!
That free Love with bondage bound.   25

                                      1794

The Chimney Sweeper

A little black thing among the snow:
Crying weep, weep, in notes of woe!
Where are thy father & mother? say?
They are both gone up to the church to pray.

Because I was happy upon the heath,   5
And smil'd among the winters snow:
They clothed me in the clothes of death,
And taught me to sing the notes of woe.

And because I am happy, & dance & sing,
They think they have done me no injury: 10
And are gone to praise God & his Priest & King
Who make up a heaven of our misery.

                                      1794

Nurses Song

When the voices of children, are heard on the green
And whisprings are in the dale:
The days of my youth rise fresh in my mind,
My face turns green and pale.

Then come home my children, the sun is gone down   5
And the dews of night arise
Your spring & your day, are wasted in play
And your winter and night in disguise.

                                      1794

10ff Earth perversely 'hears' a Father who is a distortion from the loving Word of 'Introduction'.

London

I wander thro' each charter'd street,
Near where the charter'd Thames does flow.
And mark in every face I meet
Marks of weakness, marks of woe.

In every cry of every Man,   5
In every Infants cry of fear,
In every voice: in every ban,
The mind-forg'd manacles I hear

How the Chimney-sweepers cry
Every blackning Church appalls,   10
And the hapless Soldiers sigh
Runs in blood down Palace walls

But most thro' midnight streets I hear
How the youthful Harlots curse
Blasts the new-born Infants tear   *withers* 15
And blights with plagues the Marriage hearse

1794

Holy Thursday

Is this a holy thing to see,
In a rich and fruitful land,
Babes reducd to misery,
Fed with cold and usurous hand?

Is that trembling cry a song?   5
Can it be a song of joy?
And so many children poor?
It is a land of poverty!

And their sun does never shine.
And their fields are bleak & bare.   10
And their ways are fill'd with thorns.
It is eternal winter there.

For where-e'er the sun does shine,
And where-e'er the rain does fall:
Babe can never hunger there,   15
Nor poverty the mind appall.

1794

Ah! Sun-flower

Ah Sun-flower! weary of time,
Who countest the steps of the Sun:
Seeking after that sweet golden clime
Where the travellers journey is done.

1–2 charter'd   The trade and finance interests of London Port and City operated under Royal Char-
ters guaranteeing their rights and privileges.
7 ban   official prohibition or denunciation; also summons to arms; also proclamation of marriage

Where the Youth pined away with desire,   5
And the pale Virgin shrouded in snow:
Arise from their graves and aspire,
Where my Sun-flower wishes to go.

                                                        1794

Infant Sorrow

My mother groand! my father wept.
Into the dangerous world I leapt:
Helpless, naked, piping loud;
Like a fiend hid in a cloud.

Struggling in my fathers hands: 5
Striving against my swadling bands:
Bound and weary I thought best
To sulk upon my mothers breast.

                                                        1794

The Sick Rose

O Rose thou art sick.
The invisible worm,
That flies in the night
In the howling storm:

Has found out thy bed   5
Of crimson joy:
And his dark secret love
Does thy life destroy.

                                                        1794

A Poison Tree

I was angry with my friend;
I told my wrath, my wrath did end.
I was angry with my foe:
I told it not, my wrath did grow.

And I waterd it in fears,   5
Night & morning with my tears:
And I sunned it with smiles,
And with soft deceitful wiles.

And it grew both day and night.
Till it bore an apple bright.   10
And my foe beheld it shine,
And he knew that it was mine.

And into my garden stole,
When the night had veild the pole;
In the morning glad I see,   15
My foe outstretchd beneath the tree.

                                                        1794

The Human Abstract

Pity would be no more,
If we did not make somebody Poor:
And Mercy no more could be,
If all were as happy as we;

And mutual fear brings peace;   5
Till the selfish loves increase.
Then Cruelty knits a snare,
And spreads his baits with care.

He sits down with holy fears,
And waters the ground with tears: 10
Then Humility takes its root
Underneath his foot.

Soon spreads the dismal shade
Of Mystery over his head;   *religious doctrine*
And the Catterpiller and Fly,   15
Feed on the Mystery.

And it bears the fruit of Deceit,
Ruddy and sweet to eat;
And the Raven his nest has made
In its thickest shade.   20

The Gods of the earth and sea,
Sought thro' Nature to find this Tree
But their search was all in vain:
There grows one in the Human Brain

                                                                        1794

The Tyger

Tyger Tyger, burning bright,
In the forests of the night;
What immortal hand or eye,
Could frame thy fearful symmetry?

In what distant deeps or skies,   5
Burnt the fire of thine eyes?
On what wings dare he aspire?
What the hand, dare sieze the fire?

And what shoulder, & what art,
Could twist the sinews of thy heart?   10
And when thy heart began to beat,
What dread hand? & what dread feet?

What the hammer? what the chain,
In what furnace was thy brain?
What the anvil? what dread grasp,   15
Dare its deadly terrors clasp!

The Tyger   See p. 547 for an early draft of this poem.

When the stars threw down their spears
And water'd heaven with their tears:
Did he smile his work to see?
Did he who made the Lamb make thee?   20

Tyger Tyger burning bright,
In the forests of the night:
What immortal hand or eye,
Dare frame thy fearful symmetry?

                                                    1794

From Vala, or The Four Zoas

I am made to sow the thistle for wheat; the nettle for a nourishing dainty
I have planted a false oath in the earth, it has brought forth a poison tree
I have chosen the serpent for a councellor & the dog
For a schoolmaster to my children
I have blotted out from light & living the dove & nightingale   5
And I have caused the earth worm to beg from door to door
I have taught the thief a secret path into the house of the just
I have taught pale artifice to spread his nets upon the morning
My heavens are brass my earth is iron my moon a clod of clay
My sun a pestilence burning at noon & a vapour of death in night   10

What is the price of Experience do men buy it for a song
Or wisdom for a dance in the street? No it is bought with the price
Of all that a man hath his house his wife his children
Wisdom is sold in the desolate market where none come to buy
And in the witherd field where the farmer plows for bread in vain   15

It is an easy thing to triumph in the summers sun
And in the vintage & to sing on the waggon loaded with corn
It is an easy thing to talk of patience to the afflicted
To speak the laws of prudence to the houseless wanderer
To listen to the hungry ravens cry in wintry season   20
When the red blood is filld with wine & with the marrow of lambs

It is an easy thing to laugh at wrathful elements
To hear the dog howl at the wintry door, the ox in the slaughter house moan
To see a god on every wind & a blessing on every blast
To hear sounds of love in the thunder storm that destroys our enemies 25
        house
To rejoice in the blight that covers his field, & the sickness that cuts off his
        children
While our olive & vine sing & laugh round our door & our children bring
        fruit & flowers   30

17–18 A possible reference to the surrender of the rebel angels in Milton's *Paradise Lost* V, 838–9. See also the note to line 18 of 'Introduction', p. 336.
Vala This extract is the lament of Enion at the end of 'Night the Second'.
9 See Deut. 28:23: 'And thy heaven that is over thy head shall be brass, and the earth that is under thee shall be iron.'
11–12 See Job 28: 12–13: 'Where shall wisdom be found? and where is the place of understanding? Man knoweth not the price thereof.'

Then the groan & the dolor are quite forgotten & the slave grinding at the mill
And the captive in chains & the poor in the prison, & the soldier in the field
When the shatterd bone hath laid him groaning among the happier dead

It is an easy thing to rejoice in the tents of prosperity
Thus could I sing & thus rejoice, but it is not so with me!   35

                                                   c. *1796–1807*

[Mock on Mock on Voltaire Rousseau]

Mock on Mock on Voltaire Rousseau
Mock on! Mock on! tis all in vain!
You throw the sand against the wind
And the wind blows it back again

And every sand becomes a Gem   5
Reflected in the beams divine
Blown back they blind the mocking Eye
But still in Israels paths they shine

The Atoms of Democritus
And Newtons Particles of light   10
Are sands upon the Red sea shore
Where Israels tents do shine so bright

                                        1800–08   1863

From Milton

And did those feet in ancient time,
Walk upon Englands mountains green:
And was the holy Lamb of God,
On Englands pleasant pastures seen!

And did the Countenance Divine,   5
Shine forth upon our clouded hills?
And was Jerusalem builded here,
Among these dark Satanic Mills?

Bring me my Bow of burning gold:
Bring me my Arrows of desire:
Bring me my Spear: O clouds unfold!   10
Bring me my Chariot of Fire!

I will not cease from Mental Fight,
Nor shall my Sword sleep in my hand:
Till we have built Jerusalem,   15
In Englands green & pleasant Land.

                                                              1804

---

35 See Job, 9:34–35: 'Let him take his rod away ... Then would I speak, and not fear him; but it is not so with me.'
1 **Voltaire, Rousseau**   eighteenth-century rationalist critics of the established order in France
9–10 **Democritus**   (fifth century BC) and Isaac **Newton** (1642–1727) presented mechanical models of the universe in their respective theories of atoms and light.
1–7 To Blake, who envisioned a golden age in ancient Britain, Jesus (the **Lamb of God**) is present where humankind is spiritually free. **Jerusalem** is a symbol of this freedom.
8 Mills   machines for grinding and the factories that house them; by extension, the materialist mind. A reference to industrialization

GEORGE CRABBE

1754–1832 b Aldeburgh, a remote village in Suffolk. He spent much of his life as an
Anglican priest in country places.

From The Parish Register

From *Part III. Burials*

Next died the Widow Goe, an active dame, 125
Famed ten miles round, and worthy all her fame;
She lost her husband when their loves were young,
But kept her farm, her credit, and her tongue:
Full thirty years she ruled, with matchless skill,
With guiding judgment and resistless will; 130
Advice she scorn'd, rebellions she suppress'd,
And sons and servants bow'd at her behest.
Like that great man's, who to his Saviour came,
Were the strong words of this commanding dame;—
'Come', if she said, they came; if 'go', were gone; 135
And if 'do this',—that instant it was done:
Her maidens told she was all eye and ear,
In darkness saw and could at distance hear;—
No parish-business in the place could stir,
Without direction or assent from her; 140
In turn she took each office as it fell,
Knew all their duties, and discharged them well;
The lazy vagrants in her presence shook,
And pregnant damsels fear'd her stern rebuke;
She look'd on want with judgment clear and cool, 145
She felt with reason and bestow'd by rule;
She match'd both sons and daughters to her mind,
And lent them eyes, for Love, she heard, was blind;
Yet ceaseless still she throve, alert, alive,
The working bee, in full or empty hive; 150
Busy and careful, like that working bee,
No time for love nor tender cares had she;
But when our farmers made their amorous vows,
She talk'd of market-steeds and patent-ploughs.
Not unemploy'd her evenings pass'd away, 155
Amusement closed, as business waked the day;
When to her toilet's brief concern she ran,
And conversation with her friends began,
Who all were welcome, what they saw, to share;
And joyous neighbours praised her Christmas fare, 160
That none around might, in their scorn, complain
Of Gossip Goe as greedy in her gain.   *friend*
    Thus long she reign'd, admired, if not approved;
Praised, if not honour'd; fear'd, if not beloved;—

---

133 great man   the Roman centurion of Luke 7:8
157 toilet   dressing and grooming

When, as the busy days of Spring drew near,   165
That call'd for all the forecast of the year;
When lively hope the rising crops survey'd,
And April promised what September paid;
When stray'd her lambs where gorse and greenweed grow;
When rose her grass in richer vales below;   170
When pleased she look'd on all the smiling land,
And view'd the hinds, who wrought at her command;
(Poultry in groups still follow'd where she went;
Then dread o'ercame her,—that her days were spent.
'Bless me! I die, and not a warning giv'n,—   175
With *much* to do on Earth, and ALL for Heav'n!—
No reparation for my soul's affairs;
No leave petition'd for the barn's repairs;
Accounts perplex'd, my interest yet unpaid,
My mind unsettled, and my will unmade;—   180
A lawyer haste, and in your way, a priest;
And let me die in one good work at least.'
She spake, and trembling, dropp'd upon her knees,
Heaven in her eye and in her hand her keys;
And still the more she found her life decay,   185
With greater force she grasp'd those signs of sway:
Then fell and died!—In haste her sons drew near,
And dropp'd, in haste, the tributary tear,
Then from th'adhering clasp the keys unbound,
And consolation for their sorrows found.   190

                                                        1807

CHARLOTTE SMITH

1749–1806 b London. She took up writing in order to support her twelve children and became well known as a poet and novelist.

To a nightingale

Poor melancholy bird—that all night long
    Tell'st to the Moon thy tale of tender woe;
    From what sad cause can such sweet sorrow flow,
And whence this mournful melody of song?

Thy poet's musing fancy would translate   5
    What mean the sounds that swell thy little breast,
    When still at dewy eve thou leavest thy nest,
Thus to the listening night to sing thy fate.

Pale Sorrow's victims wert thou once among,
    Tho' now released in woodlands wild to rove?   10
    Say—hast thou felt from friends some cruel wrong,
Or died'st thou—martyr of disastrous love?
Ah! songstress sad! that such my lot might be,
To sigh, and sing at liberty—like thee!

                                                        1789

The sea view

The upland Shepherd, as reclined he lies
    On the soft turf that clothes the mountain brow,
Marks the bright Sea-line mingling with the skies;
    Or from his course celestial, sinking slow,
    The Summer-Sun in purple radiance low,   5
Blaze on the western waters; the wide scene
    Magnificent, and tranquil, seems to spread
Even o'er the Rustic's breast a joy serene,
    When, like dark plague-spots by the Demons shed,
Charged deep with death, upon the waves, far seen,   10
    Move the war-freighted ships; and fierce and red,
    Flash their destructive fire—The mangled dead
And dying victims then pollute the flood.
Ah! thus man spoils Heaven's glorious works with blood!

                               1797

Written in October

The blasts of Autumn as they scatter round
    The faded foliage of another year,
And muttering many a sad and solemn sound,
    Drive the pale fragments o'er the stubble sere,
Are well attuned to my dejected mood;   5
    (Ah! better far than airs that breathe of Spring!)
    While the high rooks, that hoarsely clamouring
Seek in black phalanx the half-leafless wood,
    I rather hear, than that enraptured lay   *song*
Harmonious, and of Love and Pleasure born,   10
Which from the golden furze, or flowering thorn
    Awakes the Shepherd in the ides of May;
Nature delights *me* most when most she mourns,
For never more to me the Spring of Hope returns!

                               1797

ANNA LAETITIA BARBAULD

1743–1825 b Leicestershire. Also a literary editor she lived near London.

Washing-Day

        and their voice,
   Turning again towards childish treble, pipes
   And whistles in its sound. —

The Muses are turned gossips; they have lost   *tragic*
The buskined step, and clear high-sounding phrase,
Language of gods. Come then, domestic Muse,
In slipshod measure loosely prattling on
Of farm or orchard, pleasant curds and cream,   5

Epigraph: From *As You Like It*, II, vii, 161–163.

Or drowning flies, or shoe lost in the mire
By little whimpering boy, with rueful face;
Come, Muse, and sing the dreaded Washing-Day.
Ye who beneath the yoke of wedlock bend,
With bowed soul, full well ye ken the day   10
Which week, smooth sliding after week, brings on
Too soon;—for to that day nor peace belongs
Nor comfort;—ere the first gray streak of dawn,
The red-armed washers come and chase repose.
Nor pleasant smile, nor quaint device of mirth,   15
E'er visited that day: the very cat,
From the wet kitchen scared and reeking hearth,
Visits the parlour,—an unwonted guest.
The silent breakfast-meal is soon dispatched;
Uninterrupted, save by anxious looks   20
Cast at the lowering sky, if sky should lower.
From that last evil, O preserve us, heavens!
For should the skies pour down, adieu to all
Remains of quiet: then expect to hear
Of sad disasters,—dirt and gravel stains   25
Hard to efface, and loaded lines at once
Snapped short,—and linen horse by dog thrown down,
And all the petty miseries of life.
Saints have been calm while stretched upon the rack,
And Guatimozin smiled on burning coals;   30
But never yet did housewife notable
Greet with a smile a rainy washing-day.
—But grant the welkin fair, require not thou
Who call'st thyself perchance the master there,
Or study swept, or nicely dusted coat,   35
Or usual 'tendance;—ask not, indiscreet,
Thy stockings mended, though the yawning rents
Gape wide as Erebus; nor hope to find
Some snug recess impervious: shouldst thou try
The 'customed garden walks, thine eye shall rue   40
The budding fragrance of thy tender shrubs,
Myrtle or rose, all crushed beneath the weight
Of coarse checked apron,—with impatient hand
Twitched off when showers impend: or crossing lines
Shall mar thy musings, as the wet cold sheet   45
Flaps in thy face abrupt. Woe to the friend
Whose evil stars have urged him forth to claim
On such a day the hospitable rites!
Looks, blank at best, and stinted courtesy,
Shall he receive. Vainly he feeds his hopes   50
With dinner of roast chicken, savoury pie,
Or tart or pudding:—pudding he nor tart
That day shall eat; nor, though the husband try,

---

27 linen horse a wooden frame on which washing was hung to dry
30 Guatimozin or Cuauhtemoc (*c.* 1495–1522): last Aztec emperor, famous for his stoicism under
Spanish torture

Mending what can't be helped, to kindle mirth
From cheer deficient, shall his consort's brow   55
Clear up propitious:—the unlucky guest
In silence dines, and early slinks away.
I well remember, when a child, the awe
This day struck into me; for then the maids,
I scarce knew why, looked cross, and drove me from them: 60
Nor soft caress could I obtain, nor hope
Usual indulgencies; jelly or creams,
Relic of costly suppers, and set by
For me their petted one; or buttered toast,
When butter was forbid; or thrilling tale   65
Of ghost or witch, or murder—so I went
And sheltered me beside the parlour fire:
There my dear grandmother, eldest of forms,
Tended the little ones, and watched from harm,
Anxiously fond, though oft her spectacles   70
With elfin cunning hid, and oft the pins
Drawn from her ravelled stocking, might have soured
One less indulgent.—
At intervals my mother's voice was heard,
Urging dispatch: briskly the work went on,   75
All hands employed to wash, to rinse, to wring,
To fold, and starch, and dap, and iron, and plait.
Then would I sit me down, and ponder much
Why washings were. Sometimes through hollow bowl
Of pipe amused we blew, and sent aloft   80
The floating bubbles; little dreaming then
To see, Montgolfier, thy silken ball
Ride buoyant through the clouds—so near approach
The sports of children and the toils of men.
Earth, air, and sky, and ocean, hath its bubbles,   85
And verse is one of them—this most of all.

                                        1797   1825

WILLIAM COWPER

(pron. 'Cooper') 1731–1800 b Hertfordshire. From 1763 he was subject to intermittent depression and lived quietly in the country, cared for by friends.

Light shining out of darkness

GOD moves in a mysterious way,
    His wonders to perform;
He plants his footsteps in the sea,
    And rides upon the storm.

82 The brothers **Montgolfier**, Joseph (1740–1810) and Etienne (1745–99), conducted the first untethered, manned flights of a hot-air balloon in 1783.

Deep in unfathomable mines   5
  Of never failing skill,
He treasures up his bright designs,
  And works his sovereign will.

Ye fearful saints fresh courage take,
  The clouds ye so much dread   10
Are big with mercy, and shall break
  In blessings on your head.

Judge not the LORD by feeble sense,
  But trust him for his grace;
Behind a frowning providence,   15
  He hides a smiling face.

His purposes will ripen fast,
  Unfolding ev'ry hour;
The bud may have a bitter taste,
  But sweet will be the flow'r.   20

Blind unbelief is sure to err,
  And scan his work in vain;
GOD is his own interpreter,
  And he will make it plain.

                                1772   1774

The Cast-away

Obscurest night involved the sky,
  Th' Atlantic billows roar'd,
When such a destin'd wretch as I
  Wash'd headlong from on board
Of friends, of hope, of all bereft,   5
His floating home for ever left.

No braver chief could Albion boast
  Than He with whom he went,
Nor ever ship left Albion's coast,
  With warmer wishes sent,   10
He loved them both, but both in vain,
Nor Him beheld, nor Her again.

Not long beneath the whelming brine
  Expert to swim, he lay,
Nor soon he felt his strength decline   15
  Or courage die away;
But waged with death a lasting strife
Supported by despair of life.

The Cast-away   based on an incident in Richard Walter's memoir, *A Voyage Round the World by George Anson* (1748): during a storm near Cape Horn a sailor fell overboard, watched by helpless colleagues who remained aware of his continuing consciousness after he was lost to sight.

He shouted, nor his friends had fail'd
  To check the vessels' course,   20
But so the furious blast prevail'd
  That, pitiless perforce,
They left their outcast mate behind,
And scudded still before the wind.

Some succour yet they could afford,   25
  And, such as storms allow,
The cask, the coop, the floated cord
  Delay'd not to bestow;
But He, they knew, nor ship, nor shore,
Whate'er they gave, should visit more.   30

Nor, cruel as it seem'd, could He
  Their haste, himself, condemn,
Aware that flight, in such a sea,
  Alone could rescue *them*;
Yet bitter felt it still to die   35
Deserted, and his friends so nigh.

He long survives who lives an hour
  In ocean, self-upheld,
And so long he with unspent pow'r
  His destiny repell'd,   40
And ever, as the minutes flew,
Entreated help, or cried, Adieu!

At length, his transient respite past,
  His comrades, who before
Had heard his voice in ev'ry blast,   45
  Could catch the sound no more;
For then, by toil subdued, he drank
The stifling wave, and then he sank.

No poet wept him, but the page
  Of narrative sincere   50
That tells his name, his worth, his age,
  Is wet with Anson's tear,
And tears by bards or heroes shed
Alike immortalize the Dead.

I therefore purpose not or dream,   55
  Descanting on his fate,
To give the melancholy theme
  A more enduring date,
But Mis'ry still delights to trace
Its semblance in another's case.   60

No voice divine the storm allay'd,
  No light propitious shone,
When, snatch'd from all effectual aid,
  We perish'd, each alone;
But I, beneath a rougher sea,   65
And whelm'd in deeper gulphs than he.

MARY LEAPOR

1722–46 b Marston St Lawrence, a village in Northamptonshire. She worked for a neighbouring gentleman's family as a cook-maid.

An Essay on Woman

Woman—a pleasing, but a short-liv'd Flow'r,
Too soft for Business, and too weak for Pow'r:
A Wife in Bondage, or neglected Maid;
Despis'd, if ugly; if she's fair—betray'd.
'Tis Wealth alone inspires ev'ry Grace,   5
And calls the Raptures to her plenteous Face.
What Numbers for those charming Features pine,
If blooming Acres round her Temples twine?
Her Lip the Strawberry; and her Eyes more bright
Than sparkling *Venus* in a frosty Night.   10
Pale Lilies fade; and when the Fair appears,
Snow turns a Negro, and dissolves in Tears.
And where the Charmer treads her magic Toe,
On *English* Ground *Arabian* Odours grow;
Till mighty *Hymen* lifts his sceptred Rod,   15
And sinks her Glories with a fatal Nod;
Dissolves her Triumphs; sweeps her Charms away,
And turns the Goddess to her native Clay.

    But, *Artemisia*, let your Servant sing
What small Advantage Wealth and Beauties bring.   20
Who would be wife, that knew *Pamphilia*'s Fate?
Or who be fair, and join'd to *Sylvia*'s Mate?
Sylvia, whose Cheeks are fresh as early Day;
As Ev'ning mild, and sweet as spicy *May*:
And yet That Face her partial Husband tires,   25
And those bright Eyes, that all the World admires.
Pamphilia's Wit who does not strive to shun,
Like Death's Infection, or a Dog-Day's Sun?
The Damsels view her with malignant Eyes:
The Men are vex'd to find a Nymph so wise: 30
And Wisdom only serves to make her know
The keen Sensation of superior Woe.
The secret Whisper, and the list'ning Ear,
The scornful Eyebrow, and the hated Sneer;
The giddy Censures of her babbling Kind,   35
With thousand Ills that grate a gentle Mind,
By her are tasted in the first Degree,
Tho' overlook'd by *Simplicus*, and me.
Does Thirst of Gold a Virgin's Heart inspire,
Instill'd by Nature, or a careful Sire?   40

---

15 Hymen Greek god of marriage
19 Artemisia Artemis, Greek hunter goddess who represents female independence
28 dog-day under the dog-star, Sirius, star of summer heat and madness
39 thirst of gold in the sense of hoarding

Then let her quit Extravagance and Play;
The brisk Companion, and expensive Tea;
To feast with *Cordia* in her filthy Sty
On stew'd Potatoes, or on mouldy Pye;
Whose eager Eyes stare ghastly at the Poor,   45
And fright the Beggars from her hated Door:
In greasy Clouts she wraps her smoky Chin,   *rags*
And holds, that Pride's a never-pardon'd Sin.

If this be Wealth, no matter where it falls;
But save, ye Muses, save your *Mira*'s Walls: 50
Still give me pleasing Indolence, and Ease;
A Fire to warm me, and a Friend to please.

Since, whether sunk in Avarice, or Pride;
A wanton Virgin, or a starving Bride;
Or, wond'ring Crouds attend her charming Tongue;   55
Or deem'd an Idiot, ever speaks the Wrong:
Tho' Nature arm'd us for the growing Ill,
With fraudful Cunning, and a headstrong Will;
Yet, with ten thousand Follies to her Charge,
Unhappy Woman's but a Slave at large.   60

                                        1751

OLIVER GOLDSMITH

1730–74 b Ireland. Also a playwright and novelist, he lived in London from 1756.

[When lovely woman stoops to folly]

When lovely woman stoops to folly,
    And finds too late that men betray,
What charm can sooth her melancholy,
    What art can wash her guilt away?

The only art her guilt to cover,   5
    To hide her shame from every eye,
To give repentance to her lover,
    And wring his bosom—is to die.

                                        1766

[Ah me! when shall I marry me?]

Ah me! when shall I marry me?
    Lovers are plenty; but fail to relieve me.
He, fond youth, that could carry me,
    Offers to love, but means to deceive me.

But I will rally and combat the ruiner: 5
    Not a look, not a smile, shall my passion discover.
She that gives all to the false one pursuing her,
    Makes but a penitent, loses a lover.

                                        1774

CHRISTOPHER SMART

1722–71 b Kent. A poet, a man of learning and a religious eccentric, he worked in London as a freelance writer. *Jubilate Agno* was written during his recovery from a period of mental illness.

From Jubilate Agno

For I will consider my Cat Jeoffry.   695
For he is the servant of the Living God duly and daily serving him.
For at the first glance of the glory of God in the East he worships in his way.
For is this done by wreathing his body seven times round with elegant
      quickness.
For then he leaps up to catch the musk, which is the blessing of God
      upon his prayer.   700
For he rolls upon prank to work it in.
For having done duty and received blessing he begins to consider himself.
For this he performs in ten degrees.
For first he looks upon his fore-paws to see if they are clean.
For secondly he kicks up behind to clear away there.   705
For thirdly he works it upon stretch with the fore paws extended.
For fourthly he sharpens his paws by wood.
For fifthly he washes himself.
For Sixthly he rolls upon wash.
For Seventhly he fleas himself, that he may not be interrupted upon the beat. 710
For Eighthly he rubs himself against a post.
For Ninthly he looks up for his instructions.
For Tenthly he goes in quest of food.
For having consider'd God and himself he will consider his neighbour.
For if he meets another cat he will kiss her in kindness.   715
For when he takes his prey he plays with it to give it chance.
For one mouse in seven escapes by his dallying.
For when his day's work is done his business more properly begins.
For he keeps the Lord's watch in the night against the adversary.
For he counteracts the powers of darkness by his electrical skin and
      glaring eyes.   720
For he counteracts the Devil, who is death, by brisking about the life.
For in his morning orisons he loves the sun and the sun loves him.
For he is of the tribe of Tiger.
For the Cherub Cat is a term of the Angel Tiger.
For he has the subtlety and hissing of a serpent, which in goodness
      he suppresses.   725
For he will not do destruction, if he is well-fed, neither will he spit without
      provocation.
For he purrs in thankfulness, when God tells him he's a good Cat.
For he is an instrument for the children to learn benevolence upon.
For every house is incompleat without him and a blessing is lacking in
      the spirit.

Jubilate Agno   'Rejoice in the lamb' (i.e. Christ, the lamb of God).

For the Lord commanded Moses concerning the cats at the departure of the
 Children of Israel from Egypt.   730
For every family had one cat at least in the bag.
For the English Cats are the best in Europe.
For he is the cleanest in the use of his fore-paws of any quadrupede.
For the dexterity of his defence is an instance of the love of God to him
 exceedingly.
For he is the quickest to his mark of any creature.   735
For he is tenacious of his point.
For he is a mixture of gravity and waggery.
For he knows that God is his Saviour.
For there is nothing sweeter than his peace when at rest.
For there is nothing brisker than his life when in motion.   740
For he is of the Lord's poor and so indeed is he called by benevolence
 perpetually—Poor Jeoffry! poor Jeoffry! the rat has bit thy throat.
For I bless the name of the Lord Jesus that Jeoffry is better.
For the divine spirit comes about his body to sustain it in compleat cat.
For his tongue is exceeding pure so that it has in purity what it wants in musick.
For he is docile and can learn certain things.   745
For he can set up with gravity which is patience upon approbation.
For he can fetch and carry, which is patience in employment.
For he can jump over a stick which is patience upon proof positive.
For he can spraggle upon waggle at the word of command.
For he can jump from an eminence into his master's bosom.   750
For he can catch the cork and toss it again.
For he is hated by the hypocrite and miser.
For the former is affraid of detection.
For the latter refuses the charge.
For he camels his back to bear the first notion of business.   755
For he is good to think on, if a man would express himself neatly.
For he made a great figure in Egypt for his signal services.
For he killed the Ichneumon-rat very pernicious by land.
For his ears are so acute that they sting again.
For from this proceeds the passing quickness of his attention.   760
For by stroaking of him I have found out electricity.
For I perceived God's light about him both wax and fire.
For the Electrical fire is the spiritual substance, which God sends from
 heaven to sustain the bodies both of man and beast.
For God has blessed him in the variety of his movements.
For, tho he cannot fly, he is an excellent clamberer.   765
For his motions upon the face of the earth are more than any other
 quadrupede.
For he can tread to all the measures upon the musick.
For he can swim for life.
For he can creep.
c. *1760*   1939

729–30 See Exod. 11–12, where cats are not in fact mentioned.
756 Egypt   where cats were worshipped
758 Ichneumon-rat   mongoose-rat. The mongoose is harmless, and it is possible that Smart means
'Ichneumon-like', i.e. in appearance.

WILLIAM COLLINS

1721–59 b Chichester. He wrote a small body of poetry in his twenties before declining into mental illness.

Ode to Evening

If ought of oaten stop, or pastoral song,
May hope, chaste EVE, to sooth thy modest ear,
    Like thy own solemn springs,
    Thy springs, and dying gales,
O NYMPH reserv'd, while now the bright-hair'd sun   5
Sits in yon western tent, whose cloudy skirts,
    With brede ethereal wove,   *braid*
    O'erhang his wavy bed:
Now air is hush'd, save where the weak-ey'd bat,
With short shrill shriek flits by on leathern wing,   10
    Or where the Beetle winds   *blows*
    His small but sullen horn,
As oft he rises 'midst the twilight path,
Against the pilgrim born in heedless hum: *traveller*
    Now teach me, Maid compos'd,   15
    To breathe some soften'd strain,
Whose numbers stealing thro' thy darkning vale   *rhythms*
May not unseemly with its stillness suit,
    As musing slow, I hail
    Thy genial lov'd return!   20
For when thy folding star arising shews
His paly circlet, at his warning lamp
    The fragrant Hours, and Elves
    Who slept in flow'rs the day,
And many a Nymph who wreaths her brows with sedge,   25
And sheds the fresh'ning dew, and lovelier still,
    The PENSIVE PLEASURES sweet
    Prepare thy shadowy car.
Then lead, calm Vot'ress, where some sheety lake   *carriage*
Cheers the lone heath, or some time-hallow'd pile,   30
    Or up-land fallows grey
    Reflect its last cool gleam.
But when chill blust'ring winds, or driving rain,
Forbid my willing feet, be mine the hut,
    That from the mountain's side   35
    Views wilds, and swelling floods,
And hamlets brown, and dim-discover'd spires,
And hears their simple bell, and marks o'er all
    Thy dewy fingers draw
    The gradual dusky veil.   40

---

1 oaten stop   pastoral flute (i.e. made of oat, and having stops)
4 gales   light breezes
21 folding   indicating time to fold the sheep
30 pile   massive structure

While Spring shall pour his show'rs, as oft he wont,
And bathe thy breathing tresses, meekest Eve!
    While Summer loves to sport
    Beneath thy ling'ring light;
While sallow Autumn fills thy lap with leaves;   45
Or Winter yelling thro' the troublous air
    Affrights thy shrinking train,
    And rudely rends thy robes;
So long, sure-found beneath the Sylvan shed,
Shall FANCY, FRIENDSHIP, SCIENCE, rose-lip'd HEALTH,   50
    Thy gentlest influence own,
    And hymn thy fav'rite name!

                             1746   1746

THOMAS GRAY

1716–71 b London. He lived in Cambridge for much of his life, which was devoted largely to historical studies.

Elegy Written in a Country Church Yard

The Curfew tolls the knell of parting day,
The lowing herd wind slowly o'er the lea,
The plowman homeward plods his weary way,
And leaves the world to darkness and to me.

Now fades the glimmering landscape on the sight,   5
And all the air a solemn stillness holds,
Save where the beetle wheels his droning flight,
And drowsy tinklings lull the distant folds;

Save that from yonder ivy-mantled tow'r
The mopeing owl does to the moon complain   10
Of such, as wand'ring near her secret bow'r,
Molest her ancient solitary reign.

Beneath those rugged elms, that yew-tree's shade,
Where heaves the turf in many a mould'ring heap,
Each in his narrow cell for ever laid,   15
The rude Forefathers of the hamlet sleep.   *rustic*

The breezy call of incense-breathing Morn,
The swallow twitt'ring from the straw-built shed,
The cock's shrill clarion, or the ecchoing horn,
No more shall rouse them from their lowly bed.   20

For them no more the blazing hearth shall burn,
Or busy housewife ply her evening care:
No children run to lisp their sire's return,
Or climb his knees the envied kiss to share.

---

49 Sylvan shed i.e. the forest canopy

Oft did the harvest to their sickle yield,   25
Their furrow oft the stubborn glebe has broke;   *soil*
How jocund did they drive their team afield!
How bow'd the woods beneath their sturdy stroke!

Let not Ambition mock their useful toil,
Their homely joys, and destiny obscure;   30
Nor Grandeur hear with a disdainful smile,
The short and simple annals of the poor.

The boast of heraldry, the pomp of pow'r,
And all that beauty, all that wealth e'er gave,
Awaits alike th' inevitable hour.   35
The paths of glory lead but to the grave.

Nor you, ye Proud, impute to These the fault,
If Mem'ry o'er their Tomb no Trophies raise,
Where thro' the long-drawn isle and fretted vault
The pealing anthem swells the note of praise.   40

Can storied urn or animated bust
Back to its mansion call the fleeting breath?
Can Honour's voice provoke the silent dust,   *call forth*
Or Flatt'ry sooth the dull cold ear of Death?

Perhaps in this neglected spot is laid   45
Some heart once pregnant with celestial fire,
Hands, that the rod of empire might have sway'd,
Or wak'd to extasy the living lyre.

But Knowledge to their eyes her ample page
Rich with the spoils of time did ne'er unroll;   50
Chill Penury repress'd their noble rage,
And froze the genial current of the soul.

Full many a gem of purest ray serene,
The dark unfathom'd caves of ocean bear:
Full many a flower is born to blush unseen,   55
And waste its sweetness on the desert air.

Some village-Hampden, that with dauntless breast
The little Tyrant of his fields withstood;
Some mute inglorious Milton here may rest,
Some Cromwell guiltless of his country's blood.   60

Th' applause of list'ning senates to command,
The threats of pain and ruin to despise,
To scatter plenty o'er a smiling land,
And read their hist'ry in a nation's eyes

Their lot forbad: nor circumscrib'd alone   65
Their growing virtues, but their crimes confin'd;

57–60 Hampden John Hampden (1594–1643), prominent in the parliamentary opposition to Charles I. He was killed in the Civil War, in which **Milton** and **Cromwell** were also involved on the parliamentary side.

Forbad to wade through slaughter to a throne,
And shut the gates of mercy on mankind,

The struggling pangs of conscious truth to hide,
To quench the blushes of ingenuous shame,   70
Or heap the shrine of Luxury and Pride
With incense kindled at the Muse's flame.

Far from the madding crowd's ignoble strife,
Their sober wishes never learn'd to stray;
Along the cool sequester'd vale of life   75
They kept the noiseless tenor of their way.

Yet ev'n these bones from insult to protect
Some frail memorial still erected nigh,
With uncouth rhimes and shapeless sculpture deck'd,   *unsophisticated*
Implores the passing tribute of a sigh.   80

Their name, their years, spelt by th' unletter'd muse,
The place of fame and elegy supply:
And many a holy text around she strews,
That teach the rustic moralist to die.

For who to dumb Forgetfulness a prey,   85
This pleasing anxious being e'er resign'd,
Left the warm precincts of the chearful day,
Nor cast one longing ling'ring look behind?

On some fond breast the parting soul relies,
Some pious drops the closing eye requires;   90
Ev'n from the tomb the voice of Nature cries,
Ev'n in our Ashes live their wonted Fires.

For thee, who mindful of th' unhonour'd Dead
Dost in these lines their artless tale relate;
If chance, by lonely contemplation led,   95
Some kindred Spirit shall inquire thy fate,

Haply some hoary-headed Swain may say,   *perhaps / country man*
'Oft have we seen him at the peep of dawn
Brushing with hasty steps the dews away
To meet the sun upon the upland lawn.   100

'There at the foot of yonder nodding beech
That wreathes its old fantastic roots so high,
His listless length at noontide would he stretch,
And pore upon the brook that babbles by.

'Hard by yon wood, now smiling as in scorn,   105
Mutt'ring his wayward fancies he wou'd rove,
Now drooping, woeful wan, like one forlorn,
Or craz'd with care, or cross'd in hopeless love.

'One morn I miss'd him on the custom'd hill,
Along the heath and near his fav'rite tree;   110
Another came; nor yet beside the rill,
Nor up the lawn, nor at the wood was he,

'The next with dirges due in sad array
Slow thro' the church-way path we saw him born.
Approach and read (for thou can'st read) the lay,   115
Grav'd on the stone beneath yon aged thorn.'

The EPITAPH

Here rests his head upon the lap of Earth
A Youth to Fortune and to Fame unknown,
Fair Science frown'd not on his humble birth,   learning
And Melancholy mark'd him for her own.   120

Large was his bounty, and his soul sincere,
Heav'n did a recompence as largely send:
He gave to Mis'ry all he had, a tear,
He gain'd from Heav'n ('twas all he wish'd) a friend.

No farther seek his merits to disclose,   125
Or draw his frailties from their dread abode,
(There they alike in trembling hope repose)
The bosom of his Father and his God.

                                                 1746–50   1751

SAMUEL JOHNSON

1709–84 b Lichfield. From 1737 he lived in poverty in London as a writer of hack journalism
as well as of enduring poetry and prose, including his *Dictionary*. His famous conversation is
recorded in Boswell's biography.

From The Vanity of Human Wishes

The Tenth Satire of Juvenal Imitated

   The festal blazes, the triumphal show,   175
The ravish'd standard, and the captive foe,
The senate's thanks, the gazette's pompous tale,
With force resistless o'er the brave prevail.
Such bribes the rapid Greek o'er Asia whirl'd,
For such the steady Romans shook the world;   180
For such in distant lands the Britons shine,
And stain with blood the Danube or the Rhine;
This pow'r has praise, that virtue scarce can warm,
Till fame supplies the universal charm.
Yet Reason frowns on War's unequal game,   185
Where wasted nations raise a single name,
And mortgag'd states their grandsires wreaths regret,
From age to age in everlasting debt;
Wreaths which at last the dear-bought right convey
To rust on medals, or on stones decay.   190

Juvenal   Roman satirical poet (AD 60–*c.* 130)
179 the rapid Greek   Alexander the Great (356–23 BC)
181–82 John Churchill, the first Duke of Marlborough, received his title in the course of his successful
campaign in Austria and Bavaria in 1702–04.

On what foundation stands the warrior's pride,
How just his hopes let Swedish Charles decide;
A frame of adamant, a soul of fire,
No dangers fright him, and no labours tire;
O'er love, o'er fear, extends his wide domain,   195
Unconquer'd lord of pleasure and of pain;
No joys to him pacific scepters yield,
War sounds the trump, he rushes to the field;
Behold surrounding kings their pow'r combine,
And one capitulate, and one resign;   200
Peace courts his hand, but spreads her charms in vain;
'Think nothing gain'd, he cries, till nought remain,
On Moscow's walls till Gothic standards fly,
And all be mine beneath the polar sky.'
The march begins in military state,   205
And nations on his eye suspended wait;
Stern Famine guards the solitary coast,
And Winter barricades the realms of Frost;
He comes, not want and cold his course delay;—
Hide, blushing Glory, hide Pultowa's day: 210
The vanquish'd hero leaves his broken bands,
And shews his miseries in distant lands;
Condemn'd a needy supplicant to wait,
While ladies interpose, and slaves debate.
But did not Chance at length her error mend?   215
Did no subverted empire mark his end?
Did rival monarchs give the fatal wound?
Or hostile millions press him to the ground?
His fall was destin'd to a barren strand,
A petty fortress, and a dubious hand;   220
He left the name, at which the world grew pale,
To point a moral, or adorn a tale.

                              1749

A Short Song of Congratulation

Long-expected one and twenty
Ling'ring year at last is flown,
Pomp and Pleasure, Pride and Plenty
Great Sir John, are all your own.

Loosen'd from the Minor's tether,   5
Free to mortgage or to sell,
Wild as wind, and light as feather
Bid the slaves of thrift farewell.

Call the Bettys, Kates, and Jennys
Ev'ry name that laughs at Care,   10
Lavish of your Grandsire's guineas,
Show the spirit of an heir.

192–222 Charles XII of Sweden (1682–1718) conquered Denmark in 1700 and Poland in 1704, but was defeated by Peter the Great of Russia at Pultowa in 1709. He died in a military skirmish in Norway.

All that prey on vice and folly
Joy to see their quarry fly,
Here the Gamester light and jolly   15
There the Lender grave and sly.

Wealth, Sir John, was made to wander,
Let it wander as it will;
See the Jocky, see the Pander,
Bid them come, and take their fill.   20

When the bonny Blade carouses,
Pockets full, and Spirits high,
What are acres? What are houses?
Only dirt, or wet or dry.

If the Guardian or the Mother   25
Tell the woes of wilful waste,
Scorn the counsel and their pother,
You can hang or drown at last.

1780　1794

On the Death of Dr Robert Levet

Condemn'd to hope's delusive mine,
　As on we toil from day to day,
By sudden blasts, or slow decline,
　Our social comforts drop away.

Well tried through many a varying year,   5
　See LEVET to the grave descend;
Officious, innocent, sincere,
　Of ev'ry friendless name the friend.

Yet still he fills affection's eye,
　Obscurely wise, and coarsely kind;   10
Nor, letter'd arrogance, deny
　Thy praise to merit unrefin'd.

When fainting nature call'd for aid,
　And hov'ring death prepar'd the blow,
His vig'rous remedy display'd   15
　The power of art without the show.

In misery's darkest caverns known,
　His useful care was ever nigh,
Where hopeless anguish pour'd his groan,
　And lonely want retir'd to die.   20

Dr Robert Levet (*c.* 1701–82) a physician who worked among the poor and lodged in Johnson's house for many years. According to Boswell, his manner was 'awkward and uncouth'.
7 officious conscientious and kind　**innocent** unhurtful

No summons mock'd by chill delay,
  No petty gain disdain'd by pride,
The modest wants of ev'ry day
  The toil of ev'ry day supplied.

His virtues walk'd their narrow round,   25
  Nor made a pause, nor left a void;
And sure th' Eternal Master found
  The single talent well employ'd.

The busy day, the peaceful night,
  Unfelt, uncounted, glided by;   30
His frame was firm, his powers were bright,
  Tho' now his eightieth year was nigh.

Then with no throbbing fiery pain,
  No cold gradations of decay,
Death broke at once the vital chain,   35
  And forc'd his soul the nearest way.

                                            1783

JAMES THOMSON

1700–48 b Scotland. In London from 1725, he worked as a tutor while writing plays and poetry.

From Winter

The keener Tempests come: and fuming dun
From all the livid East, or piercing North,
Thick Clouds ascend; in whose capacious Womb   225
A vapoury Deluge lies, to Snow Congeal'd.
Heavy they roll their fleecy World along;
And the Sky saddens with the gather'd Storm.
Thro' the hush'd Air the whitening Shower descends,
At first thin-wavering; till at last the Flakes   230
Fall broad, and wide, and fast, dimming the Day,
With a continual Flow. The cherish'd Fields
Put on their Winter-Robe, of purest White.
'Tis Brightness all; save where the new Snow melts,
Along the mazy Current. Low, the Woods   235
Bow their hoar Head; and, ere the languid Sun
Faint from the West emits his Evening Ray,
Earth's universal Face, deep-hid, and chill,
Is one wild dazzling Waste, that buries wide
The Works of Man. Drooping, the Labourer-Ox   240
Stands cover'd o'er with Snow, and then demands
The Fruit of all his Toil. The Fowls of Heaven,

---

28 talent as in Christ's parable of the talents: Matt. 25: 14–30

Tam'd by the cruel Season, croud around
The winnowing Store, and claim the little Boon
Which PROVIDENCE assigns them. One alone,   245
The Red-Breast, sacred to the houshold Gods,
Wisely regardful of th' embroiling Sky,
In joyless Fields, and thorny Thickets, leaves
His shivering Mates, and pays to trusted Man
His annual Visit. Half-afraid, he first   250
Against the Window beats; then, brisk, alights
On the warm Hearth; then, hopping o'er the Floor,
Eyes all the smiling Family askance,
And pecks, and starts, and wonders where he is:
Till more familiar grown, the Table-Crumbs   255
Attract his slender Feet. The foodless Wilds
Pour forth their brown Inhabitants. The Hare,
Tho' timorous of Heart, and hard beset
By Death in various Forms, dark Snares, and Dogs,
And more unpitying Men, the Garden seeks,   260
Urg'd on by fearless Want. The bleating Kind
Eye the bleak Heaven, and next the glistening Earth,
With Looks of dumb Despair; then, sad-dispers'd,
Dig for the wither'd Herb thro Heaps of Snow.

   Now, Shepherds, to your helpless Charge be kind,   265
Baffle the raging Year, and fill their Pens
With Food at Will; lodge them below the Storm,
And watch them strict: for from the bellowing East,
In this dire Season, oft the Whirlwind's Wing
Sweeps up the Burthen of whole wintry Plains   270
In one wide Waft, and o'er the hapless Flocks,
Hid in the Hollow of two neighbouring Hills,
The billowy Tempest whelms; till, upward urg'd,
The Valley to a shining Mountain swells,
Tipt with a Wreath, high-curling in the Sky.   275

                                                    1726

MARY BARBER

? 1690–1757 b Ireland. A friend of Swift, who admired her poetry, she lived in Dublin.

To a Lady, who Invited the Author into the Country

   How gladly, Madam, would I go,
To see your Gardens, and *Chateau*;
From thence the fine Improvements view,
Or walk your verdant Avenue;
Delighted, hear the Thrushes sing,   5
Or listen to some bubbling Spring;
If Fate had giv'n me Leave to roam!
But Citizens must stay at home.

We're lonesome since you went away,
And should be dead—but for our Tea;   10
That *Helicon* of female Wits,
Which fills their Heads with rhyming Fits!
This Liquor seldom heats the Brain,
But turns it oft, and makes us vain;
With Fumes supplies Imagination,   15
Which we mistake for Inspiration,
This makes us cramp our Sense in Fetters,
And teaze our Friends with chiming Letters.

I grieve your Brother has the Gout;
Tho' he's so *stoically* stout,   20
I've heard him mourn his Loss of Pain,
And wish it in his Feet again.
What Woe poor Mortals must endure,
When Anguish is their only Cure!

Strephon is ill; and I perceive,   25
His lov'd *Elvira* grows so grave,
I fear, like *Niobe*, her Moan
Will turn herself and me to Stone.
Have I not Cause to dread this Fate,
Who scarce so much as smile of late?   30

Whilst lovely Landscapes you survey,
And peaceful pass your Hours away,
Refresh'd with various blooming Sweets;
I'm sick of Smells, and dirty Sheets,
Stifled with Smoke, and stirr'd with Noise   35
Of ev'ry thing—but my own Boys;
Thro' Rounds of *plodding* doom'd to run,
And very seldom see the Sun:
Yet sometimes pow'rful Fancy reigns,
And glads my Eyes with sylvan Scenes;   40
Where Time, enamour'd, slacks his Pace,
Enchanted by the warbling Race;
And, in Atonement for his Stay,
Thro' Cities hurries on the Day.

O! would kind Heav'n reverse my Fate,   45
Give me to quit a Life I hate,
To flow'ry Fields I soon would fly:
Let others stay—to *cheat* and *lye*.
There, in some blissful Solitude,
Where eating Care should ne'er intrude,   50
The Muse should do the Country Right,
And paint the glorious Scenes *you* slight.
     Dublin, 1728

1734

---

11 Helicon a mountain in ancient Boeotia, Greece. With its springs and fragrant plants, it was a legendary haunt of the muses.
27 Niobe a woman whom Zeus turned to stone in pity for her grief at the deaths of her twelve children. See *Metamorphoses* VI.

LADY MARY WORTLEY MONTAGU

1689–1762 b London. Essayist, letter-writer and poet, she travelled widely. She lived in Constantinople 1717–18 and in Europe—mostly Italy—from 1739 until shortly before her death.

Constantinople

To ——

Give me, Great God (said I) a Little Farm
In Summer shady and in Winter warm,
Where a clear Spring gives birth to a cool brook
By nature sliding down a Mossy rock,
Not artfully in Leaden Pipes convey'd   5
Nor greatly falling in a forc'd Cascade,
Pure and unsulli'd winding through the Shade.
All-Bounteous Heaven has added to my Prayer
A softer Climat and a Purer air.
　Our frozen Isle now chiling winter binds,   10
Deform'd with rains and rough with blasting winds,
The wither'd woods grown white with hoary froast
By driving Storms their verdent Beauty's lost,
The trembling Birds their leafless coverts shun
And seek in Distant Climes a warmer Sun,   15
The water Nimphs their Silenc'd urns deplore,
Even Thames benum'd, a river now no more;
The barren meadows give no more delight,
By Glistening Snow made painfull to the Sight.
　Here Summer reigns with one Eternal Smile,   20
And Double Harvests bless the happy Soil.
Fair, fertile, fields! to whom indulgent Heaven
Has every charm of every Season given,
No killing Cold deforms the beauteous year,
The Springing flowers no comeing winter fear,   25
But as the Parent rose decayes and dyes
The infant buds with brighter collours rise
And with fresh Sweets the Mother's-Scent Supplies.
Near them the Vi'let glows with odours blest
And blooms in more than Tyrian Purple drest,   30
The rich Jonquills their golden gleem display
And shine in glory emulating day.
These chearfull groves their Living Leaves retain,
The streams still murmur undefil'd by rain,
And rising green adorns the fruitfull plain.   35
The warbling Kind uninterrupted Sing,
Warm'd with enjoyment of perpetual Spring.
　Here from my Window I at once survey
The crouded City, and Resounding Sea,
In Distant views see Asian Mountains rise   40
And lose their Snowy Summits in the Skies.

---

30 Tyrian Purple　deep red, like the dyes of ancient Tyre

Above those Mountains high Olympus tow'rs
(The Parliamental seat of heavenly Pow'rs).
New to the sight, my ravish'd Eyes admire
Each gilded Crescent and each antique Spire,   45
The Marble Mosques beneath whose ample Domes
Fierce Warlike Sultans sleep in peacefull Tombs.
Those lofty Structures, once the Christian boast,
Their Names, their Glorys, and their Beautys lost,
Those Altars bright with Gold, with Sculpture grac'd,   50
By Barbarous Zeal of Savage Foes defac'd:
Sophia alone her Ancient Sound retains
Tho' unbeleiving Vows her shrine prophanes.
Where Holy Saints have dy'd, in Sacred Cells
Where Monarchs pray'd, the Frantic Derviche dwells.   55
How art thou falln, Imperial City, low!
Where are thy Hopes of Roman Glory now?
Where are thy Palaces by Prelates rais'd;
Where preistly Pomp in Purple Lustre blaz'd?
Where Grecian Artists all their Skill display'd   60
Before the Happy Sciences decay'd,
So vast, that youthfull Kings might there reside,
So splendid, to content a Patriarch's pride,
Convents where Emperours profess'd of Old,
The Labour'd Pillars that their Triumphs told   65
(Vain Monuments of Men that once were great!)
Sunk undistinguish'd in one common Fate!
    One Little Spot the small Fenar contains,
Of Greek Nobillity, the poor remains,
Where other Helens show like powerfull Charms   70
As once engag'd the Warring World in Arms,
Those Names which Royal Auncestry can boast
In mean Mechanic arts obscurely lost,
Those Eyes a second Homer might inspire,
Fix'd at the loom, destroy their useless Fire.   75
    Greiv'd at a view which strikes upon my Mind
The short-liv'd Vanity of Humankind,
In Gaudy Objects I indulge my Sight
And turn where Eastern Pomp gives Gay Delight.   80
See; the vast Train in Various Habits drest,
By the bright Scimetar and sable vest,
The Vizier proud, distinguish'd o're the rest,   *chief minister*
Six slaves in gay Attire his Bridle hold,
His Bridle rich with Gems, his stirrups Gold,

---

42 Olympus a mountain in northeastern Greece, home of the Greek gods
48 Christian boast Constantinople was renowned for its Christian art and architecture, particularly
of the ninth and tenth centuries. It was conquered by Muslim forces in 1453.
52 Sophia Hagia Sophia (Holy Wisdom), the great church of Constantinople built in the sixth
century. After the Muslim conquest it became a mosque. Most of its ancient Christian mosaics had been
untouched in Montagu's time.
56 Imperial City Constantinople became the centre of the Roman Empire under the Emperor
Constantine in 330.
68 Fenar the Greek quarter of Constantinople

His snowy Steed adorn'd with Lavish Pride,   85
Whole troops of Soldiers mounted by his Side,
These toss the Plumy Crest, Arabian Coursers guide.
With awfull Duty, all decline their Eyes,
No Bellowing Shouts of noisie crouds arise,
Silence, in solemn state the March attends   90
Till at the Dread Divan the slow Procession ends.   *council of state*
    Yet not these prospects, all profusely Gay,
The gilded Navy that adorns the Sea,
The rising City in Confusion fair,
Magnificently form'd irregular,   95
Where Woods and Palaces at once surprise,
Gardens, on Gardens, Domes on Domes arise,
And endless Beauties tire the wandring Eyes,
So sooths my wishes or so charms my Mind
As this retreat, secure from Human kind,   100
No Knave's successfull craft does Spleen excite,
No Coxcomb's Tawdry Splendour shocks my Sight,
No Mob Alarm awakes my Female Fears,
No unrewarded Merit asks my Tears,
Nor Praise my Mind, nor Envy hurts my Ear,   105
Even Fame it selfe can hardly reach me here,
Impertinence with all her tattling train,
Fair sounding Flattery's delicious bane,
Censorious Folly, noisy Party rage,
The thousand Tongues with which she must engage   110
Who dare have Virtue in a vicious Age.

                                                         1717   1720

ALEXANDER POPE

1688–1744 b London; moved to near Windsor in about 1700 and to Twickenham in 1718.
Although chronically ill, he dominated the literary life of his time from an early age. His
poetry earned him a comfortable living.

From An Essay on Criticism

True Ease in Writing comes from Art, not Chance,
As those move easiest who have learn'd to dance.
'Tis not enough no Harshness gives Offence,
The *Sound* must seem an *Eccho* to the *Sense*.   365
Soft is the Strain when *Zephyr* gently blows,
And the *smooth Stream* in *smoother Numbers* flows;
But when loud Surges lash the sounding Shore,
The *hoarse, rough Verse* shou'd like the *Torrent* roar.
When *Ajax* strives, some Rock's vast Weight to throw,   370
The Line too *labours*, and the Words move *slow*;
Not so, when swift *Camilla* scours the Plain,
Flies o'er th'unbending Corn, and skims along the Main.
                                                              1711

The Rape of the Lock

Canto I

What dire Offence from am'rous Causes springs,
What mighty Contests rise from trivial Things,
I sing—This Verse to *Caryll*, Muse! is due;
This, ev'n *Belinda* may vouchsafe to view:
Slight is the Subject, but not so the Praise,   5
If She inspire, and He approve my Lays.
    Say what strange Motive, Goddess! cou'd compel
A well-bred *Lord* t'assault a gentle *Belle*?
Oh say what stranger Cause, yet unexplor'd,
Cou'd make a gentle *Belle* reject a *Lord*?   10
In Tasks so bold, can Little Men engage,
And in soft Bosoms dwells such mighty Rage?
    Sol thro' white Curtains shot a tim'rous Ray,
And op'd those Eyes that must eclipse the Day;
Now Lapdogs give themselves the rowzing Shake,   15
And sleepless Lovers, just at Twelve, awake:
Thrice rung the Bell, the Slipper knock'd the Ground,
And the press'd Watch return'd a silver Sound.   *chiming watch*
Belinda still her downy Pillow prest,
Her Guardian *Sylph* prolong'd the balmy Rest.   20
'Twas he had summon'd to her silent Bed
The Morning-Dream that hover'd o'er her Head.
A Youth more glitt'ring than a *Birth-night Beau*,
(That ev'n in Slumber caus'd her Cheek to glow)
Seem'd to her Ear his winning Lips to lay,   25
And thus in Whispers said, or seem'd to say.
    Fairest of Mortals, thou distinguish'd Care
Of thousand bright Inhabitants of Air!
If e'er one Vision touch'd thy infant Thought,
Of all the Nurse and all the Priest have taught,   30
Of airy Elves by Moonlight Shadows seen,
The silver Token, and the circled Green,
Or Virgins visited by Angel-Pow'rs,
With Golden Crowns and Wreaths of heav'nly Flow'rs,
Hear and believe! thy own Importance know,   35
Nor bound thy narrow Views to Things below.
Some secret Truths from Learned Pride conceal'd,
To Maids alone and Children are reveal'd:

The Rape of the Lock This mock-epic poem was written in 1711 at the suggestion of a friend of Pope, John Caryll (see line 3), to help resolve a rift between two families which occurred when Robert, Baron Petre, cut off a lock of Arabella Fermour's hair. A first version of 334 lines in two cantos was published in 1712; the present five-canto version, which added the sylphs and expanded the epic references, was published in 1714, lines 651–80 being added in 1717. Petre married another woman, then died of smallpox in 1713. The 1714 publication mentioned Arabella Fermour by name for the first time, in a dedicatory letter; an epigraph in Latin states, 'Belinda, I did not wish to profane your locks, but am pleased to have granted this to your prayers'.
23 Birth-night Beau a gentleman dressed for the monarch's birthday celebration
32 silver Token left by the fairies for good maidservants

What tho' no Credit doubting Wits may give?
The Fair and Innocent shall still believe.   40
Know then, unnumber'd Spirits round thee fly,
The light *Militia* of the lower Sky;
These, tho' unseen, are ever on the Wing,
Hang o'er the *Box*, and hover round the *Ring*.
Think what an Equipage thou hast in Air,   45
And view with scorn *Two Pages* and a *Chair*.   *sedan chair*
As now your own, our Beings were of old,
And once inclos'd in Woman's beauteous Mold;
Thence, by a soft Transition, we repair
From earthly Vehicles to these of Air.   50
Think not, when Woman's transient Breath is fled,
That all her Vanities at once are dead:
Succeeding Vanities she still regards,
And tho' she plays no more, o'erlooks the Cards.
Her Joy in gilded Chariots, when alive,   55
And Love of *Ombre*, after Death survive.
For when the Fair in all their Pride expire,
To their first Elements the Souls retire:
The Sprights of fiery Termagants in Flame   *shrews*
Mount up, and take a *Salamander*'s Name.   60
Soft yielding Minds to Water glide away,
And sip with *Nymphs*, their Elemental Tea.
The graver Prude sinks downward to a *Gnome*,
In search of Mischief still on Earth to roam.
The light Coquettes in *Sylphs* aloft repair,   65
And sport and flutter in the Fields of Air.
   Know farther yet; Whoever fair and chaste
Rejects Mankind, is by some *Sylph* embrac'd:
For Spirits, freed from mortal Laws, with ease
Assume what Sexes and what Shapes they please.   70
What guards the Purity of melting Maids,
In Courtly Balls, and Midnight Masquerades,
Safe from the treach'rous Friend, the daring Spark,
The Glance by Day, the Whisper in the Dark;
When kind Occasion prompts their warm Desires,   75
When Musick softens, and when Dancing fires?
'Tis but their *Sylph*, the wise Celestials know,
Tho' *Honour* is the Word with Men below.
   Some Nymphs there are, too conscious of their Face,
For Life predestin'd to the *Gnomes*' Embrace.   80
These swell their Prospects and exalt their Pride,
When Offers are disdain'd, and Love deny'd.

---

44 Box   theatre box   **the Ring**   a fashionable circular drive in Hyde Park
56 Ombre   a card game
58 first Elements   In traditional cosmology (outdated by Pope's time) all things were a mixture of
four elements: earth, air, water and fire. Human temperaments were supposed to be determined by a
predominance of one of these elements.
60 The **Salamander** was reputedly able to live in fire.
62 Tea   pron. tay

Then gay Ideas crowd the vacant Brain;
While Peers and Dukes, and all their sweeping Train,
And Garters, Stars and Coronets appear,   85
And in soft Sounds, *Your Grace* salutes their Ear.
'Tis these that early taint the Female Soul,
Instruct the Eyes of young *Coquettes* to roll,
Teach Infant-Cheeks a bidden Blush to know,
And little Hearts to flutter at a *Beau*.   90
　　Oft when the World imagine Women stray,
The *Sylphs* thro' mystick Mazes guide their Way,
Thro' all the giddy Circle they pursue,
And old Impertinence expel by new.   *folly*
What tender Maid but must a Victim fall   95
To one Man's Treat, but for another's Ball?
When *Florio* speaks, what Virgin could withstand,
If gentle *Damon* did not squeeze her Hand?
With varying Vanities, from ev'ry Part,
They shift the moving Toyshop of their Heart;   100
Where Wigs with Wigs, with Sword-knots Sword-knots strive,
Beaus banish Beaus, and Coaches Coaches drive.
This erring Mortals Levity may call,
Oh blind to Truth! the *Sylphs* contrive it all.
　　Of these am I, who thy Protection claim,   105
A watchful Sprite, and *Ariel* is my Name.
Late, as I rang'd the Crystal Wilds of Air,
In the clear Mirror of thy ruling *Star*
I saw, alas! some dread Event impend,
Ere to the Main this Morning Sun descend.   110
But Heav'n reveals not what, or how, or where:
Warn'd by thy *Sylph*, oh Pious Maid beware!
This to disclose is all thy Guardian can.
Beware of all, but most beware of Man!
　　He said; when *Shock*, who thought she slept too long, 115
Leapt up, and wak'd his Mistress with his Tongue.
'Twas then *Belinda*! if Report say true,
Thy Eyes first open'd on a *Billet-doux*;   *love letter*
Wounds, Charms, and *Ardors,* were no sooner read,
But all the Vision vanish'd from thy Head.   120
　　And now, unveil'd, the *Toilet* stands display'd,
Each Silver Vase in mystic Order laid.
First, rob'd in White, the Nymph intent adores
With Head uncover'd, the *Cosmetic* Pow'rs.
A heav'nly Image in the Glass appears,   125
To that she bends, to that her Eyes she rears;
Th'inferior Priestess, at her Altar's side,
Trembling, begins the sacred Rites of Pride.

---

101 **Sword-knots** ribbons on the sword hilts
115 **Shock** a breed of longhaired lapdog; here the dog itself
121 **Toilet** the equipment for grooming
127 **inferior Priestess** i.e. the maid, Betty, mentioned in line 148

Unnumber'd Treasures ope at once, and here
The various Off'rings of the World appear;   130
From each she nicely culls with curious Toil,
And decks the Goddess with the glitt'ring Spoil.
This Casket *India*'s glowing Gems unlocks,
And all *Arabia* breathes from yonder Box.
The Tortoise here and Elephant unite,   135
Transform'd to *Combs*, the speckled and the white.
Here Files of Pins extend their shining Rows,
Puffs, Powders, Patches, Bibles, Billet-doux.
Now awful Beauty puts on all its Arms;
The Fair each moment rises in her Charms,   140
Repairs her Smiles, awakens ev'ry Grace,
And calls forth all the Wonders of her Face;
Sees by Degrees a purer Blush arise,
And keener Lightnings quicken in her Eyes.
The busy *Sylphs* surround their darling Care;   145
These set the Head, and those divide the Hair,
Some fold the Sleeve, whilst others plait the Gown;
And *Betty*'s prais'd for Labours not her own.

Canto II

Not with more Glories, in th' Etherial Plain,
The Sun first rises o'er the purpled Main,   150
Than issuing forth, the Rival of his Beams
Launch'd on the Bosom of the Silver *Thames*.
Fair Nymphs, and well-drest Youths around her shone,
But ev'ry Eye was fix'd on her alone.
On her white Breast a sparkling *Cross* she wore,   155
Which *Jews* might kiss, and Infidels adore.
Her lively Looks a sprightly Mind disclose,
Quick as her Eyes, and as unfix'd as those:
Favours to none, to all she Smiles extends,
Oft she rejects, but never once offends.   160
Bright as the Sun, her Eyes the Gazers strike,
And, like the Sun, they shine on all alike.
Yet graceful Ease, and Sweetness void of Pride,
Might hide her Faults, if *Belles* had Faults to hide:
If to her share some Female Errors fall,   165
Look on her Face, and you'll forget 'em all.
   This Nymph, to the Destruction of Mankind,
Nourish'd two Locks, which graceful hung behind
In equal Curls, and well conspir'd to deck
With shining Ringlets the smooth Iv'ry Neck.   170
Love in these Labyrinths his Slaves detains,
And mighty Hearts are held in slender Chains.

---

131 **nicely** fastidiously **curious** careful
138 **Patches** small pieces of cloth used to simulate beauty spots
139 **awful** awe-inspiring
144 **keener lightnings** by using eye shadow and/or eyedrops of belladonna

With hairy Sprindges we the Birds betray,   *snares*
Slight Lines of Hair surprize the Finny Prey,
Fair Tresses Man's Imperial Race insnare,   175
And Beauty draws us with a single Hair.
    Th' Adventrous *Baron* the bright Locks admir'd,
He saw, he wish'd, and to the Prize aspir'd:
Resolv'd to win, he meditates the way,
By Force to ravish, or by Fraud betray;   180
For when Success a Lover's Toil attends,
Few ask, if Fraud or Force attain'd his Ends.
    For this, ere *Phœbus* rose, he had implor'd
Propitious Heav'n, and ev'ry Pow'r ador'd,
But chiefly *Love*—to *Love* an Altar built,   185
Of twelve vast *French* Romances, neatly gilt.
There lay three Garters, half a Pair of Gloves;
And all the Trophies of his former Loves.
With tender *Billet-doux* he lights the Pyre,
And breathes three am'rous Sighs to raise the Fire.   190
Then prostrate falls, and begs with ardent Eyes
Soon to obtain, and long possess the Prize:
The Pow'rs gave Ear, and granted half his Pray'r,
The rest, the Winds dispers'd in empty Air.
    But now secure the painted Vessel glides,   195
The Sun-beams trembling on the floating Tydes,
While melting Musick steals upon the Sky,
And soften'd Sounds along the Waters die.
Smooth flow the Waves, the Zephyrs gently play,
Belinda smil'd, and all the World was gay.   200
All but the *Sylph*—With careful Thoughts opprest,
Th'impending Woe sate heavy on his Breast.
He summons strait his Denizens of Air:
The lucid Squadrons round the Sails repair: *gather*
Soft o'er the Shrouds Aerial Whispers breathe,   *rigging* 205
That seem'd but *Zephyrs* to the Train beneath.
Some to the Sun their Insect-Wings unfold,
Waft on the Breeze, or sink in Clouds of Gold.
Transparent Forms, too fine for mortal Sight,
Their fluid Bodies half dissolv'd in Light.   210
Loose to the Wind their airy Garments flew,
Thin glitt'ring Textures of the filmy Dew;
Dipt in the richest Tincture of the Skies,
Where Light disports in ever-mingling Dies,
While ev'ry Beam new transient Colours flings,   215
Colours that change whene'er they wave their Wings.
Amid the Circle, on the gilded Mast,
Superior by the Head, was *Ariel* plac'd;
His Purple Pinions opening to the Sun,
He rais'd his Azure Wand, and thus begun.   220
    Ye *Sylphs* and *Sylphids*, to your Chief give Ear,
Fays, *Fairies*, *Genii*, *Elves*, and *Dœmons* hear!
Ye know the Spheres and various Tasks assign'd,
By Laws Eternal, to th' Aerial Kind.

Some in the Fields of purest *Æther* play,   225
And bask and whiten in the Blaze of Day.
Some guide the Course of wandring Orbs on high,
Or roll the Planets thro' the boundless Sky.
Some less refin'd, beneath the Moon's pale Light
Pursue the Stars that shoot athwart the Night,   230
Or suck the Mists in grosser Air below,
Or dip their Pinions in the painted Bow,
Or brew fierce Tempests on the wintry Main,
Or o'er the Glebe distill the kindly Rain.   *farmland*
Others on Earth o'er human Race preside,   235
Watch all their Ways, and all their Actions guide:
Of these the Chief the Care of Nations own,
And guard with Arms Divine the *British Throne*.
   Our humbler Province is to tend the Fair,
Not a less pleasing, tho' less glorious Care.   240
To save the Powder from too rude a Gale,
Nor let th' imprison'd Essences exhale,
To draw fresh Colours from the vernal Flow'rs,
To steal from Rainbows ere they drop in Show'rs
A brighter Wash; to curl their waving Hairs,   245
Assist their Blushes, and inspire their Airs;
Nay oft, in Dreams, Invention we bestow,
To change a *Flounce*, or add a *Furbelo*.
   This Day, black Omens threat the brightest Fair
That e'er deserv'd a watchful Spirit's Care;   250
Some dire Disaster, or by Force, or Slight,   *sleight*
But what, or where, the Fates have wrapt in Night.
Whether the Nymph shall break *Diana*'s Law,
Or some frail *China* Jar receive a Flaw,
Or stain her Honour, or her new Brocade,   255
Forget her Pray'rs, or miss a Masquerade,
Or lose her Heart, or Necklace, at a Ball;   .
Or whether Heav'n has doom'd that *Shock* must fall.
Haste then ye Spirits! to your Charge repair;
The flutt'ring Fan be *Zephyretta*'s Care;   260
The Drops to thee, *Brillante*, we consign;   *diamond earrings*
And, *Momentilla*, let the Watch be thine;
Do thou, *Crispissa*, tend her fav'rite Lock;
Ariel himself shall be the Guard of *Shock*.
   To Fifty chosen *Sylphs*, of special Note,   265
We trust th' important Charge, the *Petticoat*:
Oft have we known that sev'nfold Fence to fail,
Tho' stiff with Hoops, and arm'd with Ribs of Whale.
Form a strong Line about the Silver Bound,
And guard the wide Circumference around.   270

---

225 **Æther**   the purest air, supposed to be beyond the moon
248 **Furbelo**   ornamental pleat on a dress or petticoat
253 **Diana's Law**   chastity. In classical mythology, Diana (Greek Artemis) was the chaste hunter
goddess.

Whatever Spirit, careless of his Charge,
His Post neglects, or leaves the Fair at large,
Shall feel sharp Vengeance soon o'ertake his Sins,
Be stopt in *Vials*, or transfixt with *Pins*;
Or plung'd in Lakes of bitter *Washes* lie,   275
Or wedg'd whole Ages in a *Bodkin*'s Eye:
Gums and *Pomatums* shall his Flight restrain,
While clog'd he beats his silken Wings in vain;
Or Alom-*Stypticks* with contracting Power
Shrink his thin Essence like a rivell'd Flower.   *wrinkled* 280
Or as *Ixion* fix'd, the Wretch shall feel
The giddy Motion of the whirling Mill,   *cocoa mill*
In Fumes of burning Chocolate shall glow,
And tremble at the Sea that froaths below!
He spoke; the Spirits from the Sails descend;   285
Some, Orb in Orb, around the Nymph extend,
Some thrid the mazy Ringlets of her Hair,
Some hang upon the Pendants of her Ear;
With beating Hearts the dire Event they wait,
Anxious, and trembling for the Birth of Fate.   290

Canto III

Close by those Meads for ever crown'd with Flow'rs,
Where *Thames* with pride surveys his rising Tow'rs,
There stands a Structure of Majestick Frame,
Which from the neighb'ring *Hampton* takes its Name.
Here *Britain*'s Statesmen oft the Fall foredoom   295
Of Foreign Tyrants, and of Nymphs at home;
Here Thou, Great *Anna*! whom three Realms obey,
Dost sometimes Counsel take—and sometimes *Tea*.
Hither the Heroes and the Nymphs resort,
To taste awhile the Pleasures of a Court;   300
In various Talk th' instructive hours they past,
Who gave the *Ball*, or paid the *Visit* last:
One speaks the Glory of the *British Queen*,
And one describes a charming *Indian Screen*;
A third interprets Motions, Looks, and Eyes;   305
At ev'ry Word a Reputation dies.
Snuff, or the *Fan*, supply each Pause of Chat,
With singing, laughing, ogling, and all that.
Mean while declining from the Noon of Day,
The Sun obliquely shoots his burning Ray;   310
The hungry Judges soon the Sentence sign,
And Wretches hang that Jury-men may Dine;

---

276 Bodkin a large blunt needle. The term can also apply to an ornamental hairpin or a dagger.
279 Alom-Stypticks astringent skin ointment
281 Ixion, in Greek mythology, was tied to an eternally revolving wheel for having tried to seduce the goddess Juno (Greek Hera).
293 Structure the royal palace of Hampton Court, on the Thames outside London
297 Anna Queen Anne

The Merchant from th' *Exchange* returns in Peace,
And the long Labours of the *Toilette* cease—
Belinda now, whom Thirst of Fame invites,   315
Burns to encounter two adventrous Knights,
At *Ombre* singly to decide their Doom;
And swells her Breast with Conquests yet to come.
Strait the three Bands prepare in Arms to join,
Each Band the number of the Sacred Nine.   320
Soon as she spreads her Hand, th' Aerial Guard
Descend, and sit on each important Card:
First *Ariel* perch'd upon a *Matadore*,
Then each, according to the Rank they bore;
For *Sylphs*, yet mindful of their ancient Race,   325
Are, as when Women, wondrous fond of Place.
    Behold, four *Kings* in Majesty rever'd,
With hoary Whiskers and a forky Beard;
And four fair *Queens* whose hands sustain a Flow'r,
Th' expressive Emblem of their softer Pow'r;   330
Four *Knaves* in Garbs succinct, a trusty Band,   *girded*
Caps on their heads, and halberts in their hand;
And Particolour'd Troops, a shining Train,
Draw forth to Combat on the Velvet Plain.
    The skilful Nymph reviews her Force with Care;   335
Let Spades be Trumps! she said, and Trumps they were.
    Now move to War her Sable *Matadores*,
In Show like Leaders of the swarthy *Moors*.
Spadillio first, unconquerable Lord!
Led off two captive Trumps, and swept the Board.   340
As many more *Manillio* forc'd to yield,
And march'd a Victor from the verdant Field.
Him *Basto* follow'd, but his Fate more hard
Gain'd but one Trump and one *Plebeian* Card.
With his broad Sabre next, a Chief in Years,   345
The hoary Majesty of *Spades* appears;
Puts forth one manly Leg, to sight reveal'd;
The rest his many-colour'd Robe conceal'd.
The Rebel-*Knave*, who dares his Prince engage,
Proves the just Victim of his Royal Rage.   350
Ev'n mighty *Pam* that Kings and Queens o'erthrew,
And mow'd down Armies in the Fights of *Lu*,
Sad Chance of War! now, destitute of Aid,
Falls undistinguish'd by the Victor *Spade*!

---

313 **Exchange** the Royal Exchange in London, a business centre for bankers, brokers and merchants
317 **Ombre** (pron. omber) a card game for three people, holding nine cards each, in which one player—the ombre—chooses trumps and seeks to take more tricks than either of the other two. Trumps always include the black aces. When spades are trumps (see line 336), the top three cards (known as 'matadors': line 337) in order of value are the ace of spades ('Spadille': line 339), the two of spades ('Manille': line 341) and the ace of clubs ('Basto': line 343). In the game described here, Belinda wins the first four tricks (lines 337–54) and the Baron wins the next four (lines 356–78). Belinda is in danger of being given Codille (line 382)—i.e. failing to win—but takes the final trick (line 388).
349 **Rebel-Knave** i.e. jack (or 'knave') of spades
351 **Pam** jack of clubs: the highest card in the game of loo (**Lu**: line 352)

Thus far both Armies to *Belinda* yield;   355
Now to the *Baron* Fate inclines the Field.
His warlike *Amazon* her Host invades,
Th' Imperial Consort of the Crown of *Spades*.
The *Club*'s black Tyrant first her Victim dy'd,
Spite of his haughty Mien, and barb'rous Pride: 360
What boots the Regal Circle on his Head,
His Giant Limbs in State unwieldy spread?
That long behind he trails his pompous Robe,
And of all Monarchs only grasps the Globe?
   The *Baron* now his *Diamonds* pours apace;   365
Th' embroider'd *King* who shows but half his Face,
And his refulgent *Queen*, with Pow'rs combin'd,
Of broken Troops an easie Conquest find.
Clubs, *Diamonds*, *Hearts*, in wild Disorder seen,
With Throngs promiscuous strow the level Green.   *jumbled* 370
Thus when dispers'd a routed Army runs,
Of *Asia*'s Troops, and *Africk*'s Sable Sons,
With like Confusion different Nations fly,
Of various Habit and of various Dye,
The pierc'd Battalions dis-united fall,   375
In Heaps on Heaps; one Fate o'erwhelms them all.
   The *Knave of Diamonds* tries his wily Arts,
And wins (oh shameful Chance!) the *Queen of Hearts*.
At this, the Blood the Virgin's Cheek forsook,
A livid Paleness spreads o'er all her Look;   380
She sees, and trembles at th' approaching Ill,
Just in the Jaws of Ruin, and *Codille*.
And now, (as oft in some distemper'd State)
On one nice *Trick* depends the gen'ral Fate.
An *Ace* of Hearts steps forth: The *King* unseen   385
Lurk'd in her Hand, and mourn'd his captive *Queen*.
He springs to Vengeance with an eager pace,
And falls like Thunder on the prostrate *Ace*.
The Nymph exulting fills with Shouts the Sky,
The Walls, the Woods, and long Canals reply.   390
   Oh thoughtless Mortals! ever blind to Fate,
Too soon dejected, and too soon elate!
Sudden these Honours shall be snatch'd away,
And curs'd for ever this Victorious Day.
   For lo! the Board with Cups and Spoons is crown'd,   395
The Berries crackle, and the Mill turns round.   *coffee beans*
On shining Altars of *Japan* they raise
The silver Lamp; the fiery Spirits blaze.
From silver Spouts the grateful Liquors glide,
While *China*'s Earth receives the smoking Tyde.   400

---

364 The king of clubs is depicted holding a **Globe** as an emblem of dominion.
384 nice precisely calculated
388 When the red cards are not trumps, the ace of hearts ranks behind the king, queen and jack of hearts.
397 Altars of Japan tables highly varnished in the Japanese style

At once they gratify their Scent and Taste,
And frequent Cups prolong the rich Repast.
Strait hover round the Fair her Airy Band;
Some, as she sip'd, the fuming Liquor fann'd,
Some o'er her Lap their careful Plumes display'd,   405
Trembling, and conscious of the rich Brocade.
Coffee, (which makes the Politician wise,
And see thro' all things with his half-shut Eyes)
Sent up in Vapours to the *Baron*'s Brain
New Stratagems, the radiant Lock to gain.   410
Ah cease rash Youth! desist ere 'tis too late,
Fear the just Gods, and think of *Scylla*'s Fate!
Chang'd to a Bird, and sent to flit in Air,
She dearly pays for *Nisus*' injur'd Hair!
    But when to Mischief Mortals bend their Will,   415
How soon they find fit Instruments of Ill!
Just then, *Clarissa* drew with tempting Grace
A two-edg'd Weapon from her shining Case;
So Ladies in Romance assist their Knight,
Present the Spear, and arm him for the Fight.   420
He takes the Gift with rev'rence, and extends
The little Engine on his Fingers' ends,
This just behind *Belinda*'s Neck he spread,
As o'er the fragrant Steams she bends her Head:
Swift to the Lock a thousand Sprights repair,   425
A thousand Wings, by turns, blow back the Hair,
And thrice they twitch'd the Diamond in her ear,
Thrice she look'd back, and thrice the Foe drew near.
Just in that instant, anxious *Ariel* sought
The close Recesses of the Virgin's Thought;   430
As on the Nosegay in her Breast reclin'd,
He watch'd th' Ideas rising in her Mind,
Sudden he view'd, in spite of all her Art,
An Earthly Lover lurking at her Heart.
Amaz'd, confus'd, he found his Pow'r expir'd,   435
Resign'd to Fate, and with a Sigh retir'd.
    The Peer now spreads the glitt'ring *Forfex* wide,
T'inclose the Lock; now joins it, to divide.
Ev'n then, before the fatal Engine clos'd,
A wretched *Sylph* too fondly interpos'd;   440
Fate urg'd the Sheers, and cut the *Sylph* in twain,
(But Airy Substance soon unites again)
The meeting Points the sacred Hair dissever
From the fair Head, for ever and for ever!
    Then flash'd the living Lightning from her Eyes,   445
And Screams of Horror rend th' affrighted Skies.
Not louder Shrieks to pitying Heav'n are cast,
When Husbands or when Lap-dogs breathe their last,

412–14 In Greek mythology, **Scylla** was turned into a seabird and pursued by an eagle for the treachery of cutting from the head of her father, King **Nisus**, a lock of hair (on which his life and kingdom depended) and presenting it to his enemy, King Minos. See *Metamorphoses* VIII.
437 Forfex Latin for scissors

Or when rich *China* Vessels, fal'n from high, 450
In glittring Dust and painted Fragments lie!
   Let Wreaths of Triumph now my Temples twine,
(The Victor cry'd) the glorious Prize is mine!
While Fish in Streams, or Birds delight in Air,
Or in a Coach and Six the *British* Fair,
As long as *Atalantis* shall be read, 455
Or the small Pillow grace a Lady's Bed,
While *Visits* shall be paid on solemn Days,
When numerous Wax-lights in bright Order blaze,
While Nymphs take Treats, or Assignations give,
So long my Honour, Name, and Praise shall live! 460
   What Time wou'd spare, from Steel receives its date,
And Monuments, like Men, submit to Fate!
Steel cou'd the Labour of the Gods destroy,
And strike to Dust th' Imperial Tow'rs of *Troy*;
Steel cou'd the Works of mortal Pride confound, 465
And hew Triumphal Arches to the Ground.
What Wonder then, fair Nymph! thy Hairs shou'd feel
The conqu'ring Force of unresisted Steel?

Canto IV

But anxious Cares the pensive Nymph opprest,
And secret Passions labour'd in her Breast. 470
Not youthful Kings in Battel seiz'd alive,
Not scornful Virgins who their Charms survive,
Not ardent Lovers robb'd of all their Bliss,
Not ancient Ladies when refus'd a Kiss,
Not Tyrants fierce that unrepenting die, 475
Not *Cynthia* when her *Manteau*'s pinn'd awry, *loose robe*
E'er felt such Rage, Resentment and Despair,
As Thou, sad Virgin! for thy ravish'd Hair.
   For, that sad moment, when the *Sylphs* withdrew,
And *Ariel* weeping from *Belinda* flew, 480
Umbriel, a dusky melancholy Spright,
As ever sully'd the fair face of Light,
Down to the Central Earth, his proper Scene,
Repair'd to search the gloomy Cave of *Spleen*.
   Swift on his sooty Pinions flitts the *Gnome*, 485
And in a Vapour reach'd the dismal Dome.
No cheerful Breeze this sullen Region knows,
The dreaded *East* is all the Wind that blows.
Here, in a Grotto, sheltred close from Air,
And screen'd in Shades from Day's detested Glare, 490

---

455 Atalantis *New Atalantis* (1709), scandalous memoirs by Mary De La Rivière Manley
(1672–1724)
484 Spleen the human organ associated in Pope's time with fits of melancholy, ranging in scale
from peevishness to hallucinations
486 Vapour A fit of spleen was sometimes called 'the vapours'.
488 The east wind brought rainy weather, associated with the vapours.

She sighs for ever on her pensive Bed,
Pain at her Side, and *Megrim* at her Head.
    Two Handmaids wait the Throne: Alike in Place,
But diff'ring far in Figure and in Face.
Here stood *Ill-nature* like an *ancient Maid*,   495
Her wrinkled Form in *Black* and *White* array'd;
With store of Pray'rs, for Mornings, Nights, and Noons,
Her Hand is fill'd; her Bosom with Lampoons.
    There *Affectation* with a sickly Mien
Shows in her Cheek the Roses of Eighteen,   500
Practis'd to Lisp, and hang the Head aside,
Faints into Airs, and languishes with Pride;
On the rich Quilt sinks with becoming Woe,
Wrapt in a Gown, for Sickness, and for Show.
The Fair-ones feel such Maladies as these,   505
When each new Night-Dress gives a new Disease.
    A constant *Vapour* o'er the Palace flies;
Strange Phantoms rising as the Mists arise;
Dreadful, as Hermit's Dreams in haunted Shades,
Or bright as Visions of expiring Maids.   510
Now glaring Fiends, and Snakes on rolling Spires,
Pale Spectres, gaping Tombs, and Purple Fires:
Now Lakes of liquid Gold, *Elysian* Scenes,   *heavenly*
And Crystal Domes, and Angels in Machines.   *stage machinery*
    Unnumber'd Throngs on ev'ry side are seen   515
Of Bodies chang'd to various Forms by *Spleen*.
Here living *Teapots* stand, one Arm held out,
One bent; the Handle this, and that the Spout:
A Pipkin there like *Homer's Tripod* walks;
Here sighs a Jar, and there a Goose-pye talks;   520
Men prove with Child, as pow'rful Fancy works,
And Maids turn'd Bottels, call aloud for Corks.
    Safe past the *Gnome* thro' this fantastick Band,
A Branch of healing *Spleenwort* in his hand.
Then thus addrest the Pow'r—Hail wayward Queen!   525
Who rule the Sex to Fifty from Fifteen,
Parent of Vapours and of Female Wit,
Who give th' *Hysteric* or *Poetic* Fit,
On various Tempers act by various wâys,
Make some take Physick, others scribble Plays;   *medication* 530
Who cause the Proud their Visits to delay,
And send the Godly in a Pett, to pray.
A Nymph there is, that all thy Pow'r disdains,
And thousands more in equal Mirth maintains.
But oh! if e'er thy *Gnome* could spoil a Grace,   535
Or raise a Pimple on a beauteous Face,
Like Citron-Waters Matrons' Cheeks inflame,
Or change Complexions at a losing Game;

---

519 **Pipkin**   an earthenware pot; here depicted as walking, with allusion to the wheeled three-legged
stools of the god Hephaistos in Homer's *Iliad*, XVIII.
524 **Spleenwort**   a kind of fern used to purge spleen
537 **Citron Waters**   lemon-flavoured brandy

If e'er with airy Horns I planted Heads,
Or rumpled Petticoats, or tumbled Beds, 540
Or caus'd Suspicion when no Soul was rude,
Or discompos'd the head-dress of a Prude,
Or e'er to costive Lap-Dog gave Disease,
Which not the Tears of brightest Eyes could ease:
Hear me, and touch *Belinda* with Chagrin; 545
That single Act gives half the World the Spleen.
 The Goddess with a discontented Air
Seems to reject him, tho' she grants his Pray'r.
A wondrous Bag with both her Hands she binds,
Like that where once *Ulysses* held the Winds; 550
There she collects the Force of Female Lungs,
Sighs, Sobs, and Passions, and the War of Tongues.
A Vial next she fills with fainting Fears,
Soft Sorrows, melting Griefs, and flowing Tears.
The *Gnome* rejoicing bears her Gifts away, 555
Spreads his black Wings, and slowly mounts to Day.
 Sunk in *Thalestris*' Arms the Nymph he found,
Her Eyes dejected and her Hair unbound.
Full o'er their Heads the swelling Bag he rent,
And all the Furies issued at the Vent. 560
Belinda burns with more than mortal Ire,
And fierce *Thalestris* fans the rising Fire.
O wretched Maid! she spread her Hands, and cry'd,
(While *Hampton*'s Ecchos, wretched Maid! reply'd)
Was it for this you took such constant Care 565
The *Bodkin*, *Comb*, and *Essence* to prepare; *perfume*
For this your Locks in Paper-Durance bound,
For this with tort'ring Irons wreath'd around?
For this with Fillets strain'd your tender Head, *headbands*
And bravely bore the double Loads of Lead? 570
Gods! shall the Ravisher display your Hair,
While the Fops envy, and the Ladies stare!
Honour forbid! at whose unrival'd Shrine
Ease, Pleasure, Virtue, all, our Sex resign.
Methinks already I your Tears survey, 575
Already hear the horrid things they say,
Already see you a degraded Toast,
And all your Honour in a Whisper lost!
How shall I, then, your helpless Fame defend?
'Twill then be Infamy to seem your Friend! 580
And shall this Prize, th' inestimable Prize,
Expos'd thro' Crystal to the gazing Eyes,
And heighten'd by the Diamond's circling Rays,
On that Rapacious Hand for ever blaze?
Sooner shall Grass in *Hide*-Park *Circus* grow, 585
And Wits take Lodgings in the Sound of *Bow*;

---

550 See *Odyssey* X.
557 **Thalestris** name of a queen of the Amazons
586 **Bow** the commercial area of London, within hearing of the bells of St Mary-le-Bow Church

Sooner let Earth, Air, Sea, to *Chaos* fall,
Men, Monkies, Lap-dogs, Parrots, perish all!
　She said; then raging to *Sir Plume* repairs,
And bids her *Beau* demand the precious Hairs:　　　　590
(*Sir Plume*, of *Amber Snuff-box* justly vain,
And the nice Conduct of a *clouded Cane*)
With earnest Eyes, and round unthinking Face,
He first the Snuff-box open'd, then the Case,
And thus broke out—'My Lord, why, what the Devil?　　595
Z—ds! damn the Lock! 'fore Gad, you must be civil!
Plague on't! 'tis past a Jest—nay prithee, Pox!
Give her the Hair'—he spoke, and rapp'd his Box.
　It grieves me much (reply'd the Peer again)
Who speaks so well shou'd ever speak in vain.　　　　600
But by this Lock, this sacred Lock I swear,
(Which never more shall join its parted Hair,
Which never more its Honours shall renew,
Clipt from the lovely Head where late it grew)
That while my Nostrils draw the vital Air,　　　　　605
This Hand, which won it, shall for ever wear.
He spoke, and speaking, in proud Triumph spread
The long-contended Honours of her Head.
　But *Umbriel*, hateful *Gnome*! forbears not so;
He breaks the Vial whence the Sorrows flow.　　　　610
Then see! the *Nymph* in beauteous Grief appears,
Her Eyes half-languishing, half-drown'd in Tears;
On her heav'd Bosom hung her drooping Head,
Which, with a Sigh, she rais'd; and thus she said.
　For ever curs'd be this detested Day,　　　　　615
Which snatch'd my best, my fav'rite Curl away!
Happy! ah ten times happy, had I been,
If *Hampton-Court* these Eyes had never seen!
Yet am not I the first mistaken Maid,
By Love of *Courts* to num'rous Ills betray'd.　　　620
Oh had I rather un-admir'd remain'd
In some lone Isle, or distant *Northern* Land;
Where the gilt *Chariot* never marks the Way,
Where none learn *Ombre*, none e'er taste *Bohea*!
There kept my Charms conceal'd from mortal Eye,　625
Like Roses that in Desarts bloom and die.
What mov'd my Mind with youthful Lords to rome?
O had I stay'd, and said my Pray'rs at home!
'Twas this, the Morning *Omens* seem'd to tell;
Thrice from my trembling hand the *Patch-box* fell;　630
The tott'ring *China* shook without a Wind,
Nay, *Poll* sate mute, and *Shock* was most Unkind!

---

592 clouded　fashionably veined
596 Z——ds　Zounds: a mild swearword; originally 'God's wounds'
615ff.　This speech parodies Achilles' lament for Patroclus in *Iliad* XVIII.
624 Bohea　fine Chinese tea (pron. bohay)

A *Sylph* too warn'd me of the Threats of Fate,
In mystic Visions, now believ'd too late!
See the poor Remnants of these slighted Hairs!   635
My hands shall rend what ev'n thy Rapine spares:
These, in two sable Ringlets taught to break,
Once gave new Beauties to the snowie Neck.
The Sister-Lock now sits uncouth, alone,
And in its Fellow's Fate foresees its own;   640
Uncurl'd it hangs, the fatal Sheers demands;
And tempts once more thy sacrilegious hands.
Oh hadst thou, Cruel! been content to seize
Hairs less in sight, or any Hairs but these!

Canto V

She said: the pitying Audience melt in Tears,   645
But *Fate* and *Jove* had stopp'd the *Baron*'s Ears.
In vain *Thalestris* with Reproach assails,
For who can move when fair *Belinda* fails?
Not half so fixt the *Trojan* cou'd remain,
While *Anna* begg'd and *Dido* rag'd in vain.   650
Then grave *Clarissa* graceful wav'd her Fan;
Silence ensu'd, and thus the Nymph began.
    Say, why are Beauties prais'd and honour'd most,
The wise Man's Passion, and the vain Man's Toast?
Why deck'd with all that Land and Sea afford,   655
Why Angels call'd, and Angel-like ador'd?
Why round our Coaches crowd the white-glov'd Beaus,
Why bows the Side-box from its inmost Rows?
How vain are all these Glories, all our Pains,
Unless good Sense preserve what Beauty gains: 660
That Men may say, when we the Front-box grace,
Behold the first in Virtue, as in Face!
Oh! if to dance all Night, and dress all Day,
Charm'd the Small-pox, or chas'd old Age away;
Who would not scorn what Huswife's Cares produce,   665
Or who would learn one earthly Thing of Use?
To patch, nay ogle, might become a Saint,
Nor could it sure be such a Sin to paint.
But since, alas! frail Beauty must decay,
Curl'd or uncurl'd, since Locks will turn to grey,   670
Since painted, or not painted, all shall fade,
And she who scorns a Man, must die a Maid;
What then remains, but well our Pow'r to use,
And keep good Humour still whate'er we lose?
And trust me, Dear! good Humour can prevail,   675
When Airs, and Flights, and Screams, and Scolding fail.
Beauties in vain their pretty Eyes may roll;
Charms strike the Sight, but Merit wins the Soul.

649–50 See *Aeneid* IV, where the **Trojan** Aeneas is begged by his lover **Dido** and her sister **Anna** not
to leave Carthage; when he does so, Dido kills herself.
653ff. Pope notes that this speech is a parody of that of Sarpedon in *Iliad* XII.

So spoke the Dame, but no Applause ensu'd;
Belinda frown'd, *Thalestris* call'd her Prude.   680
To Arms, to Arms! the fierce Virago cries,
And swift as Lightning to the Combate flies.
All side in Parties, and begin th' Attack;
Fans clap, Silks russle, and tough Whalebones crack;
Heroes' and Heroins' Shouts confus'dly rise,   685
And base, and treble Voices strike the Skies.
No common Weapons in their Hands are found,
Like Gods they fight, nor dread a mortal Wound.
    So when bold *Homer* makes the Gods engage,
And heav'nly Breasts with human Passions rage;   690
'Gainst *Pallas, Mars*; *Latona, Hermes* arms;
And all *Olympus* rings with loud Alarms.
Jove's Thunder roars, Heav'n trembles all around;
Blue *Neptune* storms, the bellowing Deeps resound;
Earth shakes her nodding Tow'rs, the Ground gives way;   695
And the pale Ghosts start at the Flash of Day!
    Triumphant *Umbriel* on a Sconce's Height
Clapt his glad Wings, and sate to view the Fight:
Propt on their Bodkin Spears, the Sprights survey
The growing Combat, or assist the Fray.   700
    While thro' the Press enrag'd *Thalestris* flies,
And scatters Deaths around from both her Eyes,
A *Beau* and *Witling* perish'd in the Throng,
One dy'd in *Metaphor*, and one in *Song*.
O cruel Nymph! a living Death I bear,   705
Cry'd *Dapperwit*, and sunk beside his Chair.
A mournful Glance Sir *Fopling* upwards cast,
Those Eyes are made so killing—was his last:
Thus on *Meander's* flow'ry Margin lies
Th' expiring Swan, and as he sings he dies.   710
    When bold Sir *Plume* had drawn *Clarissa* down,
Chloe stept in, and kill'd him with a Frown;
She smil'd to see the doughty hero slain,
But at her Smile, the Beau reviv'd again.
    Now *Jove* suspends his golden Scales in Air,   715
Weighs the Men's Wits against the Lady's Hair;
The doubtful Beam long nods from side to side;
At length the Wits mount up, the Hairs subside.
    See fierce *Belinda* on the *Baron* flies,
With more than usual Lightning in her Eyes;   720
Nor fear'd the Chief th' unequal Fight to try,
Who sought no more than on his Foe to die.

689ff. See the account of the war of the gods in *Iliad* XX.
691 Pallas Pallas Athene, Greek goddess of wisdom **Latona** mother of Artemis and Apollo
Hermes messenger of the gods
697 Sconce wall bracket for candles
708 Those Eyes . . . words of a song from the opera *Camilla* by Buononcini
709–10 These lines are imitated from Ovid, *Heroides* 7. The **Meander** was a winding river in ancient
Phrygia. The **Swan** was fabled to sing as it dies.

But this bold Lord, with manly Strength indu'd,
She with one Finger and a Thumb subdu'd:
Just where the Breath of Life his Nostrils drew,   725
A Charge of *Snuff* the wily Virgin threw;
The *Gnomes* direct, to ev'ry Atome just,
The pungent Grains of titillating Dust.
Sudden, with starting Tears each Eye o'erflows,
And the high Dome re-ecchoes to his Nose.   730
   Now meet thy Fate, incens'd *Belinda* cry'd,
And drew a deadly *Bodkin* from her Side.
(The same, his ancient Personage to deck,
Her great great Grandsire wore about his Neck
In three *Seal-Rings*; which after, melted down,   735
Form'd a vast *Buckle* for his Widow's Gown:
Her infant Grandame's *Whistle* next it grew,
The *Bells* she gingled, and the *Whistle* blew;
Then in a *Bodkin* grac'd her Mother's Hairs,
Which long she wore, and now *Belinda* wears.)   740
   Boast not my Fall (he cry'd) insulting Foe!
Thou by some other shalt be laid as low.
Nor think, to die dejects my lofty Mind;
All that I dread, is leaving you behind!
Rather than so, ah let me still survive,   745
And burn in *Cupid*'s Flames,—but burn alive.
   Restore the Lock! she cries; and all around
Restore the Lock! the vaulted Roofs rebound.
Not fierce *Othello* in so loud a Strain
Roar'd for the Handkerchief that caus'd his Pain.   750
But see how oft Ambitious Aims are cross'd,
And Chiefs contend 'till all the Prize is lost!
The Lock, obtain'd with Guilt, and kept with Pain,
In ev'ry place is sought, but sought in vain:
With such a Prize no Mortal must be blest,   755
So Heav'n decrees! with Heav'n who can contest?
   Some thought it mounted to the Lunar Sphere,
Since all things lost on Earth, are treasur'd there.
There Heroes' Wits are kept in pondrous Vases,
And Beaus' in *Snuff-boxes* and *Tweezer-Cases*.   760
There broken Vows, and Death-bed Alms are found,
And Lovers' Hearts with Ends of Riband bound;
The Courtier's Promises, and Sick Man's Pray'rs,
The Smiles of Harlots, and the Tears of Heirs,
Cages for Gnats, and Chains to Yoak a Flea;   765
Dry'd Butterflies, and Tomes of Casuistry.
   But trust the Muse—she saw it upward rise,
Tho' mark'd by none but quick Poetic Eyes:

733ff. Pope notes that these lines imitate the 'Progress of Agamemnon's Sceptre' in *Iliad* II; see also *Iliad* X.
758ff. In a note to these lines Pope refers the reader to Ariosto's romance poem *Orlando Furioso* (1532), Canto 34. There Astolfo finds Orlando's lost wits, among other such items, on the moon.

(So *Rome*'s great Founder to the Heav'ns withdrew,
To *Proculus* alone confess'd in view.)   770
A sudden Star, it shot thro' liquid Air,   *transparent*
And drew behind a radiant *Trail of Hair*.
Not *Berenice*'s Locks first rose so bright,
The Heav'ns bespangling with dishevel'd Light.
The *Sylphs* behold it kindling as it flies,   775
And pleas'd pursue its Progress thro' the Skies.
   This is *Beau-monde* shall from the *Mall* survey,
And hail with Musick its propitious Ray.
This, the blest Lover shall for *Venus* take,
And send up Vows from *Rosamonda*'s Lake.   780
This *Partridge* soon shall view in cloudless Skies,
When next he looks thro' *Galilæo*'s Eyes;
And hence th' Egregious Wizard shall foredoom
The Fate of *Louis*, and the Fall of *Rome*.
   Then cease, bright Nymph! to mourn thy ravish'd Hair   785
Which adds new Glory to the shining Sphere!
Not all the Tresses that fair Head can boast
Shall draw such Envy as the Lock you lost.
For, after all the Murders of your Eye,
When, after Millions slain, your self shall die;   790
When those fair Suns shall sett, as sett they must,
And all those Tresses shall be laid in Dust;
This Lock, the Muse shall consecrate to Fame,
And mid'st the Stars inscribe *Belinda*'s Name.

                                                        1714

Epistle

*To Miss BLOUNT, on her leaving
the Town, after the CORONATION*

As some fond virgin, whom her mother's care
Drags from the town to wholsom country air,
Just when she learns to roll a melting eye,
And hear a spark, yet think no danger nigh;
From the dear man unwilling she must sever,   5
Yet takes one kiss before she parts for ever:

769–70 **Founder** The mythical founder of Rome, Romulus, was said to have confirmed his status as a god by appearing in a vision to the senator **Proculus**.
773 A lost poem by Callimachus (*c.* 310–240 BC) and Poem 66 by Catullus (*c.* 84–54 BC) tell how the Egyptian queen **Berenice** pledged her hair to the gods for the safe return of her husband from war. Duly cut upon his return, the hair disappeared and was discovered by the court astronomer, Conon, changed to a constellation.
777 **Beau-monde** high society **Mall** a fashionable walk in St James's Park
780 **Rosamonda's Lake** a pond in St James's Park which was associated with lost love
781 **Partridge** John Partridge was a contemporary astrologer who, according to a note by Pope, annually predicted the downfall of Louis XIV of France and the Pope of Rome.
Miss Blount Teresa Blount, then 26, a friend of Pope
Coronation that of George I in 1714
1 **fond** foolish; also loving
7 **Zephalinda** an invented name for Miss Blount

Thus from the world fair *Zephalinda* flew,
Saw others happy, and with sighs withdrew;
Not that their pleasures caus'd her discontent,
She sigh'd not that They stay'd, but that She went.   10
  She went, to plain-work, and to purling brooks,
Old-fashion'd halls, dull aunts, and croaking rooks,
She went from Op'ra, park, assembly, play,
To morning walks, and pray'rs three hours a day;
To part her time 'twixt reading and Bohea,   15
To muse, and spill her solitary Tea,
Or o'er cold coffee trifle with the spoon,
Count the slow clock, and dine exact at noon;
Divert her eyes with pictures in the fire,
Hum half a tune, tell stories to the squire;   20
Up to her godly garret after sev'n,
There starve and pray, for that's the way to heav'n.
  Some Squire, perhaps, you take delight to rack;
Whose game is Whisk, whose treat a toast in sack,
Who visits with a gun, presents you birds,   25
Then gives a smacking buss, and cries—No words!
Or with his hound comes hallowing from the stable,
Makes love with nods, and knees beneath a table;
Whose laughs are hearty, tho' his jests are coarse,
And loves you best of all things—but his horse.   30
  In some fair evening, on your elbow laid,
You dream of triumphs in the rural shade;
In pensive thought recall the fancy'd scene,
See Coronations rise on ev'ry green;
Before you pass th' imaginary sights   35
Of Lords, and Earls, and Dukes, and garter'd Knights;
While the spread Fan o'ershades your closing eyes;
Then give one flirt, and all the vision flies.
Thus vanish sceptres, coronets, and balls,
And leave you in lone woods, or empty walls.   40
  So when your slave, at some dear, idle time,
(Not plagu'd with headachs, or the want of rhime)
Stands in the streets, abstracted from the crew,
And while he seems to study, thinks of you:
Just when his fancy points your sprightly eyes,   45
Or sees the blush of soft *Parthenia* rise,
Gay pats my shoulder, and you vanish quite;
Streets, chairs, and coxcombs rush upon my sight;   *sedan chairs*
Vext to be still in town, I knit my brow,
Look sow'r, and hum a tune—as you may now.   50

1714   1717

---

7 **Zephalinda**   an invented name for Miss Blount
15 **Bohea**   fine Chinese tea (pron. bohay)
16 **Tea**   pron. tay
24 **Whisk**   whist, unfashionable in the town   **sack**   sherry
38 **flirt**   includes a play on the literal meaning: flick, as of a fan
44 **study**   be lost in thought
46 **Parthenia**   Teresa's younger sister, Martha
47 **Gay**   John Gay, writer and friend of Pope

From An Epistle to Dr Arbuthnot

Let *Sporus* tremble—'What? that Thing of silk,   305
Sporus, that mere white Curd of Ass's milk?
Satire or Sense alas! can *Sporus* feel?
Who breaks a Butterfly upon a Wheel?'
Yet let me flap this Bug with gilded wings,
This painted Child of Dirt that stinks and stings;   310
Whose Buzz the Witty and the Fair annoys,
Yet Wit ne'er tastes, and Beauty ne'er enjoys,
So well-bred Spaniels civilly delight
In mumbling of the Game they dare not bite.
Eternal Smiles his Emptiness betray,   315
As shallow streams run dimpling all the way.
Whether in florid Impotence he speaks,
And, as the Prompter breathes, the Puppet squeaks;
Or at the Ear of *Eve*, familiar Toad,
Half Froth, half Venom, spits himself abroad,   320
In Puns, or Politicks, or Tales, or Lyes,
Or Spite, or Smut, or Rymes, or Blasphemies.
His Wit all see-saw between *that* and *this*,
Now high, now low, now Master up, now Miss,
And he himself one vile Antithesis.   325
Amphibious Thing! that acting either Part,
The trifling Head, or the corrupted Heart!
Fop at the Toilet, Flatt'rer at the Board,
Now trips a Lady, and now struts a Lord.
Eve's Tempter thus the Rabbins have exprest,   330
A Cherub's face, a Reptile all the rest;
Beauty that shocks you, Parts that none will trust,
Wit that can creep, and Pride that licks the dust.

1735

Dr Arbuthnot (1667–1735) John Arbuthnot, writer, physician and long-time friend of Pope: he had recently asked Pope to moderate his personal satire.
305 Sporus a eunuch favoured by the Roman Emperor, Nero: here Lord John Hervey (1696–1743), writer and courtier, a dedicated enemy of Pope.
318 Prompter Sir Robert Walpole, the chief minister
319 at the ear of Eve i.e. like the tempter, Satan, in Milton's *Paradise Lost* IV, 790 ff. Hervey was a confidant of Queen Caroline.
328 Toilet ritual of dressing and grooming. **Board** dinner table.
330 Rabbins rabbis; scholars of the Old Testament
332 Parts personal qualities; also, here, physical ones

JONATHAN SWIFT

1667–1745 b Dublin, of English parents. He was ordained in 1694 and lived for periods in both countries, writing satire and polemics, until appointed Anglican Dean of St Patrick's, Dublin, in 1713. There he turned his satirical gifts to the defence of the Irish against exploitation.

A Description of the Morning

Now hardly here and there an Hackney-Coach
Appearing, show'd the Ruddy Morns Approach.
Now *Betty* from her Masters Bed had flown,
And softly stole to discompose her own.
The Slipshod Prentice from his Masters Door,   5
Had par'd the Dirt, and Sprinkled round the Floor.
Now *Moll* had whirl'd her Mop with dext'rous Airs,
Prepar'd to Scrub the Entry and the Stairs.
The Youth with Broomy Stumps began to trace
The Kennel-Edge, where Wheels had worn the Place.   10
The Smallcoal-Man was heard with Cadence deep,
'Till drown'd in Shriller Notes of Chimney-Sweep,
Duns at his Lordships Gate began to meet,   *creditors*
And Brickdust *Moll* had Scream'd through half the Street.
The Turnkey now his Flock returning sees,   15
Duly let out a Nights to Steal for Fees.
The watchful Bailiffs take their silent Stands,
And School-Boys lag with Satchels in their Hands.
                                        1709   1711

A Satirical Elegy on the Death of a late Famous General

His Grace! impossible! what dead!
Of old age too, and in his bed!
And could that Mighty Warrior fall?
And so inglorious, after all!
Well, since he's gone, no matter how,   5
The last loud trump must wake him now:
And, trust me, as the noise grows stronger,
He'd wish to sleep a little longer.
And could he be indeed so old
As by the news-papers we're told?   10
Threescore, I think, is pretty high;
'Twas time in conscience he should die.
This world he cumber'd long enough;
He burnt his candle to the snuff;
And that's the reason, some folks think,   15
He left behind *so great a s——k.*

---

10 Kennel   gutter, open sewer
General   the Duke of Marlborough (1650–1722)

Behold his funeral appears,
Nor widow's sighs, nor orphan's tears,
Wont at such times each heart to pierce,   *accustomed*
Attend the progress of his herse.   20
But what of that, his friends may say,
He had those honours in his day.
True to his profit and his pride,
He made them weep before he dy'd.

Come hither, all ye empty things,   25
Ye bubbles rais'd by breath of Kings;
Who float upon the tide of state,
Come hither, and behold your fate.
Let pride be taught by this rebuke,
How very mean a thing's a Duke;   30
From all his ill-got honours flung,
Turn'd to that dirt from whence he sprung.

                                                        1722   1765

Verses on the upright Judge, who condemned the *Drapier*'s Printer

In Church your Grandsire cut his Throat;
    To do the Jobb too long he tarry'd,
He should have had my hearty Vote,
    To cut his Throat before he marry'd.

                                                        1724   1735

Stella's Birth-day

This Day, whate'er the Fates decree,
Shall still be kept with Joy by me:
This Day then, let us not be told,   *always*
That you are sick, and I grown old,
Nor think on our approaching Ills,   5
And talk of Spectacles and Pills;
To morrow will be Time enough
To hear such mortifying Stuff.
Yet, since from Reason may be brought
A better and more pleasing Thought,   10
Which can in spite of all Decays,
Support a few remaining Days:
From not the gravest of Divines,
Accept for once some serious Lines.

Although we now can form no more   15
Long Schemes of Life, as heretofore;

Judge William Whitshed, Chief Justice of Ireland, who presided at the trial for sedition of John Harding for printing Swift's anonymous *Drapier's Letters*. Despite Whitshed's browbeating of the jury, Harding was acquitted.
Stella Esther Johnson (1681–1728), Swift's close friend, whom he had known since 1689. Almost every year from 1719 he wrote a poem for her birthday, 13 March.

Yet you, while Time is running fast,
Can look with Joy on what is past.

Were future Happiness and Pain,
A mere Contrivance of the Brain,   20
As Atheists argue, to entice,
And fit their Proselytes for Vice;
(The only Comfort they propose,
To have Companions in their Woes.)
Grant this the Case, yet sure 'tis hard,   25
That Virtue, stil'd its own Reward,
And by all Sages understood
To be the chief of human Good,
Should acting, die, nor leave behind
Some lasting Pleasure in the Mind,   30
Which by Remembrance will assuage,
Grief, Sickness, Poverty, and Age;
And strongly shoot a radiant Dart,
To shine through Life's declining Part.

Say, *Stella*, feel you no Content,   35
Reflecting on a Life well spent?
Your skilful Hand employ'd to save
Despairing Wretches from the Grave;
And then supporting with your Store,
Those whom you dragg'd from Death before: 40
(So Providence on Mortals waits,
Preserving what it first creates)
Your gen'rous Boldness to defend
An innocent and absent Friend;
That Courage which can make you just,   45
To Merit humbled in the Dust:
The Detestation you express
For Vice in all its glitt'ring Dress:
That Patience under tort'ring Pain,
Where stubborn Stoicks would complain.   50

Must these like empty Shadows pass,
Or Forms reflected from a Glass?
Or mere Chimæras in the Mind,
That fly and leave no Marks behind?
Does not the Body thrive and grow   55
By Food of twenty Years ago?
And, had it not been still supply'd,
It must a thousand Times have dy'd.
Then, who with Reason can maintain,
That no Effects of Food remain?   60
And, is not Virtue in Mankind
The Nutriment that feeds the Mind?
Upheld by each good Action past,
And still continued by the last:
Then, who with Reason can pretend,   65
That all Effects of Virtue end?

Believe me *Stella*, when you show
That true Contempt for Things below,
Nor prize your Life for other Ends
Than merely to oblige your Friends; 70
Your former Actions claim their Part,
And join to fortify your Heart.
For Virtue in her daily Race,
Like *Janus*, bears a double Face; *god of doors*
Looks back with Joy where she has gone, 75
And therefore goes with Courage on.
She at your sickly Couch will wait,
And guide you to a better State.

O then, whatever Heav'n intends,
Take Pity on your pitying Friends; 80
Nor let your Ills affect your Mind,
To fancy they can be unkind.
Me, surely me, you ought to spare,
Who gladly would your Suff'rings share;
Or give my Scrap of Life to you, 85
And think it far beneath your Due;
You, to whose Care so oft I owe,
That I'm alive to tell you so.

1727   1727

ANNE FINCH, COUNTESS OF WINCHELSEA

1661–1720 b Hampshire. She was at court in London when young, then moved to Kent.
Her poetry was well known.

A Song

'Tis strange, this Heart within my breast,
    Reason opposing, and her Pow'rs,
Cannot one gentle Moment rest,
    Unless it knows what's done in Yours.

In vain I ask it of your Eyes, 5
    Which subt'ly would my Fears controul;
For Art has taught them to disguise,
    Which Nature made t' explain the Soul.

In vain that Sound, your Voice affords,
    Flatters sometimes my easy Mind; 10
But of too vast Extent are Words
    In them the Jewel Truth to find.

Then let my fond Enquiries cease,
    And so let all my Troubles end:
For, sure, that Heart shall ne'er know Peace, 15
    Which on Anothers do's depend.

1713

A Song

The Nymph, in vain, bestows her pains,
That seeks to thrive, where Bacchus reigns;
In vain, are charms, or smiles, or frowns,
All Immages his torrent drowns.

Flames to the head he may impart,   5
But makes an Island of the heart;
So inaccessible, and cold,
That to be his, is to be old.

1903

A Nocturnal Reverie

In such a *Night*, when every louder Wind
Is to its distant Cavern safe confin'd;
And only gentle *Zephyr* fans his Wings,   *warm breeze*
And lonely *Philomel*, still waking, sings;   *nightingale*
Or from some Tree, fam'd for the *Owl*'s delight,   5
She, hollowing clear, directs the Wand'rer right;
In such a *Night*, when passing Clouds give place,
Or thinly vail the Heav'ns mysterious Face;
When in some River, overhung with Green,
The waving Moon and trembling Leaves are seen;   10
When freshen'd Grass now bears it self upright,
And makes cool Banks to pleasing Rest invite,
Whence springs the *Woodbind*, and the *Bramble*-Rose,
And where the sleepy *Cowslip* shelter'd grows;
Whilst now a paler Hue the *Foxglove* takes,   15
Yet checquers still with Red the dusky brakes;
When scatter'd *Glow-worms*, but in Twilight fine,
Shew trivial Beauties watch their Hour to shine;
Whilst *Salisb'ry* stands the Test of every Light,
In perfect Charms, and perfect Virtue bright: 20
When Odours, which declin'd repelling Day,
Thro' temp'rate Air uninterrupted stray;
When darken'd Groves their softest Shadows wear,
And falling Waters we distinctly hear;
When thro' the Gloom more venerable shows   25
Some ancient Fabrick, awful in Repose,   *building*
While Sunburnt Hills their swarthy Looks conceal,
And swelling Haycocks thicken up the Vale:
When the loos'd *Horse* now, as his Pasture leads,
Comes slowly grazing thro' th' adjoining Meads,   30
Whose stealing Pace, and lengthen'd Shade we fear,
Till torn up Forage in his Teeth we hear:
When nibbling *Sheep* at large pursue their Food,
And unmolested Kine rechew the Cud;   *cows*
When *Curlews* cry beneath the Village-walls,   35
And to her straggling Brood the *Partridge* calls;

---

19 Salisb'ry   Lady Anne Salisbury, daughter of an old friend of the poet

Their shortliv'd Jubilee the Creatures keep,
Which but endures, whilst Tyrant-*Man* do's sleep;
When a sedate Content the Spirit feels,
And no fierce Light disturb, whilst it reveals;   40
But silent Musings urge the Mind to seek
Something, too high for Syllables to speak;
Till the free Soul to a compos'dness charm'd,
Finding the Elements of Rage disarm'd,
O'er all below a solemn Quiet grown,   45
Joys in th' inferiour World, and thinks it like her Own;
In such a *Night* let Me abroad remain,
Till Morning breaks, and All's confus'd again:
Our Cares, our Toils, our Clamours are renew'd,
Or Pleasures, seldom reach'd, again pursu'd.   50

                                                          1713

To Mr Pope,

In Answer to a Copy of Verses, occaisond by a little
Dispute upon four lines in the Rape of the Lock

Disarm'd, with so Genteel an Air,
    The Contest I give o're,
Yett Alexander! have a care,
    And shock the sex no more.

We rule the World, our Lives long Race,   5
    Men but assume that Right,
First Slaves to ev'ry tempting Face,
    Then Martyrs to our spight.

You of one Orpheus sure have read,
    Who wou'd, like you, have Writt,   10
Had He in London Town been bred,
    And pollish'd, too his Wit;

But He, poor Soul, thought all was Well,
    And Great shou'd be his Fame,
When he had left his Wife in Hell,   15
    And Birds and Beasts cou'd Tame.

Yett, vent'ring then with Scoffing Rimes
    The Women to Incense,
Resenting Heroines of those Times
    Soon punish'd the Offence.   20

To Mr Pope Finch had objected to some cavalier remarks on women poets in Alexander Pope's poem, *The Rape of the Lock* (lines 527–30); to which Pope replied with 'Impromptu', a short poem of compliment which wittily excepted her from the general rule. This is her answer to that poem.
9 Orpheus In Greek myth, the music of Orpheus charmed the beasts, and also persuaded the King of Hades (the underworld) to allow his dead wife, Eurydice, to return with him to the living. When he broke an agreement not to look at her following him, she was snatched back. Ultimately, he was torn to pieces by female followers of Dionysus. His severed head floated singing down the river Hebrus and out to the island of Lesbos in the Aegean, which was to become famous as the birthplace of the female poet, Sappho. See *Metamorphoses* X and XI.

And as through Hebrus rould his Scull,
  And Harpe besmear'd with Blood,
They, clashing as the Waves grew full,
  Still Harmonis'd the Flood.

But You, our Follies, gently Treat,   25
  And Spinn so fine the Thread,
You need not fear his awkward Fate;
  The *Lock* won't cost the *Head*.

Our Admiration you Command,
  For all that's gone before;   30
What next we look for at your Hand
  Can only raise itt more.

Yett Sooth the Ladies, I advise,
  As me, to Pride you've wrought;
We're born to wit, but to be wise   35
  By admonitions taught.

                              c. *1714*   1717

Melinda on an Insippid Beauty

In imitation of a fragment of Sapho's

You, when your body, life shall leave
Must drop entire, into the grave;
Unheeded, unregarded lye,
And all of you together dye;
Must hide that fleeting charm, that face in dust,   5
Or to some painted cloath, the slighted Immage trust,
Whilst my fam'd works, shall throo' all times surprise
My polish'd thoughts, my bright Ideas rise,
And to new men be known, still talking to their eyes.

                                    1903

JOHN OLDHAM

1653–83 b Gloucestershire. He worked as a tutor, while writing satire. See Dryden's elegy, p. 373

From A Satyr, in Imitation of the Third of Juvenal

  If you walk out in Bus'ness ne'er so great,
Ten thousand stops you must expect to meet:
Thick crowds in every place you must charge through,
And storm your Passage, wheresoe'er you go: 340

Sapho   Sappho, Greek poet who flourished *c*. 600 BC. See Fragment 55.
Juvenal   Roman satirical poet (AD 60–*c*. 130)

While Tides of Followers behind you throng,
And, pressing on your heels, shove you along:
One with a Board or Rafter hits your Head,
Another with his Elbow bores your side;
Some tread upon your Corns, perhaps in sport,   345
Mean while your Legs are cas'd all o'er with Dirt.
Here you the March of a slow Funeral wait,
Advancing to the Church with solemn State:
There a Sedan, and Lacquies stop your way,
That bears some Punk of Honour to the Play: *prostitute* 350
Now you some mighty piece of Timber meet,
Which tott'ring threatens ruine to the Street:
Next a huge Portland Stone, for building Pauls,
It self almost a Rock, on Carriage rowls:
Which, if it fall, would cause a Massacre,   355
And serve at once to murder, and interr.
　　If what I've said can't from the Town affright,
Consider other dangers of the Night:
When Brickbats are from upper Stories thrown,
And emptied Chamber-pots come pouring down   360
From Garret Windows: you have cause to bless
The gentle Stars, if you come off with Piss:
So many Fates attend, a man had need,
Ne'er walk without a Surgeon by his side:
And he can hardly now discreet be thought,   365
That does not make his Will, ere he go out.
　　If this you 'scape, twenty to one, you meet
Some of the drunken Scowrers of the Street,
Flush'd with success of warlike Deeds perform'd,
Of Constables subdu'd, and Brothels storm'd: 370
These, if a Quarrel or a Fray be mist,
Are ill at ease a nights, and want their Rest.
For mischief is a Lechery to some,
And serves to make them sleep like Laudanum.
Yet heated, as they are, with Youth, and Wine,   375
If they discern a train of Flamboes shine,   *torches*
If a Great Man with his gilt Coach appear,
And a strong Guard of Foot-boys in the rear,
The Rascals sneak, and shrink their Heads for fear.
Poor me, who use no Light to walk about,   380
Save what the Parish or the Skies hang out,
They value not: 'tis worth your while to hear
The scuffle, if that be a scuffle, where
Another gives the Blows, I only bear:
He bids me stand: of force I must give way,   385
For 'twere a senseless thing to disobey,
And struggle here, where I'd as good oppose
My self to P————and his Mastiffs loose.
Who's there? he cries, and takes you by the Throat,
Dog! are you dumb? Speak quickly, else my Foot   390

---

353 Pauls   St Paul's Cathedral, which was being re-built after the fire of 1666
388 P——   possibly Sir Philip Herbert, Earl of Pembroke, who had a reputation for brutality

Shall march about your Buttocks: whence d'ye come,
From what bulk-ridden Strumpet reeking home?
Saving your reverend Pimpship, where d'ye ply?
How may one have a Job of Lechery?
If you say any thing, or hold your peace,   395
And silently go off; 'tis all a case:
Still he lays on: nay well, if you scape so:
Perhaps he'l clap an Action on you too
Of Battery, nor need he fear to meet
A Jury to his turn, shall do him right,   400
And bring him in large Damage for a Shooe
Worn out, besides the pains, in kicking you.
A Poor Man must expect nought of redress,
But Patience: his best in such a case
Is to be thankful for the Drubs, and beg   405
That they would mercifully spare one leg,
Or Arm unbroke, and let him go away
With Teeth enough to eat his Meat next day.

                                                    1682   1683

JOHN WILMOT, EARL OF ROCHESTER

1647–80 b Oxfordshire. His poetry reflects his life as a libertine courtier of Charles II.

To A Lady, in A Letter

                        1
Such perfect Blisse faire Chloris, wee
    In our Enjoyment prove
'Tis pitty restless Jealiousy
    Should Mingle with our Love.
                        2
Lett us (since witt has taught us how)   5
    Raise pleasure to the Topp:
You Rivall Bottle must allow
    I'le suffer Rivall Fopp.
                        3
Thinke not in this, that I designe
    A Treason 'gainst Loves Charmes   10
When following the God of Wine
    I Leave my Chloris armes.
                        4
Since you have that for all your hast
    Att which I'le ne're repine
Will take his Likour off as fast   15
    As I can take off mine.
                        5
There's not A brisk insipid Sparke
    That Flutters in the Towne
But with your wanton eyes, you marke
    Him out to be your owne.   20

6

Nor doe you thinke it worth your care
    How empty and how dull
The heads of your Admirers are
    Soe that their Codds be full.

7

All this you freely may Confesse   25
    Yett wee nere disagree
For did you love your pleasure lesse
    You were noe Match for mee.

8

Whilst I my pleasure to pursue
    Whole nights am takeing in,   30
The Lusty Juice of Grapes, take you
    The Juice of Lusty Men.

                                                            1676

Upon Nothing

Nothing thou Elder Brother even to Shade
Thou hadst a being ere the world was made
And (well fixt) art alone of ending not afraid.

Ere Time and Place were, Time and Place were not
When Primitive nothing, somthing straight begott   5
Then all proceeded from the great united what.

Somthing, the Generall Attribute of all
Severed from thee its sole Originall
Into thy boundless selfe must undistinguisht fall:

Yet Somthing did thy mighty power Command   10
And from thy fruitfull Emptinesses hand
Snatcht, Men, Beasts, birds, fire, water, Ayre, and land.

Matter, the Wickedst offspring of thy Race
By forme assisted flew from thy Embrace
And Rebell-Light obscured thy Reverend dusky face.   15

With forme and Matter, Time and Place did joyne
Body thy foe All these did Leagues combine
To spoyle thy Peaceful Realme and Ruine all thy Line

But Turncote-time assists the foe in vayne
And Brib'd by thee destroyes their short liv'd Reign   20
And to thy Hungry wombe drives back thy slaves again.

Though Misteries are barr'd from Laick Eyes
And the Divine alone with warrant pries
Into thy Bosome, where thy truth in private lyes

Yet this of thee the wise may truly say   25
Thou from the virtuous Nothing doest delay
And to be part of thee the wicked wisely pray.

Great Negative how vainly would the wise
Enquire, define, distinguish, teach, devise,
Didst Thou not stand to poynt their blind Phylosophies.   30

Is or is not, the two great Ends of fate
And true or false the Subject of debate
That perfect or destroy the vast designes of State:

When they have wrackt the Politicians Brest
Within thy Bosome most Securely rest   35
And when reduc't to thee are least unsafe and best.

But (Nothing) why does Somthing still permitt
That Sacred Monarchs should in Councell Sitt
With persons highly thought, at best for nothing fitt

Whilst weighty Somthing Modestly abstaynes   40
From Princes Coffers and from Statesmens braines
And nothing there like Stately nothing reignes?

Nothing who dwell'st with fooles in grave disguise
For whom they Reverend Shapes and formes devise
Lawn-sleeves and furrs and Gowns, when they like thee looke wise   45

French Truth, Dutch Prowess, Brittish policy
Hibernian Learning, Scotch Civility
Spaniards Dispatch, Danes witt, are Mainly seen in thee.

The Great mans Gratitude to his best friend
Kings promises, Whors vowes towards thee they bend   50
Flow Swiftly into thee, and in thee ever end.

by 1673   1679

APHRA BEHN

1640–89 b Aphra Johnson, in Kent. She spent a year in Surinam during her twenties.
Returning to London she became a professional writer of plays and novels and an active
feminist.

Love Arm'd

Love in Fantastique Triumph satt,
Whilst Bleeding Hearts a round him flow'd,
For whom Fresh paines he did Create,
And strange Tyranick power he show'd;
From thy Bright Eyes he took his fire,   5
Which round about, in sport he hurl'd;
But 'twas from mine, he took desire,
Enough to undo the Amorous World.

From me he took his sighs and tears,
From thee his Pride and Crueltie;   10
From me his Languishments and Feares,
And every Killing Dart from thee;

---

1 Love   Eros (or Cupid), Greek god of love   Triumph   ritual celebration of a victory

Thus thou and I, the God have arm'd,
And sett him up a Deity;
But my poor Heart alone is harm'd,   15
Whilst thine the Victor is, and free.

                                                          1677

Epilogue

spoken by Mrs Gwin

I here, and there, o'reheard a Coxcomb Cry (*Looking about*)
Ah, Rott it——'tis a Womans Comedy,
One, who because she lately chanc't to please us,
With her Damn'd stuff will never cease to teaze us.
What has poor Woman done that she must be,   5
Debar'd from Sense and Sacred Poetrie?
Why in this Age has Heaven allow'd you more,
And Women less of Wit than heretofore?
We once were fam'd in Story, and cou'd write
Equall to men; cou'd Govern, nay cou'd Fight.   10
We still have passive Valour, and can show
Wou'd Custom give us leave the Active too,
Since we no provocations want from you.   *lack*
For who but we, cou'd your Dull Fopperies bear,
Your Saucy Love, and your brisk Nonsense hear;   15
Indure your worse than womanish affectation,
Which renders you the Nusance of the Nation;
Scorn'd even by all the Misses of the Town,
A jest to Vizard Mask, the *Pitt-Buffoone*;
A Glass by which th' admiring Country Fool   20
May learn to dress himself en Ridicule:
Both striving who shall most Ingenious grow
In Lewdness, Foppery, Nonsense, Noise and Show.
And yet to these fine things we must submit
Our Reason, Arms, our Lawrells, and our Wit.   25
Because we do not Laugh at you when Lewd,
And scorn and cudgell ye when you are Rude;
That we have Nobler Souls than you, we prove,
By how much more we're sensible of Love;
Quickest in finding all the subtlest waies   30
To make your Joys: why not to make you Plays?
We best can find your Feables, know our own,   *foibles*
And Gilts and Cuckolds now best please the Town;   *jilts*
Your way of writing's out of Fashion grown.
Method, and Rule—you only understand,   35
Pursue that way of Fooling, and be Damn'd.
Your Learned Cant of Action, Time, and Place,
Must all give way to the unlabour'd farce.

Epilogue   recited at the conclusion of Behn's play, *Sir Patrick Fancy* (1678), by the popular actor, Nell Gwyn (1650–87).
19 Pitt   ground floor of the theatre, occupied by the rowdiest patrons
35–37 Action, Time and Place   the classical 'unities' of drama, much discussed at the time: one action in one place in a short span of time

To all the Men of Witt we will subscribe:
But for you half Wits, you unthinking Tribe,   40
We'll let you see, what e're besides we doe,
How Artfully we Copy some of you:
And if you're drawn to th' life, pray tell me then
Why Women should not write as well as Men.

1678

And forgive us our Trespasses

How prone we are to Sin, how sweet were made
The pleasures, our resistless hearts invade!
Of all my Crimes, the breach of all thy Laws
Love, soft bewitching Love! has been the cause;
Of all the Paths that Vanity has trod,   5
That sure will soonest be forgiven of God;
If things on Earth may be to Heaven resembled,
It must be love, pure, constant, undissembled:
But if to Sin by chance the Charmer press,
Forgive, O Lord, forgive our Trespasses.   10

1685

THOMAS TRAHERNE

1636–74 b Herefordshire. He was an Anglican clergyman there and in London. His poems were discovered in 1895.

The Salutation

1
These little Limmes,
These Eys and Hands which here I find,
These rosie Cheeks wherwith my Life begins,
Where have ye been,? Behind
What Curtain were ye from me hid so long!   5
Where was? in what Abyss, my Speaking Tongue?

2
When silent I,
So many thousand thousand yeers,
Beneath the Dust did in a Chaos lie,
How could I Smiles or Tears,   10
Or Lips or Hands or Eys or Ears perceiv?
Welcome ye Treasures which I now receiv.

3
I that so long
Was Nothing from Eternitie,
Did little think such Joys as Ear or Tongue,   15
To Celebrat or See:
Such Sounds to hear, such Hands to feel, such Feet,
Beneath the Skies, on such a Ground to meet.

4
    New Burnisht Joys!
  Which yellow Gold and Pearl excell!   20
Such Sacred Treasures are the Lims in Boys,
      In which a Soul doth Dwell;
Their Organized Joynts, and Azure Veins
More Wealth include, than all the World contains.

5
    From Dust I rise,
  And out of Nothing now awake,   25
These Brighter Regions which salute mine Eys,
      A Gift from GOD I take.
The Earth, the Seas, the Light, the Day, the Skies,
The Sun and Stars are mine; if those I prize.   30

6
    Long time before
  I in my Mothers Womb was born,
A GOD preparing did this Glorious Store,
      The World for me adorne.
Into this Eden so Divine and fair,   35
So Wide and Bright, I com his Son and Heir.

7
    A Stranger here
  Strange Things doth meet, Strange Glories See;
Strange Treasures lodg'd in this fair World appear,
      Strange all, and New to me.   40
But that they mine should be, who nothing was,
That Strangest is of all, yet brought to pass.

                                                    1906

KATHERINE PHILIPS

1631–1664 b London. She was the centre of a notable literary and intellectual salon, predominantly of women.

Against Love

Hence, *Cupid*! with your cheating Toies,
Your real Griefs, and painted Joies,
Your Pleasure which it self destroies.
  Lovers like men in Feavers burn and rave,
  And only what will injure them do crave.   5
Men's weakness makes Love so severe,
They give him power by their fear,
And make the Shackles which they wear.
  Who to another does his heart submit,
  Makes his own Idol, and then worships it.   10
Him whose heart is all his own,
Peace and liberty does crown,
He apprehends no killing frown.

He feels no raptures, which are joies diseas'd,
And is not much transported, but still pleas'd.   *ecstatic* 15

1667

To the truly noble Mr Henry Lawes

Nature, which is the vast creation's soule,
That steady curious agent in the whole,
The art of Heav'n, the order of this frame,
Is onely number in another name:
For as some King, conqu'ring what was his own,   5
Hath choice of severall titles to his crown;
So harmony, on this score now, that then,
Yet still is all that takes and governs men.
Beauty is but Composure, and we find
Content is but the Concord of the mind,   10
Friendship the Unison of well-tun'd hearts,
Honour's the Chorus of the noblest parts,
And all the world on which we can reflect,
Musique to th'Eare, or to the intellect.
If then each man a little world must be,   15
How many worlds are coppy'd out in Thee?
Who art so richly formed, so compleat,
T'epitomize all that is good or great;
Whose stars this brave advantage did impart,
Thy nature's more harmonious than thy art.   20
Thou dost above the Poets praises live,
Who fetch from thee th'Eternity they give;
And as true reason triumphs over sence,
Yet is subjected to intelligence:
So Poets on the lower world look down,   25
But Lawes on them; his height is all his own.
For, like divinity it self, his Lyre
Rewards the wit it did at first inspire:
And thus by double right Poets allow
His and their Laurells should adorn his brow.   30
Live then (Great soule of nature!) to asswage
The savage dullness of this sullen age;
Charm us to sence, and though experience faile,
And reason too, thy numbers will prevaile.   *rhythm*
Then (like those Ancients) strike, and so command   35
All nature to obey thy generous hand:
None can resist, but such who needs will be
More stupid than a Stone, a Fish, a Tree.
Be it thy care our Age to new-create:
What built a world may sure repayre a state.   40

1667

Henry Lawes (1596–1662), British composer
23–24 These lines refer to the medieval hierarchy of the soul in which **intelligence**, as immediate understanding, is superior to **reason** as discursive thought, and both are superior to **sense**.
35 those ancients In Greek myth, the music of Orpheus charmed the beasts; that of Amphion charmed the walls of Thebes into place.

JOHN DRYDEN

1631–1700 b Northamptonshire. In London from 1654, he became a professional writer of poetry, plays and criticism.

From Mac Flecknoe

All humane things are subject to decay,
And, when Fate summons, Monarchs must obey:
This *Fleckno* found, who, like *Augustus*, young
Was call'd to Empire, and had govern'd long:
In Prose and Verse, was own'd, without dispute   5
Through all the Realms of *Non-sense*, absolute.
This aged Prince now flourishing in Peace,
And blest with issue of a large increase,
Worn out with business, did at length debate
To settle the succession of the State: 10
And pond'ring which of all his Sons was fit
To Reign, and wage immortal War with Wit;
Cry'd, 'tis resolv'd; for Nature pleads that He
Should onely rule, who most resembles me:
Sh—— alone my perfect image bears,   15
Mature in dullness from his tender years.
Sh—— alone, of all my Sons, is he
Who stands confirm'd in full stupidity.
The rest to some faint meaning make pretence,
But *Sh*——never deviates into sense.   20
Some Beams of Wit on other souls may fall,
Strike through and make a lucid intervall;
But *Sh*——'s genuine night admits no ray,
His rising Fogs prevail upon the Day:
Besides his goodly Fabrick fills the eye,   25
And seems design'd for thoughtless Majesty:
Thoughtless as Monarch Oakes, that shade the plain,
And, spread in solemn state, supinely reign.
Heywood and *Shirley* were but Types of thee,
Thou last great Prophet of Tautology: 30
Even I, a dunce of more renown than they,
Was sent before but to prepare thy way;
And coursly clad in *Norwich* Drugget came   *coarse cloth*
To teach the Nations in thy greater name.
My warbling Lute, the Lute I whilom strung   35
When to King *John* of *Portugal* I sung,
Was but the prelude to that glorious day,
When thou on silver *Thames* did'st cut thy way,

3 **Fleckno**   Richard Flecknoe, a little regarded contemporary poet   **Augustus**   Roman emperor
15 **Sh——**   Thomas Shadwell (?1642–92), a popular comic dramatist
29 **Heywood and Shirley**   unfashionable dramatists of an older generation
35 **whilom**   formerly (archaic)
37ff Shadwell prided himself as a musician. It is uncertain which royal occasion is referred to here.

With well tim'd Oars before the Royal Barge,
Swell'd with the Pride of thy Celestial charge;   40
And big with Hymn, Commander of an Host,
The like was ne'er in *Epsom* Blankets tost.
Methinks I see the new *Arion* Sail,
The Lute still trembling underneath thy nail.
At thy well sharpned thumb from Shore to Shore   45
The Treble squeaks for fear, the Bases roar:
Echoes from *Pissing-Ally*, *Sh*—— call,
And *Sh*——they resound from *A*——*Hall*.
About thy boat the little Fishes throng,
As at the Morning Toast, that Floats along.   50
Sometimes as Prince of thy Harmonious band
Thou weild'st thy Papers in thy threshing hand.
St *Andre*'s feet ne'er kept more equal time,
Not ev'n the feet of thy own *Psyche*'s rhime:
Though they in number as in sense excell;   55
So just, so like tautology they fell,
That, pale with envy, *Singleton* foreswore
The Lute and Sword which he in Triumph bore,
And vow'd he ne'er would act *Villerius* more.
Here stopt the good old *Syre*; and wept for joy   60
In silent raptures of the hopeful boy.
All arguments, but most his Plays, perswade,
That for anointed dullness he was made.

1678 1682

From Absalom and Achitophel

In pious times, e'r Priest-craft did begin,
Before *Polygamy* was made a sin;
When man, on many, multiply'd his kind,
E'r one to one was, cursedly, confind:
When Nature prompted, and no law deny'd   5
Promiscuous use of Concubine and Bride;
Then, *Israel's* Monarch, after Heaven's own heart,
His vigorous warmth did, variously, impart
To Wives and Slaves; And, wide as his Command,
Scatter'd his Maker's Image through the Land.   10

---

42 A character is tossed in blankets in Shadwell's *The Virtuoso*.
43 Arion in Greek myth, a poet who charmed a dolphin with his singing
50 Toast i.e. sewage
53–54 St Andre the choreographer of *Psyche*, an opera for which Shadwell was librettist
57–59 Singleton, Villerius respectively an obscure performer and a bombastic acting role
Absalom and Achitophel a royalist version of the succession crisis of 1681, based loosely on the narrative of Absalom's rebellion against King David in 2 Sam. 13–18. In the first extract here, Charles II of England (as David) is ambiguously praised: his well-known free sexuality has a criminally indulged son and a neglected kingdom as issue. The second and third extracts satirically describe two of the parliamentary leaders who worked to alter the future royal succession in favour of the king's illegitimate son, the popular and malleable Duke of Monmouth (Absalom).

Michal, of Royal blood, the Crown did wear,
A Soyl ungratefull to the Tiller's care:
Not so the rest; for several Mothers bore
To Godlike *David*, several Sons before.
But since like slaves his bed they did ascend,   15
No True Succession could their seed attend.
Of all this Numerous Progeny was none
So Beautifull, so brave as *Absolon*:
Whether, inspir'd by some diviner Lust,
His Father got him with a greater Gust;   20
Or that his Conscious destiny made way
By manly beauty to Imperiall sway.
Early in Foreign fields he won Renown,
With Kings and States ally'd to *Israel*'s Crown:
In Peace the thoughts of War he coud remove,   25
And seem'd as he were only born for love.
What e'r he did was done with so much ease,
In him alone, 'twas Natural to please.
His motions all accompanied with grace;
And *Paradise* was open'd in his face.   30
With secret Joy, indulgent *David* view'd
His Youthfull Image in his Son renew'd:
To all his wishes Nothing he deny'd,
And made the Charming *Annabel* his Bride.
What faults he had (for who from faults is free?)   35
His Father coud not, or he woud not see.
Some warm excesses, which the Law forbore,
Were constru'd Youth that purg'd by boyling o'r:
And *Amnon's* Murther, by a specious Name,
Was call'd a Just Revenge for injur'd Fame.   40
Thus Prais'd, and Lov'd, the Noble Youth remain'd,
While *David*, undisturb'd, in *Sion* raign'd.
But Life can never be sincerely blest: *completely*
Heaven punishes the bad, and proves the best.   *tests*
The *Jews*, a Headstrong, Moody, Murmuring race,   45
As ever try'd th' extent and stretch of grace;
God's pamper'd people whom, debauch'd with ease,
No King could govern, nor no God could please;
(Gods they had tri'd of every shape and size
That God-smiths could produce, or Priests devise:)   50
These *Adam*-wits, too fortunately free,
Began to dream they wanted libertie;   *lacked*
And when no rule, no president was found   *precedent*
Of men, by Laws less circumscrib'd and bound,
They led their wild desires to Woods and Caves,   55
And thought that all but Savages were Slaves.

---

39 Amnon's Murther   A decade earlier, at the age of 21, Monmouth had joined with two other
Dukes in killing a minor justice official in a dispute at a brothel; all three received royal pardons. More
recently, Monmouth's troops had beaten Sir John Coventry for a parliamentary speech in which he
mocked the king's interest in women actors. In 2 Samuel 13 Amnon ('faithful') is killed by Absalom for
raping his half sister.

They who when *Saul* was dead, without a blow,
Made foolish *Ishbosheth* the Crown forgo;
Who banisht *David* did from *Hebron* bring,
And, with a Generall Shout, proclaim'd him King: 60
Those very *Jewes*, who, at their very best,
Their Humour more than Loyalty exprest,
Now, wondred why, so long, they had obey'd
An Idoll Monarch which their hands had made: 65
Thought they might ruine him they could create;
Or melt him to that Golden Calf, a State.

★ ★ ★

Of these the false *Achitophel* was first: 150
A Name to all succeeding Ages Curst.
For close Designs, and crooked Counsells fit;
Sagacious, Bold, and Turbulent of wit:
Restless, unfixt in Principles and Place;
In Power unpleas'd, impatient of Disgrace.   155
A fiery Soul, which working out its way,
Fretted the Pigmy Body to decay:
And o'r inform'd the Tenement of Clay.
A daring Pilot in extremity;
Pleas'd with the Danger, when the Waves went high   160
He sought the Storms; but for a Calm unfit,
Would Steer too nigh the Sands, to boast his Wit.
Great Wits are sure to Madness near ally'd;
And thin Partitions do their Bounds divide:
Else, why should he, with Wealth and Honour blest,   165
Refuse his Age the needful hours of Rest?
Punish a Body which he could not please;
Bankrupt of Life, yet Prodigal of Ease?
And all to leave, what with his Toyl he won,
To that unfeather'd, two Leg'd thing, a Son: 170
Got, while his Soul did hudled Notions try;
And born a shapeless Lump, like Anarchy.
In Friendship False, Implacable in Hate:
Resolv'd to Ruine or to Rule the State.

★ ★ ★

57–60 See 2 Sam. 3–4. In contemporary terms, the regime of the Commonwealth, sustained by Oliver Cromwell, came to an end under the stewardship of his inept son. The monarchy, which had been removed by the execution of Charles I in 1649, was restored in 1660 to popular acclaim with the recall from exile of Charles II.
66 Golden Calf See Exod. 32:1–4. **State** commonwealth, republic
150 Achitophel the instigator of Absalom's rebellion: a by-word for an evil adviser. Here, Anthony Ashley Cooper, Earl of Shaftesbury, a former Lord Chancellor. The original Achitophel hanged himself; Shaftesbury, at the time of publication, was awaiting trial for treason (he was eventually acquitted by a jury of his supporters).
153 wit mental quickness
158 o'r inform'd i.e. following Aristotle's theory whereby the soul is the form of (informs) the body. Shaftesbury was short, bent with age and chronically ill.
172 shapeless Lump Shaftesbury's son was sickly.

Some of their Chiefs were Princes of the Land:
In the first Rank of these did Zimri stand:
A man so various, that he seem'd to be   545
Not one, but all Mankinds Epitome.
Stiff in Opinions, always in the wrong;
Was every thing by starts, and nothing long:
But, in the course of one revolving Moon,
Was Chymist, Fidler, States-Man, and Buffoon: 550
Then all for Women, Painting, Rhiming, Drinking;
Besides ten thousand freaks that dy'd in thinking.
Blest Madman, who could every hour employ,
With something New to wish, or to enjoy!
Rayling and praising were his usual Theams;   555
And both (to shew his Judgment) in Extreams:
So over Violent, or over Civil,
That every man, with him, was God or Devil.
In squandring Wealth was his peculiar Art:
Nothing went unrewarded, but Desert.   560
Begger'd by Fools, whom still he found too late:
He had his Jest, and they had his Estate.
He laught himself from Court, then sought Releif
By forming Parties, but coud ne're be Chief:
For, spight of him, the weight of Business fell   565
On *Absalom* and wise *Achitophel*:
Thus, wicked but in will, of means bereft,
He left not Faction, but of that was left.

                                        November 1681

From Religio Laici

Dim, as the borrow'd beams of Moon and Stars
To *lonely, weary, wandring* Travellers,
Is *Reason* to the *Soul*: And as on high,
Those rowling Fires *discover* but the Sky
Not light us *here*; So *Reason*'s glimmering Ray   5
Was lent, not to *assure* our *doubtfull* way,
But *guide* us upward to a *better Day.*
And as those nightly Tapers disappear
When Day's bright Lord ascends our Hemisphere;
So pale grows *Reason* at *Religions* sight;   10
So *dyes*, and so *dissolves* in *Supernatural Light.*
Some few, whose Lamp shone brighter, have been led
From Cause to Cause, to *Natures* secret head;
And found that *one first principle* must be:
But *what*, or *who*, that *UNIVERSAL HE*;   15
Whether some *Soul* incompassing this Ball
Unmade, unmov'd; yet *making, moving All*;

---

544 Zimri a gross violator of public decency (Num. 25:6–15) and a regicide (I Kings, 16:8–20);
here, George Villiers, Duke of Buckingham, a gifted man famous for excesses of behaviour
550 Buckingham set up a laboratory for chemical research and was also a talented violin player.
Religio Laici 'Religion of a layman'

Or various *Atom*'s interfering Dance
Leapt into *Form*, (the Noble work of *Chance*;)
Or this great *All* was from *Eternity*;   20
Not ev'n the *Stagirite* himself could see;
And *Epicurus Guess'd* as well as He:
As *blindly grop'd* they for a *future State*,
As *rashly Judg'd* of *Providence* and *Fate*:
But least of all could their Endeavours find   25
What most concern'd the good of Humane kind:
For *Happiness* was never to be found;
But vanish'd from 'em, like Enchanted ground.
One thought *Content* the Good to be enjoy'd:
This, every little *Accident* destroy'd: 30
The *wiser Madmen* did for *Vertue* toyl:
A Thorny, or at best a barren Soil:
In *Pleasure* some their glutton Souls would steep;
But found their Line too short, the Well too deep;
And leaky Vessels which no *Bliss* cou'd keep.   35
Thus, *anxious Thoughts* in *endless Circles* roul,
Without a *Centre* where to fix the *Soul*:
In this wilde Maze their vain Endeavours end:
How can the *less* the *Greater* comprehend?
Or *finite Reason* reach *Infinity*?   40
For what cou'd *Fathom GOD* were *more* than *He*.

                                                    1682

To the Memory of Mr Oldham

Farewel, too little and too lately known,
Whom I began to think and call my own;
For sure our Souls were near ally'd; and thine
Cast in the same Poetick mould with mine.
One common Note on either Lyre did strike,   5
And Knaves and Fools we both abhorr'd alike:
To the same Goal did both our Studies drive,
The last set out the soonest did arrive.
Thus *Nisus* fell upon the slippery place,
While his young Friend perform'd and won the Race.   10
O early ripe! to thy abundant store
What could advancing Age have added more?
It might (what Nature never gives the young)
Have taught the numbers of thy native Tongue.   *metre*
But Satyr needs not those, and Wit will shine   15
Through the harsh cadence of a rugged line.
A noble Error, and but seldom made,
When Poets are by too much force betray'd.

---

21 **the Stagyrite**   Aristotle (384–22 BC), Greek philosopher, born at Stageira
22 **Epicurus**   (341–270 BC), Greek philosopher
Mr Oldham   John Oldham (1653–83): see p. 393.
9–10 In *Aeneid* V, **Nisus** falls while leading in a race, then by interference helps his young friend, Euryalus, to win.

Thy generous fruits, though gather'd ere their prime
Still shew'd a quickness; and maturing time   20
But mellows what we write to the dull sweets of Rime.
Once more, hail and farewel; farewel thou young,
But ah too short, *Marcellus* of our Tongue;
Thy Brows with Ivy, and with Laurels bound;
But Fate and gloomy Night encompass thee around.   25

                                                          1684

A Song for St Cecilia's Day, 1687

                          I
From Harmony, from heav'nly Harmony
        This universal Frame began.
    When Nature underneath a heap
        Of jarring Atomes lay,
    And cou'd not heave her Head,   5
The tuneful Voice was heard from high,
        Arise ye more than dead.
Then cold, and hot, and moist, and dry,
In order to their stations leap,
        And MUSICK's pow'r obey.   10
From Harmony, from heav'nly Harmony
        This universal Frame began:
        From Harmony to Harmony
Through all the compass of the Notes it ran,
The Diapason closing full in Man.   15
                          II
What Passion cannot MUSICK raise and quell!
        When *Jubal* struck the corded Shell,
        His list'ning Brethren stood around
        And wond'ring, on their Faces fell
        To worship that Celestial Sound.
Less than a God they thought there cou'd not dwell   20
        Within the hollow of that Shell
        That spoke so sweetly and so well.
What Passion cannot MUSICK raise and quell!
                          III
    The TRUMPETS loud Clangor   25
        Excites us to Arms
    With shrill Notes of Anger
        And mortal Alarms.
    The double double double beat
        Of the thundring DRUM   30
Cryes, hark the Foes come;
Charge, Charge, 'tis too late to retreat.

---

22 **hail and farewel**   a Roman elegiac formula
23 **Marcellus**   heir to the Roman emperor Augustus: his early death is mourned in *Aeneid* VI.
St Cecilia   a martyr of the early church, whose feast day is 22 November. She is the patron saint of music, especially that of the organ (line 52).
15 **Diapason**   the entire range of tones
17 **Jubal**   'the father of all such as handle the harp and organ' (Gen. 4:21)

IV

The soft complaining FLUTE
In dying Notes discovers
    The Woes of hopeless Lovers,
Whose Dirge is whisper'd by the warbling LUTE.

V

Sharp VIOLINS proclaim
Their jealous Pangs, and Desperation,
Fury, frantick Indignation,
Depth of Pains, and height of Passion,
    For the fair, disdainful Dame.

VI

But oh! what Art can teach
    What human Voice can reach
The sacred ORGANS praise?
Notes inspiring holy Love,
Notes that wing their heav'nly ways
    To mend the Choires above.

VII

Orpheus cou'd lead the savage race;
And Trees unrooted left their place;
    Sequacious of the Lyre:
But bright *CECILIA* rais'd the wonder high'r;
When to her ORGAN, vocal Breath was giv'n
An Angel heard, and straight appear'd
    Mistaking Earth for Heaven.

Grand CHORUS

As from the pow'r of sacred Lays
    The Spheres began to move,
And sung the great Creator's praise
    To all the bless'd above;
So when the last and dreadful hour
This crumbling Pageant shall devour,
The TRUMPET *shall be heard on high,*
The Dead shall live, the Living die,
And MUSICK *shall untune the Sky.*

35

40

45

50

55

60

1687

HENRY VAUGHAN

1622–95 b Wales, in Breconshire, where he practised as a physician for much of his life.

The World

I saw Eternity the other night
Like a great *Ring* of pure and endless light,
    All calm, as it was bright,
And round beneath it, Time in hours, days, years
    Driv'n by the spheres
Like a vast shadow mov'd, In which the world
    And all her train were hurl'd;

5

The doting Lover in his queintest strain
    Did their Complain,
Neer him, his Lute, his fancy, and his flights,   10
    Wits sour delights,
With gloves, and knots the silly snares of pleasure
    Yet his dear Treasure
All scatter'd lay, while he his eys did pour
    Upon a flowr.   15

2

The darksome States-man hung with weights and woe
Like a thick midnight-fog mov'd there so slow
    He did nor stay, nor go;
Condemning thoughts (like sad Ecclipses) scowl
    Upon his soul,   20
And Clouds of crying witnesses without
    Pursued him with one shout.
Yet dig'd the Mole, and lest his ways be found
    Workt under ground,
Where he did Clutch his prey, but one did see   25
    That policie,
Churches and altars fed him, Perjuries
    Were gnats and flies,
It rain'd about him bloud and tears, but he
    Drank them as free.   30

3

The fearfull miser on a heap of rust
Sate pining all his life there, did scarce trust
    His own hands with the dust,
Yet would not place one peece above, but lives
    In feare of theeves.   35
Thousands there were as frantick as himself
    And hug'd each one his pelf,
The down-right Epicure plac'd heav'n in sense
    And scornd pretence
While others slipt into a wide Excesse   40
    Said little lesse;
The weaker sort slight, triviall wares Inslave
    Who think them brave,
And poor, despised truth sate Counting by
    Their victory.   45

4

Yet some, who all this while did weep and sing,
And sing, and weep, soar'd up into the *Ring*,
    But most would use no wing.
O fools (said I,) thus to prefer dark night
    Before true light,   50
To live in grots, and caves, and hate the day
    Because it shews the way,
The way which from this dead and dark abode
    Leads up to God,
A way where you might tread the Sun, and be   55
    More bright than he.

But as I did their madnes so discusse
      One whisper'd thus,
This Ring the Bride-groome did for none provide
      But for his bride.   60

      John Cap. 2. ver. 16, 17.
All that is in the world, the lust of the flesh, the lust of the Eys,
and the pride of life, is not of the father, but is of the world.
     And the world passeth away, and the lusts thereof, but he that
doth the will of God abideth for ever.

                                     1650

Man

      Weighing the stedfastness and state
Of some mean things which here below reside,
Where birds like watchful Clocks the noiseless date
      And Intercourse of times divide,
Where Bees at night get home and hive, and flowrs   5
         Early, aswel as late,
Rise with the Sun, and set in the same bowrs;
              2
      I would (said I) my God would give
The staidness of these things to man! for these
To his divine appointments ever cleave,   10
      And no new business breaks their peace;
The birds nor sow, nor reap, yet sup and dine,
         The flowres without clothes live,
Yet *Solomon* was never drest so fine.
              3
      Man hath stil either toyes, or Care,   15
He hath no root, nor to one place is ty'd,
But ever restless and Irregular
      About this Earth doth run and ride,
He knows he hath a home, but scarce knows where,
         He sayes it is so far   20
That he hath quite forgot how to go there.
              4
      He knocks at all doors, strays and roams,
Nay hath not so much wit as some stones have
Which in the darkest nights point to their homes,
      By some hid sense their Maker gave;   25
Man is the shuttle, to whose winding quest
         And passage through these looms
God order'd motion, but ordain'd no rest.

                                   1650

Quickness

False life! a foil and no more, when
        Wilt thou be gone?
Thou foul deception of all men
That would not have the true come on.

Thou art a Moon-like toil; a blinde
    Self-posing state;   5
A dark contest of waves and winde;
A meer tempestuous debate.

Life is a fix'd, discerning light,
    A knowing Joy;
No chance, or fit: but ever bright,   10
And calm and full, yet doth not cloy.

'Tis such a blissful thing, that still
    Doth vivifie,
And shine and smile, and hath the skill
To please without Eternity.   15

Thou art a toylsom Mole, or less
    A moving mist.
But life is, what none can express,
A quickness, which my God hath kist.   20

                  1655

[They are all gone into the world of light]

They are all gone into the world of light!
    And I alone sit lingering here;
Their very memory is fair and bright,
    And my sad thoughts doth clear.

It glows and glitters in my cloudy brest   5
    Like stars upon some gloomy grove,
Or those faint beams in which this hill is drest,
    After the Sun's remove.

I see them walking in an Air of glory,
    Whose light doth trample on my days: 10
My days, which are at best but dull and hoary,
    Meer glimering and decays.

O holy hope! and high humility,
    High as the Heavens above!
These are your walks, and you have shew'd them me   15
    To kindle my cold love,

Dear, beauteous death! the Jewel of the Just,
    Shining no where, but in the dark;
What mysteries do lie beyond thy dust;
    Could man outlook that mark!   20

He that hath found some fledg'd birds nest, may know
    At first sight, if the bird be flown;
But what fair Well, or Grove he sings in now,
    That is to him unknown.

And yet, as Angels in some brighter dreams   25
    Call to the soul, when man doth sleep:
So some strange thoughts transcend our wonted theams,
    And into glory peep.

If a star were confin'd into a Tomb
    Her captive flames must needs burn there;   30
But when the hand that lockt her up, gives room,
    She'l shine through all the sphære.

O Father of eternal life, and all
    Created glories under thee!
Resume thy spirit from this world of thrall   35
    Into true liberty.

Either disperse these mists, which blot and fill
    My perspective (still) as they pass,   *telescope*
Or else remove me hence unto that hill,
    Where I shall need no glass.   40

        1655

ANDREW MARVELL

1621–78 b Hull, which he represented in Parliament 1659–78. He was previously an assistant to Milton in Cromwell's Council of State. His poetry was published after his death.

A Dialogue between the Soul and Body

    Soul
O who shall, from this Dungeon, raise
A Soul inslav'd so many wayes?
With bolts of Bones, that fetter'd stands
In Feet; and manacled in Hands.
Here blinded with an Eye; and there   5
Deaf with the drumming of an Ear.
A Soul hung up, as 'twere, in Chains
Of Nerves, and Arteries, and Veins.
Tortur'd, besides each other part,
In a vain Head, and double Heart.   10

    Body
  O who shall me deliver whole,
From bonds of this Tyrannic Soul?
Which, stretcht upright, impales me so,
That mine own Precipice I go;
And warms and moves this needless Frame: 15
(A Fever could but do the same.)
And, wanting where its spight to try,
Has made me live to let me dye.
A Body that could never rest,
Since this ill Spirit it possest.   20

1–2 See Rom. 7:24: 'Who shall deliver me from the body of this death?'
15 needless needing nothing
17 wanting where lacking a place

Soul
What Magick could me thus confine
Within anothers Grief to pine?
Where whatsoever it complain,
I feel, that cannot feel, the pain.
And all my Care its self employes,   25
That to preserve, which me destroys:
Constrain'd not only to indure
Diseases, but, whats worse, the Cure:
And ready oft the Port to gain,
Am Shipwrackt into Health again.   30

Body
But Physick yet could never reach   *medicine*
The Maladies Thou me dost teach;
Whom first the Cramp of Hope does Tear:
And then the Palsie Shakes of Fear.
The Pestilence of Love does heat: 35
Or Hatred's hidden Ulcer eat.
Joy's chearful Madness does perplex:
Or Sorrow's other Madness vex.
Which Knowledge forces me to know;
And Memory will not foregoe.   40
What but a Soul could have the wit
To build me up for Sin so fit?
So Architects do square and hew,
Green Trees that in the Forest grew.

                                          1681

The Garden

I
How vainly men themselves amaze   *bewilder*
To win the Palm, the Oke, or Bayes;
And their uncessant Labours see
Crown'd from some single Herb or Tree,
Whose short and narrow verged Shade   5
Does prudently their Toyles upbraid;
While all Flow'rs and all Trees do close
To weave the Garlands of repose.
II
Fair quiet, have I found thee here,
And Innocence thy Sister dear!   10
Mistaken long, I sought you then
In busie Companies of Men.
Your sacred Plants, if here below,
Only among the Plants will grow.
Society is all but rude,   *uncivilised*   15
To this delicious Solitude.
III
No white nor red was ever seen
So am'rous as this lovely green.

Fond Lovers, cruel as their Flame,
Cut in these Trees their Mistress name. 20
Little, Alas, they know, or heed,
How far these Beauties Hers exceed!
Fair Trees! where s'eer your barkes I wound,
No Name shall but your own be found.

IV
When we have run our Passions heat, 25
Love hither makes his best retreat.
The *Gods*, that mortal Beauty chase,
Still in a Tree did end their race.
Apollo hunted *Daphne* so, 30
Only that She might Laurel grow.
And *Pan* did after *Syrinx* speed,
Not as a Nymph, but for a Reed.

V
What wond'rous Life is this I lead!
Ripe Apples drop about my head;
The Luscious Clusters of the Vine 35
Upon my Mouth do crush their Wine;
The Nectaren, and curious Peach, *choice*
Into my hands themselves do reach;
Stumbling on Melons, as I pass,
Insnar'd with Flow'rs, I fall on Grass. 40

VI
Mean while the Mind, from pleasure less,
Withdraws into its happiness:
The Mind, that Ocean where each kind
Does streight its own resemblance find;
Yet it creates, transcending these, 45
Far other Worlds, and other Seas;
Annihilating all that's made
To a green Thought in a green Shade.

VII
Here at the Fountains sliding foot,
Or at some Fruit-trees mossy root, 50
Casting the Bodies Vest aside,
My Soul into the boughs does glide:
There like a Bird it sits, and sings,
Then whets, and combs its silver Wings;
And, till prepar'd for longer flight, 55
Waves in its Plumes the various Light.

VIII
Such was that happy Garden-state,
While Man there walk'd without a Mate:

---

19 **Fond** both doting and foolish
29–31 In Greek myth, to escape amorous pursuit **Daphne** turned into a laurel (the bays of line 2, associated with her pursuer, **Apollo**) and **Syrinx** turned into a reed (associated with the flute of her pursuer, **Pan**). See *Metamorphoses* I.

After a Place so pure, and sweet,
What other Help could yet be meet!   60
But 'twas beyond a Mortal's share
To wander solitary there:
Two Paradises 'twere in one
To live in Paradise alone.
                    IX
How well the skilful Gardner drew   65
Of flow'rs and herbes this Dial new;   *sundial*
Where from above the milder Sun
Does through a fragrant Zodiack run;
And, as it works, th' industrious Bee
Computes its time as well as we.   70
How could such sweet and wholsome Hours
Be reckon'd but with herbs and flow'rs!

                                              ?1650–52   1681

An Horation Ode upon Cromwel's Return from Ireland

The forward Youth that would appear
Must now forsake his *Muses* dear,
    Nor in the Shadows sing
    His Numbers languishing.
'Tis time to leave the Books in dust,   *verses*
And oyl th' unused Armours rust: 5
    Removing from the Wall
    The Corslet of the Hall.
So restless *Cromwel* could not cease
In the inglorious Arts of Peace,   · 10
    But through adventrous War
    Urged his active Star.
And, like the three-fork'd Lightning, first
Breaking the Clouds where it was nurst,
    Did thorough his own Side   15
    His fiery way divide.
For 'tis all one to Courage high
The Emulous or Enemy;
    And with such to inclose
    Is more than to oppose.   20
Then burning through the Air he went,
And Pallaces and Temples rent:
    And *Cæsars* head at last
    Did through his Laurels blast.

---

60 meet fitting. See Gen. 2:20: 'But for Adam there was not found an help meet for him.'
An Horatian Ode After Charles I was beheaded in 1649, the defeat of the royalist forces and their Irish allies in 1650 by Oliver Cromwell consolidated the parliamentary revolution. He returned triumphantly from Ireland in May, and set off to subdue a revolt in Scotland in July. **Horatian** suggests the imitation of a typical verse-form—and also the urbanity—of the odes of the Roman poet, Horace (65–8 BC).
15 his own Side Cromwell emerged out of faction in the parliamentary side.
24 Laurels emblems of honour; in Roman times, laurel was also thought to protect from lightning.

'Tis Madness to resist or blame   25
The force of angry Heavens flame:
   And, if we would speak true,
   Much to the Man is due.
Who, from his private Gardens, where
He liv'd reserved and austere,   30
   As if his highest plot
   To plant the Bergamot,
Could by industrious Valour climbe
To ruine the great Work of Time,
   And cast the Kingdome old   35
   Into another Mold.
Though Justice against Fate complain,
And plead the antient Rights in vain:
   But those do hold or break
   As Men are strong or weak.   40
Nature that hateth emptiness,
Allows of penetration less:
   And therefore must make room
   Where greater Spirits come.
What Field of all the Civil Wars,   45
Where his were not the deepest Scars?
   And *Hampton* shows what part
   He had of wiser Art.
Where, twining subtile fears with hope,
He wove a Net of such a scope,   50
   That *Charles* himself might chase
   To *Caresbrooks* narrow case.
That thence the *Royal Actor* born
The *Tragick Scaffold* might adorn
   While round the armed Bands   55
   Did clap their bloody hands.
He nothing common did or mean
Upon that memorable Scene:
   But with his keener Eye
   The Axes edge did try: 60
Nor call'd the *Gods* with vulgar spight
To vindicate his helpless Right,
   But bow'd his comely Head,
   Down as upon a Bed.
This was that memorable Hour   65
Which first assur'd the forced Pow'r.
   So when they did design
   The *Capitols* first Line,

---

32 Bergamot a variety of pear
42 penetration i.e. two things occupying one space
47–56 It was popularly thought—incorrectly, it seems—that Cromwell had connived at Charles' temporary escape to Carisbrooke Castle from confinement at Hampton Court, to turn opinion against him.
68 Capitol the temple of Jupiter in Rome, named after a head (caput) which was taken as a good omen when found during the digging of foundations

A bleeding Head where they begun,
Did fright the Architects to run;   70
  And yet in that the *State*
  Foresaw its happy Fate.
And now the *Irish* are asham'd
To see themselves in one Year tam'd:
  So much one Man can do,   75
  That does both act and know.
They can affirm his Praises best,
And have, though overcome, confest
  How good he is, how just,
  And fit for highest Trust: 80
Nor yet grown stiffer with Command,
But still in the *Republick's* hand:
  How fit he is to sway
  That can so well obey.
He to the *Commons Feet* presents   85
A *Kingdome*, for his first years rents:
  And, what he may, forbears
  His Fame to make it theirs:
And has his Sword and Spoyls ungirt,
To lay them at the *Publick's* skirt.   90
  So when the Falcon high
  Falls heavy from the Sky,
She, having kill'd, no more does search,
But on the next green Bow to pearch;
  Where, when he first does lure,   95
  The Falckner has her sure.
What may not then our *Isle* presume
While Victory his Crest does plume!
  What may not others fear
  If thus he crown each Year!   100
A Cæsar he ere long to *Gaul*,
To *Italy* an *Hannibal*,
  And to all States not free
  Shall *Clymacterick* be.   *epoch-making*
The *Pict* no shelter now shall find   105
Within his party-colour'd Mind;
  But from this Valour sad   *steadfast*
  Shrink underneath the Plad: *plaid*
Happy if in the tufted brake   *bushes*
The *English Hunter* him mistake;   110
  Nor lay his Hounds in near
  The *Caledonian* Deer.   *Scottish*
But thou the Wars and Fortunes Son
March indefatigably on;
  And for the last effect   115
  Still keep thy Sword erect:

---

78 confest   This claim was made in some contemporary propaganda; its truth seems questionable.
105 Pict   a name for the ancient inhabitants of Scotland
106 party-colour'd   faction-ridden: with a play on Latin 'pictus', painted

Besides the force it has to fright
The Spirits of the shady Night,
    The same *Arts* that did *gain*
    A *Pow'r* must it *maintain*.

120

1650   1681

To his Coy Mistress

Had we but World enough, and Time,
This coyness Lady were no crime.
We would sit down, and think which way
To walk, and pass our long Loves Day.
Thou by the *Indian Ganges* side   5
Should'st Rubies find: I by the Tide
Of *Humber* would complain. I would   *lament*
Love you ten years before the Flood:
And you should if you please refuse
Till the Conversion of the *Jews*.   10
My vegetable Love should grow
Vaster than Empires, and more slow.
An hundred years should go to praise
Thine Eyes, and on thy Forehead Gaze.
Two hundred to adore each Breast: 15
But thirty thousand to the rest.
An Age at least to every part,
And the last Age should show your Heart.
For Lady you deserve this State;
Nor would I love at lower rate.   20
    But at my back I alwaies hear
Times winged Charriot hurrying near:
And yonder all before us lye
Desarts of vast Eternity.
Thy Beauty shall no more be found;   25
Nor, in thy marble Vault, shall sound
My ecchoing Song: then Worms shall try
That long preserv'd Virginity:
And your quaint Honour turn to dust;
And into ashes all my Lust.   30
The Grave's a fine and private place,
But none I think do there embrace.
    Now therefore, while the youthful hew
Sits on thy skin like morning dew,
And while thy willing Soul transpires   35
At every pore with instant Fires,

Coy   either shy or stand-offish.
7 Humber   the river at Hull
10 Conversion   This would traditionally be at the end of time.
11 vegetable   as distinct from human and animal: growing unconsciously
22 The **chariot** of the Greek sun god, Helios, was drawn by **winged** horses.
29 quaint   dainty, proud, strange; probably also a sexual pun
33–34 hew/dew   This is the common emendation of 'hew/glew', the reading of 1681. Two transcript sources have 'glew/dew' ('glew' could mean glow or glue). None of the sources is directly authorial.

Now let us sport us while we may;
And now, like am'rous birds of prey,
Rather at once our Time devour,
Than languish in his slow-chapt pow'r.   *slow-jawed* 40
Let us roll all our Strength, and all
Our sweetness, up into one Ball:
And tear our Pleasures with rough strife,
Thorough the Iron gates of Life.
Thus, though we cannot make our Sun   45
Stand still, yet we will make him run.

                                                        1681

Bermudas

Where the remote *Bermudas* ride
In th' Oceans bosome unespy'd,
From a small Boat, that row'd along,
The listning Winds receiv'd this Song.
    What should we do but sing his Praise   5
That led us through the watry Maze,
Unto an Isle so long unknown,
And yet far kinder than our own?
Where he the huge Sea-Monsters wracks,
That lift the Deep upon their Backs.   10
He lands us on a grassy Stage;
Safe from the Storms, and Prelat's rage.
He gave us this eternal Spring,
Which here enamells every thing;
And sends the Fowls to us in care,   15
On daily Visits through the Air.
He hangs in shades the Orange bright,
Like golden Lamps in a green Night.
And does in the Pomgranates close,
Jewels more rich than *Ormus* shows.   20
He makes the Figs our mouths to meet;
And throws the Melons at our feet.
But Apples plants of such a price,   *pineapples*
No Tree could ever bear them twice.
With Cedars, chosen by his hand,   25
From *Lebanon*, he stores the Land.
And makes the hollow Seas, that roar,
Proclaime the Ambergris on shoar.
He cast (of which we rather boast)
The Gospels Pearl upon our Coast.   30
And in these Rocks for us did frame
A Temple, where to sound his Name.
Oh let our Voice his Praise exalt,
Till it arrive at Heavens Vault:

---

20 Ormus   (Hormuz) an island in the Persian Gulf
28 Ambergris   a secretion left by whales, used in perfume

Which thence (perhaps) rebounding, may 35
Eccho beyond the *Mexique Bay*.
Thus sung they, in the *English* boat,
An holy and a chearful Note,
And all the way, to guide their Chime,
With falling Oars they kept the time. 40

1681

ANNE BRADSTREET

1612–72 b Northamptonshire. In 1630 she emigrated with her family to the remote new colony of Massachusetts.

A Letter to her Husband, absent upon Publick employment

As loving Hind that (Hartless) wants her Deer,
Scuds through the woods and Fern with harkning ear,
Perplext, in every bush & nook doth pry,
Her dearest Deer, might answer ear or eye;
So doth my anxious soul, which now doth miss, 5
A dearer Dear (far dearer Heart) than this.
Still wait with doubts, & hopes, and failing eye,
His voice to hear, or person to discry.
Or as the pensive Dove doth all alone
(On withered bough) most uncouthly bemoan 10
The absence of her Love, and loving Mate,
Whose loss hath made her so unfortunate:
Ev'n thus doe I, with many a deep sad groan
Bewail my turtle true, who now is gone, *turtle dove*
His presence and his safe return, still wooes, 15
With thousand dolefull sighs & mournfull Cooes.
Or as the loving Mullet, that true Fish,
Her fellow lost, nor joy nor life do wish,
But lanches on that shore, there for to dye, *launches*
Where she her captive husband doth espy. 20
Mine being gone, I lead a joyless life,
I have a loving phere, yet seem no wife: *mate*
But worst of all, to him can't steer my course,
I here, he there, alas, both kept by force:
Return my Dear, my joy, my only Love, 25
Unto thy Hinde, thy Mullet and thy Dove,
Who neither joyes in pasture, house nor streams,
The substance gone, O me, these are but dreams.
Together at one Tree, oh let us brouze,
And like two Turtles roost within one house, 30
And like the Mullets in one River glide,
Let's still remain but one, till death divide.

> *Thy loving Love and Dearest Dear,*
> *At home, abroad, and every where.*
> A.B. 35

1678

In reference to her Children, 23 June, 1656

I had eight birds hatcht in one nest,
Four Cocks there were, and Hens the rest,
I nurst them up with pain and care,
Nor cost, nor labour did I spare,
Till at the last they felt their wing,   5
Mounted the Trees, and learn'd to sing;
Chief of the Brood then took his flight,
To Regions far, and left me quite:
My mournful chirps I after send,
Till he return, or I do end,   10
Leave not thy nest, thy Dam and Sire,   *Dame*
Fly back and sing amidst this Quire.
My second bird did take her flight,
And with her mate flew out of sight:
Southward they both their course did bend,   15
And Seasons twain they there did spend: *two*
Till after blown by *Southern* gales,
They *Norward* steer'd with filled sayles.
A prettier bird was no where seen,
Along the Beach among the treen.   *trees* 20
I have a third of colour white,
On whom I plac'd no small delight;
Coupled with mate loving and true,
Hath also bid her Dam adieu:
And where *Aurora* first appears,   *Dawn* 25
She now hath percht, to spend her years;
One to the Academy flew
To chat among that learned crew:
Ambition moves still in his breast
That he might chant above the rest,   30
Striving for more than to do well,
That nightingales he might excell.
My fifth, whose down is yet scarce gone
Is 'mongst the shrubs and bushes flown,
And as his wings increase in strength,   35
On higher boughs he'l perch at length.
My other three, still with me nest,
Untill they'r grown, then as the rest,
Or here or there, they'l take their flight,
As is ordain'd, so shall they light.   40
If birds could weep, then would my tears
Let others know what are my fears
Lest this my brood some harm should catch,
And be surpriz'd for want of watch,
Whilst pecking corn, and void of care   45
They fall un'wares in Fowlers snare:
Or whilst on trees they sit and sing,
Some untoward boy at them do fling:

Or whilst allur'd with bell and glass,
The net be spread, and caught, alas.   50
Or least by Lime-twigs they be foyl'd,   *lest*
Or by some greedy hawks be spoyl'd.
O would my young, ye saw my breast,
And knew what thoughts there sadly rest,
Great was my pain when I you bred,   55
Great was my care, when I you fed,
Long did I keep you soft and warm,
And with my wings kept off all harm,
My cares are more, and fears than ever,
My throbs such now, as 'fore were never: 60
Alas my birds, you wisdome want,   *lack*
Of perils you are ignorant,
Oft times in grass, on trees, in flight,
Sore accidents on you may light.
O to your safety have an eye,   65
So happy may you live and die:
Mean while my dayes in tunes Ile spend,
Till my weak layes with me shall end.
In shady woods I'le sit and sing,
And things that past, to mind I'le bring.   70
Once young and pleasant, as are you,
But former toyes (no joyes) adieu.
My age I will not once lament,
But sing, my time so near is spent.
And from the top bough take my flight,   75
Into a country beyond sight,
Where old ones instantly grow young,
And there with Seraphims set song:
No seasons cold, nor storms they see;
But spring lasts to eternity,   80
When each of you shall in your nest
Among your young ones take your rest,
In chirping language, oft them tell,
You had a Dam that lov'd you well,
That did what could be done for young,   85
And nurst you up till you were strong,
And 'fore she once would let you fly,
She shew'd you joy and misery;
Taught what was good, and what was ill,
What would save life, and what would kill.   90
Thus gone, amongst you I may live,
And dead, yet speak, and counsel give:
Farwel my birds, farewel adieu,
I happy am, if well with you.
                                    A.B.   95
                                          1678

JOHN MILTON

1608–74 b London, where he lived for much of his life. A writer of civil and religious polemics in prose throughout the 1640s, he became a secretary to Cromwell's Council of State in the 1650s, despite being blind by 1652. His epic poetry was composed mainly after that date and was written down by his daughters at his dictation.

Lycidas

In this Monody the Author bewails a learned Friend, unfortunately drown'd in his passage from Chester *on the* Irish Seas, 1637. *And by occasion foretells the ruine of our corrupted Clergie then in their height.*

Yet once more, O ye Laurels, and once more
Ye Myrtles brown, with Ivy never sear,
I com to pluck your Berries harsh and crude,
And with forc'd fingers rude,
Shatter your leaves before the mellowing year.   5
Bitter constraint, and sad occasion dear,
Compells me to disturb your season due:
For *Lycidas* is dead, dead ere his prime,
Young *Lycidas*, and hath not left his peer:
Who would not sing for *Lycidas*? he knew   10
Himself to sing, and build the lofty rhyme.
He must not flote upon his watry bear   *bier*
Unwept, and welter to the parching wind,
Without the meed of som melodious tear.   *reward*
   Begin then, Sisters of the sacred well,   15
That from beneath the seat of *Jove* doth spring,
Begin, and somewhat loudly sweep the string.
Hence with denial vain, and coy excuse,
So may some gentle Muse
With lucky words favour my destin'd Urn,   20
And as he passes turn,
And bid fair peace be to my sable shrowd.
For we were nurst upon the self-same hill,
Fed the same flock, by fountain, shade, and rill.
   Together both, ere the high Lawns appear'd   25
Under the opening eye-lids of the morn,
We drove a field, and both together heard
What time the Gray-fly winds her sultry horn,   *blows*
Batt'ning our flocks with the fresh dews of night,   *feeding*
Oft till the Star that rose at Ev'ning, bright,   30
Toward Heav'ns descent had slop'd his westering wheel.

Lycidas   A formal lament for Edward King, a student acquaintance of Milton at Cambridge; cast in the classical form of a pastoral, i.e. using idealised rural images to speak about personal and public affairs. Lycidas is a name used by the Roman poet, Virgil (70–90 BC), for a young shepherd: appropriate here, since King had intended becoming a pastor of the Church.
Monody   an ode for single voice in Greek drama
2 sear   withered
3 crude   unripe
6 dear   heartfelt; also dire
15 Sisters   muses, who in Greek myth were said to dwell near various springs

Mean while the Rural ditties were not mute,
Temper'd to th' Oaten Flute,
Rough *Satyrs* danc'd, and *Fauns* with clov'n heel,
From the glad sound would not be absent long,   35
And old *Damœtas* lov'd to hear our song.
    But O the heavy change, now thou art gon,
Now thou art gon, and never must return!
Thee Shepherd, thee the Woods, and desert Caves,
With wilde Thyme and the gadding Vine o'regrown,   *straggling* 40
And all their echoes mourn.
The Willows, and the Hazle Copses green,
Shall now no more be seen,
Fanning their joyous Leaves to thy soft layes.
As killing as the Canker to the Rose,   45
Or Taint-worm to the weanling Herds that graze,
Or Frost to Flowers, that their gay wardrop wear,
When first the White Thorn blows;   *blooms*
Such, *Lycidas*, thy loss to Shepherds ear.
    Where were ye Nymphs when the remorseless deep   50
Clos'd o're the head of your lov'd *Lycidas*?
For neither were ye playing on the steep,
Where your old *Bards*, the famous *Druids* ly,
Nor on the shaggy top of *Mona* high,
Nor yet where *Deva* spreads her wisard stream: 55
Ay me, I fondly dream!
Had ye bin there—for what could that have don?
What could the Muse her self that *Orpheus* bore,
The Muse her self for her inchanting son
Whom Universal nature did lament,   60
When by the rout that made the hideous roar,
His goary visage down the stream was sent,
Down the swift *Hebrus* to the *Lesbian* shore.
    Alas! What boots it with uncessant care
To tend the homely slighted Shepherds trade,   65
And strictly meditate the thankless Muse,
Were it not better don as others use,
To sport with *Amaryllis* in the shade,
Or with the tangles of *Neœra*'s hair?
Fame is the spur that the clear spirit doth raise   70
(That last infirmity of Noble mind)
To scorn delights, and live laborious dayes;

---

33 Oaten of oat stalk
50 Nymphs female deities of the countryside
52–55 Mona (Anglesey, on whose 'steep' the **Druids**, Celtic magician-poet-priests, are buried) and **Deva** (the river Dee) are both in the west of Britain near where King drowned.
58 Muse Calliope, muse of epic. The musician **Orpheus** was torn to pieces by drunken followers of Dionysus; his head floated singing down the river Hebrus and out to the island of Lesbos in the Aegean. See *Metamorphoses* XI.
59 inchanting singing; also magically enchanting
64 What boots it what good is it
65 Shepherds trade In pastoral, the shepherd is a poet.
68–69 Amaryllis, Neæra shepherdesses

But the fair Guerdon when we hope to find,   *reward*
And think to burst out into sudden blaze,
Comes the blind *Fury* with th' abhorred shears,   75
And slits the thin spun life. But not the praise,
Phœbus repli'd, and touch'd my trembling ears;
Fame is no plant that grows on mortal soil,
Nor in the glistering foil
Set off to th' world, nor in broad rumour lies,   80
But lives and spreds aloft by those pure eyes,
And perfet witnes of all-judging *Jove*;
As he pronounces lastly on each deed,
Of so much fame in Heav'n expect thy meed.
   O Fountain *Arethuse*, and thou honour'd floud,   85
Smooth-sliding *Mincius*, crown'd with vocal reeds,
That strain I heard was of a higher mood:
But now my Oat proceeds,
And listens to the Herald of the Sea
That came in *Neptune*'s plea,   90
He ask'd the Waves, and ask'd the Fellon Winds,
What hard mishap hath doom'd this gentle swain?   *young shepherd*
And question'd every gust of rugged wings
That blows from off each beaked Promontory;
They knew not of his story,   95
And sage *Hippotades* their answer brings,
That not a blast was from his dungeon stray'd,
The Air was calm, and on the level brine,
Sleek *Panope* with all her sisters play'd.
It was that fatal and perfidious Bark   *small ship* 100
Built in th' eclipse, and rigg'd with curses dark,
That sunk so low that sacred head of thine.
   Next *Camus*, reverend Sire, went footing slow,
His Mantle hairy, and his Bonnet sedge,
Inwrought with figures dim, and on the edge   105
Like to that sanguine flower inscrib'd with woe.
Ah; Who hath reft (quoth he) my dearest pledge?
Last came, and last did go,
The Pilot of the *Galilean* lake,

---

75 Fury Atropos, third of the three Fates, or Furies, who in Greek myth control a person's destiny: she cuts life off.
77 Phœbus Apollo
79 foil metal set beneath a gem to make it glitter
85 Arethuse a spring of Ortygia, off Sicily: here representing the Sicilian pastoral of the Greek poet Theocritus, who flourished *c.* 270 BC. See note to line 132.
86 Mincius Virgil's native river in Lombardy: representing Virgilian pastoral
88 Oate rustic flute
89 Herald Triton, attendant to the sea god, Neptune
96 Hippotades Aeolus, the wind god
99 Panope a sea nymph
103 Camus the river Cam and Cambridge: his costume is an emblem of the academic (fur-trimmed academic hood) and of the river (sedge).
106 that sanguine flower the hyacinth sprung from the blood of Apollo's dear friend, Hyacinthus; it is inscribed 'ai' ('alas'). See *Metamorphoses* X.
109–10 Pilot St Peter, a fisherman of Galilee and chief of the apostles, to whom Christ gave the **keys** of heaven. See Matt. 16:19.

Two massy Keyes he bore of metals twain,   110
(The Golden opes, the Iron shuts amain)
He shook his Miter'd locks, and stern bespake,
How well could I have spar'd for thee, young swain,
Anow of such as for their bellies sake,   *enough*
Creep and intrude, and climb into the fold?   115
Of other care they little reck'ning make,
Than how to scramble at the shearers feast,
And shove away the worthy bidden guest;
Blind mouthes! that scarce themselves know how to hold
A Sheep-hook, or have learn'd ought els the least   120
That to the faithfull Herdmans art belongs!
What recks it them? What need they? They are sped;   *like*
And when they list, their lean and flashy songs   *scrawny*
Grate on their scrannel Pipes of wretched straw,   125
The hungry Sheep look up, and are not fed,
But swoln with wind, and the rank mist they draw,
Rot inwardly, and foul contagion spread:
Besides what the grim Woolf with privy paw   *secret*
Daily devours apace, and nothing sed,   130
But that two-handed engine at the door,
Stands ready to smite once, and smite no more.
    Return *Alpheus*, the dread voice is past,
That shrunk thy streams; Return *Sicilian* Muse,
And call the Vales, and bid them hither cast   135
Their Bells, and Flourets of a thousand hues.
Ye valleys low where the milde whispers use,
Of shades and wanton winds, and gushing brooks,
On whose fresh lap the swart Star sparely looks,
Throw hither all your quaint enameld eyes,   140
That on the green terf suck the honied showres,
And purple all the ground with vernal flowres.
Bring the rathe Primrose that forsaken dies,   *early*
The tufted Crow-toe, and pale Gessamine,
The white Pink, and the Pansie freakt with jeat,   145
The glowing Violet,
The Musk-rose, and the well attir'd Woodbine,
With Cowslips wan that hang the pensive head,
And every flower that sad embroidery wears:
Bid *Amarantus* all his beauty shed,   150
And Daffadillies fill their cups with tears,
To strew the Laureat Herse where *Lycid* lies.
For so to interpose a little ease,
Let our frail thoughts dally with false surmise.
Ay me! Whilst thee the shores, and sounding Seas

---

120 **Sheep-hook** symbolising pastoral care
122 **What recks it them?** What do they care?
132 **Alpheus** an Arcadian river god who chased the nymph, Arethuse, below the sea to the Sicilian
island of Ortygia; there, where his waters emerge, she became a spring. See *Metamorphoses* V.
138 **swart Star** Sirius, associated with withering summer heat
149 **Amaranthus** legendary never-fading flower

Wash far away, where ere thy bones are hurl'd,   155
Whether beyond the stormy *Hebrides*
Where thou perhaps under the whelming tide
Visit'st the bottom of the monstrous world;
Or whether thou to our moist vows deny'd,
Sleep'st by the fable of *Bellerus* old,   160
Where the great vision of the guarded Mount
Looks toward *Namancos* and *Bayona*'s hold;
Look homeward Angel now, and melt with ruth.
And, O ye *Dolphins*, waft the haples youth.
　　Weep no more, woful Shepherds weep no more,   165
For *Lycidas* your sorrow is not dead,
Sunk though he be beneath the watry floar,
So sinks the day-star in the Ocean bed,
And yet anon repairs his drooping head,
And tricks his beams, and with new spangled Ore,   *dresses*   170
Flames in the forehead of the morning sky:
So *Lycidas* sunk low, but mounted high,
Through the dear might of him that walk'd the waves
Where other groves, and other streams along,
With *Nectar* pure his oozy Locks he leaves,   175
And hears the unexpressive nuptial Song,   *inexpressible*
In the blest Kingdoms meek of joy and love.
There entertain him all the Saints above,
In solemn troops, and sweet Societies
That sing, and singing in their glory move,   180
And wipe the tears for ever from his eyes.
Now *Lycidas* the Shepherds weep no more;
Henceforth thou art the Genius of the shore,
In thy large recompense, and shalt be good
Too all that wander in that perilous flood.   185
　　Thus sang the uncouth Swain to th' Okes and rills, *unsophisticated*
While the still morn went out with Sandals gray,
He touch'd the tender stops of various Quills,
With eager thought warbling his *Dorick* lay: *song*
And now the Sun had stretch'd out all the hills,   190
And now was dropt into the Western Bay;
At last he rose, and twitch'd his Mantle blew:
To morrow to fresh Woods, and Pastures new.

　　　　　　　　　　　　　　　　　　　　　　　1637   1637

---

156 **Hebrides**   islands west of Scotland
160 **Bellerus**   Bellerium is a name for Land's End in Cornwall.
161 **guarded Mount**   St Michael's Mount in Cornwall
162 **Namancos and Bayona**   both in north-west Spain: here representing the threat of Spanish Catholicism   **hold**   fortress
163 **Angel**   i.e. St Michael
173 **him**   Christ. See Matt. 14:25–33.
183 **Genius**   guardian deity
189 **Dorick**   i.e. pastoral

On the late Massacher in Piemont

Avenge O Lord thy slaughter'd Saints, whose bones
  Lie scatter'd on the Alpine mountains cold,
  Ev'n them who kept thy truth so pure of old
  When all our Fathers worship't Stocks and Stones,
Forget not: in thy book record their groanes   5
  Who were thy Sheep and in their antient Fold
  Slayn by the bloody *Piemontese* that roll'd
  Mother with Infant down the Rocks. Their moans
The Vales redoubl'd to the Hills, and they
  To Heav'n. Their martyr'd blood and ashes sow   10
  O're all th'*Italian* fields where still doth sway
The triple Tyrant: that from these may grow
  A hunderd-fold, who having learnt thy way
  Early may fly the *Babylonian* wo.

                    1655   1673

[When I consider how my light is spent]

When I consider how my light is spent,
  Ere half my days, in this dark world and wide,
  And that one Talent which is death to hide,
  Lodg'd with me useless, though my Soul more bent
To serve therewith my Maker, and present   5
  My true account, least he returning chide;   *lest*
  Doth God exact day-labour, light deny'd,
  I fondly ask; But patience to prevent   *foolishly*
That murmur, soon replies, God doth not need
  Either man's work or his own gifts, who best   10
  Bear his milde yoak, they serve him best, his State
Is Kingly. Thousands at his bidding speed
  And post o're Land and Ocean without rest:
  They also serve who only stand and waite.

                 ?1655   1673

[*Lawrence* of vertuous Father vertuous Son]

Lawrence of vertuous Father vertuous Son,
  Now that the Fields are dank, and ways are mire,
  Where shall we sometimes meet, and by the fire
  Help wast a sullen day; what may be won

Massacher   The Vaudois, whose Protestant-like ways had been tolerated in north-western Italy (Piedmont) since the twelfth century, were attacked by the army of the Catholic Duke of Savoy in 1655.
12 triple Tyrant   The Pope wore a triple crown.
14 Babylonian   i.e. the Babylon of the Old Testament and Revelations, applied to the Roman Church
2 half my days   Milton was blind by the age of 43.
3 Talent   as in Christ's parable of the talents: Matt. 25:14–30
13 post   travel quickly
Lawrence   Edward Lawrence (1633–57), son of Henry Lawrence, Lord President of Cromwell's Council of State

From the hard Season gaining: time will run   5
   On smoother, till *Favonius* re-inspire
   The frozen earth; and cloth in fresh attire
   The Lillie and Rose, that neither sow'd nor spun.
What neat repast shall feast us, light and choice,
   Of Attick tast, with Wine, whence we may rise   10
   To hear the Lute well toucht, or artfull voice
Warble immortal Notes and *Tuskan* Ayre?
   He who of those delights can judge, and spare
   To interpose them oft, is not unwise.

                                1655   1673

[Methought I saw my late espoused Saint]

Methought I saw my late espoused Saint
   Brought to me like *Alcestis* from the grave,
   Whom *Joves* great Son to her glad Husband gave,
   Rescu'd from death by force though pale and faint.
Mine as whom washt from spot of child-bed taint,   5
   Purification in the old Law did save,
   And such, as yet once more I trust to have
   Full sight of her in Heaven without restraint,
Came vested all in white, pure as her mind:
   Her face was vail'd, yet to my fancied sight,   10
   Love, sweetness, goodness, in her person shin'd
So clear, as in no face with more delight.
   But O as to embrace me she enclin'd,
   I wak'd, she fled, and day brought back my night.

                                  1673

From Paradise Lost

From *Book IV*

O for that warning voice, which he who saw
Th' *Apocalyps*, heard cry in Heaven aloud,
Then when the Dragon, put to second rout,
Came furious down to be reveng'd on men,
Wo to the inhabitants on Earth! that now,   5

---

6 **Favonius** the west wind
8 See Matt. 6:28: 'And why take ye thought for raiment? Consider the lilies of the field, how they grow: they toil not, neither do they spin.'
10 **Attick** Athenian: simple and elegant
2–3 **Alcestis** in Greek myth, a woman who gave her life for her husband, but was restored by Hercules, **Joves great Son**, who wrestled with Death for her. See the play by Euripides (c. 480–406 BC).
6 **Purification** as required after childbirth in Mosaic law: see Lev. 12. Milton's first wife, Mary (d. 1652) and his second, Katherine (d. 1657) both died not long after giving birth: it is uncertain which is the subject of the poem.
10 **vail'd** as Alcestis was on her return; also a reference to Milton's blindness
Paradise Lost In the earlier Books of this epic on the fall of Adam and Eve from Paradise, the rebel angels have responded to their expulsion from Heaven into Chaos by seeking for means to recover from their loss. Their leader, Satan, makes a long journey to Earth to confirm rumours of a new creation, mankind. At the end of Book III he lands on Mt Niphates in Assyria, near the modern border of Iran and Turkey: the land of Eden lies to the south.
5 See Rev. 12:7–12.

While time was, our first Parents had bin warnd
The coming of thir secret foe, and scap'd,
Haply so scap'd his mortal snare; for now   *by good luck*
Satan, now first inflam'd with rage, came down,
The Tempter ere th' Accuser of man-kind,   10
To wreck on innocent frail man his loss
Of that first Battel, and his flight to Hell:
Yet not rejoycing in his speed, though bold,
Far off and fearless, nor with cause to boast,
Begins his dire attempt, which nigh the birth   15
Now rowling, boiles in his tumultuous brest,
And like a devillish Engine back recoiles
Upon himself; horror and doubt distract
His troubl'd thoughts, and from the bottom stirr
The Hell within him, for within him Hell   20
He brings, and round about him, nor from Hell
One step no more than from himself can fly
By change of place: Now conscience wakes despair
That slumberd, wakes the bitter memorie
Of what he was, what is, and what must be   25
Worse; of worse deeds worse sufferings must ensue.
Sometimes towards *Eden* which now in his view
Lay pleasant, his grievd look he fixes sad,
Sometimes towards Heav'n and the full-blazing Sun,
Which now sat high in his Meridian Towre: *noon*   30
Then much revolving, thus in sighs began.   *pondering*
    O thou that with surpassing Glory crownd,
Look'st from thy sole Dominion like the God
Of this new World; at whose sight all the Starrs
Hide thir diminisht heads; to thee I call,   35
But with no friendly voice, and add thy name
O Sun, to tell thee how I hate thy beams
That bring to my remembrance from what state
I fell, how glorious once above thy Spheare;
Till Pride and worse Ambition threw me down   40
Warring in Heav'n against Heav'ns matchless King:
Ah wherefore! he deserved no such return
From me, whom he created what I was
In that bright eminence, and with his good
Upbraided none; nor was his service hard.   45
What could be less than to afford him praise,
The easiest recompence, and pay him thanks,
How due! yet all his good prov'd ill in me,
And wrought but malice; lifted up so high
I sdeind subjection, and thought one step higher   *disdained*   50
Would set me highest, and in a moment quit
The debt immense of endless gratitude,
So burthensome, still paying, still to ow;
Forgetful what from him I still receivd,

---

17 Engine   i.e. cannon; also plot

And understood not that a grateful mind   55
By owing owes not, but still pays, at once
Indebted and dischargd; what burden then?
O had his powerful Destiny ordaind
Me some inferiour Angel, I had stood
Then happie; no unbounded hope had rais'd   60
Ambition. Yet why not? som other Power
As great might have aspir'd, and me though mean
Drawn to his part; but other Powers as great
Fell not, but stand unshak'n, from within
Or from without, to all temptations arm'd.   65
Hadst thou the same free Will and Power to stand?
Thou hadst: whom hast thou then or what to accuse,
But Heav'ns free Love dealt equally to all?
Be then his Love accurst, since love or hate,
To me alike, it deals eternal woe.   70
Nay curs'd be thou; since against his thy will
Chose freely what it now so justly rues.
Me miserable! which way shall I flie
Infinite wrauth, and infinite despaire?
Which way I flie is Hell; my self am Hell;   75
And in the lowest deep a lower deep
Still threatning to devour me opens wide,
To which the Hell I suffer seems a Heav'n.
O then at last relent: is there no place
Left for Repentance, none for Pardon left?   80
None left but by submission; and that word
Disdain forbids me, and my dread of shame
Among the Spirits beneath, whom I seduc'd
With other promises and other vaunts
Than to submit, boasting I could subdue   85
Th' Omnipotent. Ay me, they little know
How dearly I abide that boast so vaine,
Under what torments inwardly I groane:
While they adore me on the Throne of Hell,
With Diadem and Scepter high advanc't   90
The lower still I fall, onely supream
In miserie; such joy Ambition findes.
But say I could repent and could obtaine
By Act of Grace my former state; how soon
Would higth recal high thoughts, how soon unsay   95
What feign'd submission swore: ease would recant
Vows made in pain, as violent and void.
For never can true reconcilement grow
Where wounds of deadly hate have peirc'd so deep:
Which would but lead me to a worse relapse,   100
And heavier fall: so should I purchase deare
Short intermission bought with double smart.
This knows my punisher; therefore as farr

---

94 Act of Grace favour, as distinct from right

From granting hee, as I from begging peace:
All hope excluded thus, behold in stead   105
Of us out-cast, exil'd, his new delight,
Mankind created, and for him this World.
So farwel Hope, and with Hope farwel Fear,
Farwel Remorse: all Good to me is lost;
Evil be thou my Good; by thee at least   110
Divided Empire with Heav'ns King I hold
By thee, and more than half perhaps will reigne;
As Man ere long, and this new World shall know.
    Thus while he spake, each passion dimm'd his face
Thrice chang'd with pale, ire, envie and despair,   115
Which marrd his borrow'd visage, and betraid
Him counterfet, if any eye beheld.
For heav'nly mindes from such distempers foule
Are ever cleer. Whereof hee soon aware,
Each perturbation smooth'd with outward calme,   120
Artificer of fraud; and was the first
That practisd falshood under saintly shew,
Deep malice to conceale, couch't with revenge:
Yet not anough had practisd to deceive
Uriel once warnd; whose eye pursu'd him down   125
The way he went, and on th' *Assyrian* mount
Saw him disfigur'd, more than could befall
Spirit of happie sort: his gestures fierce
He markd and mad demeanour, then alone,
As he suppos'd, all unobserv'd, unseen.   130
So on he fares, and to the border comes
Of *Eden*, where delicious Paradise,
Now nearer, Crowns with her enclosure green,   *open land*
As with a rural mound the champain head   135
Of a steep wilderness, whose hairie sides   *romantic*
With thicket overgrown, grottesque and wilde,
Access deni'd; and over head up grew
Insuperable highth of loftiest shade,
Cedar, and Pine, and Firr, and branching Palm,   140
A Silvan Scene, and as the ranks ascend
Shade above shade, a woodie Theatre
Of stateliest view. Yet higher than thir tops
The verdurous wall of Paradise up sprung:
Which to our general Sire gave prospect large   145
Into his neather Empire neighbouring round.
And higher than that Wall a circling row
Of goodliest Trees loaden with fairest Fruit,
Blossoms and Fruits at once of golden hue
Appeerd, with gay enameld colours mixt: 150
On which the Sun more glad impress'd his beams

---

125 Uriel   the archangel by whom Satan, disguised as a good angel, was directed to Earth at the end of Book III
144 Sire   i.e. Adam

Than in fair Evening Cloud, or humid Bow,   *rainbow*
When God hath showrd the earth; so lovely seemd
That Lantskip: And of pure now purer aire   *landscape*
Meets his approach, and to the heart inspires
Vernal delight and joy, able to drive   155
All sadness but despair: now gentle gales
Fanning thir odoriferous wings dispense
Native perfumes, and whisper whence they stole
Those balmie spoiles. As when to them who saile
Beyond the *Cape of Hope*, and now are past   160
Mozambic, off at Sea North-East windes blow
Sabean Odours from the spicie shoare
Of *Arabie* the blest, with such delay
Well pleas'd they slack thir course, and many a League
Cheard with the grateful smell old Ocean smiles.   165
So entertaind those odorous sweets the Fiend
Who came thir bane, though with them better pleas'd
Than *Asmodeus* with the fishie fume,
That drove him, though enamourd, from the Spouse
Of *Tobits* Son, and with a vengeance sent   170
From *Media* post to *Ægypt*, there fast bound.
    Now to th' ascent of that steep savage Hill   *wild*
Satan had journied on, pensive and slow;
But further way found none, so thick entwin'd,
As one continu'd brake, the undergrowth   175
Of shrubs and tangling bushes had perplext
All path of Man or Beast that past that way:
One Gate there only was, and that look'd East
On th' other side: which when th' arch-fellon saw
Due entrance he disdaind, and in contempt,   180
At one slight bound high over leap'd all bound
Of Hill or highest Wall, and sheer within
Lights on his feet. As when a prowling Wolfe,
Whom hunger drives to seek new haunt for prey,
Watching where Shepherds pen thir Flocks at eeve   185
In hurdl'd Cotes amid the field secure,   *shelters*
Leaps o're the fence with ease into the Fould:
Or as a Thief bent to unhoord the cash
Of some rich Burgher, whose substantial dores,
Cross-barrd and bolted fast, fear no assault,   190
In at the window climbs, or o're the tiles;
So clomb this first grand Thief into Gods Fould:
So since into his Church lewd Hirelings climbe.   *ignorant*
Thence up he flew, and on the Tree of Life,
The middle Tree and highest there that grew,   195
Sat like a Cormorant; yet not true Life
Thereby regaind, but sat devising Death

---

162 **Sabean** of Saba (now Yemen)
170 **Tobits Son** Tobias, who made a 'fishie fume' to drive away the jealous spirit, Asmodeus, the killer of his wife's seven previous husbands: the spirit was caught and bound by the archangel Raphael. See Tobit 8.

To them who liv'd; nor on the vertue thought
Of that life-giving Plant, but only us'd
For prospect, what well us'd had bin the pledge   *for a lookout* 200
Of immortality. So little knows
Any, but God alone, to value right
The good before him, but perverts best things
To worst abuse, or to thir meanest use.
Beneath him with new wonder now he views   205
To all delight of human sense expos'd
In narrow room Natures whole wealth, yea more,
A Heav'n on Earth: for blissful Paradise
Of God the Garden was, by him in the East
Of *Eden* planted; *Eden* stretched her Line   210
From *Auran* Eastward to the Royal Towrs
Of great *Seleucia*, built by *Grecian* Kings,
Or where the Sons of *Eden* long before
Dwelt in *Telassar*: in this pleasant soile
His farr more pleasant Garden God ordaind;   215
Out of the fertil ground he caus'd to grow
All Trees of noblest kind for sight, smell, taste;
And all amid them stood the Tree of Life,
High eminent, blooming Ambrosial Fruit
Of vegetable Gold; and next to Life   220
Our Death the Tree of Knowledge grew fast by,
Knowledge of Good bought dear by knowing ill.
Southward through *Eden* went a River large,
Nor chang'd his course, but through the shaggie hill
Pass'd underneath ingulft, for God had thrown   225
That Mountain as his Garden mould high rais'd
Upon the rapid current, which through veins
Of porous Earth with kindly thirst up drawn,   *natural*
Rose a fresh Fountain, and with many a rill
Waterd the Garden; thence united fell   230
Down the steep glade, and met the neather Flood,
Which from his darksom passage now appeers,
And now divided into four main Streams,
Runs divers, wandring many a famous Realme
And Country whereof here needs no account,   235
But rather to tell how, if Art could tell,
How from that Saphire Fount the crisped Brooks,
Rowling on Orient Pearl and sands of Gold,
With mazie error under pendant shades   *meander*
Ran Nectar, visiting each plant, and fed   240
Flours worthy of Paradise, which not nice Art   *elaborate*
In Beds and curious Knots, but Nature boon   *bountiful*
Powrd forth profuse on Hill and Dale and Plaine,
Both where the morning Sun first warmly smote
The open field, and where the unpierc't shade   245
Imbround the noontide Bowrs: Thus was this place,   *darkened*

211–14 The area would cover much of modern Syria and Iraq.
234 divers variously

A happy rural seat of various view;
Groves whose rich Trees wept odorous Gumms and Balme,
Others whose fruit burnisht with Golden Rinde
Hung amiable, *Hesperian* Fables true,   *lovely*   250
If true, here only, and of delicious taste:
Betwixt them Lawns, or level Downs, and Flocks
Grasing the tender herb, were interpos'd,
Or palmie hilloc, or the flourie lap
Of som irriguous Valley spred her store,   *watered* 255
Flours of all hue, and without Thorn the Rose:
Another side, umbrageous Grots and Caves   *shady*
Of coole recess, o're which the mantling Vine
Layes forth her purple Grape, and gently creeps
Luxuriant; mean while murmuring waters fall   260
Down the slope hills, disperst, or in a Lake,
That to the fringed Bank with Myrtle crownd,
Her chrystal mirror holds, unite thir streams.
The Birds thir quire apply; aires, vernal aires,
Breathing the smell of field and grove, attune   265
The trembling leaves, while Universal *Pan*
Knit with the *Graces* and the *Hours* in dance
Led on th' Eternal Spring. Not that faire field
Of *Enna*, where *Proserpin* gathering flours
Her self a fairer Floure by gloomie *Dis*   270
Was gatherd, which cost *Ceres* all that pain
To seek her through the world; nor that sweet Grove
Of *Daphne* by *Orontes*, and th' inspir'd
Castalian Spring, might with this Paradise
Of *Eden* strive; nor that *Nyseian* Ile   275
Girt with the River *Triton*, where old *Cham*,
Whom Gentiles *Ammon* call and *Libian Jove*,
Hid *Amalthea* and her Florid Son
Young *Bacchus* from his Stepdame *Rhea*'s eye;
Nor where *Abassin* Kings thir issue Guard,   280
Mount *Amara*, though this by som suppos'd
True Paradise under the *Ethiop* Line
By *Nilus* head, enclos'd with shining Rock,
A whole dayes journey high, but wide remote
From this *Assyrian* Garden, where the Fiend   285
Saw undelighted all delight, all kind
Of living Creatures new to sight and strange:

---

250 Hesperian Fables   i.e. of the literally golden fruit of the fabled islands of the Hesperides
266–68 Pan, Graces, Hours   classical figures for nature, beauty and recurring time, whose dance of unity here is the emblem of an **Eternal Spring**
269 Enna   in Sicily: whence, in Roman and Greek myth, **Proserpina** (or Persephone) was abducted by **Dis** (or Hades), god of the underworld, and made his queen for half of each year. Her mother, **Ceres** (or Demeter), goddess of harvest and fertility, searched for her, and still grows desolate until Proserpina's return each spring. See *Metamorphoses* V.
273 Daphne   a grove by the river **Orontes** near Antioch, with an oracle of Apollo and a stream named after the **Castalian** spring of the muses on Mt Parnassus.
275 Nyseian Ile   Nysa, where Dionysus (**Bacchus**) grew up, is located variously, in this version near modern Tunis. The conflation of his father, Zeus (**Libian Jove**) with **Cham**, son of Noah, and **Ammon**, god of the Egyptians, was traditional.
281 Amara   a mountain famous for its palaces and pleasure gardens

Two of far nobler shape erect and tall,
Godlike erect, with native Honour clad
In naked Majestie seemd Lords of all,   290
And worthie seemd, for in thir looks Divine
The image of thir glorious Maker shon,
Truth, Wisdome, Sanctitude severe and pure,
Severe, but in true filial freedom plac't;
Whence true autoritie in men; though both   295
Not equal, as thir sex not equal seemd;
For contemplation hee and valour formd,
For softness shee and sweet attractive Grace,
Hee for God only, shee for God in him:
His fair large Front and Eye sublime declar'd   *forehead* 300
Absolute rule; and Hyacinthin Locks
Round from his parted forelock manly hung
Clustring, but not beneath his shoulders broad:
Shee as a vail down to the slender waste
Her unadorned golden tresses wore   305
Dissheveld, but in wanton ringlets wav'd
As the Vine curles her tendrils, which impli'd
Subjection, but requir'd with gentle sway,
And by her yeilded, by him best receivd,
Yeilded with coy submission, modest pride,   *shy* 310
And sweet reluctant amorous delay.
Nor those mysterious parts were then conceald,
Then was not guiltie shame, dishonest shame
Of natures works, honor dishonorable,
Sin-bred, how have ye troubl'd all mankind   315
With shews instead, meer shews of seeming pure,
And banisht from mans life his happiest life,
Simplicitie and spotless innocence.
So passd they naked on, nor shund the sight
Of God or Angel, for they thought no ill: 320
So hand in hand they passd, the lovliest pair
That ever since in loves imbraces met,
Adam the goodliest man of men since borne
His Sons, the fairest of her Daughters *Eve*.
Under a tuft of shade that on a green   325
Stood whispering soft, by a fresh Fountain side
They sat them down, and after no more toil
Of thir sweet Gardning labour than suffic'd
To recommend coole *Zephyr*, and made ease
More easie, wholsom thirst and appetite   330
More grateful, to thir Supper Fruits they fell,
Nectarine Fruits which the compliant boughes
Yeilded them, side-long as they sat recline
On the soft downie Bank damaskt with flours:

---

299 See 1 Cor. 11:3: 'The head of every man is Christ; and the head of the woman is the man; and the head of Christ is God.'
313 dishonest   unchaste
329 Zephyr   the west wind

The savourie pulp they chew, and in the rinde   335
Still as they thirsted scoop the brimming stream;
Nor gentle purpose, nor endearing smiles
Wanted, nor youthful dalliance as beseems   *lacked*
Fair couple, linkt in happie nuptial League,
Alone as they. About them frisking playd   340
All Beasts of th' Earth, since wilde, and of all chase
In Wood or Wilderness, Forrest or Den;
Sporting the Lion rampd, and in his paw
Dandl'd the Kid; Bears, Tygers, Ounces, Pards   *lynxes, leopards*
Gambold before them, th' unwieldy Elephant   345
To make them mirth us'd all his might, and wreathd
His Lithe Proboscis; close the Serpent sly
Insinuating, wove with Gordian twine
His breaded train, and of his fatal guile   *braided*
Gave proof unheeded; others on the grass   350
Couch't, and now field with pasture gazing sat,
Or Bedward ruminating: for the Sun
Declin'd was hasting now with prone carreer
To th' Ocean Iles, and in th' ascending Scale
Of Heav'n the Starrs that usher Evening rose: 355
When *Satan* still in gaze, as first he stood,
Scarce thus at length faild speech recoverd sad.
    O Hell! what doe mine eyes with grief behold,
Into our room of bliss thus high advanc't
Creatures of other mould, earth-born perhaps,   360
Not Spirits, yet to heav'nly Spirits bright
Little inferior; whom my thoughts pursue
With wonder, and could love, so lively shines
In them Divine resemblance, and such grace
The hand that formd them on thir shape hath pourd.   365
Ah gentle pair, yee little think how nigh
Your change approaches, when all these delights
Will vanish and deliver ye to woe,
More woe, the more your taste is now of joy;
Happie; but for so happie ill secur'd   370
Long to continue, and this high seat your Heav'n
Ill fenc't for Heav'n to keep out such a foe
As now is enterd; yet no purpos'd foe
To you whom I could pittie thus forlorne
Though I unpittied: League with you I seek,   375
And mutual amitie so streight, so close,
That I with you must dwell, or you with me
Henceforth; my dwelling haply may not please   *perchance*
Like this fair Paradise, your sense, yet such
Accept your makers work; he gave it me,   380
Which I as freely give; Hell shall unfold,
To entertain you two, her widest Gates,

---

337 purpose conversation
348 Gordian twine tied tightly, as in the Gordian knot which had to be cut
376 streight intimate; also honest

And send forth all her Kings; there will be room,
Not like these narrow limits, to receive
Your numerous ofspring; if no better place, 385
Thank him who puts me loath to this revenge
On you who wrong me not for him who wrongd.
And should I at your harmless innocence
Melt, as I doe, yet public reason just,
Honour and Empire with revenge enlarg'd, 390
By conquering this new World, compels me now
To do what else though damnd I should abhorre.
  So spake the Fiend, and with necessitie,
The Tyrants plea, excus'd his devilish deeds.
Then from his loftie stand on that high Tree 395
Down he alights among the sportful Herd
Of those fourfooted kinds, himself now one,
Now other, as thir shape serv'd best his end
Neerer to view his prey, and unespi'd
To mark what of thir state he more might learn 400
By word or action markt: about them round
A Lion now he stalks with fierie glare,
Then as a Tiger, who by chance hath spi'd
In some Purlieu two gentle Fawns at play,
Strait couches close, then rising changes oft 405
His couchant watch, as one who chose his ground
Whence rushing he might surest seise them both
Grip't in each paw.

                 c. *1642–65*   1667

EDMUND WALLER

1606–87 b Buckinghamshire. He was a Member of Parliament for much of his adult life.

Song

  Go lovely Rose,
Tell her that wastes her time and me,
  That now she knows
When I resemble her to thee,
  How sweet and fair she seems to be. 5

  Tell her that's young,
And shuns to have her graces spy'd,
  That hadst thou sprung
In desarts, where no men abide,
  Thou must have uncommended dy'd. 10

  Small is the worth
Of beauty from the light retir'd;
  Bid her come forth,
Suffer her self to be desir'd,
  And not blush so to be admir'd. 15

Then die, that she
The common fate of all things rare
,   May read in thee,
How small a part of time they share,
That are so wondrous sweet and fair.   20

1645

Of the last Verses in the Book

When we for Age could neither read nor write,
The Subject made us able to indite.
The Soul with Nobler Resolutions deckt,
The Body stooping, does Herself erect:
No Mortal Parts are requisite to raise   5
Her, that Unbody'd can her Maker praise.

   The Seas are quiet, when the Winds give o're;
So calm are we, when Passions are no more:
For then we know how vain it was to boast
Of fleeting Things, so certain to be lost.   10
Clouds of Affection from our younger Eyes
Conceal that emptiness, which Age descries.

   The Soul's dark Cottage, batter'd and decay'd,
Lets in new Light thro' chinks that time has made.
Stronger by weakness, wiser Men become   15
As they draw near to their Eternal home:
Leaving the Old, both Worlds at once they view,
That stand upon the Threshold of the New.

1686

THOMAS CAREW

(pron. 'Carey') 1598–1640. He was attached to the court of Charles I.

A Song

Aske me no more where JOVE bestowes,
When JUNE is past, the fading rose:
For in your beauties orient deepe,
These flowers as in their causes, sleepe.

Aske me no more whither doth stray,   5
The golden Atomes of the day:
For in pure love heaven did prepare,
Those powders to inrich your haire.

Of the last Verses   This poem was apparently written very late in Waller's life; it was added to the
corpus of his work in the first posthumous edition.

Aske me no more whither doth hast,
The Nightingale when May is past: 10
For in your sweet dividing throat,
She winters and keepes warme her note.

Aske me no more where those starres light,
That downewards fall in dead of night:
For in your eyes they sit, and there,   15
Fixed become as in their sphere.

Aske me no more if East or West,
The Phenix builds her spicy nest:
For unto you at last shee flies,
And in your fragrant bosome dyes.   20

        1640

Maria Wentworth,

Thomæ Comitis Cleveland, filia præmortua prima
Virgineam animam exhalauit. An. Dom. 1632 Æt. suae 18.

And here the precious dust is layd;
Whose purely-tempered Clay was made
So fine, that it the guest betray'd.

Else the soule grew so fast within,
It broke the outward shell of sinne,   5
And so was hatch'd a Cherubin.

In heigth, it soar'd to God above;
In depth, it did to knowledge move,
And spread in breadth to generall love.

Before, a pious duty shind   10
To Parents, courtesie behind,
On either side an equall mind,

Good to the Poore, to kindred deare,
To servants kind, to friendship cleare,
To nothing but her selfe, severe.   15

So though a Virgin, yet a Bride
To every Grace, she justifi'd
A chaste Poligamie, and dy'd.

Learne from hence (Reader) what small trust
We owe this world, where vertue must   20
Fraile as our flesh, crumble to dust.

        1640

---

11 **dividing** In music, divisions are quick, elaborate variations on the notes of a melody.
18 **Phenix** (Phoenix) a legendary Arabian bird, the only one of its kind, which burns and is reborn from the ashes. Its nest is of spices.
'**Maria Wentworth,** pre-deceased first daughter of Sir Thomas Cleveland, breathed out her virgin soul AD 1632, aged 18.'

GEORGE HERBERT

1593–1633 b Wales. A brilliant scholar with prospects of public preferment, he opted for pastoral work, and from 1630 was Anglican rector at Bemerton, Wiltshire.

Prayer (I)

Prayer the Churches banquet, Angels age,
    Gods breath in man returning to his birth,
    The soul in paraphrase, heart in pilgrimage,
The Christian plummet sounding heav'n and earth;

Engine against th' Almightie, sinners towre,   5
    Reversed thunder, Christ-side-piercing spear,
    The six-daies world transposing in an houre,
A kinde of tune, which all things heare and fear;

Softnesse, and peace, and joy, and love, and blisse,
    Exalted Manna, gladnesse of the best,   10
    Heaven in ordinarie, man well drest,
The milkie way, the bird of Paradise,

    Church-bels beyond the starres heard, the souls bloud,
    The land of spices; something understood.

        1633

The Temper (I)

How should I praise thee, Lord! how should my rymes
    Gladly engrave thy love in steel,
    If what my soul doth feel sometimes,
        My soul might ever feel!

Although there were some fourtie heav'ns, or more,   5
    Sometimes I peere above them all;
    Sometimes I hardly reach a score,
        Sometimes to hell I fall.

O rack me not to such a vast extent;
    Those distances belong to thee: 10
    The world's too little for thy tent,
        A grave too big for me.

Wilt thou meet arms with man, that thou dost stretch
    A crumme of dust from heav'n to hell?
    Will great God measure with a wretch?   15
        Shall he thy stature spell?

O let me, when thy roof my soul hath hid,
    O let me roost and nestle there:
    Then of a sinner thou art rid,
        And I of hope and fear.   20

Yet take thy way; for sure thy way is best:
    Stretch or contract me, thy poore debter:
    This is but tuning of my breast,
        To make the musick better.

Whether I flie with angels, fall with dust,   25
    Thy hands made both, and I am there:
    Thy power and love, my love and trust
       Make one place ev'ry where.

             1633

Church-monuments

While that my soul repairs to her devotion,
Here I intombe my flesh, that it betimes
May take acquaintance of this heap of dust;
To which the blast of deaths incessant motion,
Fed with the exhalation of our crimes,   5
Drives all at last. Therefore I gladly trust

My bodie to this school, that it may learn
To spell his elements, and finde his birth
Written in dustie heraldrie and lines;
Which dissolution sure doth best discern,   10
Comparing dust with dust, and earth with earth.
These laugh at Jeat and Marble put for signes,

To sever the good fellowship of dust,
And spoil the meeting. What shall point out them,
When they shall bow, and kneel, and fall down flat   15
To kisse those heaps, which now they have in trust?
Deare flesh, while I do pray, learn here thy stemme
And true descent; that when thou shalt grow fat,

And wanton in thy cravings, thou mayst know,
That flesh is but the glasse, which holds the dust   20
That measures all our time; which also shall
Be crumbled into dust. Mark here below
How tame these ashes are, how free from lust,
That thou mayst fit thy self against thy fall.

             1633

Vertue

Sweet day, so cool, so calm, so bright,
The bridall of the earth and skie:
The dew shall weep thy fall to night;
       For thou must die.

Sweet rose, whose hue angrie and brave   5
Bids the rash gazer wipe his eye:
Thy root is ever in its grave,
       And thou must die.

Sweet spring, full of sweet dayes and roses,
A box where sweets compacted lie;   *perfumes* 10
My musick shows ye have your closes,   *cadences*
       And all must die.

Onely a sweet and vertuous soul,
Like season'd timber, never gives;
But though the whole world turn to coal,   15
          Then chiefly lives.

                                                            1633

The Collar

                                                            table
I struck the board, and cry'd, No more.
          I will abroad.
What? shall I ever sigh and pine?
My lines and life are free; free as the rode,
Loose as the winde, as large as store.   *abundance* 5
          Shall I be still in suit?
Have I no harvest but a thorn
To let me bloud, and not restore
What I have lost with cordiall fruit?
          Sure there was wine   10
Before my sighs did drie it: there was corn
          Before my tears did drown it.
Is the yeare onely lost to me?
          Have I no bayes to crown it?
No flowers, no garlands gay? all blasted?   15
          All wasted?
Not so, my heart: but there is fruit,
          And thou hast hands.
Recover all thy sigh-blown age
On double pleasures: leave thy cold dispute   20
Of what is fit, and not. Forsake thy cage,
          Thy rope of sands,
Which pettie thoughts have made, and made to thee
Good cable, to enforce and draw,
          And be thy law,   25
While thou didst wink and wouldst not see.
          Away; take heed:
          I will abroad.
Call in thy deaths head there: tie up thy fears.
          He that forbears   30
      To suit and serve his need,
          Deserves his load.
But as I rav'd and grew more fierce and wilde
          At every word,
Me thoughts I heard one calling, *Child!*   35
          And I reply'd, *My Lord.*

                                                            1633

---

6 still in suit   always in attendance
29 deaths head   skull, kept as a reminder of death

Bitter-sweet

Ah my deare angrie Lord,
Since thou dost love, yet strike;
Cast down, yet help afford;
Sure I will do the like.

I will complain, yet praise;   5
I will bewail, approve:
And all my sowre-sweet dayes
I will lament, and love.

                                    1633

HENRY KING

1592–1669 b London. He was a friend of Donne, his fellow cleric for a time at St Paul's, and became Bishop of Chichester in 1642.

The Exequy

Accept thou Shrine of my dead Saint,
Insteed of Dirges this complaint;   *lament*
And for sweet flowres to crown thy hearse,
Receive a strew of weeping verse
From thy griev'd friend, whom thou might'st see   5
Quite melted into tears for thee.

   Dear loss! since thy untimely fate
My task hath been to meditate
On thee, on thee: thou art the book,
The library whereon I look   10
Though almost blind. For thee (lov'd clay)
I languish out not live the day,
Using no other exercise
But what I practise with mine eyes:
By which wet glasses I find out   15
How lazily time creeps about
To one that mourns: this, onely this
My exercise and bus'ness is:
So I compute the weary houres
With sighs dissolved into showres.   20

   Nor wonder if my time go thus
Backward and most preposterous;
Thou hast benighted me, thy set
This Eve of blackness did beget,
Who was't my day, (though overcast   25
Before thou had'st thy Noon-tide past)

The Exequy a poem written on the death of King's wife, Anne (1600–24). They had been married eight years.

And I remember must in tears,
Thou scarce had'st seen so many years
As Day tells houres. By thy cleer Sun
My love and fortune first did run;   30
But thou wilt never more appear
Folded within my Hemisphear,
Since both thy light and motion
Like a fled Star is fall'n and gon,
And twixt me and my soules dear wish   35
The earth now interposed is,
With such a strange eclipse doth make
As ne're was read in Almanake.

    I could allow thee for a time
To darken me and my sad Clime,   40
Were it a month, a year, or ten,
I would thy exile live till then;
And all that space my mirth adjourn,
So thou wouldst promise to return;
And putting off thy ashy shrowd   45
At length disperse this sorrows cloud.

    But woe is me! the longest date
Too narrow is to calculate
These empty hopes: never shall I
Be so much blest as to descry   50
A glimpse of thee, till that day come
Which shall the earth to cinders doome,
And a fierce Feaver must calcine   *burn to ashes*
The body of this world like thine,
(My Little World!) that fit of fire   55
Once off, our bodies shall aspire
To our soules bliss: then we shall rise,
And view our selves with cleerer eyes
In that calm Region, where no night
Can hide us from each others sight.   60

    Mean time, thou hast her earth: much good
May my harm do thee. Since it stood
With Heavens will I might not call
Her longer mine, I give thee all
My short-liv'd right and interest   65
In her, whom living I lov'd best:
With a most free and bounteous grief,
I give thee what I could not keep.
Be kind to her, and prethee look
Thou write into thy Dooms-day book   70
Each parcell of this Rarity
Which in thy Casket shrin'd doth ly:
See that thou make thy reck'ning streight,
And yield her back again by weight;

For thou must audit on thy trust 75
Each graine and atome of this dust,
As thou wilt answer *Him* that lent,
Not gave thee my dear Monument.

So close the ground, and 'bout her shade
Black curtains draw, my *Bride* is laid. 80

Sleep on my *Love* in thy cold bed
Never to be disquieted!
My last good night! Thou wilt not wake
Till I thy fate shall overtake:
Till age, or grief, or sickness must 85
Marry my body to that dust
It so much loves; and fill the room
My heart keeps empty in thy Tomb.
Stay for me there; I will not faile
To meet thee in that hollow Vale. 90
And think not much of my delay;
I am already on the way,
And follow thee with all the speed
Desire can make, or sorrows breed.
Each minute is a short degree, 95
And ev'ry houre a step towards thee.
At night when I betake to rest,
Next morn I rise neerer my West
Of life, almost by eight houres saile,
Than when sleep breath'd his drowsie gale. *breeze* 100

Thus from the Sun my Bottom stears, *hull*
And my dayes Compass downward bears:
Nor labour I to stemme the tide
Through which to *Thee* I swiftly glide.

'Tis true, with shame and grief I yield, 105
Thou like the *Vann* first took'st the field, *vanguard*
And gotten hast the victory
In thus adventuring to dy
Before me, whose more years might crave 110
A just precedence in the grave.
But heark! My pulse like a soft Drum
Beats my approach, tells *Thee* I come;
And slow howere my marches be,
I shall at last sit down by *Thee*.

The thought of this bids me go on, 115
And wait my dissolution
With hope and comfort. *Dear* (forgive
The crime) I am content to live
Divided, with but half a heart,
Till we shall meet and never part. 120

1657

ROBERT HERRICK

1591–1674 b London. Most of his published poems are from 1629–47, when he was
Anglican parish priest at the remote village of Dean Prior, Devon.

Delight in Disorder

A sweet disorder in the dresse
Kindles in cloathes a wantonnesse:
A Lawne about the shoulders thrown   *fine linen*
Into a fine distraction:
An erring Lace, which here and there   5
Enthralls the Crimson Stomacher:
A Cuffe neglectfull, and thereby
Ribbands to flow confusedly:
A winning wave (deserving Note)
In the tempestuous petticote: 10
A carelesse shooe-string, in whose tye
I see a wilde civility:
Doe more bewitch me, than when Art
Is too precise in every part.

                                                         1648

To Daffadills

Faire Daffadills, we weep to see
        You haste away so soone:
As yet the early-rising Sun
        Has not attain'd his Noone.
                Stay, stay,   5
        Untill the hasting day
                Has run
        But to the Even-song;
And, having pray'd together, we
        Will goe with you along.   10

We have short time to stay, as you,
        We have as short a Spring;
As quick a growth to meet Decay,
        As you, or any thing.
                We die,   15
        As your hours doe, and drie
                Away,
        Like to the Summers raine;
Or as the pearles of Mornings dew
        Ne'r to be found againe.   20
                                                         1648

---

6 Stomacher   ornamental vest worn under the laced front of a bodice

Corinna's going a Maying 449

Upon Julia's Clothes

When as in silks my *Julia* goes,
Then, then (me thinks) how sweetly flowes
That liquefaction of her clothes.

Next, when I cast mine eyes and see
That brave Vibration each way free;   5
O how that glittering taketh me!

1648

To Dianeme

Sweet, be not proud of those two eyes,
Which Star-like sparkle in their skies:
Nor be you proud, that you can see
All hearts your captives; yours, yet free:
Be you not proud of that rich haire,   5
Which wantons with the Love-sick aire:
When as that *Rubie*, which you weare,
Sunk from the tip of your soft eare,
Will last to be a precious Stone,
When all your world of Beautie's gone.   10

1648

Corinna's going a Maying

Get up, get up for shame, the Blooming Morne
Upon her wings presents the god unshorne.
        See how *Aurora* throwes her faire
        Fresh-quilted colours through the aire:
        Get up, sweet-Slug-a-bed, and see   5
        The Dew-bespangling Herbe and Tree.
Each Flower has wept, and bow'd toward the East,
Above an houre since; yet you not drest,
        Nay! not so much as out of bed?
        When all the Birds have Mattens seyd,   10
        And sung their thankfull Hymnes: 'tis sin,
        Nay, profanation to keep in,
When as a thousand Virgins on this day,
Spring, sooner than the Lark, to fetch in May.

Rise; and put on your Foliage, and be seene   15
To come forth, like the Spring-time, fresh and greene;
        And sweet as *Flora*. Take no care
        For Jewels for your Gowne, or Haire:
        Feare not; the leaves will strew
        Gemms in abundance upon you: 20

Corinna's going a Maying   May branches were gathered on May Day to deck the houses and streets.
2 the god   i.e. the sun god
3 Aurora   Greek goddess of dawn
10 Mattens   (matins) morning prayers
17 Flora   goddess of flowers

Besides, the childhood of the Day has kept,
Against you come, some *Orient Pearls* unwept:
  Come, and receive them while the light
  Hangs on the Dew-locks of the night:
  And *Titan* on the Eastern hill
  Retires himselfe, or else stands still   25
Till you come forth. Wash, dresse, be briefe in praying:
Few Beads are best, when once we goe a Maying.

Come, my *Corinna*, come; and comming, marke
How each field turns a street; each street a Parke 30
  Made green, and trimm'd with trees: see how
  Devotion gives each House a Bough,
  Or Branch: Each Porch, each doore, ere this,
  An Arke a Tabernacle is
Made up of white-thorn neatly enterwove; 35
As if here were those cooler shades of love.
  Can such delights be in the street,
  And open fields, and we not see't?
  Come, we'll abroad; and let's obay
  The Proclamation made for May: 40
And sin no more, as we have done, by staying:
But my *Corinna*, come, let's goe a Maying.

There's not a budding Boy, or Girle, this day,
But is got up, and gone to bring in May.
  A deale of Youth, ere this, is come 45
  Back, and with *White-thorn* laden home,
  Some have dispatcht their Cakes and Creame,
  Before that we have left to dreame:
And some have wept, and woo'd, and plighted Troth,
And chose their Priest, ere we can cast off sloth: 50
  Many a green-gown has been given;
  Many a kisse, both odde and even:
  Many a glance too has been sent
  From out the eye, Loves Firmament:
Many a jest told of the Keyes betraying 55
This night, and Locks pickt, yet w'are not a Maying.

Come, let us goe, while we are in our prime;
And take the harmlesse follie of the time.
  We shall grow old apace, and die
  Before we know our liberty. 60
  Our life is short; and our dayes run
  As fast away as do's the Sunne:
And as a vapour, or a drop of raine
Once lost, can ne'r be found againe:
  So when or you or I are made 65
  A fable, song, or fleeting shade;

---

22 Against you come against your coming
25 Titan Helios, Greek sun god
28 Beads rosaries, i.e. prayers

All love, all liking, all delight
Lies drown'd with us in endlesse night.
Then while time serves, and we are but decaying;
Come, my *Corinna*, come, let's goe a Maying.   70

1648

LADY MARY WROTH

?1586–1652 b Penshurst, Kent, a member of the Sidney family. Frequently at the court of
James II, she was both a poet and a patron of poets.

From The Countesse of Mountgomeries Urania

Blame me not dearest, though grieved for your sake,
    Love mild to you, on me triumphing sits,
    Sifting the choysest ashes of my wits,
    Burnt like a Phœnix, change but such could shake.

And a new heat, given by your eyes did make   5
    Embers dead cold, call Spirits from the pits
    Of darke despaire, to favour newfelt fits,
    And as from death to this new choice to wake.

Love thus crownes you with power, scorne not the flames,
    Though not the first, yet which as purely rise   10
    As the best light, which sets unto our eyes,
    And then againe ascends free from all blames.

Purenesse is not alone in one fix'd place,
Who dies to live, finds change a happy grace.

★ ★ ★

Losse my molester at last patient be,
    And satisfied with thy curst selfe, or move
    Thy mournefull force thus oft on perjurd love,
    To wast a life which lives by mischeifes fee.

Who will behould true misery, view me,   5
    And find what wit hath fain'd, I fully prove;
    A heaven-like blessing chang'd throwne from above,
    Into Dispaire, whose worst ill I doe see.

Had I not happy beene, I had not knowne
    So great a losse, a King depos'd, feeles most   10
    The torment of a Throne-like-want when lost,
    And up must looke to what late was his owne.

Lucifer downe cast, his losse doth grieve,
    My Paradice of joy gone, doe I live?

1621

The Countesse of Mountgomeries Urania   a romance written in prose, sonnets and lyrics. The
poems are spoken by various characters.
2 Love   Eros (or Cupid), Greek god of love
4 Phœnix   a legendary Arabian bird, the only one of its kind, which burns and is reborn from the ashes
6 fain'd   feigned, as in the writing of fiction, in prose or poetry

JOHN WEBSTER

?1580–?1625 b London; playwright. Little is known of his life.

[Call for the Robin-Red-brest and the wren]

Call for the Robin-Red-brest and the wren,
Since ore shadie groves they hover,
And with leaves and flowres doe cover
The friendlesse bodies of unburied men.
Call unto his funerall Dole   *lamentation* 5
The Ante, the field-mouse, and the mole
To reare him hillockes, that shall keepe him warme,
And (when gay tombes are rob'd) sustaine no harme,
But keepe the wolfe far thence: that's foe to men,
For with his nailes hee'l dig them up agen.   10

                                              1612

ANONYMOUS

Tom o' Bedlam's Song

From the hagg and hungrie Goblin
That into raggs would rend ye,
And the spirit that stands by the naked man
In the Book of Moones defend yee.
That of your five sounde sences   5
You never be forsaken,
Nor wander from your selves with Tom
Abroad to begg your bacon.

   While I doe sing, any foode any feeding,
   Feedinge drinke or clothing,   10
   Come dame or maid, be not afraid,
   Poore Tom will injure nothing.

Of thirty bare years have I
Twice twenty bin enraged,   *mad*
And of forty bin three tymes fifteene   15
In durance soundlie caged.
On the lordlie loftes of Bedlam,
With stubble softe and dainty,
Brave braceletts strong, sweet whips ding dong
With wholsome hunger plenty.   20

   And nowe I sing, etc.

Call for the Robin-Red-brest a song sung by a mother over the body of her murdered son in the play, *The White Divel.*
17 Bedlam hospital for the insane in London

With a thought I tooke for Maudline — *Magdalen*
And a cruse of cockle pottage, — *bowl / soup*
With a thing thus tall, skie blesse you all,
I befell into this dotage.   25
I slept not since the Conquest,
Till then I never waked,
Till the rogysh boy of love where I lay
Mee found and strip't mee naked.

    And nowe I sing, etc.   30

When I short have shorne my sowce face — *sow's*
And swigg'd my horny barrell,
In an oaken Inne I pound my skin — *impound*
As a suite of guilt apparell. — *gilt*   35
The moon's my constant Mistresse,
And the lowlie owle my morrowe,
The flaming Drake and the Nightcrowe make — *dragon*
Mee musicke to my sorrowe.

    While I doe sing, etc.

The palsie plagues my pulses   40
When I prigg your pigs or pullen, — *steal / poultry*
Your culvers take, or matchles make — *doves / mate-less*
Your Chanticleare or sullen. — *rooster / goose*
When I want provant, with Humfrie — *food*   45
I sup, and when benighted,
I repose in Powles with waking soules — *St Paul's*
Yet never am affrighted.

    But I doe sing, etc.

I knowe more than Apollo,
For oft, when hee ly's sleeping,   50
I see the starres att bloudie warres
In the wounded welkin weeping; — *sky*
The moone embrace her shepheard,
And the quene of love her warryer,
While the first doth horne the star of morne,   55
And the next the heavenly Farrier.

    While I doe sing, etc.

The Gipsie snap and Pedro — *swindler*
Are none of Tom's comradoes.
The punk I skorne and the cutpurse sworn — *prostitute*   60
And the roaring boyes bravadoes.

---

26 **Conquest**   the Norman conquest of Britain, 1066
28 **boy of love**   Eros (or Cupid), Greek god of love
44–45 **with Humfrie I sup**   I go without dinner (colloquial).
53 **her shepheard**   Endymion, in Greek myth a shepherd loved by the moon
54 **queene of love**   In Roman myth, Venus loved the warrior god, Mars.
55 **doth horne**   is unfaithful to   **the star of morne**   Hesperus, here the moon's husband
56 **heavenly farrier**   Vulcan, husband of Venus

The meeke, the white, the gentle,
Me handle touch and spare not
But those that crosse Tom Rynosseross
Doe what the Panther dare not.   65

   Although I sing, etc.

With an hoast of furious fancies,
Whereof I am comaunder,
With a burning speare, and a horse of aire,
To the wildernesse I wander.   70
By a knight of ghostes and shadowes
I summon'd am to Tourney
Ten leagues beyond the wide world's end
Me thinke it is noe journey.

   Yet will I sing, etc   75

                By 1615   1660

BEN JONSON

1572–1637 b London. He was a bricklayer, soldier and actor before becoming a writer of
plays, court masques and poems which are influenced by a deep classical learning.

On Lucy Countesse of Bedford

This morning, timely rapt with holy fire,
  I thought to forme unto my zealous *Muse*,
What kinde of creature I could most desire,
  To honor, serve, and love; as *Poets* use.
I meant to make her faire, and free, and wise,   5
  Of greatest bloud, and yet more good than great;
I meant the day-starre should not brighter rise,
  Nor lend like influence from his lucent seat.
I meant shee should be curteous, facile, sweet,
  Hating that solemne vice of greatnesse, pride;   10
I meant each softest vertue, there should meet,
  Fit in that softer bosome to reside.
Onely a learned, and a manly soule
  I purpos'd her; that should, with even powers,
The rock, the spindle, and the sheeres controule   15
  Of destinie, and spin her owne free houres.
Such when I meant to faine, and wish'd to see,   *portray*
  My *Muse* bad, *Bedford* write, and that was shee.   *bade*

                1616

Lucy Countesse of Bedford   (?1581–1627) friend and patron of poets, including Jonson and Donne
9 facile affable
15 In Greek mythology a person's life was determined by three Fates, who respectively started it on a
distaff ('rock'), spun it, and cut it off.

Inviting a friend to supper

To night, grave sir, both my poore house, and I
    Doe equally desire your companie:
Not that we thinke us worthy such a ghest,
    But that your worth will dignifie our feast,
With those that come; whose grace may make that seeme   5
    Something, which, else, could hope for no esteeme.
It is the faire acceptance, Sir, creates
    The entertaynment perfect: not the cates.   *food*
Yet shall you have, to rectifie your palate,
    An olive, capers, or some better sallade   10
Ushring the mutton; with a short-leg'd hen,
    If we can get her, full of egs, and then,
Limons, and wine for sauce: to these, a coney   *rabbit*
    Is not to be despair'd of, for our money;
And, though fowle, now, be scarce, yet there are clarkes,   *scholars* 15
    The skie not falling, thinke we may have larkes.
Ile tell you of more, and lye, so you will come:
    Of partrich, pheasant, wood-cock, of which some
May yet be there; and godwit, if we can:
    Knat, raile, and ruffe too. How so ere, my man   20
Shall reade a piece of VIRGIL, TACITUS,
    LIVIE, or of some better booke to us,
Of which wee'll speake our minds, amidst our meate;
    And Ile professe no verses to repeate:
To this, if ought appeare, which I know not of,   25
    That will the pastrie, not my paper, show of.
Digestive cheese, and fruit there sure will bee;
    But that, which most doth take my *Muse*, and mee,
Is a pure cup of rich *Canary*-wine,
    Which is the *Mermaids*, now, but shall be mine: 30
Of which had HORACE, or ANACREON tasted,
    Their lives, as doe their lines, till now had lasted.
Tabacco, Nectar, or the *Thespian* spring,
    Are all but LUTHERS beere, to this I sing.
Of this we will sup free, but moderately,   35
    And we will have no *Pooly'*, or *Parrot* by;
Nor shall our cups make any guiltie men:
    But, at our parting, we will be, as when
We innocently met. No simple word,
    That shall be utter'd at our mirthfull boord,   40
Shall make us sad next morning: or affright
    The libertie, that wee'll enjoy to night.

        1616

19–20 godwit, knat, raile, ruffe wading birds
21–22 Virgil (70–19 BC), **Tacitus** (*c.* AD 55–117) and Livy (**Livie**: 59 BC–AD 17) were notable writers of classical Rome.
30 Mermaid famous tavern
31 Horace (65–8 BC) urbane poet of classical Rome **Anacreon** (sixth century BC) pastoral poet of early classical Greece
33 Thespian spring the sacred spring of the muses at the foot of Mt Helicon in Greece
34 Luthers beere German beer, weaker than English
36 Pooly, Parrot notorious informers. Pooly was present at the murder of Christopher Marlowe.

To Penshurst

Thou art not, PENSHURST, built to envious show,
    Of touch, or marble; nor canst boast a row
Of polish'd pillars, or a roofe of gold:
    Thou hast no lantherne, whereof tales are told;
Or stayre, or courts; but stand'st an ancient pile,   5
    And these grudg'd at, art reverenc'd the while.
Thou joy'st in better markes, of soyle, of ayre,
    Of wood, of water: therein thou art faire.
Thou hast thy walkes for health, as well as sport:
    Thy *Mount*, to which the *Dryads* doe resort,   *tree nymphs* 10
Where PAN, and BACCHUS their high feasts have made,
    Beneath the broad beech, and the chest-nut shade;
That taller tree, which of a nut was set,
    At his great birth, where all the *Muses* met.
There, in the writhed barke, are cut the names   15
    Of many a SYLVANE, taken with his flames.
And thence, the ruddy *Satyres* oft provoke
    The lighter *Faunes*, to reach thy *Ladies oke*.
Thy copp's, too, nam'd of GAMAGE, thou hast there,   *copse*
    That never failes to serve thee season'd deere,   20
When thou would'st feast, or exercise thy friends.
    The lower land, that to the river bends,
Thy sheepe, thy bullocks, kine, and calves doe feed: *cows*
    The middle grounds thy mares, and horses breed.
Each banke doth yeeld thee coneyes; and the topps   *rabbits* 25
    Fertile of wood, ASHORE, and SYDNEY's copp's,
To crowne thy open table, doth provide
    The purpled pheasant, with the speckled side:
The painted partrich lyes in every field,
    And, for thy messe, is willing to be kill'd.   30
And if the high swolne *Medway* faile thy dish,
    Thou hast thy ponds, that pay thee tribute fish,
Fat, aged carps, that runne into thy net.
    And pikes, now weary their owne kinde to eat,
As loth, the second draught, or cast to stay,   35
    Officiously, at first, themselves betray.   *obligingly*
Bright eeles, that emulate them, and leape on land,
    Before the fisher, or into his hand.
Then hath thy orchard fruit, thy garden flowers,
    Fresh as the ayre, and new as are the houres.   40
The earely cherry, with the later plum,
    Fig, grape, and quince, each in his time doth come:

Penshurst   the estate of the Sidney family in Kent
2 touch   black marble
4 lantherne   turreted skylight
14 great birth   i.e. of the poet, Sir Philip Sidney. See p. 486.
16 Sylvane   forest dweller
18 thy Ladies oke   an oak under which Barbara Gamage, the then lady of Penshurst, was said to
have begun labour

The blushing apricot, and woolly peach
  Hang on thy walls, that every child may reach.
And though thy walls be of the countrey stone,   45
  They'are rear'd with no mans ruine, no mans grone,
There's none, that dwell about them, wish them downe;
  But all come in, the farmer, and the clowne: *rustic*
And no one empty-handed, to salute
  Thy lord, and lady, though they have no sute.   50
Some bring a capon, some a rurall cake,
  Some nuts, some apples; some that thinke they make
The better cheese, bring 'hem; or else send
  By their ripe daughters, whom they would commend
This way to husbands; and whose baskets beare   55
  An embleme of themselves, in plum, or peare.
But what can this (more than expresse their love)
  Adde to thy free provisions, farre above
The neede of such? whose liberall boord doth flow,
  With all, that hospitalitie doth know!   60
Where comes no guest, but is allow'd to eate,
  Without his feare, and of thy lords owne meate:
Where the same beere, and bread, and selfe-same wine,
  That is his Lordships, shall be also mine.
And I not faine to sit (as some, this day,   65
  At great mens tables) and yet dine away.
Here no man tells my cups; nor, standing by,
  A waiter, doth my gluttony envy:
But gives me what I call, and lets me eate,
  He knowes, below, he shall finde plentie of meate,   70
Thy tables hoord not up for the next day,
  Nor, when I take my lodging, need I pray
For fire, or lights, or livorie: all is there;   *provision*
  As if thou, then, wert mine, or I raign'd here:
There's nothing I can wish, for which I stay.   75
  That found King JAMES, when hunting late, this way,
With his brave sonne, the Prince, they saw thy fires
  Shine bright on every harth as the desires
Of thy *Penates* had beene set on flame,
  To entertayne them; or the countrey came,   80
With all their zeale, to warme their welcome here.
  What (great, I will not say, but) sodayne cheare   *prompt*
Did'st thou, then, make 'hem! and what praise was heap'd
  On thy good lady, then! who, therein, reap'd
The just reward of her high huswifery,   85
  To have her linnen, plate, and all things nigh,
When shee was farre: and not a roome, but drest,
  As if it had expected such a guest!

---

50 sute (suit) attendance required of a tenant; also petition
65 faine obliged; also willing
79 Penates Roman household gods

These, PENSHURST, are thy praise, and yet not all.
  Thy lady's noble, fruitfull, chaste withall.   90
His children thy great lord may call his owne:
  A fortune, in this age, but rarely knowne.
They are, and have beene taught religion: Thence
  Their gentler spirits have suck'd innocence.
Each morne, and even, they are taught to pray,   95
  With the whole houshold, and may, every day,
Reade, in their vertuous parents noble parts,
  The mysteries of manners, armes, and arts.
Now, PENSHURST, they that will proportion thee   *compare*
  With other edifices, when they see   100
Those proud, ambitious heaps, and nothing else,
  May say, their lords have built, but thy lord dwells.

          By 1612 1616

On my first Sonne

Farewell, thou child of my right hand, and joy;
  My sinne was too much hope of thee, lov'd boy,
Seven yeeres tho'wert lent to me, and I thee pay,
  Exacted by thy fate, on the just day.
O, could I loose all father, now. For why   *lose* 5
  Will man lament the state he should envie?
To have so soone scap'd worlds, and fleshes rage,
  And, if no other miserie, yet age?
Rest in soft peace, and, ask'd, say here doth lye
  BEN. JONSON his best piece of *poetrie*.   10
For whose sake, hence-forth, all his vowes be such,
  As what he loves may never like too much.

          1603 1616

To Celia

Kisse me, sweet: The warie lover
Can your favours keepe, and cover,
When the common courting jay
All your bounties will betray.
Kisse againe: no creature comes.   5
Kisse, and score up wealthy summes
On my lips, thus hardly sundred,
While you breath. First give a hundred,
Then a thousand, then another
Hundred, then unto the tother   10
Adde a thousand, and so more:
Till you equall with the store,

---

91 thy great lord i.e. Sir Robert Sidney (1563–1626), younger brother of Sir Philip
On my first Sonne Benjamin (in Hebrew, child of the right hand), who died in 1603 on his seventh birthday

All the grasse that *Rumney* yeelds,
Or the sands in *Chelsey* fields,
Or the drops in silver *Thames*,   15
Or the starres, that guild his streames,
In the silent sommer-nights,
When youths ply their stolne delights.
That the curious may not know
How to tell 'hem, as they flow,   20
And the envious, when they find
What their number is, be pin'd.   *pained*

1616

Her Triumph

See the Chariot at hand here of Love
    Wherein my Lady rideth!
Each that drawes, is a Swan, or a Dove,
    And well the Carre Love guideth.
As she goes, all hearts doe duty   5
                Unto her beauty;
And enamour'd, doe wish, so they might
                But enjoy such a sight,
    That they still were to run by her side,
Through Swords, through Seas, whither she would ride.   10

Doe but looke on her eyes, they doe light
    All that Loves world compriseth!
Doe but looke on her Haire, it is bright
    As Loves starre when it riseth!
Doe but marke her forhead's smoother   15
                Than words that sooth her!
And from her arched browes, such a grace
                Sheds it selfe through the face,
    As alone there triumphs to the life
All the Gaine, all the Good, of the Elements strife.   20

Have you seene but a bright Lillie grow,
    Before rude hands have touch'd it?
Ha' you mark'd but the fall o'the Snow
    Before the soyle hath smutch'd it?
Ha' you felt the wooll o' the Bever?   25
                Or Swans Downe ever?
Or have smelt o'the bud o'the Brier?
                Or the Nard in the fire?
Or have tasted the bag of the Bee?
O so white! O so soft! O so sweet is she!   30

By 1616   1640

13–14 Rumney Romney was a town in grassy country in Kent **Chelsey** (Chelsea), on the Thames, was then outside London.
Triumph victory procession
28 Nard an aromatic ointment

My Picture left in Scotland

I now thinke, Love is rather deafe, than blind,
  For else it could not be,
        That she,
Whom I adore so much, should so slight me,
  And cast my love behind: 5
I'm sure my language to her, was as sweet,
        And every close did meet
        In sentence, of as subtile feet,
              As hath the youngest Hee,
    That sits in shadow of *Apollo*'s tree.   10
Oh, but my conscious feares,
        That flie my thoughts betweene,
        Tell me that she hath seene
        My hundreds of gray haires,
        Told seven and fortie yeares,   *counted* 15
  Read so much wast, as she cannot imbrace
    My mountaine belly, and my rockie face,
And all these through her eyes, have stopt her eares.

                                        1619   1640

JOHN DONNE

1572–1631 b London. He took part in expeditions against the Spanish in Cadiz and the
Azores in the 1590s. An impolitic secret marriage in 1602 (which produced twelve children) ended hopes of political preferment. He was ordained in 1615 and made Dean of St
Paul's in 1621. Most of his poems were circulated in manuscript form and were printed
after his death.

The Flea

Marke but this flea, and marke in this,
How little that which thou deny'st me is;
It suck'd me first, and now sucks thee,
And in this flea, our two bloods mingled bee;
Thou know'st that this cannot be said   5
A sinne, nor shame nor losse of maidenhead,
    Yet this enjoyes before it wooe,
    And pamper'd swells with one blood made of two,
    And this, alas, is more than wee would doe.

Oh stay, three lives in one flea spare,   10
Where wee almost, yea more than maryed are.
This flea is you and I, and this
Our mariage bed, and mariage temple is;

---

7 **close**   the conclusion of a phrase, sentence or cadence
8 **sentence**   includes the sense of judicious thought

Though parents grudge, and you, w'are met,
And cloysterd in these living walls of Jet.   15
   Though use make you apt to kill mee,
   Let not to that, selfe murder added bee,
   And sacrilege, three sinnes in killing three.

Cruell and sodaine, hast thou since
Purpled thy naile, in blood of innocence?   20
Wherein could this flea guilty bee,
Except in that drop which it suckt from thee?
Yet thou triumph'st, and saist that thou
Find'st not thy selfe, nor mee the weaker now;
   'Tis true, then learne how false, feares bee;   25
   Just so much honor, when thou yeeld'st to mee,
   Will wast, as this flea's death tooke life from thee.

                                               1633

Song

Goe, and catche a falling starre,
   Get with child a mandrake roote,
Tell me, where all past yeares are,
   Or who cleft the Divels foot,
Teach me to heare Mermaides singing,   5
Or to keep off envies stinging,
         And finde
         What winde
Serves to advance an honest minde.

If thou beest borne to strange sights,   10
   Things invisible to see,
Ride ten thousand daies and nights,
   Till age snow white haires on thee,
   Thou, when thou retorn'st, wilt tell mee
All strange wonders that befell thee,   15
         And sweare
         No where
Lives a woman true, and faire.

If thou findst one, let mee know,
   Such a Pilgrimage were sweet,   20
Yet doe not, I would not goe,
   Though at next doore wee might meet,
Though shee were true, when you met her,
And last, till you write your letter,
         Yet shee   25
         Will bee
False, ere I come, to two, or three.

                                               1633

---

2 The **mandrake roote** is forked, as if with legs.

To his Mistris Going to Bed

Come, Madam, come, all rest my powers defie,
Until I labour, I in labour lie.
The foe oft-times having the foe in sight,
Is tir'd with standing though they never fight.
Off with that girdle, like heavens Zone glistering,   5
But a far fairer world incompassing.
Unpin that spangled breastplate which you wear,
That th'eyes of busie fooles may be stopt there.
Unlace your self, for that harmonious chyme
Tells me from you, that now tis your bed time.   10
Off with that happy busk, whom I envie,   *corset*
That still can be, and still can stand so nigh.
Your gown going off, such beautious state reveals,
As when from flowry meads th'hills shadow steales.
Off with your wyerie Coronet and shew   15
The haiery Diadem which on you doth grow:
Now off with those shooes, and then safely tread
In this loves hallow'd temple, this soft bed.
In such white robes, heaven's Angels us'd to be
Receavd by men: Thou Angel bring'st with thee   20
A heaven like Mahomets Paradice, and though
Ill spirits walk in white, we easly know,
By this these Angels from an evil sprite,
They set our hairs, but these our flesh upright.
    Licence my roaving hands, and let them go,   25
Behind, before, above, between, below.
Oh my America! my new-found-land,
My kingdome, safeliest when with one man man'd,
My Myne of precious stones, my Emperie,
How blest am I in this discovering thee!   30
To enter in these bonds, is to be free;
Then where my hand is set, my seal shall be.
    Full nakedness! All joyes are due to thee,
As souls unbodied, bodies uncloth'd must be,
To taste whole joyes. Gems which you women use   35
Are as Atlanta's balls, cast in mens views,
That when a fools eye lighteth on a Gem,
His earthly soul may covet theirs, not them.
Like pictures, or like books gay coverings made
For lay-men, are all women thus array'd;   40

To his Mistris   The first printing of this poem (1669) is somewhat corrupt; the version here accepts several readings from earlier transcripts.
9 chyme   possibly from a chiming watch
21 Mahomets Paradice   i.e. sensual
27 new-found-land   a reference to contemporary exploration (but not to Newfoundland, which did not yet have that name)
30 discovering   includes the sense of uncovering
36 Atlanta's balls   Hippomenes, while racing with the swift Atalanta for her hand, won by throwing three golden apples in her path, which she stopped to pick up. See *Metamorphoses* X.

Themselves are mystick books, which only wee
(Whom their imputed grace will dignifie)
Must see reveal'd. Then since I may know,
As liberally as to a Midwife shew
Thy self: cast all, yea, this white lynnen hence,   45
Here is no pennance, much less innocence:
   To teach thee I am naked first; why than   *then*
What needst thou have more covering than a man?

                                        1669

The Sunne Rising

    Busie old foole, unruly Sunne,
      Why dost thou thus,
Through windowes, and through curtaines call on us?
Must to thy motions lovers seasons run?
      Sawcy pedantique wretch, goe chide   5
      Late schoole boyes, and sowre prentices,
   Goe tell Court-huntsmen, that the King will ride,
   Call countrey ants to harvest offices;   *duties*
Love, all alike, no season knowes, nor clyme,
Nor houres, dayes, moneths, which are the rags of time.   10

    Thy beames, so reverend, and strong   *harmless*
      Why shouldst thou thinke?
I could eclipse and cloud them with a winke,
But that I would not lose her sight so long:
      If her eyes have not blinded thine,   15
      Looke, and to morrow late, tell mee,
   Whether both the'Indias of spice and Myne
   Be where thou leftst them, or lie here with mee.
Aske for those Kings whom thou saw'st yesterday,
And thou shalt heare, All here in one bed lay.   20

    She'is all States, and all Princes, I,
      Nothing else is.
Princes doe but play us; compar'd to this,
All honor's mimique; All wealth alchimie.   *alchemy*
      Thou sunne art halfe as happy'as wee,   25
      In that the world's contracted thus.
Thine age askes ease, and since thy duties bee
To warme the world, that's done in warming us.
Shine here to us, and thou art every where;
This bed thy center is, these walls, thy spheare.   30

                                          1633

---

42 imputed grace i.e. as in Calvinist doctrine: grace applied to the elect without any merit of their own
46 The garbs of innocence and of penance are both white. 1669 and some mss: 'There is no penance due to innocence.'
7 Court-huntsmen courtiers who reluctantly attended King James I in his enthusiastic early-morning hunting
17 Indias East Indies for spice; West Indies for gold

The good-morrow

I wonder by my troth, what thou, and I
Did, till we lov'd? were we not wean'd till then?
But suck'd on countrey pleasures, childishly?   *rustic*
Or snorted we i'the seaven sleepers den?   *snored*
T'was so; But this, all pleasures fancies bee.   5
If ever any beauty I did see,
Which I desir'd, and got, t'was but a dreame of thee.

And now good morrow to our waking soules,
Which watch not one another out of feare;
For love, all love of other sights controules,   10
And makes one little roome, an every where.
Let sea-discoverers to new worlds have gone,
Let Maps to others, worlds on worlds have showne,
Let us possesse one world, each hath one, and is one.

My face in thine eye, thine in mine appeares,   15
And true plaine hearts doe in the faces rest,
Where can we finde two better hemispheares
Without sharpe North, without declining West?
What ever dyes, was not mixt equally;
If our two loves be one, or, thou and I   20
Love so alike, that none doe slacken, none can die.

                                                    1633

The Canonization

For Godsake hold your tongue, and let me love,
    Or chide my palsie, or my gout,
My five gray haires, or ruin'd fortune flout,
    With wealth your state, your minde with Arts improve,
        Take you a course, get you a place,   5
        Observe his honour, or his grace,
Or the Kings reall, or his stamped face
    Contemplate; what you will, approve,   *try out*
    So you will let me love.

Alas, alas, who's injur'd by my love?   10
    What merchants ships have my sighs drown'd?
Who saies my teares have overflow'd his ground?
    When did my colds a forward spring remove?
        When did the heats which my veines fill
        Adde one more to the plaguie Bill?   15

---

4 seaven sleepers   seven young Christian men of the third century, who were said to have slept nearly 200 years in a cave where they hid from persecutors, until wakened into a Christian world
5 But this   except for this
18 sharpe   very cold   **declining**   descending, as of the sun.
19 not mixt equally   In the medical theory of the time, decay was attributed to an imbalance of constitutive physical elements.
5 course   course of action
7 stamped   i.e. on a coin
15 plaguie Bill   published list of plague victims

Soldiers finde warres, and Lawyers finde out still
    Litigious men, which quarrels move,
Though she and I do love.

Call us what you will, wee'are made such by love;
    Call her one, mee another flye,   20
We'are Tapers too, and at our owne cost die,
    And wee in us finde the'Eagle and the Dove.
        The Phœnix ridle hath more wit
        By us, we two being one, are it.
So, to one neutrall thing both sexes fit.   25
    Wee dye and rise the same, and prove
Mysterious by this love.

Wee can dye by it, if not live by love,
    And if unfit for tombes or hearse
Our legend bee, it will be fit for verse;   30
    And if no peece of Chronicle wee prove,
        We'll build in sonnets pretty roomes;
        As well a well wrought urne becomes   *befits*
The greatest ashes, as halfe-acre tombes,
    And by these hymnes, all shall approve   35
Us *Canoniz*'d for Love.

And thus invoke us: You whom reverend love
    Made one anothers hermitage;
You, to whom love was peace, that now is rage,
    Who did the whole worlds soule extract, and drove 40
        Into the glasses of your eyes,
        So made such mirrors, and such spies,
That they did all to you epitomize,
    Countries, Townes, Courts: Beg from above
A patterne of your love!   45
                                        1633

A Valediction forbidding mourning

As virtuous men passe mildly'away,
    And whisper to their soules, to goe,
Whilst some of their sad friends doe say,
    The breath goes now, and some say, no:

So let us melt, and make no noise,   5
    No teare-floods, nor sigh-tempests move,
T'were prophanation of our joyes
    To tell the layetie our love.

---

20 flye any flying insect; flies were proverbially immodest in sex.
21 die Death was a common metaphor for orgasm.
23 Phoenix a legendary Arabian bird, the only one of its kind, which burns and is reborn from its own ashes
32 sonnets little songs (here not necessarily of 14 lines)

Moving of th'earth brings harmes and feares,
  Men reckon what it did and meant,   ·   10
But trepidation of the spheares,
  Though greater farre, is innocent.   *harmless*

Dull sublunary lovers love
  (Whose soule is sense) cannot admit
Absence, because it doth remove   15
  Those things which elemented it.

But we by'a love, so much refin'd,
  That our selves know not what it is,
Inter-assured of the mind,
  Care lesse, eyes, lips, and hands to misse.   20

Our two soules therefore, which are one,
  Though I must goe, endure not yet
A breach, but an expansion,
  Like gold to ayery thinnesse beate.

If they be two, they are two so   25
  As stiffe twin compasses are two,
Thy soule the fixt foot, makes no show
  To move, but doth, if the'other doe.

And though it in the center sit,
  Yet when the other far doth rome,   30
It leanes, and hearkens after it,
  And growes erect, as that comes home.

Such wilt thou be to mee, who must
  Like th'other foot, obliquely runne.
Thy firmnes makes my circle just,   35
  And makes me end, where I begunne.

                                                              1633

Song

Sweetest love, I do not goe,
  For wearinesse of thee,
Nor in hope the world can show
  A fitter Love for mee,
    But since that I   5
Must dye at last, 'tis best,
To use my selfe in jest
  Thus by fain'd deaths to dye.

---

10 moving of th'earth earthquake; also possibly the impact of the relatively recent Copernican theory that the earth moves around the sun
11 In the older, Ptolemaic system of astronomy, a trembling of the ninth—the outermost—sphere of the universe was postulated to account for the precession of the equinoxes, i.e. the gradual shift over millennia in the sun's place of entry to the constellations of the zodiac.
13 sublunary below the moon, i.e. earthly

Yesternight the Sunne went hence,
　　And yet is here to day,　　　　　　　　　　　　　　　10
He hath no desire nor sense,
　　Nor halfe so short a way:
　　　Then feare not mee,
But beleeve that I shall make
Speedier journeyes, since I take　　　　　　　　　　　15
　　More wings and spurres than hee.

O how feeble is mans power,
　　That if good fortune fall,
Cannot adde another houre,
　　Nor a lost houre recall!　　　　　　　　　　　　　20
　　　But come bad chance,
And wee joyne to'it our strength,
And wee teach it art and length,
　　It selfe o'r us to'advance.

When thou sigh'st, thou sigh'st not winde,　　　　　25
　　But sigh'st my soule away,
When thou weep'st, unkindly kinde,
　　My lifes blood doth decay.
　　　It cannot bee
That thou lov'st mee, as thou say'st,　　　　　　　　30
If in thine my life thou waste,
　　Thou art the best of mee.

Let not thy divining heart
　　Forethinke me any ill,
Destiny may take thy part,　　　　　　　　　　　　　35
　　And may thy feares fulfill,
　　　But thinke that wee
Are but turn'd aside to sleepe;
They who one another keepe
　　Alive, ne'r parted bee.　　　　　　　　　　　　　40

　　　　　　　　　　　　　　　　　　　1633

A nocturnall upon S. Lucies day,

Being the shortest day

Tis the yeares midnight, and it is the days,
Lucies, who scarce seaven houres herself unmaskes,
　　The Sunne is spent, and now his flasks
　　Send forth light squibs, no constant rayes;
　　　The world's whole sap is sunke:　　　　　　　5
The generall balme th'hydroptique earth hath drunk,　　*thirsty*
Whither, as to the beds-feet, life is shrunke

S. Lucies day　December 13. The eve, December 12, was thought to be the winter solstice. St Lucy
is the patron saint of light and of sight.
3 flasks　gunpowder flasks: here, the stars

Dead and enterr'd; yet all these seeme to laugh,
Compar'd with mee, who am their Epitaph.

Study me then, you who shall lovers bee   10
At the next world, that is, at the next Spring:
   For I am every dead thing,
   In whom love wrought new Alchimie.
    For his art did expresse   *press out*
A quintessence even from nothingnesse,   15
From dull privations, and leane emptinesse:
He ruin'd mee, and I am re-begot
Of absence, darknesse, death; things which are not.

All others, from all things, draw all that's good,
Life, soule, forme, spirit, whence they beeing have;   20
   I, by loves limbecke, am the grave
   Of all, that's nothing. Oft a flood
    Have wee two wept, and so
Drownd the whole world, us two; oft did we grow
To be two Chaosses, when we did show   25
Care to ought else; and often absences
Withdrew our soules, and made us carcasses.

But I am by her death, (which word wrongs her)
Of the first nothing, the Elixer grown;
   Were I a man, that I were one,   30
   I needs must know; I should preferre,
    If I were any beast,
Some ends, some means; Yea plants, yea stones detest,
And love; all, all some properties invest;   *put on*
If I an ordinary nothing were,   35
As shadow,'a light, and body must be here.

But I am None; nor will my Sunne renew.
You lovers, for whose sake, the lesser Sunne
   At this time to the Goat is runne
   To fetch new lust, and give it you,   40
    Enjoy your summer all;
Since shee enjoyes her long nights festivall,
Let mee prepare towards her, and let mee call
This houre her Vigill, and her Eve, since this
Both the yeares, and the dayes deep midnight is.   45

                1633

---

15 **quintessence**   in alchemy, the most concentrated essence of a substance
21 **limbecke**   distilling apparatus
29 **Elixer**   quintessence
30–34 A commonplace hierarchy: a man has self-knowledge, a beast has perception of ends and means, plants and stones have attractions and repulsions.
39 The sun enters Capricorn (the goat) on St Lucy's Day. Goats were proverbially lecherous.
44 **Vigill**   the night of prayer before the day of a religious festival

From Holy Sonnets

VII

At the round earths imagin'd corners, blow
Your trumpets, Angells, and arise, arise
From death, you numberlesse infinities
Of soules, and to your scattred bodies goe,
All whom the flood did, and fire shall o'erthrow,   5
All whom warre, dearth, age, agues, tyrannies,
Despaire, law, chance, hath slaine, and you whose eyes
Shall behold God, and never tast deaths woe.
But let them sleepe, Lord, and mee mourne a space,
For, if above all these, my sinnes abound,   10
'Tis late to aske abundance of thy grace,
When wee are there; here on this lowly ground,
Teach mee how to repent; for that's as good
As if thou'hadst seal'd my pardon, with thy blood.

                                                      1633

X

Death be not proud, though some have called thee
Mighty and dreadfull, for, thou art not soe,
For, those, whom thou think'st, thou dost overthrow,
Die not, poore death, nor yet canst thou kill mee;
From rest and sleepe, which but thy pictures bee,   5
Much pleasure, then from thee, much more must flow,
And soonest our best men with thee doe goe,
Rest of their bones, and soules deliverie.
Thou'art slave to Fate, chance, kings, and desperate men,
And dost with poyson, warre, and sicknesse dwell,   10
And poppie, 'or charmes can make us sleepe as well,
And better than thy stroake; why swell'st thou then?
One short sleepe past, wee wake eternally,
And death shall be no more, Death thou shalt die.

                                                      1633

XIV

Batter my heart, three person'd God; for you
As yet but knocke, breathe, shine, and seeke to mend;
That I may rise, and stand, o'erthrow mee,'and bend
Your force, to breake, blowe, burn and make me new.
I, like an usurpt towne, to'another due,   5
Labour to'admit you, but Oh, to no end,
Reason your viceroy in mee, mee should defend,
But is captiv'd, and proves weake or untrue,

---

1 imagin'd as on a flat map **corners** See Rev. 7:1: 'I saw four angels standing on the four corners of the earth, holding the four winds of the earth'.
8 never tast a reference to those still alive when the world ends. See 2 Peter 3:10.
1 three person'd God the Trinity: Father, Son and Holy Spirit

Yet dearely'I love you, and would be lov'd faine,   *gladly*
But am betroth'd unto your enemie,   10
Divorce mee,'untie, or breake that knot againe,
Take mee to you, imprison mee, for I
Except you'enthrall mee, never shall be free,
Nor ever chast, except you ravish mee.

                                                        1633

Hymne to God my God, in my sicknesse

Since I am comming to that Holy roome,
   Where, with thy Quire of Saints for evermore,
I shall be made thy Musique; As I come
    I tune the Instrument here at the dore,
    And what I must doe then, thinke here before.   5

Whilst my Physitians by their love are growne
   Cosmographers, and I their Mapp, who lie
Flat on this bed, that by them may be showne
    That this is my South-west discoverie
    Per fretum febris, by these streights to die,   10

I joy, that in these straits, I see my West;
   For, though theire currants yeeld returne to none,
What shall my West hurt me? As West and East
    In all flatt Maps (and I am one) are one,
    So death doth touch the Resurrection.   15

Is the Pacifique Sea my home? Or are
   The Easterne riches? Is *Jerusalem*?
Anyan, and *Magellan*, and *Gibraltare*,
    All streights, and none but streights are wayes to them,
    Whether where *Japhet* dwelt, or *Cham*, or *Sem*.   20

We thinke that *Paradise* and *Calvarie*,
   Christs Crosse, and *Adams* tree, stood in one place;
Looke Lord, and finde both *Adams* met in me;
    As the first *Adams* sweat surrounds my face,
    May the last *Adams* blood my soule embrace.   25

So, in his purple wrapp'd receive mee Lord,
   By these his thornes give me his other Crowne;
And as to others soules I preach'd thy word,
    Be this my Text, my Sermon to mine owne,
    Therefore that he may raise the Lord throws down.   *in order that* 30

                                                        ?1623 1635

---

9 South-west discoverie the Straits of Magellan, discovered in 1520. Feverish heat (south) and decline (west) are also implied.
10 Per fretum febris through the raging (also the straits) of fever
11 these straits See Matt. 7:14: 'Strait is the gate, and narrow is the way, which leadeth unto life, and few there be that find it.'
20 Japhet, Cham, Sem Noah's sons, who populated Europe, Africa and Asia respectively.
23 both Adams i.e. Adam and Christ
26 purple here crimson, the royal colour. See Mark 15:17: 'And they clothed him with purple, and plaited a crown of thorns, and put it about his head.'
30 See Psalm 146:8: 'The Lord raiseth them that are bowed down.'

A Hymne to God the Father

Wilt thou forgive that sinne where I begunne,
  Which is my sin, though it were done before?
Wilt thou forgive those sinnes through which I runne,
  And do them still: though still I do deplore?
    When thou hast done, thou hast not done,   5
      For, I have more.

Wilt thou forgive that sinne by which I wonne
  Others to sinne? and, made my sinne their doore?
Wilt thou forgive that sinne which I did shunne
  A yeare, or two: but wallowd in, a score?   10
    When thou hast done, thou hast not done,
      For I have more.

I have a sinne of feare, that when I'have spunne
  My last thred, I shall perish on the shore;
Sweare by thy selfe, that at my death thy Sunne   15
  Shall shine as it shines now, and heretofore;
    And, having done that, Thou haste done,
      I have no more.
                     ?1623   1633

THOMAS NASHE

1567–1601 b Suffolk. He was active in London as a satirist, playwright and writer of prose fiction.

Song

Adieu, farewell earths blisse,
This world uncertaine is,
Fond are lifes lustfull joyes,   *foolish*
Death proves them all but toyes,
None from his darts can flye,   5
I am sick, I must dye.
    Lord have mercy on us.

Rich men, trust not in wealth,
Gold cannot buy you health,
Phisick himselfe must fade.   10
All things, to end are made,
The plague full swift goes bye,
I am sick, I must dye,
    Lord have mercy on us.

Beauty is but a flowre   15
Which wrinckles will devoure,
Brightnesse falls from the ayre,
Queenes have died yong and faire,
Dust hath closde *Helens* eye.
I am sick, I must dye,   20
    Lord have mercy on us.

Strength stoopes unto the grave,
Wormes feed on *Hector* brave,
Swords may not fight with fate,
Earth still holds ope her gate,   25
Come, come, the bells do crye.
I am sick, I must dye,
    Lord have mercy on us.

Wit with his wantonnesse
Tasteth deaths bitternesse,   30
Hels executioner
Hath no eares for to heare
What vaine art can reply.
I am sick, I must dye,
    Lord have mercy on us.   35

Haste therefore eche degree,
To welcome destiny:
Heaven is our heritage,
Earth but a players stage,
Mount wee unto the sky.   40
I am sick, I must dye,
    Lord have mercy on us.

           c. *1592*   1600

THOMAS CAMPION

1567–1620. He was the composer of music for his poems; also a physician.

[My sweetest Lesbia, let us live and love]

My sweetest Lesbia, let us live and love,
And, though the sager sort our deedes reprove,
Let us not way them: heav'ns great lampes doe dive
Into their west, and strait againe revive,
But, soone as once set is our little light,   5
Then must we sleepe one ever-during night.

If all would lead their lives in love like mee,
Then bloudie swords and armour should not be,
No drum nor trumpet peaceful sleepes should move,
Unles alar'me came from the campe of love: 10
But fooles do live, and wast their little light,
And seeke with paine their ever-during night.

When timely death my life and fortune ends,
Let not my hearse be vext with mourning friends,
But let all lovers, rich in triumph, come,   15
And with sweet pastimes grace my happie tombe;
And, Lesbia, close up thou my little light,
And crowne with love my ever-during night.

           1601

My sweetest Lesbia   The first stanza is based on the opening lines of the poem, 'Vivamus mea Lesbia', by the Roman poet, Catullus (*c.* 84–*c.* 54 BC).

[Shall I come, sweet Love, to thee]

Shall I come, sweet Love, to thee,
   When the ev'ning beames are set?
Shall I not excluded be?
   Will you finde no fained lett?   *feigned hindrance*
      Let me not, for pitty, more,   5
      Tell the long houres at your dore.   *count*

Who can tell what theefe or foe,
   In the covert of the night,
For his prey, will worke my woe,
   Or through wicked foule despight: 10
      So may I dye unredrest,
      Ere my long love be possest.

But, to let such dangers passe,
   Which a lovers thoughts disdaine,
'Tis enough in such a place   15
   To attend loves joyes in vaine.
      Doe not mocke me in thy bed,
      While these cold nights freeze me dead.

1617

WILLIAM SHAKESPEARE

1564–1616 b Stratford-upon-Avon. He was in London by 1592. Beginning as an actor, he became a prolific playwright and a stage director, and retired to Stratford in about 1611.

From Sonnets

18

Shall I compare thee to a Summers day?
Thou art more lovely and more temperate:
Rough windes do shake the darling buds of Maie,
And Sommers lease hath all too short a date:
Sometime too hot the eye of heaven shines,   5
And often is his gold complexion dimm'd,
And every faire from faire some-time declines,
By chance, or natures changing course untrim'd:
But thy eternall Sommer shall not fade,
Nor loose possession of that faire thou ow'st,   *lose / ownest* 10
Nor shall death brag thou wandr'st in his shade,
When in eternall lines to time thou grow'st,
   So long as men can breath or eyes can see,
   So long lives this, and this gives life to thee.

Sonnets   Shakespeare's sonnets form a loose progression. 1–18 are graceful compliments to a young nobleman; 19–126 trace the development of a more passionate attachment to this man; 127–54 explore an obsessive affair with a woman. Although there is no hard evidence, the sonnets are often taken to be autobiographical. Most were probably written 1592–98.
8 untrim'd   stripped of ornament

20

A womans face with natures owne hand painted,
Haste thou the Master Mistris of my passion,   *hast*
A womans gentle hart but not acquainted
With shifting change as is false womens fashion,
An eye more bright than theirs, lesse false in rowling: 5
Gilding the object where-upon it gazeth,
A man in hew all *Hews* in his controwling,   *hue*
Which steales mens eyes and womens soules amaseth.
And for a woman wert thou first created,
Till nature as she wrought thee fell a dotinge,   10
And by addition me of thee defeated,
By adding one thing to my purpose nothing.
    But since she prickt thee out for womens pleasure,
    Mine be thy love and thy loves use their treasure.

29

When in disgrace with Fortune and mens eyes,
I all alone beweepe my out-cast state,
And trouble deafe heaven with my bootlesse cries,   *useless*
And looke upon my selfe and curse my fate.
Wishing me like to one more rich in hope,   5
Featur'd like him, like him with friends possest,
Desiring this mans art, and that mans skope,
With what I most injoy contented least,
Yet in these thoughts my selfe almost despising,
Haplye I thinke on thee, and then my state,   *perchance* 10
(Like to the Larke at breake of day arising)
From sullen earth sings himns at Heavens gate,
    For thy sweet love remembred such welth brings,
    That then I skorne to change my state with Kings.

65

Since brasse, nor stone, nor earth, nor boundlesse sea,
But sad mortallity ore-swaies their power,
How with this rage shall beautie hold a plea,
Whose action is no stronger than a flower?
O how shall summers hunny breath hold out,   5
Against the wrackfull siedge of battring dayes,
When rocks impregnable are not so stoute,
Nor gates of steele so strong but time decayes?
O fearefull meditation, where alack,
Shall times best Jewell from times chest lie hid?   10
Or what strong hand can hold his swift foote back,
Or who his spoile of beautie can forbid?
    O none, unlesse this miracle have might,
    That in black inck my love may still shine bright.

---

13 prickt   picked; also a sexual pun

66

Tyr'd with all these for restfull death I cry,
As to behold desert a begger borne,   *merit*
And needie Nothing trimd in jollitie,   *festively*
And purest faith unhappily forsworne,
And gilded honor shamefully misplast,   5
And maiden vertue rudely strumpeted,
And right perfection wrongfully disgrac'd,
And strength by limping sway disabled,
And arte made tung-tide by authoritie,
And Folly (Doctor-like) controuling skill,   10
And simple-Truth miscalde Simplicitie,
And captive-good attending Captaine ill.
 Tyr'd with all these, from these would I be gone,
 Save that to dye, I leave my love alone.

71

Noe Longer mourne for me when I am dead,
Than you shall heare the surly sullen bell
Give warning to the world that I am fled
From this vile world with vildest wormes to dwell:
Nay if you read this line, remember not,   5
The hand that writ it, for I love you so,
That I in your sweet thoughts would be forgot,
If thinking on me then should make you woe.
O if (I say) you looke upon this verse,
When I (perhaps) compounded am with clay,   10
Do not so much as my poore name reherse;
But let your love even with my life decay.
 Least the wise world should looke into your mone,   *lest*
 And mocke you with me after I am gon.

73

That time of yeeare thou maist in me behold,
When yellow leaves, or none, or few doe hange
Upon those boughes which shake against the could,   *cold*
Bare ruin'd quiers, where late the sweet birds sang.
In me thou seest the twi-light of such day,   5
As after Sun-set fadeth in the West,
Which by and by blacke night doth take away,
Deaths second selfe that seals up all in rest.

---

6 **strumpeted** called a strumpet
8 **limping sway** weak leadership
10 **Doctor-like** with an expert's manner
11 **Simplicitie** naivety
4 **quiers** The choir is the place for the singers in a church or monastery chapel. Many monasteries
were pillaged in the Reformation under Henry VIII some decades previously.

In me thou seest the glowing of such fire,
That on the ashes of his youth doth lye,   10
As the death bed, whereon it must expire,
Consum'd with that which it was nurrisht by.
      This thou percev'st, which makes thy love more strong,
      To love that well, which thou must leave ere long.

87

Farewell thou art too deare for my possessing,
And like enough thou knowst thy estimate,
The Charter of thy worth gives thee releasing:
My bonds in thee are all determinate.
For how do I hold thee but by thy granting,   5
And for that ritches where is my deserving?
The cause of this faire guift in me is wanting,
And so my pattent back againe is swerving.   *patent*
Thy selfe thou gav'st, thy owne worth then not knowing,
Or mee to whom thou gav'st it, else mistaking,   10
So thy great guift upon misprision growing,   *error*
Comes home againe, on better judgement making.
      Thus have I had thee as a dreame doth flatter,
      In sleepe a King, but waking no such matter.

94

They that have powre to hurt, and will doe none,
That doe not do the thing, they most do showe,
Who moving others, are themselves as stone,
Unmooved, could, and to temptation slow: *cold*
They rightly do inherrit heavens graces,   5
And husband natures ritches from expence,
They are the Lords and owners of their faces,
Others, but stewards of their excellence:
The sommers flowre is to the sommer sweet,
Though to it selfe, it onely live and die,   10
But if that flowre with base infection meete,
The basest weed out-braves his dignity: *its*
      For sweetest things turne sowrest by their deedes,
      Lillies that fester, smell far worse than weeds.

110

Alas 'tis true, I have gone here and there,
And made my selfe a motley to the view,
Gor'd mine own thoughts, sold cheap what is most deare,
Made old offences of affections new.

---

3 **releasing**   i.e. from obligation
4 **determinate**   expired (a legal term)
6 **husband**   manage prudently   **expence**   squandering
2 **motley**   the parti-coloured costume of a professional fool

Most true it is, that I have lookt on truth   5
Asconce and strangely: But by all above,
These blenches gave my heart an other youth,   *side glances*
And worse essaies prov'd thee my best of love,
Now all is done, have what shall have no end,
Mine appetite I never more will grin'de   *grind* 10
On newer proofe, to trie an older friend,
A God in love, to whom I am confin'd.
    Then give me welcome, next my heaven the best,
    Even to thy pure and most most loving brest.

116

Let me not to the marriage of true mindes
Admit impediments, love is not love
Which alters when it alteration findes,
Or bends with the remover to remove.
O no, it is an ever fixed marke   *sea-mark* 5
That lookes on tempests and is never shaken;
It is the star to every wandring barke,   *small ship*
Whose worths unknowne, although his higth be taken.
Lov's not Times foole, though rosie lips and cheeks
Within his bending sickles compasse come,   10
Love alters not with his breefe houres and weekes,
But beares it out even to the edge of doome:
    If this be error and upon me proved,
    I never writ, nor no man ever loved.

120

That you were once unkind be-friends mee now,
And for that sorrow, which I then didde feele,
Needes must I under my transgression bow,
Unlesse my Nerves were brasse or hammered steele.
For if you were by my unkindnesse shaken   5
As I by yours, y'have past a hell of Time,
And I a tyrant have no leasure taken
To waigh how once I suffered in your crime.
O that our night of wo might have remembred
My deepest sence, how hard true sorrow hits,   10
And soone to you, as you to me then tendred
The humble salve, which wounded bosomes fits!
    But that your trespasse now becomes a fee,
    Mine ransoms yours, and yours must ransome mee.

---

8 essaies attempts, i.e. with others

129

Th'expence of Spirit in a waste of shame
Is lust in action, and till action, lust
Is perjurd, murdrous, blouddy full of blame,
Savage, extreame, rude, cruell, not to trust,
Injoyd no sooner but dispised straight,   5
Past reason hunted, and no sooner had
Past reason hated as a swollowed bayt,
On purpose layd to make the taker mad.
Mad in pursut and in possession so,
Had, having, and in quest, to have extreame,   10
A blisse in proofe and provd a very wo,
Before a joy proposd behind a dreame,
    All this the world well knowes yet none knowes well,
    To shun the heaven that leads men to this hell.

130

My Mistres eyes are nothing like the Sunne,
Currall is farre more red, than her lips red,   *coral*
If snow be white, why then her brests are dun:
If haires be wiers, black wiers grow on her head: *filigree*
I have seene Roses damaskt, red and white,   5
But no such Roses see I in her cheekes,
And in some perfumes is there more delight,
Than in the breath that from my Mistres reekes.
I love to heare her speake, yet well I know,
That Musicke hath a farre more pleasing sound: 10
I graunt I never saw a goddesse goe,
My Mistres when shee walkes treads on the ground.
    And yet by heaven I thinke my love as rare,
    As any she beli'd with false compare.   *belied*
1609

138

When my love sweares that she is made of truth,
I do beleeve her though I know she lyes,
That she might thinke me some untuterd youth,
Unlearned in the worlds false subtilties.
Thus vainely thinking that she thinkes me young,   5
Although she knowes my dayes are past the best,
Simply I credit her false speaking tongue,
On both sides thus is simple truth supprest:
But wherefore sayes she not she is unjust?
And wherefore say not I that I am old?   10
O loves best habit is in seeming trust,
And age in love, loves not t'have yeares told.
    Therefore I lye with her, and she with me,
    And in our faults by lyes we flattered be.

1599

146

Poore soule the center of my sinfull earth,
Foil'd by these rebell powres that thee array,
Why dost thou pine within and suffer dearth
Painting thy outward walls so costlie gay?
Why so large cost having so short a lease,   5
Dost thou upon thy fading mansion spend?
Shall wormes inheritors of these excesse
Eate up thy charge? is this thy bodies end?
Then soule live thou upon thy servants losse,
And let that pine to aggravat thy store;   10
Buy tearmes divine in selling houres of drosse:
Within be fed, without be rich no more,
    So shalt thou feed on death, that feeds on men,
    And death once dead, ther's no more dying then.

                                        1609

[When Isacles hang by the wall]

When Isacles hang by the wall,
And Dicke the Sheepheard blowes his naile:
And Thom beares Logges into the hall,
And Milke coms frozen home in paile:
When Blood is nipt, and wayes be full,   5
Then nightly singes the staring Owle
Tu-whit to-who.
    A merrie note,
    While greasie Jone doth keele the pot.   *stir*

When all aloude the winde doth blow,   10
And coffing drownes the Parsons saw;   *proverb*
And Birdes sit brooding in the Snow,
And Marrians nose lookes red and raw:
When roasted Crabbs hisse in the bowle,
Then nightly singes the staring Owle,   15
Tu-whit to-who.
    A merrie note,
    While greasie Jone doth keele the pot.

                                        1598

[When that I was and a little tine boy]

When that I was and a little tine boy,
    with hey, ho, the winde and the raine:
A foolish thing was but a toy,
    for the raine it raineth every day.

---

2 1609 reads: 'My sinfull earth these rebell powres that thee array.' The repetition of 'My sinfull earth' from the first line seems to be a compositor's error, and editors generally invent a substitution. 'Foil'd by' is from Geoffrey Hiller (1977).
When Isacles hang from *Loves Labors Lost, c.* 1594
When that I was from *Twelfth Night, c.* 1601: sung by Feste, the Fool, at the end of the play

But when I came to mans estate,   5
    with hey, ho, the winde and the raine:
Gainst Knaves and Theeves men shut their gate,
    for the raine it raineth every day.

But when I came alas to wive,
    with hey, ho, the winde and the raine: 10
By swaggering could I never thrive,
    for the raine it raineth every day.

But when I came unto my beds,
    with hey, ho, the winde and the raine:
With tospottes still had drunken heades,   15
    for the raine it raineth every day.

A great while ago the world begon,
    hey, ho, the winde and the raine:
But that's all one, our Play is done,
    and wee'l strive to please you every day.   20
                                              1623

[Feare no more the heate o'th'Sun]

Feare no more the heate o'th'Sun,
Nor the furious Winters rages,
Thou thy worldly task hast don,
Home art gon, and tane thy wages.
Golden Lads, and Girles all must,   5
As Chimney-Sweepers come to dust.

Feare no more the frowne o'th'Great,
Thou art past the Tirants stroake,
Care no more to cloath and eate,
To thee the Reede is as the Oake: 10
The Scepter, Learning, Physicke must,
All follow this and come to dust.

Feare no more the Lightning flash,
Nor th'all-dreaded Thunderstone,
Feare not Slander, Censure rash,   15
Thou hast finish'd Joy and mone:
All Lovers young, all Lovers must,
Consigne to thee and come to dust.

No Exorciser harme thee,
Nor no witch-craft charme thee.   20
Ghost unlaid forbeare thee.
Nothing ill come neere thee.
Quiet consumation have,
And renowned be thy grave.
                                            1623

Feare no more   from *Cymbeline, c.* 1610

[When Daffadils begin to peere]

When Daffadils begin to peere,
With heigh the Doxy over the dale,
Why then comes in the sweet o'the yeere,
For the red blood raigns in the winters pale.

The white sheete bleaching on the hedge,   5
With hey the sweet birds, O how they sing:
Doth set my pugging tooth an edge,   *thieving*
For a quart of Ale is a dish for a King.

The Larke, that tirra-Lyra chaunts,
With heigh, the Thrush and the Jay: 10
Are Summer songs for me and my Aunts   *sweethearts*
While we lye tumbling in the hay.

                                                           1623

[Full fadom five thy Father lies]

Full fadom five thy Father lies,
Of his bones are Corrall made:
Those are pearles that were his eies,
Nothing of him that doth fade,
But doth suffer a Sea-change   5
Into something rich, and strange:
Sea-Nimphs hourly ring his knell.
                    Burthen: ding dong
Hearke now I heare them, ding dong bell.

                                                           1623

CHRISTOPHER MARLOWE

1564–93 b Canterbury. A leading playwright of the Elizabethan stage, he died in a tavern quarrel.

The passionate Sheepheard to his love

Come live with mee, and be my love,
And we will all the pleasures prove,
That Vallies, groves, hills and fieldes,
Woods, or steepie mountaine yeeldes.

And wee will sit upon the Rocks,   5
Seeing the Sheepheards feede theyr flocks,
By shallow Rivers, to whose falls
Melodious byrds sing Madrigalls.

When Daffadils begin   from *The Winters Tale, c.* 1611
2 Doxy   mistress or young woman (slang)
4 pale   pale colour; also territory
Full fadom five   from *The Tempest*, 1611: sung by a spirit, Ariel, to Prince Ferdinand, alone on the shore of an enchanted island after he and his father, Alonso, have been shipwrecked. It turns out that Alonso is not drowned, but the experience is the beginning of his moral regeneration.
The passionate Sheepheard   See Ralegh's reply, p. 497.

And I will make thee beds of Roses,
And a thousand fragrant posies,   10
A cap of flowers, and a kirtle,   *gown*
Imbroydred all with leaves of Mirtle.

A gowne made of the finest wooll,
Which from our pretty Lambes we pull,
Fayre lined slippers for the cold: 15
With buckles of the purest gold.

A belt of straw, and Ivie buds,
With Corall clasps and Amber studs,
And if these pleasures may thee move,
Come live with mee, and be my love.   20

The Sheepheards Swaines shall daunce and sing,
For thy delight each May-morning.
If these delights thy minde may move,
Then live with mee, and be my love.

                                                                   1600

MICHAEL DRAYTON

1563–1631 b Warwickshire. He lived mainly in London. He was a versatile and prolific
poet who saw poetry as his profession.

To the Virginian Voyage

You brave Heroique Minds,
Worthy your Countries Name,
    That Honour still pursue,
    Goe, and subdue,
Whilst loyt'ring Hinds   5
Lurke here at home, with shame.

Britans, you stay too long,
Quickly aboord bestow you,
    And with a merry Gale
    Swell your stretch'd Sayle,   10
With Vowes as strong
As the Winds that blow you.

Your Course securely steere,
West and by South forth keepe,
    Rocks, Lee-shores, nor Sholes,   15
    When EOLUS scowles,
You need not feare,
So absolute the Deepe.

Virginian Voyage   an expedition of 1606
5 Hinds   menials, i.e. unspirited men
16 Eolus   Greek god of winds

And cheerefully at Sea,
Successe you still intice
    To get the Pearle and Gold,
    And ours to hold,
VIRGINIA,
Earth's onely Paradise.

Where Nature hath in store
Fowle, Venison, and Fish,
    And the fruitfull'st Soyle,
    Without your Toyle,
Three Harvests more,
All greater than your Wish.

And the ambitious Vine
Crownes with his purple Masse
    The Cedar reaching hie
    To kisse the Sky,
The Cypresse, Pine
And use-full Sassafras.

To whose, the golden Age
Still Natures lawes doth give,
    No other Cares that tend,
    But Them to defend
From Winters age,
That long there doth not live.

When as the Lushious smell
Of that delicious Land,
    Above the Seas that flowes,
    The cleere Wind throwes,
Your Hearts to swell
Approching the deare Strand.

In kenning of the Shore
(Thanks to God first given,)
    O you the happy'st men,
    Be Frolike then,
Let Cannons roare,
Frighting the wide Heaven.

And in Regions farre
Such *Heroes* bring yee foorth,
    As those from whom We came,
    And plant Our name,
Under that Starre
Not knowne unto our North.

20
25
30
35
40
45

sighting
50
55
60

---

36 use-full   i.e. medicinally

And as there Plenty growes
Of Lawrell every where,
   APOLLO's Sacred tree,
   You it may see,
A Poets Browes   65
To crowne, that may sing there.

Thy Voyages attend,
Industrious HACKLUIT,
   Whose Reading shall inflame
   Men to seeke Fame,   70
And much commend
To after-Times thy Wit.   *intelligence*
                              1606 1606

From Idea

61

Since ther's no helpe, Come let us kisse and part,
Nay, I have done: You get no more of Me,
And I am glad, yea glad with all my heart,
That thus so cleanly, I my Selfe can free,
Shake hands for ever, Cancell all our Vowes,   5
And when We meet at any time againe,
Be it not seene in either of our Browes,
That We one jot of former Love reteyne;
Now at the last gaspe, of Loves latest Breath,
When his Pulse fayling, Passion speechlesse lies,   10
When Faith is kneeling by his bed of Death,
And Innocence is closing up his Eyes,
   Now if thou would'st, when all have given him over,
   From Death to Life, thou might'st him yet recover.

                              1619

[Soe well I love thee, as without thee I]

These verses weare made By Michaell Drayton Esquier
Poett Lawreatt the night before hee dyed.

Soe well I love thee, as without thee I
Love Nothing; yf I might Chuse, I'de rather dye
Than bee one day debarde thy companye.

Since Beasts, and plantes doe growe, and live and move,
Beastes are those men, that such a life approve: 5
Hee onlye Lives, that Deadly is in Love.

---

68 **Richard Hakluyt**   a writer on exploration, and a backer of the expedition
Soe well I love thee   This poem was written for Anne Rainsford (born Goodere), whom Drayton
addressed as 'Idea' in love poetry throughout his life.

The Corne that in the grownd is sowen first dies   *grain*
And of one seed doe manye Eares arise;
Love this worldes Corne, by dying Multiplies.

The seeds of Love first by thy eyes weare throwne   10
Into a grownd untild, a harte unknowne
To beare such fruitt, tyll by thy handes t'was sowen.

Looke as your Looking glass by Chance may fall,
Devyde and breake in manye peyces smale
And yett shewes forth, the selfe same face in all,   15

Proportions, Features, Graces just the same;
And in the smalest peyce as well the name
Of Fayrest one deserves, as in the richest frame.

Soe all my Thoughts are peyces but of you
Whiche put together makes a Glass soe true   20
As I therin noe others face but yours can Veiwe.

                                                    1895

CHIDIOCK TICHBORNE

1558–86 Nothing is known of him except that he was executed for his part in the Babington plot against Queen Elizabeth.

Tychbornes Elegie,

written with his owne hand in the Tower
before his execution

My prime of youth is but a frost of cares,   *spring*
    my feast of joy is but a dish of paine:
My Crop of corne is but a field of tares,
    and al my good is but vaine hope of gaine.
The day is past, and yet I saw no sunne,   5
And now I live, and now my life is done.

My tale was heard, and yet it was not told,
    my fruit is falne, and yet my leaves are greene:
My youth is spent, and yet I am not old,
    I saw the world, and yet I was not seene.   10
My thred is cut, and yet it is not spunne,
And now I live, and now my life is done.

I sought my death, and found it in my wombe,
    I lookt for life and saw it was a shade:
I trod the earth, and knew it was my Tombe,   15
    and now I die, and now I was but made.
My glasse is full, and now my glasse is runne,
And now I live, and now my life is done.

                                    1586

SIR PHILIP SIDNEY

1554–86 b Penshurst, Kent. A courtier, diplomat and writer of poetry and prose, he died in
the Netherlands from a battle wound. His poetry circulated in manuscript form.

From Astrophil and Stella

1

Loving in truth, and faine in verse my love to show,   *eager*
That the deare She might take some pleasure of my paine:
Pleasure might cause her reade, reading might make her know,
Knowledge might pitie winne, and pitie grace obtaine,
　　I sought fit words to paint the blackest face of woe,   5
Studying inventions fine, her wits to entertaine: *ideas*
Oft turning others leaves, to see if thence would flow
Some fresh and fruitfull showers upon my sunne-burn'd braine.
　　But words came halting forth, wanting Inventions stay,   *support*
Invention, Natures child, fled step-dame Studies blowes,   10
And others feete still seem'd but strangers in my way.
Thus great with child to speake, and helplesse in my throwes,
　　Biting my trewand pen, beating my selfe for spite,   *truant*
　　Foole, said my Muse to me, looke in thy heart and write.

5

It is most true, that eyes are form'd to serve
The inward light: and that the heavenly part   *reason*
Ought to be king, from whose rules who do swerve,
Rebels to Nature strive for their own smart.
　　It is most true, what we call *Cupids* dart,   5
An image is, which for our selves we carve;
And, fooles, adore in temple of our hart,
Till that good God make Church and Churchman starve.
　　True, that true Beautie Vertue is indeed,
Whereof this Beautie can be but a shade,   10
Which elements with mortall mixture breed:
True, that on earth we are but pilgrims made,
　　And should in soule up to our countrey move:
　　True, and yet true that I must *Stella* love.

6

Some Lovers speake when they their Muses entertaine,
Of hopes begot by feare, of wot not what desires,
Of force of heav'nly beames, infusing hellish paine: *I know not*
Of living deaths, deare wounds, fair stormes and freezing fires:
　　Someone his song in *Jove*, and *Joves* strange tales attires,   5
Broadred with buls and swans, powdred with golden raine: *embroidered*
Another humbler wit to shepheards pipe retires,
Yet hiding royall bloud full oft in rurall vaine.

To some a sweetest plaint, a sweetest stile affords,
  While teares powre out his inke, and sighs breathe out his words: 10
His paper pale dispaire, and paine his pen doth move.
  I can speake what I feele, and feele as much as they,
  But thinke that all the Map of my state I display,
When trembling voice brings forth that I do *Stella* love.

45

Stella oft sees the verie face of wo
  Painted in my beclowded stormie face:
  But cannot skill to pitie my disgrace,
Not though thereof the cause her selfe she know:
  Yet hearing late a fable, which did show   5
    Of Lovers never knowne, a grievous case,
    Pitie thereof gate in her breast such place,   *got*
That from that sea deriv'd teares spring did flow.
    Alas if Fancy drawne by imag'd things,
Though false, yet with free scope more grace doth breed   10
Than servants wracke, where new doubts honour brings;
Then thinke my deare, that you in me do reed
  Of Lovers ruine some sad Tragedie:
  I am not I, pitie the tale of me.

49

I on my horse, and *Love* on me doth trie
  Our horsmanships, while by strange worke I prove
  A horsman to my horse, a horse to *Love*;
And now mans wrongs in me poore beast descrie.
  The raines wherewith my Rider doth me tie,   5
    Are humbled thoughts, which bit of Reverence move,
    Curb'd in with feare, but with guilt bosse above
Of Hope, which makes it seeme faire to the eye.
    The Wand is Will, thou Fancie Saddle art,
Girt fast by memorie, and while I spurre   10
My horse, he spurres with sharpe desire my hart:
He sits me fast, how ever I do sturre:
  And now hath made me to his hand so right,
  That in the Manage myselfe takes delight.

71

Who will in fairest book of Nature know,
  How Vertue may best lodg'd in beautie be,
  Let him but learne of *Love* to reade in thee
Stella, those faire lines, which true goodnesse show.

---

7 **guilt bosse**   ornamental gilt stud on the curb

There shall he find all vices overthrow,   5
   Not by rude force, but sweetest souveraigntie
   Of reason, from whose light those night-birds flie;
That inward sunne in thine eyes shineth so.
   And not content to be Perfections heire
Thy selfe, doest strive all minds that way to move,   10
Who marke in thee what is in thee most faire.
So while thy beautie drawes the heart to love,
   As fast thy Vertue bends that love to good:
   But ah, Desire still cries, give me some food.

1591

EDMUND SPENSER

?1552–99 b London. He wrote most of his poetry in Ireland, where he served as a senior official of the crown, 1580–98.

From Amoretti

LXVII

Lyke as a huntsman after weary chace,
   seeing the game from him escapt away,
   sits downe to rest him in some shady place,
   with panting hounds beguiled of their pray:
So after long pursuit and vaine assay,   5
   when I all weary had the chace forsooke,
   the gentle deare returned the self-same way,
   thinking to quench her thirst at the next brooke.
There she beholding me with mylder looke,
   sought not to fly, but fearelesse still did bide: 10
   till I in hand her yet halfe trembling tooke,
   and with her owne goodwill hir fyrmely tyde.
Strange thing me seemd to see a beast so wyld,
   so goodly wonne with her owne will beguyld.

LXXV

One day I wrote her name upon the strand,
   but came the waves and washed it away:
   agayne I wrote it with a second hand,
   but came the tyde, and made my paynes his pray.
Vayne man, sayd she, that doest in vaine assay,   5
   a mortall thing so to immortalize,
   for I my selve shall lyke to this decay,
   and eek my name bee wyped out lykewize.   *also*
Not so, (quod I) let baser things devize
   to dy in dust, but you shall live by fame: 10
   my verse your vertues rare shall eternize,
   and in the hevens wryte your glorious name.

Where whenas death shall all the world subdew,
our love shall live, and later life renew.

1594–95 1595

Prothalamion

1

Calme was the day, and through the trembling ayre,
Sweete breathing *Zephyrus* did softly play
A gentle spirit, that lightly did delay
Hot *Titans* beames, which then did glyster fayre:
When I whom sullein care,   5
Through discontent of my long fruitlesse stay
In Princes Court, and expectation vayne
Of idle hopes, which still doe fly away,
Like empty shaddowes, did aflict my brayne,
Walkt forth to ease my payne   10
Along the shoare of silver streaming *Themmes*,
Whose rutty Bancke, the which his River hemmes,
Was paynted all with variable flowers,
And all the meades adornd with daintie gemmes,
Fit to decke maydens bowres,   15
And crowne their Paramours,   *lovers*
Against the Brydale day, which is not long:
   Sweete *Themmes* runne softly, till I end my Song.

2

There, in a Meadow, by the Rivers side,
A Flocke of *Nymphes* I chaunced to espy,   20
All lovely Daughters of the Flood thereby,
With goodly greenish locks all loose untyde,
As each had bene a Bryde,
And each one had a little wicker basket,
Made of fine twigs entrayled curiously,   25
In which they gathered flowers to fill their flasket:
And with fine Fingers, cropt full feateously   *deftly*
The tender stalkes on hye.
Of every sort, which in that Meadow grew,
They gathered some; the Violet pallid blew,   30
The little Dazie, that at evening closes,
The virgin Lillie, and the Primrose trew,
With store of vermeil Roses,
To decke their Bridegromes posies,
Against the Brydale day, which was not long: 35
   Sweete *Themmes* runne softly, till I end my Song.

Prothalamion   literally: 'before the bridal chamber'. The poem was written for the double wedding of
Elizabeth and Katherine Somerset, daughters of the Earl of Worcester.
2 Zephyrus   the west wind
4 Titan   Helios, Greek sun god

3

With that, I saw two Swannes of goodly hewe,
Come softly swimming downe along the Lee;
Two fairer Birds I yet did never see:
The snow which doth the top of *Pindus* strew,   40
Did never whiter shew,
Nor *Jove* himselfe when he a Swan would be
For love of *Leda*, whiter did appeare:
Yet *Leda* was they say as white as he,
Yet not so white as these, nor nothing neare;   45
So purely white they were,
That even the gentle streame, the which them bare,
Seem'd foule to them, and bad his billowes spare
To wet their silken feathers, least they might
Soyle their fayre plumes with water not so fayre,   50
And marre their beauties bright,
That shone as heavens light,
Against their Brydale day, which was not long:
　　Sweete *Themmes* runne softly, till I end my Song.

4

Eftsoones the *Nymphes*, which now had Flowers their fill,   *at once* 55
Ran all in haste, to see that silver brood,
As they came floating on the Christal Flood.
Whom when they sawe, they stood amazed still,
Their wondring eyes to fill,
Them seem'd they never saw a sight so fayre,   60
Of Fowles so lovely, that they sure did deeme
Them heavenly borne, or to be that same payre
Which through the Skie draw *Venus* silver Teeme,
For sure they did not seeme
To be begot of any earthly Seede,   65
But rather Angels or of Angels breede:
Yet were they bred of *Somers-heat* they say,
In sweetest Season, when each Flower and weede
The earth did fresh aray,
So fresh they seem'd as day,   70
Even as their Brydale day, which was not long:
　　Sweete *Themmes* runne softly, till I end my Song.

5

Then forth they all out of their baskets drew
Great store of Flowers, the honour of the field,
That to the sense did fragrant odours yeild,   75
All which upon those goodly Birds they threw,
And all the Waves did strew,
That like old *Peneus* Waters they did seeme,
When downe along by pleasant *Tempes* shore
Scattred with Flowres, through *Thessaly* they streeme,   80

---

38 Lee a river which at that time flowed into the Thames
40 Pindus a mountain range in Greece
78 Peneus a river in the valley of **Tempe** in **Thessaly**, northern Greece

That they appeare through Lillies plenteous store,
Like a Brydes Chamber flore:
Two of those *Nymphes*, meane while, two Garlands bound,
Of freshest Flowres which in that Mead they found,
The which presenting all in trim Array, 85
Their snowie Foreheads therewithall they crownd,
Whil'st one did sing this Lay,
Prepar'd against that Day,
Against their Brydale day, which was not long:
    Sweete *Themmes* runne softly, till I end my Song 90

      6
Ye gentle Birdes, the worlds faire ornament,
And heavens glorie, whom this happie hower
Doth leade unto your lovers blisfull bower,
Joy may you have and gentle hearts content
Of your loves couplement: 95
And let faire *Venus*, that is Queene of love,
With her heart-quelling Sonne upon you smile,
Whose smile they say, hath vertue to remove
All Loves dislike, and friendships faultie guile
For ever to assoile. *absolve* 100
Let endlesse Peace your steadfast hearts accord,
And blessed Plentie wait upon your bord,
And let your bed with pleasures chast abound,
That fruitfull issue may to you afford,
Which may your foes confound, 105
And make your joyes redound,
Upon your Brydale day, which is not long:
    Sweete *Themmes* runne softly, till I end my Song.

      7
So ended she; and all the rest around
To her redoubled that her undersong, *refrain* 110
Which said, their bridale daye should not be long.
And gentle Eccho from the neighbour ground,
Their accents did resound.
So forth those joyous Birdes did passe along,
Adowne the Lee, that to them murmurde low, 115
As he would speake, but that he lackt a tong
Yeat did by signes his glad affection show,
Making his streame run slow.
And all the foule which in his flood did dwell
Gan flock about these twaine, that did excell 120
The rest, so far, as *Cynthia* doth shend *moon goddess / shame*
The lesser starres. So they enranged well, *arranged*
Did on those two attend,
And their best service lend,
Against their wedding day, which was not long: 125
    Sweete *Themmes* runne softly, till I end my Song.

---

120 Gan flock flocked

8

At length they all to mery *London* came,
To mery London, my most kyndly Nurse,
That to me gave this Lifes first native sourse:
Though from another place I take my name,   130
An house of auncient fame.
There when they came, whereas those bricky towres,
The which on *Themmes* brode aged backe doe ryde,
Where now the studious Lawyers have their bowers
There whylome wont the Templer Knights to byde,   *formerly* 135
Till they decayd through pride:
Next whereunto there standes a stately place,
Where oft I gayned giftes and goodly grace
Of that great Lord, which therein wont to dwell,
Whose want too well now feeles my freendles case: 140
But Ah here fits not well
Olde woes but joyes to tell
Against the bridale daye, which is not long:
    Sweete *Themmes* runne softly, till I end my Song.

9

Yet therein now doth lodge a noble Peer,   145
Great *Englands* glory and the Worlds wide wonder,
Whose dreadfull name, late through all *Spaine* did thunder,
And *Hercules* two pillors standing neere,
Did make to quake and feare:
Faire branch of Honor, flower of Chevalrie,   150
That fillest *England* with thy triumphs fame,
Joy have thou of thy noble victorie,
And endlesse happinesse of thine owne name
That promiseth the same:
That through thy prowesse and victorious armes,   155
Thy country may be freed from forraine harmes:
And great *Elisaes* glorious name may ring
Through al the world, fil'd with thy wide Alarmes,
Which some brave muse may sing
To ages following,   160
Upon the Brydale day, which is not long:
    Sweete *Themmes* runne softly, till I end my Song.

10

From those high Towers, this noble Lord issuing,
Like Radiant *Hesper* when his golden hayre
In th' *Ocean* billowes he hath Bathed fayre,   165
Descended to the Rivers open viewing,

---

135 The Temple, a law college, was named for the military and religious order of Knights Templars which originally occupied it.
137 **stately place**   Essex House, which, as Leicester House, was the home of Spenser's patron, the Earl of Leicester, until his death in 1588.
145 **noble Peer**   the Earl of Essex, stepson of Leicester and friend of the Earl of Worcester. He had recently returned from a successful campaign in Spain.
148 **pillors**   the rocks on both sides of the Straits of Gibraltar
158 **Alarmes**   calls to arms
164 **Hesper**   the evening star

With a great traine ensuing.
Above the rest were goodly to bee seene
Two gentle Knights of lovely face and feature
Beseeming well the bower of anie Queene,   170
With gifts of wit and ornaments of nature,
Fit for so goodly stature:
That like the twins of *Jove* they seem'd in sight,
Which decke the Bauldricke of the Heavens bright.
They two forth pacing to the Rivers side,   175
Received those two faire Brides, their Loves delight,
Which at th'appointed tyde,
Each one did make his Bryde,
Against their Brydale day, which is not long:
    Sweet *Themmes* runne softly, till I end my Song.   180

                  1596   *1596*

From The Faerie Queene

From *Book VII, Canto vii*

        28
So, forth issew'd the Seasons of the yeare;
   First, lusty *Spring*, all dight in leaves of flowres   *dressed* 245
   That freshly budded and new bloosmes did beare
   (In which a thousand birds had built their bowres
   That sweetly sung, to call forth Paramours):
   And in his hand a javelin he did beare,
   And on his head (as fit for warlike stoures)   *conflicts* 250
   A guilt engraven morion he did weare;   *helmet*
That as some did him love, so others did him feare.
        29
Then came the jolly *Sommer*, being dight
   In a thin silken cassock coloured greene,
   That was unlyned all, to be more light: 255
   And on his head a girlond well beseene
   He wore, from which as he had chauffed been   *heated*
   The sweat did drop; and in his hand he bore
   A boawe and shaftes, as he in forrest greene
   He hunted late the Libbard or the Bore,   *Leopard* 260
And now would bathe his limbes, with labor heated sore.
        30
Then came the *Autumne* all in yellow clad,
   As though he joyed in his plentious store,
   Laden with fruits that made him laugh, full glad
   That he had banisht hunger, which to-fore   265
   Had by the belly oft him pinched sore.

---

173 twins   Castor and Pollux, who, in Greek myth, after death became the Gemini of the zodiac
174 Bauldricke   a belt worn diagonally from the shoulder: here, the zodiac
The Faerie Queene   In this extract from Spenser's allegorical epic, the goddess Mutabilitie (Change) has prevailed upon Nature to summon a pageant which, as she thinks, will prove her dominion. In the event, it shows that within the sub-lunary world she is part of the process of divinely sanctioned order. The poem at times uses deliberately archaic language.

Upon his head a wreath that was enrold
With eares of corne, of every sort he bore:
And in his hand a sickle he did holde,
To reape the ripened fruits the which the earth had yold.   *yielded* 270

31

Lastly, came *Winter* cloathed all in frize,   *coarse wool*
 Chattering his teeth for cold that did him chill,
 Whil'st on his hoary beard his breath did freese;
 And the dull drops that from his purpled bill   *nose*
 As from a limbeck did adown distill.   275
 In his right hand a tipped staffe he held,
 With which his feeble steps he stayed still:
 For, he was faint with cold, and weak with eld;   *age*
That scarse his loosed limbes he hable was to weld.   *control*

32

These, marching softly, thus in order went,   280
 And after them, the Monthes all riding came;
 First, sturdy *March* with brows full sternly bent,
 And armed strongly, rode upon a Ram,
 The same which over *Hellespontus* swam:
 Yet in his hand a spade he also hent,   *held* 285
 And in a bag all sorts of seeds ysame,   *together*
 Which on the earth he strowed as he went,
And fild her womb with fruitfull hope of nourishment.

33

Next came fresh *Aprill* full of lustyhed,
 And wanton as a Kid whose horne new buds: 290
 Upon a Bull he rode, the same which led
 Europa floting through th' *Argolick* fluds: *Greek*
 His hornes were gilden all with golden studs
 And garnished with garlonds goodly dight   *decked*
 Of all the fairest flowres and freshest buds   295
 Which th'earth brings forth, and wet he seem'd in sight
With waves, through which he waded for his loves delight.

34

Then came faire *May*, the fayrest mayd on ground,
 Deckt all with dainties of her seasons pryde,
 And throwing flowres out of her lap around: 300
 Upon two brethrens shoulders she did ride,
 The twinnes of *Leda*; which on eyther side
 Supported her like to their soveraine Queene.
 Lord! how all creatures laught, when her they spide,
 And leapt and daunc't as they had ravisht beene!   *entranced* 305
And *Cupid* selfe about her fluttred all in greene.

---

275 **limbeck** distilling apparatus
283 **Ram** Aries (a sign of the zodiac is assigned to each month in the pageant); also the ram of the golden fleece, Jove in disguise, who lost Helle in the sea of the Hellespont while carrying her on his back.
291–92 Jove, in the form of a bull, carried **Europa** across the sea to Crete and seduced (or raped) her.
302 **twinnes** Castor and Pollux, fathered on **Leda** by Jove in the form of a swan

35

And after her, came jolly *June*, arrayd
  All in greene leaves, as he a Player were;
  Yet in his time, he wrought as well as playd,
  That by his plough-yrons mote right well appeare: *must*   310
  Upon a Crab he rode, that him did beare
  With crooked crawling steps an uncouth pase,
  And backward yode, as Bargemen wont to fare
  Bending their force contrary to their face,
Like that ungracious crew which faines demurest grace.   *feigns*   315

36

Then came hot *July* boyling like to fire,
  That all his garments he had cast away:
  Upon a Lyon raging yet with ire
  He boldly rode and made him to obay:
  It was the beast that whylome did forray   *formerly*   320
  The Nemæan forrest, till th' *Amphytrionide*
  Him slew, and with his hide did him array;
  Behinde his back a sithe, and by his side
Under his belt he bore a sickle circling wide.

37

The sixt was *August*, being rich arrayd   325
  In garment all of gold downe to the ground:
  Yet rode he not, but led a lovely Mayd
  Forth by the lilly hand, the which was cround
  With eares of corne, and full her hand was found;
  That was the righteous Virgin, which of old   330
  Liv'd here on earth, and plenty made abound;
  But, after Wrong was lov'd and Justice solde,
She left th'unrighteous world and was to heaven extold.   *raised*

38

Next him, *September* marched eeke on foote;   *also*
  Yet was he heavy laden with the spoyle   335
  Of harvests riches, which he made his boot,   *booty*
  And him enricht with bounty of the soyle:
  In his one hand, as fit for harvests toyle,
  He held a knife-hook; and in th'other hand
  A paire of waights, with which he did assoyle   *resolve*   340
  Both more and lesse, where it in doubt did stand,
And equall gave to each as Justice duly scann'd.

39

Then came *October* full of merry glee:
  For, yet his noule was totty of the must,
  Which he was treading in the wine-fats see,   *wine-vat's see*   345
  And of the joyous oyle, whose gentle gust   *taste*
  Made him so frollick and so full of lust:

---

308 greene leaves   the stage-dress of a wild man
313 backward yode   went backward; i.e. as the sun in the zodiac after the June solstice
321 th'Amphytrionide   Hercules, supposedly the son of Amphytrion, but in reality of Jove
330 righteous Virgin   Astræa, goddess of justice
344 For yet his head was tipsy with the new wine.

Upon a dreadfull Scorpion he did ride,
The same which by *Dianaes* doom unjust
Slew great *Orion*: and eeke by his side   350
He had his ploughing share, and coulter ready tyde.

           40
Next was *November*, he full grosse and fat,
    As fed with lard, and that right well might seeme;
    For, he had been a fatting hogs of late,
    That yet his browes with sweat, did reek and steem,   355
    And yet the season was full sharp and breem;   *bitter*
    In planting eeke he took no small delight:
    Whereon he rode, not easie was to deeme;
    For it a dreadfull *Centaure* was in sight,
The seed of *Saturne*, and faire *Nais*, *Chiron* hight.   *named* 360

           41
And after him, came next the chill *December*:
    Yet he through merry feasting which he made,
    And great bonfires, did not the cold remember;
    His Saviours birth his mind so much did glad:
    Upon a shaggy-bearded Goat he rode,   365
    The same wherewith *Dan Jove* in tender yeares,
    They say, was nourisht by th'*Idæan* mayd;
    And in his hand a broad deepe boawle he beares;
Of which, he freely drinks an health to all his peeres.

           42
Then came old *January*, wrapped well   370
    In many weeds to keep the cold away;   *clothes*
    Yet did he quake and quiver like to quell,   *quail*
    And blow his nayles to warme them if he may:
    For, they were numbd with holding all the day
    An hatchet keene, with which he felled wood,   375
    And from the trees did lop the needlesse spray:
    Upon an huge great Earth-pot steane he stood;   *jar*
From whose wide mouth, there flowed forth the Romane floud.

           43
And lastly, came cold *February*, sitting
    In an old wagon, for he could not ride;   380
    Drawne of two fishes for the season fitting,
    Which through the flood before did softly slyde
    And swim away: yet had he by his side
    His plough and harnesse fit to till the ground,
    And tooles to prune the trees, before the pride   385
    Of hasting Prime did make them burgein round: *spring*
So past the twelve Months forth, and their dew places found.

348–50 Orion was killed by a **Scorpion** sent by **Diana** after he boasted of his ability to kill any earthly creature.
367 Idæn   from Mt Ida, in Crete
378 Romane floud   the river Tiber: its significance here is uncertain.
381 the season   that of Lent

44

And after these, there came the *Day*, and *Night*,
  Riding together both with equall pase,
  Th'one on a Palfrey blacke, the other white;   390
  But *Night* had covered her uncomely face
  With a blacke veile, and held in hand a mace,
  On top whereof the moon and stars were pight,   *placed*
  And sleep and darknesse round about did trace:
  But *Day* did beare, upon his scepters hight,   395
The goodly Sun, encompast all with beames bright.

45

Then came the *Howres*, faire daughters of high *Jove*,
  And timely *Night*, the which were all endewed   *temporal*
  With wondrous beauty fit to kindle love;
  But they were Virgins all, and love eschewed,   400
  That might forslack the charge to them fore-shewed
  By mighty *Jove*; who did them Porters make
  Of heavens gate (whence all the gods issued)
  Which they did dayly watch, and nightly wake
By even turnes, ne ever did their charge forsake.   405

46

And after all came *Life*, and lastly *Death*;
  Death with most grim and griesly visage seene,
  Yet is he nought but parting of the breath;
  Ne ought to see, but like a shade to weene,   *imagine*
  Unbodied, unsoul'd, unheard, unseene.   410
  But *Life* was like a faire young lusty boy,
  Such as they faine *Dan Cupid* to have beene,   *portray / master*
  Full of delightfull health and lively joy,
Deckt all with flowres, and wings of gold fit to employ.

                         c. 1598   1609

SIR WALTER RALEGH

?1552–1618 b Devon. A soldier and leader of voyages of discovery and warfare, he spent thirteen years in prison for treason and was beheaded.

The Nimphs reply to the Sheepheard

If all the world and love were young,
And truth in every Sheepheards tongue,
These pretty pleasures might me move,
To live with thee, and be thy love.

Time drives the flocks from field to fold,   5
When Rivers rage, and Rocks grow cold,
And *Philomell* becommeth dombe,
The rest complaines of cares to come.

---

401 forslack cause neglect of
The Nimphs reply A reply to Marlowe's poem (p. 481)
7 Philomell the nightingale See *Metamorphoses* VI; and note, p. 141.

The flowers doe fade, and wanton fieldes,
To wayward winter reckoning yeeldes;   10
A honny tongue, a hart of gall,
Is fancies spring, but sorrowes fall.

Thy gownes, thy shooes, thy beds of Roses,
Thy cap, thy kirtle, and thy posies,   *overskirt*
Soone breake, soone wither, soone forgotten: 15
In follie ripe, in reason rotten.

Thy belt of straw and Ivie buddes,
Thy Corall claspes and Amber studdes,
All these in mee no meanes can move,
To come to thee, and be thy love.   20

But could youth last, and love still breede,
Had joyes no date, nor age no neede,
Then these delights my minde might move,
To live with thee, and be thy love.

                                                        1600

The Lie

Goe soule the bodies guest
    upon a thankelesse arrant,   *errand*
Feare not to touch the best,
    the truth shall be thy warrant:
Goe since I needs must die,   5
    and give the world the lie.

Say to the Court it glowes,
    and shines like rotten wood,
Say to the Church it showes
    whats good, and doth no good.   10
If Church and Court reply,
    then give them both the lie.

Tell Potentates they live
    acting by others action,
Not loved unlesse they give,   15
    not strong but by affection.
If Potentates reply,
    give Potentates the lie.

Tell men of high condition,
    that mannage the estate,   20
Their purpose is ambition,
    their practise onely hate:
And if they once reply,
    then give them all the lie.

Tell them that brave it most,   25
    they beg for more by spending,
Who in their greatest cost
    like nothing but commending.
And if they make replie,
    then give them all the lie.   30

Tell zeale it wants devotion,
  tell love it is but lust,
Tell time it meets but motion,   *measures*
  tell flesh it is but dust.
And wish them not replie   35
  for thou must give the lie.

Tell age it daily wasteth,
  tell honour how it alters,
Tell beauty how she blasteth,   *withers*
  tell favour how it falters.   40
And as they shall reply,
  give every one the lie.

Tell wit how much it wrangles
  in tickle points of nycenesse,
Tell wisedome she entangles   *subtlety*
  her selfe in over wisenesse.   45
And when they doe reply
  straight give them both the lie.

Tell Phisicke of her boldnes,   *medicine / arrogance*
  tell skill it is prevention: 50
Tell charity of coldnes,
  tell law it is contention,
And as they doe reply
  so give them still the lie.

Tell fortune of her blindnesse,   55
  tell nature of decay,
Tell friendship of unkindnesse,
  tell justice of delay.
And if they will reply,
  then give them all the lie.   60

Tell Arts they have no soundnesse,
  but vary by esteeming,
Tell schooles they want profoundnes
  and stand too much on seeming.
If Arts and schooles reply,   65
  give arts and schooles the lie.

Tell faith its fled the Citie,
  tell how the country erreth,
Tell manhood shakes off pittie,
  tell vertue least preferreth.   70
And if they doe reply,
  spare not to give the lie.

So when thou hast as I
  commanded thee, done blabbing,
Although to give the lie,   75
  deserves no lesse than stabbing,
Stab at thee he that will,
  no stab thy soule can kill.

?1593–96 1608

[As you came from the holy land]

As you came from the holy land
   Of Walsinghame
Mett you not with my true love
   By the way as you came?

'How shall I know your trew love   5
   That have mett many one
As I went to the holy lande
   That have come, that have gone?'

She is neyther whyte nor browne
   Butt as the heavens fayre;   10
There is none hathe a forme so divine
   In the earth or the ayre.

'Such an one did I meet, good Sir,
   Suche an Angelyke face,
Who lyke a queene, lyke a nymph, did appere   15
   By her gate, by her grace.'   *gait*

She hath lefte me here all alone,
   All allone as unknowne,
Who somtymes did me lead with her selfe
   And me lovde as her owne.   20

'Whats the cause that she leaves you alone
   And a new waye doth take;
Who loved you once as her owne
   And her joye did you make?'

I have lovde her all my youth,   25
   Butt now ould as you see,
Love lykes not the fallyng frute
   From the wythered tree:

Know that love is a careless chylld
   And forgets promyse paste,   30
He is blynd, he is deaff when he lyste   *wants to be*
   And in faythe never faste:

His desyre is a dureless contente   *unlasting*
   And a trustless joye,
He is wonn with a world of despayre   35
   And is lost with a toye:

Of women kynde suche indeed is the love
   Or the word Love abused,
Under which many chyldysh desyres
   And conceytes are excusde: 40

Butt true Love is a durable fyre
   In the mynde ever burnynge:
Never sycke, never ould, never dead,
   From itt selfe never turnynge.

                 By 1600   1631

As you came   This poem is generally attributed to Ralegh. It may be partly based on an older ballad.
2 Walsinghame   famous shrine of Mary in Norfolk

[What is our life? a play of passion]

What is our life? a play of passion,
Our mirth the musicke of division;
Our mothers wombes the tyring houses be,
Where we are drest for this short Comedy,
Heaven the Judicious sharpe spectator is,   5
That sits and markes still who doth act amisse,
Our graves that hide us from the searching Sun,
Are like drawne curtaynes when the play is done.
Thus march we playing to our latest rest,
Onely we dye in earnest, that's no Jest.   10
                                    1612

GEORGE GASCOIGNE

?1539–77 b Bedford. He attempted careers in the law and as a soldier, but attended principally to writing.

Gascoignes Lullabie

Sing lullabie, as women do,
Wherewith they bring their babes to rest,
And lullabie can I sing too
As womanly as can the best.
With lullabie they still the childe,   5
And if I be not much beguilde,
Full many wanton babes have I
Which must be stilld with lullabie.

    First lullaby my youthfull yeares,
It is now time to go to bed,   10
For crooked age and hoarie heares,
Have wonne the haven within my head:
With Lullabye then youth be still,
With Lullabye content thy will,
Since courage quayles, and coomes behynde,   15
Goe sleepe, and so beguyle thy mynde.

    Next Lullabye my gazing eyes,
Whiche woonted were to glaunce apace:
For every glasse maye nowe suffise,
To shewe the furrowes in my face: 20
With Lullabye then wynke a whyle,
With Lullabye youre lookes beguyle:
Lette no fayre face, nor beautie bryghte
Entice you efte with vayne delyght.   *after*

    And Lullabye my wanton will,   25
Lette reasons rule nowe reigne thy thought,
Since all too late I fynde by skill,
Howe deare I have thy fansies bought:

With Lullabye nowe take thyne ease,
With Lullabye thy doubtes appease: 30
For trust to this, if thou be still,
My bodie shall obeye thy will.

   Eke Lullabye my loving boye,   *also*
My little Robyn take thy rest,   *penis*
Synce Age is colde, and nothyng coye,   *amorous* 35
Keepe close thy coyne, for so is beste:
With Lullabye bee thou content,
With Lullabye thy lustes relente,
Lette others paye whiche have mo pence,   *more*
Thou arte too poore for suche expense.   40

   Thus Lullabie my youth, myne eyes,
My will, my ware, and all that was,
I can no mo delayes devise,
But welcome payne, lette pleasure passe:
With Lullabye nowe take your leave,   45
With Lullabye youre dreames deceyve,
And when you rise with waking eye,
Remembre *Gascoignes* Lullabye.

                1573

[And if I did what then?]

And if I did what then?
Are you agreev'd therfore?
The Sea hath fishe for every man,
And what would you have more?

Thus did my Mistresse once,   5
Amaze my mind with doubt:
And popt a question for the nonce,
To beate my braynes about.

Whereto I thus replied,
Eche fisherman can wishe,   10
That all the Sea at every tyde,
Were his alone to fishe.

And so did I (in vaine,)
But since it may not be:
Let such fishe there as finde the gaine,   15
And leave the losse for me.

And with such lucke and losse,
I will content my selfe:
Till tydes of turning time may tosse,
Such fishers on the shelfe.   20

And when they sticke on sandes,
That every man may see:
Then will I laugh and clappe my handes,
As they doe now at mee.

                1573

QUEEN ELIZABETH I

1533–1603 b Greenwich. Her upbringing included a thorough renaissance education.

[I grieve, and dare not show my Discontent]

I grieve, and dare not show my Discontent;
I love, and yet am forc'd to seem to hate;
I do, yet dare not say I ever meant;
I seem stark mute, but inwardly do prate:
       I am, and not; I freez, and yet am burn'd   5
       Since from my Self another Self I turn'd.

My Care is like my Shadow in the Sun,
Follows me flying, flies when I pursue it,
Stands, and lies by me, doth what I have done;
His too familiar Care doth make me rue it.   10
       No means I find to ridd him from my Breast,
       Till by the End of things it be supprest.

Some gentler Passion slide into my Mind,
For I am soft, and made of melting Snow;
Or be more cruel Love, and so be kind;   15
Let me or float or sink, be high or low;
       Or let me Live with some more sweet Content,   *either*
       Or Die, and so forget what Love e're meant.   1823

SIR THOMAS WYATT

1503–42 b Kent. A diplomat who experienced the Italian renaissance at first hand, he was
in and out of favour at the court of Henry VIII. His poetry circulated in manuscript form.

[The longe love that in my thought doeth harbar]

The longe love that in my thought doeth harbar   *harbour*
    and in myn hert doeth kepe his residence,   *heart*
    into my face preseth with bold pretence
    and therin campeth, spreding his baner.
She that me lerneth to love and suffre   *teaches* 5
    and will that my trust and lustes negligence
    be rayned by reason, shame and reverence,
    with his hardines taketh displeasur.
Wherewithall unto the hertes forrest he fleith,
    leving his entreprise with payne and cry,   10
    and there him hideth and not appereth.
What may I do when my maister fereth,   *fears*
    but in the feld with him to lyve and dye?
    for goode is the liff ending faithfully.   1557

The longe love   The poem is based on *Rime 140* by the Italian poet, Petrarch (1304–74).
7 rayned   reined; also reigned

[They fle from me, that sometyme did me seke]

They fle from me, that sometyme did me seke	*flee*
with naked fote stalking in my chambre.	
I have sene theim gentill tame and meke	
that nowe are wyld, and do not remember	
that sometyme they put theimself in daunger	5
to take bred at my hand; and nowe they raunge	
besely seking with a continuell chaunge.	*busily seeking*

Thancked be fortune, it hath ben othrewise	
twenty tymes better; but ons in speciall,	
in thyn arraye after a pleasant gyse,	*thin / style* 10
when her lose gowne from her shoulders did fall,	*loose*
and she me caught in her armes long and small,	
therewithall swetely did me kysse,	
and softely saide 'dere hert, howe like you this?'	*heart*

It was no dreme: I lay brode waking.	*broad* 15
But all is torned thorough my gentilnes	*turned*
into a straunge fasshion of forsaking;	
and I have leve to goo of her goodenes,	*go*
and she also to use new fangilnes.	*fickleness* 20
But syns that I so kyndely ame served,	
I would fain knowe what she hath deserved.	

1557

[Who so list to hounte I know where is an hynde]

Who so list to hounte I know where is an hynde,	*wants to hunt / hind*
but as for me, helas, I may no more.	*alas*
The vayne travaill hath weried me so sore,	
I ame of theim that farthest cometh behinde.	
Yet may I by no meanes my weried mynde	5
drawe from the Diere, but as she fleeth afore	
faynting I folowe; I leve off therefore,	
sithens in a nett I seke to hold the wynde.	*since*
Who list her hount I put him owte of dowbte,	
as well as I may spend his tyme in vain:	10
and graven with Diamondes in letters plain	
There is written her faier neck rounde abowte:	
'noli me tangere for Cesars I ame,	
and wylde for to hold though I seme tame'.	

[Madame, withouten many wordes]

Madame, withouten many wordes	
ons I ame sure ye will or no.	*once*
And if ye will then leve your bordes	*jests*
and use your wit and shew it so	

---

21 kyndely   according to her nature; also kindly, in the modern sense
Who so list   The poem is based on *Rime 190* by Petrarch.
13 noli me tangere   'touch me not': see John 20:17.   **Cesars I ame**   Wyatt was at one time involved with Anne Boleyn, who married Henry VIII.

And with a beck ye shall me call: 5
  and if of oon that burneth alwaye   *one*
  ye have any pitie at all
  aunswer him faire with yea or nay.

Yf it be yea, I shalbe fayne,   *glad*
  if it be nay, frendes as before: 10
  ye shall an othre man obtain
  and I myn owne and yours no more.

1557

[Stond who so list upon the Slipper toppe]

Stond who so list upon the Slipper toppe   *likes / slippery*
of courtes estates, and lett me heare rejoyce   *here*
and use me quyet without lett or stoppe,   *hindrance*
unknowen in courte, that hath suche brackishe joyes.
In hidden place so lett my dayes forthe passe   5
that when my yeares be done withouten noyse,
I may dye aged after the common trace.
For hym death greep'the right hard by the croppe   *grippeth*
that is moche knowen of other; and of him self alas,   *to others / to himself*
doth dye unknowen, dazed with dreadfull face.   10

1557

JOHN SKELTON

1460–1529 b Cumberland (or possibly Norfolk). A scholar and satirist, he was a parish
priest in Norfolk and later public orator at the court of Henry VIII.

Uppon a deedmans hed   *dead*

> *Skelton Laureat, uppon a deedmans hed, that was sent to hym from an
> honorable Jentyllwoman for a token, Devysyd this gostly medytacyon
> in Englysh: Covenable in sentence, Comendable, Lamentable, Lacrymable,
> Profytable for the soule.*

Youre ugly tokyn
My mynd hath brokyn
From worldly lust;
For I have dyscust
We ar but dust,   5
And dy we must.
  It is generall
To be mortall:
I have well espyde
No man may hym hyde   10
From deth holow-eyed,
With synnews wyderyd,   *withered*
With bonys shyderyd,   *shattered*

With hys worme-etyn maw
And hys gastly jaw   15
Gaspyng asyde,
Nakyd of hyde,
Neyther flesh nor fell.   *skin*
   Then by my councell,
Loke that ye spell   20
Well thys gospell;
For wherso we dwell,
Deth wyll us quell
And with us mell.   *mingle*
   For all oure pamperde paunchys   25
Ther may no fraunchys,
Nor worldly blys
Redeme us from this.
Our days be datyd
To be chekmatyd,   30
With drawttys of deth
Stoppyng oure breth,
Oure eyen synkyng,   *eyes*
Oure bodys stynkyng,
Oure gummys grynnyng,   35
Oure soulys brynnyng.   *burning*
To whom then shall we sew   *sue*
For to have rescew,
But to swete Jesu
On us then for to rew?   40
   O goodly chyld
Of Mary mylde,
Then be oure shylde:
That we be not exylyd
To the dyne dale   *dark* 45
Of boteles bale,   *useless grief*
Nor to the lake
Of fendys blake.   *fiends black*
   But graunt us grace
To se thy face,   50
And to purchace
Thyne hevenly place
And thy palace,
Full of solace,
Above the sky   55
That is so hy;
Eternally
To beholde and se
The Trynyte.
   Amen.   60
Myrres vous y.

        c. *1500*   1527

---

26 fraunchys franchise, i.e. privilege
32 drawttys chess moves
61 Look at yourself there.

WILLIAM DUNBAR

?1460–?1525 b East Lothian. He was a mendicant friar in France and later court poet to
James IV of Scotland.

[I that in heill wes and gladnes]

I that in heill wes and gladnes	*health was*
Am trublit now with gret seiknes	*sickness*
And feblit with infermite.	
Timor mortis conturbat me.	
Our plesance heir is all vane glory,	*here*
This fals warld is bot transitory,	
The flesch is brukle, the fend is sle.	*brittle / fiend is sly*
Timor mortis conturbat me.	
The stait of man dois change and vary,	
Now sound, now seik, now blith, now sary,	10
Now dansand mery, now like to dee.	*dancing / die*
Timor mortis conturbat me.	
No stait in erd heir standis sickir.	
As with the wind wavis the wickir,	*willow twig*
Wavis this warldis vanite.	15
Timor mortis conturbat me.	
On to the ded gois all estatis,	
Princis, prelotis and potestatis,	*potentates*
Baith riche and pur of all degre.	
Timor mortis conturbat me.	20
He takis the knythis in to feild,	*takes*
Anarmyt under helme and scheild.	
Victour he is at all melle.	*melee*
Timor mortis conturbat me.	
That strang unmercifull tyrand	25
Takis on the moderis breist sowkand	*mother's / sucking*
The bab full of benignite.	
Timor mortis conturbat me.	
He takis the campion in the stour,	*champion / conflict*
The capitane closit in the tour,	30
The lady in bour, full of bewte.	
Timor mortis conturbat me.	
He sparis no lord for his piscence,	*power*
Na clerk for his intelligence.	
His awful strak may no man fle.	35
Timor mortis conturbat me.	

---

4 The fear of death confounds me (from the *Office for the Dead*).
13 No state on earth here stands secure.

Art magicianis and astrologgis,
Rethoris, logicianis and theologgis,   *rhetoricians*
Thame helpis no conclusionis sle.   *them*
Timor mortis conturbat me.   40

In medicyne the most practicianis,   *greatest*
Lechis, surrigianis and physicianis,   *leeches / surgeons*
Thame self fra ded may not supple.   *death / help*
Timor mortis conturbat me.

I se that makaris amang the laif   *rest*   45
Playis heir ther pageant, syne gois to graif;   *then / grave*
Sparit is nought ther faculte.   *procession*
Timor mortis conturbat me.

He has done petuously devour
The noble Chaucer of makaris flour,   *flower*   50
The Monk of Bery, and Gower, all thre.
Timor mortis conturbat me.

The gud Syr Hew of Eglintoun,
And eik Heryot, and Wyntoun,   *also*
He has tane out of this cuntre.   *taken*   55
Timor mortis conturbat me.

That scorpion fell has done infek
Maister Johne Clerk and James Afflek
Fra ballat making and trigide.   *ballad*
Timor mortis conturbat me.   60

Holland and Barbour he has berevit;
Allace, that he nought with us levit   *alas / left*
Schir Mungo Lokert of the Le.
Timor mortis conturbat me.

Clerk of Tranent eik he has tane   65
That maid the Anteris of Gawane;   *adventures*
Schir Gilbert Hay endit has he.
Timor mortis conturbat me.

He has Blind Hary and Sandy Traill
Slaine with his schour of mortall haill,   70
Quhilk Patrik Johnestoun mycht nought fle.   *which*
Timor mortis conturbat me.

He has reft Merseir his endite   *writing*
That did in luf so lifly write,   *love*
So schort, so quyk, of sentence hie.   *high*   75
Timor mortis conturbat me.

---

37 **Art magicianis**   practitioners of magic arts
45 **makaris**   makers; a term for poets
50ff **Chaucer**, John Lydgate (the **Monk of Bery**), John **Gower** and a few of the others mentioned were prominent poets, but not all.
81 **done roune**   conversed

He has tane Roull of Aberdene
And gentill Roull of Corstorphin.
Two bettir fallowis did no man se.
Timor mortis conturbat me.   80

In Dunfermelyne he has done roune
With Maister Robert Henrisoun;
Schir Johne the Ros enbrast has he.
Timor mortis conturbat me.

And he has now tane last of aw   *all* 85
Gud gentill Stobo and Quintyne Schaw.
Of quham all wichtis has pete.   *people / pity*
Timor mortis conturbat me.

Gud Maister Walter Kennedy
In poynt of dede lyis veraly.   90
Gret reuth it wer that so suld be.   *grief*
Timor mortis conturbat me.

Sen he has all my breyer tane,   *since*
He will naught lat me lif alane:
On forse I man his nyxt pray be.   *must* 95
Timor mortis conturbat me.

Sen for the ded remeid is none,   *remedy*
Best is that we for dede dispone,   *prepare*
Eftir our deid that lif may we.
Timor mortis conturbat me.   100
                                                        1508

ANONYMOUS LYRICS

[Westron wynde, when wyll thow blow]

Westron wynde, when wyll thow blow,   *western*
The smalle rayne downe can rayne.
Cryst if my love were in my armys,   *arms*
And I yn my bed agayne.
                        ?Early 16th century 1792

A Lyke-wake Dirge

This ae nighte, this ae nighte,   *one*
    Every night and alle;
Fire and fleet, and candle lighte,
    And Christe receive thye saule.   *soul*

---

81 **done roune**   conversed
Lyke-wake   body-watch: nightwatch over a dead body
3 **Fire and fleet**   fire and house room (legal phrase); fleet means floor

When thou from hence away are paste,   5
  Every nighte and alle;
To Whinny-muir thou comest at laste;   *Gorse-moor*
  And Christe receive thye saule.

If ever thou gavest hosen and shoon,   *stockings / shoes*
  Every nighte and alle,   10
Sit thee down, and put them on;
  And Christe receive thye saule.

If hosen and shoon thou ne'er gavest nane,
  Every nighte and alle:
The whinnes shall pricke thee to the bare bane   *bone*   15
  And Christe receive thye saule.

From Whinny-muir when thou mayst passe,
  Every nighte and alle;
To Brigg o'Dread thou comest at laste;   *bridge*
  And Christe receive thye saule.   20

From Brigg o'Dread when thou mayst passe,
  Every nighte and alle;
To purgatory fire thou comest at laste;
  And Christe receive thye saule.

If ever thou gavest meate or drinke,   25
  Every night and alle;
The fire shall never make thee shrinke;
  And Christe receive thye saule.

If meate or drinke thou never gavest nane,
  Every nighte and alle;
The fire will burn thee to the bare bane;   30
  And Christe receive thye saule.

This ae nighte, this ae nighte,
  Every nighte and alle;
Fire and fleet, and candle lighte,
  And Christe receive thye saule.   35

           ?Early 16th century   1802

The Corpus Christi Carol

Lully lulley lully lulley
The fawcon hath born my mak away.   *mate*

He bare hym up, he bare hym down,   *bore*
He bare hym into an orchard brown.

In that orchard ther was an hall,   5
That was hangid with purpill and pall.

And in that hall ther was a bede,
Hit was hangid with gold so rede.

---

6 purpill and pall rich, purple cloth (formulaic phrase): purple included crimson, the colour of royalty.

And yn that bed ther lythe a knyght,
His wowndes bledyng day and nyght.   10

By that bedes side ther kneleth a may,   *maiden*
And she wepeth both nyght and day.

And by that beddes side ther stondith a ston,
'Corpus Christi' wreten theron.   *body of Christ*

                  Early 16th century   1903

[Farewell this world, I take my leve for ever]

Farewell this world, I take my leve for ever,
I am arrestid to appere affore Godis face.
O mercyfull God, thow knowest that I had lever   *rather*
Than all this worldis good to have an owre space   *hour*
For to make aseth for my gret trespace.   *reparationy* 5
My harte, alas, is brokyn for that sorow.
Som be this day that shall not be tomorrow.

This world, I see, is but a chery fayre,
All thyngis passith and so moste I algate.   *must / indeed*
This day I satt full royally in a chayre   10
Tyll sotyll deth knokkid at my gate   *subtle*
And unavised he said to me, 'Chekmate.'   *with no warning*
Loo, how sodynly he maketh a devorce
And wormes to fede, here he hath layde my corse.   *corpse*

Speke softe, ye folkis, for I am layde aslepe.   15
I have my dreme, in truste is myche treason.
From dethis hold fayn wold I make a lepe   *gladly*
But my wisdom ys torned into feble reason:
I see this worldis joye lastith but a season.
Wold God I had remembrid this beforne.   20
I say no more but beware of an horne.   *trumpet*

This fekyll world, so false and so unstable,
Promoteth his lovers but for a lytill while,
But at the last he geveth them a bable   *bauble*
Whan his payntid trowth is torned into gile.   *turned / guile* 25
Experyence cawsith me the trowth to compile,   *formulate*
Thynkyng this: too late, alas, that I began,
For foly and hope disseyveth many a man.   *deceives*

Farewell my frendis, the tide abidith no man.
I moste departe hens and so shall ye,   30
But in this passage the beste songe that I can   *know*
Is Requiem Eternam. I pray God grant it me.   *rest eternal*

Farewell this world   Versions of the last stanza of this poem can still be seen on some early gravestones.
8 chery fayre   fair held in the brief cherry season
25 payntid   painted, i.e. artificial   **trowth**   both pledge and truth
29 tide   both time and tide

Whan I have endid all myn adversite
Graunte me in paradise to have a mancyon,
That shede his blode for my redempcion.   35
    Beati mortui qui in domino moriuntur.
    Humiliatus sum vermis.

Late 15th century

[I syng of a myden]

I syng of a myden   *maiden*
That is makeles,
Kyng of alle kynges
To here sone che ches.   *her / she chose*

He cam also stylle   *just as*   5
Ther his moder was   *where / mother*
As dew in Aprylle
That fallyt on the gras.

He cam also stylle
To his moderes bowr   10
As dew in Aprille
That fallyt on the flour.   *flower*

He cam also stylle
Ther his moder lay
As dew in Aprille   15
That fallyt on the spray.

Moder and maydyn
Was never non but che,
Wel may swych a lady   *such*
Godis moder be.   20

Early 15th century

[I have a gentil cok]

I have a gentil cok   *noble*
Crowyt me day;   *crows*
He doth me rysyn erly
My matyins for to say.

I have a gentil cok,   5
Comyn he is of gret;
His comb is of reed corel   *red coral*
His tayil is of get.   *jet*

I have a gentyl cok,
Comyn he is of kynde;   10
His comb is of red corel
His tayl is of inde.   *indigo*

36–37 'Blessed are the dead who die in the Lord. I am brought low with the worms.' (From the *Office for the Dead.*)
2 makeless   immaculate; also matchless, in both senses: peerless and mate-less
4 matyins   (matins) morning prayer
6 He comes of great lineage.
10 He comes of good natural stock.

His legges ben of asor	*azure*
So geintil and so smale;	*slender*
His spores arn of sylver qwyt	*spurs / white* 15
Into the wortewale.	*root*

His eynyn arn of cristal,	*eyes are*
Lokyn al in aumbyr;	*set / amber*
And every nyht he perchit hym	
In myn ladyis chaumbyr.	20

Early 15th century

[Sumer is icumen in]

Sumer is icumen in:	*has come*
Lhude sing cuccu.	*loudly*
Groweth sed and bloweth med	
And springth the wde nu.	*wood now*
Sing cuccu.	5

Awe bleteth after lomb,	*ewe*
Lhouth after calve cu,	*lows / cow*
Bulluc sterteth, bucke verteth.	*leaps / farts*
Murie sing cuccu.	
Cuccu, cuccu,	10
Wel singes thu cuccu.	*thou*
Ne swik thu naver nu.	*nor cease*

Sing cuccu nu, sing cuccu.
Sing cuccu, sing cuccu nu.

Mid 13th century

[Foweles in the frith]

Foweles in the frith,	*birds / wood*
The fisses in the flod,	
And I mon waxe wod.	*must grow mad*
Mulch sorw I walke with	*much sorrow*
For beste of bon and blod.	5

Early 13th century

[Nou goth sonne under wod]

Nou goth sonne under wod:	
Me reweth, Marie, thi faire rode.	*I pity / face*
Nou goth sonne under tre:	
Me reweth, Marie, thi sone and thee.	

Early 13th century

---

3 Seed grows and meadow blooms
Foweles in the frith   Taken by some to be a courtly lyric of unrequited love; by others, to refer to Christ, as in Matt. 8:20: 'The foxes have holes and the birds of the air have nests; but the Son of man hath not where to lay his head.'
5 **For** because of **beste** best; also beast.
1 Now goes sun under wood; also son
2 **rode** complexion (i.e. face); also cross

GEOFFREY CHAUCER

?1343–1400 b London. He spent much of his life in senior government service, in London, and in a number of visits abroad to Italy and France.

From The Canterbury Tales

From *The General Prologue*

Whan that Averyll with his shoures soote — *April / sweet*
The droghte of March hath perced to the roote
And bathed every veyne in swich lycour — *such / liquid*
Of which vertu engendred is the flour, — *power / flower*
Whan zephirus eek with his sweete breeth — *western breeze* 5
Inspired hath in every holt and heeth — *wood*
The tendre croppes, and the yonge sonne — *shoots*
Hath in the Ram his half cours yronne,
And smale foweles maken melodye — *birds*
That slepen al the nyght with open eye— 10
So priketh hem nature in hir corages— — *them / hearts*
Thanne longen folk to goon on pilgrymages, — *then / go*
And Palmeres for to seeken straunge strondes — *foreign shores*
To ferne halwes, kouthe in sondry londes, — *distant shrines / known*
And specially from every shyres ende 15
Of Engelond to Caunterbury they wende, — *go*
The holy blisful martir for to seke
That hem hath holpen whan that they weere seeke. — *helped / sick*
Bifel that in that sesoun on a day — *it befell*
In Southwerk at the Tabard as I lay — *lodged* 20
Redy to weenden on my pilgrymage
To Caunterbury with ful devout corage,
At nyght was come in to that hostelrye
Wel nyne and twenty in a compaignye,
Of sondry folk, by aventure yfalle — *chance / fallen* 25
In felaweshipe, and pilgrymes weere they alle
That toward Caunterbury wolden ryde. — *would*
The chambres and the stables weeren wyde, — *bedrooms*
And wel we weeren esed at the beste, — *given best comforts*
And shortly whan the sonne was to reste, — *sun* 30
So hadde I spoken with hem everichoon — *every one*
That I was of hir felaweshipe anon, — *their / at once*
And maade forward erly for to ryse — *agreed*
To take oure wey ther as I yow devyse. — *will relate*

* * *

The Canterbury Tales   These are tales told by pilgrims riding together to the shrine of St Thomas à Becket at Canterbury.
7–8 The sun starts the solar year in Aries (the Ram).
13 palmeres   professional pilgrims
20 Tabard   name of an inn   **Southwerk**   a district at the edge of London

The Nun's Priest's Tale

A poore widwe somdel stape in age	*widow somewhat advanced*
Was whilom dwellynge in a narwe cotage	*once / small*
Biside a grove, stondyng in a dale.	
This widwe of which I telle yow my tale	
Syn thilke day that she was last a wyf	*since that* 5
In pacience ladde a ful symple lyf,	*led*
For litel was hir catel and hir rente.	*possessions / income*
By housbondrye of swich as god hir sente	*careful use / such*
She foond hirself and eek hir doghtren two.	*provided for / also*
Thre large sowes hadde she and namo,	*no more* 10
Thre kyn and eek a sheep that highte Malle.	*cows / was named*
Ful sooty was hir bour and eek hir halle	*bower*
In which she eet ful many a sklendre meel.	*slender*
Of poynaunt sawce hir neded never-a-deel,	*pungent*
No deyntee morsel passed thurgh hir throte:	15
Hir diete was acordant to hir cote.	*cottage*
Repleccioun ne made hir nevere syk:	*surfeit*
Attempree diete was al hir phisyk	*temperate / medication*
And exercise and hertes suffisaunce.	*heart's*
The gowte lette hir nothyng for to daunce,	*gout hindered* 20
N'apoplexie shente nat hir heed.	*injured / head*
No wyn ne drank she, neither whit ne reed.	
Hir bord was served moost with whit and blak,	*table*
Milk and broun breed in which she foond no lak,	
Seynd bacoun, and somtyme an ey or tweye	*Singed / egg / two* 25
For she was as it were a maner deye.	*kind of dairywoman*
A yeerd she hadde enclosed al aboute	*yard*
With stikkes and a drye dych withoute	*stakes*
In which she hadde a cok heet Chauntecler.	*named*
In al the land of crowyng nas his peer.	*was not* 30
His voys was murier than the myrie orgon	
On massedayes that in the chirche gon.	*goes*
Wel sikerer was his crowyng in his logge	*truer / lodge*
Than is a clokke or any abbey-orlogge.	*abbey-clock*
By nature he krew ech ascencioun	35
Of equinoxial in thilke town:	
For whan degrees XV were ascended	
Thanne krew he that it myghte nat ben amended.	*crowed / improved*
His komb was redder than the fyn coral	
And batayled as it were a castel-wal,	*crenellated* 40
His byle was blak and as the jeet it shoon,	*bill / jet*
Lyk asure were hise legges and his toon,	*toes*
Hise nayles whitter than the lylye-flour	
And lyk the burned gold was his colour.	*burnished*

---

23 whit and blak i.e. milk and bread
35–36 By nature he knew each step in the equinoxial (i.e. each hour).
37 i.e. one hour: fifteen degrees in the revolution of the celestial equator

This gentil cok hadde in his governaunce   45
Sevene hennes for to doon al his plesaunce
Whiche were hise sustres and his paramours
And wonder lyke to hym as of colours.
Of whiche the faireste hewed on hire throte   *hued*
Was clepid faire damoysele Pertelote.   *named* 50
Curteys she was, discret and debonaire,
And compaignable, and bar hirself so faire
Syn thilke day that she was seven nyght oold
That trewely she hath the herte in hoold   *hold*
Of Chauntecler, loken in every lyth.   *locked / limb* 55
He loved hir so that wel was hym therwith.
But swich a joye was it to here hem synge,
Whan that the brighte sonne gan to sprynge,
In swete acord, 'My leef is faren in londe':
For thilke tyme as I have understonde   60
Beestes and briddes kouden speke and synge.   *birds*
    And so bifel that in a dawenynge,   *dawning*
As Chauntecler among his wyves alle
Sat on his perche that was in the halle
And next hym sat this faire Pertelote,   65
This Chauntecler gan gronen in his throte   *began to groan*
As man that in his dreem is drecched soore.   *troubled*
    And whan that Pertelote thus herde hym rore
She was agast, and seyde, 'Herte deere,
What eyleth yow to grone in this manere?   70
Ye ben a verray sleper, fy for shame.'
    And he answerde and seyde thus: 'Madame,
I pray yow that ye take it nat agrief.
By god me mette I was in swich meschief
Right now that yet myn herte is soore afright.   75
Now god,' quod he, 'my swevene recche aright   *dream / interpret*
And kepe my body out of foul prisoun.
Me mette how that I romed up and doun
Withinne oure yeerd where as I say a beest
Was lyk an hound and wolde han maad arest   *would have* 80
Upon my body and han had me ded.   *have had*
His colour was bitwixe yelow and red
And tipped was his tayl and bothe hise erys   *ears*
With blak, unlik the remenaunt of hise herys.   *hairs*
His snowte smal with glowyng eyen tweye.   85
Yet of his look for fere almoost I deye.
This caused me my gronyng douteles.'
    'Avoy,' quod she 'fy on yow hertelees.
Allas,' quod she, 'for by that god above
Now han ye lost myn herte and al my love.   90

---

59 'My love is gone away': a popular song
71 You are a true sleeper
74 **me mette** I dreamed
88 **avoy** fie

I kan nat love a coward by my feith.
For certes whatso any womman seith,   *certainly*
We alle desiren if it myghte be
To han housbondes hardy, wise and fre,   *generous*
And secree and no nygard ne no fool,   *discreet* 95
Ne hym that is agast of every tool,   *weapon*
Ne noon avauntour. By that god above   *no boaster*
How dorste ye seyn for shame unto youre love   *dare*
That anythyng myghte make yow aferd?
Have ye no mannes herte and han a berd?   *beard* 100
Allas and konne ye ben agast of swevenys?
    'Nothyng, god woot, but vanytee in swevene is.   *knows*
Swevenes engendren of replexions
And ofte of fume, and of complexions   *vapour / mixed humours*
Whan humours ben to habundant in a wight.   *too / person* 105
Certes this dreem which ye han met tonyght   *dreamed*
Comth of the grete superfluitee
Of youre rede colera pardee,   *assuredly*
Which causeth folk to dreden in hir dremes
Of arwes and of fyr with rede lemes,   *arrows / flames* 110
Of rede bestes that they wol hem byte,
Of contek and of whelpes grete and lyte;   *strife / whelps*
Right as the humour of malencolie
Causeth ful many a man in sleep to crie
For fere of blake beres or boles blake,   *bears / bulls* 115
Or ellis blake develes wol hem take.   *else / will*
Of othere humours koude I telle also
That werken many a man in sleep ful wo,
But I wol passe as lightly as I kan.
Lo Catoun which that was so wys a man   120
Seyde he nat thus: Ne do no fors of dremes?   *give no attention*
    'Now, sire,' quod she, 'whan we fle fro thise bemes   *fly / beams*
For goddes love as taak som laxatif.
Up peril of my soule and of my lif   *upon*
I conseile yow the beste, I wol nat lye,   125
That bothe of coler and of malencolye
Ye purge yow. And for ye shal nat tarye,
Thogh in this town is noon apothecarye,   *no*
I shal myself to herbes techen yow
That shul ben for youre heele and for youre prow;   *health / benefit* 130
And in oure yerd tho herbes shal I fynde   *those*
The whiche han of hir propretee by kynde
To purge yow bynethe and eek above.
Foryet nat this for goddes owene love.   *forget*

---

103 Dreams spring from overeating.
105 ff. Pertelote's diagnosis follows the contemporary theory that a predominance of one of the four humours in the body is the cause of each of the four basic temperaments—in Chauntecler's case the choleric, from red choler, or red bile (line 108).
113 humour of malencolie i.e. black bile
120 Catoun Dionysius Cato, supposed author of *Disticha Catonis*, a book of maxims

Ye ben ful colerik of complexioun: 135
Ware the sonne in his ascencioun   *beware*
Ne fynde yow nat replet of humours hote;   *hot*
And if it do, I dar wel leye a grote   *lay a coin*
That ye shul have a fevere terciane
Or an agew that may be youre bane. 140
A day or two ye shul han degestyves
Of wormes, er ye take youre laxatyves
Of lauriol, centaur and fumetere,
Or ellis of ellebor that groweth there,
Of katapuce or of gaytrys beryis, 145
Of herbe-yve growyng in oure yerd ther merye is.
Pekke hem up right as they growe and ete hem in.
Be myrie, housbonde, for youre fader kyn.   *father*
Dredeth no dreem. I kan sey yow namoore.'
   'Madame,' quod he, 'grant mercy of youre loore. 150
But nathelees as touchyng daun Catoun   *nevertheless*
That hath of wisdom swich a gret renoun
Thogh that he bad no dremes for to drede,   *bade*
By god men may in olde bokes rede
Of many a man moore of auctoritee 155
Than evere Caton was, so mote I thee,   *may I thrive*
That al the revers seyn of his sentence   *opinion*
And han wel founden by experience
That dremes ben signyficaciouns
As wel of joye as tribulaciouns 160
That folk enduren in this lyf present.
Ther nedeth make of this noon argument;
The verray preve sheweth it in dede.   *very experience*
   'Oon of the gretteste auctour that men rede
Seith thus: that whilom two felawes wente 165
On pilgrymage in a ful good entente,
And happed so they coomen in a town
Where as ther was swich congregacioun
Of peple and eek so streit of herbergage   *restricted of lodging*
That they ne founde as muche as o cotage   *one* 170
In which they bothe myghte ylogged be.   *lodged*
Wherfore they mosten of necessitee   *must*
As for that nyght departe compaignye;
And ech of hem gooth to his hostelrye
And took his loggyng as it wolde falle. 175
That oon of hem was logged in a stalle
Fer in a yeerd with oxen of the plow.   *far*
That oother man was logged wel ynow   *enough*
As was his aventure or his fortune   *chance*
That us governeth alle as in commune.   *in general* 180

---

139 fevere terciane tertian fever: a fever occurring every other day
146 Ther merye is where it is pleasant
150 Thank you for your advice.
164 ff. This story could be from either Cicero or Valerius Maximus, both classical Latin authors.

And so bifel that longe er it were day
This man mette in his bed ther as he lay   *dreamed*
How that this felawe gan upon hym calle
And seyde, "Allas for in an oxes stalle
This nyght I shal be mordred ther I lye.   *murdered where* 185
Now help me, deere brother, or I dye.
In alle haste com to me," he sayde.
 'This man out of his sleep for feere abrayde.   *started up*
But whan that he was wakned of his sleep
He turned hym and took of this no keep: 190
Hym thoughte his dreem nas but a vanytee.   *was not*
Thus twies in his slepyng dremed he,
And atte thridde tyme yet his felawe
Cam as hym thoughte and seyde, "I am now slawe.   *slain*
Bihoold my blody woundes depe and wyde.   195
Arys up erly in the morewe tyde   *morning time*
And atte west gate of the town," quod he,   *said*
"A carte ful of donge ther shaltow se   *dung / shall you see*
In which my body is hyd ful prively.
Do thilke cart aresten boldely.   200
My gold caused my mordre sooth to seyn,"   *truth to say*
And tolde hym every poynt how he was sleyn
With a ful pitous face pale of hewe.
And truste wel his dreem he fond ful trewe,
For on the morwe as soone as it was day   205
To his felawes in he took the way;   *inn*
And whan that he cam to this oxes stalle
After his felawe he bigan to calle.
 'The hostiler answerde hym anon
And seyde: "Sire, youre felawe is agon.   210
As soone as day he wente out of the town."
 'This man gan fallen in suspecioun
Remembrynge on hise dremes that he mette,
And forth he goth, no lenger wolde he lette,   *delay*
Unto the west gate of the town and fond   215
A dong-carte wente as it were to donge lond   *land*
That was arrayed in that same wise
As ye han herd the dede man devyse.
And with an hardy herte he gan to crye
"Vengeaunce and justice of this felonye.   220
My felawe mordred is this same nyght
And in this cart heere he lyth gapyng upright.
I crye on the mynystres," quod he,
"That sholde kepe and rulen this citee:
Harrow, allas heere lyth my felawe slayne."   *help* 225
What sholde I moore unto this tale sayn?
The peple up sterte and caste the cart to grounde.   *started*
And in the myddel of the dong they founde

---

190 turned hym   i.e. turned in bed

The dede man that mordred was al newe.
'O blisful god that art so just and trewe,   230
Lo how that thow biwreyest mordre alway.   *disclose*
Mordre wol out, that se we day by day.
Mordre is so wlatsom and abhomynable   *loathsome*
To god, that is so just and resonable,
That he ne wol nat suffre it helyd be   *concealed* 235
Though it abyde a yeer or two or thre.
Mordre wol out, this my conclusioun.
And right-anon ministres of that town
Han hent the cartere and so soore hym pyned   *seized / tortured*
And eek the hostiler so sore engyned   *racked* 240
That they biknewe hir wikkednesse anon   *confessed their*
And were anhanged by the nekke-bon.   *bone*
Heere may men sen that dremes ben to drede.   *to be dreaded*
    'And certes in the same book I rede
Right in the nexte chapitre after this   245
(I gabbe nat so have I joye or blys)   *lie*
Two men that wolde han passed over see   *sea*
For certeyn cause into a fer contree
If that the wynd ne hadde ben contrarie
That made hem in a citee for to tarie   250
That stood ful myrie upon an haven-syde.   *harbour*
But on a day agayn the even-tyde   *toward*
The wynd gan chaunge and blew right as hem leste.   *they wished*
Jolif and glad they wenten unto reste
And casten hem ful erly for to sayle.   *arranged* 255
But herkneth, to that o man fil a gret mervaille.   *fell*
    'That oon of hem in slepyng as he lay
Hym mette a wonder dreem agayn the day.
Hym thoughte a man stood by his beddes syde
And hym comanded that he sholde abyde,   260
And seyde hym thus: "If thow tomorwe wende,
Thow shalt be dreynt. My tale is at an ende."
    'He wook and tolde his felawe what he mette
And preyde hym his viage to lette.   *voyage*
As for that day he preyde hym to byde.   265
    'His felawe that lay by his beddes syde
Gan for to laughe and scorned hym ful faste.
"No dreem," quod he, "may so myn herte agaste
That I wol lette for to do my thynges.
I sette nat a straw by thy dremynges   270
For swevenes ben but vanytees and japes.
Men dreme al day of owles or of apes,
And of many a maze therwithal.
Men dreme of thyng that nevere was ne shal.
But sith I see that thow wolt here abyde   275
And thus forslewthen wilfully thy tyde,   *idle away*
God woot it reweth me and have good day."   *I'm sorry*
And thus he took his leve and wente his way.
But er that he hadde half his cours yseyled,
Noot I nat why ne what meschaunce it eyled   *I don't know / ailed* 280

But casuelly the shippes botme rente	*by chance*
And ship and man under the water wente	
In sighte of othere shippes it bisyde	
That with hem seyled at the same tyde.	
'And therfore, faire Pertelote so deere,	285
By swiche ensamples old maystow leere	*may you learn*
That no man sholde ben to recchelees	*too reckless*
Of dremes, for I sey thee doutelees	
That many a dreem ful soore is for to drede.	
'Lo in the lyf of seint Kenelm I rede,	290
That was Kenulphus sone, the noble kyng	
Of Mercenrike, how Kenelm mette a thyng	*Mercia*
A lite er he was mordred on a day.	*little before*
His mordre in his avysion he say.	*saw*
His norice hym expowned every del	*nurse explained / detail* 295
His swevene and bad hym for to kepe hym wel	
For traysoun. But he nas but vii yeer old	*from*
And therfore litel tale hath he told	
Of any dreem, so holy was his herte.	
By god I hadde levere than my sherte	300
That ye hadde rad his legende as have I.	
Dame Pertelote, I sey yow trewely	
Macrobeus, that writ the avysioun	
In Affrike of the worthy Cipioun,	
Affermeth dremes and seith that they ben	305
Warnynge of thynges that men after sen.	*see*
'And forthermoore I pray yow looketh wel	
In the Olde Testament of Danyel	
If he heeld dremes any vanytee.	
Rede eek of Joseph and there shul ye see	310
Wher dremes be somtyme, I sey nat alle,	*whether*
Warnynge of thynges that sul after falle.	
Looke of Egipte the kyng, daun Pharao,	*master*
His bakere and his butiller also	*butler*
Wher they ne felte noon effect in dremes.	315
'Whoso wol seke actes of sondry remes	*realms*
May rede of dremes many a wonder thyng.	
Lo Cresus which that was of Lyde kyng	*Lydia*
Mette he nat that he sat upon a tree	
Which signyfide he sholde anhanged be.	320
Lo here Andromacha, Ectores wyf,	*Hector's*
That day that Ector sholde lese his lyf	*lose*
She dremed on the same nyght biforn	
How that the lyf of Ector sholde be lorn	*lost*

300 I had rather than my shirt: i.e. I'd give my shirt.
303–4 Macrobeus Macrobius, author of a commentary on Cicero's *Dream of Scipio* (**Cipioun**)
308 See Daniel 7.
310–15 See Genesis 37, 40 and 41.
321–28 This story from the Trojan War is from medieval (not classical) accounts.

If thilke day he wente into bataille.   325
She warned hym but it myghte nat availle:
He wente for to fighte natheless,
But he was slayn anon of Achilles.   *by*
   'But thilke tale is al to long to telle,
And eek it is ney day, I may nat dwelle.   *near* 330
Shortly I seye as for conclusion
That I shal han of this avysioun
Adversitee. And I seye forthermoor
That I ne telle of laxatyves no stoor,
For they ben venymes I woot it wel.   335
I hem deffie, I love hem never-a-del.   *them not a bit*
   'Now lat us speke of myrthe and stynte al this.   *stop*
Madame Pertelote, so have I blys
Of o thyng god hath sent me large grace.
For whan I se the beautee of youre face   340
Ye ben so scarlet reed aboute youre eyen
It maketh al my drede for to dyen:
For also siker as *In principio*   *sure*
Mulier est hominis confusio.
Madame, the sentence of this Latyn is: 345
Womman is mannes joye and al his blys.
For whan I feele a nyght youre softe syde,   *at*
Al be it that I may nat on yow ryde
For that oure perche is maad so narwe allas,
I am so ful of joye and of solas   350
That I deffie bothe swevene and dreem.'
   And with that word he fley doun fro the beem
For it was day, and eke hise hennes alle,
And with a chuk he gan hem for to calle
For he hadde founde a corn lay in the yerd.   355
Real he was, he was namoore aferd.   *regal / no more*
He fethered Pertelote twenty tyme
And trad as ofte er it was pryme.   *trod*
He looketh as it were a grym leoun,
And on hise toos he rometh up and doun.   360
Hym deyned nat to sette his foot to grounde
And chukketh whan he hath a corn yfounde
And to hym rennen thanne hise wyves alle.   *ran then*
Thus real as a prince is in his halle
Leve I this Chauntecler in his pasture,   365
And after wol I telle his aventure.
   Whan that the monthe in which the world bigan,
That highte March, whan god first maked man,

---

332 avysioun   vision: a divinely inspired dream, as distinct from the merely human swevene or dreem
343–44   In the beginning, woman is man's ruin (Latin). 'In principio' is biblical (John 1:1) and a familiar phrase from the Mass; Chauntecler adds the rest.
358 pryme   the hour of morning prayer, at dawn.
367–77   i.e. 9 a.m., 3 May

Was complet and passed were also
Syn March bigan 30 dayes and two,   370
Bifel that Chauntecler in al his pryde
Hise sevene wyves walkyng hym bisyde
Caste up hise eyen to the brighte sonne
That in the signe of Taurus hadde yronne   *run*
XX degrees and oon and somwhat moore,   375
And knew by kynde and by noon oother loore   *nature*
That it was pryme and krew with blisful stevene.   *voice*
'The sonne,' he seyde, 'is clomben upon hevene
40 degrees and oon and moore ywis.   *for certain*
Madame Pertelote my worldes blys,   380
Herkneth thyse blisful bryddes how they synge,   *birds*
And se the fresshe floures how they sprynge.
Ful is myn herte of revel and solas.'
But sodeynly hym fil a sorweful cas,   *befell / chance*
For evere the latter ende of joye is wo.   385
God woot that worldly joye is soone ago,
And if a rethor koude faire endite,   *rhetorician / compose*
He in a cronycle saufly myghte it write   *safely*
As for a sovereyn notabilitee.   *fact*
Now every wys man lat hym herkne me: *hearken to* 390
This storie is also trewe I undertake   *as*
As is the book of Launcelot de Lake
That wommen holde in ful gret reverence.
Now wol I torne agayn to my sentence.   *main point*
   A colfox ful of sley iniquitee   395
That in the grove hadde woned yeres thre,   *dwelt*
By heigh ymaginacioun forncast   *foreplanned*
The same nyght thurghout the hegges brast   *hedges / burst*
Into the yerd ther Chauntecler the faire   *where*
Was wont and eek hise wyves to repaire,   400
And in a bed of wortes stille he lay   *cabbages*
Til it was passed undren of the day,   *midmorning*
Waitynge his tyme on Chauntecler to falle
As gladly doon thise homycides alle   *do*
That in awayt liggen to mordre men.   *lie* 405
O false mordrour lurkynge in thy den,
O newe Scariot, newe Genylon,
False dissimilour, o Greek Synoun   *dissembler*
That broghtest Troye al outrely to sorwe.   *utterly*
O Chauntecler acursed be that morwe   410
That thow into the yerd flaugh fro the bemys: *beams*
Thow were ful wel ywarned by thy dremys

---

392 **Launcelot de Lake**   a popular romance
395 **colfox**   fox with black-tipped ears and tail
407 **Scariot**   Judas Iscariot   **Genylon**   Genelon, the betrayer of Roland in the medieval French
epic *The Song of Roland*
408 **Synoun**   Sinon, originator of the ruse of the Trojan horse: see *Aeneid* II.

That thilke day was perilous to thee.
But what that god forwoot moot nedes be,   *foreknew / must*
After the opynyoun of certeyn clerkis.   *clerics*   415
Witnesse on hym that any parfit clerk is   *perfect*
That in scole is gret altercacioun   *university*
In this matere and gret disputisoun
And hath ben of an hundred thousand men.
But I ne kan nat bulte it to the bren   *sift / husks*   420
As kan the holy doctour Augustyn
Or Boece or the bisshop Bradwardyn
Wheither that goddes worthy forewityng   *foreknowing*
Streyneth me nedely for to doon a thyng   *constrains / necessarily*
('Nedely' clepe I symple necessitee)   *call*   425
Or ellis if fre choys be graunted me   *else*
To do that same thyng or do it noght
Though god forwoot it er that I was wroght;   *wrought*
Or if his wityng streyneth never-a-del   *knowing*
But by necessitee condicionel.   430
I wol nat han to do of swich matere:
My tale is of a cok, as ye may heere,
That took his conseil of his wyf with sorwe
To walken in the yerd upon that morwe
That he hadde met the dreem that I yow tolde.   435
Wommens conseils be ful ofte colde:
Wommannes conseil broghte us first to wo
And made Adam fro paradys to go
Ther as he was ful myrie and wel at ese.
But, for I noot to whom it myghte displese   *I don't know*   440
If I conseil of wommen wolde blame,
Passe over, for I seyde it in my game.   *sport*
Rede auctours where they trete of swich matere
And what they seyn of wommen ye may heere;
Thise ben the cokkes wordes and nat myne.   445
I kan noon harm on no womman devyne.   *guess*
   Faire in the sond to bathe hir myrily   *sand*
Lyth Pertelote and alle hir sustres by
Agayn the sonne. And Chauntecler so free   *in*
Song myrier than the mermayde in the see,   450
For Phisiologus seith sikerly   *certainly*
How that they syngen wel and myrily.
And so bifel that as he caste his eye
Among the wortes on a boterflye
He was war of this fox that lay ful lowe.   *aware*   455
Nothyng ne liste hym thanne for to crowe,

420–21 Augustyn (St Augustine, 354–430), **Boece** (Boethius, c. 470–525) and **Bradwardyn**
(Thomas Bradwardine, c. 1290–1349, an archbishop of Canterbury) all wrote on the theological question of God's fore-knowledge and human free will.
430 necessitee condicionel Boethius' theory of a necessity which included the operation of free
will
451 Phisiologus supposed author of a popular medieval bestiary
456 Nothyng ne liste hym nothing he wished

But cryde anon, 'Cok, cok', and up he sterte
As man that was affrayd in his herte,
For naturelly a beest desireth flee
Fro his contrarie if he may it see   460
Though he nevere erst hadde seye it with his eye.   *before / seen*
This Chauntecler whan he gan hym espye,
He wolde han fled but that the fox anon
Seyde, 'Gentil sire, allas wher wol ye gon?
Be ye affrayd of me that am youre freend?   465
Now certes I were worse than a feend
If I to yow wolde harm or vileynye.
I am nat come youre conseil for t'espye,   *private affairs*
But trewely the cause of my comynge
Was oonly for to herkne how that ye synge: 470
For trewely ye han as myrie a stevene
As any angel hath that is in hevene.
Therwith ye han in musyk moore feelynge
Than hadde Boece or any that kan synge.
My lord youre fader (god his soule blesse)   475
And eek youre moder of hir gentillesse   *gentility*
Han in myn hous yben to my gret ese.
And certes, sire, ful fayn wolde I yow plese.   *gladly*
    'But for men speke of syngynge I wol seye,
So mote I browke wel myne eyen tweye,   480
Save ye I herde nevere man so synge
As dide youre fader in the morwenynge.
Certes it was of herte al that he song.
And for to make his voys the moore strong
He wolde so peyne hym that with bothe hise eyen   *pain* 485
He moste wynke, so loude he wolde cryen,   *close*
And stonden on his typton therwithal
And strecche forth his nekke long and smal.
And eek he was of swich discrecioun
That ther nas no man in no regioun   490
That hym in song or wisdom myghte passe.
I have wel rad in daun Burnell the asse
Among hise vers how that ther was a cok,
For a preestes sone yaf hym a knok   *gave*
Upon his leg whil he was yong and nyce   *foolish* 495
He made hym for to lese his benefice.   *lose*
But certeyn ther nys no comparisoun   *is not*
Bitwix the wisdom and discrecioun   *discernment*
Of youre fader and of his subtiltee.
Now syngeth, sire, for seynte charitee.   *holy* 500

---

474 Boethius wrote a treatise on music.
480 browke wel   retain the use of
492 daun Burnell the asse   title of a twelfth-century satirical poem by Nigel Wiriker
496 In Wiriker's poem, the disaffected cock crows late, so that his master misses the occasion of his ordination and hence a benefice (an income as a priest).

Lat se konne ye youre fader countrefete.'   *imitate*
  This Chauntecler hise wynges gan to bete
As man that koude his trayson nat espie,
So was he ravysshed with his flaterie.
  Allas ye lordes, many a fals flatour   505
Is in youre court and many a losengeour   *liar*
That Plesen yow wel moore by my feyth
Than he that soothfastnesse unto yow seith.   *truth*
Redeth Ecclesiaste of flaterye.
Beth war, ye lordes, of hir trecherye.   510
  This Chauntecler stood hye upon his toos
Strecchynge his nekke and heeld hise eyen cloos
And gan to crowe lowde for the nones.   *for the occasion*
And daun Russell the fox stirte up atones   *at once*
And by the gargat hente Chauntecler   *throat* 515
And on his bak toward the wode hym beer   *wood*
For yet ne was ther no man that hym sewed.   *pursued*
  O destynee that mayst nat ben eschewed.
Allas that Chauntecler fly fro the bemes.
Allas his wif ne roghte nat of dremes.   *cared* 520
And on a Friday fil al this meschaunce.
  O Venus that art goddesse of plesaunce,
Syn that thy servant was this Chauntecler
And in thy servyce dide al his power
Moore for delit than world to multiplie,   525
Why woldestow suffre hym on thy day to dye?
  O Gaufred, deere maister soverayn,
That whan thy worthy kyng Richard was slayn
With shot, compleynedest his deth so soore,   *missile*
Why ne hadde I now thy sentence and thy loore   *wisdom / learning* 530
The Friday for to chide as diden ye?
For on a Friday soothly slayn was he.
Thanne wolde I shewe yow how that I kowde pleyne   *lament*
For Chaunteclerys drede and for his peyne.
  Certes swich cry ne lamentacioun   535
Was nevere of ladyes maad whan Ylioun
Was wonne and Pirrus with his streite swerd
Whanne he hadde hent kyng Priam by the berd
And slayn hym, as seith us Eneydos,   *Aeneid*
As maden alle the hennes in the cloos   540
Whan they hadde seyn of Chauntecler the sighte.
But sovereynly dame Pertelote shrighte

---

509 See Eccles. 12:10–18.
526 Friday was Venus' day, considered a day of bad luck.
527 Gaufred Geoffrey de Vinsauf, a medieval rhetorician whose works included a lament for the death of Richard I by a poisoned arrow
536 Ylioun Ilium, i.e. Troy
537 Pirrus Pyrrhus, the killer of Priam: see *Aeneid* II.

Ful louder than dide Hasdrubales wyf
Whan that hire housbonde hadde ylost his lyf
And that the Romayns hadden brend Cartage.   *burned*   545
She was so ful of torment and of rage   *madness*
That wilfully unto the fyr she sterte
And brende hirselven with a stedefast herte.
O woful hennes, right so cryden ye
As, whan that Nero brende the citee   550
Of Rome, cryden the senatours wyves
For that hir housbondes losten all hir lyves.
Withouten gilt this Nero hath hem slayn.
Now wol I turne to my tale agayn.
The sely widwe and eek hire doghtres two   *innocent*   555
Herden thise hennes crye and maken wo.
And out at dores stirten they anon
And seyen the fox toward the grove gon
And bar upon his bak the cok away
And criden, 'Out, harrow and weilaway,   560
Ha, ha, the fox.' And after hym they ran,
And eek with staves many another man.
Ran Colle oure dogge and Talbot and Gerland
And Malkyn with a distaf in hir hand.
Ran cow and calf and eek the verray hogges   565
So fered for berkynge of the dogges
And showtynge of the men and wommen eek:
They ronne so hem thoughte hir herte breek,
They yelleden as fendes doon in helle,
The dokes cryden as men wolde hem quelle   *ducks / kill*   570
The gees for feere flowen over the trees,   *flew*
Out of the hyve cam the swarm of bees.
So hydous was the noyse, a, benedicite,   *bless me*
Certes he, Jakke Straw, and his meynee   *company*
Ne made nevere showtes half so shrille   575
Whan that they wolden any Flemyng kille
As thilke day was maad upon the fox.
Of bras they broghten bemys and of box,
Of horn, of boon, in whiche they blewe and powped   *bone / tooted*
And therwithall they skryked and they howped.   580
It seemed as that hevene sholde falle.
Now, goode men, I prey yow herkneth alle
Lo how fortune turneth sodeynly.
The hope and pryde eek of hire enemy,
This cok that lay upon the foxes bak,   585
In al his drede unto the fox he spak

---

543 Hasdrubales wyf   the wife of Hasdrubal, the king of Carthage; they were both killed when the
Romans sacked the city in 146 BC.
574 Jakke Straw   Jack Straw, a leader of the Peasants' Revolt in 1381, which was partly directed
against immigrant Flemings
578 bemys trumpets   **box** boxwood

And seyde, 'Sire, if that I were as ye
Yit sholde I seyn, as wys god helpe me: *as surely as*
"Turneth ayein, ye proude cherles alle,   *turn back*
A verray pestilence upon yow falle.   590
Now I am come unto this wodes syde,
Maugree youre heed the cok shal here abyde.   *despite*
I wol hym ete in feith and that anon."'
   The fox answerde, 'In feith it shal be don.'
And as he spak that word, al sodeynly   595
This cok brak from his mouth delyverly   *deftly*
And hye upon a tree he fley anon.
   And whan the fox say that he was gon,   *saw*
'Allas,' quod he, 'o Chauntecler, allas
I have to yow,' quod he, 'ydon trespas   *done* 600
In as muche as I maked yow aferd
Whan I yow hente and broghte into this yerd.
But, sire, I dide it in no wikke entente.   *wicked intent*
Com doun and I shal telle yow what I mente.
I shal seye sooth to yow god help me so.'   605
   'Nay, thanne,' quod he, 'I shrewe us bothe two.   *curse*
And first I shrewe myself bothe blood and bones,
If thow bigile me any ofter than ones.
Thow shalt namoore thurgh thy flaterye
Do me to synge and wynken with myn eye,   *cause me* 610
For he that wynketh whan he sholde see
Al wilfully, god lat hym nevere thee.'   *thrive*
   'Nay,' quod the fox, 'but god yeve hym meschaunce
That is so undiscret of governaunce   *self-control*
That jangleth whan he sholde holde his pees.'   *chatters* 615
   Lo swich it is for to be recchelees
And necligent and truste on flaterye.
But ye that holden this tale a folye
As of a fox or of a cok and hen,
Taketh the moralitee, goode men.   620
For seint Poul seith that al that writen is
To oure doctryne it is ywrite ywis.
Taketh the fruyt and lat the chaf be stille.
Now goode god, if that it be thy wille,
As seith my lord so make us alle goode men   625
And bring us to his heye bliss. Amen.

1390s *?1478*

621–22 See Rom. 15:4.

WILLIAM LANGLAND

?1330–?1390 b Shropshire (possibly). Nothing certain is known about his life.

From Piers Plowman

In a somer seson whan soft was the sonne	
I shope me in shroudes as I a shepe were;	
In habite as an heremite unholy of workes	
Went wyde in this world wondres to here.	*hear*
Ac on a May mornynge on Malverne hulles	*but / hills* 5
Me byfel a ferly, of fairy me thoughte:	
I was wery forwandred and went me to reste	
Under a brode banke bi a bornes side,	*stream's*
And as I lay and lened and loked in the wateres,	
I slombred in a slepyng, it sweyved so merye.	*sounded* 10
Thanne gan I to meten a merveilouse swevene,	
That I was in a wildernesse, wist I never where.	*knew*
As I bihelde into the est, an hiegh to the sonne,	
I seigh a toure on a toft, trielich ymaked;	
A depe dale binethe, a dongeon thereinne	15
With depe dyches and derke and dredful of sight.	
A faire felde ful of folke fonde I there bytwene,	*found*
Of alle maner of men, the mene and the riche,	*poor*
Worchyng and wandryng as the worlde asketh.	*requires*
Some putten hem to the plow, pleyed ful selde,	*seldom* 20
In settyng and in sowyng swonken ful harde,	
And wonnen that wastours with glotonye destruyeth.	
And some putten hem to pruyde, apparailed hem thereafter,	*pride / accordingly*
In contenaunce of clothyng comen disgised.	*display / came*
In prayers and in penance putten hem manye,	25
Al for love of owre Lorde lyveden ful streyte,	*rigorously*
In hope forto have heveneriche blisse;	*kingdom of heaven's*
As ancres and heremites that holden hem in here selles,	*anchorites / their cells*
And coveiten nought in contre to kairen aboute,	*desire / travel*
For no likerous liflode her lykam to plese.	30
And somme chosen chaffare; they cheven the bettere,	*trade / prosper*
As it semeth to owre syght that suche men thryveth;	

Piers Plowman A long allegorical fusion of satire, mysticism and theology, which exists in three versions now considered to be by one author. The extract here is the opening of the poem, from the B-text.
2 I dressed in garments as if I were a shepherd (or a sheep).
6 ferly marvel **of fairy** magic
7 forwandred gone astray
11 Then I dreamed a dream of marvels.
14–17 The **toure** is an emblem of heaven, the **depe dale** of hell, and the **faire felde** of the world.
14 I saw a tower on a hill, elegantly made.
20 hem them; i.e. themselves
22 And produced what wastrels destroy in gluttony.
30 likerous liflode luxurious living **her lykam** their body

And somme murthes to make as mynstralles conneth,   *mirth / know how to*
And geten gold with here glee giltles, I leve.   *their music / believe*
Ac japers and jangelers, Judas chylderen,   *jesters and chatterers* 35
Feynen hem fantasies and foles hem maketh,
And han here witte at wille to worche, yif thei sholde;
That Poule precheth of hem I nel nought preve it here;   *Paul / will not prove*
Qui turpiloquium loquitur etc. is Luciferes hyne.   *servant*
   Bidders and beggeres fast about yede   *went* 40
With her bely and her bagge of bred ful ycrammed;
Fayteden for here fode, foughten atte ale;   *alehouse*
In glotonye, God it wote, gon hij to bedde,
And risen with ribaudye, tho roberdes knaves;   *debauchery / robbers*
Slepe and sori sleuthe seweth hem evre.   *wretched sloth / pursue* 45
   Pilgrymes and palmers plighted hem togidere   *pledged*
To seke seynt James and seyntes in Rome.
Thei went forth in here wey with many wise tales,
And hadden leve to lye al here lyf after.
I seigh somme that seiden thei had ysought seyntes: *said* 50
To eche a tale that thei tolde here tonge was tempred to lye
More than to sey soth, it semed bi here speche.   *truth*
   Heremites on an heep, with hoked staves,
Wenten to Walsyngham, and here wenches after;
Grete lobyes and longe that loth were to swynke   *lubbers / tall* 55
Clotheden hem in copis, to ben knowen fram othere,   *copes*
And shopen hem heremites here ese to have.
   I fonde there freris, alle the foure ordres,   *friars*
Preched the peple for profit of hemselven,
Glosed the gospel as hem good lyked,   *interpreted* 60
For coveitise of copis construed it as thei wolde.
Many of this maistres freris mowe clothen hem at lykyng,   *these master friars can*
For here money and marchandise marchen togideres,
For sith charite hath be chapman and chief to shryve lordes
Many ferlis han fallen in a fewe yeris.   *happened* 65
But holychirche and hij holde better togideres,
The most myschief on molde is mountyng wel faste.   *greatest / on earth*
   There preched a pardonere as he a prest were;   *as if*
Broughte forth a bulle with bishopes seles,   *proclamation*
And seide that hymself myghte assoilen hem alle   *absolve* 70
Of falshed of fastyng, of vowes ybroken.

---

36 Invent outlandish tales and make fools of themselves.
37 han here witte have their intelligence   **yif thei sholde** if they would
39 Adapted from Eph. 5:4: 'Neither filthiness, nor foolish talking ... but rather the giving of thanks.'
40 Bidders beadsmen, i.e. professional prayer-sayers
43 it wote knows it   **hij** they
46 palmers those who have been on pilgrimage to the Holy Land, whose emblem is a palm; also any continually travelling pilgrim
47 seynte James the shrine of Santiago at Compostella in Spain
54 Walsyngham a famous shrine of Mary in Norfolk
58 foure ordres Carmelites, Augustinians, Dominicans and Franciscans
64 Since Charity has been a peddler, and especially to shrive lords.
66 But unless
68 pardonere one who sells indulgences

Lewed men leved hym wel and lyked his wordes;   *ignorant men believed*
Comen up knelyng to kissen his bulles.
He bonched hem with his brevet and blered here eyes   *banged / dimmed*
And raughte with his ragman rynges and broches.   75
Thus they geven here golde glotones to kepe.   *give*
And leveth such loseles that lecherye haunten.
Were the bischop yblissed and worth bothe his eres,   *ears*
His seel shulde nought be sent to deceyve the peple.
Ac it is naught by the bischop that the boy precheth,   *fellow* 80
For the parisch prest and the pardonere parten the silver
That the poraille of the parish sholde have, yif thei nere.   *poor*

ANONYMOUS BALLADS

These narrative poems were composed for singing, over a period that reaches from medieval times to the eighteenth century. They were transmitted orally in a non-literate culture, and polished and altered over generations: the versions presented here come from the end of that period, from collections such as those by Bishop Thomas Percy (1765) and Sir Walter Scott (1802), both of whom sometimes amended the material. Numberings are given from the standard collection by Francis James Child, *The English and Scottish Popular Ballads* (1882–98).

The Three Ravens

There were three Ravens sat on a tree,
    Down a downe, hay down, hay downe,
There were three Ravens sat on a tree,
    With a downe
There were three Ravens sat on a tree,   5
They were as blacke as they might be,
    With a downe derrie, derrie, derrie, downe, downe.

The one of them said to his make,   *mate*
Where shall we our breakefast take?

Downe in yonder greene field   10
There lies a Knight slain under his shield.

His hounds they lie downe at his feete,
So well they can their Master keepe.

His Haukes they flie so eagerly
There's no fowle dare him come nie.   15

---

74 **brevet** letter of indulgence
75 And raked in with his roll rings and brooches.
77 And believe such wastrels that practise lechery.
82 **yif thei nere** if they (i.e. these individuals) were not

Downe there comes a fallow Doe
As great with yong as she might goe.

She lift up his bloudy hed
And kist his wounds that were so red.

She got him up upon her backe   20
And carried him to earthen lake.

She buried him before the prime,
She was dead her selfe ere even-song time.

God send every gentleman
Such haukes, such hounds, and such a Leman.   *lover*

Child no. 26 1611

The Twa Corbies

As I was walking all alane,
I heard twa corbies making a mane;   *ravens / moan*
The tane unto the t'other say,   *the one*
Where sall we gang and dine to-day?   *go*

In behint yon auld fail dyke,   *turf ditch* 5
I wot there lies a new-slain knight;   *know*
And naebody kens that he lies there,   *knows*
But his hawk, his hound, and his lady fair.

His hound is to the hunting gane,
His hawk, to fetch the wild-fowl hame,   10
His lady's ta'en another mate,
So we may mak our dinner sweet.

Ye'll sit on his white hause-bane,   *neck-bone*
And I'll pike out his bonny blue een.   *eyes*
Wi' ae lock o' his gowden hair,   *with one* 15
We'll theek our nest when it grows bare.   *thatch*

Mony a one for him makes mane,
But nane sall ken whare he is gane:
O'er his white banes, when they are bare,
The wind sall blaw for evermair.   20

Child no. 26   Scott 1803

Edward, Edward

Quhy dois your brand sae drop wi' bluid,   *why*
    Edward, Edward?
Quhy dois your brand sae drop wi' bluid?
    And quhy sae sad gang yee, O?   *go*
O, I hae killed my hauke sae guid,   *good* 5
    Mither, mither:
O, I hae killed my hauke sae guid:
    And I had nae mair bot hee, O.   *more*

---

16 fallow of a species of light-coloured deer
22 prime the time of monastic morning prayer, 6 am

Your haukis bluid was nevir sae reid,
        Edward, Edward: 10
Your haukis bluid was nevir sae reid,
        My deir son I tell thee, O.
O, I hae killed my reid-roan steid,
        Mither, mither:
O, I hae killed my reid-roan steid,   15
        That erst was sae fair and free, O.   *before*

Your steid was auld, and ye hae gat mair,
        Edward, Edward:
Your steid was auld, and ye hae gat mair,
        Sum other dule ye drie, O.   *grief / suffer* 20
O, I hae killed my fadir deir,
        Mither, mither:
O, I hae killed my fadir deir,
        Alas! and wae is me, O!

And quhatten penance wul ye drie for that,   *what* 25
        Edward, Edward?
And quhatten penance will ye drie for that?
        My deir son, now tell me, O.
Ile set my feit in yonder boat,
        Mither, mither: 30
Ile set my feit in yonder boat,
        And Ile fare ovir the sea, O.

And quhat wul ye doe wi' your towirs and your ha', *hall*
        Edward, Edward?
And quhat wul ye doe wi' your towirs and your ha,' 35
        That were sae fair to see, O?
Ile let them stand til they doun fa',
        Mither, mither:
Ile let them stand til they doun fa',
        For here nevir mair maun I bee, O.   *must* 40

And quhat wul ye leive to your bairns and your wife,
        Edward, Edward?
And quhat wul ye leive to your bairns and your wife,
        Quhan ye gang ovir the sea, O?
The warldis room, let thame beg throw life,   *world's* 45
        Mither, mither:
The warldis room, let thame beg throw life,
        For thame nevir mair wul I see, O.

And quhat wul ye leive to your ain mither deir,
        Edward, Edward?   50
And quhat wul ye leive to your ain mither deir?
        My deir son, now tell me, O.
The curse of hell frae me sall ye beir,
        Mither, mither:
The curse of hell frae me sall ye beir,   55
        Sic counseils ye gave to me, O.   *such*

Child no. 13B Percy 1765

Battle of Otterbourne

It fell about the Lammas tide   *time*
  When the muir-men win their hay,   *moor / dry*
The doughty Douglas bound him to ride
  Into England, to drive a prey.

He chose the Gordons and the Graemes,   5
  With them the Lindesays light and gay;
But the Jardines wald not with him ride
  And they rue it to this day.

And he has burn'd the dales of Tyne
  And part of Bambrough shire;   10
And three good towers on Reidswire fells,
  He left them all on fire.

And he march'd up to Newcastle
  And rode it round about:
O wha's the lord of this castle,   15
  Or wha's the lady o't?

But up spake proud Lord Percy then,
  And O but he spake hie: *high*
I am the lord of this castle,
  My wife's the lady gay.   20

If thou'rt the lord of this castle
  Sae weel it pleases me;
For ere I cross the Border fells
  The tane of us shall die.   *the one*

He took a lang spear in his hand,   25
  Shod with the metal free,
And for to meet the Douglas there
  He rode right furiouslie.

But O how pale his lady look'd
  Frae aff the castle wa',   30
When down before the Scottish spear
  She saw proud Percy fa'.

Had we twa been upon the green,
 • And never an eye to see,
I wad hae had you, flesh and fell;   *skin* 35
  But your sword sall gae wi' me.

But gae ye up to Otterbourne
  And wait there dayis three,
And if I come not ere three dayis end
  A fause knight ca' ye me.   *false* 40

Battle of Otterbourne Fought on 19 August, 1388, between the Scottish forces of James, Earl of Douglas, and Henry Percy (Hotspur), son of the Earl of Northumberland. Otterbourne is about 50 km. from Newcastle, in England.
1 Lammas harvest festival, 1 August

The Otterbourne's a bonnie burn,
  'Tis pleasant there to be;
But there is nought at Otterbourne
  To feed my men and me.

The deer rins wild on hill and dale,   45
  The birds fly wild from tree to tree,
But there is neither bread nor kale   *greens*
  To fend my men and me.   *support*

Yet I will stay at Otterbourne
  Where you shall welcome be,   50
And if ye come not at three dayis end
  A fause lord I'll ca' thee.

Thither will I come, proud Percy said,
  By the might of our Ladye:
There will I bide thee, said the Douglas,   *await* 55
  My troth I plight to thee.

They lighted high on Otterbourne
  Upon the bent sae brown;   *coarse grass*
They lighted high on Otterbourne
  And threw their pallions down.   *tents* 60

And he that had a bonnie boy
  Sent out his horse to grass;
And he that had not a bonnie boy,
  His ain servant he was.

But up then spake a little page   65
  Before the peep of dawn:
O waken ye, waken ye, my good lord,
  For Percy's hard at hand.

Ye lie, ye lie, ye liar loud,
  Sae loud I hear ye lie;   70
For Percy had not men yestreen   *last evening*
  To dight my men and me.   *deal with*

But I have dream'd a dreary dream
  Beyond the Isle of Sky;
I saw a dead man win a fight,   75
  And I think that man was I.

He belted on his guid braid sword
  And to the field he ran;
But he forgot the helmet good
  That should have kept his brain.   80

When Percy wi' the Douglas met
  I wat he was fu' fain: *know / eager*
They swakked their swords till sair they swat,   *sweated*
  And the blood ran down like rain.

But Percy with his good broad sword   85
   That could so sharply wound
Has wounded Douglas on the brow
   Till he fell to the ground.

Then he call'd on his little foot-page
   And said, Run speedilie,   90
And fetch my ain dear sister's son
   Sir Hugh Montgomery.

My nephew good, the Douglas said,
   What recks the death of ane: *matters*
Last night I dream'd a dreary dream   95
   And I ken the day's thy ain.   *own*

My wound is deep, I fain would sleep;
   Take thou the vanguard of the three,
And hide me by the braken bush
   That grows on yonder lilye lee.   100

O bury me by the braken bush,
   Beneath the blooming brier;
Let never living mortal ken   *know*
   That ere a kindly Scot lies here.   *native*

He lifted up that noble lord   105
   Wi the saut tear in his e'e';
He hid him in the braken bush
   That his merrie men might not see.

The moon was clear, the day drew near,
   The spears in flinders flew,   *splinters* 110
But mony a gallant Englishman
   Ere day the Scotsmen slew.

The Gordons good, in English blood
   They steep'd their hose and shoon;   *shoes*
The Lindsays flew like fire about   115
   Till all the fray was done.

The Percy and Montgomery met
   That either of other were fain;
They swapped swords, and they twa swat,
   And aye the blude ran down between.   120

Yield thee, O yield thee, Percy, he said,
   Or else I vow I'll lay thee low:
Whom to shall I yield, said Earl Percy,
   Now that I see it must be so?

Thou shalt not yield to lord nor loun   *low-born* 125
   Nor yet shalt thou yield to me;
But yield thee to the braken bush
   That grows upon yon lilye lee.

I will not yield to a braken bush
  Nor yet will I yield to a brier;   130
But I would yield to Earl Douglas,
  Or Sir Hugh the Montgomery, if he were here.

As soon as he knew it was Montgomery
  He struck his sword's point in the gronde;
The Montgomery was a courteous knight   135
  And quickly took him by the honde

This deed was done at the Otterbourne
  About the breaking of the day;
Earl Douglas was buried at the braken bush
  And the Percy led captive away.   140

Child no. 161   Scott 1833

Sir Patrick Spence

The king sits in Dumferling toune,
  Drinking the blude-reid wine:
O quhar will I get a guid sailor,   *where*
  To sail this schip of mine?

Up and spak an eldern knicht,   5
  Sat at the kings richt kne:
Sir Patrick Spence is the best sailor
  That sails upon the se.

The king has written a braid letter,   *broad*
  And sign'd it wi' his hand;   10
And sent it to Sir Patrick Spence,
  Was walking on the sand.

The first line that Sir Patrick red,
  A loud lauch lauched he: *laugh*
The next line that Sir Patrick red,   15
  The teir blinded his ee.

O quha is this has don this deid,   *who*
  This ill deid don to me;
To send me out this time o' the yeir
  To sail upon the se?   20

Mak haste, mak haste, my mirry men all,
  Our guid schip sails the morne.   *in the morning*
O say na sae, my master deir,   *so*
  For I feir a deadlie storme.

Late, late yestreen I saw the new moone   *last evening* 25
  Wi' the auld moone in hir arme;
And I feir, I feir, my deir master,
  That we will com to harme.

---

1 **Dumferling** Dunfermline, on the north shore of the Firth of Forth, was a residence of the Kings of Scotland from the late eleventh century.

O our Scots nobles wer richt laith   *loth*
  To weet their cork-heil'd schoone;   *wet / shoes*   30
Bot lang owre a' the play wer play'd,   *before all*
  Thair hats they swam aboone.   *above*

O lang, lang may thair ladies sit
  Wi' thair fans into their hand,
Or eir they se Sir Patrick Spence   *before ever*   35
  Cum sailing to the land.

O lang, lang may the ladies stand
  Wi' thair gold kems in their hair,   *combs*
Waiting for thair ain deir lords,
  For they'll se thame na mair.   40

Haf owre, haf owre to Aberdour,   *half over*
  It's fiftie fadom deip:
And thair lies guid Sir Patrick Spence,
  Wi' the Scots lords at his feit.

Child no. 58A   Percy 1765

The Wife of Usher's Well

There lived a wife at Usher's Well
  And a wealthy wife was she;
She had three stout and stalwart sons
  And sent them o'er the sea.

They hadna been a week from her,   5
  A week but barely ane,   *one*
Whan word came to the carline wife   *old woman*
  That her three sons were gane.

They hadna been a week from her,
  A week but barely three,   10
Whan word came to the carline wife
  That her sons she'd never see.

I wish the wind may never cease,
  Nor fashes in the flood,   *disturbance*
Till my three sons come hame to me   15
  In earthly flesh and blood.

It fell about the Martinmas
  Whan nights are lang and mirk,
The carline wife's three sons came hame
  And their hats were o' the birk.   20

It neither grew in syke nor ditch   *marsh*
  Nor yet in ony sheugh,   *trench*
But at the gates o' Paradise
  That birk grew fair eneugh.

---

41 **Aberdour**   on the south side of the Firth, about 15 km. east of Dunfermline
14 **fashes**   1802 reads: 'fishes'. The emendation is suggested by Lockhart in the second edition of Scott, 1833.
20 **birk**   birch, associated with the dead

Blow up the fire, my maidens,
  Bring water from the well;
For a' my house shall feast this night
  Since my three sons are well.   25

And she has made to them a bed,
  She's made it large and wide,
And she's ta'en her mantle her about,   30
  Sat down at the bed-side.

Up then crew the red, red cock
  And up and crew the gray;
The eldest to the youngest said,   35
  'Tis time we were away.

The cock he hadna craw'd but once
  And clapp'd his wings at a'
Whan the youngest to the eldest said,
  Brother, we must awa'.   40

The cock doth craw, the day doth daw,
  The channerin' worm doth chide;   *fretting*
Gin we be mist out o' our place   *if*
  A sair pain we maun bide.   *sore / must*

Fare ye weel, my mother dear;   45
  Fareweel to barn and byre;
And fare ye weel, the bonny lass
  That kindles my mother's fire.

                     Child no. 79A   Scott 1802

Bonny Barbara Allan

It was in and about the Martinmas time,
  When the green leaves were a-falling,
That Sir John Graeme in the west country
  Fell in love with Barbara Allan.

He sent his man down through the town,   5
  To the place where she was dwelling,
O haste and come to my master dear,
  Gin ye be Barbara Allan.   *if*

O hooly, hooly rose she up,   *gently*
  To the place where he was lying,   10
And when she drew the curtain by,
  Young man, I think you're dying.

O it's I'm sick, and very very sick,
  And 'tis a' for Barbara Allan.
O the better for me ye's never be,   15
  Tho' your heart's blood were a-spilling.

---

1 Martinmas   feast of St Martin, 11 November

O dinna ye mind, young man, said she,   *don't you remember*
    When ye was in the tavern a-drinking,
That ye made the healths gae round and round,
    And slighted Barbara Allan?   20

He turn'd his face unto the wall,
    And death was with him dealing;
Adieu, adieu, my dear friends all,
    And be kind to Barbara Allan.

And slowly, slowly raise she up,   25
    And slowly, slowly left him;
And sighing said, she cou'd not stay,
    Since death of life had reft him.

She had not gane a mile but twa,
    When she heard the dead-bell ringing,   30
And every jow that the dead-bell gied,   *stroke / gave*
    It cry'd, Woe to Barbara Allan.

O mother, mother, make my bed,
    O make it saft and narrow,
Since my love dy'd for me to-day,   35
    I'll die for him to-morrow.

          Child no. 84A   Tea Table Miscellany 1740

The Unquiet Grave

The wind doth blow today, my love,
    And a few small drops of rain;
I never had but one true-love,
    In cold grave she was lain.

I'll do as much for my true-love   5
    As any young man may;
I'll sit and mourn all at her grave
    For a twelvemonth and a day.

The twelvemonth and a day being up,
    The dead began to speak: 10
Oh who sits weeping on my grave
    And will not let me sleep?

'Tis I, my love, sits on your grave
    And will not let you sleep;
For I crave one kiss of your clay-cold lips   15
    And that is all I seek.

You crave one kiss of my clay-cold lips,
    But my breath smells earthy strong;
If you have one kiss of my clay-cold lips
    Your time will not be long.   20

'Tis down in yon garden green,
  Love, where we used to walk,
The finest flower that ere was seen
  Is withered to a stalk.

The stalk is withered dry, my love,   25
  So will our hearts decay;
So make yourself content, my love,
  Till God calls you away.

                              Child no. 78A 1868

Lady Maisry

The young lords o' the north country
  Have all a wooing gone
To win the love of Lady Maisry;
  But o' them she wou'd hae none.

O they hae courted Lady Maisry   5
  Wi' a' kin kind of things,
An' they hae sought her Lady Maisry
  Wi' brotches an' wi' rings.

An' they ha' sought her Lady Maisry
  Frae father and frae mother,   *from* 10
An' they ha' sought her Lady Maisry
  Frae sister an' frae brother.

An' they ha' follow'd her Lady Maisry
  Thro' chamber an' thro' ha';
But a' that they cou'd say to her,   15
  Her answer still was Na.

O had your tongues, young men, she says,   *hold*
  An' think nae mair o' me;
For I've gien my love to an English lord,
  An' think nae mair o' me.   20

Her father's kitchy boy heard that—
  And ill death may he dee—
An' he is on to her brother
  As fast as gang cou'd hee.   *go*

O is my father an' my mother well,   25
  But an' my brothers three?
Gin my sister Lady Maisry be well   *if*
  There's naething can ail me.

Your father and your mother is well,
  But an' your brothers three;   30
Your sister Lady Maisry's well
  So big wi' bairn gangs she.   *child*

Gin this be true you tell to me,
  My mailison light on thee;   *curse*
But gin it be a lie you tell   35
  You sal be hangit hie.   *high*

He's done him to his sister's bow'r   *taken himself*
 Wi' meikle doole an' care,   *much grief*
An' there he saw her Lady Maisry
 Kembing her yallow hair.   40

O wha is aught that bairn, he says,   *who's is*
 That ye sae big are wi'?
And gin ye winna own the truth   *won't*
 This moment ye sall dee.

She turn'd her right an' roun' about   45
 An' the kem fell frae her han';
A trembling seiz'd her fair body
 An' her rosy cheek grew wan.

O pardon me, my brother dear,
 An' the truth I'll tell to thee;   50
My bairn it is to Lord William
 An' he is betroth'd to me.

O cou'd na ye gotten dukes or lords
 Intill your ain country,   *within*
That ye draw up wi' an English dog   55
 To bring this shame on me?

But ye maun gi' up the English lord
 Whan youre young babe is born,
For gin you keep by him an hour langer
 Your life sall be forlorn.   *lost* 60

I will gi' up this English blood
 Till my young babe be born,
But the never a day nor hour langer
 Tho' my life should be forlorn.

O whare is a' my merry young men   65
 Whom I gi' meat and fee,   *wage*
To pu' the thistle and the thorn
 To burn this wile whore wi'?   *vile*

O whare will I get a bonny boy
 To help me in my need,   70
To rin wi' haste to Lord William
 And bid him come wi' speed?

O out it spake a bonny boy,
 Stood by her brother's side:
O I would rin your errand, Lady,   75
 O'er a' the world wide.

Aft have I run your errands, Lady,
 Whan blawn baith win' and weet;   *wind / wet*
But now I'll rin your errand, Lady,   80
 Wi' sat tears on my cheek.   *salt*

O whan he came to broken briggs
 He bent his bow and swam,
An' whan he came to the green grass growin
 He slack'd his shoone and ran.   *slipped off / shoes* 85

O whan he came to Lord William's gates
 He baed na to chap or ca',   *stayed / knock*
But set his bent bow till his breast   *to*
 An' lightly lap the wa';   *leapt*
An' or the porter was at the gate   *ere* 90
 The boy was i' the ha'.   *hall*

O is my biggins broken, boy?   *bridges*
 Or is my towers won?
Or is my Lady lighter yet
 Of a dear daughter or son?   95

Your biggin is na broken, Sir,
 Nor is your towers won;
But the fairest Lady in a' the lan'
 For you this day maun burn.   *must*

O saddle me the black, the black,   100
 Or saddle me the brown;
O saddle me the swiftest steed
 That ever rade frae a town.

Or he was near a mile awa   *ere*
 She heard his wild horse sneeze: 105
Mend up the fire, my false brother,
 It's na come to my knees.

O whan he lighted at the gate
 She heard his bridle ring:
Mend up the fire, my false brother,   110
 It's far yet frae my chin.

Mend up the fire to me, brother,
 Mend up the fire to me;
For I see him comin hard an' fast
 Will soon men' 't up to thee.   115

O gin my hands had been loose, Willy,
 Sae hard as they are boun',
I would have turn'd me frae the gleed   *blaze*
 And castin out your young son.

O I'll gar burn for you, Maisry,   *make* 120
 Your father an' your mother;
An' I'll gar burn for you, Maisry,
 Your sister an' your brother.

An' I'll gar burn for you, Maisry,
 The chief of a' your kin;   125
An' the last bonfire that I come to
 Mysel I will cast in.

    Child no. 65A Jamieson 1806

May Colven

False Sir John a wooing came
  To a maid of beauty fair,
May Colven was this lady's name,
  Her father's only heir.

He woo'd her butt, he woo'd her ben,   5
  He woo'd her in the ha',   *hall*
Until he got this lady's consent
  To mount and ride awa',

He went down to her father's bower,
  Where all the steeds did stand;   10
And he's taken one of the best steeds,
  That was in her father's land.

He's got on and she's got on,
  And fast as they could flee,
Until they came to a lonesome part,   15
  A rock by the side of the sea.

Loup off the steed, says false Sir John,
  Your bridal bed you see;
For I have drowned seven young ladies,
  The eight one you shall be.   20

Cast off, cast off, my May Colven,
  All and your silken gown,
For it's o'er good, and o'er costly,
  To rot in the salt sea foam.

Cast, cast off, my May Colven,   25
  All and your embroider'd shoen,   *shoes*
For they're o'er good, and o'er costly
  To rot in the salt sea foam.

O turn you about O false Sir John,
  And look to the leaf of the tree;   30
For it never became a gentleman,
  A naked woman to see.

He turned himself straight round about,
  To look to the leaf of the tree;
So swift as May Colven was,   35
  To throw him in the sea.

O help, O help my May Colven,
  O help, or else I'll drown;
I'll take you home to your father's bower
  And set you down safe and sound.   40

---

5 **butt**   in the kitchen   **ben**   in the parlour

No help, no help O false Sir John,
   No help nor pity thee;
Tho' seven king's daughters you have drown'd
   But the eight shall not be me.

So she went on her father's steed,   45
   As swift as she could flee;
And she came home to her father's bower
   Before it was break of day.

Up then and spoke the pretty parrot,
   May Colven where have you been,   50
What has become of false Sir John,
   That woo'd you so late the streen.   *last evening*

He woo'd you butt, he woo'd you ben,
   He woo'd you in the ha',
Until he got your own consent   55
   For to mount and gang awa'.   *go*

O hold your tongue my pretty parrot,
   Lay not the blame upon me,
Your cup shall be of the flowered gold,
   Your cage of the root of the tree.   60

Up then spake the king himself,
   In the bed chamber where he lay,
What ails the pretty parrot,
   That prattles so long or day.   *before*

There came a cat to my cage door,   65
   It almost a worried me,
And I was calling on May Colven,
   To take the cat from me.

Child no. 4C   Herd 1776

The Cherry-tree Carol

Joseph was an old man,
   And an old man was he,
When he wedded Mary
   In the land of Galilee.

Joseph and Mary walked   5
   Through an orchard good,
Where was cherries and berries
   So red as any blood.

Joseph and Mary walked
   Through an orchard green,   10
Where was berries and cherries
   As thick as might be seen.

O then bespoke Mary
  So meek and so mild:
Pluck me one cherry, Joseph,   15
  For I am with child.

O then bespoke Joseph
  With words most unkind:
Let him pluck thee a cherry
  That brought thee with child.   20

O then bespoke the Babe
  Within his mother's womb:
Bow down then the tallest tree
  For my mother to have some.

Then bowed down the highest tree   25
  Unto his mother's hand;
Then she cried, See, Joseph,
  I have cherries at command.

O then bespake Joseph:
  I have done Mary wrong;   30
But cheer up, my dearest,
  And be not cast down.

Then Mary plucked a cherry
  As red as the blood,
Then Mary went home   35
  With her heavy load.

Then Mary took her babe
  And sat him on her knee,
Saying, My dear son, tell me
  What this world will be.   40

O I shall be as dead, mother,
  As the stones in the wall;
O the stones in the streets, mother,
  Shall mourn for me all.

Upon Easter-day, mother   45
  My uprising shall be;
O the sun and the moon, mother,
  Shall both rise with me.

                              Child no. 54A   Sandys 1833

AN EARLY DRAFT OF A POEM BY WILLIAM BLAKE

The Tyger

1
Tyger Tyger burning bright
In the forests of the night
What immortal hand or eye
~~Dare~~ ~~Could~~ frame thy fearful symmetry

Burnt in
2
~~In what~~ distant deeps or skies
~~The cruel~~ ~~Burnt the~~ fire of thine eyes
On what wings dare he aspire
What the hand dare sieze the fire

3
And what shoulder & what art
Could twist the sinews of thy heart
And when thy heart began to beat
What dread hand & what dread feet

Could fetch it from the furnace deep
And in thy horrid ribs dare steep
In the well of sanguine woe
In what clay & what mould
Were thy eyes of fury rolld

~~Where~~   ~~where~~
4
~~What~~ the hammer ~~what~~ the chain
In what furnace was thy brain

dread grasp
What the anvil what the ~~arm arm grasp clasp~~
Dare   ~~Could~~ its deadly terrors ~~clasp grasp~~ clasp

6
Tyger Tyger burning bright
In the forests of the night
What immortal hand & eye
frame
Dare ~~form~~ thy fearful symmetry

★   ★   ★

dare he ~~smile laugh~~
5 ̷3
And ~~did he laugh~~ his work to see
ankle
What the shoulder what the knee
Dare
4
~~Did~~ he who made the lamb make thee
1
When the stars threw down their spears
2
And waterd heaven with their tears

This early draft, taken from Blake's *Notebook*, includes his own
numbering and deletions. See p. 340.

PARODIES

Waste Land Limericks

I

In April one seldom feels cheerful;
Dry stones, sun and dust make me fearful;
    Clairvoyantes distress me,
    Commuters depress me—
Met Stetson and gave him an earful.   5

II

She sat on a mighty fine chair,
Sparks flew as she tidied her hair;
    She asks many questions,
    I make few suggestions—
Bad as Albert and Lil—what a pair!   10

III

The Thames runs, bones rattle, rats creep;
Tiresias fancies a peep—
    A typist is laid,
    A record is played—
Wei la la. After this it gets deep.   15

IV

A Phoenician called Phlebas forgot
About birds and his business—the lot,
    Which is no surprise
    Since he'd met his demise
And been left in the ocean to rot.   20

V

No water. Dry rocks and dry throats,
Then thunder, a shower of quotes
    From the Sanskrit and Dante.
    Da. Damyata. Shantih.
I hope you'll make sense of the notes.   25

by Wendy Cope (b. 1945)
See p. 138. First published 1986.

If Pope Had Written 'Break, Break, Break'

Fly, Muse, thy wonted themes, nor longer seek
The consolations of a powder'd cheek;
Forsake the busy purlieus of the Court
For calmer meads where finny tribes resort.
So may th' Almighty's natural antidote   5
Abate the worldly tenour of thy note,
The various beauties of the liquid main
Refine thy reed and elevate thy strain.

See how the labour of the urgent oar
Propels the barks and draws them to the shore.   10
Hark! from the margin of the azure bay
The joyful cries of infants at their play.
(The offspring of a piscatorial swain,
His home the sands, his pasturage the main.)
Yet none of these may soothe the mourning heart,   15
Nor fond alleviation's sweets impart;
Nor may the pow'rs of infants that rejoice
Restore the accents of a former voice,
Nor the bright smiles of ocean's nymphs command
The pleasing contact of a vanished hand.   20
So let me still in meditation move,
Muse in the vale and ponder in the grove,
And scan the skies where sinking Phoebus glows
With hues more rubicund than Cibber's nose . . . .

(*After which the poet gets into his proper stride.*)   25

1917

by J. C. Squire (1884–1958)
See p. 251. Colley Cibber (line 24) was a critic satirised by Alexander Pope.

From Variations of an Air:

*Composed on having to appear in a pageant
as Old King Cole.*

Old King Cole was a merry old soul,
And a merry old soul was he;
He called for his pipe,
He called for his bowl,
And he called for his fiddlers three.   5

After W.B. Yeats

Of an old King in a story
   From the grey sea-folk I have heard,
Whose heart was no more broken
   Than the wings of a bird.

As soon as the moon was silver   5
  And the thin stars began,
He took his pipe and his tankard,
  Like an old peasant man.

And three tall shadows were with him
  And came at his command;   10
And played before him for ever
  The fiddles of fairyland.

And he died in the young summer
  Of the world's desire;
Before our hearts were broken   15
  Like sticks in a fire.

After Robert Browning

Who smoke-snorts toasts o' My Lady Nicotine,
Kicks stuffing out of Pussyfoot, bids his trio
Stick up their Stradivarii (that's the plural)
Or near enough, my fatheads; *nimium*
Vicina Cremonæ; that's a bit too near).   5
Is there some stockfish fails to understand?
Catch hold o' the notion, bellow and blurt back 'Cole'?
Must I bawl lessons from a horn-book, howl,
Cat-call the cat-gut 'fiddles'? Fiddlesticks!

After Walt Whitman

Me clairvoyant,
Me conscious of you, old camarado,
Needing no telescope, lorgnette, field-glass, opera-glass, myopic pince-nez,
Me piercing two thousand years with eye naked and not ashamed;
The crown cannot hide you from me;   5
Musty old feudal-heraldic trappings cannot hide you from me,
I perceive that you drink.
(I am drinking with you. I am as drunk as you are.)
I see you are inhaling tobacco, puffing, smoking, spitting
(I do not object to your spitting)   10
You prophetic of American largeness,
You anticipating the broad masculine manners of these States;
I see in you also there are movements, tremors, tears, desire for the
        melodious,
I salute your three violinists, endlessly making vibrations,
Rigid, relentless, capable of going on for ever;   15
They play my accompaniment; but I shall take no notice of any
        accompaniment;
I myself am a complete orchestra.
So long.

by G.K. Chesterton (1874–1936).
Published in 1932.

RHYTHM, FORM AND METRE

We value poetry for many reasons. It involves philosophy and feeling, it is a cultural record, it both concentrates and extends language. It is also, like singing, an art which centres language in our bodies. Rhythm is of prime importance in the speaking of poetry—even in the speaking of a silent reading.

Compared with the immediate pleasure of reading poetry, the study of rhythm and metre is technical. Yet the enjoyment of any art is generally enhanced by an understanding of some of its techniques. Poets themselves, who may have begun by writing well with an internalised understanding but only a hazy formal knowledge of rhythm and metre, often turn in mid-career to a study of the principles, to sharpen their perception of what they do.

Rhythm in poetry formalises and tightens ordinary speech rhythm, and like the rhythm of all spoken language, it is learned by hearing. As children, we imitated speech rhythms even before we learned words, and in learning to speak we adapted rhythm as well as vocabulary and syntax to the purpose of communication. At the same time, most of us internalised the four-beat line of poetry from hearing children's rhymes. Later, if we learned to appreciate the more subtle five-beat line (the pentameter) and the variable line of free verse, this also would have been influenced by hearing others. The analysis of rhythm, whether of conversation or of poetry, therefore draws upon reflection; it brings to light knowledge which we implicitly possess. In a way, it might follow that analysis is superfluous; a thorough enjoyment of poetry is possible without it. Yet it is the very entrenchment of rhythm and metre in our intimate experience of language that makes them worth studying.

The discussion of rhythm applies to all speech; that of rhythm in metre applies to poetry alone.

Rhythm

RHYTHM   a perceived pattern of repetition in time. The term has wide reference, from the cycles of the seasons to the pulse of an atomic clock. As applied to language, 'rhythm' refers to a timing which is not exact, but rather fluent, like that of the heartbeat, breathing and walking. The BEAT of a rhythm in English is normally carried by stressed syllables.

STRESS   Whenever we speak, we stress some syllables more than others by giving an extra squeeze to the air in the lungs. This lengthens the syllable, or raises the pitch of the voice, or both. Sometimes we use EMPHATIC stress—'*you* can go', 'you *can* go', 'you can *go*'—the stress depending on the nuance being signalled. More fundamental, however, is NORMAL stress—the stress we give to a syllable because the pronunciation of the word requires it. 'Requires' is not pronounced '*re*quires' ('ˊ ˘) but 're*quires*' (˘ ˊ); it has an unstressed syllable followed by a stressed syllable, a nonstress (˘) followed by a stress (ˊ).

Some monosyllabic words are normally stressed: 'hówl', 'míne', 'clípped', 'báck'. Others are normally unstressed—'thĕ', 'ă', 'ŏf', 'ĭn', 'ĭs', 'ănd'—but may be stressed for emphasis.

Single words of two syllables have one normal stress, on either syllable: 'úndĕr', 'bĕlów', 'pérmĭt' (noun), 'pĕrmít' (verb). In a compound word of two syllables, however, both syllables are stressed: 'éyesíght', 'bláckbírd'.

In words of more than two syllables, various combinations of normal stress occur: 'kángăróo', 'rĕvérsăl', 'tímŏrŏus', 'héavĭlÿ'; 'ănálÿsĭs', 'íncŭbátŏr'; 'rĕfrígĕrátŏr,' 'ĕléctrícĭtÿ'. (Note: An ending in '-ous', '-is' or '-y' is a nonstress: 'tímŏrŏus', 'ănálÿsĭs', 'ĕléctrícĭtÿ'.)

Usually, words cannot lose their normal stress. The only exception occurs when we under-emphasise a normally stressed one-syllable word ('gó', 'twó'), or a two-syllable preposition ('bĕtwéen', 'íntŏ') or auxiliary verb ('cánnŏt', 'dóesn't'), in order to throw emphasis onto a following word: we may say 'gó físhĭng' or 'gŏ físhĭng'; 'bĕtwéen twó wárs' or 'bĕtwĕen twó wárs'.

Of two neighbouring stresses, one is usually more prominent than the other. Within a phrase, the second of two stresses is normally the more prominent: 'púsh a bárrow', 'líghtly ríse', 'ríse líghtly', 'bláck bírd'. In a compound word, the first stress is always more prominent: '*éye*síght', *bláck*bírd'. In a single word with two stresses, either the first stressed syllable ('*ín*cubátor') or the second ('élec*trí*city') may take the more prominent normal stress.

However, whatever the relation of prominence between two neighbouring stresses, they tend to remain stresses: the lesser one rarely becomes a nonstress. The pulse—the rhythmic beat—of English has a simple basis in the mind's clear distinction between stress and nonstress. This distinction is intimately physical in origin, being based on our experience of stresses as strong pulses (literally, stresses) of muscular energy in the chest wall when we speak—an experience which is recognised even in silent reading. Stresses normally make the BEAT of a rhythm; nonstresses normally make the OFFBEAT.

The TIMING of the beat occurs at approximately equal intervals. 'Rát-tráp' and 'ráttlĕtráp' in a sentence take a roughly equal time to say: to keep the beat of a rhythm we tend to lengthen the one syllable of 'rat' and correspondingly compress the two syllables of 'rattle'. We keep a beat in daily speech by occasionally slurring (or 'eliding') unstressed syllables. We keep a beat also when we articulate more carefully, as in public speaking and the speaking of poetry. Timing is usually broken, however, by pauses and hesitations (that is, we rarely incorporate pauses into our timing).

If we reflect on our own speech, we may notice that frequently a SINGLE BEAT (stressed) will alternate with a SINGLE OFFBEAT (nonstressed) to form a DUPLE RHYTHM. 'Tŏ fórm ă dúplĕ rhýthm' is itself an example. Since timing is never quite exact—some stresses are hit sharply ('hít'), and others are slightly held ('hèld')—a duple rhythm will be full of small quickenings and slowings. Even so, an unrelieved duple rhythm would be monotonous. In practice it is varied structurally in two ways: by double offbeats and by double beats.

A DOUBLE OFFBEAT consists of *two nonstresses together* (^{xx}), as in 'músĭcăl cháirs'. Compared with the single offbeat in 'músĭc cháirs', the double offbeat is light and quick, since to keep a rhythm we cover two syllables in roughly the timing of one (perhaps assisted by a slight rushing of the preceding stressed syllable—'mu-' may be fractionally shorter in 'musical' than in 'music').

A DOUBLE BEAT consists of two beats formed by *two stresses together* ($^{\prime\prime}$) and is precisely opposite in effect. The two stresses are lengthened to compensate for the lack of an offbeat between, thus maintaining the timing of two beats. The result is emphasis. Often, one of the pair may be especially lengthened, as for example 'fine' in the double beat, 'fíne mèss': 'yŏu've máde ă fíne mèss'.

The rhythm of English may be described as the alternation of single beat and single offbeat in a basic *duple rhythm*, varied by the quick skip of a *double offbeat* or the weighty dwelling of a *double beat*. (For example 'thĕ áltĕrnátiŏn ŏf sínglĕ béat ănd sínglĕ óffbéat' is in duple rhythm, varied by one double offbeat and one double beat.) These effects depend on identity between a stress and a beat: a BEAT here is simply a STRESS, considered in its function of beating out a rhythm.

What happens when there are not one or two but *three* in a row, of either stresses ($^{\prime\prime\prime}$) or nonstresses (^{xxx})? The answer seems to be that the mind will maintain the feeling of a duple rhythm by making the middle the odd one out in each case. The middle of three stresses is felt as an offbeat, and the middle of three nonstresses is felt as a beat, to keep a duple rhythm going. Here the usual rule does not apply: stress and beat do *not* coincide. These are effects of mental adjustment; the mind fabricates or 'feels' a duple rhythm even though the stress pattern does not warrant it. We are all aware of the mind's tendency to create a duple rhythm with little or no excuse: for example, in hearing 'tick-tock' in the even ticking of a clock.

Thus the MIDDLE OF THREE STRESSES IN A ROW functions as a STRESSED OFFBEAT. It remains a stress, with the weight of a stress, and therefore slows the rhythmic timing, but it is *felt* as an offbeat. This can be indicated on the page by marking stresses and beats separately—the stresses as usual above the syllables, and the beats by underlining: 'thĕ rŏad bĕhínd thĕ ŏld stóne púb'. Here, the stress pattern and the beat pattern coincide (as we would expect) at most points, but not on 'stone'. As the middle of three stresses, this is not a beat (unless it is slowed down to an extra strong emphasis). It is a slow, stressed offbeat, the rhythmic recoil between two beats: 'ŏld stone púb', 'tĭck tock tĭck'. The mind maintains a duple rhythm against the stress pattern. We usually signal this by raising or lowering the pitch of the voice on the offbeat syllable.

Conversely, the MIDDLE OF THREE NONSTRESSES IN A ROW functions as an UNSTRESSED BEAT. It remains a nonstress, with the lightness of a nonstress—and therefore quickens the rhythmic timing—but it is *felt* as a beat. Take the phrase 'hídděn ĭn ă cúpbŏard'. Here the mind maintains a duple rhythm by lightly registering the unstressed 'in' as the beat between nonstresses on either side, but without stressing it. 'In' becomes a stressed beat only if we emphasise it, as a child might do by chanting. In normal conversation, of course, we may keep the timing of a rhythm by slurring (or 'eliding') the three unstressed syllables down to a double offbeat ('híd ĭn ă cúpbŏard') or one offbeat ('hídnă cúpbŏard'). However, if we articulate all three unstressed syllables (as we generally do in public speaking, or in speaking poetry), the mind will find a beat, however barely registered, in the middle. There are *never* more than two offbeats between beats.

Stressed offbeats and unstressed beats are exceptions: generally, beat pattern and stress pattern coincide.

The effects of rhythm are delicate, but we use them all the time. They give resiliency and expressive point to our daily conversations, and we instinctively improvise our speech to take advantage of them. A three-year-old knows the subtle difference in practice between 'Í wánt ă bíscŭit, múmmў' and 'Múmmў, Í wánt ă bíscŭit'. The first sounds reasonable, the second is more peremptory. The more peremptory effect follows not only from the prominent opening placement 'mummy', but also from its rhythm. 'Múmmў Í wánt', which begins immediately with the beat and follows up with a quick double offbeat ($^{\prime\,x\,x\,\prime}$) is a more explosive opening than 'Í wánt ă bíscŭit', where a soft initial offbeat opens out into an even, duple rhythm ($^{x\,\prime\,x\,\prime\,x}$). This explosive opening, as we shall see, has the same configuration as 'initial inversion' in a line of poetry, but it is plainly not a mystery known only to poets. POETRY works on the same principle as all speech (and prose): that of creating interesting and expressive tension out of variations on a basic rhythm. The organisation, however, is more subtle and complex, as the rhythm of dancing is, compared with that of walking.

Turning to duple rhythm in poetry, consider these lines by Wordsworth:

> Bŭt nŏw thĕ sún ĭs rísĭng cálm ănd bríght;
> Thĕ bírds ăre síngĭng ĭn thĕ dístănt wŏods.

The first line is in duple rhythm. An offbeat alternates with a beat throughout, and we may read the evenness of this rhythm as enacting a confidence in the steadiness and calm of the sun's arrival. The second line is also in duple rhythm, but its third beat is an unstressed beat—the middle of three nonstresses in a row. This quickens the line for a moment at its centre; in context it suggests a lightening of spirit, and perhaps also a quickening of attention to the sounds in the 'distant woods' (an unstressed beat often has the effect of focusing attention onto the stressed beats that follow). It also introduces a touch of informality as compared with the more regular previous line. Even one unstressed beat, as here, can introduce into a line a tone of easy conversation.

The duple rhythm in the following line from Auden slows down at its end, by means of three stresses in a row, with a stressed offbeat on 'help'. In context, this reinforces a sense of desolation:

> And cŏuld nŏt hópe fŏr hélp ănd nó help cáme.

The following line from Yeats, describing his friend, Maud Gonne, begins with a beat followed by a quick double offbeat ('Hóllŏw ŏf')—exploding with a quick urgency, before settling into the steady pace of a regular duple rhythm:

> Hóllŏw ŏf chéek ăs thŏugh ĭt dránk thĕ wínd.

In this line from Milton, 'fresh Woods' has the lingering emphasis typical of a double beat:

> Tŏ mórrŏw tŏ frésh Wóods, ănd Pástŭres néw.

In context, the effect is of savouring a joy—and all the more so because of the weighty contrast with the quickening double offbeat ('mórrŏw tŏ') which leads into it.

The basic effects of stress and nonstress in duple rhythm are easy to comprehend. Where they alternate, the movement is steady; where stresses predominate, the rhythmic effect is weighty; where nonstresses predominate, the rhythmic effect is light. This rule applies both in conversation and in those forms of poetry—namely *duple metre* and *free verse*—which (as we shall see) take duple rhythm as a basis. With such poetry, the marking of stresses and nonstresses on the page enables us to see patterns of steadiness, weightiness and lightness in the language. This basic perception does not strictly require the additional underlining of beats; for example, the lightening effect of three nonstresses in a row is evident even without the understanding that, rhythmically, the middle of these catches the beat. However, both stresses and beats will be marked in the examples given on these pages, for a full understanding of rhythmic pattern.

Form

'Poetry' may refer simply to evocative language. Hence a short piece of evocative prose is sometimes called a 'prose poem'. However, the LINE is so powerful an instrument for organising language evocatively, through rhythm and other effects of repetition, that most people think of a 'poem' automatically as being in VERSE (which originally meant 'line', and is the term for poetry in lines). Following this usage, poetry and verse are considered here as synonymous.

The rhythmic shaping of each line echoes subtly in our reading of the next. Line is measured against line, making palpable any shifts or contrasts or parallels of rhythm and phrasing. In reading, it is therefore important to register each line-ending, either by a pause or by holding on slightly to a final syllable. In this way, the line that follows will begin with its proper cadence—a CADENCE being the particular rhythm of a group of words. We risk swallowing the opening of a line if we rush into it, and this destroys the rhythm.

END-STOPPED LINE   a line which has a natural pause at the end, its closure coinciding with the closure of a phrase or clause. This may or may not be indicated by punctuation. Most lines are end-stopped.

ENJAMBED LINE (enjambment)   where a line closes in the middle of a phrase. This creates a strong tension between our sense that the line has finished and our sense that the phrase has not. If we register this tension in our reading, rather than run on as if reading prose, it can produce delicate effects. (The term sometimes used, 'run-on line', is therefore somewhat misleading.) In the following quotation, a lingering on the enjambed 'I' prepares for the energetic beat on the first syllable, 'Did', in the subsequent line:

> I wonder by my troth, what thou, and I
> Did, till we lov'd? were we not wean'd till then?   Donne

Depending on the sense of the words, a particular enjambment may suggest a barely checked energy (as above) or, alternatively, a tentativeness; it may shape a pause in mid phrase as if weighing a word or idea; it may involve proceeding with a statement while quietly placing a key word in a key position at the end or beginning of a line; or its pause or lingering may closely support the sense—as here, where the line is suspended on 'hange':

> When yellow leaves, or none, or few doe hange
> Upon those boughes which shake against the could.
>   Shakespeare

CAESURA   a pause *within* the line at the completion of a phrase or clause, or for emphasis. This is normally indicated by punctuation, but not necessarily. In the lines quoted above, there is a light caesura (pause or mental check) after 'boughes', which closes a phrase even though a comma is not marked. The varying position of a çaesura within a line allows phrases to expand or contract expressively in relation to the fixed extremities of the line. The nearer to the centre of the line a caesura occurs, the more balanced the line will feel. A caesura near the line's extremities tends to invoke disturbance and energy, as in the quotation from Donne. Some lines have more than one caesura; a few have none.

STANZA (Italian for *room*) a regular grouping of three lines or more, marked off on a page by a space. In rhymed, metrical verse, each stanza usually repeats the same rhyme-scheme and metre. Regular groupings of lines without metre or rhyme, however, are also referred to as stanzas. Irregular groupings of lines are usually called 'verse paragraphs'.

COUPLET a unit of two lines.
TERCET or TRIPLET a stanza of three lines.
QUATRAIN a stanza of four lines.

A sample of stanza rhyme-schemes:
Terza Rima (with concluding couplet) See 'Ode to the West Wind' (Shelley).
Rhyme Royal See 'They fle from me' (Wyatt).
Ottava Rima See 'Don Juan' (Byron) and 'Sailing to Byzantium' (Yeats).
Spenserian Stanza See 'The Faerie Queene' (Spenser).

SONNET a fourteen-line rhymed poem, usually in pentameter and usually divided into an OCTAVE (eight lines) and a SESTET (six lines). Typically, the octave states a theme and the sestet resolves or varies it in some way. The *Italian* sonnet is rhymed abbaabba/cdcdcd (although the rhyme-scheme in the sestet may vary). The *English* sonnet, which is by far the most common form of sonnet in English, is rhymed ababcdcd/efefgg; note that here the rhyme-scheme creates a second structure of three quatrains and a final couplet, superimposed on that of the octave and sestet. The *Spenserian* sonnet is similar, but its rhyme-scheme knits the quatrains together: ababbcbc/cdcdee. The sonnet has remained a popular form with poets because, it seems, it is of sufficient length to develop a complex theme and yet short enough and strict enough in its formal restraint to allow a sharpness of focus.
A LYRIC is a fairly short poem which directly expresses or explores an emotion. For example, a sonnet is usually a form of lyric. An ODE is a particularly formal lyric which has some length and complexity.
A BALLAD is a narrative poem in popular metre which tells a story tersely through snatches of dialogue and brief, dramatic scenes. The form was first developed in the anonymous traditional ballads which were composed for singing in medieval times.

SOUND EFFECTS As a rough generalisation, *soft* consonants may sometimes convey generous or gentle associations from their fleshy formation in the mouth or on the lips, and from the fact that they can be held: *l, m, n, r, w, f, v.* Unvoiced, airy *h* and *th* are also gentle. By contrast, *hard* consonants, formed with a small explosion on the palate or teeth (and hence called 'plosives') have a more brisk effect: *d, g, k, t;* on the lips, *p* is a soft plosive; its voiced counterpart, *b,* is harder. However, the ways in which the sound of a word may reinforce the sense, or not, are labyrinthine. The sound effect of many words is rather neutral; with others it is contrary—'hammer' has deceptively soft consonants. Unvoiced *s* tends to be neutral, gaining any suggestiveness from other consonants with which it may be combined. Nevertheless, poetry, as an art which foregrounds language, will pick up suggestiveness of sound where this is possible and appropriate.

REPETITION OF SOUND may bind words significantly:
Assonance   echoing of vowels in stressed syllables: for example, 'lay'/'awake'.
Alliteration   echoing of consonants: for example, 'table'/'tree'; 'work'/'picking'.
Rhyme   where two words have identical final segments (the last stressed vowel and whatever follows it): for example, 'pine'/'divine'; 'feather'/'whether'; 'amorous'/'glamorous'. The last two pairs are examples of double and triple rhyme respectively, which are used mainly in light verse. Rhyme may be internal to a line or at the end of a line.
Half-Rhyme   echoing of a final consonant but not of the preceding vowel: for example, 'join'/'divine'. Sometimes, apparent half-rhymes were full rhymes when the poem was written; 'join'/'divine' was a full rhyme in the eighteenth century.

Metre

METRE (from the Greek, *metron,* measure)   a regular and recurring pattern that can be abstracted from the rhythmical organisation of lines of poetry.

The SCANSION, or metrical analysis,* of a written line of poetry is done by marking stresses (thús) and nonstresses (thŭs). The beats in a rhythm, which mostly coincide with stressed syllables but sometimes do not, may also be marked

---

*Metrical analysis may be approached according to any one of a number of systems. The discussion of rhythm and metre here is indebted to the approach taken in the influential study by Derek Attridge, *The Rhythms of English Poetry,* 1982, although it differs in important respects. Some of the insights of traditional scansion are incorporated here; however, the traditional division of a line into 'feet' of two or three syllables is discarded, as it is in most contemporary studies. Although foot-division can be useful for isolating a variation within a line, it tends to cut artificially across cadences. Attridge's terms, 'stress' and 'nonstress', are adopted here for their sharpness of distinction, in preference to the more biologically accurate alternatives also in use, 'strong stress' and 'weak stress' (a twitch of the diaphragm is required even for a nonstress). The descriptive terms, 'popular metre', 'unstressed beat' and 'stressed offbeat' have been coined here; Attridge prefers 'four-beat metre', 'promoted nonstress' and 'demoted stress'. The traditional marks for stress and nonstress, and underlining for a beat, replace Attridge's more elaborate notation. Earlier editions of this anthology used the terms 'light beat' and 'slow offbeat' as alternatives for 'unstressed beat' and 'stressed offbeat'; although they remain good terms for describing rhythmic effects, they have been omitted here to minimise terminology. I am grateful to Peter Groves of Monash University for a number of particular suggestions, including the succinct short definition of metre.

(th<u>u</u>s). If beats are marked, the offbeats are thereby obvious and rarely require marking.

There are two broad categories of metre in poetry in English: stress metre and duple metre.

1. Stress metre where the line has a *fixed number of stressed beats* (usually four) *with an optional number of offbeats.* Note that the beats are always stressed.

POPULAR METRE has been the principal form of stress metre in use during the last seven centuries: basically, *lines of four beats, stressed and strongly timed, arranged in rhymed quatrains.* It is the metre of much popular poetry, including children's rhymes, ballads (bush, folk and traditional), hymns, limericks and rap. It has more affinity with the strong 4:4 timing of popular music than with the flexible rhythms of conversation, being easily set to music and, in many cases, composed for it.

Some forms of popular metre include the equivalent of a rest note in the timing of a song: a line of only three stressed beats may have a rest beat—a final silent pause marking the timing of a fourth beat. This occurs regularly in the second and fourth lines of BALLAD METRE, also called COMMON METRE, the metre of most ballads and hymns. In the following example of ballad metre, only three beats are marked within the second and fourth lines, but the timing of a fourth, silent beat at the end can be registered by reciting the quatrain while tapping out a four-beat rhythm with the hand:

> Fár ånd féw, fár ånd féw,
> Åre thĕ lánds whĕre thĕ Júmblĭes lĭve;   (*beat*)
> Thĕir héads åre gréen, ånd thĕir hánds åre blúe,
> Ånd thĕy wént tŏ séa ĭn å síeve.   (*beat*)   Lear

CONVERSATIONAL STRESS METRE should be mentioned here: a line of four stressed beats (or three, or any suitable number) in the flexible rhythm of clearly spoken conversation. An example is the line in Old English and medieval alliterative verse, where, out of four stressed beats, at least three are picked out for attention by alliteration. (See Langland, *Piers Plowman*: 'Ĭn å sómĕr sésŏn whån sóft wås thĕ sónne'.) Conversational stress metre has been little used since medieval times, although, as we will see, it has a kind of shifting presence in some free verse. It will not be examined further here.

2. Duple metre where the line has an *equal number of offbeats and beats,* usually 5 + 5 = 10 syllables, called PENTAMETER, or 4 + 4 = 8 syllables, called TETRAMETER. The beats are not always stressed. This metre formalises the basic alternation of offbeat and beat in the duple rhythm of conversational speech in English: 'Ĭf Wíntĕr cómes, cån Spríng bĕ fár bĕhínd?' (Shelley).

Duple metre allows the conversational flexibility of an occasional unstressed beat. This is because the beat occurs regularly on every second syllable (with only very brief variations) and is therefore recognisable without emphasis. Yet duple metre is a little more taut than the rhythm of normal conversation. Whereas conversation can vary its rhythm by introducing extra offbeats and beats loosely into the rhythm, duple metre must balance exactly the number of offbeats and beats in a given line. Hence a double beat will need to be balanced by a double offbeat to maintain an equal count, as in the pentameter line, 'Tŏ mŏrrŏw tŏ frĕsh Wŏods, ănd Pắstŭres nĕw' (Milton).

Duple metre (sometimes called 'accentual-syllabic' metre) was the principal metre in the literary tradition from the sixteenth to the late nineteenth century and is still often used. Apart from pentameter and tetrameter, it includes some forms used more often for variation than for whole poems: *dimeter* (2 beats + 2 offbeats = 4 syllables), *trimeter* (3 + 3 = 6) and *alexandrine* (6 + 6 = 12). Examples of alexandrine are sonnets 1 and 6 from Sidney's *Astrophil and Stella*, and the final line in each stanza of 'The Faerie Queene' by Spenser and of 'Resolution and Independence' by Wordsworth.

Pentameter is the metre of much of the poetry of Keats, Wordsworth, Pope, Milton, Donne, Chaucer and many others. It is the metre of the verse dialogue in Shakespeare's plays, and of most sonnets.

Although most poems in duple metre use either pentameter or tetrameter throughout, some use a variety of line lengths: pentameter, tetrameter, trimeter etc. These may form recurrent stanza patterns, as in 'The Sunne Rising' (Donne). Or (more rarely) they may form no recurrent pattern, as in 'A Song for St Cecilia's Day, 1687' (Dryden) and 'Dover Beach' (Arnold). 'Goblin Market' (Rossetti) is a rare example of a poem which irregularly mingles pentameter lines with lines in popular metre, to a continually disjointing effect.

An IAMBIC line is a line in the regular pattern of duple metre beginning with the offbeat (ˣ′ˣ′ˣ′ˣ′ˣ′). A TROCHAIC line is a line in the regular pattern of duple metre beginning with the beat (′ˣ′ˣ′ˣ′ˣ). *Pentameter is always iambic* (with the rarest of exceptions). *Tetrameter may be either iambic or trochaic.*

We need to add a third form, which is not a metre:

3. Free verse   where the lines have *no regular count of beats or offbeats*. They are therefore of irregular length. Free verse is free of metre (measure).

Free verse improvises on a basic duple rhythm, much as conversational speech does, only more tightly and attentively. According to the demands of tone and sense, it may set up a cadence, vary it, discard it and perhaps return to it. It may incorporate recognisable fragments of duple metre or stress metre into the weave.

Free verse was rarely used until Whitman took it up in the mid-nineteenth century. It has been the most commonly used form for poetry in the twentieth century, although popular metre and duple metre have also thrived. Most of the poems by Plath, Eliot, Pound, Williams and many other poets in the first 170 pages of the present anthology are in free verse.

We can sum up by stating that most of the poems composed in English in the last seven centuries are in one of the following forms:

1. Popular metre four-beat strongly timed stress metre line, in four-line stanzas

2. Tetrameter four-beat, eight-syllable duple metre line (less common than pentameter)

3. Pentameter five-beat, ten-syllable duple metre line

4. Free verse no metre; lines of irregular length

Each will now be examined in more detail. In the order given, they represent a sliding scale of metrical influence. The children's rhyme and the rap poem in popular metre are extreme examples of metre dominating the normal speech rhythms, distorting them for the sake of a strongly timed and stressed beat. In pentameter, speech rhythms are maintained in tension with metre. In free verse, speech rhythms are usually dominant.

1. Popular metre four beats in the line, stressed and strongly timed, almost to a musical exactness; with an optional number of offbeats. The lines are usually arranged in rhymed quatrains.

The following stanza has the full pattern of popular metre, four lines of four stressed beats with an optional number of offbeats (here from four to seven):

> When my mother died I was very young,
> And my father sold me while yet my tongue,
> Could scarcely cry weep weep weep weep.
> So your chimneys I sweep and in soot I sleep.   Blake

Notice how, in the third line, the four-beat pattern allows only two of the four stressed 'weeps' to make the beat.

In popular metre the *fourth* beat may be a silent REST BEAT, a pause at the end of a line of three beats, incorporated into the rhythm like a rest note in music. (This effect is confined to popular metre. In pentameter, free verse and normal conversation, a pause, however significant, usually breaks a rhythm and is not part of it.) Hence in BALLAD METRE (also called 'common metre') the *metrical pattern* remains 4444 (four beats to the line in a four-line stanza) while the *realised pattern* is 4343 (three beats in the utterance of the second and fourth lines, requiring a rest beat to complete the metrical pattern). See the example from Lear on p. 559.

Other realised patterns are possible: a limerick is in 3343, with an internal rhyme in the third line.

Even 3333 is possible. The mind which has been attuned since childhood to four-beat metre is always likely to feel something incomplete—at least the ghost of a final, silent beat—at the end of any three-beat line: hence the persistent check that may be felt at the line endings of 'Easter, 1916' (Yeats), 'Neither Out Far Nor In Deep' (Frost), 'As I Walked Out One Evening' (Auden) and 'My Papa's Waltz' (Roethke). These poems are in three-beat lines, which we may term 'three-beat metre'. However, we may equally consider them as having—or tending towards—the four-beat metrical timing of popular metre, with the fourth beat a rest beat. The following quatrain displays such metre at full stretch:

> Bréak, bréak, bréak,
> Ŏn thy̌ cóld gráy stónes, Ŏ̌ Séa!
> Ǎnd Ĭ wóuld thǎt my̌ tóngue cŏuld úttěr
> Thě thóughts thǎt ǎríse ĭn mé.   Tennyson

Although it is possible to read straight through the endings of these three-beat lines, the effect is more powerful if we feel the tension of a fourth, silent beat holding us back. Notice how the beats in the first line are slow, in the absence of offbeats, whereas six offbeats in the third line require a quicker and more urgent speaking to maintain the timing. Notice also how the stress on the offbeat, 'gray', drags at the timing to expressive effect in the second line.

The quatrain structure of popular metre may be modified. For example, it may be written as eight lines of two beats, as in 'The Sick Rose' (Blake). Or the four lines of ballad metre (4343) may be written as two lines of seven beats; such a line is called a 'septenary':

> Thě Láird ŏ̌' Phélps spént Hógmǎnáy děcláriňg hé wǎs sóběr,
> Cóuntěd hǐs féet tŏ próve thě fáct ǎnd fóund hě hǎd óne fóot óvěr.
>   MacNeice

In some poems the quatrain may be extended by extra lines to delay a conclusion, or cap a climax, as in 'Three Blind Mice' and 'Edward, Edward' (Anon.) and the occasional lengthened stanzas in 'The Ancient Mariner' (Coleridge). But the overall principle in popular metre remains one of doubling: paired beats bound into a line, lines bound variously into pairs, and pairs of lines bound into four in the quatrain. These doublings are supported by rhyme-schemes, whether abab, aabb, abba or abcb.

TRIPLE METRE is a form of popular metre in which the line gathers a busy and sometimes galloping rhythm by the regular inclusion of double offbeats:

> 'Wě névěr dŏ wórk whěn wě're rúiněd', sǎid shé   Hardy

Triple metre is generally confined to comical poetry and children's poetry; elsewhere it risks monotony. However, in brief touches it can be an effective variation, as for example in its evocation of the innocence of children's rhymes in the opening line of the following quatrain:

> Whĕn thĕ vǫ́icĕs ŏf chĭldrĕn, ăre hę́ard ŏn thĕ grę́en
> And whĭsprĭngs ăre ĭn thĕ dạ́le:
> Thĕ dạ́ys ŏf mў̆ yǫ́uth ríse frę́sh ĭn mў̆ mį̆nd,
> Mў̆ fạ́ce túrns grę́en ănd pạ́le.   Blake

Notice here also how stressed offbeats, 'rise' and 'turns', drag in tension with the strong timing.

A note on finding the beat: When we first read a poem, the beat is immediately obvious in some lines, and it is these which indicate the metre to expect in a poem. There are four unmistakable stressed beats in the line 'Ŏ hạ́ste ănd cǫ́me tŏ mў̆ mạ́stĕr dę́ar':

> Hĕ sę́nt hĭs mạ́n dǫ́wn thrŏ́ugh thĕ tǫ́wn,
>   Tŏ thĕ plạ́ce whĕre shę́ wăs dwę́llĭng,
> Ŏ hạ́ste ănd cǫ́me tŏ mў̆ mạ́stĕr dę́ar,
>   Gĭn yę́ bĕ Bạ́rbără Ạ́llăn.   Anon.

With some lines, however, we have to search for the place of the beat. This may be optional. Keeping to four beats, do we say, 'Hĕ sę́nt his mạ́n dǒwn thrǫ́ugh thĕ tǫ́wn', or 'Hĕ sę́nt hĭs mạ́n dǫ́wn thrŏ́ugh thĕ tǫ́wn'? The first is steady, the second is energetic. It depends on what emphasis we prefer.

In the following line in popular metre, a search for four realized beats has to find a beat on 'up' where conversation would probably not put one: 'Shĕ lĭft ụ́p hĭs blǫ́udў̆ hę́d' ('The Three Ravens', Anon.). Again, in the third line of the following 3343 quatrain, the stressed beat on 'in' is demanded purely by the metre: 'Pę́as pǫ́rrĭdge hǫ́t / Pę́as pǫ́rrĭdge cǫ́ld / Pę́as pǫ́rrĭdge ĭn thĕ pǫ́t / Níne dạ́ys ǫ́ld'. Children's rhymes and contemporary rap poetry work consistently with such musically timed distortion of normal speech. In pentameter, by contrast, the metre is contained within a clear, conversational speaking of the words.

2. Tetrameter (from the Greek, *tetra*, four)   four beats and four offbeats in the line, making eight syllables. Various stanza forms may be used, or none. The lines are usually rhymed.

> Thĭs Líquŏr sę́ldŏm hę́ats thĕ Brạ́in   Barber

Tetrameter has a duple metre's capacity for the conversational lightness of an occasional unstressed beat:

> Fŏr Ạ́rt hăs tạ́ught thĕm tŏ̆ dĭsguíse   Finch

Here the unstressed beat on 'tŏ' makes the rhythm of the line quicker, lighter and nearer to conversation than the always stressed beat of a popular metre line would allow. We could emphasise that beat artificially—the popular metre of a children's chant could do so—but delicacy would be lost. Even so, it is important to note that a tetrameter line in which all four beats happen to be stressed is indistinguishable from a line in popular metre.

The affinity between tetrameter and popular metre has led some scholars, such as Derek Attridge, to put both under the heading FOUR-BEAT METRE, as distinguished from FIVE-BEAT METRE (pentameter). Such a distinction recognises that any four-beat line, with its two pairs of beats, invites strong timing—a repetitive insistence that a line of five beats escapes. 'Four-beat metre' and 'five-beat metre' can thus be useful covering terms—but with the understanding that tetrameter, as a duple metre form, is a special case of four-beat metre, able to moderate its timing with an unstressed beat. THREE-BEAT METRE can likewise be a useful term to cover both trimeter and the three-beat variation in popular metre.

Tetrameter feels closest to popular metre when cast into quatrains. Indeed, more often than not, tetrameter in quatrains alternates with trimeter lines in a duple metre version of *ballad metre* (4343). Here the subtlety available to duple metre is combined with the robust drive of a popular metre form, including the timing of a rest beat at the end of the second and fourth lines. See for example 'The Ancient Mariner' (Coleridge), 'I heard a Fly buzz—when I died' (Dickinson) and many of Blake's *Songs*.

Tetrameter is most conversational in longer stanza or paragraph forms: for example, 'Fourth of July in Maine' (Lowell), 'In reference to her Children, 23 June 1656' (Bradstreet), 'The Exequy' (King) and many of the poems of Swift and Marvell. The tetrameter line is most often iambic (regular pattern beginning with an offbeat)—for example, *In Memorium A. H. H.* (Tennyson). It can also be trochaic (regular pattern beginning with a beat)—either a regular eight syllables, ending on an offbeat:

Pŏmp ănd Plĕasŭre, Prĭde ănd Plĕntў   Johnson

or seven syllables, ending on a beat (SHORT TETRAMETER):

Rŭns ĭn blŏod dŏwn Păláce wălls   Blake

The third part of 'In Memory of W.B. Yeats' (Auden) is entirely in short tetrameter lines. 'A Short Song of Congratulation' (Johnson) is in trochaic tetrameter, alternating eight-syllable with seven-syllable (short tetrameter) lines.

The structure of duple metre allows specific metrical variations. These are explained with examples from both tetrameter and pentameter on pp. 565–67.

3. Pentameter (from the Greek, *penta*, five)   five beats and five offbeats in the line, making ten syllables. Various stanza forms may be used, or none. Rhyme is optional.

> Bŭt nǫw thĕ sún ĭs rísĭng cálm ănd bríght;
> Thĕ bírds ăre síngĭng ĭn thĕ dístănt wǫods.   Wordsworth

A five-beat line is rhythmically more flexible than a four-beat line, partly because five beats provide more space for rhythmic variation, and partly because five is an odd number: it escapes the insistent doublings to which a four-beat metre is prone. For example, a caesura after the fifth syllable of a pentameter line divides it into two unequal halves, one with two beats and one with three. Moreover, pentameter (like tetrameter) has a duple metre's capacity for the lightness of an occasional unstressed beat. It is suited to a wide range of conversational effects. Yet the metre provides a formality—something tauter than conversation—for these effects to tug against: the equal count of beats and offbeats, and the shaping of phrases in relation to regular line endings.

The following is a regular pentameter line—duple rhythm, starting with the offbeat:

> Ĭf Wíntĕr cómes, căn Spríng bĕ fár bĕhínd?   Shelley

Most lines enliven this pattern by varying it, creating a tension between the regular pattern that the mind expects and the actual pattern that emerges from a natural clear speaking of the line. There are only a handful of variations, as listed below. Since these variations are common to duple metre, *each second example given is in tetrameter*. Notice that the equal ratio of beats to offbeats in a line remains constant; what varies is their strength (a, b and c) or their disposition (d and e). The hats that appear over each example are not metrical marks, but simply indicators of the point of variation.

a. UNSTRESSED BEAT   This is the most common variation. It holds the pulse of the beat, but lightens and quickens it by being unstressed. It may occur as the *middle of three nonstresses in a row* or (more rarely) as the final beat of a line. The first of the following examples illustrates both positions:

> Thĕ wǫrks ǒf wǫmĕn ăre sўmbólĭcăl   Barrett Browning

> Sǒ ínăccéssĭblĕ, ănd cóld   Finch

Deliberate emphasis would optionally turn the unstressed beat marked on 'ăre' in the first example into a stressed beat. Note that, in a trochaic line, an unstressed beat may occur also as the opening beat:

Ănd thĕ sĕas ŏf pítў líe   Auden

b. INTERNAL STRESSED OFFBEAT   the *middle of three stresses in a row.* This slows the timing:

Ănd cŏuld nŏt hŏpe fŏr hĕlp ănd nŏ hélp cáme   Auden

Úpŏn thĕ grĕat wórld's áltăr-stáirs   Tennyson

c. INITIAL STRESSED OFFBEAT   the *first of two consecutive stresses at the opening of a line.* In duple metre, as in normal conversation, a pair of consecutive stresses are usually felt as two beats in the rhythm—a double beat. The opening two syllables of a line, however, provide an exception. When two consecutive stresses open a line in duple metre, the first stress normally functions as a slow, preparatory offbeat. The second stress is the beat which rhythmically propels the rest of the line:

Púffs, Pówdĕrs, Pátchĕs, Bíblĕs, Bíllĕts-dóux   Pope

Shíne fŏrth ŭpŏn ŏur clŏudĕd hílls   Blake

Such a line reads best if we drive it rhythmically from the stress on the second syllable—'Pow-' and 'forth'. This confirms the metrical expectation of a regular (that is, iambic) five beat line, beginning—though massively—with an offbeat.

d. INITIAL INVERSION   *beat on the first syllable of a line, followed by double offbeat.* The regular iambic pattern is 'inverted' for the first two syllables—normal ˣ´ becomes ´ˣ—before reasserting itself: ´ˣˣ´ˣ´ˣ´ˣ´. The beat on the first syllable combines with the quick double offbeat to form an explosive opening:

Hóllŏw ŏf chĕek ăs thŏugh it dránk thĕ wínd   Yeats

Túrn'd tŏ thăt dírt frŏm whĕnce hĕ sprúng   Swift

Occasionally, the second offbeat in initial inversion is stressed:

Gíve mĕ, Gréat Gód (săid Í) ă Líttlĕ Fárm   Montagu

e. PAIRING: DOUBLE BEAT and DOUBLE OFFBEAT   When a double beat occurs in a duple metre line, a double offbeat must also occur, to maintain an equal count of beats and offbeats. The pairs are nearly always adjacent—either double offbeat followed by double beat:

Tŏ mórrŏw tŏ frĕsh Wŏods, ănd Pástŭres nĕw   Milton

    ⌐‾‾‾‾‾‾‾‾‾⌐‾‾‾‾‾‾‾‾‾‾‾
    Tŏ ă gréen Thóught ĭn ă gréen Sháde   Marvell

or double beat followed by double offbeat:

    ⌐ˣ‾‾‾‾‾‾‾‾‾‾‾‾‾‾⌐
    Ĭ wóke, ónce, wĭth mў pálm ăcróss yŏur móuth   Harwood

    ⌐ˣ‾‾‾‾‾‾‾‾‾‾‾⌐
    Ĭn spríng-tíme frŏm thĕ Cúckŏo-bírd   Wordsworth

This variation creates cadences full of movement.

Some lines incorporate more than one of the above variations. A sample:

    Góod stróng thíck stúpĕfýĭng íncénse-smóke   Browning

    Thĕ stíll, sád músĭc óf hŭmánĭtў   Wordsworth

    Báre rúĭn'd quíers, whĕre láte thĕ swéet bírds sáng   Shakespeare

    thĕ prĕcíse crýstăls óf ŏur éyes   Wright

    Sometimes the reader has a choice. The Donne line below begins with either initial stressed offbeat or initial inversion. The Marvell line begins with either a regular opening or initial inversion.

    Lóve, áll álĭke, nŏ séasŏn knówes, nŏr clýme
    Lóve, ăll álĭke, nŏ séasŏn knówes, nŏr clýme   Donne

    Hăd wé bŭt Wórld ĕnóugh, ănd Tíme
    Hád wĕ bŭt Wórld ĕnóugh, ănd Tíme   Marvell

The decision will depend on what tone and degree of emphasis we prefer.

ELISION   the gliding of two adjacent syllables into one. For example, in conversation we often elide 'we are' to 'we're'. Adjacent vowels, as in 'we are', are particularly prone to elision. Although such vowels may retain a degree of separateness, in the absence of a dividing consonant they can sometimes be felt as one continuing syllable.

    Duple metre (both pentameter and tetrameter) sometimes includes elision in the count of syllables. Thus two adjacent unstressed vowels ('th'entire') or two unstressed vowels separated by a lightly stressed consonant such as *h* ('th'horizon'), *l* ('trav'ling'), *n* ('op'ning') or *r* ('am'rous') may count as one. In the English of Shakespeare's time, *v* was only slightly pronounced: hence the elisions 'o'er', 'e'er', 'e'en' and 'heav'n', which thereafter for three centuries were used as poeticisms.

Until about the first decades of the nineteenth century, most elisions in poetry were marked on the page by an apostrophe, as in the examples given above. Since then, the apostrophe has been used more sparely, but elision has continued to be current in duple metre, as a count of syllables in some lines will confirm. Elisions (marked ⁀) in the following pentameter lines reduce the syllable count respectively from eleven, eleven and twelve to a regular ten:

> Thánks tŏ thĕ mĕans whĭch Nátŭre dĕigns to ĕmplóy   Wordsworth
>
> Ópeñing thĕ pĕaceful clóuds; ŏr shĕ măy úse   Wordsworth
>
> The hŏrĭzŏn's útmŏst bŏundarý; fŏr ăbŏve   Wordsworth

Note that elision need not always occur where it may. It depends on the rhythmical requirement of a particular line. A count of ten syllables makes it plain that, in the following pentameter line, 'to a' is not elided:

> Ă líttlĕ bŏat tĭed tŏ ă wíllŏw trĕe   Wordsworth

Final '-ed' was a separate syllable in early English. By Shakespeare's time it was often elided; today we elide it in most cases. From Shakespeare's time up to about the first decades of the nineteenth century, '-ed' spelling indicated a separate syllable, and ''d' indicated elision, as a count of ten syllables (in a pentameter line) will almost invariably confirm:

> Cŏol'd ă lóng áge ĭn thĕ dĕep-dĕlvĕd ĕarth   Keats

The present anthology keeps to this spelling; editions which print all such endings as '-ed' in the name of modernised spelling unfortunately blur a crucial rhythmic distinction.

BLANK VERSE is *unrhymed pentameter*, as for example 'The Bishop Orders His Tomb' (Browning), *Aurora Leigh* (Barrett Browning), 'Tintern Abbey' and *The Prelude* (Wordsworth), *Paradise Lost* (Milton) and the verse dialogue in Shakespeare's plays. This should not be confused with 'free verse'.

4. Free verse   irregular number of beats and offbeats in the line; hence without metre. Various stanza forms may be used, or none. The lines are rarely rhymed.

Free verse was very little used until Whitman developed it in the latter half of the nineteenth century, taking as a model the long, freely cadenced line used in the Authorised Version of the Bible (1611). Since Whitman, it has been adapted to wide use.

Since free verse is without the regular repetitions of metre, other repetitions are important: of words, of cadence, of patterns of syntax, and of sounds—alliteration and assonance—as in the following lines:

> Sŏmethǐng stártlĕs mĕ whére Ĭ thóught Ĭ wăs sáfĕst,
> Ĭ wǐthdráw frŏm thĕ stíll wŏods Ĭ lóved,
> Ĭ wǐll nót gŏ nŏw ŏn thĕ pástŭres tŏ wálk,
> Ĭ wǐll nót stríp thĕ clóthes frŏm mў bódў tŏ méet mў lóvĕr thĕ séa,
> Ĭ wǐll nót tóuch mў flĕsh tŏ thĕ éarth ăs tŏ óthĕr flĕsh tŏ rĕnéw mĕ.
>
> Whitman

The end-stopped lines here are typical of long lines of free verse. Shorter lines often work rather through delicate shapings and tensions on enjambed line-endings:

> Sŭch púre léaps ănd spírăls—
> Súrelў thĕy trávĕl
>
> Thĕ wórld fŏrévĕr, Ĭ shăll nót ĕntírelў
> Sǐt émptǐed ŏf beaútǐes, thĕ gíft
>
> Ŏf yŏur smáll bréath, thĕ drénched gráss
> Smĕll ŏf yŏur sléeps, lǐlǐes, lǐlǐes
>
> Plath

A well-made poem in free verse will feel more active if read with attention to the checks at the line-endings than if read straight through as fluent prose. In this respect it is worth reflecting on our own speech: something like enjambment operates in normal conversation, where we frequently linger, or even pause, at odd places in the middle of a phrase, to shape and point our language.

Unlike duple metre, with its requirement for an equal count of offbeats and beats, free verse may include the more *ad hoc* variations of conversational speech, such as the casual addition of double offbeats (abetted by the fact that normally unstressed syllables are slightly more prevalent in the vocabulary than stressed syllables). Inevitably, however, tightenings of rhythm will produce frequent echoes of duple metre. Effects of a conversational stress metre may also be present: in the Whitman example above, a clear, conversational speaking of the second and third lines produces four stressed beats, and the next two lines echo each other similarly with seven. Indeed the conversational stress metre of some Old English and medieval poets, such as Langland, finds its modern legacy, not so much in experiments with alliteration, as in its persistence—albeit in a shifting form—in much free verse. Some free verse poems might be better termed 'free stress metre'. For example, 'Love Poem for a Wife' (Ramanujan) uses three stressed beats in a conversational line, varying intermittently to four, with mostly two in the final line of each stanza. This is a loose form, but it develops a particular rhythm.

SYLLABIC VERSE is kin to free verse in having no regular number of beats within the line, and its rhythm is therefore improvised; however, it does have regular line-endings, lightly defined by a regular count of syllables. The following lines all have seven syllables, but no regular pattern of beats or offbeats:

> Thǐs tómcát cúts ǎcróss thě
> zónes ǒf thě rěspéctǎbḷe
> thrǒugh fénces, wạlls, fóllǒwǐng
> óthěr róutes, hǐs ówn. Ǐ sẹe
> hǐs sạd whǐskěred skụ́ll-móuth fạll
> wịde, cǒmplaịnǐnglỷ, ạskǐng   Baxter

Usually the syllable count is of an odd number (for example, 5, 7, 9, 11), which effectively disallows the evenly balanced line of most duple metre. Poems in syllabic verse include 'An Introduction' and 'The Inheritance' (Das), 'Mushrooms' (Plath), 'Fern Hill' (D. Thomas), 'In Praise of Limestone', 'Prime', 'Since', 'Old People's Home' (Auden), 'Bird-Witted' and 'The Mind Is an Enchanting Thing' (Moore). It is almost exclusively a twentieth-century form.

A final note

In all metres and forms, most lines have a STRONG ENDING, an ending on a stressed beat:

> Fǒr Gódsáke hóld yǒur tóngue, ǎnd lẹt mě lóve   Donne

A WEAK ENDING is a line-ending on an unstressed beat:

> Whǒ stánds cǒnfírm'd ǐn fụll stǔpídǐtỷ   Dryden

This is not the same as an OFFBEAT ENDING (traditionally termed a 'feminine ending'), which is an extra offbeat after the final beat. In pentameter, an offbeat ending is an eleventh syllable. Being added at the end, it does not affect the internal metre of the line:

> Thére Hérǒes' Wịts ǎre képt ǐn póndrǒus Vásěs   Pope

A pattern of alternate offbeat and strong endings is used in 'An Impromptu for Ann Jennings' (Harwood) and 'A Short Song of Congratulation (Johnson). The softness of weak and offbeat endings may have varying effects—such as expansiveness or quietness—depending on the verbal context.

ACKNOWLEDGMENTS

FLEUR ADCOCK: 'The Soho Hospital for Women', 'Crab' from *Selected Poems* (1983), © Fleur Adcock 1983, reprinted from Fleur Adcock's *Selected Poems* (1982) by permission of Oxford University Press. JOHN ASHBERY: 'Some Trees' from *Some Trees* (1956), 'Paradoxes and Oxymorons' from *The Shadow Train* (1981) reprinted by permission of Carcanet Press Ltd. MARGARET ATWOOD: 'She considers evading him' from *Power Politics* (1971), reprinted by permission of House of Anansi Press, Toronto; 'You Begin' reprinted by permission of Virago Press Ltd, from *Selected Poems II*, published by Houghton Mifflin, USA and McClelland Stewan Canada, © 1978. W.H. AUDEN: 'Song — For what as easy', 'As I Walked Out One Evening', 'Musée des Beaux Arts', 'In Memory of W.B. Yeats', 'Prime', 'Lullaby', 'The Shield of Achilles', 'Old People's Home', 'Song: Say this city has ten million souls', From 'Sonnets from China: X: So an age ended, and the last deliver', 'In Praise of Limestone' from *Collected Poems* (1976) by W.H. Auden, edited by Edward Mendelson, reprinted by permission of Faber & Faber Ltd; 'Since' from *City Without Walls* (1969) published by Faber & Faber Ltd copyright © 1969 by W.H. Auden, reprinted by permission of Curtis Brown Ltd, New York. JAMES K. BAXTER: 'The Beach House', 'Lament for Barney Flanagan', 'Tomcat', 'The Ikons' from *Collected Poems* (1979), 'The Beach House' from *Collected Poems of James K. Baxter* (1980), edited by J.E. Weir reprinted by permission of Mrs Baxter and Oxford University Press. SIR JOHN BETJEMAN: 'Indoor Games near Newbury', 'Devonshire Street W.1.' from *Collected Poems* (1958), reprinted by permission of John Murray Publishers Ltd. ELIZABETH BISHOP: 'Sestina', 'One Art', 'The Moose' from *The Complete Poems 1927–1979*, copyright © 1947, 1956, 1965, 1972, 1974, 1976 by Elizabeth Bishop, copyright © 1979, 1983 by Alice Helen Methtessel; originally appeared in *The New Yorker*, reprinted by permission of Farrar, Straus and Giroux Inc. KAMAU BRATHWAITE: 'Ogun' from *Islands* (1969), © Oxford University Press, reprinted by permission of Oxford University Press, extract from 'Sun Poem', © Edward Kamau Brathwaite 1982, reprinted from *Sun Poem* (1982) by permission of Oxford University Press. EMILY BRONTE: 'The starry night shall tidings bring', 'There was a time when my cheek burned' from *Emily Jane Bronte: The Complete Poems*, 1992, edited by Janet Gezari, 1992, © Janet Gezari, reprinted with permission of Janet Gezari, and Penguin Books Publishers. DENNIS BRUTUS: 'A simple lust is all my woe', extract from 'Letter to Martha', from *A Simple Lust* (1973), reprinted by permission of Heinemann Publishers (Oxford) Ltd. ROBERT BURNS: 'Song — for a' that' and a' that' from *The Poems and Songs of Robert Burns* (1958), edited by James Kinsley, reprinted by permission of Oxford University Press. ROY CAMPBELL: 'The Zulu Girl', 'The Serf' from *Collected Works*, Volume I (1985), reprinted by permission of Francisco Campbell Custodio and Ad.Donker (Pty). JOHN CLARE: 'Winter Fields', 'I Am' from *Selected Poems and Prose of John Clare*, edited by Eric Robinson and Geoffrey Summerfield, Oxford University Press, Eric Robinson 1967, reprinted by permission of Curtis Brown Ltd, London. WENDY COPE: 'Waste

Land Limericks' from *Making Cocoa for Kingsley Amis* by Wendy Cope, reprinted by permission of Faber & Faber Ltd. HART CRANE: Selections from 'Voyages', reprinted from *The Complete Poems and Selected Letters and Prose of Hart Crane*, edited by Brom Weber, with the permission of Liveright Publishing Corporation, copyright 1933, 1958, 1966 by Liveright Publishing Corporation. E.E. CUMMINGS: 'next to of course god america I', 'my sweet old etcetera', 'these children singing in stone a' 'I(a' from *Complete Poems 1913–1962* reprinted by permission of Grafton Books. ALLEN CURNOW: 'House and Land', 'Wild Iron', 'The Kitchen Cupboard', 'Continuum' from *Selected Poems 1940–1989* (1990), reprinted by permission of the author, Auckland University Press, Penguin Books Ltd and Viking. KAMALA DAS: 'An Introduction' from *Summer in Calcutta*, New Delhi: Rajinder Paul & Everest Press, 1965 'The Inheritance' from *The Old Play House and Other Poems* (1973), © Orient Longman Ltd, reprinted by permission of Orient Longman Ltd. BRUCE DAWE: 'Soliloquy for one Dead', 'Drifters' from *Sometimes Gladness: Collected Poems 1954–1982*, revised edition, reprinted by permission of the author and Addison Wesley Longman. EMILY DICKINSON: 'I dreaded that first Robin so', 'What soft cherubic creatures', 'I heard a Fly buzz — when I died', 'I cannot live with you', 'Because I could not stop for Death', 'As imperceptibly as Grief', 'The last Night that She lived', 'There came a Wind like a Bugle', 'Wild nights — Wild nights', 'I felt a funeral in my brain', 'The Soul selects her own Society', 'I died for Beauty — but was scarce', 'I gave myself to him', 'A still — Volcano — Life', 'I dwell in Possibility', reprinted by permission of the publishers and the Trustees of Amherst College, from *The Poems of Emily Dickinson* (1951), edited by Thomas H. Johnson, Cambridge, Mass., The Belknap Press of Harvard College; 'After great pain, a formal feeling comes' from *The Complete Works of Emily Dickinson* edited by Thomas H. Johnson, copyright 1929, 1935 by Martha Dickinson Bianchi, copyright © renewed 1957, 1963 by Mary L. Hampson, reprinted by permission of Little, Brown and Company. PAUL DURCAN: 'Irish Church Comes in from the Cold' from *Going Home to Russia*, reprinted by permission of Blackstaff Press. T.S. ELIOT: 'The Love Song of J. Alfred Prufrock', 'The Waste Land', 'Journey of the Magi', 'Marina' from *Collected Poems 1909–1962*, reprinted by permission of Faber & Faber Ltd. NISSIM EZEKIEL: 'Background, Casually' from *Hymns in Darkness* (1976), reprinted by permission of Oxford University Press, India. ROBERT FROST: 'Neither Out Far Nor In Deep', 'Design', 'The Most of it', 'The Subverted Flower', 'Out, Out' from *The Poetry of Robert Frost* (1971), edited by Edward Connery Lathem, reprinted by permission of the Estate of Robert Frost and Jonathan Cape Ltd; 'In White' from *Robert Frost — The Early Years 1874–1915*, by Lawrence Thompson (1966), reprinted by permission of the Estate of Robert Frost, Lawrence Thompson and Jonathan Cape Ltd. ALLEN GINSBERG: 'An Open Window on Chicago' from *Collected Poems 1947–1980* (Viking Books, 1985), text copyright © Allen Ginsberg, 1984, reprinted by permission of Penguin Books Ltd. DENIS GLOVER: 'The Magpies' from *Selected Poems* (1981), reprinted by permission of the Estate of Denis Glover. ROBERT GRAVES: 'The Cool Web', 'Nature's Lineaments', 'With a Gift of Rings' from *Collected Poems 1975*, reprinted by permission of A.P. Watt Ltd on behalf of the Executors of the Estate of Robert Graves. TONY HARRISON: 'Divisions I', 'Book Ends I' from *Selected Poems* (1984), reprinted by permission of the author and Penguin Books Ltd. GWEN HARWOOD: 'An Impromptu for Ann Jennings', 'Suburban Sonnet', 'Nasturtiums' from *Selected Poems* © Gwen Harwood, 1975; 'The Sea Anemones' from *The Lion's Bride* © Gwen Harwood, 1981, reprinted by permission ETT Imprint. H.D.: From 'Toward the Piraeus', From 'The Master' from *Collected Poems 1912–1944* (1984), reprinted with permission from Carcanet Press Ltd. SEAMUS HEANEY: 'Homecoming', 'Casualty' from *Field Work* (1979) and 'The Railway Children' from *Station Island* (1984), reprinted by permission of Faber & Faber Ltd. A.D. HOPE: 'X-Ray Photograph', 'The Death of the Bird', 'Paradise Saved' from *Collected Poems 1930–1970*, © A.D. Hope, 1966, reprinted by permission of HarperCollins Publishers Australia. TED HUGHES: 'Bride and Groom Lie Hidden for Three Days' from *Cave Birds* (1978), 'Ravens' from *Moortown* (1979), 'The Thought Fox' from *The Hawk in the Rain*, 'Full Moon and Little

Frieda' from *Wodwo*, reprinted by permission of Faber & Faber Ltd. RANDALL JARRELL: 'The Death of the Ball Turret Gunner', 'The Truth' from *The Complete Poems of Randall Jarrell* (1971), reprinted by permission of Faber & Faber Ltd. GALWAY KINNELL: 'After Making Love We Hear Footsteps' from *Moral Acts, Mortal Words* by Galway Kinnell, copyright © 1980 by Galway Kinnell, reprinted by permission of Houghton Mifflin Co. All rights reserved; 'The Man Splitting Wood in the Daybreak', 'Prayer' from *The Past* by Galway Kinnell, © Galway Kinnell, reprinted by permission of Houghton Mifflin Co. All rights reserved. WILLIAM LANGLAND: 'Piers Plowman' from *Langland: Piers Plowman*, edited by J.A.W. Bennett, 1972, reprinted by permission of Oxford University Press, London. PHILIP LARKIN: 'Lines on a Young Lady's Photograph Album', 'Going' from *The Less Deceived* (1955), reprinted by permission of The Marvell Press, England and Australia; 'The Explosion' from *High Windows* (1974), 'The Whitsun Weddings', 'Aubade' from *Collected Poems* by Philip Larkin (1964), reprinted by permission of Faber & Faber Ltd. AUDRE LORDE: 'Coal' from *Chosen Poems — Old and New* (1982) reprinted with permission of Virago Press, 'The Art of Response' from *Our Dead Behind Us* (1986) reprinted with permission of Sheba Press. ROBERT LOWELL: 'Memories of West Street and Lepke' from *Life Studies* (1959), 'Fourth of July in Maine' from *Near the Ocean* (1967), 'For the Union Dead' from *For the Union Dead* (1964), reprinted by permission of Faber & Faber Ltd. EDGAR LEE MASTERS: 'The Hill' from *The Spoon River Anthology* (1915), reprinted by permission of Ellen C. Masters and The Macmillan Company, New York. JAMES McAULEY: 'Because' from *Collected Poems 1936–1970*, © Norma McAuley 1971, reprinted by permission of HarperCollins Publishers Australia. HUGH MacDIARMID: 'Crystals like Blood', 'Another Epitaph on an Army of Mercenaries' from *The Complete Poems of Hugh MacDiarmid* (1978), reprinted by permission of Mr Michael Grieve and Martin O'Keeffe Ltd. MEDBH McGUCKIAN: 'The War Ending', 'A Different Same' from *Marconi's Cottage* (1991), by kind permission of the author and The Gallery Press, Loughcrew, Oldcastle, County Meath, Ireland. LOUIS MacNEICE: 'Conversation', 'Bagpipe Music' from *The Collected Poems of Louis MacNeice* (1966) edited by E.R. Dobbs, reprinted by permission of Faber & Faber Ltd. ELMA MITCHELL: 'Thoughts After Ruskin', 'At First, My Daughter' © Elma Mitchell, from *People Etcetera: Poems New & Selected* (1987), reproduced by permission of Peterloo Poets. LADY MARY WORTLY MONTAGU: 'Constantinople' from *Essays and Poems and Simplicity, A Comedy*, 1977, edited by Robert Halsband and Isabel Grundy, © Isabel Grundy, reprinted with permission of Oxford University Press Publishers, London; MARIANNE MOORE: 'The Mind is an Enchanting Thing', 'Bird-witted' from *The Complete Poems of Marianne Moore* (1968) by Marianne Moore, reprinted by permission of Faber & Faber Ltd. EDWIN MORGAN: 'Opening the Cage' from *Poems of Thirty Years* (1982), © 1984 by Carcanet Press Ltd, reprinted by permission of Carcanet Press Ltd. MUDROOROO: 'Aussie Dreams a Wakey-wake Time 2', 'A Mouth' from *The Garden of Gesthemane*, reproduced by permission of Hyland House. LES A. MURRAY: 'The Conquest', 'The Broad Bean Sermon', 'Driving through Sawmill Towns' from *The Vernacular Republic, Poems 1961–1981*, © Les A. Murray, 1982, HarperCollins Publishers Australia, reprinted by permission of Margaret Connolly. FRANK O'HARA: 'Why I Am Not a Painter' from *The Collected Poems of Frank O'Hara*, reprinted by permission of Alfred A. Knopf Inc.; 'The Day Lady Died' from *Lunch Poems*, copyright © 1983 by Sharon Olds, 'The Food Thief' from *The Gold Cell* by Sharon Olds, © 1987 by Sharon Olds, reproduced by permission of Alfred A. Knopf Inc. WILFRED OWEN: 'Dulce et Decorum Est', 'Strange Meeting' from *Collected Poems* (1963), edited by C. Day Lewis, reprinted by permission of Chatto and Windus Ltd. OKOT P'BITEK: 'Return the Bridewealth', reprinted by permission of East African Publishing House and the Estate of Okot p'Bitek. KATHERINE PHILIPS: 'To the truly noble Mr Henry Lawes' from *The Collected Works of Katherine Philips*, Vol. 1, *The Poems*, 1990, edited by Patrick Thomas, © Patrick Thomas and Stump Cross Books, reprinted with permission of Patrick Thomas and Stump Cross Books. SYLVIA PLATH: 'Morning Song', 'Tulips', 'The Applicant', 'The Night Dances' from *Ariel* (1965) by Sylvia Plath, published by

'Woman to Man', 'Train Journey', 'Naked Girl and Mirror' from *Collected Poems 1942–1970*, 'Smalltown Dance' from *A Human Pattern: Selected Poems* (1990), © Judith Wright, 1971, reprinted by permission of ETT Imprint. W.B. YEATS: 'A Prayer for My Daughter', 'The Stare's Nest by My Window', 'After Long Silence', 'The Circus Animals' Desertion' from *The Collected Poems of W.B. Yeats*; 'The Song of Wandering Aengus', 'The Wild Swans at Coole', 'Easter 1916', 'Leda and the Swan', 'Among School Children', 'Sailing to Byzantium', 'Crazy Jane Talks with the Bishop', 'Long-legged Fly' from *The Poems: A New Edition* (1984), reprinted by permission of A.P. Watt Ltd on behalf of Michael B. Yeats and Macmillan London Ltd.

Acknowledgment is due to the following libraries for permission to reproduce manuscript sources:

The Master and Scholars of Balliol College, Oxford: 'The Corpus Christi Carol' (MS 354 f. 165b); 'Farewell this world' (MS f. 199). Bodleian Library, Oxford: M. Drayton, 'Soe well I love thee' (MS Ashmole 38); Queen Elizabeth I, 'I grieve, and dare not show my Discontent' (MS Tanner 76, p. 162); Sir Walter Ralegh, 'As you came from the holy land' (MS Rawl. Poet. 85, f. 123); T. Traherne, 'The Salutation' (Dobell Folio MS Eng. Poet. C.42); Anon., 'Foweles in the frith' (Douce MS 139); 'Nou goth sonne under wod' (Arch. Selden, MS supra 74). National Library of Wales, Aberystwyth: Selections from *The Canterbury Tales* (Peniarth 392).

Details for the acknowledgments are supplied by copyright-holders. Every effort has been made to trace the original source of all material contained in this book. Where the attempt has been unsuccessful, the editor and publisher would be pleased to hear from the author/publisher concerned, to rectify any omission.

INDEX OF FIRST LINES AND TITLES

INDEX OF POETS